THE PROBLEMS
OF A
CHANGING POPULATION

•

REPORT OF THE
COMMITTEE ON POPULATION PROBLEMS
TO THE
U.S NATIONAL RESOURCES COMMITTEE
MAY 1938

SECOND PRINTING

UNITED STATES GOVERNMENT PRINTING OFFICE   WASHINGTON : 1938

For sale by the Superintendent of Documents, Washington, D. C. - - - - - - - Price 75 cents (paper cover)

National Resources Committee

North Interior Building

Washington

May 14, 1938.

The President,
The White House.

My Dear Mr. President:

We have the honor to transmit herewith a report on the "Problems of a Changing Population," prepared by a special subcommittee set up for this purpose by our Science Committee.

This report discusses some of the major problems of our human resources on a basis comparable with previous studies of the National Resources Committee and its predecessors. It presents significant data in regard to population trends, anticipated stable population, changing age groups, migration within the country, health, education, economic opportunity, and other similar problems which must be faced within the next generation.

The members of the Committee desire to indicate to you their belief in the basic significance of the problems set forth in this report. The report represents the results of many months of intensive study and research. We consider it an important step in gaining wider and deeper knowledge in this field.

Sincerely yours,

HAROLD L. ICKES,
Secretary of the Interior, Chairman.

HARRY H. WOODRING,
Secretary of War.

HENRY A. WALLACE,
Secretary of Agriculture.

DANIEL C. ROPER,
Secretary of Commerce.

FRANCES PERKINS,
Secretary of Labor.

HARRY L. HOPKINS,
Works Progress Administrator.

FREDERIC A. DELANO.
CHARLES E. MERRIAM.

●

HENRY S. DENNISON.
BEARDSLEY RUML.

NATIONAL RESOURCES COMMITTEE

HAROLD L. ICKES, *Chairman*
Secretary of the Interior

FREDERIC A. DELANO
Vice Chairman

DANIEL C. ROPER
Secretary of Commerce

HARRY H. WOODRING
Secretary of War

HARRY L. HOPKINS
Works Progress Administrator

CHARLES E. MERRIAM

HENRY A. WALLACE
Secretary of Agriculture

FRANCES PERKINS
Secretary of Labor

ADVISORY COMMITTEE

FREDERIC A. DELANO, *Chairman*

CHARLES E. MERRIAM

HENRY S. DENNISON

BEARDSLEY RUML

STAFF

CHARLES W. ELIOT, 2ND
Executive Officer

HAROLD MERRILL
Assistant Executive Officer

SCIENCE COMMITTEE

FRANK R. LILLIE
EDWIN B. WILSON
JOHN C. MERRIAM

WILLIAM F. OGBURN
HARRY A. MILLIS
CARTER GOODRICH,
Resigned

EDWARD C. ELLIOTT
WALTER D. COCKING
CHARLES H. JUDD

COMMITTEE ON POPULATION PROBLEMS

EDWIN B. WILSON, *Chairman*
DAVID L. EDSALL

L. C. GRAY
CHARLES H. JUDD

WILLIAM F. OGBURN
WARREN S. THOMPSON

TECHNICAL STAFF

FRANK LORIMER, *Director*
HAROLD F. DORN

LOUISE P. BLODGET
MILDRED HARTSOUGH

RUPERT B. VANCE
ROBERT M. WOODBURY

SPECIAL CONTRIBUTORS

B. A. BOTKIN
NINA COLLIER
NEWTON EDWARDS

CLYDE E. KEELER
CLYDE V. KISER
SAMUEL A. STOUFFER

IRENE B. TAEUBER
DOROTHY S. THOMAS

This report was prepared under the direction of a subcommittee of the Science Committee. The latter group is made up of designees from the National Academy of Sciences, the Social Science Research Council, and the American Council of Education. These organizations assume no responsibility for the views and opinions expressed by their designees.

CONTENTS

FOREWORD

THE PROBLEM

In the foreword to the Report of the National Resources Board on National Planning and Public Works in Relation to Natural Resources and including land use and water resources, dated December 1, 1934, were the following two paragraphs:

The problems centering around land and water cannot be solved in these terms alone, but require for their practical and successful treatment a full consideration of the broader but closely related aspects of agriculture, industry, labor, transportation, communication, health, education, public finance, and government organization.

Finally, human resources and human values are more significant than the land, water, and minerals on which men are dependent. The application of engineering and technological knowledge to the reorganization of the natural resources of the Nation is not an end in itself, but is to be conceived as a means of progressively decreasing the burdens imposed upon labor, raising the standard of living, and enhancing the well-being of the masses of the people. It follows that the social directives back of such technical programs should be developed by persons competent by training and point of view to appraise the human values involved.

Many substantial investigations have been directed by biological, medical, psychological, educational, and other experts toward one or another aspect of the problems connected with the American population problem. It is important that there should be widespread recognition that there are a great many emerging problems in this field of population which deserve attention and that a great many experts in the country are studying them. The results of inquiry need to be thoroughly absorbed by a much larger number of our people to the end that action taken in the furtherance of American interests shall be based upon as much information and wisdom as may be available, and that the further development of such information and wisdom be encouraged.

METHOD OF STUDY

The National Resources Committee presented this problem to its science committee, designated by the National Academy of Sciences, the Social Science Research Council, and the American Council on Education. This Committee, looking at the problem from the point of view of the natural, social, and educational sciences, all of which are severally and jointly interested in any broad picture of population problems, recommended that a special population committee be set up to supervise the preparation of this report and that the details of the plan be worked out by a technical staff. The topics treated are summed up under the following heads:

The Trend of Population: Economic Aspects

Regional Distribution of Economic Opportunity

Trends in Population Redistribution

Regional and Racial Differences in Reproduction Rates

Social Conditions Affecting Birth Rates

Physical Characteristics and Biological Inheritance

Health and Physical Development

Social Development and Education

Cultural Diversity in American Life

Government Research on Population

The supervising committee consisted of Edwin B. Wilson, chairman, professor of vital statistics in the school of public health of Harvard University; William F. Ogburn, professor of sociology in the University of Chicago; Charles H. Judd, head of the department of education in the University of Chicago; Warren S. Thompson, director of the Scripps Foundation for Research in Population Problems at Miami University; David L. Edsall, M. D., dean of the medical school, of the school of public health and of the faculty of dentistry, *emeritus*, of Harvard University, and Lewis C. Gray, economist in charge of the division of land economics of the United States Bureau of Agricultural Economics, and past director of the land use section of the National Resources Committee. The technical staff was under the direction of Frank Lorimer, secretary of the Population Association of America.

SIGNIFICANCE

In general and without endorsement of all details, we commend this report to the consideration of the several agencies most directly concerned with the problems involved, with a view to such legislation and administration as may be appropriate; and further to the consideration of the American people in shaping broad national policies regarding our population problems. Some of these policies may, of course, center around the National Government; others around State and local governments; and still others around the family, the

4

home, and voluntary associations of various kinds.

It cannot be too strongly emphasized, however, that this report deals not merely with problems regarding the quantity, quality, and distribution of population, important as they are, but also with the widening of opportunities for the individuals making up this population, no matter how many or where they are. In our democratic system we must progressively make available to all groups what we assume to be American standards of life. The gains of the Nation are essentially mass gains, and the birthright of the American citizen should not be lost by indifference or neglect. Foremost among all the gains of civilization are health and education, and in our land we cannot long continue to deny the opportunity for an American minimum of health and education to any of our fellow citizens. This is one of the first great goals to which a national program for the use of our natural resources must lead.

ACKNOWLEDGMENTS

The committee on population problems and its technical staff have received generous cooperation from many organizations and individuals. The preparation of the chapter on "Social Development and Education", by Newton Edwards, assisted by Mabel Waltz, was arranged through the courtesy of the American Council on Education. The chapter on "Social Conditions Affecting Birth Rates", by Clyde V. Kiser, was provided by the Milbank Memorial Fund. The Committee is also indebted for special contributions or consultation services to B. A. Botkin, University of Oklahoma; Nina Collier, arts projects, Works Progress Administration; Samuel A. Stouffer, University of Chicago; Irene B. Taeuber, Population Association of America; Dorothy S. Thomas, Institute of Human Relations, Yale University.

The estimates of future population used in this report were prepared under the direction of Warren S. Thompson and P. K. Whelpton, of the Scripps Foundation for Research in Population Problems. The distribution of gainful workers by social-economic classes for States were prepared, under the direction of Alba M. Edwards, by the Bureau of the Census. The Central Statistical Board cooperated in the preparation of the guide to Government serial reports and current research in population and related fields.

The Committee is indebted for valuable suggestions or unpublished material to O. E. Baker, John Bennett, John D. Black, Horace R. Cayton, Joseph Chassell, M. D., Robert E. Cook, Donald H. Davenport, Edwin R. Embree, Philip Hauser, Charles S. Johnson, Nolan D. C. Lewis, Frederick Osborn, Gladys Palmer, Hazel K. Stiebeling, George Terborgh, Caroline F. Ware, Louis I. Wirth, J. J. Woodall, Lawrence Woolley, M. D., W. S. Woytinsky, Sewall Wright, and to officers of the health departments of Alabama, Delaware, Maine, Massachusetts, and Michigan. The technical staff has been assisted throughout its work by Ezra Glaser, Luella McFaddin, and Helen Shaw. The original maps and diagrams presented in the report were prepared under the direction of Charles Faunce.

STATEMENT OF THE COMMITTEE ON POPULATION PROBLEMS

It is apparent that great changes are taking place in the population of the United States: transition from an era of rapid growth to a period of stationary or decreasing numbers, increase in the proportion of children surviving to maturity, limitation of births in varying degrees among different groups, redistribution of people in relation to natural resources and social institutions. Some of these are the culmination of tendencies that have long been at work. They affect the foundations of human experience in biological inheritance, family relations, and the conditions of daily living. Many of these changes, already in force or appearing on the horizon, are very encouraging, bringing enhanced opportunity for good living to millions of people who would be severely handicapped if the population trends of the nineteenth century were projected without change far into the future. Some changes, such as the increase in the proportion of aged persons, while gratifying, raise problems of considerable difficulty and importance. Other tendencies, revealed by an analysis of the rates of increase and decrease of different population groups, lead to very serious questions regarding the biological and cultural forces now operative in American life.

The committee on population problems of the National Resources Committee has sought to explore these problems with the aid of a technical staff and through conferences with scholars in related fields. On some points, the evidence is adequate and decisive. On other points, definite conclusions are impossible because of deficiencies and inaccuracies in the source data on population now available in this country. The committee has investigated the relation of population changes to physical welfare, education, and cultural life, reaching beyond pure demography and vital statistics into the analysis and interpretation of various conditions affecting the conservation and development of human resources in this country. In these fields the procedure is frankly exploratory, raising many problems that are left unanswered. The committee has attempted to formulate some of the main implications or corollaries of population studies for social action, relative to such objectives as the general increase of health and intelligence, and the provision of greater opportunities for economic and cultural advance; but all such formulations are obviously tentative and experimental, to be confirmed or revised in the light of new evidence.

1. The Trend of the National Population

The settling of Europeans in America coincided with an acceleration of population growth in Europe. Natural increase of European stocks rose continuously through the eighteenth and nineteenth centuries. Population growth is now, however, slowing down in western Europe, while it continues with full force in eastern Europe, and is rising in some parts of Asia. The great increase of world population during the last few centuries resulted from the lowering of death rates, increases in production and trade, the opening up of new areas, and the introduction of sanitary measures. A slowing down of population growth is now in evidence.

These general trends are clearly reflected in the course of population change in the United States. It is likely that population growth was never more rapid in any nation than among the youthful population of this New World, from the days of colonial settlement to the time of the Civil War—with an increase of 35 percent per decade. The signs of an approaching change were already present, however, in the gradual lowering of ratios of children to women in the northeastern States during the early nineteenth century; but these signs passed unnoticed for many decades.

Crude rates of natural increase now register the slowing down of population growth in the United States, and more refined analysis yields even more striking results. The birth *rate* has been declining for many decades; the total *number* of births per year reached a peak in the years 1921–25. Since 1929 there has been a general trend toward decrease in the number of births each year. Moreover, when "true rates" are computed to eliminate the temporary effects of variations in age distribution, it is found that the intrinsic reproductive trend is already slightly below that required for permanent population replacement. In other words, if no change occurred in the proportions of persons surviving from birth to different ages or in fertility rates of women at different ages, population growth would gradually cease. Actually there is good reason to expect that further decline in fertility rates will be more rapid than the rise in survival rates. Furthermore, there will be a peak in the number of young persons of marriageable age about 1945 (about 20 years after the peak in the number of births already mentioned). Therefore, after the middle of the century further decrease must be expected in the number of births each year unless present trends in fertility are reversed or unless the population is augmented by heavy immigration.

The most recent estimates of future population change, prepared for this report by Warren S. Thompson and P. K. Whelpton, are based on three sets of hypotheses for birth rates and for death rates. On the assumption of medium fertility and mortality rates, population will continue to grow for 50 years but at a constantly decreasing rate, reaching 153,000,000 in 1980. Assuming a net immigration of 100,000 persons per year from 1940 on, the figure for 1980 is raised to 158,000,000. Even with the highest rates that can reasonably be assumed, there would be a natural increase of less than 50,000,000 from 1935 to 1980. The minimum estimate assumes a decline of about one-third in the fertility of native white women from the 1930–34 level to 1980, with no net accession of immigrants. This estimate gives a peak population of 138,000,000 in 1955, with a decrease of 10,000,000 during the next quarter century.

A change in age distribution is accompanying the change in trend of total population. The estimates for 40 years hence, based on "medium" assumptions as regards births and deaths and with no allowance for immigration, indicate the presence of an approximately equal number of persons—about 2 million—at each year of age from birth to 60 years. There will be a smaller number of persons at the later ages, but they will form a much larger proportion of the total than at present. In 1900 there were 90 persons under 20 years of age for each 100 persons aged 20 to 60 years, whereas the corresponding ratio in 1935 was only 68 and by 1975 will be about 48. Conversely, where there were 13 persons over 60 years of age per 100 persons aged 20 to 60 years in 1900, the corresponding ratio in 1935 was 17 and in 1975 will be about 34.

These changes present a whole new set of national problems, the problems of a "mature population." This characterization of the situation in Minnesota by the planning board of that State is applicable to the Nation as a whole:

Minnesota has come of age and is reaching a period of maturity * * * This is in no sense a cause for gloom. The period of middle age may be for a nation as for an individual, the most productive and happiest period of existence. We are, however, face to face with the sober and thought-provoking necessity of developing a way of life for a mature community.[1]

The urban population of the Nation is already so great in relation to the rural population that future growth of cities will be much slower and more uncertain than in the past. Urban growth will probably expand the periphery of existing industrial and commercial centers faster than the central cities. The population of the Nation appears to be approaching stabilization both in number and in geographical distribution.

The change from an expanding to a stabilized or slowly decreasing national population entails new economic and social problems, but it also opens up new possibilities of orderly progress. This is especially important in view of our changed economic situation. Practically all of the good land available for agriculture has been settled, the best timber stands have been exploited, and some types of mining already show diminishing returns. Probably there will be some further discovery of minerals and reclamation of land, but future economic progress must be achieved for the most part by the conservation and better use of natural resources already tapped.

It must be emphasized, however, that the approaching equilibrium thus indicated is not a static but a dynamic equilibrium, in which some large groups are increasing rapidly while other large groups are tending toward extinction. The passing of the frontier also accentuates the sharp contrasts in opportunity and levels of living now existing among people in different regions of the United States. Furthermore, with increased facilities for transportation and communication there is likely to be a greater shuttling of migrants back and forth between communities. The whole tempo of social change is becoming increasingly rapid. After the stabilization of national population growth, we shall still be confronted with important problems of internal shifts and adjustments.

The transition from an increasing to a stationary or decreasing population may on the whole be beneficial to the life of the Nation. It insures the continuance of a favorable ratio of population to natural resources in the United States. Each citizen of this country will continue to have, on the average, a larger amount of arable land, minerals, and other natural resources at his disposal than the citizen of any of the countries of the Old World. This supplies the material basis for a high level of living, if these resources are used wisely and if cultural conditions are favorable to initiative and cooperative endeavor.

The gradual decrease in the proportion of children, at least in many sections of the population, raises problems of major national interest. This aspect of the situation has been treated, especially in European writings, under such captions as *A Nation Without Youth*. We shall return to this question in a later section. Here we may simply sound a warning against the hasty projection of past trends into the future, without taking into account new conditions that may arise to change these trends. Questions relating to changing reproductive tendencies call for very careful analysis, but there is no occasion for hysteria. Even on the minimum assumptions described above, the population of the United States in 1980 would be equal to that of today.

The Population Committee has given some attention to the question as to whether or not the slowing down of population may have been a factor of any considerable importance in the onset and course of the depression. The answer to this question seems to be mainly negative. The housing shortage which developed during the war and the subsequent spurt in urban population growth in the early twenties stimulated a boom in the building industry, from which the recession in 1928–29 may have been one of the contributory factors to the depression. But this cannot be attributed primarily to a change in the trend of total population.

The slowing down of population growth will not cause any sudden economic disturbances. The population at ages 20–45 years was and still is steadily increasing, and will not reach its peak until about 1950. Obviously, speculations based on continued rapid expansion of population would be hazardous. Changes in population trends must be taken realistically into account, and this is possible because of the gradual character of these changes and the time interval between birth and economic productivity.

It follows from an analysis of the trend of the Nation's population that continued expansion of the domestic market for American goods and services must be sought through the increase of effective consumer demand, through increased productivity and broadened distribution of income, rather than in the numerical increase of population. This has important implications regarding the relative demand for different types of products, but these have not been elaborated in this report—except with reference to the division of population between farming and industrial-commercial communities.[2] There is certainly ample opportunity for the improvement of levels of living among large population groups in the United States. Clearly the main implication of this analysis is a constructive emphasis on the community of interests of the American people, in economic as well as in cultural matters.

The economic problems of persons who have passed the period of gainful productivity have been brought to the attention of the Nation through social security legislation and related issues. There is need, however, for calling attention to some of the neglected aspects of the changing age distribution. The most striking feature of this shift, to be expected during the next few decades, is the increase in the number of older workers relative to the number of younger adults. Between 1935 and 1975, the estimated increase in the number of persons 20–44 years of age, on the "medium" hypothesis, amounts to only 6 percent, whereas an increase of 69 percent is expected in the number of persons 45–64 years. The analysis of the age distribution of workers in different industries shows that occupations that have been declining hold older workers, but that the personnel of new industries is heavily weighted with young people. These findings suggest the importance to national economy and individual morale of greater consideration of conditions affecting the employment of older workers, and of provisions for retraining and increasing the adaptability of individual workers displaced from their usual occupations by technological change.[3]

The increasing proportion of aged persons in the population raises cultural as well as economic problems. Vigor and contentment in old age rest on the foundations of good health and intellectual vitality in youth. Education has commonly been viewed chiefly as preparation for the middle years of maximum productivity. Educators now insist that it must also interpret the immediate experiences of childhood and youth, and there is a growing idea that education should make possible an intellectual development continuing throughout life. The place of aged persons in the family has received little attention from American psychologists and sociologists. Here, as in relations between parents and children, mutual tolerance and appreciation may contribute to a greater sense of personal security, the enlargement of individual experience, and the increase of human happiness. Thus the changing population pattern in the United States carries far reaching implications for education, recreation, conditions of labor, and family living.

The gradual slowing down of population growth is due to social changes taking place throughout the whole civilized world. The trend toward cessation of natural increase and toward an increase in the proportion of older people will not necessarily lead to unhappy results, though these changes raise problems that need careful consideration. There is no reason for the hasty adoption of any measures designed to stimulate population growth in this country.

Problems relating to the welfare of persons past middle life are becoming increasingly urgent. In addition to provisions for insurance and other old age benefits, attention should be given to opportunities for and conditions of employment of older workers not ready for retirement. There should be consideration of further possibilities for adult education and other measures for enhancing the usefulness and increasing the joy of persons in the later middle and last years of life.

---

[2] See ch. III, sec. 6.

[3] See ch. I, sec. 4.

2. Population Distribution and Redistribution

People have entered the United States (1) by various routes as colonists or immigrants and (2) by birth. The first of these primary forces influencing the distribution of population in this country brought people to points along the whole Atlantic seaboard at first, and then led to concentration of immigrants in certain areas of expanding industrial opportunity, notably in the Northeast, with areas of secondary concentration in other sections, in the Middle States, Northwest, Far West, and Southwest. The second of the primary forces in population distribution (differential natural increase among regions and types of community) has tended toward accumulation of population in the most rural sections of the country. Immigration is now relatively unimportant, but differential natural increase is still an active force. During the years 1930–34, 55 percent of the total natural increase occurred in the States of the South and Northwest, which contain only about one-third of the total population.

Internal migration constantly modifies the accumulation of population that would otherwise result in certain areas from immigration or differential natural increase. In many cases it brings about new concentrations of population in response to economic opportunities or other attractions. In 1930, about 23 percent of the total native white population and 25 percent of the total Negro population were living outside the States in which they were born. There has been a constant interchange of population between different areas, but two main movements have predominated: (1) the movement to new lands, mines, and jobs in the West—across the Alleghenies into the Ohio and Mississippi valleys, the prairies, the Pacific coast, and finally to dry-farming areas in the Great Plains; (2) the movement to industrial and commercial opportunities in various parts of the country but most notably in the Middle Atlantic, southern New England, Great Lakes, and Pacific areas. The second type of movement drew people from the very areas previously regarded as areas of new opportunity. Thus, in 1930, 5,000,000 persons born east of the Mississippi were living west of that river; but the States in the northeast quadrant contained more than 1,650,000 people born west of the Mississippi River, as well as more than 3,000,000 born south of the Mason-Dixon line.

In recent decades the dominant feature of internal migration has been the movement from farms to cities. This movement is, in large part, an expression of shifts in industrial production made possible by improvements in technology. Between 1880 and 1930 the proportion of gainful workers employed in the extractive industries (agriculture, mining, forestry, and fishing) declined from over 45 to under 25 percent, the proportion in manufacturing and mechanical industries increased from 20 to 29 percent, and that in the distributive and service trades from 34 to 47 percent. Movement out of agricultural areas has also been forced, in part, by the high reproductive rates that have been and still are characteristic of rural communities. Contrary to a popular impression, this movement has continued even through the depression. There was a net migration of more than half a million people from farms to cities and villages between 1930 and 1935—2,600,000 out-migrants from farms, as compared with 1,995,000 in-migrants—but this movement was insufficient to offset continued rapid natural increase of farm population (estimated at 2,023,000), so that the farm population enumerated on January 1, 1935, was 1,356,000 in excess of that enumerated on April 1, 1930. Furthermore, the apparent movement to "farms" was largely to places in the vicinity of large cities, manufacturing or mining areas. Emigration from farms in the typical agricultural counties was sufficiently heavy to offset their rapid natural increase even during this period, 1930–35.

During the nineteenth century most of the people in some isolated areas—notably in the southern Appalachians—were quite unaffected by the appeal of new opportunities elsewhere. Railroads, automobiles, busses, and radios have now established lines of migration and intercommunication that are all but ubiquitous. There are no longer any self-contained areas in the United States. During the decade 1920–30 people were moving in very considerable numbers from rural areas of meager opportunity all over the country, particularly from central Georgia and from Montana and eastern Washington. There was, in fact, a net decrease of population in 41 percent of the counties in the United States during this 10-year interval.

In spite of the tendency for internal migration to effect a balance between the distribution of population and the distribution of economic resources, there remain in this country large areas of overpopulation relative to developed resources, resulting in chronic poverty and cultural stagnation for millions of people. Comparing the six main regions of the United States, as defined in the Southern Regional Study, we find that in the middle twenties the average annual gross value-productivity of each farm worker in the Southeast was less than half that for all the rest of the United States, and well below that for the average agricultural worker in England.[4] There are other examples of maldistribution of population in this country. Variations in level of living in rural areas, as revealed by various indices, show a significant relation to varia-

---

[4] See ch. I, table 5.

tions in density of farm population relative to quantity units of arable land or value units of total farm land.

There are three ways in which population and basic economic resources may be maladjusted:[5]

1. The natural resources of an area, its population, its geographical situation, and the level of technical development already reached may provide the basis for economic progress at a relatively high level of living—and yet economic unbalance may result in mass unemployment, widespread underemployment, severe need, and social conflict. The parts are all there, but they are badly adjusted and the machine will not run. The acute disturbance of our national economy in 1929 was of this nature, and similar disturbances have occurred at many times and in many places. Millions of workers in industry, trade, and the service occupations may be reduced to part-time work or thrown out of employment in a few months. Such a situation is a disturbance of economic operation, rather than one of chronic disparity in the relation of people to resources.

2. Fundamental maladjustment of population to resources may be caused by the exhaustion of the natural resources on which the whole economy of a region or nation depends.

The situation of forest lands that formerly yielded great wealth and gave employment to many, but are now stripped of the best stands, is exemplified in the Great Lakes cut-over region of northern Michigan, Wisconsin, and Minnesota. The forests in this region once seemed almost inexhaustible, and were exploited without regard to principles of sustained yield. As the land was cleared and employment in lumbering grew less, the settlers turned to agriculture, but found that much of the land was not really fit for cultivation and returned only a meager subsistence. Now isolated farmsteads prevail, agricultural returns are small, and opportunities for profitable supplementary employment are scarce. At present less than 15 percent of the land in this region is covered with merchantable timber. Only in the past few years has any widespread effort been made to replenish the stand. Rehabilitation of this region depends chiefly on development of a long-time plan for restoration and maintenance of forest resources. Such a plan will necessarily be slow and costly to operate.

Tremendous waste of soil resources through erosion or overgrazing has occurred in many parts of the United States. The Great Plains area, extending from the Dakotas and Montana to northern Texas, was originally brought into use as range country. As cultivation was extended westward, much of the plains area was plowed and planted to crops—especially the cash-grain crop, wheat. With the tremendously increased demand and accompanying high prices for food crops during the World War, the Great Plains were brought more and more completely under cultivation. Much of the area was farmed in parcels too small for efficient management under prevailing conditions of soil and climate. It is a region of sun and high wind, and of little and irregular rain. Once it was denuded of its sod covering, the soil was left unprotected from wind erosion; severe droughts have been followed by dust storms that have carried away the surface soil, ruined millions of acres, and driven thousands of farm families away from their homesteads. Plans are now being formed for this area, based on principles of soil conservation, in an effort to check this wastage. The development of a sound regional economy will involve far-reaching changes in the present land-use system.

The Great Plains is not the only region to suffer serious effects from soil erosion. In many parts of the country, intensive cultivation of slopes has caused the washing away of millions of tons of topsoil during periods of heavy run-off. The whole agricultural program has been oriented to the idea of soil conservation. Arresting the wholesale destruction of the resources basic to our vaunted prosperity depends on scientific conservation programs. In some instances these programs will require considerable changes in the location of population, as poor farm areas are transferred to forest use, or as eroded lands are shifted from an agricultural to a pastoral economy.

3. The relation between the number of people in an area and its characteristic occupations may be such as to hold the level of living relatively low.

This is likely to occur in a region dominated by agriculture, forestry, or mining, especially if demand for its characteristic products is inelastic or declining, and if it is a region of high reproduction rates. In such a situation a vicious circle may be set up which is extremely hard to break. Low average income, lack of contact with outside developments, meager and ineffective education—these conditions are conducive to high birth rates. They may also retard the introduction of new industries or methods of production, and hamper movement to other places where opportunity is greater. Thus areas of inadequate opportunity may develop an accumulation of population which is only partly relieved by emigration. Theoretically, such situations might be greatly improved by increased production of supplementary goods and services to meet local needs. Actually, however, low cash income has a discouraging effect on production for home use as well as for sale.

[5] The term "economic resources" is used to cover institutional factors such as transportation facilities and established means of providing goods and services, as well as natural resources.

The two types of maladjustment just described are closely related. The distinction is one of emphasis on the primary causal factor. Pressure of population on natural resources often leads to the exhaustion of these resources through bad management or excessive use. Conversely, maladjustment due primarily to the rapid depletion of natural resources brings about overpopulation.

In some parts of the world overpopulation is a cause of mass poverty for millions of people—for example, China, India, Japan, Java, Egypt, and Puerto Rico. Such a situation is clearly not characteristic of the continental United States as a whole. Relative excess of population in relation to present use of economic resources, however, does seriously affect the outlook for some agricultural, mining, and forest areas in this country.

Several constructive approaches are possible in meeting the problems presented by this situation:

Free movement of workers from agricultural areas of limited opportunity should be encouraged, through the United States Employment Service and other agencies, in the interest of a higher average level of living for families now suffering from chronic poverty.

The same objective may be furthered by governmental purchase of lands unsuited to agriculture, and the diversion of such lands to forestry, recreation, and other conservational uses.

Efforts should be directed to the development of new enterprises, including diversified types of agricultural production. To this end, attention should be directed to the prevention of any artificial barriers, such as differential freight rates or trade agreements, prejudicial to such areas. Direct or indirect subsidies for the development of new industries in areas of retarded economic development would appear to be justified only insofar as there are reasonable prospects of sound, independent development.

Emphasis may also be placed in matters relating to the development of power, transportation, communication, and housing on the facilitation of residence outside the central areas of large cities, where such encouragement is supported by a realistic analysis of economic and social opportunity.

A sound program of national development favors the maintenance of a conservative immigration policy. So long as there is a large surplus population in some rural areas in this country, it seems unnecessary and inadvisable to encourage the immigration of persons initially equipped for unskilled rather than for technical production.

3. The Conservation of Human Resources

The protection and promotion of the interests of the people who comprise a nation are the sole ends of organized national life. Natural resources, industrial institutions, and all forms of social cooperation are valuable only insofar as they contribute to the welfare of the people. The conservation of human resources is therefore a matter of primary national importance.

There are obvious differences in the developed abilities of individuals. These can now be given quantitative expression, to a significant though imperfect degree, through the use of standardized psychological tests. People differ in abilities, not merely because of differences in genetic constitution, but also because of childhood differences in nutrition, family life and conversation, formal education, conditions of work, and opportunities for recreation.

It is evident that, at present, families in the occupational groups characterized by superior education and enlarged opportunities have on the average fewer children than families handicapped by meager education and limited economic and cultural resources. This contrast is characteristic of most communities today, though it is not found in the oldest surviving patriarchal societies.[7] A negative relationship between level of cultural-intellectual development and reproduction may operate as an imperceptible drag on cultural advance. This drag can be offset by ameliorative social action, extensive provisions for public education, and the stimulating impact of technological advance. But no civilization can be stable or progressive over a long period unless it is able to establish a positive relation between reproduction and health, culture, and social ideals. Emphasis on the importance of the family and informal community contacts does not gainsay the importance of formal education. It rather suggests that educational influences are cumulative in their effects, reaching beyond the individuals immediately affected, and building cultural patterns that from the fabric of civilization. Family traditions and schoolroom practices interact and reinforce each other. Weakness in either of these great cultural forces is likely to vitiate the influence of the other.

There is absolutely no doubt about the existence generally at present of a negative rela-

---

[7] On the basis of his own and other investigations, Lamson attempts to show "that in China the upper economic classes have more children per family than the lower economic classes; that modern education tends to increase rather than decrease the number of offspring per family." See Lamson, Herbert D., "Differential Reproduction in China," *Quarterly Review of Biology*, X: 308–321, September 1935. There is also some suggestion from data supplied by Frank W. Notestein, of the Milbank Memorial Fund, that fertility increases slightly with size of farm among rural Chinese completed families. (See ch. XIII in Buck, J. L.: *Land Utilization in China*, Shanghai, 1936.)

tionship in the United States between fertility and social or economic status. There is, for example, a pronounced tendency toward net reproductive loss among the families of urban workers in occupations that usually require high school training or its equivalent, causing a net decrease of 10 to 35 percent per generation among these groups. Furthermore, it is well established that families on relief are on the average more fertile than nonrelief families in the same community, although there is no evidence that relief status as such has any influence on this differential. This is a striking illustration of the general finding that families on the margin of decent subsistence or actually submerged in poverty are often characterized by high fertility. It is hardly necessary to argue the fact that poverty means handicapped child development. Present differential birth rates subject a disproportionately large number of children in each succeeding generation to the blighting effects of poverty. Furthermore, the larger average number of children born to poor parents places an unequal share of the economic burden of replacing the Nation's population on the very families that are least able to bear this special responsibility.

Evidence regarding the reproductive tendencies of persons affected by severe physical or mental handicaps, which in some cases may be hereditary, is meager. The institutional care of persons suffering from mental breakdown at an early age obviously restricts their fertility. Furthermore, extreme handicaps may often prove a bar to marriage and reproduction. A study of data on the number of brothers or sisters of children examined at a Chicago clinic shows that, whereas the children with low normal intelligence come on the average from larger families than those with high intelligence ratings, the number of brothers and sisters in the families of children classified as imbeciles or idiots was no higher than the general average. Nevertheless, it seems clear that the prevention of reproduction by persons handicapped by severe mental deficiency or by disabling physical conditions that appear to be hereditary is socially desirable.

Questions relating to qualitative population trends call for more extensive scientific study. There is need for further definition and measurement of physical and mental characteristics influencing health and personality, and study of conditions affecting individual development. There is also need for the systematic investigation of the influence on the size of family of various economic, social, and psychological factors, about which very little is known at the present time.

4. Opportunity for Individual Development

Opportunity for individual development has been suggested as an American ideal that might be used as a test of population policies. An associated idea, equality of opportunity, has been set forth as the final test of good government by American statesmen.

Popular attention is now centered on the question of economic opportunity. It has already been shown that the outlook in certain areas is limited by the unfavorable relation of population to the natural resources and characteristic occupations of these regions. The possibility of raising levels of living in such places depends either on the movement of part of the present population to other places or on the development of new types of economic adjustment. But any effective movement of population from areas of low opportunity must depend upon an expansion of industry and commerce elsewhere. A general increase in opportunities for employment is therefore fundamental, if the problems of regional overpopulation are to be solved.

Security of the opportunity to work for all who are able and willing to do so is coming to be recognized as a major responsibility, perhaps the first responsibility, of civilized government. Millions of unemployed workers represent a tragic, obvious waste of human resources. Potential contributions to the common good are left unrealized, and individual development and happiness are impaired. The need is for economic adjustment that will stabilize economic development in relation to long-time trends. The actual mechanisms for accomplishing this purpose involve problems in the field of economics beyond the scope of this report. Sound distribution of population, healthy reproduction trends, and opportunities for individual development depend on the establishment of a more adaptable and progressive economy.

Tremendous advances have been made during the past few decades in improving physical development and health. There is evidence that people are actually taller and more broad-shouldered today than 50 years ago.[8] The control of sources of infection and the care of tubercular patients has reduced the death toll of tuberculosis from 201 deaths per 100,000 population in 1900 to 57 deaths in 1934.[9] The death rate from typhoid fever has been reduced to one-tenth of that prevailing in 1900. Using data for Massachusetts, which are available for earlier years, we find that, whereas 158 out of every 1,000 infants born alive in 1890 died

[8] Ch. VI, sec. 2.
[9] Ch. VII, sec. 2.

within 1 year, the frequency of such deaths (Massachusetts, white population) had been reduced to 59 in 1929–31. During the same interval more than 17 years were added to the total expectation of life at birth.[10] These recent advances are due chiefly to improved economic conditions, sanitation, and public health measures. The possibility of further gains through the application of knowledge already attained is shown by the fact that the expectation of life at birth is now about 6 years higher in New Zealand than in the United States. In fact, the extension to all groups in all parts of the country of conditions most favorable to health already enjoyed by the white population in some parts of the United States would effect a reduction of some 400,000 deaths each year.

In theory, the ideal of equal opportunity for health receives very general support. Medical ethics recognizes no distinction between individuals except as to their health needs. Generous efforts have been made by public and private agencies, aided by the voluntary support of individual practitioners, to supply medical care for those who cannot pay for it. Provision for nutrition is generally considered the first necessity in relief. Nevertheless, there still remain among American groups large differences in mortality rates, physical development, and health which have, at least in part, an economic basis. Some of the problems raised by such differences in health fall within the recognized sphere of public health responsibility; others relate to the treatment of individuals. The present cost of adequate medical care is often beyond the reach of persons in moderate circumstances. This raises problems of difficulty and importance.

Public health responsibility for control of epidemic diseases such as smallpox, cholera, diphtheria, yellow fever, and typhoid fever has long been recognized. The field of public health has been gradually extended to include dissemination of health information, provision for public health nurses, and establishment of public clinics. With respect to many diseases, however, the responsibility of the community is still insufficiently recognized.

Special attention is needed for the diseases which lower vitality and which require control of environmental conditions. Malaria is foremost among such diseases at the present time. The fundamental attack on malaria is eradication of mosquito breeding grounds in affected areas, through drainage or the spraying of large bodies of stagnant water where drainage is impracticable. Typhoid fever still takes an unnecessarily large toll in certain localities. This might be eliminated by the systematic application of methods for control already well established elsewhere. The common cold

makes a terrific drain on the efficiency and comfort of the population. Related diseases, especially pneumonia, are a major cause of death. The whole field of the respiratory diseases is one in which great progress may be expected in the near future.

Little progress has been made in the United States toward the control of venereal disease. The experience of Sweden and Denmark in effecting marked reduction of these diseases through the adoption of simple public health measures shows what might be done here within a relatively short time.

The problem of mental disease is perhaps the most baffling in the entire field of health at the present time. Sixty percent of all occupied hospital beds in the United States are now assigned to patients suffering from nervous and mental diseases. The causes of mental breakdown are still largely obscure. Hereditary factors play an important, though possibly a minor, part in the most common types of mental disease. The problem of mental illness is sometimes confused in public discussion with the problem of mental deficiency, although little relation exists between them. Present evidence indicates that hereditary factors play a very important role in causing mental deficiency. Data as to the extent and distribution both of mental deficiency and of mental disease are extremely meager at present. There is therefore need for an extensive series of mental health surveys in sample communities, with uniform procedures, to supply accurate information. Such surveys might throw great light on conditions affecting various types of mental disorder.

There are many other possibilities for great improvement of physical well-being, the prevention of disease, and the saving of life—through better nutrition, improvement of working conditions and safeguards against accidents, provision for healthier ways of life and more adequate medical care for the whole population, as well as through further advance in medical science.

Application of the idea of equal opportunity to the problems of cultural relations, personality, and education has important implications—though the fact of individual differences in equipment and interest must always be taken into account. There is not and cannot be equality among individuals with regard to hereditary capacities. The chance distribution of genes must always give rise to diversity of natural endowment. This is in large part beyond human control, although the proportion of persons handicapped by hereditary deficiencies might be reduced by intelligent social action. Variations in environmental situations must always give rise to infinite variety of personality. We should not want this to

---

[10] Ch. VII, sec. 6.

be otherwise, except as regards conditions that definitely thwart personality development or lead to serious strains or mental breakdown.

The failure of the traditional public school programs to provide for the unusual child may leave capacities for leadership in science, art, and public affairs unrecognized and undeveloped. Furthermore, if education is to be a vital part of the experience of growing boys and girls and of mature adults, it must be elastic and intelligently related to the real needs of individuals in their particular communities.

It is possible, though unproved, that there may be significant differences in average vitality or hereditary capacity for intellectual development between large population groups in this country at present. Whether or not this is true, environmental situations creating unequal opportunity play a far greater role at present in causing group variations in levels of cultural-intellectual development. Such differences must always be taken into account in interpreting statistical data on population trends, health, intelligence, and personality traits.

The areas having a high ratio of children to adult population are usually also areas of meager economic resources. Analysis of the tax resources of many rural areas shows that they cannot be expected to maintain, at local expense, educational facilities equal to those in regions of greater natural resources or more advanced economic development.[11] In many States where expenditure for education per child is lower than the national average, this expenditure represents a relatively large percentage of the total taxable resources of the State. There is no significant correlation between adequacy of financial support for education and the effort made to supply such support.

The recent increase in the number of young people continuing their education beyond the elementary grades puts a heavy strain on the facilities of the secondary schools. The proportion of children 14 to 17 years of age enrolled in high schools rose from about 32 percent in 1920 to 51 percent in 1930; by 1936 the figure had risen to more than 60 percent. Educational progress has been made even more difficult by the presence of many young people who might prefer to be gainfully employed but who continue schooling in preference to idleness. The situation would, of course, be improved by greater opportunities for employment. It is also possible that other types of educational experience may be developed. Some aspects of the Civilian Conservation Corps are suggestive in this connection.

Secondary education in the United States was formerly organized as preparation for ad-

vanced study along classical lines. Then there came a strong reaction in the direction of specific training for jobs. The idea of education as the organization and enlargement of experience has not made great headway. Much classroom performance has been unrelated to community situations outside; the irrelevance of much classical education is widely recognized. It is perhaps not so well recognized that much vocational training offered in secondary schools is equally irrelevant to the needs of individuals in a period of specialization and frequent occupational shifts, by reason of failure to base the training program on the occupational needs of the community. Too often such programs are merely amplifications and expansions of former manual training or industrial arts programs.

The field of vocational education is one that merits and is receiving intensive and critical study. Training for specialized machine tending, unless related to broader education in technical principles and industrial processes, may well be treated as the responsibility of the industries requiring this training, to be carried out at their expense at the time of actual placement, under some measure of government supervision. On the other hand, instruction in basic principles underlying many operations may be regarded as an important function in public education. Specifically, two sets of such principles may be cited: (1) the mechanical principles fundamental to machine processes; and (2) the linguistic and numerical processes that underlie various clerical operations. Such widely applicable vocational training would help to prepare the individual for transfer from one job to another. Fundamental educational values can be realized as well by this kind of training as by traditional courses. Work is a part of life; education should help to make possible effective work and the securing of satisfaction from it.

There is a wealth of material in scientific discovery, economic and social studies, the history of civilization, and the best literary and artistic creations, to arouse the imaginations of American children. Each is now called upon to play a part in a stirring period when the Nation must adapt itself to rapidly changing conditions. The school should prepare him for his part in this drama. Teaching of the physical and social sciences has importance far beyond the accumulation of facts. It should be the means of training young people to think scientifically. The field of the social sciences offers a special challenge to the educator. If he can convey to the child a realization of actual working and living conditions, and develop an objective attitude toward them, he will fulfill an important social function.

There is an inevitable lag in integrating scientific and social advance into the formal educational system. Traditional materials become

---

[11] The detailed discussion of this question in ch. VIII is summarized in table 13 in that chapter.

entrenched in the curriculum and many teachers know how to use only these materials. A further lag is occasioned by the necessity of translating scientific and social research into educational procedures, and the need for experiment with new methods of presentation. It is important that educators in all parts of the country should be kept in close touch with significant developments relating to their work and aided in appraising such developments and applying them in different situations. The United States Office of Education, in addition to its assigned administrative responsibilities, can play a far larger role than at present in furthering the progress of American education. A more extensive, imaginative, and critical program of inquiry and leadership is needed. This is dependent on increased financial support. The role of the Federal Office of Education can be enlarged in this way without raising the question of State jurisdiction and control of educational procedures, while encouraging the provision by each State of adequate and equal educational opportunities.

The whole course of American development has been conditioned by geographic variety and by diversity of cultural background. Old-world cultures have been run into new molds, and have given rise to new patterns of living. Any attempt to force uniformity of ideas and behavior involves the subordination of all other interests to some dominant pattern. Religious toleration and insistence on local responsibility have been cardinal principles in the American tradition, but these principles have been threatened at times by repressive movements advanced in the name of Americanism. Frequently, too, these principles have not been extended to minority groups. Intolerance of cultural differences may damage the self-respect and conflict with the family loyalties of children brought up in traditions that differ from those of the dominant group in their community. Furthermore, the attempt to create uniformity usually results in spiritual impoverishment. It is easier to destroy old loyalties and artistic interests than to build new ones. The appreciation of cultural diversity protects individual interests and enhances the cultural resources of the Nation.

Respect for cultural diversity must, however, be distinguished from arbitrary or romantic antiquarianism. The customs of some isolated rural groups, which outsiders may regard as quaint or picturesque, are likely to disappear as the lines of communication are extended. So far as such regional characteristics are rooted in poverty or isolation, they may be expected to wither with the extension of communication and transportation. Much that is good may be lost in this process but artificial attempts to prevent such changes are certain to prove futile. On the other hand, so far as local customs, traditions, art forms, and social patterns can be preserved along with rising standards of living and the extension of communication, such diversity should be encouraged. Both the particular groups concerned and the common cultural heritage will benefit.

The problems of the adjustment of immigrants in American communities and problems of the cultural interaction between rural and urban areas have a closer relationship than is usually realized. Most of the immigrants to the United States came from rural communities, bringing with them rural habits of living, respect for tradition, strong family loyalties, and high birth rates. They settled chiefly in industrial centers. Accordingly, their relations with older American families were marked from the start by much cultural isolation. There was some mutual appreciation, but apprehension and conflict were more common. The cultural situation in many industrial areas has been further complicated by the presence of new native groups. Negroes from the rural South have migrated cityward, along with whites of Anglo-Saxon origin from the cotton and tobacco areas, the coastal plains, isolated Appalachian districts, the prairie States and the far West. The processes of cultural assimilation in American cities have been more rapid than has sometimes been supposed. The recent rapid decline in the birth rate among immigrants and in rural areas, and the low birth rate of urban Negroes, are evidences of this change.

In many cases, however, the assimilation of traditional cultures has not been accompanied by any lessening of social tension, but rather by a shift of conflict from cultural to economic and social issues. New lines of division differentiate agricultural and industrial groups, commercial and subsistence farmers, owners and tenants, machine operatives and white-collar workers, families having hereditary wealth and families having none, and persons of varying degrees of education.

The cultural significance of the new instruments of mass communication, notably the movies and the radio, and the influence of mass production on personal tastes, remain obscure. There appears to be a strong trend toward standardization, more or less at a dead level of artistic production, but there is also clear evidence of important movements in the direction of experimentation and diversity.

The machine age has brought new cultural needs, with possibilities for richer and better ordered living, as well as for increasing disorder. In this situation there is need for emphasis on the development of scientific habits of thought, the encouragement of a diversity of cooperative activities, and the reinforcement of conditions favorable to family life.

The health of the country has been greatly improved by advances in medical science and their application through public health administration. Notable further improvement could be accomplished by introducing into more communities, city and rural, methods for the conservation of life and health which have already been shown to be successful elsewhere. Furthermore, the continued advance in medical science is constantly bringing forward new leads which may result in improvement in directions not yet pursued. There are clear opportunities for great advances in the further control of common infectious diseases, especially those of the respiratory organs, the control of venereal disease, and the elimination of typhoid fever and malaria. Improvement in the prognosis for cancer through more prompt diagnosis, the removal of industrial hazards, and the improvement of nutrition likewise offer great possibilities.

More than half the occupied hospital beds in this country are assigned to patients suffering from mental diseases. The social, economic, and medical aspects of these diseases, whereof the causes are still largely unknown, are very serious. They deserve the most intensive study.

Attempts to insure medical, surgical, and hospital care of individuals through organized group services have been made, in one way or another, in various communities here and in other countries with much success. Wider extension of such arrangements in the United States should be actively encouraged.

There is clear evidence of gross inequality in educational opportunity in different parts of the country. In general, facilities are most meager in the very areas where there is the highest ratio of children to adults. The fact that these areas are sources of out-migration to other parts of the country makes these inequalities of more than local interest. Especially is it important that good schools should be provided for rural youth. Analysis shows that local tax resources in many areas are insufficient for the maintenance of adequate school opportunities, judged by national standards. This handicap applies in some cases to whole States.

Social forces affecting the life of the people of the United States today are of the greatest complexity. The traditional ways of living of those who comprise the Nation have been in many cases destroyed by migration to new scenes, the conditions of urban living, and the impact of new techniques of production and communication. In this situation, there is need for emphasis above all else on conditions enhancing cultural progress, the mutual understanding and tolerance of diverse groups, and opportunities for the free intellectual and spiritual development of individuals.

With local control of education in this country, there has developed a great variety of experiment and research in this field. There is need for the coordination, critical interpretation, and dissemination to the whole country of *the results of significant advances in educational research and administration. It is recommended that the United States Office of Education be organized and equipped to carry out these important functions.*

5. Research on Population Problems

The investigation of population problems having broad social significance was in the past carried on largely, if at all, by individual scholars or small research groups. By reason of changing conditions, there is now a more widespread interest in these subjects. In fact, in some countries extreme population policies have been adopted hastily and uncritically. The scientific development of this subject is therefore a matter of great importance.

Research in population and in other social science fields has been advanced by a new sense of public responsibility for conditions affecting human welfare. The results of this are seen in the extension of public health activities, education, the social security program, and in many other developments. The need for more systematic investigation relating to the soundness of public works planned for future needs, as well as that relating to private enterprises, creates further demand for more extensive and more accurate demographic data. These changes are leading to an increased emphasis on population research, both in the work of governmental agencies and in the plans of foundations, universities, and various local agencies.

Governmental needs, responsibilities, and opportunities in this field are described in appendix A of this report, supplemented by a guide to serials and current research projects on population and related subjects by Federal agencies (appendix B). A description of the continuous register system of population accounting now in use in several European countries is also presented here (appendix C).

The Federal Government has primary responsibility for the collection and presentation of many types of basic demographic data and shares responsibility with local and private agencies for their elaboration and interpretation. Several specific suggestions are offered in line with this objective.

There is great need for strengthening the regular research agencies in the Federal Government concerned with population studies, especially the Population and Research Divisions of the Bureau of the Census and the Division of Farm Population and Rural Life of the Bureau of Agricultural Economics. All of these divisions are making valuable contributions, but lack sufficient funds to carry out effectively the programs for which they are responsible.

It is advisable that the Federal census of population be established on a 5-year basis, with continued efforts to secure more accurate and more complete enumeration.

The regular census of population should be supplemented by sampling studies in selected areas to supply information (1) regarding intercensal trends in population movements, and (2) on special topics not covered by the regular census.

In view of the importance of regional and local studies, provisions should be made for more extensive analysis and presentation of population data for standard areas. Such areas should be drawn within State boundaries (or divided between areas in several States) and wherever possible should be composed of county units. It is probable that 300 to 400 such areas, including the metropolitan districts (or State divisions thereof) as separate units, would serve this purpose. It is recommended that the Central Statistical Board give attention to the problem of preparing such a series of areas for statistical purposes, in cooperation with the agencies primarily concerned with social statistics.

In view of the importance of independent regional and local initiative in so large and varied a country as the United States, special effort should be directed toward strengthening local research agencies concerned with population studies. Such local agencies may be expected to carry out significant researches on the relation of demographic data to economic and social conditions affecting migration, reproduction, and health. Special attention should be directed to enhancing the work of the State planning boards as coordinating agencies in this field.

No definite recommendation is made at this time regarding the possible adoption of the continuous-register system of population accounting, now in use in Sweden, Belgium, and The Netherlands. It is, however, recommended that further investigation be made of the advantages and disadvantages of this procedure and its possible application to the situation in this country.

EDWIN B. WILSON, *Chairman.*
DAVID L. EDSALL.
L. C. GRAY.
CHARLES H. JUDD.
WILLIAM F. OGBURN.
WARREN S. THOMPSON.
FRANK LORIMER, *Technical Secretary.*

I. THE TREND OF POPULATION: ECONOMIC ASPECTS

1. Historical Background

Population Increase in the Eighteenth and Nineteenth Centuries

It is likely that colonial America was the scene of the most rapid natural increase of population in human history. There was a large proportion of young adults of reproductive age in the Colonies. Conditions of living, after the perilous period of first settlement was over, were relatively healthful. The colonists were imbued with the enthusiasm of a new world. The biblical admonition, "Be fruitful, multiply and replenish the earth", seemed peculiarly appropriate to their situation. Before them stretched the wilderness to be possessed and cultivated. The young Nation responded exuberantly to this ideal, more than doubling itself in each generation.

Each fertile married woman in the Revolutionary period, according to an estimate by Lotka, bore on the average eight children (the exact estimate for the year 1790 is 7.76, with an inference that at an earlier date the figure may have been even higher). After 1810 the ratio of children to women of childbearing age was lower, with one exception, at each succeeding census; but the rate of natural increase remained high throughout the eighteenth, nineteenth, and early twentieth centuries. Rapid natural increase in the New World was supplemented by a constant inflow of immigrants, which rose to large proportions during the latter half of the nineteenth and the first quarter of the twentieth century.

The colonial population increased from about 275,000 in 1700 to 2,200,000 in 1770, an average increase of 34.7 percent per decade.[1] A similar rate of growth marked the period between the Revolutionary and Civil Wars. The absolute population added to the Nation each decade increased until the World War, although the rate of decennial increase gradually declined.

---

[1] See table 1.

Population growth in America was not an isolated phenomenon. It was the expression, in its most acute form, of the general trend toward increase of population characteristic of all European peoples in this period. The medieval period had been marked by local advances and recessions of population, which probably resulted in net increase; but it is extremely difficult to obtain any reliable estimate of population changes in Europe from classical to early modern times. The development of science and trade in the seventeenth century stimulated a remarkable population growth, so that the people of Europe and their descendants in other lands increased from about 100 million persons in 1650 to 642 million in 1929. This expansion is represented graphically in figure 1, where the land area of each continent is proportional to the estimated total number of white inhabitants at each date. During the same period the non-European stocks apparently increased about threefold, or half as fast as the peoples of Europe. Thus the nineteenth and twentieth centuries probably witnessed the greatest expansion of world population in all time. The spearhead of this thrust appears in American population growth.

Relation of Population Growth to Economic Expansion in the United States

Population growth in America supplied the basis for an equally remarkable expansion of economic activity. The early American situation placed a high premium on energy and initiative. The opening up of new areas, the expansion of population, and establishment of new industries covered the scars of mistaken undertakings. The whole American economy, as André Siegfried has pointed out, was based on an abundance of resources and a scarcity of labor. Local excesses of labor supply could be relieved by migration to other areas, as illustrated by old tobacco-growing counties in tidewater Virginia that have a smaller population today than in 1790.

The best vacant lands had been ceded by 1890, but the Far West remained an area of special opportunity, attracting a great stream of migrants through the next four decades. In fact, the largest addition through internal migration to the population of any State in any decade is represented by the net movement of 1,650,000 persons from other States to California between 1920 and 1930. Although there have been gradual accumulations of population without adequate economic resources in some parts of the United States, the spread of population and economic exploitation of natural resources, and the development of new enterprises in the West, have supplied a safety valve for economic disorders in other parts of the country.

This era has apparently come to an end. The posting of guards on the California border in the last few years symbolizes the fact that free expansion into undeveloped areas has ceased to be an automatic-adjustment-mechanism for the maladjustments of a planless economy.

The idea that we are approaching an era of stationary or decreasing population comes as something of a shock to most Americans. The dividends of population expansion in America have naturally accrued in greatest measure to the owners of established enterprises and to persons of unusual initiative among those first on the scene. American families that found themselves in possession of property located along the main lines of population advance or had acquired shares in enterprises serving an expanding market, through the sound judgment of their founders or sheer good luck, have enjoyed the most privileged economic position of any large group in the world. The advantages of population growth have also been shared by American wage earners and their families in areas serving growing populations. Thus, the idea that population growth is a boon has become firmly rooted in our thinking. "Bigger" has come to be regarded as a synonym for "better." Even in the sober language of the census, a population increase is a "gain", a decrease is a "loss." Some demographers almost unconsciously speak of a trend toward natural increase as "favorable", and the term "population decline" carries a sinister note.

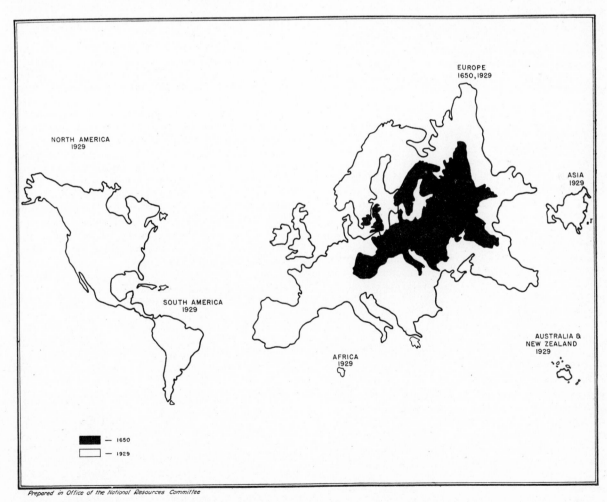

FIGURE 1.—The expansion of Europe. Land areas proportional to unmixed European stocks in 1650 and in 1929. Based on estimates by Willcox in *International Migrations*, vol. II, Interpretations.

The question of whether a further increase or decrease of population would be generally advantageous or harmful is one that should be approached in the spirit of critical inquiry rather than on the basis of preconceived assumptions.

World Population Problems

In Europe, too, the history of the last few centuries has established the idea that natural increase is the normal characteristic of a healthy nation. The increase of European population during the last two centuries, while the economic level was also rising, was sustained by technological advances in agriculture, industry, and medicine and by the development of an elaborate structure of specialized production and international trade.

This structure involves serious economic and political hazards in a world at war or disturbed by the threat of war. The volume of foreign trade for European countries was greater on the eve of the depression than the total volume of primary domestic production. In 1929, the value of foodstuffs and industrial raw materials produced in Europe was equivalent to 21 billion dollars.[2] Imports to European countries that year amounted to 19.7 billion and exports to 16.1 billion dollars (total, 35.8 billion).[3] An index for world trade (1929 base) fell to 68 in 1932, but rose again to 83 in 1935. Meanwhile the production of foodstuffs for the world as a whole remained practically constant through this period, while the index of industrial production (1929 base), after declining to 66 in 1932, passed the 100 mark again in 1935 and reached 105 toward the end of the year.[4] Europe and the Americas can produce enough materials to support their present great populations. The problem has become one of ensuring efficient distribution, stability, and orderly progress.

Commerce and imperialism have also stimulated population growth in oriental lands. Although in some instances conquest has resulted in the destruction of primitive peoples, in other cases it has imposed peace on lands formerly subject to frequent tribal conflicts. The economic organization established by imperialist nations, while not such as to bring about a high standard of living for the native populations, has tended to maintain the food supply and sanitary control. These effects are strikingly illustrated in the case of India, where the enumerated population increased from 318,900,000 in 1921 to 352,800,000 in 1931. The result was a population density of over 200 persons per square mile (five times as great as in the United States). The nineteenth century was the period of maximum population growth

for Europe. It seems likely that, barring some tremendous disaster, the twentieth century will be the period of maximum population growth for Asia. This continent already contains over 1,000 million people, or more than half of the population of the globe. The figure set opposite Asia in the last *Statistical Year Book of the League of Nations* is 1,121,200,000, but no exact statement is possible, as the best estimates of the population of China are subject to a margin of error of a hundred million or so.

The decline in international trade resulting from the World War and its attendant economic maladjustments, including a feverish insistence on economic nationalism, the increasing density of population in some areas, and the growing political power of nations with few colonial possessions, give rise to world problems of staggering proportions. But such problems lie mainly outside the scope of this report. The geographic position of the United States makes it possible to give attention to the objectives of national development in this country with less anxiety than is possible for nations not so fortunately situated, and to pursue those objectives largely in isolation, if that should be necessary.

2. The Trend of Total Population

Factors Affecting Number of Births and Deaths

It is important to bear in mind that the number of births and deaths is affected by (1) the size of the base population, (2) fertility and mortality rates at specific ages, and (3) the age and sex distribution of the population. Due to the effects of past immigration and previous rapid population growth, the age distribution of the present population of the United States is temporarily characterized by an abnormal proportion of young adults, at the very ages that are biologically productive and at which death comes less frequently than in the early or in the late years of life. The forces now at work will inevitably result in a gradual increase in the proportion of aged people. As this comes about, the crude death rate (i. e., deaths per 1,000 total population) will tend to rise. This trend may be partially offset by further decreases in age-specific death rates, but not to such an extent as to prevent an increase in the total number of deaths each year. At the same time, a gradual decrease after about 1945 in the number of young females at the most fertile childbearing ages, even if there were no further decrease in age-specific fertility rates, would cause a continued decrease after this time in the number of births occurring each year.

The Peak of Population Growth

Due to the rapidity with which the original population of the United States has increased,

[2] *League of Nations. World Production and Prices, 1925–1933*, p. 113.
[3] *League of Nations. Review of World Trade, 1923*, p. 15.
[4] International Labour Conference, Twentieth Session, *Report of the Director*, Geneva (1936), p. 6.

it is not commonly realized that the birth rate has been declining for nearly a century. Until recently its effects have been counterbalanced by a decided decrease in mortality rates, by heavy immigration of adults, and by the fact that there has been a large proportion of the females in the childbearing ages. It is evident, however, that since the mortality rate cannot decline indefinitely, and since immigration is now drastically restricted, the decline in the birth rate must soon outweigh the factors tending to increase the population and bring about a decline in annual increments of population growth. In fact this turning point was reached about 1925. In the early twenties (1920–24) about 1,880,000 persons were being added to the population each year. Ten years later (1930–34) the increase averaged less than half as many—about 900,000 persons per year. Part of this spectacular change in the rate of increase was due to the decline in net immigration from about 400,000 per year to a net emigration of nearly 60,000 per year; but the major factor has been the decrease in the excess of births over deaths.

Changes in the total number of births, deaths, and natural increase per year in the United States during the last 25 years are shown in figure 2. It should be noted that the values in this chart represent absolute total numbers, and not rates. Decrease in rates of birth, death, and natural increase have been much more rapid, but these changes have until recently been offset by continual increases in the total population subject to these rates. It may be noted that the yearly number of deaths has been fairly constant during this period; the drop in the death rates at particular ages has been offset by the increase and gradual aging of the total population. The recent decline in net excess of births over deaths has come about chiefly from a gradual decrease in the absolute number of births each year.

The record of population growth in this country from 1650 to 1935 is shown in table 1 (see also fig. 5 below). The absolute numbers for all dates after 1850 represent estimates as of July 1 for each census year. The number for 1870 has been adjusted in accordance with a census estimate for underenumeration.[5] A similar adjustment has also been made in accordance with an estimate by this committee of apparent underenumeration in 1920. The number shown here for that year is derived from the 1930 population, after making allowance for age-specific death rates of native whites and Negroes, and assuming a proportional correction factor for underenumeration of foreign-born whites and other races.[6] These

[5] See *Fourteenth Census, Population*, vol. 2, pp. 15–29.
[6] The procedure followed in this estimate is presented in the *Statistical Supplement*. It may be noted that the results obtained by this process could be ascribed to a fictitious addition of native elements in 1930, resulting from the reporting of foreign-born persons as native in excess of any correspond-

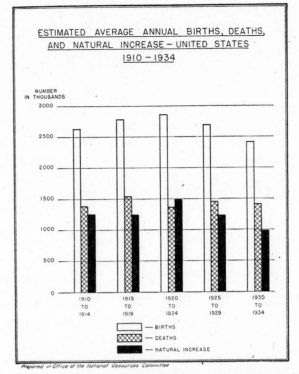

FIGURE 2.—Natural increase of total population, United States, 1910–34 Data for 1910–29 are from estimates prepared by the Scripps Foundation for Research in Population Problems. Data for 1930–34 estimated from current reports of the Bureau of the Census.

TABLE 1.—*Population, amount of increase and percent of increase, United States, 1650–1935* [1]

Year	Population (thousands)	Increase (thousands)	Decennial percent increase
1650	52		
1660	85	33	64.0
1670	114	30	35.0
1680	156	41	35.9
1690	214	58	37.2
1700	275	62	28.8
1710	358	82	30.0
1720	474	117	32.7
1730	655	181	38.1
1740	889	234	35.7
1750	1,207	318	35.8
1760	1,610	403	33.4
1770	2,205	595	37.0
1780	2,781	576	26.1
1790	3,929	1,148	41.3
1800	5,308	1,379	35.1
1810	7,240	1,931	36.4
1820	9,638	2,399	33.1
1830	12,866	3,228	33.5
1840	17,069	4,203	32.7
1850	23,260	6,191	36.3
1860	31,502	8,242	35.4
1870	39,904	8,402	26.7
1880	50,262	10,358	26.0
1890	63,056	12,794	25.5
1900	76,129	13,073	20.7
1910	92,267	16,138	21.2
1920	107,190	14,923	16.2
1930	123,091	15,901	14.8
1935 [2]	[2] 127,521	[2] 4,430	[3] 7.2

[1] See text.
[2] 5-year interval.
[3] Decennial percentage increase corresponding to increase of 3.6 percent in 5-year interval.

ing fictitious addition to native elements in 1920, or to an increase in native elements resulting from unrecorded immigration. It is possible, but hardly probable that such defects in the basic data are of sufficient magnitude to account entirely for the discrepancy between the population figures for native elements in 1920 and in 1930.

figures do not include any correction for under-enumeration of children under 5 years of age (amounting to about 5 percent for whites and to about 15 percent for Negroes), as this is assumed to be a fairly constant error in the entire series.

Estimates of Future Population

The estimates of future population presented here were prepared for this report by Warren S. Thompson and P. K. Whelpton, of the Scripps Foundation for Research in Population Problems. They represent a revised application of the methods used in preparing estimates for the President's Research Committee on Social Trends. The detailed estimates, by age, sex, and race-nativity groups, will be presented in a statistical supplement to this report.

The figures for the future population of the United States prepared by the Scripps Foundation for Research in Population Problems for the National Resources Committee do not represent prophecies—the result of "second sight"—but only what will occur if birth rates, death rates, and immigration follow certain assumed trends. In fact, it is possible that their greatest value lies not in indicating what the population may be, but in showing the effect on future growth of different trends of birth rates, death rates, and immigration. From either viewpoint, however, a brief description of the trends used should make the figures on population more significant to the reader.

DEATH RATES

For several generations the prevention of death and the prolonging of human life have been looked upon as greatly to be desired in time of peace, and have been the goal of much public and private effort. Chiefly as a result of these endeavors death rates have been lowered greatly, and the length of life increased correspondingly. In Massachusetts, for example, the average new-born boy baby would live

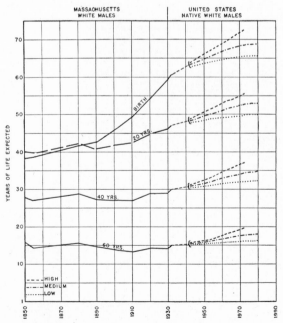

FIGURE 3.—Expectation of life at birth, at age 20, at age 40, and at age 60, Massachusetts, 1789–1931, and estimated future trend for United States. White males.

34.5 years according to death rates of 1789, but this was lengthened to 46.1 years by 1900–1902, and to 59.3 years by 1929–1931. Births and deaths were not registered in all the States before 1933, but judging from the information that is available, mortality conditions have been improved in the Nation about as much as in Massachusetts, and expectation of life at birth has been almost doubled in the last 140 years.

Other nations under the influence of western civilization also have made much progress in lowering death rates and lengthening life, New Zealand, Australia, and Sweden having even surpassed the United States. According to 1931 death rates in New Zealand, the expectation of life at birth was 65 years for males and 67.9 years for females compared with 59.1 and 62.7 for white males and females in the United States during 1929–31.

Looking ahead 50 years in the United States, there seems no likelihood that the desire to postpone death and prolong life will weaken. It is to be expected, therefore, that the increase in longevity will be limited only by human ability to bring about such change. Because of the success that has rewarded efforts to lower death rates in the past, and because New Zealand is ahead of the United States at present, it seems almost certain that by 1980 people will be longer lived here than they now are, and that native white males will live at least to 65.6 years and females to 68.4 years as an average. These represent the low assumptions for expectation of life at birth—the high assumptions for mortality—used in the present calculations of future population (see fig. 3).

In choosing the opposite assumptions—high expectation of life and low mortality—it is necessary to consider several conditions. There is no evidence that people are going to live forever—that the span of life (which is about 100 years) has been increasing—but only that a larger proportion of the population may live to a ripe old age. The rapid increase in expectation of life at birth during past decades has resulted from large reductions in death rates of infants and young children, mortality at ages between 10 and 60 having declined only slightly, and little if any improvement having been made at ages over 60. Looking at Massachusetts again, the male expectation of life at birth increased 13.2 years from 1900–1902 to 1929–31 (46.1 to 59.3), but life expectancy at age 20 increased by only 4.3 years (41.8 to 46.1), at age 40 by only 1.8 years (27.2 to 29.0), while at age 60 there was practically no change (13.9 to 14.3). Death rates at ages under 25 are already so low that if all deaths below this age could be prevented and mortality conditions at other ages remain unchanged, the expectation of life at birth would be lengthened by only 6.3 years. Larger increases, therefore, will require the lowering of death rates among adults, particularly among the middle aged, where progress heretofore has not been so easy. One of the leading causes of death in this group—pneumonia—is likely to be reduced rapidly in the future as the serum treatment which has been developed comes into general use. But the other important causes, heart disease, cancer, nephritis, and cerebral hemorrhage are likely to prove much more difficult to control than such former scourges as smallpox, tuberculosis, typhoid fever, and diarrhea and enteritis. In view of the entire situation, it will be surprising if the native white expectation of life reaches the high figures assumed for 1980, namely 72 years for males and 74 years for females.

The medium assumptions are midway between the extremes just described. It seems probable to the staff of the Scripps Foundation that the actual life expectancy of native whites in 1980 will be nearer the medium figures of 68.8 years for males and 71.2 years for females than either the high or low values mentioned above.

Because death rates of foreign-born whites, Negroes, and other colored persons are higher than those of native whites and thus offer greater chance for improvement, they are reduced more rapidly than those for native whites in the high, medium, and low assumptions.

BIRTH RATES

Judging from past events, it would seem that the forces making for decline in the birth rate are even more potent than those making for decline in the death rate, since the former has fallen much more than the latter. The Federal birth registration area was not organized until 1915, but according to the number of children and women enumerated by the census, birth rates in 1800 were about 3½ times as large as in 1930, and even as late as 1880 women were twice as prolific as today. Moreover, at no time in the past does the decline in fertility seem to have been as rapid as from 1925–29 to 1930–34, when a drop of 16.8 percent took place. It is possible that part of the past decrease has come about through physiological changes causing a reduction in the chances of pregnancy, and through changes in such matters as diet and mode of life. The preponderance of evidence, however, is to the effect that the most important cause has been control of family size.

With the present state of knowledge it is apparent that birth rates are subject to human control to a greater extent than death rates; they vary more from year to year with prosperity and depression, and may be reduced more rapidly and to a greater extent if desired. In considering the future trend of death rates the uncertainty is how much reduction it is humanly possible to bring about through control of disease and prevention of accidents and war. With birth rates, on the other hand, the unknown factor is how many children will be wanted. It seems far easier to judge what can be done in lowering death rates in the future than to judge what people may want to do regarding the size of their families; hence the relative difference between the high and low birth rate assumptions which are described below is roughly four times as great as that between the high and low death rate assumptions presented above.

With birth rates at each age of life as they were during 1930–34, 1,000 native white women living through the childbearing period bear 2,158 children). Counting only women who marry (before age 50), there are about 2,410 births per 1,000 married women. Decreasing the number of women still further by excluding those who bear no children (estimated at about one-sixth of the group) raises the expected number of births to approximately 2,900 per 1,000 fertile women. In other words, under birth rates of recent years the average native white woman living to age 50 bears approximately 2⅕ children; if only those to whom births occur are counted, the average does not rise quite to 3 children per woman. In view of the past trend in the United States, and the lower rates that prevail in certain other nations, the highest assumption that seems justified for native white women in the future is a continuation of the present rates (see "high" assumption, as shown by bottom lines for whites and for Negroes in fig. 4).

As a probable lower limit, it is assumed that the decline in birth rates will continue until 1980, although at a rapidly diminishing rate. For native whites the maximum decrease anticipated in the 50 years after 1930–34 amounts to 31 percent compared with the 34 percent decline in the 25 years prior to 1930–34. According to this low assumption there will be about 1,500 births per 1,000 women living to age 50, or 1½ births to the average woman (see "low" assumption, fig. 4). Allowing for childless women raises this to about two births to the average fertile woman. This is approximately the present situation in California and Washington, D. C., as well as in all of England.

The medium assumption for native whites continues the past decline in birth rates, but slows it up much more rapidly than the low, the 1980 rate be-

ing somewhat nearer the high than the low. It anticipates a decrease of about 13 percent in the next 50 years, with 1,000 women living through the child-bearing period having about 1,900 births. This is slightly less than an average of two births for all women, and slightly more than 2½ per fertile woman. It is approximately the 1930 rate in Massachusetts, Connecticut, Washington, and Oregon, and also in Sweden. In the opinion of the staff of the Scripps Foundation these medium birth rate assumptions are more likely to be followed than either the high or the low. It is admitted, however, that there must be a rather rapid change in attitude regarding the desirability of 3- and 4-child families if this medium trend is not to prove too high.

Birth rates to native white women are somewhat lower than those to foreign-born white, Negro, and other colored women. In the high assumptions this differential is maintained but in the medium assumption it is reduced by one-fourth, and in the low by one-half on the basis that the higher the rate the greater the opportunity for loss in a period of general decline.

IMMIGRATION

During recent years the general attitude toward immigration has been one of disapproval. Permission to enter the United States has been so restricted by laws and regulations that in each year from 1931 to 1935 more people left the Nation than entered. As economic conditions improve, however, there is no assurance that this situation will not change. The present quota laws permit 153,714 immigrants to enter from quota countries, and set no limit on those from other countries. They may be made more or less restrictive by Congress. The administrative regulations which have limited immigration much more rigidly during the depression may be relaxed by the President and Secretary of Labor as easily as they were imposed.

In view of these uncertainties regarding the movement of people in the future the desirable plan in these calculations seems to be to show how the population will grow according to certain trends of birth and death rates if no immigration occurs, and then to show how much larger it will be with the net arrival of 100,000 immigrants annually. Adding to this "with immigration" series the difference between it and the "no immigration" series will give the population if immigration amounts to 200,000 annually. In a similar manner the effect of other amounts of immigration may easily be obtained.[7]

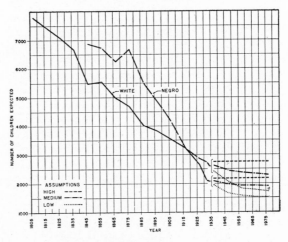

FIGURE 4.—Number of births expected per 1,000 women living through the childbearing ages at estimated birth rates for successive periods, 1810–1980.

---

[7] Statement prepared by Scripps Foundation.

In the judgment of this Committee, the analysis of regional trends in birth rates leads to the conclusion that in some parts of the country where birth rates are still high there will be further decline during the next few decades. Furthermore, it seems extremely unlikely that this decline will be offset by increases of such magnitude, in areas where birth rates are low, as to cause fertility rates for the Nation as a whole to remain constant. Accordingly, emphasis is here placed on the estimates based on "medium" and "low" assumptions as regards fertility, combined with the "medium" assumption as regards mortality (see fig. 5). The results obtained by various hypotheses are shown in table 2.

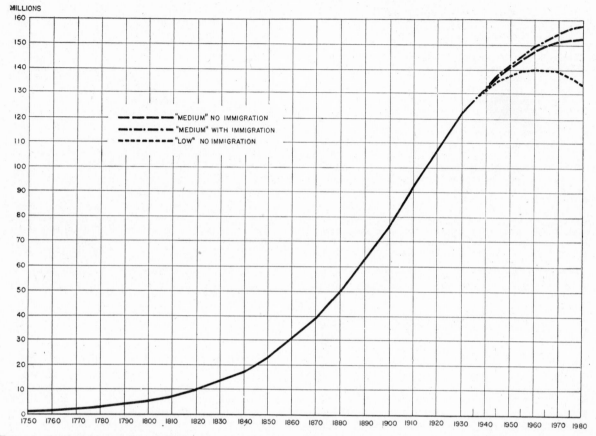

FIGURE 5.—Trend of total population. Actual 1750–1930, estimated 1930–80. "Medium" and "Low" refer to fertility. Both have been combined with "Medium" mortality.

TABLE 2.—*Estimates of total population, at 5-year intervals, Apr. 1, 1930–Apr. 1, 1980* [1]

HYPOTHESES

Mortality	Medium	Medium	Medium	High	Low	Medium	Medium.
Fertility	Low	Medium	Medium	Low	High	High	High.
Annual net immigration after 1940	None	None	100,000 [2]	None	None	None	100,000. [2]
	A	B	C	D	E	F	G
	Thousands	*Thousands*	*Thousands*	*Thousands*	*Thousands*	*Thousands*	*Thousands*
1930	122,775	122,775	122,775	122,775	122,775	122,775	122,775
1935	127,354	127,354	127,354	127,354	127,354	127,354	127,354
1940	131,308	131,993	131,993	131,157	132,613	132,496	132,496
1945	134,586	136,447	136,957	134,139	138,210	137,854	138,363
1950	137,084	140,561	141,645	136,177	143,898	143,154	144,247
1955	138,721	144,093	145,808	137,172	149,353	148,042	149,786
1960	139,457	146,987	149,372	137,089	154,564	152,494	154,941
1965	139,372	149,341	152,421	136,026	159,720	156,696	159,882
1970	138,455	151,170	154,969	134,049	164,836	160,712	164,672
1975	136,680	152,433	156,977	131,221	169,779	164,490	169,269
1980	133,993	153,022	158,335	127,571	174,330	167,899	173,541

[1] See text for description of hypotheses, designated here as "high," "medium," "low." The estimates of future population have been adjusted to correspond to previous census data by the use of constant underenumeration factors for children under 5 years of age. As this adjustment is not made in table 3, the sums of figures for age groups differ somewhat from the totals shown here. Hypotheses A, B, and C are exhibited in fig. 5.
[2] The influence of larger net immigration can be estimated by multiplying the differences between figures with no immigration and figures with 100,000 immigration by corresponding proportions. For example, these differences would be doubled by a net immigration of 200,000 per year.

Future Population by Age Groups

Change in age distribution is a fundamental feature of current population trends. Estimates of changes in numbers of persons in different age classes from 1900 through 1980 are shown in figure 6, on two hypotheses: (A) Medium mortality, low fertility, and no immigration; (B) medium mortality, medium fertility, and no immigration. The corresponding absolute numbers for 1930–80, and those obtained from the third set of assumptions, medium mortality, medium fertility, net immigration of 100,000 per year after 1940 (hypothesis C) are shown in table 3.

TABLE 3.—*Estimated number of persons (in thousands) in specified age classes, 1930–80*

HYPOTHESIS A: LOW FERTILITY, MEDIUM MORTALITY, NO IMMIGRATION

Year	0–4	5–19	20–44	45–64	65 and over
1930	12,143	36,192	47,059	21,431	6,639
1935	10,912	36,370	49,374	23,845	7,482
1940	10,303	35,052	51,396	26,730	8,419
1945	9,983	32,658	54,273	28,517	9,732
1950	9,521	30,623	56,030	30,258	11,205
1955	8,942	29,295	55,810	32,369	12,828
1960	8,319	27,979	54,496	34,335	14,818
1965	7,781	26,357	52,525	36,822	16,347
1970	7,303	24,654	49,636	39,301	17,995
1975	6,872	23,047	46,798	40,366	20,008
1980	6,464	21,627	44,432	39,807	22,051

HYPOTHESIS B: MEDIUM FERTILITY, MEDIUM MORTALITY, NO IMMIGRATION

1930	12,143	36,192	47,059	21,431	6,639
1935	10,912	36,370	49,374	23,845	7,482
1940	11,031	35,052	51,396	26,730	8,419
1945	11,197	33,377	54,273	28,517	9,732
1950	11,181	32,539	56,030	30,258	11,205
1955	10,884	32,842	55,810	32,369	12,828
1960	10,538	32,721	55,199	34,335	14,818
1965	10,302	32,090	54,396	36,822	16,347
1970	10,156	31,237	53,094	39,301	17,995
1975	10,042	30,530	52,098	40,366	20,008
1980	9,906	30,046	51,818	39,807	22,051

HYPOTHESIS C: MEDIUM FERTILITY, MEDIUM MORTALITY, NET IMMIGRATION 100,000 PER YEAR AFTER 1940

1930	12,143	36,192	47,059	21,431	6,639
1935	10,912	36,370	49,374	23,845	7,482
1940	11,031	35,052	51,396	26,730	8,419
1945	11,216	33,498	54,622	28,535	9,736
1950	11,281	32,735	56,774	30,299	11,213
1955	11,050	33,159	56,956	32,450	12,843
1960	10,756	33,202	56,706	34,505	14,842
1965	10,559	32,766	56,169	37,180	16,381
1970	10,454	32,067	55,078	39,958	18,043
1975	10,389	31,489	54,298	41,351	20,083
1980	10,305	31,134	54,247	41,091	22,180

The change in age distribution is a function of two different factors that are not necessarily related. Improvement in conditions affecting health is causing an increase in the proportion of those born alive who reach maturity and survive to more advanced ages. At the same time we are passing out of the period when infants entered the scene in larger numbers each year, while the mature population was made up of the survivors of a much smaller number of infants. For both reasons, the percentage of children in the total population is decreasing, while the percentage of aged persons is growing. Thus in 1900, 44 percent of the population was under 20 years of age; the corresponding figure for 1935 is 37 percent; that for 1980 on hypothesis A is 21 percent, on hypothesis C 25 percent. Conversely, the proportion of those over 65 years has risen from 4 percent in 1900 to 6 percent in 1935 and may be expected to rise to about 15 percent in 1980 (hypothesis A, 16 percent; hypothesis C, 14 percent).

The number of families is determined by the number of persons, their distribution by age and sex, and their habits and economic conditions. In the years preceding 1930 there was a tendency toward earlier marriages and toward the division of larger family groups into smaller units.[8] During the early depression years there was a deficit in marriages and a tendency toward the doubling up of families. It is impossible to measure accurately the influence of these changing conditions on family formation, or to forecast their future course. The figures for the period 1930–80 in table 4 show expected numbers of "private families" (including persons living alone and boarding houses with not over 10 persons) on the arbitrary hypothesis that proportion of persons of each age and sex to be classified as heads of families remain constant, as of 1930.[9] The figure thus obtained for 1935 is certainly above the actual number of private families at that time. The rather large increases indicated by this analysis for the next decade may, however, have more positive significance.

TABLE 4.—*Estimated number of private families in the United States 1900–1980*

	Hypothesis A [2]	Hypothesis C [2]
1900	[1] 16,147,200	
1910	[1] 20,204,900	
1920	[1] 24,290,800	
1930	29,904,663	
1935	31,982,200	31,982,200
1940	34,367,600	34,367,600
1945	36,823,900	36,930,500
1950	39,265,800	39,524,800
1955	41,368,700	41,814,100
1960	43,133,400	43,883,400
1965	44,590,300	45,863,400
1970	45,660,400	47,624,000
1975	46,302,800	49,173,600
1980	46,405,600	50,327,700

[1] Assuming constant ratio of private families to total families, as of 1930. The census reports 15,963,965 private families in 1900, but the definition of quasi-families at that time was more inclusive.

[2] Assuming same ratio of male and female heads of families to total number of male and female persons in each age class as in 1930, using Scripps estimates, assuming medium mortality. See table 3 and accompanying text for description of hypotheses.

[8] If the proportion of persons in each age and sex class reportable as heads of families had been the same in each previous census as in 1930, the number of private families would have exceeded the figure shown here for 1920 by 2.6 percent, that for 1910 by 3.5 percent, and that for 1900 by 1.3 percent.

[9] Somewhat lower estimates were obtained by George Terborgh through another, but similar, method. He estimated future populations by sex and marital status for each race-nativity group (all ages) by applying age-specific marital status ratios to 5-year age classes as given by hypothesis B (table 3 above, with detailed breakdown). He then applied 1930 head-of-family ratios to each of these estimated populations. The results, in thousands, are as follows: 1935, 31,855; 1940, 34,122; 1945, 36,463; 1950, 38,758.

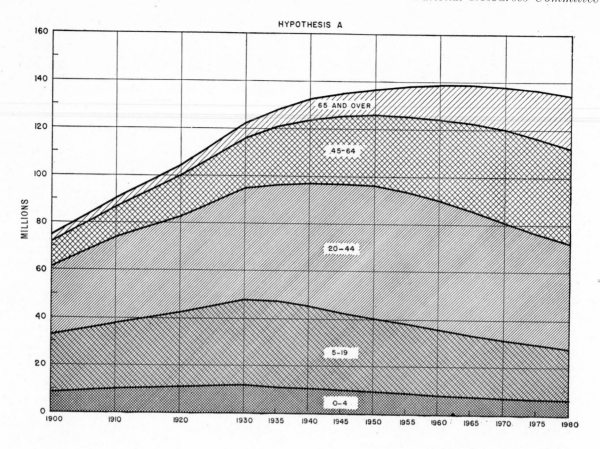

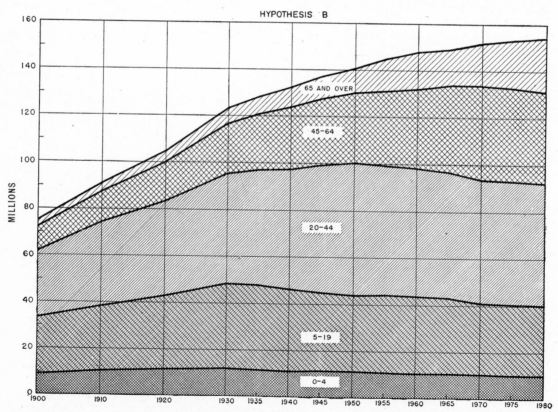

FIGURE 6.—Trend of population by broad age classes, 1900–80. Hypothesis A: medium mortality, low fertility, no immigration, 1935–80.
Hypothesis B: medium mortality, medium fertility, no immigration, 1935–80.

Immigration

It is difficult to forecast the outlook as to immigration, because this depends primarily on public opinion and consequent political action. The restriction of immigration altered one of the most characteristic features of the earlier American scene. Migrants from European countries have come to the United States in waves of varying magnitude. The earliest peaks—approximately 400,000 immigrants annually—appeared in 1854 (about 1.5 percent of the population) and in the early seventies (about 1 percent of the population at this time). A still higher peak of 790,000 immigrants (again about 1.5 percent) was reached in 1882. Through the nineties a fairly low average—under 400,000 per year—prevailed, but the number of immigrants rose rapidly to cross the million mark (but only about 1 percent of the population) in 1905–07, 1910, and 1913–14. A temporary law to restrict immigration, passed in 1921, was succeeded by permanent legislation in 1924. According to the 1924 act, immigration from most countries was limited in direct relation to the estimated numerical contribution of each nation to the population of the United States prior to 1920, allowing a total of about 150,000 immigrants annually from all "quota countries." This restriction does not apply to Canada, Mexico, Cuba, Haiti, countries of Central and South America, or to United States dependencies.

An Executive order of September 1930 instructed consular officers to take into account depression conditions in application of the clause excluding persons likely to become a public charge. As a result of this policy, the number of immigrants entering this country during the past few years has been less than the number of emigrants.

As economic conditions improve, it is probable that the extreme immigration policy of the depression years will be relaxed. It is possible, however, that the experience of the depression may lead to further permanent restrictions. The most likely of these is an extension of the quota principle to countries in the Western Hemisphere. There can be little doubt that all the considerations originally leading to the passage of the Immigration Act of 1924 can be applied with equal or greater force to mass immigration from Mexico: low standards of living, difficulties of cultural adjustment, high reproduction rates. But a general extension of the quota system would still allow a net immigration sufficient to have an appreciable effect on future population growth.

3. Population, Production, and Consumption

International Variations in Agricultural and Industrial Productivity per Worker

It is well known that there are wide variations among nations in average productivity per worker. Some idea of the range of such variations for agriculture is afforded by table 5. The values shown here are derived from data on quantity of production in each country, weighted in accordance with a uniform price scale (United States average farm prices for the years 1917–26), except in the case of Japan where it was necessary to use Japanese prices adjusted in accordance with exchange rates. It should be noted that in each case the value-productivity figure represents total productivity of workers, land, and machinery per worker. It is therefore always higher than a true figure for the value-productivity of each worker. Figures are shown per male worker and per worker (both sexes). In the former case the contribution of female workers is included in the numerator but not in the denominator; their labor, in other words, is "thrown in." Thus the figures "per worker" differ much more between England and Germany than the figures "per male worker", because the proportion of female workers is high in Germany. The figures on proportion of gainfully occupied persons engaged in agriculture are more satisfactory than the figures on farm population for some countries, especially in the case of England. Accordingly, the uniform but somewhat inaccurate procedure is followed of applying the former proportion (derived from data on occupations) to figures on density of total population, to obtain an index of density of farm population.

TABLE 5.—*Population density and value productivity per agricultural worker, England, Germany, Japan proper, and the United States* [1]

Country	Percent of male workers in agriculture	Population per square mile	Index of density of farm population	Value of farm products per year per agricultural worker	
				Males only	All workers
England	8.4	685	58	$1,208	$1,142
Germany	22.7	348	79	803	389
Japan proper	40.8	434	177	214	134
United States	25.1	41	10	[2] 1,370	[2] 1,224
Southeast				[2] 768	[2] 631
All other regions				[2] 1,726	[2] 1,626

[1] Quantity production figures for staple crops, livestock and dairy items, fruits, and vegetables, were used for all countries except Japan. Production figures for England were for 1930–31; for Germany, the average for the years 1925–29; for the United States, the average for the years 1924–28. These quantities were evaluated at United States average farm prices, 1917–26. In the case of Japan yen values for the year 1927 were used, translated into dollars on the basis of the current exchange value of the yen. The committee is indebted to O. E. Baker of the United States Department of Agriculture for suggestions regarding procedure and for many of the data used in this computation.

[2] In this table, no allowance is made for expenditures for fertilizer, machinery, or purchased feed. Estimated expenditures for these items are deducted from the values presented in ch. II, for United States regions.

The values shown here are at best mere approximations, although computed at considerable pains. They should be used with caution, and merely as a rough index of certain significant variations. The relation of population engaged in agriculture to land resources is undoubtedly one major factor influencing variations in agricultural productivity, but other important factors must be taken into account: soil, climate, topography, agricultural techniques, relation of agriculture to industry and commerce, and relation to foreign markets. For example, the German policy of land settlement and protective tariffs for farm products has undoubtedly tended to increase the proportion of all workers in agriculture, and to decrease the average quantity productivity per farm worker. It may be surprising at first to find that the value-productivity figures per male worker for England and the United States are not widely different. However, when comparison is made between England and the United States outside of the Southeast,[10] the figure for the latter area is appreciably higher than that for England. These figures suggest that the United States still enjoys real advantages in ratio of farm population to land resources, as compared with many other countries.

A few studies have been made of the relative productivity of industrial workers in various countries. The results obtained in one of the most careful comparisons of this sort, relating to conditions in the pre-war period, are shown in table 6. Flux reached the conclusion that, as of about 1910, industrial productivity per capita was about 2.82 times as high in the United States as in Great Britain. Since that time, in his estimation, efficiency had increased about 25 percent more in the United States than in Great Britain.[11]

TABLE 6.—*Average value of output per industrial worker in the United Kingdom, British Dominions, and the United States, as estimated by Flux* [1]

Country	Period	Estimated average annual net output per worker (in dollars)
United Kingdom	1907	$495
Canada	1910	1,095
South Africa	1915–16	811
Australia	1910	767
New Zealand	1910–11	1,020
United States	1909	1,087

[1] Based on estimates reported by A. W. Flux in "The Census of Production," *Journal of the Royal Statistical Society*, LXXXVII: 351–375, 1924. Comparisons were made between net output per person employed for England (1907 census of production) and value added by manufacture per worker engaged in manufacture for the United States. In both cases proprietors and firm members were included among persons engaged in manufacture. Net output in the English figures differs from value added by manufactures in that the expenses item relating to contract work was included with cost of materials and deducted from value of product to secure net output. In mining and quarrying, cost of fuel and power and of ores purchased was subtracted from value of product in the English figures. In comparing the United Kingdom and the United States, Flux computed quantity as well as value of output per worker in four industries: iron and steel, tinplate, gloves, and cement. He found that, in each of these industries, the differences between the two countries in output per industrial worker were larger when measured in units of quantity than when measured in value of product.

[10] For description of regions and examination of regional variations in the United States, see ch. II.
[11] Flux, A. W., Industrial Productivity in Great Britain and the United States, *Quarterly Journal of Economics*, November 1933, pp. 1–38.

Workers in the United States have been and still are in an especially favorable position as regards their command over material resources. The slowing down of population growth will tend toward the maintenance of this advantageous situation. Clearly there are ample resources in the country, if wisely used, to support at a high level of living a population as large as or larger than that to be expected in the near future.

It is, however, not too soon to sound the warning that the ratio of population to natural resources may be lowered by a wasteful economy, even more rapidly than by the multiplication of population. In fact, our resources have already undergone serious depletion.

The process of depletion has been accompanied by waste so serious as to raise conservation of resources to an issue of first rank. . . .

Unless these wastes are controlled, they will handicap the economic position of the United States. The significant result of depletion is not ultimate exhaustion but a tendency to increasing cost. The national resources are still abundant. The danger to be averted is not a day of wrath centuries hence when all the coal and iron shall be gone and all the upland farms washed away. It is rather a period of diminishing yield and increasing cost, a surrender of the margin of natural advantage which in the past has aided us in foreign trade and at home helped to maintain a high material standard of life.[12]

The Problem of an Optimum Population

There has been considerable discussion but very little scientific research on the question of the ideal relation of total population to material resources from the standpoint of average productivity per worker and levels of living, at any given stage of technical development and industrial organization. An approach to this question could be made through an analysis of conditions affecting different industries, which might lead to interesting results. At present, however, it is impossible to add greatly to such meager data and inferences as have already been presented with reference to the economic situation of the United States at the present time.

There is even less decisive evidence on the relation of population to military power, although assumptions on this subject are frequently made in popular discussion, and sometimes in governmental programs. It appears that, within wide limits, the relation is an extremely dubious one. Wealth, technical skill, organization, and morale are probably more important in all military affairs than mere numerical strength today. This is obviously so in aerial and naval operations. It may be true to such an extent that a population policy aimed purely at increasing the general level of well-being would be most advantageous from the standpoint of increasing potential military

[12] Goodrich, Carter, and others, *Migration and Economic Opportunity*, University of Pennsylvania Press (1936), pp. 283, 285.

resources. A policy aimed at increasing population at the cost of lowered economic level might, in the long run, defeat its own purpose.

Other considerations affecting any final evaluation of optimum population are even more elusive. Few have ventured to appraise the aesthetic and spiritual significance of numbers of people in relation to natural resources.[13]

Even on the highest reasonable assumptions with regard to fertility and survival rates, population growth is definitely slowing down in this country. But, on the lowest reasonable assumptions, there will be as many people in the United States 50 years hence as there are today. Accordingly, there does not seem to be any substantial basis for agitation about the trend of total population in the United States during the next few decades. It should, however, be noted that present conditions appear to be working against, rather than reinforcing, the factors making for permanent population replacement. Thoughtful consideration should therefore be given to the analysis of these tendencies, and to the determination of conditions most favorable both for population replacement in the future and for continued

[13] There have been a few such attempts. See, for example, Mukherjee, Radhakamal, "On the Criterion of Optimum Population", *American Journal of Sociology*, xv: 344–348. November 1934.

progress in opportunities for individual development and family welfare.

The Relation Between the Trend of Population and Business Fluctuations

The slow change in the trend of total population in recent years, in contrast to the more erratic movement of various indices of industrial income, appears in figure 7. There has been, to be sure, considerable variation in the annual increments of population growth (as shown by the lowest line in the chart); but their effect on the trend of total population is very gradual. The change in the adult population, which alone is economically productive and is also most important from the standpoint of consumption requirements, is even more gradual. There has been a decline, since about 1925, in the number of births; but the number of young people entering the economically productive age classes will continue to increase until about 1945. Furthermore, the decline in the number of dependent children has been in part offset by an increase in the number of the dependent aged. Clearly, the causes of cyclical depressions must be sought primarily in the analysis of industrial and financial relations, both national and international, rather than in the short-time effects of changing trends in total population.

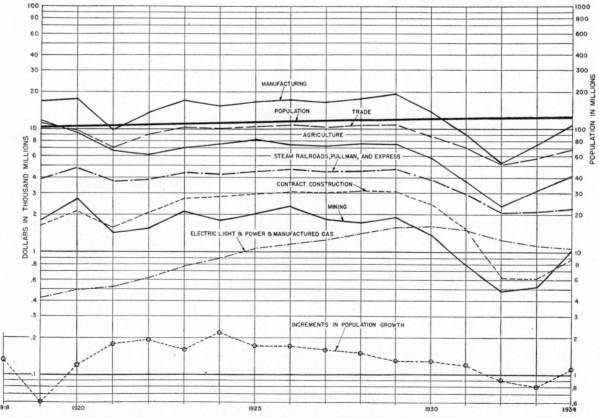

FIGURE 7.—Trends of total population and of income produced in seven industrial branches, 1919–34. Data on income from Kuznets, Simon, "Income Originating in Nine Basic Industries, 1919–1934", *National Bureau of Economic Research, Bulletin 59*, May 4, 1936.

Consideration of changes in number of families in relation to volume of residential construction affords a critical test of this thesis, and leads to an important modification. Here it is possible only to measure changes taking place in urban areas. The marriage data relate to total population, but the secular trend in age-specific marriage rates was presumably similar in urban and in rural areas. If we then compare the trend of marriages in the total population with an index of urban residential construction, the movement of the latter appears quite independent of the former. The downward trend in residential construction began well before the downward trend of marriages during the depression (see fig. 8). The peak and decline of residential construction, however, may be explained as the reaction to an urban housing shortage in the early twenties—due to (*a*) interruption of normal activity during the war, (*b*) immigration, and (*c*) movement from farms to cities—which overshot the mark, and led to a recession. This appeared first in residential and later in other forms of construction in the late twenties, but well before the collapse of the stock market in the fall of 1929.[14] This recession was most marked in the case of residential building; the index of urban residential construction for the second quarter of 1929 was 25 percent below that for the second quarter of 1928. Here local population movements appear as a factor, though an indirect and secondary factor, lead-

ing toward the economic disorder of 1929 and later years.

All sorts of changes are constantly introducing strains in the national economy that test its flexibility and adequacy in meeting human needs. This is true of changes in the number, age composition, and distribution of population, as well as of international trade movements, credit, technological processes, and the distribution of income. But most of the population changes are so gradual that they are relatively unimportant in interpreting cyclical or irregular fluctuations in business activity.

The primary importance of technological and organizational changes, as contrasted with changes in population, in determining fluctuations of business is also shown by data on output per worker and productivity per capita of total population. Estimates from various sources, reported by Ezekiel, show an increase of 143 percent from 1870 to 1930 in the average output per agricultural worker, and a corresponding increase of 155 percent in the average output per industrial worker (in manufacturing and mining). Although the proportion of all workers who were engaged in agriculture declined from 53 percent in 1870 to 21 percent in 1930, the volume of agricultural production per capita of the total population shows an estimated increase of 22 percent. The combined effect of the release of workers from agriculture into industry and the increase in the average productivity of industrial workers made possible an estimated increase of 350 percent, from 1870 to 1930, in the physical volume of industrial production

---

[14] The committee is indebted for suggestions on this topic to George Terborgh, formerly of the Brookings Institution, now with the Division of Research and Statistics of the Federal Reserve Board. See forthcoming study, *The Problems of Recovery*, by the staff of the Brookings Institution.

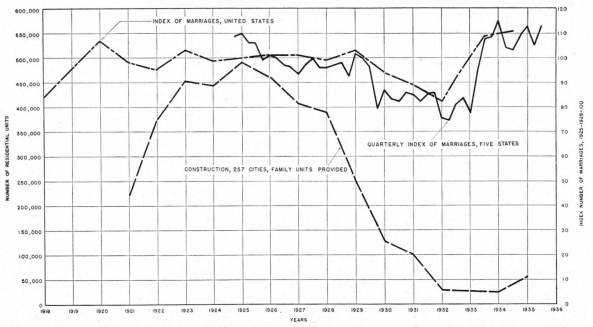

FIGURE 8.—Trend in Number of Marriages, United States, 1918–1935, and in Urban Residential Construction, 1921–1935. The index of marriages for the United States for the years 1932–35 is based on estimates by Stouffer, Samuel A. and Spencer, Lyle M. The five States represented in the quarterly index of marriage are Alabama, Delaware, Maine, Massachusetts, Michigan. The data on residential construction are those of the Bureau of Labor Statistics.

per capita of the population (see table 7). It is, therefore, apparent that changes in agricultural and industrial techniques, in financial organization, and in organization of industry, trade, and the service occupations are directly responsible for the major economic changes of recent years.

TABLE 7.—*Physical volume of production per capita of total population, by census periods, 1870 to 1930 (total farm and industrial production in 1900 = 100)*[1]

Census year	Farm products	Industrial products	All products
1870	27.4	27.0	54.4
1880	33.6	37.1	70.7
1890	32.6	53.3	85.9
1900	36.0	64.0	100.0
1910	28.4	90.7	119.1
1920	32.6	101.5	134.1
1930	33.3	121.5	154.8

[1] From Ezekiel, Mordecai, Population and Unemployment, in *Annals of the American Academy of Political and Social Science*, 188: 230–242, Nov. 1936.

The problems of depression and recovery have been intensified, both from the standpoint of opportunity for individuals and that of national economic stability, by a further concentration of production during this period. The result has been that, whereas three-fifths of the reduction from 1929 to 1933 in the annual volume of industrial production was recovered during the next 3 years (1933 to 1936), less than two-fifths of the decline in man-hours of employment was recovered. Furthermore, making allowance for increase in the employable population, it appears that only about one-quarter of those who became unemployed during the depression have been restored to work (see table 8).

TABLE 8.—*Indices of industrial employment and production, 1929, 1933, 1936* [1]

Year	Persons at work in factories, index	Average number of factory hours per week	Man-hours of employment per week, index	Physical Production indices		Estimated number of unemployed persons
				Total volume	Per man-hour	
1929	100	50	100	100	100	2,696,000
1933	60	37.55	45	53	117	15,316,000
1936	84	38.65	65	81	124	12,226,000

[1] Adapted from Ezekiel, *op. cit.*

In addition to the army of the unemployed, data to be presented in the following chapter reveal other millions of chronically underemployed persons in rural areas with meager resources. One sort of approach to these situations, the defeatist approach, proceeds on the assumption that there is no longer enough work to be done to keep everyone fully occupied. Various alternatives are then proposed, such as (1) restriction on the introduction of machinery, (2) the spreading of work (not merely as an emergency measure, where it may be of real value, but as a permanent solution to

the problem of overproduction), (3) the perpetual maintenance of a large relief population, or (4) the routing of a large population into economically unproductive or subsistence occupations, chiefly farming in regions of low land values. Both of the last two alternatives envisage the permanent retirement of large numbers of families from participation in economically effective activities. However, in view of the fact that in this country during the past 60 years the average per capita consumption of the products of farms, factories, and mines has been multiplied nearly threefold (see last column, table 7), and the further fact that large numbers of people are clearly in need of more goods and services than they are now able to purchase, there is good reason to believe that the Nation can well absorb all the economic goods that may be supplied through efficient organization of production and distribution, and the full participation of the whole population in effective enterprise or service of various sorts. The constructive suggestions relating to population problems, presented in this report, have been developed on the positive thesis of the possibility of continued national advance and widespread equalization of opportunity.

4. Economic Aspects of Changing Age Distribution

New problems are arising from the changing age distribution of the people of the United States. This change is closely related to the slowing down of population growth. Here, too, the problems are real but not so overwhelming as sometimes represented. We are not rapidly becoming a Nation in wheel chairs, dependent for support on a vanishing company of productive workers. In fact the proportion of the total population in the productive age classes, 20–64 years, will apparently be greater throughout the twentieth century than during the nineteenth.

In planning institutional facilities, it is important to recognize that for the Nation as a whole the number of children of school age will not increase, but the age classes most heavily represented in certain types of institutions, for example, homes for the aged and hospitals for mental patients, will greatly increase. The shift in age distribution also has many broad implications for our whole economic and social life. Only a few of these can be developed in this report.

Changes in the Population at Productive Ages

The proportion of the total population in the economically productive age classes, 20–64 years, is expected to rise gradually during the next few decades from slightly over 55 percent in 1930 to a plateau of about 61 to 63 percent from 1950 through 1970. Thereafter it will probably decline gradually, as the expected increase in the proportion of the aged begins to outweigh the expected decrease in the proportion of minors. The proportion included in this group (aged 20–64 years) was relatively low 50 years ago (about 40 percent, 1880–90). It then rose rapidly to 54.5 percent in 1920 but, as has been shown, it will presumably change only gradually during the next 50 years. Meanwhile, however, there will be a decided increase in the percentage of older persons within this total productive age group, as well as in the proportion of aged people.

The Problem of Economic Security for the Aged

It is clear that there will be an increasing number of aged persons, many of whom will need to be released from productive activity (see table 9). There are now (in the middle of the decade, 1930–40) about 7,500,000 people over 65 years of age. Forty-five years hence, in 1980 (according to the Scripps estimates, with medium mortality rates and no immigration), there will be 22,000,000 in this age class. The number of those 20–64 years will, on the same hypothesis, have increased from 73,200,000 to 91,600,000; but 87 percent of the increase in this broad age group will be concentrated in the age class 45–64 years. If all those over 65 years then received cash benefits, raised by direct taxation, the average tax on each man and woman in the productive age classes would be $24 for each $100 paid to an older person. If only those over 70 received such benefits, the corresponding tax on each man and woman aged 20–64 years would be $15 per $100 received by each aged person. It is obvious that the problems raised by this situation require both courageous and realistic treatment. The social security program is an attempt to deal with these problems on a broad national basis. Many problems in this field still remain to be solved through further research and experimentation.

TABLE 9.—*Expected number of persons (in thousands) over specified ages, on hypothesis of medium mortality rates and no immigration, 1930–80*

Year	60	65	70
1930	10,456	6,702	3,929
1940	13,307	8,419	4,936
1950	17,221	11,205	6,542
1960	21,584	14,818	8,856
1970	26,193	17,995	11,473
1980	31,308	22,051	14,086

Problems Presented by the Increase of Older Persons Within the Productive Age Classes

One major aspect of the problem of economic and social security for older persons has as yet received relatively little attention: The question of opportunities for the employment of older workers who are still able and willing to work. Since the average age of the population is increasing, it follows that the labor

supply available in the future will be, on the average, older than in the past. Industry will have to adapt itself to this change in the labor supply or society will be faced with an enormous burden. Much has been heard of a tendency of industrial management to set an age deadline at 40, at least for the employment of new workers. Such a policy is directly contrary to the tendency of the population toward increase at the older ages and decrease at the younger ages. Evidently the question of the occupational adjustment of older workers is becoming a major problem.

A comparison of changes from 1910 to 1930 in the proportion of persons over 45 years engaged in different occupations throws valuable light on shifts in opportunities for older workers in different fields. Table 10 presents such a comparison for gainfully occupied males. Since the proportion of adults over 45 years was increasing in the total population during this period, at the same time that there was a trend toward reducing child labor, it is not surprising to find that the percentage of gainfully employed workers over 45 years of age increased for all industries combined, from 26.1 percent in 1910 to 32.7 percent in 1930. Various industries, however, show very different tendencies in this respect.

TABLE 10.—*Changes in proportions of male workers 45 years of age and over in selected occupations, 1910 to 1930, United States*

Industry and service group	Percent of male workers 45 years of age and over		
	1910	1930	Percent in 1930 minus percent in 1910
All occupations	26.1	32.7	6.6
Agriculture and forestry:			
Agriculture	29.3	37.9	8.6
Forestry	30.2	31.8	1.6
Extraction of minerals:			
Coal mines	17.3	29.4	12.1
Copper mines	16.0	28.8	12.8
Gold and silver mines	34.6	49.9	15.3
Iron mines	13.2	31.0	17.8
Lead and zinc mines	17.8	27.3	9.5
Quarries	21.9	30.1	8.2
Oil wells and gas wells	20.4	22.6	2.2
Manufacturing and mechanical industries:			
Building industry	32.7	39.1	6.4
Gas works	21.1	27.4	6.3
Paint and varnish factories	16.7	29.5	12.8
Petroleum refineries	21.4	19.9	−1.5
Rayon factories		13.2	
Soap factories	21.9	27.8	5.9
Cigar and tobacco factories	25.6	37.4	11.8
Brick, tile, and terra cotta factories	19.1	28.7	9.6
Glass factories	15.4	27.5	12.1
Marble and stone yards	29.1	37.7	8.6
Potteries	19.1	31.5	12.4
Corset factories	18.4	33.5	15.1
Glove factories	21.7	36.5	14.8
Hat (felt) factories	21.5	31.0	9.5
Shirt, collar, and cuff factories	13.6	23.1	9.5
Suit, coat, and overalls factories	21.0	42.4	21.4
Other clothing factories	14.2	27.8	13.6
Bakeries	19.3	23.0	3.7
Candy factories	16.2	27.7	11.5
Fish canning and packing	30.8	34.3	3.5
Flour and grain mills	36.4	38.8	2.4
Fruit and vegetable canning, etc.	28.6	32.7	4.1
Slaughter and packing houses	19.1	25.8	6.7
Sugar factories and refineries	19.6	31.9	12.3
Liquor and beverage industries	25.2	30.9	5.7
Agricultural implement factories	23.3	30.2	6.9
Automobile factories	12.0	19.6	7.6
Automobile repair shops		12.8	
Blast furnaces and steel rolling mills	16.0	26.6	10.6
Car and railroad shops	20.4	34.3	13.9

TABLE 10.—*Changes in proportions of male workers 45 years of age and over in selected occupations, 1910 to 1930, United States—Continued*

Industry and service group	Percent of male workers 45 years of age and over		
	1910	1930	Percent in 1930 minus percent in 1910
Manufacturing and mechanical industries—Continued.			
Ship and boat building	30.3	34.4	4.1
Wagon and carriage factories	31.6	46.6	15.0
Brass mills	18.2	33.2	15.0
Clock and watch factories	24.7	31.4	6.7
Jewelry factories	19.3	29.8	10.5
Harness and saddle factories	38.1	68.9	30.8
Leather goods, etc., factories	28.4	31.1	2.7
Shoe factories	17.7	26.0	8.3
Tanneries	23.1	35.8	11.7
Furniture factories	27.6	34.2	6.6
Piano and organ factories	21.9	45.6	23.5
Saw and planing mills	18.2	28.1	9.9
Paper and pulp mills	20.4	28.8	8.4
Printing, publishing, and engraving	17.6	26.3	8.7
Carpet mills	21.0	31.9	10.9
Cotton mills	16.4	25.6	9.2
Knitting mills	14.0	14.0	---
Lace and embroidery mills	15.1	32.3	17.4
Silk mills	16.2	22.6	5.2
Textile, dyeing, finishing, etc., mills	23.1	31.5	7.4
Woolen and worsted mills	21.6	37.2	15.6
Electric light and power plants	14.4	20.1	5.7
Electric machinery and supply factories	12.3	18.8	6.5
Rubber factories	16.8	21.1	4.3
Transportation and communication:			
Air transportation	---	9.3	---
Construction and maintenance of roads, etc.	28.8	31.5	2.7
Express companies	15.1	25.5	10.4
Livery stables	29.2	52.6	23.4
Postal service	26.9	35.3	8.4
Radio broadcasting	---	5.5	---
Steam railways	18.7	34.7	16.0
Street railways	16.0	36.1	20.1
Telephone and telegraph	9.6	18.6	9.0
Truck, transfer and cab companies	22.1	19.8	−2.3
Water transportation	25.5	29.7	4.2
Trade and service industries:			
Banking and brokerage	26.8	27.5	0.7
Grain elevators	29.4	41.1	11.7
Insurance	31.4	31.5	0.1
Real estate	45.6	55.0	9.4
Stockyards	23.5	34.4	10.9
Warehouse and cold storage	26.1	32.7	6.6
Public service (not elsewhere)	36.6	35.0	−1.6
Professional service	30.3	37.6	7.3

For all occupations combined, the proportion of gainful workers over 45 years of age rose 6.6 points (as noted in the preceding paragraph) from 1910 to 1930. Therefore, increases of more than this amount show occupations with a tendency to increased concentration in the older ages. Among these are, for example, agriculture with 8.6 points increase; all mining operations (except oil and gas wells which showed a great expansion during the period in question and only a slight increase in the percentage of workers over 45); certain manufacturing and mechanical industries; candy factories; sugar factories and refineries; blast furnaces and steam rolling mills; car and railroad shops; wagon and carriage factories; brass mills; and jewelry factories. The tendency of declining industries to hold an unusually high proportion of older workers is strikingly revealed by the fact that the greatest increases, from 1910 to 1930, in percentage of male workers over 45 years of age are found in the case of harness and saddle factories (30.8 points), livery stables (23.4 points), and street railways (20.1 points). A few industries showed little

or no change in the age distribution of male workers during this period, for example, public service (not elsewhere classified), knitting mills, and insurance.

Study of these changes and of the differences in the proportion of workers over 45 years of age suggests the operation of certain important causes, including relative growth or decay of the industry; technological changes; character of occupation, whether skilled or unskilled; unionization; and immigration.

The factor of technological change.—The influence of relative growth or decline of an industry is strikingly exhibited in the table. Many declining industries show very large proportions of workers over 45 years of age—for example, harness factories (68.9 percent), livery stables (52.6 percent), piano and organ factories (45.6 percent). Rapidly expanding industries show low proportions of workers past the 45-year line—for example, automobile factories (19.6 percent), rubber products (21.1 percent), petroleum refineries (19.9 percent), and radio broadcasting (5.5 percent). New industries, established usually in urban communities, draw upon young persons who have not become attached to an established industry, as the most available labor supply. Declining industries that do not need to expand their labor force tend to keep their old employees who have become skilled in their special requirements. However, where the continuing demand is not sufficiently great, some of the old employees in these industries may be retired, or forced to change their occupations.

Technological change, it seems, brings special problems to older workers. Where technical improvements supplant an old established craft with machinery, the newly employed semiskilled machine operatives will tend to be recruited from the younger ages; but the rapidity of the change may be influenced by many factors, including strength of labor organization and severity of competition. When improvements cut down the labor force required but increase the degree of skill or responsibility for those employed, as in the flour and grain mills, these changes appear less likely to lead to supplanting older with younger workers. In this industry, however, the relatively high average age of workers may be affected by the existence of many small mills operated by independents. Skilled occupations tend to have high and increasing proportions of workers over 45, but, as a group, these occupations are declining in relative importance.

Unionization.—Union organization may be a factor in protecting the position of the worker already in an industry against pressure for displacement of older employees by machinery or by younger workers. The skilled operatives are more largely unionized than are the semiskilled or the unskilled, and the influence of unionization may therefore be partly responsible for the high average age of the skilled labor group. The same applies to railway employees. Locomotive engineers and firemen show an increase in median age between 1910 and 1930 of 6.9 years, as compared with an average increase of only 2.6 years for all occupied males.[15] The evidence on this subject, however, is inconclusive because many of the most thoroughly organized industries are in the older branches of industry.

Other factors.—The decrease at successive age levels in the number of persons engaged in certain major occupational classes is shown in figure 9. It is apparent that agriculture holds a large proportion of the older workers; conversely it has lost a large proportion of young persons to nonfarm occupations. The professional group also tends to hold workers at the older age levels. The self-employed apparently continue longer in active occupations than the employed.

The retirement policies of corporations vary widely in different fields. Barkin found for New York State that, of 911 concerns which reported, 6 percent had formal and 15 percent had informal maximum age hiring policies cov-

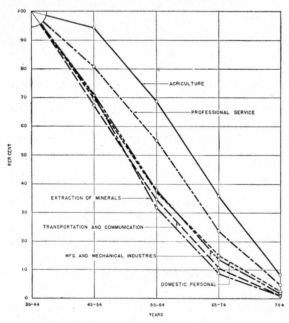

FIGURE 9.—Number of gainfully occupied persons at later ages per 100 workers aged 35–44 in different industry groups.

[15] See Smith, Mapheus, "Trends in the Ages of Gainful Workers, by Occupation, 1910–30", *Journal of the American Statistical Association*, XXX: 680, December 1935.

ering the entire concerns, 39 percent had an informal maximum age hiring policy for selected jobs, and 12 percent had a "special case age hiring policy." [16]

It is clear that occupational opportunities for older workers are affected by a wide variety of factors. In the case of women, the situation is even more complicated than for men, especially for the older woman who seeks to enter a new occupation after a long period devoted to household duties. The whole subject is one that calls for careful study, in view of its increasing economic and social importance.

5. Summary

Population trends have a profound influence, in the long run, on economic activity, through changes in the basic relations of people, natural resources, and social institutions.

Changes in population trends, however, because of their gradual development, do not play a large part in causing cyclical and irregular fluctuations in business activity. The only exception to this general statement is found in the case of large-scale, rapid migratory movements. And even here, the role of population change is similar to that of changes of other sorts—simply presenting new conditions that call for accurate analysis and appropriate economic adjustments.

The trend of the national population has been reviewed in some detail, with estimates of future numbers on various hypotheses. The outlook is in many ways distinctly gratifying. Some of the worst fears that have haunted population theorists in earlier periods are proving groundless. It is apparent, too, that the slowing down of population growth in the United States will leave this Nation in a peculiarly advantageous position, as to the relation of total population to total natural resources. The situation is one that opens great possibilities for further economic and social advances.

The changing age distribution presents certain difficult and important problems, both with respect to the increase in the proportion of aged persons, and with respect to the approaching large increase in the proportion of older people within the broad age groups commonly classed as economically productive.

[16] Barkin, Solomon, *The Older Worker in Industry.* A study of New York State manufacturing industries. A report of the first legislative committee on unemployment. Prepared under the auspices of the continuation committee of the New York State Commission on Old Age Security. Studies of New York Legislative Document (1933) No. 66.

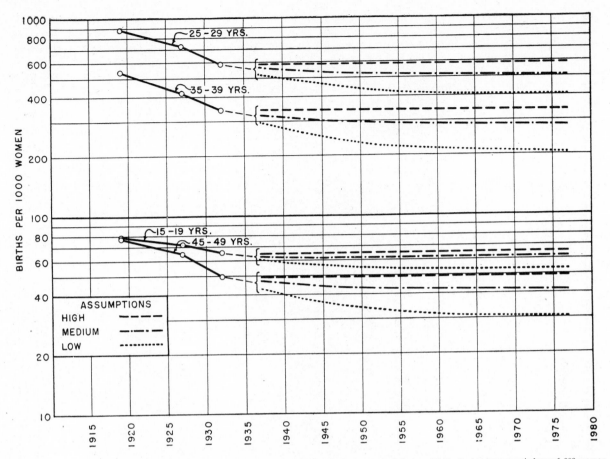

FIGURE 10.—Estimated fertility rates for native white women, 1917–80, selected age classes, United States. Births during 5-year periods per 1,000 women by age at end of period. Based on recorded births, 1917–21 to 1930–34; hypothetical 1935–39 to 1975–79.

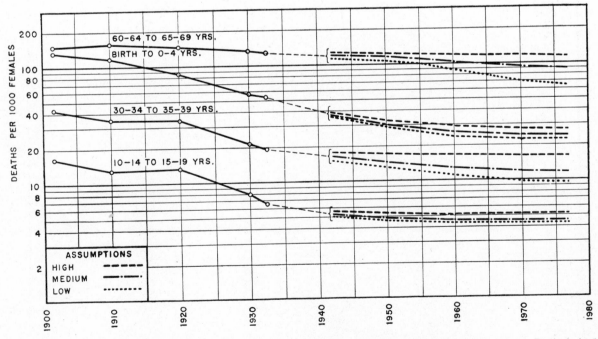

FIGURE 11.—Estimated death rates for white women, 1900–34 and for native white women 1935–80, selected age classes, United States. Deaths during 5 year periods per 1,000 females by age at beginning of period. Based on recorded deaths, 1900–02 to 1929–34; hypothetical 1940–44 to 1975–7.9

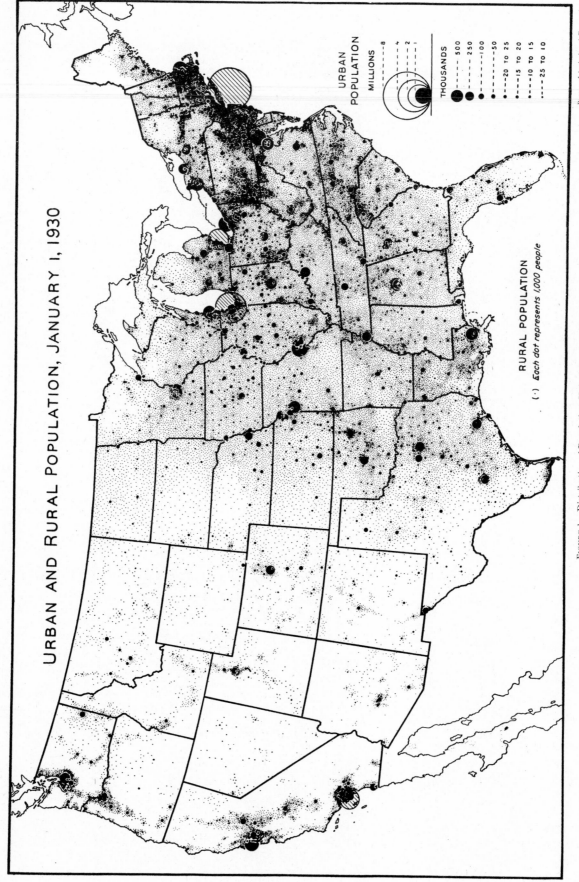

URBAN AND RURAL POPULATION, JANUARY 1, 1930

URBAN POPULATION
MILLIONS

THOUSANDS

RURAL POPULATION
(·) *Each dot represents 1,000 people*

Bureau of Agricultural Economics.

FIGURE 1.—Distribution of Population, United States, 1930.

II. REGIONAL DISTRIBUTION OF ECONOMIC OPPORTUNITY

1. The Pattern of Population Distribution

Spotted on the map, the location of population in our country does not appear as evenly distributed pepper dots. On the contrary, the shaker appears to have passed lightly over large areas, to have released great heaps at certain strategic locations, and to have scattered the rest of its contents here and there at random (fig. 1). Superficially this distribution suggests a combination of rational design and of accident. Closer analysis shows that this superficial impression has far more validity than one might expect.

Population distribution is usually ascribed, in economic treatises as well as in local guidebooks, to the rational selection of residence in relation to economic opportunity, cultural advantages, or climate. Such conscious preferences do exert a powerful force in the continuous redistribution of population. But in spite of the conspicuous mobility of the American people, historical accident and differential reproduction rates have played a far larger part in determining population distribution in this country than is generally supposed. The sheer size of our land area, its geographical diversity, and the variety of cultural patterns controlling our interests and attitudes have served to intensify the force of these irrational factors.

The Balance of Population and Economic Resources

This chapter will be devoted to an examination of the present distribution of the population of the United States in relation to regional resources. We shall inquire to what extent geographic differences in levels of living and opportunity for economic progress may be influenced by relation of population to economic resources. The term "economic resources" is here used to refer to the possibilities of an area as regards (*a*) natural resources, (*b*) present economic development, (*c*) known possibilities for new developments, and (*d*) the economic relationship of this to other areas. All these factors must be taken into account in studying the balance of population in relation to economic opportunity. A patch of fertile land lying over a natural gas reservoir outside of Cleveland may offer very different economic possibilities from a parcel of land of the same size with similar natural resources located somewhere in Arizona. The economic possibilities of a tract of sandy land in the Florida lake region may be transformed by the development of orange groves and the attraction of winter tourists. We may say that a given area is "overpopulated" in relation to its economic resources when economic progress comparable to that possible in other parts of the country is blocked there by the size of present population relative to present occupations and industries and recognized possibilities in that area. The answer to "overpopulation" in this sense might be either emigration or the development of new agricultural, industrial, or service opportunities.

Evidence already presented shows that the United States as a whole is not overpopulated, relative to other nations. Pressure of total population on natural resources in this country is not so great as seriously to hamper continued economic expansion and a rise in the general level of living, through more efficient economy. The data on regional variations in the distribution of goods and services to be introduced in this chapter will show, however, that in some parts of the country the pressure of population on economic resources is already a basic factor in causing low levels of living or even widespread chronic poverty.

The emphasis in this chapter may produce a pessimistic impression, as though there were too many people everywhere and too few opportunities anywhere. That is not the intent. It is indeed the case at the present time, due to present economic disorders. There is obviously a general scarcity of opportunities for employment. But economic revival may be expected to open new opportunities where circumstances are favorable to the development of mechanical industries, to the extension of trade and service occupations, and in some cases to the development of new types of agricultural, forest, and mineral production. It is not possible to locate "areas of opportunity" with the same exactness that is sometimes possible in the case of "problem areas", just because opportunity is more diffuse than the sort of specific limitations which mark off areas of overpopulation. This does not mean, however, that the potential opportunities are less real than these negative conditions.

Variations in Crude Population Density

We shall begin with a brief survey of crude density of population relative to land area. Population densities, by counties, are shown in figures 2a–c for 1870, 1900, and 1930. The rapid expansion of the West is clearly indicated. One finds, however, that the areas of early colonial settlement are still, in general, more densely populated than the newer parts of the country. This contrast is also apparent in figure 3, showing the distribution of land area and of population among the six major regions of the United States, in 1900, 1930, and 1935.[1]

Despite the westward trend of population, the three western regions had only one-fifth of

[1] The six regions used here are those used in Odum, Howard W., *Southern Regions of the United States*, University of North Carolina Press (1936). For detailed treatment of types of regional analysis, see *Regional Factors in National Planning and Development*, National Resources Committee (1935).

the Nation's total population in 1935, in comparison with three-fifths of the total land area. The proportion of the total population living in the Southeast was reduced between 1900 and 1930, but increased slightly between 1930 and 1935, due largely to the reduced emigration of farm population from that area since the onset of the depression.

The question as to whether or not there still is, in general, greater opportunity in the newer West than in the older East is interesting but difficult to answer. Maps of crude population density are particularly deceptive in this respect, because the greatest mountain and desert areas happen to lie in the more recently settled parts of the country. If population density were evened off all over the country the result would obviously be disastrous. Clearly we must resort to more refined analysis of the functional relations of population to economic resources in order to gain any true insight into the significance of population distribution in the United States at the present time.

Variations in Levels of Living

The Study of Population Redistribution has provided a serviceable map of county variations in plane of living in the United States. The composite index used for this map is admittedly a crude measure, but it does clearly

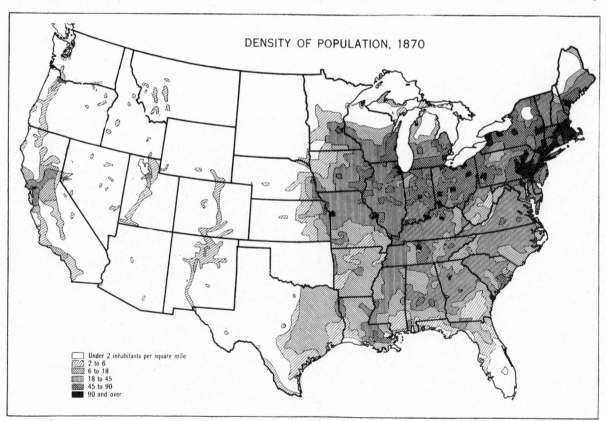

DENSITY OF POPULATION, 1870

Under 2 inhabitants per square mile
2 to 6
6 to 18
18 to 45
45 to 90
90 and over

FIGURE 2a.—From *Atlas of Historical Geography of the United States.*

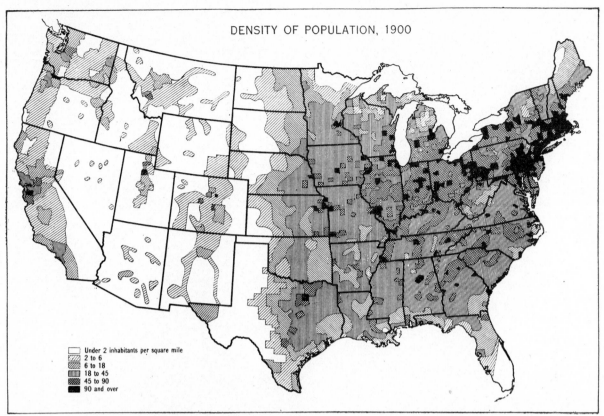

FIGURE 2b.—From *Atlas of Historical Geography of the United States.*

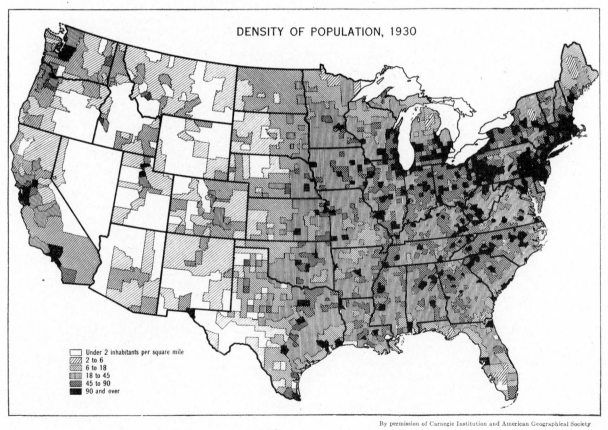

FIGURE 2c.—From *Atlas of Historical Geography of the United States.*

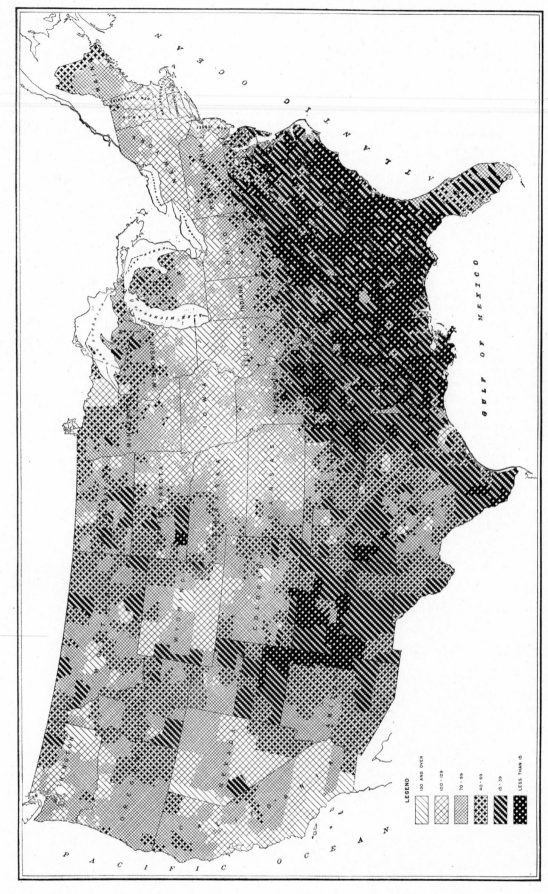

FIGURE 3.—Plane of living, 1928–29.   Adapted from Goodrich and Others, *Migration and Economic Opportunity* (University of Pennsylvania Press).

portray gross differences in material conditions of life across the whole nation. It is based on three variables measured in relation to the total population of each county; this relationship is then expressed in each case as a percentage of the national average. The three variables are: number of individual Federal income-tax returns in 1928, number of residence telephones in use January 1, 1930, and number of radio sets in use reported to the 1930 Census.[2] A glance at this map (fig. 3) shows a light band representing the highest plane of living, which extends from southern New England through New York, south of the Great Lakes and across the plains as far as Nebraska and Kansas. The same shading appears again in part of Wyoming and in considerable sections of the far west. In contrast to these fortunate areas,

[2] Goodrich, Carter, and others, *Migration and Economic Opportunity*, University of Pennsylvania Press (1936), pp. 14, 19, 20. When these three factors had been selected they were combined as follows: The population of each county in 1930 was found, together with its number of income tax returns, home telephones, and radios, on the dates noted above. The percentage of the number of income tax returns to the county population was computed, and the same was done for telephones and for radios. In the Nation as a whole the number of income tax returns was 3.31 percent of the 1930 population (4,059,610 to 122,775,046). There were 13,177,885 telephones, 1 for every 9 persons, and 12,048,762 radios, 1 for every 10. The county's percentage of income tax returns to population was now expressed as a proportion of the national average, 3.31 percent. If a county had about the average number of returns, its reading would then be near 100 percent (of the national average). Similar percentages of their national averages were computed for telephones and radios. The resulting figures were, for instance, 95 percent for income-tax returns, 167 percent for telephones, and 180 percent of the national average for radios; or, to cite another actual example, 8, 11, and 6 percent. These three percentages were next averaged to give a final index for the county: 147 in the first, 8 in the second instance.

almost the entire southeast, except for Florida, falls into one of the two lowest groups. Not more than half a dozen counties in the northeast (and these are all in West Virginia) drop into the lowest group; only one county in the southeast reaches the highest group. The west central portion of the country, from Montana and the Dakotas south to Texas, New Mexico, and Arizona, is more spotty, most of it being in one or the other of the middle groups.

The great majority of the counties classed as having the highest plane of living are either urban or industrial in character. Some contain governmental, resort, or educational centers. A few farming counties and one mining county belong in the highest group. Almost all of those in the lowest group are poor farming counties.

Variations in per Capita Income

Figures on the regional distribution of the Nation's income account in large measure for the differences in level of living described above (see table 1). The income estimates for 1929 used here were prepared by Brookings Institution. The figures represent per capita personal income, including income from profits from the sale of property and imputed rent on owned homes, but excluding imputed income from durable consumption goods other than homes. Farm incomes include allowances for rent and for food produced and consumed on

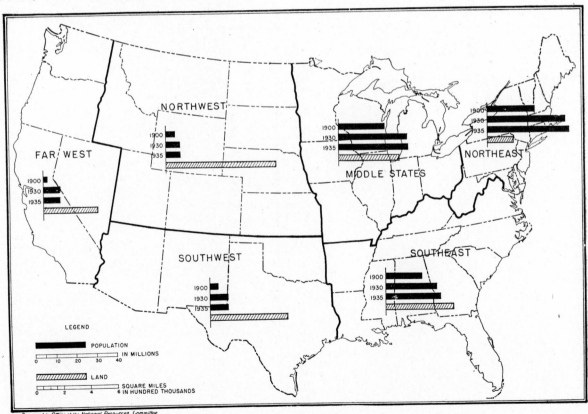

FIGURE 4.—Regional distribution of total population, 1900, 1930, 1935, and of total land.

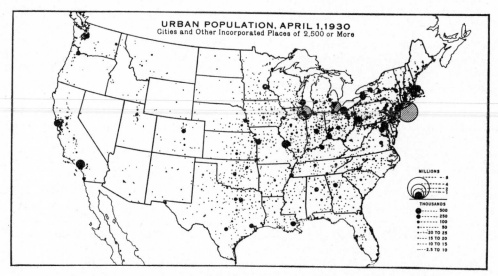

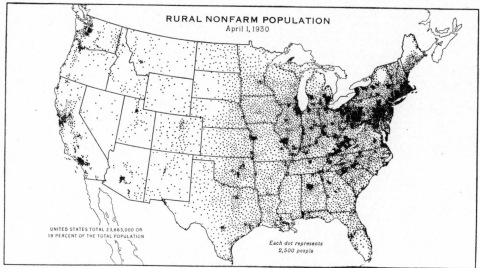

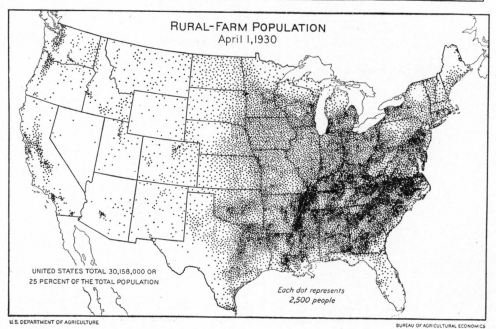

FIGURE 5.—Distribution of urban, rural-farm, and rural-nonfarm population, 1930.

the farm, the prices used being farm rather than city prices.[3]

The Northeast and the Far West have higher average per capita incomes than the next most favored region, the Middle States (the difference being $166 in the first instance, $206 in the second). The average per capita income in the Northwest and Southwest come next. The lowest per capita income is found in the Southeast, where the figure is less than half of that for the Nation as a whole.

The differences between per capita farm and nonfarm incomes are also striking. For the nation as a whole, nonfarm incomes are estimated as being more than three times as great as farm incomes, and in only one region (the far West) do farm incomes approach the nonfarm in size. The regional variations in farm incomes are greater than those in nonfarm incomes. The latter run from $535 in the Southeast to $953 in the Far West. The per capita farm incomes range from less than $200 in the Southeast to over $800 in the far West, a ratio of 4½ to 1; thus the same regions occupy the first and the last rank with respect to both types of income.

TABLE 1.—*Average annual per-capita income by regions, 1929* [1]

	General average	Average for non-farm population	Average for farm population
United States	$750	$908	$273
Northeast	881	946	366
Middle States	715	854	262
Northwest	590	703	426
Southeast	365	535	183
Southwest	564	683	366
Far West	921	953	818

[1] Based on estimates for separate States, in *America's Capacity to Consume*, Brookings Institution (1934).

Such great regional variations in incomes and levels of living call for a searching investigation of data that may throw light on underlying causes, social effects, and possibilities of readjustment.

2. The Main Industrial Divisions of the Population

Distribution of Farm and Nonfarm Populations

The distribution of urban, rural-nonfarm, and rural-farm population in 1930 is shown in figures 5 a–c. The major part of the urban population, including the largest cities, is in the Northeast and Middle States. In the

[3] This method of estimating farm incomes corresponds to the methods used by the Department of Agriculture in making its estimates of farm income. The use of farm prices of course reduces the dollar incomes of farmers. In comparing the relative position of farm and nonfarm elements in the population, it should be remembered that in 1929 the share of the nonfarm population contained a considerable amount of realized profits from the sale of securities—profits used in the main for reinvestment in securities which shortly declined in value.

Northwest particularly, cities are small and scattered. The distribution of the rural-nonfarm population for the most part follows the pattern of urban concentration rather strikingly, the outstanding exception being the mining population of West Virginia and Kentucky.

The map of rural-farm population, however, shows the heaviest shading in the Southeast, with a rather even distribution throughout the Northeast and Middle States, and a progressively lighter shading to the west except for the Pacific coast area.

The Northeast and the Middle States show a rough balance between farm population and total land in farms (fig. 6). Together they include 28 percent of the farm land and 34 percent of the farm population. The Northwest has less than 10 percent of the farm population and 28 percent of the farm land. Together the Far West and Southwest have 15 percent of the farm population and almost twice that proportion of the farm land. The Southeast, on the other hand, where the average incomes and levels of living are below the average for the Nation, has 40 percent of the farm population but only 17 percent of the total land in farms. While large allowance must be made for differences in quality of land, climate, agricultural techniques, and proximity to markets in the various regions, it is quite clear that the farmers generally in the northern and western portions of the United States are in a position to win a much more adequate living from the soil than those in the Old South.

Regional variations in the distribution of farm and nonfarm population, also shown in figure 6, must be taken into account here. The northeast has less than 10 percent of the farm population, but close to 40 percent of the nonfarm. In sharp contrast, the Southeast, with 40 percent of the farm population of the country, has only 14 percent of the nonfarm. Just where there is evidence of greatest pressure of farm population on soil resources we also find the largest proportion of the population directly dependent on agriculture for a living. These findings suggest large differences in the basic relation of population to economic resources in different parts of the country, and lead on to further and more analytical inquiry.

Regional Distribution of Workers in Three Main Industrial Groups

One of the most significant indices of contrast in regional development is supplied by an examination of trends in the distribution of gainful workers in three broad industry classes: (1) Extractive (agriculture, mining, and forestry), (2) mechanical and manufacturing, and (3) trade and service (figs. 7a–b). It is instructive, before considering regional variations, to take account of major changes in this regard in the country as a whole. For the total United States, the proportion engaged in extractive industries declined steadily from over 45 percent in 1880 to just under 25 percent in 1930. At the same time the proportion engaged in the distributive and service trades increased from 34 to over 47 percent. The number employed in the latter occupational group in 1930 was almost a third greater than the number of all gainfully employed persons in 1880. There was less change in the proportion of persons engaged in manufacturing and mechanical industries during the same period, from 20 percent in 1880 to 29 percent in 1930. Furthermore, during the decade 1920–30 the proportion engaged in manufacturing and mechanical industries actually declined, while the proportion in trade, professional, and service occupations rose sharply. These figures are a striking reflection of the transformation of our economic system from one organized around the exploitation of natural resources to one in which the chief stress is on mechanical, managerial, professional, and service functions. Employment opportunities are, to an increasing extent, in the factory, store, and office. If the trend established in the past decade continues in the future, most of the new jobs must be sought where there is opportunity for taking part in complex industrial and commercial processes or in servicing community needs. This has important implications for population redistribution.

In the Northeast in 1880 about one-fourth of the gainfully employed were in the extractive industries, just over one-third were in manufacturing, and well over 40 percent were in distributive and service occupations. The proportion in the extractive industries has declined steadily since that time, and between 1920 and 1930 there was a decline in the actual number of those engaged in agriculture and forestry. The proportion employed in manufacturing increased up to 1920, but declined somewhat between 1920 and 1930. The distributive and service occupations increased steadily in relative importance, except for a slight drop between 1900 and 1920; by 1930 this group included well over half the total gainfully employed in the region.

The extractive industries of the Middle States declined steadily in relative importance from almost one-half of the gainfully employed in 1880 to less than one-fifth in 1930. Manufacturing increased in relative importance in each State up to 1920, but declined slightly during the following decade. The distributive and service occupations included about one-third of the total gainfully employed in the region in 1880. In 1930 this group of occupations included over 40 percent of the total in every State.

It was in the Southeast that extractive industries were of most outstanding importance in 1880, and that is the region where least

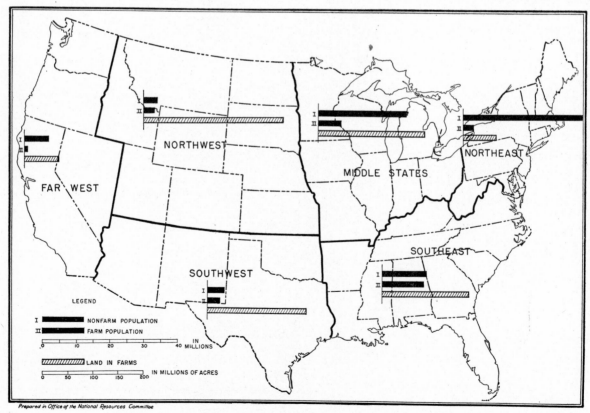

FIGURE 6.—Regional distribution of farm and nonfarm population and of land in farms, 1930.

change has occurred. From 52 to 83 percent of the total gainfully employed in each State were in the extractive industries in 1880. In 1930 this group still included 46 percent of the total for the region.

Manufacturing was insignificant in the Southeast in 1880, only 7 percent of the total gainfully employed falling into this group. While it has increased constantly in relative importance, in no State did it account for more than one-fourth of the total employed in 1930. The distributive and service group also is less important here than in any other region, but the proportion of gainful workers so employed has risen from less than one-fourth of the total in 1880 to about one-third in 1930. Florida, where the tourist industry ranks high, is exceptional among southeastern States in this respect, with over one-half of the total in trade and service occupations. The continued predominance of the extractive industries in the Southeast is in accordance with our earlier findings that the regional share of the Nation's farm population was more than twice as great as its share of the total nonfarm population. The trend toward increase in the importance of the other two main occupational groups has taken place more slowly in the Southeast than in any other region.

The extractive industries are still more important than manufacturing as a source of employment in the Northwest and in the Southwest; but in both of these regions the number engaged in the distributive and service industries is now equal to or greater than the number engaged in agriculture, mining, and forestry.

In the Far West, as in the Northeast, the extractive industries were less important as a source of employment than the distributive and service occupations even in 1880. The former group has declined from 36 percent of the total in 1880 to 18 percent in 1930, while the latter has increased from 45 to 56 percent. Manufacturing increased up to 1920 and then, as in the

Middle States and the Northwest, declined slightly in relative importance.

It is thus apparent that the Southeast has followed a course of development, with respect to the distribution of employment between the three major groups, different from that of any other region. It had in 1880 a larger proportion of its gainfully employed in the extractive industries than had any other region, and the shifts between the three occupational groups have been less rapid there than elsewhere. Since the increasing numbers of gainfully employed in the Southeast have continued to go chiefly into agriculture, it is not surprising that the ratio of farm population to land in farms is much greater there than in any other region. The continued reliance on agriculture as the chief source of employment in the Southeast should also be borne in mind in connection with the later discussion of agricultural productivity per worker in the various regions of the United States.

The Distribution of the Extractive Industries

From a population standpoint, agriculture is far more important than mining and forestry. The distribution of workers in the major types of extractive industries, by regions, is shown in table 2. In 1930, in the United States as a

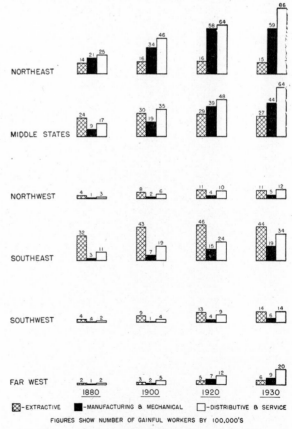

FIGURE 7b.—Trend of three major occupational groups, by regions, 1880, 1900, 1920, 1930.

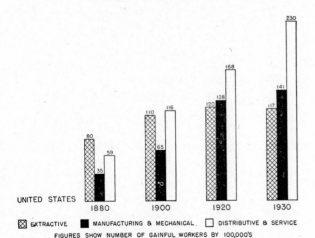

FIGURE 7a.—Trend of three major occupational groups, United States 1880, 1900, 1920, 1930.

115961°—38——4

whole, nearly 10,500,000 persons of both sexes were employed in agriculture. In contrast to this figure, all the other important extractive industries included only 1,235,000 persons, a ratio of more than 8 to 1. Nevertheless, mine workers and their families in the United States comprise some 5 million people; and well over a million people are normally dependent for their support on forestry and fishing.

Table 2.—*Extractive occupations, 1930, by regions and sex*

	Agriculture		Forestry and Fishing		Mining	
	Males	Females	Males	Females	Males	Females
United States	9, 562, 059	909, 939	250, 140	329	983, 564	759
Northeast	984, 363	31, 294	47, 152	38	433, 459	251
Middle States	2, 389, 811	66, 685	36, 225	36	180, 324	208
Northwest	989, 278	25, 602	10, 965	6	72, 232	54
Southeast	3, 543, 179	669, 942	81, 681	181	148, 049	124
Southwest	1, 148, 198	96, 763	10, 545	23	96, 936	56
Far West	507, 230	19, 653	63, 572	45	52, 564	66

The population problems raised by the extractive industries are closely related. Not only are all three based on the direct exploitation of natural resources; all three give rise to the same type of scattered settlement. In contrast to people in urban communities, workers in these industries have fewer alternative opportunities for employment open to them. At the same time, they tend to have less mobility than people in urban centers. They are usually attached to their present locations both by tradition and by economic ties.

A further relationship between the extractive industries lies in the fact that there is considerable interchange of workers between them. A combination of part-time farming with work in the lumber industry or at the mines is quite common. Also, men who can no longer find employment as lumbermen or miners often turn to farming in the area where they live in preference to migrating a long distance in search of other kinds of work.

The Northeast had slightly more than a million persons engaged in agriculture; this figure represented just under 10 percent of the total for the United States. Later discussion will show how agriculture in the Northeast is integrated into the economy of the region. The number engaged in forestry and fishing in the Northeast was 19 percent of the national total. Distribution of these workers throughout the region was fairly even. No striking geographic concentration was apparent. The situation for those engaged in mining presented an entirely different aspect. The whole region included 44 percent of the total 1 million miners in the country; 94 percent of the region's total was concentrated in Pennsylvania and West Virginia. Those two States include

the only anthracite coal field of any importance, and part of the most important bituminous field.

In the Middle States, agriculture is of prime importance among the extractive industries. Nearly two and a half million persons—23 percent of the total for the United States—were in 1930 gainfully employed in agriculture in this region. Neither forestry nor mining was inconsiderable, however. The Middle States had 14 percent of those engaged in forestry and fishing throughout the country, and 18 percent of the miners.

The Southeast is unique in that there all three extractive industries are both vital and troublesome. The region in 1930 had 40 percent of all agricultural workers, 33 percent of those in forestry, and 15 percent of the miners. The percentage in mining was relatively small; but geographic concentration, combined with other factors to be described below, has resulted in stranded communities presenting serious problems. Nearly three-fourths of all the miners in the region were in three States— Kentucky, Tennessee, and Alabama.

Agriculture also leads the other extractive industries in both the Northwest and the Southwest. The Far West, however, which includes only 5 percent of the Nation's workers in agriculture and mining, had more than 25 percent of the total workers in forestry in 1930.

The Study of Population Redistribution found that only 9 percent of all miners lived in cities of 25,000 or over; 25 percent more lived in towns between 2,500 and 25,000 population; 59 percent lived in villages, camps, or "patches" of less than 2,500; the remaining 7 percent lived on farms.[4]

The accompanying map (fig. 8) shows graphically the distribution of those engaged in mining, the farm population, and cities of 25,000 or more population. This indicates more clearly than can any verbal description the relation between the population employed in the principal extractive industries and the contrast between their distribution and that of the urban population.

Workers in lumbering or mining, living in small settlements, are faced with a serious situation when the nearby mine or mill that is their only source of work closes down because of exhaustion of the raw material or for some other reason. Such stranded communities were known long before the depression. They are more common in lumbering and mining than in other industries. In some cases the situation affects an entire district—for instance, the case of copper mining in Michigan. Stranded populations dependent on single mines are not uncommon in the case of other metals, and they are found in both anthracite and bituminous coal districts.

[4] Goodrich, *op. cit.,* p. 303.

3. The Situation in Forestry and Mining

The situation of the quarter-million gainful workers employed in forestry and fishing presents especially interesting problems. The most important aspects of the forest industries have been their progressive movement westward as the country was opened up, and the extremely rapid depletion of a rich natural resource so that relatively little virgin forest now remains in the United States.

The plight of workers and their families who were dependent upon lumbering became serious some years before the onset of the depression. Many of the lumber workers moved on with the cut. Many others, as the timber resources neared exhaustion in the isolated areas in which they lived, turned to agriculture in the cut-over lands. They found that much of the land was unsuitable for farms and yielded only a very meager subsistence. Vivid insight into the difficulties of such groups is afforded by a recent study of a cut-over area in Louisiana:

> This area was chosen for special study because of the serious situation confronting its population. The timber resources are now about depleted. Two sawmills have already "cut out" and shut down. The remaining mills are operating at from 35 to 45 percent of capacity and even at this have only a few years left to run. Many of the people who formerly obtained a livelihood from the lumber industry are left stranded in the rural sawmill villages. Others are "squatting" on company land. Still others are confronted with loss of employment in the very near future. Obviously the people in the area are facing an immediate readjustment, and agricultural pursuits are those most frequently mentioned as an alternative. But the entire Ward is included in the area recommended for retirement from agricultural purposes, making the prospects of gaining a livelihood from agriculture in the surrounding territory very slender. Besides agriculture, lumbering, and one small gravel pit, there is at present no basis for the support of the people in the region. Trade within the area is negligible.[5]

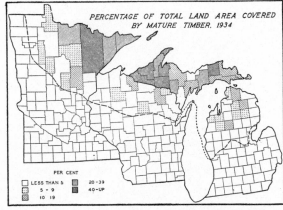

PERCENTAGE OF TOTAL LAND AREA COVERED BY MATURE TIMBER, 1934

PER CENT

☐ LESS THAN 5   ▨ 20 - 39
▧ 5 - 9   ■ 40 - UP
▨ 10 - 19

University of Pennsylvania Press.

FIGURE 9.—From Goodrich and others, *Migration and Economic Opportunity*.

[5] Smith, T. Lynn, and Fry, Martha R., *The Population of a Selected "Cut-Over" Area in Louisiana*, Louisiana State University and Agricultural and Mechanical College, Bulletin No. 268 (January 1936), p. 4.

The Great Lakes Cut-over Region

A similar situation, on a more extensive scale and dating from a somewhat earlier period, is found in the Great Lakes cut-over area stretching from northern Michigan across Wisconsin and Minnesota. The outlook for population in this area has been examined by the Study of Population Redistribution. Lumbering, mining, and agriculture have been the chief sources of income in this area, and have given rise to scattered settlements dependent on a single occupation. Employment in lumbering and mining has been declining for a decade or so. Figure 9 shows how little mature timber is now standing. Many of the displaced workers turned to agriculture, but found that most of the land would yield no adequate return. Rural poverty and local government units unable to finance themselves are chronic problems in this region. To these more permanent difficulties new troubles have been added since 1929 by acute unemployment at the mines and in nearby industrial areas. There has been a resultant pressure on poor land that makes even subsistence agriculture a problem.

From 1880 to 1900, while the rich timber resources were being rapidly exploited, the population of this region more than tripled (increasing from 280,933 to 970,235). After 1900, however, the increase slowed down; between 1920 and 1930 the 76 counties of this area showed a net loss in population.[6] In 1930, 11 percent of the gainful workers in this region were employed in forestry, fishing, and allied industries, and 27 percent were in agriculture. About 250,000 workers and their families, altogether a million or more persons, are now dependent on extractive industries in this area. A large proportion of these people are in serious straits. Emigration has practically ceased during the depression, and in some sections many persons have returned to try to wring the means of subsistence from the soil.

The authors of *Migration and Economic Opportunity* point out that a constructive program for the future of those engaged in forestry and agriculture must have as its central objective the establishment of a permanent forest-farm economy, supplemented by recreational development. This involves public ownership or public control of the land, so as to make possible a long-range program. The basis for such a development is being laid in the Great Lakes cut-over region at the present time, through Federal acquisition of large tracts and the passage of rural zoning legislation, to prevent agricultural settlement of land recommended for permanent forestation. The application of a long-range program for restoration and maintenance of timber resources on a sustained-yield basis, together with the development of the recreational and resort pos-

[6] Goodrich, *op. cit.*, p. 178.

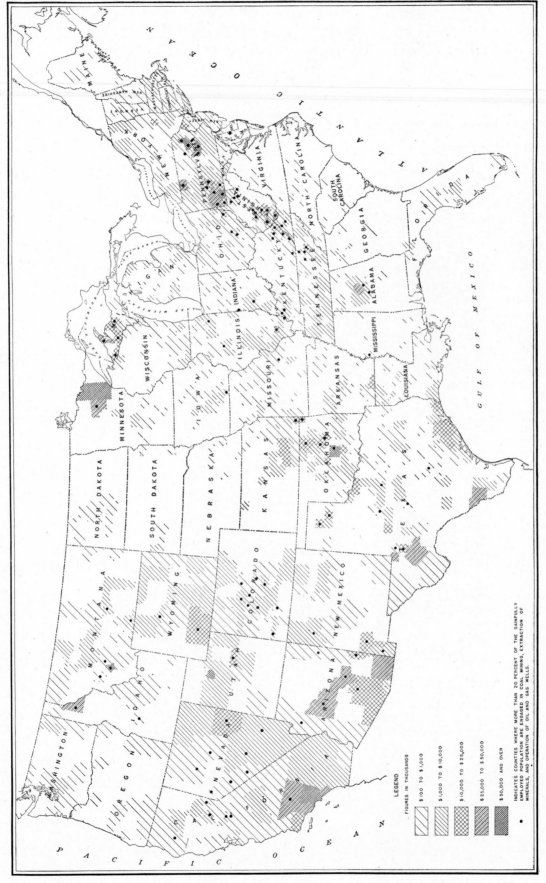

FIGURE 10.—Value of mineral products by counties, 1930.

sibilities of the area, would yield employment to a considerably larger number of people than are at present engaged in forestry in this region (54,000 workers in 1930). On the other hand, a large proportion of the 137,000 workers who were engaged in agriculture in 1930 would probably either have to find employment under the new program or be forced to migrate to some other area. It is estimated that the total farm population in the Great Lakes cut-over area increased by more than 80,000 persons between 1930 and 1935. It is safe to say that most of these people, in addition to the surplus already there, will be at least partly dependent on public support until some other economic opportunity opens to them.

The situation in the northern counties of Wisconsin, Michigan, and Minnesota exemplifies in intense form the general problem presented by the depletion of forest resources on which the population of some parts of the country has been economically dependent. Comparable situations on a smaller scale are found in northern New England and parts of the Southeast.

In the Great Lakes region the situation is further complicated by difficulties in the iron and copper industries. Next to agriculture, mining offers the chief source of employment in this region. More than three-quarters of all the iron ore mined in the United States comes from northern Minnesota, and there are iron and copper mines in Michigan. In mining, as in forestry, serious difficulties antedate the depression. It is difficult for the deep high-cost copper mines of Michigan to be worked in competition with mines in the western United States and in Africa. The depression has greatly accentuated the problem by driving a number of mines out of operation. In 1935 production of copper ore in Michigan was less than 40 percent of the 1929 level. At the same time employment was less than 20 percent of the 1929 figure. Prospects of increased employment in these mines are poor, and many of the unemployed copper miners and their families who are now stranded in this vicinity must seek employment elsewhere. The outlook for the iron miners in this region is somewhat more favorable. A considerable amount of readjustment, required by technological changes, took place in this industry during the twenties, when opportunities for other employment were relatively great. Unemployment during the depression was very serious, and affected a much larger number of people than those engaged in copper mining—the 1929 employment figures were 6,790 in copper mining and 21,811 in iron mining—but recovery since 1933 has been encouraging. It seems reasonable to expect that, as business conditions improve, iron mining in the Lake Superior region will return to approximately its 1929 level, although individual mines may encounter more permanent difficulties due to high production costs or to a reduced demand for particular types of ore. Employment prospects are by no means the same as the prospects for the industry, because of the effects of continuous technological changes. The total number of miners permanently displaced from iron mining in this region may be absolutely as great as in copper mining, although proportionately less.

The Situation in the Mineral Industries

The plight of the mining population of the Great Lakes cut-over area is part of the larger national problem of the whole mineral industry. The present conditions and the outlook for population in the principal mining areas have been investigated during recent months by the sectional economic research unit of the Federal Emergency Relief Administration and by the Study of Population Redistribution. The latter study points out, by way of summary, that the westward march of mining and lumbering has been continuous, and that the extractive industries—except for coal—have moved more rapidly than have manufactures and population. This westward movement, which is now slowing down, has resulted from four chief factors: (1) Exploration and discovery, (2) expanding transport, (3) developing technology, and (4) not least, depletion of our immensely rich natural resources. The value of mineral products by counties in 1930 is shown in figure 10. The conclusion as to employment prospects in mining as a whole is that, from the short-time point of view, technological changes bringing about increased productivity per worker will probably be the most significant factor. Even with the revival of general business conditions, there is little likelihood that employment will rise much above the 1929 levels. Regional shifts in opportunity in the near future will create local hardships and bring about gradual movements of population. From the long-time point of view, however, the outlook is quite different, since the factor of depletion will inevitably become the dominant one. This will create a marked, though gradual, increase in the demand for labor, as the less rich resources in one field after another have to be drawn upon.

Coal mining greatly overshadows all other mining operations in immediate human importance. The workers engaged in coal mining in 1920 made up 67 percent of all gainful workers engaged in the extraction of minerals, including fuels; but during the next decade this percentage declined 4 points to 63 percent of the total in 1930. These workers are rooted to the industry and area of their occupation both by residence in isolated, single-industry regions and by the development of special skills not easily transferable to other fields of activity. In 1920, approximately the peak of employment in the industry, there were altogether 733,936 workers, who with their families made

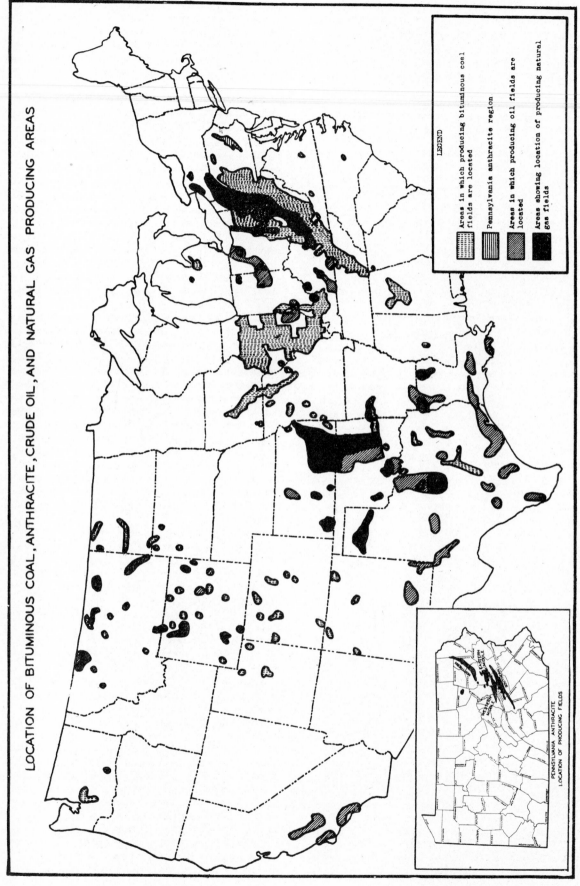

LOCATION OF BITUMINOUS COAL, ANTHRACITE, CRUDE OIL, AND NATURAL GAS PRODUCING AREAS

LEGEND

Areas in which producing bituminous coal fields are located

Pennsylvania anthracite region

Areas in which producing oil fields are located

Areas showing location of producing natural gas fields

PENNSYLVANIA ANTHRACITE
LOCATION OF PRODUCING FIELDS

FIGURE 11.—Location of bituminous coal, anthracite, crude oil, and natural gas producing areas. From *The Bituminous Coal Industry with Survey of Competing Fuels,* Sectional Economic Research, Works Progress Administration.

up some 3 million persons supported by this industry.

Anthracite coal.—Figure 11 shows the geographic distribution of coal mines and oil and gas wells. Anthracite mining is almost entirely concentrated in a small area in Pennsylvania. The production of hard coal has increased little since 1910, except for the peak during the war years. Since 1918 the decline in production has been rather marked, due chiefly to the competition of other fuels. In anthracite mining there has been a net decline since 1929 of over 42,000 jobs—28 percent.[7] At the same time the average number of days worked per year fell from 225 to 207, so that the number of man-days in the industry declined by one-third.

There is little chance that many of these men will be reemployed. The 10 counties where there is anthracite mining constitute practically a single-industry region. Of the total number gainfully employed here in 1929, almost one-third were associated with anthracite production. The possibilities of full-time agricultural employment in this region for those permanently displaced from mining is slight. Their reabsorption into industry seems to depend either on migration or on the attraction of other industries to this locality.

Bituminous coal.—With respect to bituminous coal the situation is more complicated. There are three principal producing regions:[8]

1. The Appalachian, which produces about 75 percent of the total volume of bituminous coal, and includes mines in Pennsylvania, West Virginia, Ohio, Maryland, Virginia, eastern Kentucky, Tennessee, and Alabama.

2. The eastern interior, which produces about 15 percent of the total, and includes Illinois, Indiana, and western Kentucky.

3. The western, including all mines west of the Mississippi, which produce about 10 percent of the total.

The competition between these areas has added to the difficulties of the bituminous coal industry. Prior to the war, Pennsylvania and Ohio produced the largest share of the country's bituminous coal. The stimulus of the war brought about increased production and capacity in all fields. This led, during the period of decreased demand after 1920, to intensified competition for markets. In this situation the unionized fields of the northern Appalachians and the eastern interior found themselves at a disadvantage in competition with the nonunion southern Appalachian mines, which were located in an area of surplus farm population. The latter were able to produce at lower costs, due chiefly to low wage

rates. They secured an increasing share of the market, and in 1925 their production exceeded that of Pennsylvania and Ohio. Since that time the advantage of the southern Appalachians has been somewhat reduced. This has come about partly through wage cuts in the union fields, partly through the equalizing effect on wages of the National Recovery Administration, partly through increased freight differentials favoring the northern fields, and partly through the rapid introduction there of mechanized processes that have increased labor productivity.

Approximately half a million workers are engaged in the mining of bituminous coal. Their prospects of future employment are adversely affected by several factors: (1) Technological economies in the use of fuel, which counterbalance the increasing demand for energy; (2) displacement of coal by competing fuels; (3) overcapacity of the mines, which destroys the stability of the industry and makes for irregularity of employment and earnings of the workers; (4) wide seasonal variation in the demand for coal, which increases the irregularity of employment; and (5) displacement of labor through the adoption of mechanized processes of production. Enumeration of these factors helps to make it clear why coal mining was regarded as one of the "sick industries" even before the onset of the depression. In 1929, 30,000 workers in this industry were entirely unemployed and part-time employment was widespread. The peak in the demand for bituminous coal was reached in 1918; since that time the trend in the number of man-days worked has been generally downward. The peak in the number of commercial mines, however, and in the number of employees was not reached until 1923, the discrepancy being accounted for by the fact that after 1918 the mines operated fewer days in the year.

Many of the miners who were displaced before 1930 sought and found other occupations. Those who did not and those who were dropped after 1930 have much more limited possibilities of finding other employment. It is estimated that a total of 75,000 jobs have been lost, to say nothing of those who, because of the prevailing part-time employment in the mines, can make only the most meager living. There is a consensus of opinion that, even with a return to 1929 business levels, the demand for bituminous coal will probably be 5 to 7 percent below the output of 1929. This will result chiefly from increasing fuel efficiency, and the shift toward forms of energy affording a larger yield relative to the amount of labor required for production. The progress of this shift from 1870 to 1930 is indicated in figure 12. Employment will probably drop even more than output, due to the introduction of mechanized methods of production. At present 80 percent of the national coal output is under-

[7] *The Employment Situation in the Pennsylvania Anthracite Region*, Sectional Economic Research, Works Progress Administration, October 1935, pp. 15 and A-3.
[8] *The Bituminous Coal Industry with a Survey of Competing Fuels*, Sectional Economic Research, Works Progress Administration, December 1935, p. 58 and maps on pp. A-2 and A-3.

cut by machine (as compared with about 58 percent in 1918), but only about 12 percent is machine loaded. The possibilities of labor displacement are considerable, in view of the fact that loaders comprise the largest group of workers in the industry, and that the introduction of machine loading has to date been largely confined to the mines of Illinois, Indiana, and the Far West. Any factor which tends to increase production costs in the Appalachian bituminous fields will stimulate the adoption of mechanized processes and thus increase the displacement of workers. On the other hand, where production costs are high, as they are in Maryland, and geological factors make it impossible to introduce mechanization, the loss of all except a local market must be anticipated. The workers thus seem to be faced with a Hobson's choice. Many of them will lose their jobs either through displacement by machines or through the closing down of mines unable to compete with coal produced at lower cost.

The most extensive recent study of the bituminous coal industry reaches the conclusions that, on the basis of increased mechanization between 1927 and 1931, and assuming a maximum production of 500 million tons when business conditions are similar to 1929, mechanization and lessened demand for bituminous coal will displace from 80,000 to 136,000 men—leaving employment for 429,000 to 483,000 men. The lower limit of employment supposes no changes in productivity between the 8-hour day

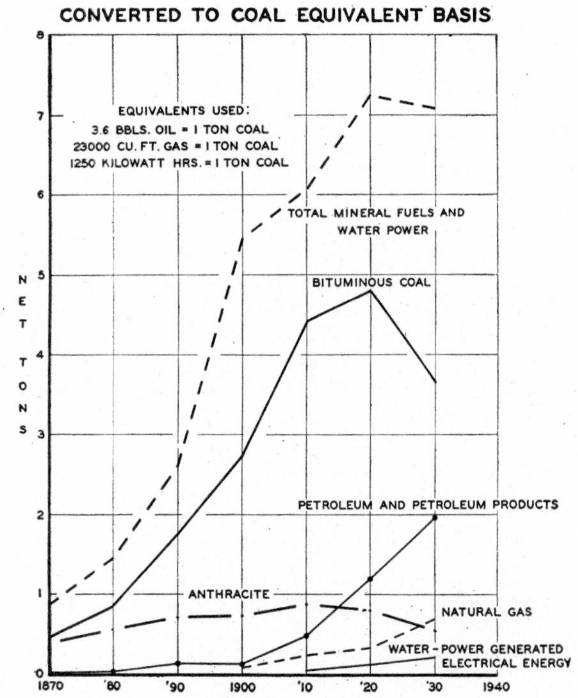

FIGURE 12.—Per capita consumption of energy sources, United States, 1870–1930. From *The Bituminous Coal Industry with Survey of Competing Fuels*, Sectional Economic Research, Works Progress Administration.

current in 1929 and the 7-hour day now becoming general. The upper limit of employment postulates the maximum decrease in productivity. In addition to those permanently displaced, the soft coal industry has been characterized by a large proportion of part-time workers, many of whom cannot earn an adequate living from the amount of employment available to them in the mines. Exact figures are not available, but in 1929 about 8 percent of the total employees in bituminous coal mining earned less than $46 per month, while in 1932 almost 30 percent earned less than $28 per month.[9]

It is thus clear that a large number of miners will need to find a means of livelihood other than, or supplementary to, bituminous coal mining. The seriousness of their situation is intensified by the fact that most of these people are located in the Appalachian region, already overpopulated in relation to its economic opportunities. The agricultural resources of this area are insufficient to support the present farm population, as will be shown below, and alternative industrial opportunities are very limited. For many of the surplus miners, migration seems to be the most promising possibility.

Mineral industries other than coal.—For the one-third of a million workers engaged in mining other than coal, prospects are varied. Iron and copper mining have already been touched upon. With respect to iron, the opinion seems to be that, granted generally satisfactory business conditions, employment will not be widely different from that prevailing in the twenties. Copper, which is especially subject to foreign competition, will probably offer only reduced opportunities in the near future. Apparently many of the men who have been copper miners in the Michigan and Butte, Mont., fields must seek other lines of employment. As to the precious metals, recent economic events have increased demand, and employment prospects at present are better than in most other types of mining, though the number of workers affected is relatively small.

Technological changes had brought about a drop in employment in quarries, and a consequent readjustment of workers, before 1929; the present prospects are that with improvement in business conditions employment will once more approach pre-depression levels. Workers in oil and gas wells have perhaps the most encouraging outlook of any in the mineral industries, at least for the next few decades. Employment in this field may increase further as secondary methods of recovery come into use.[10]

The Study of Population Redistribution calls attention to two factors which have an important bearing on the location of those en-

9 *Ibid.*, pp. 3–4.
10 Goodrich, *op. cit.*, ch. VII, pp. 303–314, passim.

gaged in the mineral industries. One is the marked tendency toward concentration, with a reduction in the number and a corresponding increase in the average size of mines. The other is the widening radius of daily travel possible for miners with improvements in transportation. These two influences tend to stabilize employment and to concentrate job opportunities geographically. At the same time they make it possible for the worker to live, in either town or country, at a greater distance from his job. The company town is gradually becoming less common in mining districts, since it is now feasible for the worker to live in a rural area, where, if suitable land is available, he can combine part-time farming with the aid of other members of the family with his work in the mine, or in an incorporated town from which he can travel daily to any of several mines and where he has greater possibilities of alternative employment in other occupations. In accordance with these tendencies, we shall expect in the future to see a slow decline in the large percentage of mine workers living in villages and small settlements immediately adjacent to the mine, and an increase in the percentages living both in larger towns and on farms.

The immediate outlook both for forestry and mining is full of uncertainties but the situation presents interesting and bright possibilities. The displacement of workers from extractive industries is a characteristic of the technological progress which makes possible the development of new goods and services, and rising levels of living. Long-time planning in the interest of conservation of natural resources and efficient management with reference both to productivity and to the human interests that are immediately at stake may provide more stable employment, though in somewhat lesser volume, in forestry and mining than ever before. This would result in far better conditions of living for the workers in these industries and for their families.

4. The Situation in Agriculture

A study of conditions affecting the farm population has peculiar interest for the student of population problems, for two reasons. In the first place, the relation of farm population to natural resources affects the welfare of 30 million people directly and vitally, and indirectly exerts a profound influence on the economic life of the whole Nation. In the second place, whereas the total nonfarm population of the United States in 1930 already lacked a sufficient number of children to be self-replacing, there were enough children in the farm population to supply an increase of 62 percent in the number of persons of reproductive age in this group.[11] Trends in farm population

---

[11] Based on census data for children under 5 years of age in 1930, and life table values for 1930.

are extremely important, therefore, both from the standpoint of economic balance in the distribution of population and from that of differential reproduction.

Three-quarters of the total farm population of the United States is concentrated in three of the six major regions. These regions are, in order of importance: the Southeast (containing 40 percent of the total farm population); the Middle States (23 percent); the Southwest (12 percent). Regional analysis reveals opportunities and problems in large perspective. Such analysis should, of course, be supplemented by a more intensive examination of local variations. Some attention will be paid to both types of analysis, but the chief emphasis here will be placed on broad regional treatment.

The farm population of the Northeast may be thought of as comprising three main groups: (1) Commercial farms serving nearby urban markets, truck gardens, milk sheds, etc.; (2) part-time subsistence and suburban farms; and (3) general farms, frequently located in more or less isolated areas (the Adirondacks, northern New England, western Pennsylvania, lower Delaware, etc.). The situation in this region is dominated in large part by proximity to urban industrial and commercial centers. The farms of this region feed and offer a retreat for urban residents, and thus have an assured place in the national economy. The great increase of nonproductive farm population in the areas surrounding the great cities in this region during the depression has been a symptom rather than a cause of the reduction of these families to a status of poverty and privation. It may be expected that recovery will induce the return of these families to industry, leaving the normal farm population of the area in a favorable position.

The Northwest is naturally divided into three quite different segments: the eastern parts of the Dakotas, Nebraska, and Kansas, which in their economy resemble the tier of middle States lying west of the Mississippi River; the Great Plains; and the Rocky Mountain States. Attention is centered at present on the Great Plains, the problem area in this region. This area yielded large returns in the years following the World War and as a whole makes a good showing in the farm statistics for 1929 and 1930. But a movement out of this region was already in progress during the twenties. Montana was the only 1 of the 48 States to show a net loss in population between 1920 and 1930. The severe droughts of recent years, especially in 1934 and 1936, have revealed the irreparable damage to the soil resources in some parts of this area that have resulted from overgrazing and from plowing up land best adapted to grazing. The region as a whole presents large possibilities as well as large problems. It is hoped that the present tragic

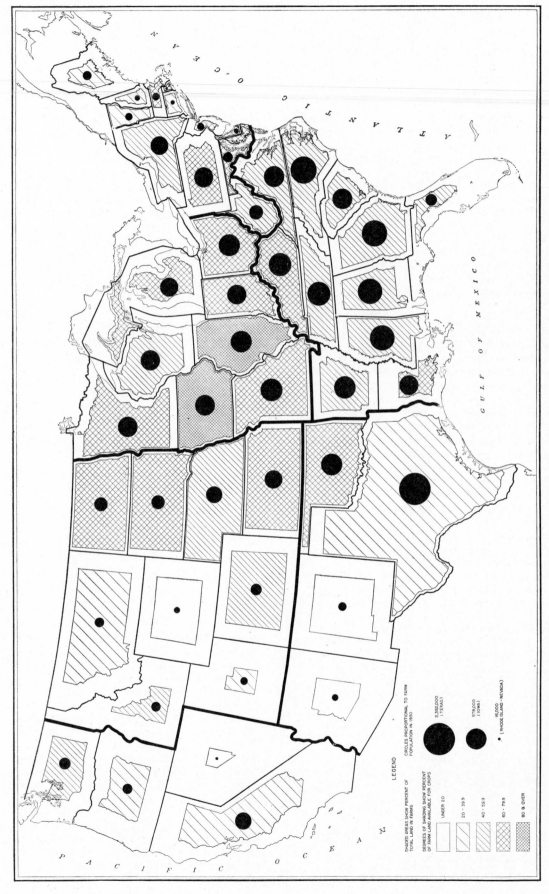

LEGEND

SHADED AREAS SHOW PERCENT OF TOTAL LAND IN FARMS

DEGREES OF SHADING SHOW PERCENT OF FARM LAND AVAILABLE FOR CROPS

UNDER 20

20 - 39.9

40 - 59.9

60 - 79.9

80 & OVER

CIRCLES PROPORTIONAL TO FARM POPULATION IN 1930

2,350,000 (TEXAS)

978,000 (IOWA)

16,000 (RHODE ISLAND - NEVADA)

situation will lead to the formulation and application of a scientific long-time land use program for this part of the country.

The problems of the Southeast are very different in character. Here, too, there are some prosperous areas, and great possibilities for new developments. Nevertheless, we have already seen that in many sections of this region there is widespread and chronic poverty. The basic reason for this is not the racial composition of the population in the southeastern States, nor can it be attributed primarily to events of 70 years ago. Poverty blights a large proportion of the white as well as the Negro families, and retarded development of the region in recent decades must be interpreted in terms of the present structure of southern economy. In examining the distribution of farm population in relation to economic resources, we shall therefore give special attention to conditions affecting the situation of the 12½ million people living on farms in the Southeast.

Variations in the Density of Farm Population

The first step in the study of farm population problems is the quantitative analysis of variations in density of farm population relative to land resources. The major features of such analysis may be set forth by the use of three maps (figs. 13, 14, and 15). In figure 13 the black circles are proportional to the size of the farm population and the shaded areas within each State are proportional to the total quantity of land in farms in that State. These areas are shaded to represent degrees in the proportion of total land that may be classified as "arable" (harvest land plus idle or fallow crop land plus "plowable pasture").

The reasons for some of the most conspicuous variations in gross density of farm population, shown in the first part of this chapter, are immediately apparent in figure 13. The very small farm population in some of the Rocky Mountain States must be interpreted both in the light of the relatively small amount of land in farms and of the small proportion of farm land classified as arable. The same consideration applies, in lesser degree, to parts of New England and to Florida. In Illinois and Iowa the high proportion of farm land adapted to cultivation affords an adequate physical basis for the large farming population. But in some of the Southeast States there are even larger farm populations, with somewhat smaller amounts of land in farms and much lower proportions of arable land.

Quantity of "arable land"—a term used extensively in European studies—represents the most useful single measure of absolute land resources. This leaves out of account the dry pasture and range land of the western States; but if such land were included, the apparent disparity between sections would be increased considerably. Thus, regional variations in agricultural density are in general understated by the criterion here adopted.

There is no wholly satisfactory measure of absolute land resources in the United States in view of the great variety of existing soils and crops. An acre of corn in tidewater Virginia is not the same as an acre of corn in central Iowa, and neither is equivalent to an acre of rich truck land in New Jersey or an acre of oranges in Florida. Accordingly, the map (fig. 15) showing the relation of farm population to land values by counties gives a more reliable picture of the relation of farm population to "economic resources." Economic resources in this sense include social factors such as demand for farm products in different regions. In general the counties with greatest resources per capita of farm population measured by current farm values are also those characterized by large average holdings of land fit for cultivation. Figures 14 and 15, showing density of farm population in relation to acres of arable land and to land values, should be compared with the county map showing planes of living presented above[12] (see fig. 4).

The most striking feature about these maps is the contrast between most of the Southeast and the other main agricultural areas. On the population density maps large areas in the Southeast are characterized by dark colors, revealing the presence of a large farming population in an area where much of the land is of poor quality, or at least where much of the land yields low returns as it is now being used. However, several fairly prosperous agricultural areas in the Southeast stand out in the map showing density of farm population relative to land values, in contrast to the high density of farm population characteristic of most of this region. These are: a dairy, fruit and estate area in western and northern Virginia; sections in central Kentucky and central Tennessee; the Yazoo-Mississippi Delta area; and the fruit and vegetable lands in Florida.

The Northeast, much of which appears in a favorable light on the plane of living map, is heavily shaded on the two density maps. This is notably the case in the first of these maps (fig. 14) showing density of farm population measured in relation to acreage of arable land. According to this criterion, the entire Northeast, except one county in New York and two in Maryland, belongs in that half of the scale indicating relatively high densities but it has a smaller proportion of counties in the two highest density classes than has the Southeast. Density of farm population, even in relation to land values, has of course a different mean-

---

[12] They may also be compared with a county map showing absolute values of farm property per acre, regardless of population. See National Resources Committee, *Maladjustments in Land Use in the United States*, Supplementary Report of the Land Planning Committee, pt. VI (1935), p. 14.

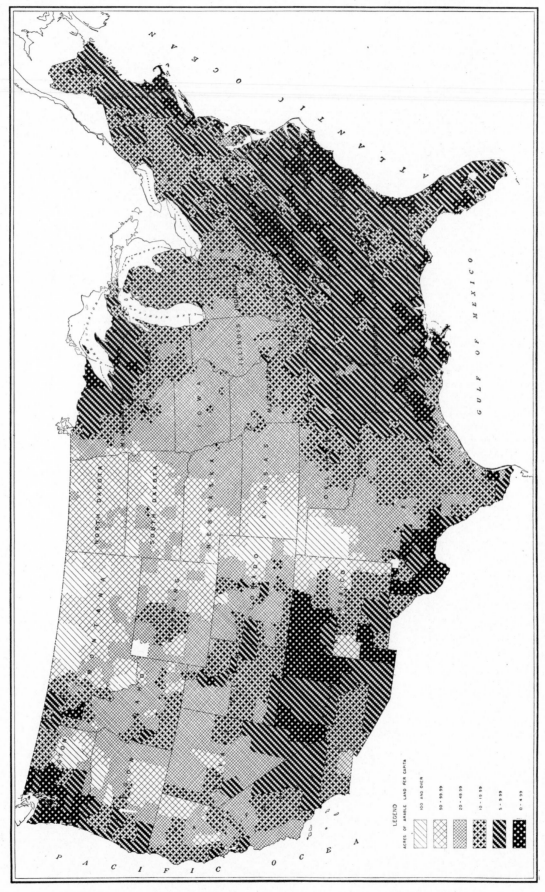

FIGURE 14.—Density of farm population by counties, I: acres of arable land per capita of the farm population, 1935.

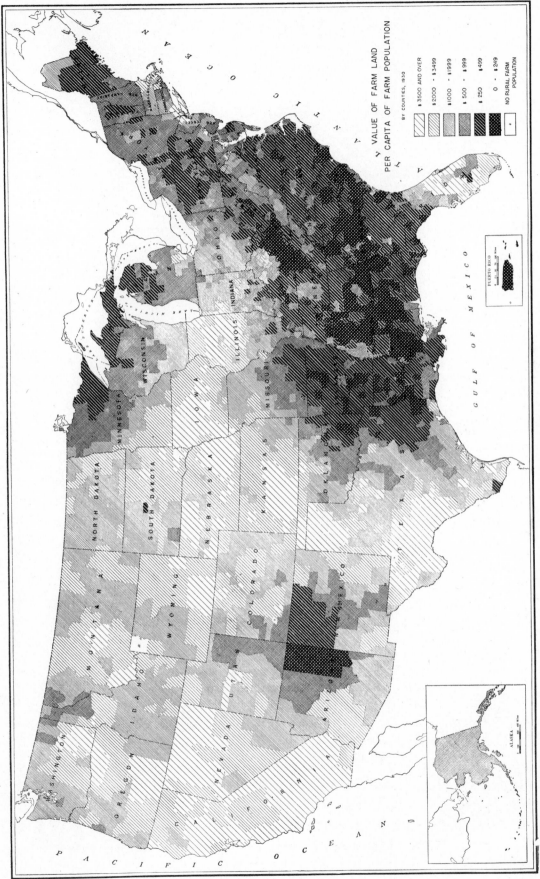

FIGURE 15.—Density of farm population by counties, II: value of farm land per capita of the farm population, 1930.

ing in the vicinity of large cities than in more isolated rural regions. Near cities there is more possibility that farmers have supplementary occupations, and also that farms are used for recreation or retirement.

Most of the Middle States region belongs in the medium classes, with two exceptions, on all three maps. In the vicinity of cities, the farm population is more dense; and in the cut-over region of the Great Lakes, much of the land is not arable. In spite of the rather sparse population in the Great Plains area, recent events indicate that much of this area is actually over-populated from the standpoint of soil conservation. In the Southwest and Far West, all the shades from lightest to darkest appear. There are considerable quantities of land in both regions suitable only for range. In these places the population is thinly scattered. There are other sections where, due to high fertility of soil or proximity to cities, intensive agriculture is practiced and the farm population is dense. The area showing black in Arizona and New Mexico on the density maps corresponds to a dark area on the plane of living map. It represents chiefly the unfortunate situation of the reservation Indians in this region, but includes some poor "squatter" communities.

Throughout New England, per capita values run between $250 and $1,000, except in Massa-chusetts and the potato-growing section in Maine. Sections of Connecticut, New York, Pennsylvania, and New Jersey appear in a lighter shade than the rest of the Northeast. This is due chiefly (as in Massachusetts) to the influence of urbanization. These sections are in the same value group as two patches along the northern boundary of Virginia, where fertile soil and suburban advantages account for relatively high land values. Beginning in Ohio, the shading to the west grows much lighter, except in southern Indiana, Illinois, Missouri, and the Great Lakes region. The Far West has the largest proportion of land valued at $3,500 or more per capita of the farm population. Nowhere in the whole region do values fall below $500 and in California practically all the land is above $2,000 per capita.

The most striking feature of these maps is their revelation of the prevalence of dense agricultural population in the Southeast, except in Florida. This is true both for absolute amounts of land adapted for cultivation and for land values. The majority of the counties in this region show average per capita land values of less than $500. These findings clearly indicate the presence of a large population engaged in farming in areas where much of the land yields low returns, at least as used and valued at the present time.

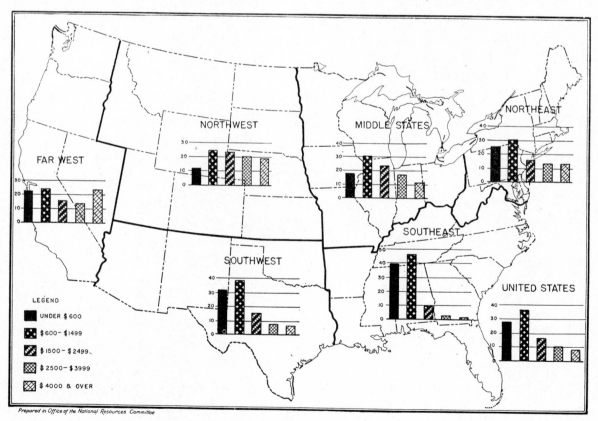

FIGURE 16.—Percentage distribution of farms by value of product classes, by regions, 1930.

Variations in Average Value of Products per Farm

A general idea of regional differences in basic conditions affecting farm income is obtained when farms are grouped into classes according to the value of their products, including home products consumed by the farm family. For more than one-fourth of all the farms in the United States, the value of all products sold or consumed at home in the year 1929 was under $600 per farm. At the other end of the scale, one-fifth of the country's farms had an annual value of products of over $2,500 each. These figures both refer to gross value of products, with no allowance for expenditure for feed, seed, machines, tools, or interest on investment.

If the farms of the United States are divided into two nearly equal groups, on the basis of the value of their products, it is found that the poorer half (49 percent of the total) produces only 11 percent of the total value of all agricultural goods that are sold or traded. This half of the Nation's farms also produces less than half (42 percent) of all products consumed at home—in spite of the fact that much of the effort of this group must be directed toward producing things for home use. Thus it appears that the farms sometimes designated as "subsistence farms" actually grow less, on the average, for home use than do the "commercial farms."

An examination of the regional figures reveals some striking differences. In the Northeast, 25 percent of the farms fall into the group producing less than $600 worth of products annually; in the Far West 23 percent; in the Middle States 18 percent; and in the Northwest only 12 percent. In the Southeast, on the other hand, 40 percent of the farms produce less than $600 worth of products annually. The situation in the Southwest is intermediate between that in the north and west and that in the Southeast (see fig. 16).

Figure 17, showing cumulative percentage distributions of the total number of farms and of the total value of farm products, also reveals, in another way, significant variations between different parts of the country. In the United States as a whole, approximately 50 percent of the farms having the lowest value of products (all under $1,000 per year) produce only 15 percent of the total value of all crops and animal products. In the Southeast, the corresponding 50 percent of the farms (all with production values under $800) produce almost one-fourth of the total value of agricultural products for the region. In the Far West, the poorer half of the farms (including those with average values up to nearly $1,500) produce only about 12 percent of the region's products.

At the upper end of the scale, we find that less than a fourth of the agricultural output of

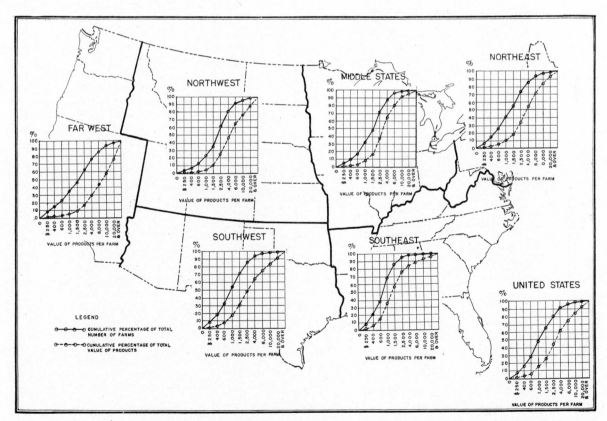

FIGURE 17.—Cumulative percentage distribution, by value of product classes, of number of farms and total value of products, by regions. 1930.

the Southeast comes from farms that yielded more than $2,500 worth of products in 1929. This fact destroys the persistent notion of the South as a region of great plantations with large annual yields.

The income derived from land and labor in farms with total products under $600 must often be divided between landlord and tenant, and a considerable portion of the landlord's share must go to payment of interest on crop advances. A large proportion of farm families in the South are thus forced to a position at or near a low subsistence level; distribution of a more generous share of this income to tenant families would still leave many of them in poverty. Real prosperity for farm families in some sections of the country is absolutely dependent on large increases in average productivity, measured in terms of value.[13]

Many of the low-value farms are part-time enterprises; but the extent to which this is

true varies greatly in different regions. In 1930 there were approximately 340,000 part-time farms in the United States.[14] Assuming that nine-tenths of these part-time farms in each region fall in the class with annual value of products under $600, the proportion of farms with very low productivity in each region that are accounted for in this way can be estimated. This explanation is found to account for 44 percent of the low-productivity farms in the Northeast, but for only about 10 percent of the low-productivity farms in the Southeast and in the Southwest (see table 3).

TABLE 3.—*Relation of number of part-time farms to number of farms with annual value of products under $600, by regions*

Region	Number of farms having a value of products under $600	Total number of part-time farms	Estimated percent of low value-of-product farms that are part-time enterprises
United States	1,681,667	339,207	18
Northeast	151,162	73,370	44
Middle States	275,483	89,170	29
Northwest	75,079	22,267	27
Southeast	901,348	108,703	11
Southwest	221,731	21,092	9
Far West	56,864	24,605	39

Colored farm families in the South have, on the average, much lower incomes than white farm families, but it would be a mistake to suppose that rural poverty in the South is a race phenomenon. The lowest average values, either of farm property or of farm productivity, frequently appear in areas where there are few colored people. It is impossible to measure incomes or productivity directly for the two racial groups in the South. Some insight into the situation, however, can be gained by analyzing the figures on average value of land per farm by color of operator, regardless of ownership. We find that average land values are distinctly lower in the South for farms operated by colored persons than for farms operated by white persons. Nevertheless, the average value of land in farms with white operators is much lower in the Southeast than in any other part of the United States (see fig. 18).

Relative amounts of supplementary labor in other enterprises by owners and by tenants, classified by color, are shown by regions in table 4. The importance of supplementary occupations for farm owners in the Northeast and in the Far West is immediately apparent. Those who combine part-time farming with other occupations are more likely to appear as farm owners. Apparently such combination is found with unusually high frequency among those reported as colored operators who

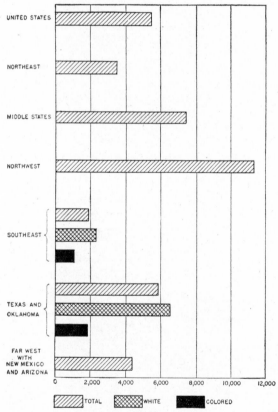

FIGURE 18.—Average value of land per farm by regions, 1930, with classification by color of operator in the South.

[13] These figures represent value of products per farm, without reference to the number of persons per farm. The question must then be raised as to whether or not more people are, on the average, supported by each farm in the regions where average value of products per farm runs high. Actually, we find the reverse to be true. The population per farm is greatest in the Southeast, and lowest in the Far West.

	Farm population per farm, 1930
Region:	
United States	4.84
Northeast	4.88
Middle States	4.61
Northwest	4.54
Southeast	5.11
Southwest	4.88
Far West	4.38

[14] A part-time farm was defined in the 1930 Census as one where the farm operator worked for pay at work not connected with the farm for 150 days or more, or reported an occupation other than farmer, provided the value of farm products did not exceed $750.

TABLE 4.—*Days of other occupation of farm operators, with percentages so reporting by regions, and days of other occupation by color and tenure, 1929* [1]

Region	Percentage of operators reporting other occupations (A)	Average number of days worked in other occupations by those reporting such occupation (B)	Average number of days worked in other occupations per farm operator [2] (A × B)	Average number of days worked in other occupations per white operator [2]		Average number of days worked in other occupations per colored operator [2]	
				Owners and managers	Tenants	Owners and managers	Tenants
United States_____	30.3	100	30	35	26	33	19
Northeast_____	38.4	130	50	51	45	73	41
Middle States_____	26.6	99	26	29	21	48	26
Northwest_____	26.6	85	23	24	20	25	27
Southeast_____	31.5	91	29	35	28	35	18
Southwest_____	28.4	89	25	27	24	21	24
Far West_____	37.1	145	54	57	44	30	19

[1] Based on Fifteenth Census, Agriculture, vol. IV, tables 23 and 25.

[2] The base figures here included operators reporting no supplementary employment as well as those reporting other occupations.

own farms in the Northeast. Supplementary work in other enterprises is relatively more important in the Southeast than in any other region, except the Northeast and the Far West. Comparing the Southeast and the Middle States in this respect, we find an average of 29 days of supplementary occupation for each farm operator in the Southeast, as compared with 26 days for each farm operator in the Middle States. The regional difference in the case of the white operators amounts to 6 or 7 days, when computed separately for owners and tenants. A large amount of supplementary work (48 days) is reported by colored operators in the Middle States; a small amount (18 days) by colored tenants in the Southeast.

Prevalence of Tenancy and Mortgage Indebtedness

Farm tenancy, which is widespread in the South, is most common in the case of Negro operators, but it also characterizes the situation of many white farm families. The proportion of tenants among farm operators in the United States has increased steadily in the last four decades, from 28 percent in 1890 to 42 percent in 1930. During the whole period, tenancy has been most prevalent in the two southern regions. By 1930, well over half the farmers in these two regions were renters or sharecroppers. Outside the South, tenancy has increased most rapidly in the Northwest. The proportion of all farms operated by tenants actually declined in the Northeast between 1900 and 1930.

In 1890 almost 71 percent of the farms operated by owners in the United States were reported as free of mortgage indebtedness. By 1930 the proportion had fallen to just over half. In all regions except the Southeast, mortgage indebtedness was reported among a

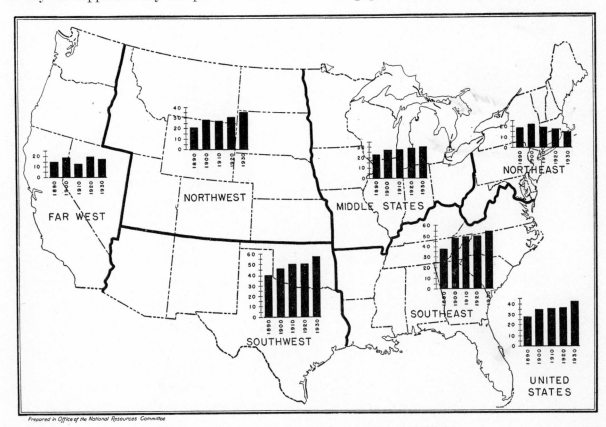

Prepared in Office of the National Resources Committee

FIGURE 19a.—Percentage of farms operated by tenants, by regions, 1890–1930.

smaller proportion of the colored than of the white owners in 1930. The percentage of owners reporting mortgages in 1890 was very much smaller in the two southern regions than in any other part of the country. In 1930 the farm owners in the Southeast still reported the smallest percentage of mortgages, followed by the Northeast and the Southwest. The percentages for the other three regions were above the national average. In the Far West and the Northwest, over half the farm owners reported mortgages.

To a considerable extent, the increasing prevalence of tenancy and of mortgage indebtedness is a reflection of the increasing maturity of the country—the disappearance of free land and the growing capital investment required to purchase and operate a farm. Students have, however, long since called attention to the fact that tenancy is no longer primarily a step in the agricultural ladder toward ownership. There has been a growing tendency for farm tenants to remain permanently in that class. There has been resulting loss in the incentive to preserve or increase the productivity of the soil, and in the personal sense of security and independence that may come from ownership of the land.

Regional trends in tenancy and in the encumbrance of farms by mortgages from 1890 to 1930 are shown in figures 19a and 19b.

Variations in Farm Wages

Variations in monthly wage rates for farm laborers in different parts of the United States, during the predepression period, afford a useful index of relative opportunities for agricultural workers. Unfortunately it is impossible to secure reliable information on this subject with a differentiation by race or color. Related data indicate that, if such analytical treatment were possible, the difference between wage rates for white workers in Northern and in Southern States would be much less than the difference for all workers. A very large differential would, however, still remain. Farm wage levels, of course, reflect both the demand for farm labor, or the productivity to be expected from each additional farm laborer, and the alternative opportunities in other types of employment open to unskilled or semiskilled workers. Data on this topic, for the predepression period, are shown in table 5.

Variations in Average Agricultural Productivity per Worker

Measurement of the actual productivity of farm workers gives the most significant index of regional differences in agricultural opportunity under existing conditions in the United States. It is possible to obtain an appropriate index of this sort in terms of average value of

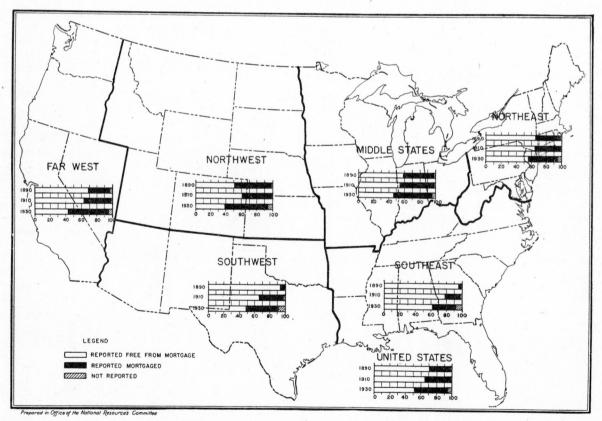

Prepared in Office of the National Resources Committee

FIGURE 19b.—Percentage distribution by mortgage status of owner-operated farms, by regions, 1890, 1910, 1930.

TABLE 5.—*Average monthly farm wages paid, 1926–28, by States and regions* [1]

Region or State	Average wages of farm labor for 1926, 1927, 1928; rate per month with board	Region or State	Average wages of farm labor for 1926, 1927, 1928; rate per month with board
United States	$34.91	Northwest—Con.	
		Montana	$53.38
Northeast	44.09	Idaho	54.96
Maine	44.69	Wyoming	47.99
New Hampshire	46.50	Colorado	40.01
Vermont	47.65	Utah	56.40
Massachusetts	50.93	Southeast	24.61
Rhode Island	53.85	Virginia	29.40
Connecticut	53.29	North Carolina	27.83
New York	49.46	South Carolina	20.63
New Jersey	49.47	Georgia	20.23
Delaware	33.61	Florida	25.90
Pennsylvania	39.74	Kentucky	27.15
Maryland	36.31	Tennessee	24.22
West Virginia	33.96	Alabama	21.40
Middle States	41.49	Mississippi	22.43
Ohio	38.90	Arkansas	24.83
Indiana	36.64	Louisiana	23.46
Illinois	42.92	Southwest	29.36
Michigan	42.19	Oklahoma	29.45
Wisconsin	47.20	Texas	27.73
Minnesota	44.10	New Mexico	34.43
Iowa	47.36	Arizona	46.27
Missouri	33.36	Far West	58.14
Northwest	44.17	Nevada	60.58
North Dakota	43.22	California	61.78
South Dakota	45.85	Washington	51.42
Nebraska	42.25	Oregon	48.83
Kansas	36.41		

[1] Compiled from data furnished by the Bureau of Agricultural Economics.

products per year per farm worker in different regions for the period of the middle twenties.[15] The regional variations obtained by the use of this index are shown in figure 20 (see also table 6). The final figures for States are given in the Statistical Supplement.

The figures given in table 6 indicate variations in the average annual value-productivity per worker in agriculture. They differ from the figures given in chapter I (see table 5 in that chapter), since a sum is deducted from

[15] An average figure for production by States (based on the 5 years 1924–28) was secured for 20 grain and hay crops; 14 livestock and dairy items; cotton, tobacco, potatoes; 11 miscellaneous crops; 14 truck crops; and 20 fruit items (a total of 82 items). The production figures include quantities used in the farm home and sold or for sale, but do not include quantities used as feed or seed on the farm. The quantities were priced at United States average farm prices for the years 1917–26. The resulting figure was taken as the "gross agricultural productivity" per State. From this figure was subtracted three items: (1) An average figure for purchases of feed, by States, (2) an average figure for expenditures for fertilizer by States, and (3) an allowance for machinery expenditures. The figure remaining when these three items had been subtracted was taken as "net productivity." To secure productivity per worker, the number of farm operators per State was secured, a working year of 310 days was assumed, and an allowance was made for supplementary work, based on the number of days of such work reported in the 1930 Census. The number of days of hired labor in 1929 (secured from the 1930 Census) was computed into man-years, also on the basis of 310 days per year, and this figure was added to the one for farm operators to give a figure for man-years in agriculture, by States. The figure on productivity was then divided by the number of man-years, and the resulting sum taken as the "net agricultural productivity per worker." It should be noted that this is productivity per worker, but not productivity by worker, because it includes not only labor productivity but also that of capital investments in land, buildings, and machinery. The Committee is indebted to Dr. O. E. Baker of the United States Bureau of Agricultural Economics for suggestions regarding method and for many of the data used in this computation. Two figures were computed, one for male workers and one for all workers in agriculture, by States and by regions, as well as for the United States.

the gross value figures to represent the annual cost of fertilizer, machinery, and purchased feed. They still indicate productivity per worker rather than productivity by workers, since no allowance is made for differences in soil quality, climate, farm management techniques, and similar factors. In the first column, the farm labor performed by women is "thrown in"—that is, the total value of agricultural products is divided by the number of males employed in agriculture. For the second column, the value figure is divided by the total number of persons engaged in agriculture.[16]

The highest values of products per year per farm worker during the years 1924–28 are found for workers in the Northwest and Far West, on fertile soil divided in large holdings, and aided by a large investment in machinery. The Middle States come next, followed by the Southwest; then comes the Northeast. The Southeast is found to be far below any other region. The average net productivity per agricultural worker in that region is only 45 percent of the figure for the rest of the country, when only male workers are considered. When productivity per worker is computed, including females as well as males, the figure for the United States outside the Southeast is reduced by about 6 percent. The proportion of female farm labor is much larger in the Southeast than in any other region, and productivity there is reduced almost 20 percent when computed per worker. It thus falls to 40 percent of the figure for the rest of the country on this basis.

Some of the State variations are also highly significant. Productivity per male worker is considerably higher for New York and for Maine than for the Northeast as a whole. For Rhode Island and Connecticut it is much lower, due to the larger proportion of part-time, urban, and subsistence farms in these States. The figure for Iowa is considerably above that for the Middle States as a whole, but no State in this area falls more than 25 percent below the regional average. The States of the North-

TABLE 6.—*Average net value of agricultural products per year per agricultural worker, by regions, 1924–28*

	Net value of products per male worker	Net value of products per worker
United States	$1,189	$1,063
Northeast	960	878
Middle States	1,508	1,438
Northwest	2,099	2,044
Southeast	672	552
Southwest	1,267	1,160
Far West	1,780	1,685
United States, except the Southeast	1,495	1,408

[16] In both cases an allowance is made for days of supplementary work reported by farm operators, as given in the 1930 Census.

west also appear reasonably uniform in this series. There is a difference of only about 25 percent between the lowest and the highest. One must remember, of course, that these figures refer to years which were not disturbed by any serious droughts. The percentage variation is also fairly low between the States in the Southeast. The two other western regions, although they include only four States each, show a wider variation, particularly in the Far West, where Nevada is 30 percent above the regional average and Oregon is more than 50 percent below.

From a population standpoint these differences, particularly as between regions, have a good deal of significance. It was suggested earlier, on the basis of regional distribution of farm population and farm land, that the farmers in the Middle and Western States had on the average a much better opportunity of winning an adequate living from the soil than did those in the Old South. The figures on value of products per farm confirm this. The productivity data show that the average agricultural worker in the Southeast produces goods that have less than half as much money value as those raised by his fellows in the rest of the country. A part of this difference is the result of less efficient agricultural techniques in the South; but this in itself is partly because the farm population in that area is so large that holdings are too small for efficient management. Efficiency is further lowered, as we shall

see, by education that is far less adequate than in other parts of the United States. This again must be largely attributed to the low income and relatively meager tax resources of many communities in the Southeast. Furthermore, it is impossible to measure the psychological effects of poverty continued through successive decades.

Agricultural Problem Areas

The main rural problem areas, as delimited by the Federal Emergency Relief Administration—differentiated primarily by high relief rates—are shown in figure 21. The two most populous of these areas lie within the Southeast: the Appalachian-Ozark area and the Eastern Cotton Belt. Beginning in Virginia and North Carolina, these sections extend west and south to the Mississippi River. Together they cover much of the Southeast as we have been studying it. These areas present the most long-standing and serious problems of adjustment of population to economic resources and opportunity that exist in the United States.

The Southeast.—The seriousness of the problems now confronting the Southeast is clearly recognized by the social scientists who know this region most intimately.[17] These

[17] See especially Odum, Howard W., *Southern Regions of the United States*, University of North Carolina Press (1936); Vance, Rupert B., *Human Geography of the South*, University of North Carolina Press (1932); Woofter, T. J., Jr., "Southern Population and Social Planning", in *Social Forces*, 14: 16–22, October 1935.

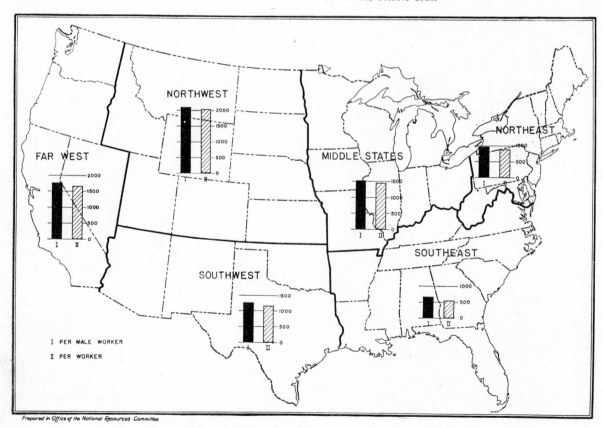

FIGURE 20.—Average net value of products (in dollars) per year per agricultural worker, by regions, 1924–28.

Population Problems 65

problems are national in character, because the destiny of the Nation cannot be divorced from that of its constituent regions. The Southeast is a principal area of population replacement for the rest of the country (see ch. IV). The solution of its problems calls for the intel- ligent understanding, good will and energy of the entire Nation. It is essential for all concerned to realize that any fundamental solution of the problems presented here must involve a very considerable change in the ratio of population to economic resources in the Southeast,

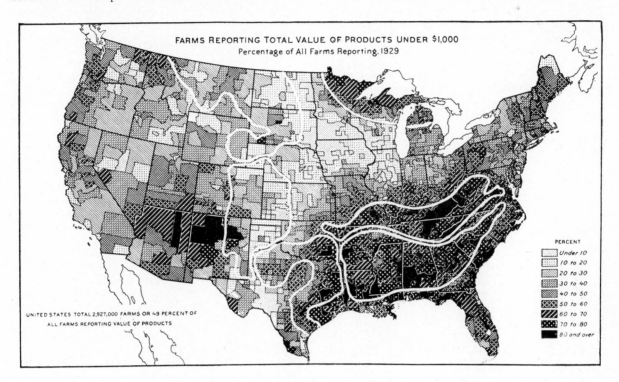

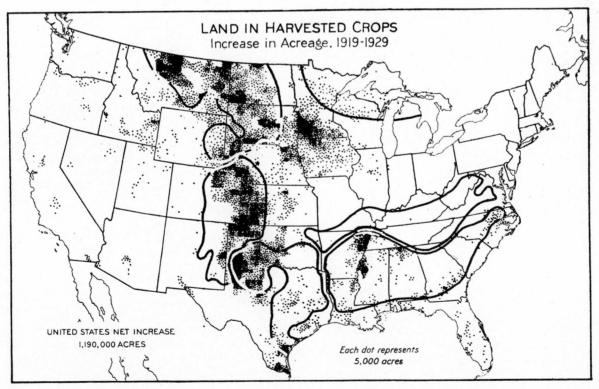

FIGURE 21.—Rural problem areas. From *Six Rural Problem Areas*, Federal Emergency Relief Administration, February 1936.

and in some other rural parts of the country, by either (1) large emigration from these regions, or (2) the development of new economic opportunities there, or by both.

We can get some insight into the amount of surplus farm population in the Southeast by asking a question to which it is possible to give a quantitative answer. If new opportunities in other industries attracted workers from the rural South until the average value-productivity (per male worker) became as high for those remaining in agriculture in this area as for farm workers in other parts of the country, what percentage of the present farm population of the Southeast would still be needed to supply farm commodities worth as much as those now produced by this region? This question may be answered first on the basis of quantities and price levels prevailing in the period 1924–28. If we assume that increased efficiency would involve greater use of farm machinery, we must therefore assume that operating expenses would be substantially as large as in other sections. The average gross productivity per male worker in agriculture (not deducting expenses for purchased feed, machinery, or fertilizer, and including supplementary labor of women) was $1,726 per year for all sections outside the Southeast. At this rate of value-productivity, the products of about 1½ million male workers would equal the current value of all farm commodities produced in the Southeast. This would release nearly 2 million male workers and their families for other lines of enterprise, involving a total of some 9 million people. If we assume that half of the population thus released found new opportunities for support in the same region—in meeting the increased demand for goods and services brought about by a general rise in levels of living in southern communities, and through developing new enterprises in southern States—we get a hypothetical surplus of 4½ million for whom opportunities would need to be found in other parts of the country. Obviously any such calculation is wholly hypothetical, but it serves to bring us to grips with the magnitude of the problems raised by the present situation.

The world cotton market is not so favorable now as in the period considered above (1924–28). The percentage of total population living on farms in the Southeast has increased somewhat since 1930. The authors of *Migration and Economic Opportunity* define the present situation of the old Cotton Belt thus:

> The gravest calamity that might befall the region would be the loss of the world market; at present, the happiest fate would seem to be the return of pre-depression conditions.[18]

If world markets are to be retained, the prices of cotton and tobacco cannot be lifted

---

[18] Goodrich, *op. cit.*, p. 155.

arbitrarily, except by subsidy from other areas. If a large share of the potential foreign market is sacrificed in the interest of higher prices, there would be need for a still greater reduction in farm population in this region. Accordingly, the situation in the Southeast seems to present the following choices, or a combination of them: (1) Continuance of widespread poverty; (2) large subsidies from other areas; (3) development of extensive new industries (either agricultural or mechanical); (4) development of extensive lines of production for home use, or some sort of cooperative enterprises; or (5) emigration within the near future of 3 to 6 million people to seek new opportunities in other regions.

The Northwest.—Next to the Southeast, in size of population and of area involved, come the problem areas of the Northwest. The Federal Emergency Relief Administration study mentioned above delimits two problem areas in this region: (1) The spring wheat area, extending from North Dakota and Montana south into northern Nebraska and eastern Wyoming, and (2) the winter wheat area, reaching from Nebraska and Colorado into northwest Texas and eastern New Mexico (see fig. 21). Both lie in the short-grass semiarid belt where dry-farming methods are practised. The first settlers who moved into this region found the land covered with grass which served very well as range for cattle and sheep. As lands to the east were more completely taken up and railroad lines were extended westward, the ranchers in the western plains were followed by farmers who broke up the sod and planted cash grain crops, chiefly wheat. This process was accelerated by the introduction of farm machinery such as the tractor and the combine, and was greatly stimulated by the tremendous demand for food crops of the World War years. A glance at figure 21 shows that the chief increase in farm acreage during the twenties took place in this region, where new land was being broken up and farmsteads established whose occupants were gambling for high profits in good years against the periods of insufficient rainfall which brought about crop shortages or complete failure. Meanwhile, the remaining unplowed land was being overgrazed, while the cropped land, deprived of its natural grass covering, was exposed to erosion by the prevailing high winds and frequent torrential rains. These cumulative evils were not recognized even by the farmers of the area until the recent succession of severe drought years brought not only widespread crop failure, but dust storms which afflicted man and beast and removed fertile top soil from millions of acres of land, reducing or destroying its arable qualities. It is now beginning to be understood that, relatively sparse as the farming population of this region is, it is still too large to be adequately supported on the land, much of which should be returned to range and protected by grass or forage cover crops.

It has been estimated that with such transformations in land use as are desirable to restore and maintain soil qualities, the Great Plains area would support only two-thirds of its present population.[19] This would mean a reduction of the 1930 population by about 900,000.

The Great Lakes cut-over area.—Another area of maladjustment of population to present economic resources is the cut-over region of the Great Lakes, which has already been touched upon. This is an agricultural problem area chiefly insofar as the workers displaced from lumbering and mining in the region, and from nearby manufacturing enterprise since the beginning of the depression, have turned to farming in the cut-over land. Figure 21 indicates a considerable increase in farm acreage in the section during the twenties. Much of the land, even when cleared of stumps, is stony and infertile; this, coupled with a short growing season and light rainfall, reduces agricultural returns for most of the would-be farmers to a subsistence level. Revival of industry will draw away many of those who in the past few years have resorted to agriculture as a stopgap. An extended plan for reforestation and sustained-yield management of forest lands, together with development of the resort possibilities of the area, would eventually furnish part-time employment to some hundred thousand workers. Even taking full account of these factors, there remains a considerable number of people for whom no prospect of profitable employment exists within the region.

The Southwest.—The western cotton area, covering a considerable part of Texas and Oklahoma, is included among the problem areas delimited by the Federal Emergency Relief Administration. Cotton cultivation increased rapidly in this section during the twenties, helping to make Texas and Oklahoma the leading cotton-producing States of the country. Many of the evils of farm management and tenure characteristic of the old South have been reproduced in this newer section, including a one-crop system, tenancy and share-cropping, and a large share of farms with a low annual value of products. Drought in the western part of the area and prevailing low prices for the chief cash crop have combined in the past few years to make the lot of the marginal farmers and farm laborers a hard one. The basic problem in this area, however, is not so much one of absolute pressure of population on agricultural resources as of alteration in farm management techniques, to make possible a readier adjustment to periodic

lean years in agriculture and to more permanent changes in market conditions.

A recent study of geographic variations in the relation between agricultural population and agricultural resources [20] contains the following statement: "The conclusion is inescapable from the foregoing that at least some sections of the United States are well past the optimum point, and probably all of them are past it, in the present state of the arts. This does not mean, however, that improvements in the arts will not raise the average for any or all sections." Geographical variations in per capita returns are attributed to differences in the distribution of resources, in the standard of living, and to similar factors, as well as to absolute pressure of population. Among suggested methods for achieving greater equality in per capita returns are emphasis on improvements in production techniques, particularly in the least favorably situated areas, migration of capital, and continual population redistribution through migration.

There are undoubtedly great possibilities for the development of more diversified agriculture and more production for home use by American farm families. In view of the apparent fact that at present the farms with higher than average value of cash crops also produce more for home use than the farms that produce little for sale, it seems likely that this beneficial development will be hastened by any improvement that may be effected in opportunities for commercial production.

5. Regional Distribution of Industrial Employment

From a consideration of the regional variations in extractive industries we turn now to the second of the major occupational groups—manufacturing and mechanical industries. For the Nation as a whole, this group has remained fairly constant in relative importance, in contrast to the decline of the extractive industries and the rise in the distributive and service occupations. In all the regions except the two southern, the proportion engaged in manufacturing increased from 1890 to 1920 and then decreased in the decade of the twenties. In the southern regions, where manufacturing was of much less importance, it continued to increase throughout the period.

Manufacturing is concentrated chiefly in the northeastern part of the United States. In 1880 it accounted for one-third of the gainfully employed in the Northeast, while in no other region did it include as many as one-fifth. Industry showed a tendency to move

---

[19] *Ibid.*, ch. V.

[20] Black, John D., "Agricultural Population in Relation to Agricultural Resources". *Annals of the American Academy of Political and Social Science*, 188 : 205–217 (November 1936).

southward and westward during the twentieth century. In 1930, however, manufacturing was still relatively more important in the Northeast than in any other region, the Middle States approaching it most closely.

For the student of population problems there are several ways of measuring regional variations in industry. The number of wage jobs gives an idea of the number of people supported by employment in the factories. The amount of wages paid indicates how adequate that support is (without, however, taking into account regional variations in the cost of living). The value of products per wage earner gives some idea of the productivity of factory workers, but this measure ignores differences in the value of raw materials used. It is therefore much less satisfactory than the value added by manufacture per wage earner. This latter figure is in some degree comparable to the figures on average gross productivity per worker in agriculture in indicating variations in the value-productivity of labor.

The most striking feature of the distribution of wage jobs in the United States is their concentration in a relatively few areas. (See table 7.) Although manufacturing, which first became important in New England, gradually spread westward with the movement of population, it has never really crossed the Mississippi, so that the northeastern part of the country still retains a large lead. The chief manufacturing and industrial belt of the Nation comprises 11 States,[21] extending from southern New England through the Middle Atlantic States and westward beyond the Great Lakes. In 1933 nearly 70 percent of all the wage jobs of the country were located within this relatively limited area. The only important industrial areas west of the Mississippi River are the Seattle-Tacoma area, the Los Angeles and San Francisco-Oakland areas, and the Kansas City area.

Table 7 shows a relative decline during the twentieth century in the importance of the Northeast and a relative increase in the importance of the Middle States and the Southeast, with reference to total number of wage jobs in manufacturing, but a high degree of concentration in the older region still persists. It accounted for 56 percent of the jobs in 1899. Even when the proportion was the lowest, in 1929, over 44 percent of all the wage jobs were located in the Northeast.

Outside the two regions comprising the manufacturing belt, the Southeast is the only one having a large percentage of the Nation's wage jobs. In 1933 these three regions together included more than 90 percent of the total. Although the number of wage jobs in the Far

[21] Massachusetts, Connecticut, New York, New Jersey, Pennsylvania, Maryland, Ohio, Indiana, Illinois, Michigan, and Wisconsin.

West more than trebled in the 30 years between 1899 and 1929, at the latter date this region still had only about 5 percent of the total.

TABLE 7.—*Regional percentages of total wage jobs and of total wages paid in manufacturing, 1899–1933*

Region	A. Wage jobs				B. Wages paid			
	1899	1919	1929	1933	1899	1919	1929	1933
Northeast	55.65	49.33	44.24	45.18	57.77	49.38	45.57	47.34
Middle States	27.76	30.65	33.15	30.78	28.32	32.34	36.26	32.77
Northwest	2.08	2.20	1.94	1.83	2.56	2.39	2.02	2.05
Southeast	10.76	11.34	13.26	15.22	7.00	8.72	8.51	10.41
Southwest	1.06	1.66	2.05	2.00	1.11	1.61	1.84	1.91
Far West	2.69	4.82	5.36	4.99	3.24	5.56	5.80	5.52

The regional concentration of manufacturing is even more apparent when measured in terms of total wages paid. The 11 States previously referred to as the manufacturing belt had 72 percent of all the wage jobs in the country in 1899. At the same date those States paid 75 percent of the wages. For the next 30 years, while the section's percentage of total wage jobs was declining slightly, its share of wages paid increased to 82 percent. During the depression years, wages dropped much more rapidly here than elsewhere but even in 1933, when the region had 67 percent of all the wage jobs in the country, it still paid 71 percent of the wages.

The Northeast has paid about one-half of the Nation's wages in manufacturing ever since 1899. Its share of wages, as of wage earners, declined up to 1929, and then increased slightly to 1933. The opposite tendency has been evident in the Middle States— a relative increase in both wage earners and wages between 1899 and 1929, followed by a slight decrease in 1933. Its share of wages has been consistently somewhat larger than its share of wage earners. The Southeast has shown a steady increase during the twentieth century, but the lower wages prevailing there are reflected in the fact that that region's percentage of wages has always been smaller than its percentage of wage jobs.

Wages paid in these three regions amounted to more than nine-tenths of the total for the country. The Far West, where the share of wages paid is somewhat larger than its share of wage earners, showed a relative increase in both up to 1929, with a slight drop during the depression.

The average value of products per wage earner in 1929 varied from $5,000 in the Southeast to almost $14,000 in the Northwest—a difference of more than 60 percent. This wide range reflects chiefly differences in the value of raw materials used and in the degree of mechanization of industrial processes. The value added by manufacture per wage earner varies less widely from region to region (see

TABLE 8.—*Regional variations in value added by manufacture per wage earner, 1929–33*

Region	1929	1933
United States	$3,615	$2,401
Northeast	3,674	2,452
Middle States	3,881	2,601
Northwest	4,011	2,848
Southeast	2,481	1,603
Southwest	3,760	2,647
Far West	4,097	2,847

table 8). The figure for the Southeast in 1929 was 30 percent below that for the country as a whole, whereas figures for the other regions were 2 to 13 percent above the national average. These differences, furthermore, have been widened by the depression. The figure for the Southeast in 1933 was 33 percent below the national average, while for the other regions they were 2 to 19 percent above.

The geographic distribution of manufacturing establishments by industries is shown in table 9. The important factor of size of establishment is ignored, but in general the average size of establishment in any industry is probably largest in the area of concentration of that industry. In each of the 13 industrial groups, except for forest products, the North-

TABLE 9.—*Regional distribution of manufacturing establishments by industries, 1930*

Industry	United States	North-east	Middle States	South-east
Textiles and their products	27,404	20,439	3,535	1,870
Forest products	26,912	6,211	4,857	11,555
Paper and allied products	3,126	1,848	895	165
Printing, publishing, and allied industries	27,522	10,263	8,822	2,623
Chemical and allied products	8,278	3,267	2,341	1,342
Products of petroleum and coal	1,497	504	409	174
Leather and its manufactures	4,277	2,953	850	153
Stone, clay, and glass products	8,514	3,431	2,739	943
Iron and steel and products [1]	6,640	3,071	2,537	304
Nonferrous metals and their products	7,522	3,761	2,340	236
Machinery [2]	12,955	5,024	5,201	729
Transportation equipment	2,550	922	974	238
Railroad repair shops	2,297	653	791	317
Miscellaneous industries	14,620	8,429	4,006	647
Total	154,114	70,776	40,297	21,296

Industry	South-west	North-west	Far West
Textiles and their products	242	168	1,150
Forest products	791	612	2,886
Paper and allied products	22	25	171
Printing, publishing, and allied industries	1,311	1,792	2,711
Chemical and allied products	423	225	680
Products of petroleum and coal	159	118	133
Leather and its manufactures	52	65	204
Stone, clay, and glass products	313	344	744
Iron and steel and products [1]	94	89	545
Nonferrous metals and their products	157	144	884
Machinery [2]	345	321	1,335
Transportation equipment	46	59	311
Railroad repair shops	171	200	165
Miscellaneous industries	273	256	1,009
Total	4,399	4,418	12,928

[1] Not including machinery.
[2] Not includi gtransportation equipment.

east and the Middle States have much the largest share of the factories, their combined proportion in no case falling below 60 percent.

The Trend of Manufacturing in Massachusetts

The Northeast, where manufacturing first developed, has retained its predominance with a considerable degree of stability, though it has already been noted that other sections of the country have gradually absorbed an increasing share of the Nation's industry. It is possible to get some understanding of the factors at work in this gradual shift by taking account of recent changes in manufacturing employment and production in one of the States of the old manufacturing belt. An analysis of trends in manufacturing since 1909 in Massachusetts, as compared with the rest of the country,[22] has recently been made by Donald H. Davenport and John J. Croston, of the Harvard Graduate School of Business Administration.

The number of wage earners in manufacturing industries in Massachusetts rose from 1909 to 1919, but at a slower rate than in the total United States; the State's percentage of all industrial wage jobs declined during this interval from 8.8 to 7.9 percent. There was somewhat less recession in Massachusetts in 1921 than in the rest of the Nation. But from 1923 to 1929, while the number of wage earners in manufacturing in the United States remained fairly constant, there was a gradual decline in Massachusetts; the State's percentage of all industrial wage jobs fell to 6.3 percent in 1929. The relative figures for 1931 and 1933 were slightly higher, indicating that industry in Massachusetts was not so adversely affected by the depression as in many other areas. This is understandable in view of the relatively greater importance of consumer goods, such as shoes and textiles, in Massachusetts. The general trend during the last 25 years, however, shows a decrease in the relative importance of Massachusetts industries.

An examination of statistics for particular industries reveals some interesting variations. In the leather goods industry, which employs a larger number of wage earners than any other industrial group in Massachusetts, the level of employment in the State was significantly lower during 1925–29 than in 1909, after having risen to a peak in 1919. In the rest of the United States, however, the level of employment during 1925–29 was somewhat higher than in 1909. From 1909 to 1929, Massachusetts' share of the total employment in leather goods fell from 31 percent to 24 percent. Similarly there was a general expansion in the production of cotton goods from 1909 to 1919, but the rise in Massa-

[22] Unemployment and Prospects for Reemployment in Massachusetts, Publication of the Graduate School of Business Administration, vol. XXIII, no. 6 (August 1936).

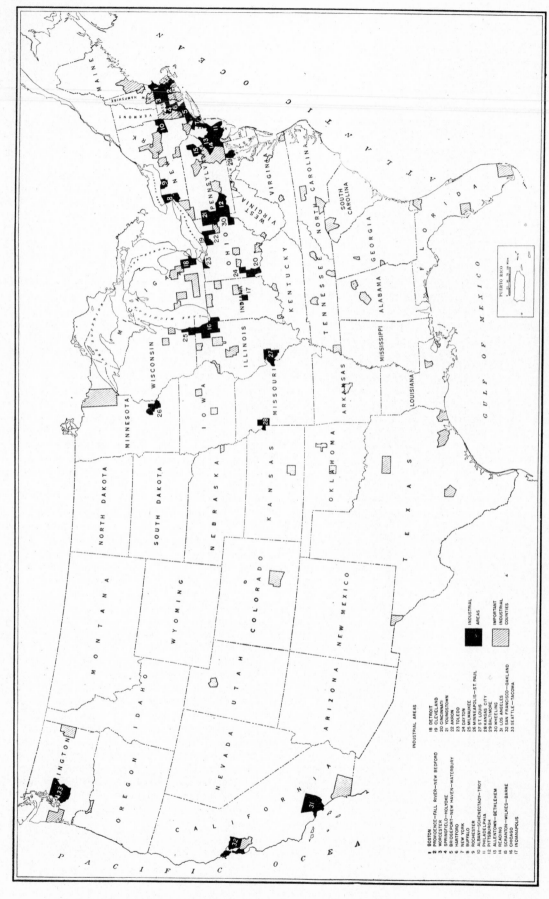

INDUSTRIAL AREAS

1 BOSTON
2 PROVIDENCE—FALL RIVER—NEW BEDFORD
3 WORCESTER
4 SPRINGFIELD—HOLYOKE
5 BRIDGEPORT—NEW HAVEN—WATERBURY
6 HARTFORD
7 NEW YORK
8 BUFFALO
9 ROCHESTER
10 ALBANY—SCHENECTADY—TROY
11 PHILADELPHIA
12 PITTSBURGH
13 ALLENTOWN—BETHLEHEM
14 READING
15 SCRANTON—WILKES—BARRE
16 CHICAGO
17 INDIANAPOLIS

18 DETROIT
19 CLEVELAND
20 CINCINNATI
21 YOUNGSTOWN
22 AKRON
23 TOLEDO
24 DAYTON
25 MILWAUKEE
26 MINNEAPOLIS—ST. PAUL
27 ST. LOUIS
28 KANSAS CITY
29 BALTIMORE
30 WHEELING
31 LOS ANGELES
32 SAN FRANCISCO—OAKLAND
33 SEATTLE—TACOMA

INDUSTRIAL
AREAS

IMPORTANT
INDUSTRIAL
COUNTIES

FIGURE 22.—Industrial areas and important industrial counties, as defined in the Census of Manufactures, 1929.

chusetts did not keep pace with that in the rest of the United States. Comparing numbers of wage earners in the cotton textile industry in 1919 and in 1929, we find little change in the United States total, but the number so employed in Massachusetts dropped during this period from 125,000 to 74,000. In this industry the relative position of Massachusetts continued to decline between 1929 and 1933. Massachusetts' percentage of wage earners in the cotton industry was 29 percent in 1909, 27 percent in 1919, 16 percent in 1929, but only 11.7 percent in 1933. Meanwhile mechanization as measured by horsepower installed per wage earner proceeded somewhat more rapidly in Massachusetts than elsewhere, while the value of production per wage earner did not increase quite as rapidly in Massachusetts as in the total industry. Massachusetts has not shared in the expansion of "other textiles" (exclusive of cotton and woolen).[23] While the number of wage earners so employed in the total United States increased from 356,000 in 1909 to 547,000 in 1929, the corresponding figure for Massachusetts was only 15 percent higher in 1929 than in 1909. In the rubber goods industry there was a steady increase during the years 1923–31 in the number of wage earners employed in the total United States; there was a gradual decline in the number so employed in Massachusetts during the same period. The relative position of Massachusetts as regards number of wage earners also declined during the twenties in iron and steel products, heavy machinery, paper and allied products, and clothing.

The situation in the woolen industry presents an interesting contrast. Nearly a third of all wage earners in this industry are located in Massachusetts; this percentage has remained fairly constant during the last 25 years. The industry as a whole, however, reached its peak in 1923; it has been decreasing in value of products and number of wage earners since that time. Improvement in the woolen industry since the early years of the depression has been far greater than in general business. Massachusetts has also shared in the advance of some expanding industries, notably electrical machinery, and chemicals, and has maintained a fairly steady position in printing, jewelry production, and some other industries.

Three out of four industrial wage earners in Massachusetts in 1929 were in industries that showed downward trends in employment in the preceding decade. It is therefore likely that the migration of native-born population out of the State, which began in the 1920's but was largely stopped by the depression, will again become evident and will increase in volume as business conditions in the Nation as a whole improve.

Prospects for Wide Dispersion of Industry

Another important phase of industrial location is the counterbalancing forces of concentration and scatter. It is scarcely necessary to point out the influence which the tendency toward concentration has already had, in the development of huge industrial centers. Examples at once spring to mind—iron and steel around Pittsburgh and Gary, textiles in Manchester, New Bedford, Lawrence, and Fall River, automobiles in Detroit, meat packing in Chicago.

Students have for some time now been calling attention to an opposite tendency toward decentralization—the spread of industry to locations outside these main centers. The belief has been expressed that this newer development will gradually distribute industry much more widely and more evenly over the country, with corresponding effects on the distribution of population. Some even look toward a sort of ruralization of manufactures, with many industrial plants located in the smaller towns. The workers could then combine factory labor with part-time farming to give them a buffer against fluctuations in industrial employment.

Trends in the location of industrial wage jobs have been analyzed in detail, with special attention to tendencies toward centralization and decentralization, by the Study of Population Redistribution. The authors distinguish between two different tendencies: (1) Dispersion, by which is meant movement of industries to scattered towns and villages outside the areas of industrial concentration, and (2) diffusion, which refers to the movement of industries within or between industrial areas. This includes both the location of establishments in the periphery of a central city and transfer of operations from old industrial regions (e. g., in eastern Massachusetts) to less developed industrial areas (e. g., in the Carolina Piedmont or an industrial section of the Pacific coast). There has been more of the latter type of movement, but even this is less marked than is often supposed.[24] The manufacturing belt extending from the Atlantic coast beyond the Great Lakes retained a large measure of its predominance during the first three decades of this century, with a decline of less than 5 percent in its share of the Nation's wage jobs between 1899 and 1933.

The absence of any marked trend toward dispersion of industry is shown by noting the constant proportion of wage jobs and the increasing share of total wages reported for the 200 counties comprising the industrial areas as defined by the Census of Manufactures in 1929 (see fig. 22).

For the past 30 years these 200 counties (out of the more than 3,000 counties in the

---

[23] "Other textiles" includes dyeing and finishing, knit goods, silk, and rayon, and the manufacture of rugs.

[24] See Goodrich, *op. cit.*, chap. VII, "The Changing Pattern of Industrial Location."

TABLE 10.—*Percentage of total wage jobs and wages paid located in 200 selected counties, 1899–1933*

Year	Percent of wage jobs	Percent of total wages paid
1899	73.2	76.1
1919	74.5	76.3
1929	74.0	78.5
1931	74.6	78.8
1933	73.0	78.9

United States) have provided nearly three-fourths of the total manufacturing employment and more than three-fourths of the total wages paid. The stability of these percentages is as remarkable as their size.

A more complete analysis of the trend in the dispersion of industries into places outside areas of high concentration, and their diffusion to the periphery of large congested cities and into newer industrial areas, is made possible by the classification of the counties of the Nation into the following groups:

A. Principal city of an industrial area.

B. Large satellite cities in the industrial area.

C. Remainder of the industrial area.

D. Cities of 100,000 or more inhabitants outside an industrial area.

E. Remainder of counties in which these cities are located.

F. Important industrial counties without a city as large as 100,000 inhabitants.

G. Remainder of the United States.

Groups A through F represent areas of concentration and diffusion, while group G represents the area of dispersion. The relative concentration of wage jobs in these areas affords interesting contracts.

The old manufacturing belt is an area of concentration, with relatively few jobs located in the nonindustrial "all-the-rest" counties. All the Southern States and the Mountain States of the West are areas of wide dispersion of wage jobs. One-half to two-thirds of the jobs are in counties outside the industrial areas. On the Pacific coast there is more concentration than in the South but less than in the East. About one-third of the manufacturing employment is in the nonindustrial counties. How has this general pattern of concentration and dispersion varied during the past 34 years?

For the entire country the period from 1899 to 1933 witnessed a relative decline in the proportion of total wage jobs in manufacturing supplied by the principal industrial cities and their large satellite cities. The industrial peripheries of these cities, other large cities, and the important industrial counties showed a steady increase. The trend in the remaining 2,800 counties—the area of dispersion—was irregular, the proportion of wage jobs generally decreasing until 1931, but increasing somewhat in the next 2 years. There was little net change between 1899 and 1933.

There was the same general trend throughout the United States, with two important exceptions. In New England there was a definite increase in the proportion of wage jobs located in the principal cities of the industrial areas and an even more marked decrease in the relative importance of the nonindustrial counties. This reveals an unequivocal tendency toward centralization in this area. This is especially interesting in view of the fact that scattered mill towns have been characteristic of New England for a long time. Evidently this historic decentralization did not mean stability. On the other hand, in the South Atlantic States the proportion of all wage jobs that were located in the principal industrial cities was reduced one-half between 1899 and 1933. The important industrial counties without a city of more than 100,000 population had the largest relative increase in their proportion of the total manufacturing employment (from 8 to 18 percent of the total for the region). The Mountain States were the only other region where the areas of dispersion became relatively more important. However, the number of wage jobs in these States is small. Outside of the South Atlantic States the proportion of the total manufacturing employment in the United States located in the nonindustrial counties decreased steadily from 24 percent in 1899 to a low point of 21 percent in 1931. Between 1931 and 1933 there was an increase of 1 point.

Implications of the Industrial Analysis for Future Population Movements

The implications of this analysis have considerable significance for future trends in population distribution. The extractive industries have had the effect of scattering the Nation's people. Trade and industry and large-scale commercial operations have brought them together again. From both movements important national problems have arisen. The westward movement of lumbering and agriculture resulted in deforestation of large areas unsuitable for farming and unnecessary for production of an adequate food supply. Problems of soil depletion, erosion, and flood control resulted. The development of industry, by concentrating large numbers of people in a few large cities, not only created the problems associated with high density of population, but also left these people absolutely dependent on the orderly operation of a complicated industrial and commercial structure.

The significance of the two lines of development were not generally appreciated until the coming of the depression. Almost overnight the Nation was faced with the problem of providing food, clothing, and shelter for nearly one-sixth of its people, whose independence had been destroyed by conditions beyond their control. As relief costs mounted and as the outlook for employment in industry appeared uncertain and discouraging, strong sentiment developed for a movement of population back to the land, where food and shelter could be secured more easily and cheaply. Such a movement did offer a way of escape for many individuals. To some, this trend seemed to afford the basis for better living and a more stable economic order.

In view of the facts that an expansion of commercial agriculture at the present time would be definitely harmful, and that any great increase in subsistence farming would have the effect of lowering the level of living of our rural population and thus of threatening continued national development, the incomes of these new rural families would need to be supplemented by cash earnings in industry. Advocates of this back-to-the-farm movement do in fact propose that supplementary income be obtained from part-time employment in rural or suburban industrial establishments. This would make it possible, they hope, for a large proportion of the Nation's population to enjoy the combined advantages of agriculture and industry without the disadvantages of either.

The prospects for part-time industrial employment.—The foregoing analysis, however, offers little support for a belief that opportunities for part-time or full-time industrial employment can be widely distributed geographically in the near future. The records both of past migration and of industrial expansion show that workers have usually moved to the factory, rather than the factory to the workers. There is little evidence that there will be widespread development of combined industrial-farming employment, as the basis for a better national economy, although there may be important developments of this sort in certain favored localities.

It is impossible to make any reliable prediction about future changes in the location of industry. The analyses reported here strongly suggest that it will be predominantly centered in fairly well-defined industrial areas. But it is impossible to say to what extent some of the more established industrial areas may decline in importance, or to what extent there may be a development of certain new industrial areas.

The evidence as to trends in the location of industrial employment have still further significance in relation to the location of the future potential labor supply. Since industry reveals little tendency to decentralize, what adjustments in population distribution seem most likely to occur? What adjustments seem most desirable? In view of present reproduction trends, a large proportion of the future labor supply will be born in areas far removed from centers of employment. To what extent can rates of reproduction and trends in migration be expected to maintain an adjustment

between population distribution and opportunities for employment? Examination of these questions will be undertaken in later chapters.

6. Regional Variations in Social-Economic Groups

In an earlier section of this chapter an analysis was made of regional trends in the major occupational groups: Extractive industries, manufacturing and mechanical industries, and the trade and service occupations. Following that came an examination of regional differences in economic opportunity in agriculture and industry. The evidence presented, including data on income and level of living, shows wide variations between different sections of the country in the relation between population and developed economic resources.

The Social-Economic Classification of Gainful Workers

A somewhat different approach to the problem of regional differences is possible through an analysis of data on gainful workers by States, classified by race, sex, and social-economic groups.[25] The results are summarized by geographic regions in tables 11–14. The detailed data for States are presented in the Statistical Supplement. Two sorts of percentage distribution are presented for the gainfully occupied workers of each sex and of each main racial group in each region: (1) The distribution of all workers into the main farm and nonfarm social-economic groups, and (2) separate distributions of (*a*) farm workers into their main social-economic groups, and (*b*) nonfarm workers into their main social-economic groups.

The predominance of nonfarming occupations among male workers in the Northeast (92 percent), Far West (82 percent), and Middle States (78 percent) is immediately apparent. Even in the Southeast somewhat less than one-half of all male workers are engaged in farming (42 percent). In the "rural" Northwest and Southwest only 43.5 percent and 42 percent, respectively, work on farms. Less than one-tenth of all gainfully occupied women in the United States are engaged in farming. Less than 1 percent of the female workers in the Northeast are so occupied but, at the other extreme, about 30 percent of those in the Southeast. The proportions of Negroes and those of other races engaged in farming are much higher than the corresponding proportion for white workers. Among male workers, 42 percent of the Negroes and 47.5 percent of those of other races are farmers or farm laborers. Less than 5 percent of all gainfully occupied white women work on farms, but 27.5

[25] Based on special computation of occupational data by States, prepared for this report in the Bureau of the Census, under the direction of Alba M. Edwards.

percent of the gainfully occupied Negro women and 21 percent of those of other races are agricultural workers.

The Professions

Professional work holds more than three times as large a proportion of the gainfully occupied among women as among men.[26] However, there are about three and one-half times as many men as women gainfully occupied in all classes in the total United States. In absolute numbers there are more professional men than women in the country as a whole, and in the Northeast, the Middle States, and the Far West. In the Southwest the numbers are almost equal, and in the Northwest and the Southeast the women in this group outnumber the men.

The location of professional workers is influenced by location of trade and governmental centers, but still more by the levels and standards of living of the general population in different areas. Thus we find that the proportion of male workers listed in the professional group is higher in the "urban" Far West (5.2) than in the "urban" Northeast (4.7) and much

[26] Over half of the women classed as professional, but only an eighth of the professional men, are occupied as teachers.

higher in the "rural" Northwest (3.6) than in the "rural" Southeast (2.5). Although the percentage of Negro males in the professions in the Southeast is very low, the proportion of white males in the professions also remains distinctly lower here than in any other region.

Slightly more than one in every six gainfully occupied women in the United States is classified as a professional worker. The regional proportions vary from 23 percent in the Northwest to under 10 percent in the Southeast. The low percentage in the Southeast is due to the large number of Negro women engaged in agriculture there. The proportion of the gainfully occupied white women in the professional group is slightly higher in the Southeast than in the total United States, though much lower than in the Northwest. The relative frequency of professional workers among all gainfully occupied Negro women is low in all regions, but it is as high in the Southeast as in the total United States.

Trade

The percentage of male workers engaged in wholesale and retail trade is somewhat larger than the percentage in the professions in every region except in the Far West. Again, the

TABLE 11a.—*Percentage distribution of male workers (all races) by social-economic groups, United States and regions, 1930*

	United States	Northeast	Middle States	Northwest	Southeast	Southwest	Far West
Total workers _____ number __	38,077,804	12,047,213	10,742,787	2,273,542	7,427,885	2,739,548	2,846,829
	Percent 100.0	*Percent* 100.0	*Percent* 100.0	*Percent* 100.0	*Percent* 100.0	*Percent* 100.0	*Percent* 100.0
Farm _____	25.1	8.2	22.2	43.5	47.7	41.9	17.9
Owners and managers [1] _____	8.6	3.7	9.5	17.3	12.4	10.7	7.0
Tenants, including croppers [1] _____	6.7	.7	4.6	10.5	16.9	15.3	1.6
Croppers [2]	*1.9*				*8.1*	*3.8*	
Laborers _____	9.8	3.8	8.1	15.7	18.4	15.9	9.3
Nonfarm _____	74.9	91.8	77.8	56.5	52.3	58.1	82.1
Professional persons _____	3.9	4.7	4.0	3.6	2.5	3.4	5.2
Wholesale and retail dealers _____	4.4	5.2	4.3	4.0	3.3	4.2	4.9
Other proprietors, managers, and officials _____	4.6	5.3	4.7	4.5	2.9	4.1	6.0
Clerks and kindred workers _____	12.8	15.8	13.4	10.2	7.7	10.1	15.8
Skilled workers and foremen _____	16.1	20.0	18.2	11.2	9.4	11.0	17.7
Semiskilled workers _____	14.3	19.6	15.0	7.8	9.3	8.2	13.3
Laborers _____	16.1	17.8	15.7	13.4	15.3	14.8	15.4
Service workers _____	2.7	3.4	2.5	1.8	1.9	2.3	3.8
Farm workers _____	100.0	100.0	100.0	100.0	100.0	100.0	100.0
Owners and managers _____	34.2	45.2	42.8	39.7	26.1	25.5	29.2
Tenants, including croppers _____	26.6	8.8	20.8	24.2	35.4	36.5	8.7
Croppers _____	*7.4*				*16.9*	*9.1*	
Laborers _____	39.2	46.0	36.4	36.1	38.5	38.0	52.1
Nonfarm workers _____	100.0	100.0	100.0	100.0	100.0	100.0	100.0
Professional persons _____	5.2	5.1	5.1	6.3	4.8	5.8	6.3
Wholesale and retail dealers _____	5.9	5.7	5.5	7.1	6.2	7.2	5.9
Other proprietors, managers, and officials _____	6.1	5.7	6.0	8.0	5.5	7.0	7.3
Clerks and kindred workers _____	17.1	17.2	17.3	18.0	14.7	17.5	19.3
Skilled workers _____	21.5	21.8	23.4	19.8	18.1	19.0	21.5
Semiskilled workers _____	19.1	21.4	19.3	13.8	17.9	14.1	16.3
Laborers _____	21.5	19.4	20.2	23.8	29.2	25.5	18.7
Service workers _____	3.6	3.7	3.2	3.2	3.6	3.9	4.7

[1] Figures for owners and tenants by sex are not available in the 1930 Census of Agriculture. The number of tenants and of croppers, white and Negro, by States, was supplied from unpublished data by the census. The number of owners, white and Negro, was derived by deducting the number of tenants (including croppers) from the figure for owners and tenants combined, given in the 1930 Census of Population (Vol. IV). The number of owners and tenants, by sex, was estimated by applying to the figures for owners and tenants separately the sex ratio for owners and tenants combined. The figures for farm managers are also based on unpublished data, adjusted to give sex distribution by race, on the assumption that the number of female Negro managers is negligible.

[2] White and Negro croppers only, in Southeast and Southwest.

TABLE 11b.–*Percentage distribution of female workers (all races) by social-economic groups, United States, and Regions, 1930*

	United States	Northeast	Middle States	Northwest	Southeast	Southwest	Far West
Total workers..............number..	10,752,116	3,926,788	2,729,135	459,720	2,262,273	603,126	771,074
	Percent 100.0	*Percent* 100.0	*Percent* 100.0	*Percent* 100.0	*Percent* 100.0	*Percent* 100.0	*Percent* 100.0
Farm	8.5	.8	2.4	5.6	29.6	16.0	2.5
Owners and managers [1]	1.4	.4	1.2	2.3	2.6	1.8	1.3
Tenants, including croppers [1]	1.1	.1	.6	1.4	3.5	2.6	.3
Croppers [2]	.5				*2.0*	.8	
Laborers	6.0	.3	.6	1.9	23.5	11.6	.9
Nonfarm	91.5	99.2	97.6	94.4	70.4	84.0	97.5
Professional persons	13.5	12.8	14.7	23.2	9.5	15.1	17.5
Wholesale and retail dealers	1.0	1.1	1.1	1.2	.7	1.1	1.5
Other proprietors, managers and officials	1.2	.9	1.3	2.6	.9	1.9	2.1
Clerks and kindred workers	28.6	32.7	34.5	29.3	12.6	23.6	36.9
Skilled workers and foremen	.7	.9	1.0	.5	0.3	.3	.8
Semiskilled workers	23.5	30.7	23.3	16.1	16.0	14.7	21.3
Laborers	1.5	1.2	1.8	1.0	1.8	1.1	1.0
Service workers	21.5	18.9	19.9	20.5	28.6	26.2	16.4
Farm workers	100.0	100.0	100.0	100.0	100.0	100.0	100.0
Owners and managers	16.2	55.6	48.8	41.4	8.7	11.2	52.8
Tenants, including croppers	12.8	11.1	23.8	25.1	11.9	16.3	12.4
Croppers	*5.4*				*2.0*	*5.1*	
Laborers	71.0	33.3	27.4	33.5	79.4	72.5	34.8
Nonfarm workers	100.0	100.0	100.0	100.0	100.0	100.0	100.0
Professional persons	14.7	12.9	15.0	24.6	13.4	18.0	18.0
Wholesale and retail dealers	1.2	1.1	1.1	1.3	1.0	1.4	1.5
Other proprietors, managers, and officials	1.3	.9	1.4	2.7	1.3	2.3	2.2
Clerks and kindred workers	31.2	32.9	35.4	31.0	17.9	28.1	37.9
Skilled workers	.8	1.0	1.0	.5	.4	.3	.7
Semiskilled workers	25.7	30.9	23.8	17.1	22.8	17.4	21.8
Laborers	1.6	1.2	1.9	1.1	2.6	1.3	1.0
Service workers	23.5	19.1	20.4	21.7	40.6	31.2	16.9

[1] Figures for owners and tenants by sex are not available in the 1930 Census of Agriculture. The number of tenants and of croppers, white and Negro, by States, was supplied from unpublished data by the census. The number of owners, white and Negro, was derived by deducting the number of tenants (including croppers) from the figures for owners and tenants combined, given in the 1930 Census of Population (Vol. IV). The number of owners and tenants, by sex, was estimated by applying to the figures for owners and tenants separately the sex ratio for owners and tenants combined.
[2] White and Negro croppers only, in Southeast and Southwest.

TABLE 12a.—*Percentage distribution of white male workers by social-economic groups, United States and regions, 1930*

	United States	Northeast	Middle States	Northwest	Southeast	Southwest	Far West
Total workers..............number..	33,766,933	11,446,743	10,282,495	2,188,307	5,127,522	2,128,463	2,593,403
	Percent 100.00	*Percent* 100.00	*Percent* 100.00	*Percent* 100.00	*Percent* 100.00	*Percent* 100.00	*Percent* 100.00
Farm	23.1	8.2	23.0	43.9	44.4	39.5	16.1
Owners and managers	9.2	3.8	9.9	17.6	15.7	11.8	7.4
Tenants, including croppers	5.5	.7	4.8	10.8	13.4	14.8	1.6
Croppers	*1.0*				*5.5*	*3.1*	
Laborers	8.4	3.7	8.3	15.5	15.3	12.9	7.1
Nonfarm	76.9	91.8	77.0	56.1	55.6	60.5	83.9
Professional persons	4.3	4.8	4.0	3.6	3.1	3.9	5.6
Wholesale and retail dealers	4.8	5.5	4.4	4.2	4.5	5.0	5.1
Other proprietors, managers, and officials	5.0	5.5	4.9	4.7	4.0	5.0	6.4
Clerks and kindred workers	14.2	16.4	13.9	10.5	10.8	12.4	16.9
Skilled workers	17.6	20.7	18.6	11.5	12.0	12.9	18.9
Semiskilled workers	15.0	19.8	15.0	7.8	10.6	8.7	13.8
Laborers	14.1	16.5	14.4	12.4	10.1	11.5	14.3
Service workers	1.9	2.6	1.8	1.4	.5	1.1	2.9
Farm workers	100.00	100.00	100.00	100.00	100.00	100.00	100.00
Owners and managers	39.6	46.6	43.2	40.2	35.4	29.8	46.0
Tenants, including croppers	23.8	8.9	20.7	24.6	30.1	37.6	9.9
Croppers	*4.5*				*12.4*	*8.0*	
Laborers	36.6	44.5	36.1	35.2	34.5	32.6	44.1
Nonfarm workers	100.00	100.00	100.00	100.00	100.00	100.00	100.00
Professional persons	5.5	5.3	5.3	6.5	5.6	6.5	6.6
Wholesale and retail dealers	6.3	5.9	5.7	7.4	8.1	8.3	6.1
Other proprietors, managers, and officials	6.5	5.9	6.3	8.3	7.1	8.3	7.6
Clerks and kindred workers	18.5	17.9	18.0	18.7	19.4	20.6	20.2
Skilled workers	22.8	22.6	24.2	20.5	21.6	21.3	22.6
Semiskilled workers	19.5	21.6	19.5	14.0	19.0	14.3	16.5
Laborers	18.4	18.0	18.7	22.1	18.2	18.9	17.0
Service workers	2.5	2.8	2.3	2.5	1.0	1.8	3.4

TABLE 12b.—*Percentage distribution of white female workers by social-economic groups, United States and regions, 1930*

	United States	Northeast	Middle States	Northwest	Southeast	Southwest	Far West
Total workers _____ number__	8,817,564	3,619,991	2,553,116	442,313	1,072,573	401,040	728,531
	Percent 100.00	*Percent* 100.00	*Percent* 100.00	*Percent* 100.00	*Percent* 100.00	*Percent* 100.00	*Percent* 100.00
Farm_____	4.5	.8	2.6	5.4	19.4	12.5	2.2
Owners and managers_____	1.3	.5	1.3	2.4	3.5	2.1	1.4
Tenants, including croppers_____	.8	.1	.6	1.4	2.9	2.5	.3
Croppers_____	*.2*				*1.2*	*.5*	
Laborers_____	2.4	.2	.7	1.6	13.0	7.9	.5
Nonfarm_____	95.5	99.2	97.4	94.6	80.6	87.5	97.8
Professional persons_____	15.7	13.6	15.5	24.0	16.4	20.6	18.3
Wholesale and retail dealers_____	1.2	1.2	1.1	1.2	1.3	1.5	1.5
Other proprietors, managers, and officials__	1.4	.9	1.4	2.6	1.7	2.6	2.1
Clerks and kindred workers_____	34.5	35.3	36.6	30.3	25.9	34.0	38.7
Skilled workers_____	.9	1.0	1.0	.5	.5	.4	.8
Semiskilled workers_____	26.3	31.7	23.4	16.2	26.4	15.8	20.8
Laborers_____	1.4	1.2	1.8	1.0	1.8	.9	.9
Service workers_____	14.1	14.3	16.6	18.8	6.6	11.7	14.7
Farm workers_____	100.00	100.00	100.00	100.00	100.00	100.00	100.00
Owners and managers_____	29.6	57.6	50.4	44.0	18.1	16.5	63.3
Tenants, including croppers_____	17.4	11.2	23.4	25.9	14.9	20.2	14.2
Croppers_____	*3.8*				*6.1*	*4.3*	
Laborers_____	53.0	31.2	26.2	30.1	67.0	63.3	22.5
Nonfarm workers_____	100.00	100.00	100.00	100.00	100.00	100.00	100.00
Professional persons_____	16.4	13.7	15.8	25.3	20.4	23.6	18.7
Wholesale and retail dealers_____	1.3	1.2	1.2	1.3	1.6	1.7	1.6
Other proprietors, managers, and officials__	1.5	.9	1.4	2.8	2.1	3.0	2.2
Clerks and kindred workers_____	36.1	35.6	37.6	32.1	32.2	38.8	39.5
Skilled workers_____	.9	1.0	1.1	.6	.6	.4	.8
Semiskilled workers_____	27.5	32.0	24.0	17.1	32.8	18.0	21.2
Laborers_____	1.5	1.2	1.9	1.0	2.2	1.1	.9
Service workers_____	14.8	14.4	17.0	19.8	8.1	13.4	15.1

TABLE 13a.—*Percentage distribution of Negro male workers by social-economic groups, United States and regions, 1930*

	United States	Northeast	Middle States	Northwest	Southeast	Southwest
Total workers _____ number__	3,570,946	543,396	398,520	21,977	2,289,815	317,238
	Percent 100.00	*Percent* 100.00	*Percent* 100.00	*Percent* 100.00	*Percent* 100.00	*Percent* 100.00
Farm_____	41.6	6.9	5.4	9.4	55.2	51.0
Owners and managers_____	4.4	.8	.8	2.8	5.6	7.3
Tenants, including croppers_____	17.9	.5	1.4	1.7	24.3	22.7
Croppers_____	*10.0*				*13.9*	*11.9*
Laborers_____	19.3	5.6	3.2	4.9	25.3	21.0
Nonfarm_____	58.4	93.1	94.6	90.6	44.8	49.0
Professional persons_____	1.5	2.1	2.1	2.7	1.1	1.9
Wholesale and retail dealers_____	.7	.9	1.2	1.0	.5	.5
Other proprietors, managers, and officials__	.6	.9	1.2	.9	.4	.6
Clerks and kindred workers_____	1.6	4.4	3.4	2.3	.8	.9
Skilled workers_____	4.7	6.9	8.5	6.4	3.7	2.9
Semiskilled workers_____	8.8	15.2	14.5	13.6	6.6	6.2
Laborers_____	31.7	44.4	45.6	45.9	26.9	26.7
Service workers_____	8.8	18.3	18.1	17.8	4.8	9.3
Farm workers_____	100.00	100.00	100.00	100.00	100.00	100.00
Owners and managers_____	10.7	11.9	14.3	29.3	10.1	14.3
Tenants, including croppers_____	43.0	7.8	25.7	18.2	44.1	44.5
Croppers_____	*24.0*				*25.2*	*23.3*
Laborers_____	46.3	80.3	60.0	52.5	45.8	41.2
Nonfarm workers_____	100.00	100.00	100.00	100.00	100.00	100.00
Professional persons_____	2.5	2.3	2.3	3.0	2.6	3.8
Wholesale and retail dealers_____	1.1	.9	1.2	1.1	1.2	1.1
Other proprietors, managers, and officials__	1.0	.9	1.2	1.1	.8	1.2
Clerks and kindred workers_____	2.8	4.7	3.6	2.5	1.8	1.9
Skilled workers_____	8.0	7.5	9.0	7.0	8.2	5.9
Semiskilled workers_____	15.1	16.3	15.3	15.0	14.7	12.7
Laborers_____	54.3	47.7	48.2	50.6	59.9	54.4
Service workers_____	15.2	19.7	19.2	19.7	10.8	19.0

[1] Figures used in this table are for those States in which 3 percent or more of the total population is Negro.

TABLE 13b.—*Percentage distribution of Negro female workers by social-economic groups, United States and Regions, 1930* [1]

	United States	Northeast	Middle States	Northwest	Southeast	Southwest
Total workers _____ number __	1, 797, 100	289, 572	168, 338	8, 310	1, 187, 109	143, 771
	Percent 100. 00	*Percent* 100. 00	*Percent* 100. 00	*Percent* 100. 00	*Percent* 100. 00	*Percent* 100. 00
Farm _____	27. 5	.4	.6	.9	38. 7	23. 2
Owners and managers _____	.8	.1	.1	.3	1. 0	1. 2
Tenants, including croppers _____	3. 4	(2)	.1	.2	4. 8	3. 6
Croppers _____	*1. 9*				*2. 7*	*1. 9*
Laborers _____	23. 3	.3	.4	.4	32. 9	18. 4
Nonfarm _____	72. 5	99. 6	99. 4	99. 1	61. 3	76. 8
Professional persons _____	3. 3	3. 1	3. 2	5. 7	3. 2	4. 4
Wholesale and retail dealers _____	.2	.2	.3	.6	.2	.2
Other proprietors, managers, and officials _____	.3	.3	.8	1. 3	.2	.5
Clerks and kindred workers _____	1. 1	1. 9	3. 1	2. 1	.6	.7
Skilled workers _____	.1	.2	.2	.1	(2)	.1
Semiskilled workers _____	10. 0	18. 6	20. 4	13. 3	6. 7	6. 7
Laborers _____	1. 7	1. 2	2. 1	3. 1	1. 8	1. 1
Service workers _____	55. 8	74. 1	69. 3	72. 9	48. 6	63. 1
Farm workers _____	100. 00	100. 00	100. 00	100. 00	100. 00	100. 00
Owners and managers _____	2. 8	11. 7	11. 5	31. 6	2. 6	5. 0
Tenants, including croppers _____	12. 6	7. 6	20. 8	19. 7	12. 4	15. 5
Croppers _____	*7. 0*				*7. 0*	*8. 2*
Laborers _____	84. 6	80. 7	67. 7	48. 7	85. 0	79. 5
Nonfarm workers _____	100. 00	100. 00	100. 00	100. 00	100. 00	100. 00
Professional persons _____	4. 5	3. 1	3. 3	5. 8	5. 2	5. 7
Wholesale and retail dealers _____	.3	.2	.3	.6	.3	.3
Other proprietors, managers, and officials _____	.5	.3	.8	1. 3	.4	.6
Clerks and kindred workers _____	1. 5	1. 9	3. 1	2. 1	1. 0	1. 0
Skilled workers _____	.1	.2	.2	.1	(2)	.1
Semiskilled workers _____	13. 7	18. 7	20. 5	13. 4	11. 0	8. 7
Laborers _____	2. 3	1. 2	2. 1	3. 2	3. 0	1. 5
Service workers _____	77. 1	74. 4	69. 7	73. 5	79. 1	82. 1

[1] Figures used in this table are for those States in which 3 percent or more of the total population is Negro.
[2] Less than 0.1 percent.

TABLE 14a.—*Percentage distribution of other than white and Negro male workers, by social-economic groups, United States and regions, 1930* [1]

	United States	Northwest	Southwest	Far West
Total workers _____ number __	522, 881	32, 449	288, 130	202, 302
	Percent 100. 00	*Percent* 100. 00	*Percent* 100. 00	*Percent* 100. 00
Farm _____	47. 5	58. 7	50. 5	41. 5
Owners, managers, and tenants _____	12. 1	17. 3	17. 3	4. 0
Laborers _____	35. 4	41. 4	33. 2	37. 5
Nonfarm _____	52. 5	41. 3	49. 5	58. 5
Professional persons _____	1. 0	.8	.9	1. 2
Wholesale and retail dealers _____	2. 4	.4	2. 3	3. 0
Other proprietors, managers, and officials _____	1. 2	1. 0	.9	1. 7
Clerks and kindred workers _____	3. 7	.9	3. 5	4. 5
Skilled workers _____	5. 2	2. 6	6. 2	4. 1
Semiskilled workers _____	6. 9	3. 4	6. 3	8. 2
Laborers _____	26. 7	29. 7	26. 8	26. 1
Service workers _____	5. 4	2. 5	2. 6	9. 7
Farm workers _____	100. 00	100. 00	100. 00	100. 00
Owners, managers, and tenants _____	25. 5	29. 4	34. 3	9. 5
Laborers _____	74. 5	70. 6	65. 7	90. 5
Nonfarm workers _____	100. 00	100. 00	100. 00	100. 00
Professional persons _____	2. 0	1. 9	1. 9	2. 1
Wholesale and retail dealers _____	4. 7	.9	4. 6	5. 1
Other proprietors, managers, and officials _____	2. 3	2. 4	1. 9	2. 8
Clerks and kindred workers _____	7. 0	2. 1	7. 0	7. 6
Skilled workers _____	9. 8	6. 2	12. 5	7. 1
Semiskilled workers _____	13. 1	8. 2	12. 7	14. 0
Laborers _____	50. 9	72. 2	54. 1	44. 7
Service workers _____	10. 2	6. 1	5. 3	16. 6

[1] Figures used in this table are for only those States in which 3 percent or more of the total population are "Other races."

TABLE 14b.—*Percentage distribution of other than white and Negro female workers by social-economic groups, United States and regions, 1930* [1]

	United States	Northwest	Southwest	Far West
Total workers......................number..	83,249	2,823	56,691	23,735
	Percent 100.00	*Percent* 100.00	*Percent* 100.00	*Percent* 100.00
Farm..	21.3	45.4	23.5	13.0
Owners, managers, and tenants...............	2.2	6.4	2.5	0.8
Laborers..	19.1	39.0	21.0	12.2
Nonfarm...	78.7	54.6	76.5	87.0
Professional persons.........................	3.0	2.7	3.0	3.2
Wholesale and retail dealers.................	1.3	0.3	1.4	1.2
Other proprietors, managers, and officials...	1.0	0.7	0.9	1.4
Clerks and kindred workers...................	8.9	3.4	8.7	10.0
Skilled workers...............................	0.3	0.2	0.2	0.6
Semiskilled workers..........................	30.7	11.8	26.8	42.3
Laborers......................................	2.6	2.6	2.1	3.6
Service workers...............................	30.9	32.9	33.4	24.7
Farm workers......................................	100.00	100.00	100.00	100.00
Owners, managers and tenants.................	10.2	14.0	10.6	6.5
Laborers......................................	89.8	86.0	89.4	
Nonfarm workers...................................	100.00	100.00	100.00	100.00
Professional persons.........................	3.9	4.9	3.9	3.7
Wholesale and retail dealers.................	1.6	0.6	1.8	1.4
Other proprietors, managers, and officials...	1.3	1.2	1.1	1.6
Clerks and kindred workers...................	11.3	6.3	11.4	11.5
Skilled workers...............................	0.4	0.3	0.3	0.6
Semiskilled workers..........................	39.0	21.7	35.1	48.6
Laborers......................................	3.3	4.8	2.8	4.2
Service workers...............................	39.2	60.2	43.6	28.4

[1] Figures used in this table are for only those States in which 3 percent or more of the total population are "Other races."

percentage of male workers classed as "other proprietors, managers, and officials", is somewhat larger than the percentage either of those in trade or of those in the professions everywhere except in the two southern regions.

When males engaged in the professional, proprietary, and managerial occupations are considered as a combined group, they constitute 15 percent of the total in the Northeast, 13 percent in the Middle States, 12 percent in the Northwest, 9 percent in the Southeast, 12 percent in the Southwest, and 16 percent in the Far West.

Some indication as to the relative importance of retail trade in different parts of the country is furnished by figure 24, showing per-capita retail sales by States for 1929 and 1933.[27] In New York, California, and Nevada retail sales had a per-capita value of over $500 in 1929. In most of the rest of the Northeast and the Far West, and in the Middle States, per-capita sales at this time ran above $400. In the Northwest they ranged between $340 and $480; in the Southwest between $270 and $440. In the Southeast the average value of per-capita sales was much lower, only Florida going above $300, while South Carolina and Georgia fell below $200. For the 1933 map, the figures marking the class intervals were divided in half, corresponding to the drop of 50 percent in dollar retail sales between 1929 and 1933. The relative ranking of the States

[27] See Goodrich, *op. cit.*, pp. 33–37, for a discussion of these maps.

changed but little, particularly in the Far West and the Northwest. No State changed its position by more than one interval. The States of the Northeast make a somewhat better showing in 1933. The Southeast shows more variation; but, with the exception of West Virginia, all the States with the lowest per-capita sales are still in that region.

Classes of Agricultural Workers.

Data on the situation of agricultural workers in different parts of the United States have already been given in considerable detail. Here it is necessary only to add a brief consideration of variations in the proportions of farm operators and farm laborers in different regions. The farm labor group comprised nearly 40 percent of all males engaged in agriculture in 1930. If the cropper group is added, the combined total (46.6 percent) is nearly equal to the combined total of owners, managers, and renters other than croppers.

The proportions of laborers among all male farm workers in the Northeast and in the Far West are very high (46 and 52 percent, respectively), as compared with corresponding proportions in the Middle States and in the Northwest (36 percent). When the comparison on this point is limited to white workers, the figures for the Middle States and the Northwest remain practically unchanged, but the figures for both the Northeast and the Far West drop to 44 percent in the labor group. The conspicuous drop in the latter case is due to the importance of Mexican and Japanese farm laborers in that region.

The analysis of farm labor in the Southern States is complicated by the cropper group, propertyless farm operators working on a share basis with implements supplied by the landlord. If croppers are classed with the farm laborers, the relative figure for this combined labor group rises to 55 percent of all male agricultural workers in the Southeast and to 47 percent in the Southwest—working, as was shown in a previous section, at very low monthly wages. Even when the analysis is limited to white workers, 47 percent of the male agricultural workers in the Southeast and 41 percent of those in the Southwest are reported either as farm laborers or as croppers.

As already noted, only one in 12 of all gainfully occupied women is engaged in farming in the country as a whole. In the Southeast, however, well over one-fourth are so occupied. Furthermore, in the Northern and Western States, from 66 to 72 percent of all paid women workers in agriculture are farm operators, but 79 percent of all female farm workers in the Southeast and 72 percent in the Southwest are classed as laborers. If the analysis is limited to white workers, the figures are reduced to 67 percent in the Southeast and 63 percent in the Southwest.

The prospects of farm laborers rise and fall, in large part, in relation to general conditions in agriculture and general industrial conditions. These workers, farm laborers and croppers, with their families, constitute a considerable segment of the American public—a group which deserves greater attention than it has usually been accorded.

Classes of Industrial, Clerical, and Service Workers

Turning to the consideration of the distribution of nonfarm workers in occupations outside of the professions, trade, and managerial positions, we find that in the total United States each of four main classes absorbs about one-fifth of all nonfarm male workers: clerks and kindred workers (17 percent), skilled workers (21.5 percent), semiskilled workers (19 percent), unskilled workers (21.5 percent). These ratios show surprisingly little variation among regions. The principal deviations are found in the relatively small proportion of semiskilled workers in the Northeast and in the Southeast (14 percent in both cases), and in the rather low proportion of skilled (15 percent) and the correspondingly high proportion of unskilled workers (29 percent) in the Southeast. Only a small proportion of all nonfarm male workers in any region are engaged in personal and domestic service. The percentages range from 3.2 in the Middle States and in the Northwest to 4.7 in the Far West.

Much greater regional variations are found in the percentage distribution of female workers (exclusive of those on farms). Clerical positions hold more than 30 percent of the gainfully occupied nonfarm women in the Northeast, Middle States, Northwest, and Far West, and nearly this proportion in the Southwest (28 percent), but only 18 percent in the

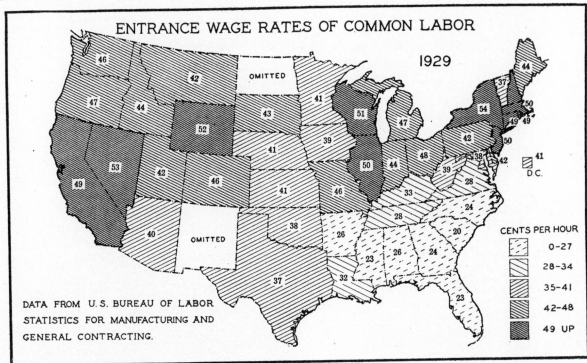

University of Pennsylvania Press.

FIGURE 23.—Entrance wage rates of common labor, by States, 1929. From Goodrich and others, *Migration and Economic Opportunity.*

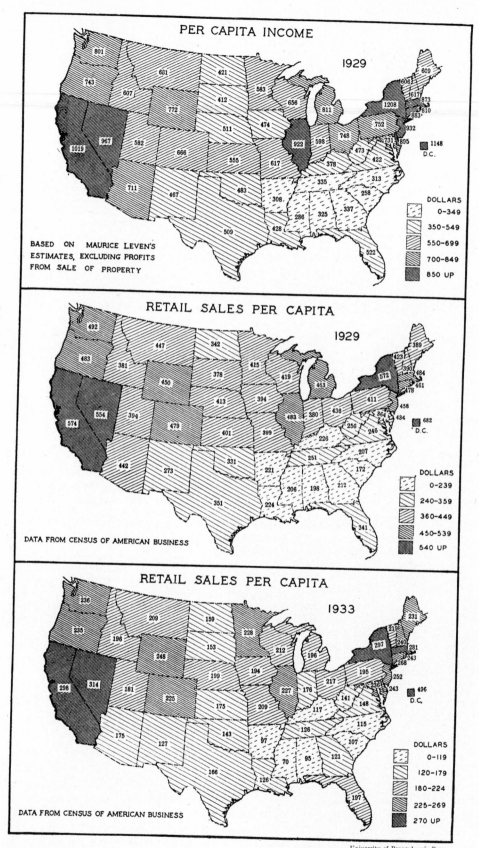

FIGURE 24.—Estimated retail sales per capita, by States, 1929 and 1933; also income per capita, 1929. From Goodrich and others, *Migration and Economic Opportunity*.

Southeast. In the Northeast the proportion of the semiskilled (31 percent) almost equals that of the clerks (33 percent), but the semiskilled constitute less than 25 percent of all nonfarm women workers in other sections, and only 17 percent in the Northwest and in the Southeast. The service occupations account for about one-fifth of the gainfully occupied women in the nonfarm group in the Northeast, Middle States, and Northwest. The corresponding proportions are much larger in the Southeast (41 percent) and Southwest (31 percent), but smaller in the Far West (17 percent).

It would be illuminating if data on variations in average wage rates could be added to the figures showing geographical variations in occupational distribution. Reliable data of this character are, however, almost completely lacking—due to lack of comparability of operations, hours of employment, and other variables. Figure 23, showing entrance wage rates of common labor by States in 1929, definitely suggests wide average differences.[28] Average rates in most States of the Southeast were below 30 cents an hour, while rates running up to 50 cents and more were paid in States along the Atlantic coast, around the Great Lakes, and in the Far West. Wyoming constitutes an island of high rates in the Northwest.

Occupational Opportunities of Racial Minorities in Different Parts of the United States

There is less regional variation than might be expected in the distribution of Negro male workers in nonfarm occupations. Together, laborers and service workers make up 67 percent of the total in the Northeast and in the Middle States, 70 percent in the Northwest and in the Southeast, and 73 percent in the Southwest.[29] The ratio of unskilled to service workers, among Negro males, is about 5 to 2 in all sections except in the Southeast, where it is 6 to 1. Relatively, the greatest regional variation is found in the group designated as "clerks and kindred workers." This class constitutes 4.7 percent of the nonfarm male Negro group in the Northeast (and 4.4 percent of all gainfully occupied Negro males in that region), 3.6 percent in the Middle States, 2.5 percent in the Northwest, but only 1.8 percent in the Southeast (only 0.8 percent of all gainfully occupied Negro males in that region).

In the case of male Negro workers, the big difference between North and South is found in the division between the farm and nonfarm occupations. Farms hold 55 percent of all gainfully occupied Negro males in the Southeast and 51 percent in the Southwest, but only 7 percent in the Northeast, 5 percent in the Middle States, and 9 percent in the Northwest.

Among gainfully occupied Negro women not on farms, the proportion in service occupations ranges from 70 percent in the Middle States to 82 percent in the Southwest. The group which shows the widest variations is that of semiskilled workers, who make up 19 percent of the Negro women workers in the Northeast and 20 percent in the Middle States, but only 11 percent in the Southeast and 9 percent in the Southwest.

Opportunities for professional work for Negro women are relatively greater in the Southeast, Southwest, and Northwest (accounting for over 5 percent of the nonfarm Negro women workers in each of these regions) than in the Northeast and in the Middle States (where the corresponding proportion is 3 percent).

The data for racial groups other than whites and Negroes are too heterogeneous to yield very significant results. The proportion of the males in this group found in nonfarm occupations is somewhat smaller than in the Negro group. But the occupational distribution of the nonfarm workers in the former group is somewhat more varied, with 5 percent in trade, 7 percent in clerical occupations, 10 percent classified as skilled, 13 percent as semiskilled, 51 percent as laborers, and 10 percent as service workers.

Among Negroes the ratio of gainfully occupied men to gainfully occupied women is just 2 to 1, in contrast to a corresponding ratio of nearly 4 to 1 among whites. There are nearly 7 gainfully occupied men to every gainfully occupied woman among other racial groups. The relatively few occupied women in these other racial groups are principally distributed between three classes: Farm laborers (19 percent), semiskilled workers (31 percent), and service workers (31 percent); but 3 percent are professional workers, and 9 percent are clerks.

The data presented in this section show clearly the influence both of regional situation and of racial status on the occupations of American workers. Although the former influence may have greater effect in determining general levels of living, it would appear that traditional attitudes associated with racial divisions are quite as powerful in creating or limiting occupational opportunity for the members of racial minorities in the United States.

Perhaps the most interesting conclusion which emerges from the regional-racial comparisons is the discovery that the white population of the Southeast does not enjoy a privileged position as regards occupational distribution, in spite of the large proportion of Negroes there engaged as laborers and in service

---

[28] See Goodrich, *op. cit.*, p. 30, for a discussion of the data used in this map.

[29] No data are presented for Negro workers in the far West, because the treatment is here limited to States in which Negroes are more than 3 percent of the total population.

occupations. It seems evident that a general increase in economic level for all groups in the South would broaden the opportunities in the more privileged occupations for whites as well as for Negroes.

The development of new industrial, commercial, and professional enterprises in the United States, and the full interchange of population among regions in response to emerging opportunities in different localities may bring future economic progress for the United States as a Nation. It is hoped that such developments will also afford a solid basis for the progress of the various regions, each responding to its particular resources and opportunities, and in accordance with its own traditions and genius.

7. Summary

Every type of analysis that has been undertaken in this chapter has indicated wide geographical variations in the relation between population and developed economic resources. The historical trend in the Nation as a whole during the past 50 years has been toward a decline in the extractive industries and an increase in the trade and service occupations, while the relative importance of the manufacturing and mechanical industries has remained fairly constant. The Northeast, the Middle States, and the Far West have shared in this national trend to a much more marked degree than the other regions. In spite of the movement away from the extractive industries, that part of the population still employed in them is in a number of sections among the least favorably situated economically. This is due in part to the destruction of natural resources (forests, mines, soil fertility) and in part to the increasing pressure of population in some sections where the chief employment opportunities are in the extractive industries. Among such areas are the Great Lakes cut-over region, some of the bituminous coal mining regions, a considerable part of the Southeast, and parts of the Great Plains area.

A number of measures were applied in the analysis of regional variations in the agricultural situation, culminating in estimates of the average productivity per worker in agriculture. They uniformly indicated the Southeast to be in the least favorable position, average productivity per worker there being less than half the figure for any other region. The significance of these findings is intensified by the consideration that it is in the Southeast that the largest proportion of the workers are engaged in agriculture.

Manufacturing and mechanical industries are concentrated chiefly in the Northeast and the Middle States. Analysis of recent trends indicates some movement away from the old manufacturing centers, but the main trend seems to be toward a persistence of the general pattern of concentration and dispersion as found at present, with slow diffusion of industry within the principal industrial areas and the occasional emergence of new industrial centers, rather than toward any general dispersion of industry across the whole country.

The general picture which emerges is corroborated by an examination of the regional distribution of gainful workers by social-economic classes. The opportunity for employment in the more desirable and more remunerative occupations is greatest in the Northeast and the Far West, and most restricted in the Southeast.

Variations in the plane of living, in average per-capita incomes and in per-capita retail sales serve to clarify further the contrasts in economic well-being between different parts of the United States. An equalization of opportunity involves "leveling up" the less favored groups and sections to correspond more closely to what is usually thought of as the American standard of living. This appears to depend in part upon a stimulation of more varied economic development in regions where the plane of living is low, with emphasis on a well-rounded agricultural system as well as upon the development of manufacturing and the trade and service occupations. It also depends upon continued redistribution of population, with movement from the less favorably situated areas to those of greater opportunity.

III. TRENDS IN POPULATION REDISTRIBUTION

1. Changing Tides of Internal Migration

The Westward Movement

From the date of first settlement along the Atlantic seaboard, the population of the United States has been on the move. By the close of the Revolutionary War, a considerable number of hardy individuals had already penetrated the forests of the Appalachian and Allegheny Mountains, and were claiming the territory immediately to the west for the new Nation. The westward trek continued with such rapidity that by 1850 the original colonies had lost more than 2 million people to the States between the Appalachians and the Mississippi River. With the close of the Civil War, the residents of Ohio and the Southern States, except Florida, joined the westward movement in increasing numbers. By 1930, 5 million persons born east of the Mississippi were living somewhere to the west of that river.

The settling of Oklahoma between 1890 and 1910 filled the last vacant space in the Southwest, and the American people began to look about for new places to live. The first wave of migration to the undeveloped lands of the West was over. The frontier was closed. There were no new fields to conquer. Consolidation of farm land in the West continued, but population increase, except in California, now proceeded at a much slower pace.

A temporary resurgence of the agricultural migration occurred during the World War. The cry "Wheat will win the war" sent thousands to the range land of the Great Plains. Hundreds of thousands of acres of grassland were plowed for the first time. Waving heads of wheat sprang up where buffalo and cattle had grazed. The war ended. Soldiers turned from the trenches to the wheat fields, and the foreign demand for American grain declined rapidly. The last agricultural migration ended in disappointment and hardship, as dry seasons parched the soil of the Great Plains no longer protected by grass. The population of Montana, which increased 46 percent between 1910

and 1920, decreased 2 percent between 1920 and 1930. The rate of growth of North Dakota dropped from 12 to 5 percent, that of Wyoming from 33 to 16 percent, that of Colorado from 18 to 10 percent, and that of Nebraska from 9 to 6 percent.

The Attraction of Northern Industrial Centers

Meanwhile a new attraction, which had developed slowly at first, made rapid gains. The new industrial economy drew large numbers of migrants to sections that had previously been areas of emigration. By 1900, New England and the Middle Atlantic States were attracting more people than they were losing. Between 1910 and 1920, westward migration across the Mississippi River was insufficient to balance deaths among those who had previously moved from Eastern to Western States, so that the number of those born in the East but living in the West began to decline. People in the cotton States of the South were going north rather than west. By 1930, the States in the northeast quadrant contained more than 3,000,000 persons who were born south of the Mason-Dixon Line and nearly 1,650,000 persons who were born west of the Mississippi River. The general pattern of migration had completely changed. The surge of population westward from the Atlantic seaboard had given way to a general movement from the interior to the States of the Pacific coast, the Great Lakes, and the North Atlantic seacoast.

Main Channels of Movement

It would be incorrect to assume that all migration, even at any given period, has been in one direction. There have been certain main paths of travel, but there have always been strong counter-currents and a considerable number of migrants have struck out in other directions. Figure 1 shows currents of internal migration as evidenced by the distribution in 1930 of white and Negro persons relative to their States of birth. It should be noted that the data on which this map is based do not record intermediate stages and trial

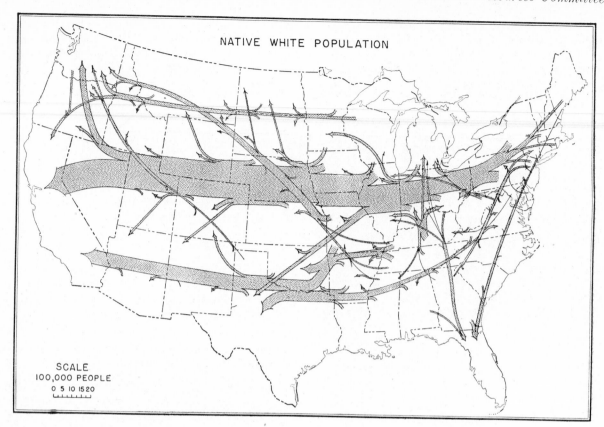

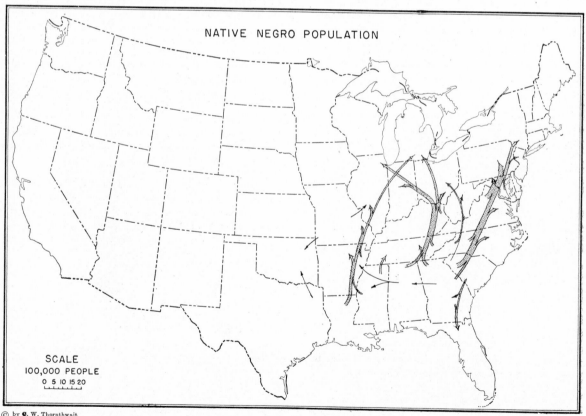

FIGURE 1.—Net migration since birth of native population, 1930.   Adapted from Goodrich and others in *Migration and Economic Opportunity.*

moves, and leave quite out of account those who ventured away but then returned to their home States. Since this map reflects net migratory movements since the Civil War period, the westward movement still predominates in the redistribution record of the native white population, but the new industrial attraction is apparent in the migration record of the Negro population. The mobility of the American people has been so great that almost every State has both gained and lost a considerable proportion of its native-born population. In 1930 every State except California had sent forth more than 15 percent of the population born within its boundaries. Conversely, every State, with five exceptions (Maine, Vermont, Delaware, Utah, and Nevada), included more than 100,000 residents born in other States. In the country as a whole, about 23 percent of the total native population—22,000,000 native whites and 3,000,000 native Negroes—were at this time living outside the States where they were born.

Farming communities have in the past been the principal source from which migrants have gone out to other farms, or to cities, just because the people of previous generations in this country have been predominantly agricultural, and because the birth rate has always been highest in farming communities. Movement from farms to cities and villages has assumed major proportions in recent decades. The period of the twenties witnessed a net decrease of more than a million persons in the farm population of the Nation. There was a net migration away from the farms of every State except California, Massachusetts, and Rhode Island. Moreover, in two-thirds of the States the net migration from farms exceeded the natural increase, so that the farm population actually decreased in number (see fig. 2).

It is clear that economic motives have played the major role in the redistribution of population in this country—the search for new land in the earlier movement to the West, the hope of new, more highly paid jobs in later movements to industrial and commercial centers. The desire for adventure also has undoubtedly played a real part in setting these people on the move. Those who went west were looking for rich soils to crop, but many of them were also responding to the appeal of the frontier with its unknown horizons. Similarly, young men and women setting out for cities are mindful of more varied and freer opportunities for living. The appeal of New York, Washington, Cleveland, and Los Angeles is not wholly economic. Others have moved from cities to farms, not merely in search of economic security, but also because of a longing for contact with the soil and the society of friendly neighbors.

Migration During the Depression

The economic depression distinctly changed the pattern of internal migration in the United States, at least for a time. But its effects are more complicated than is sometimes supposed.

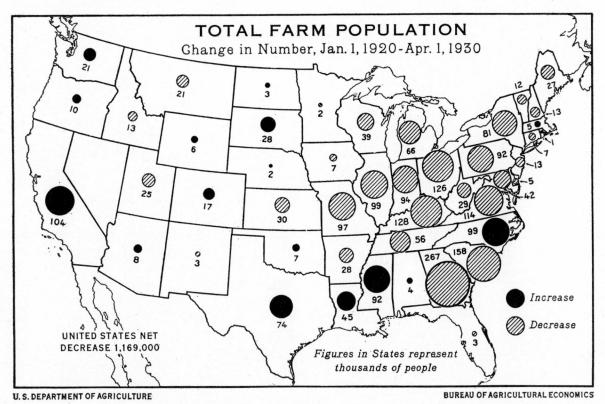

FIGURE 2.—Total farm population: change in number, January 1, 1920–April 1, 1930.

The actual movement to farms was never large, even during the early years of the depression, and this movement, since 1933, has averaged only one-half to two-thirds of that occurring in the years 1925 to 1929. This is what might be expected. The first impulse of many unemployed was to return to friends or relatives in the country, or to cultivate a small plot of land where a portion of the food necessary for existence could be raised. But the welcome of friends and relatives who were already near the subsistence level was soon ex-

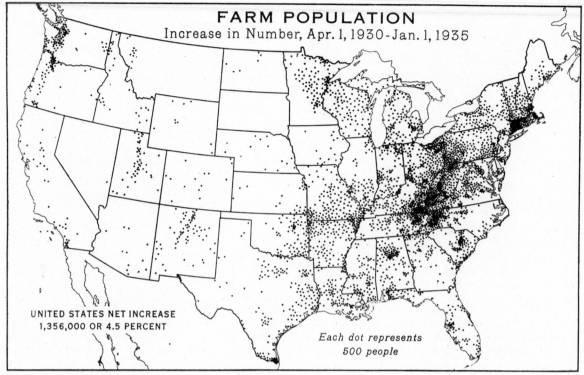

FARM POPULATION
Increase in Number, Apr. 1, 1930 - Jan. 1, 1935

UNITED STATES NET INCREASE
1,356,000 OR 4.5 PERCENT

*Each dot represents
500 people*

U.S. DEPARTMENT OF AGRICULTURE   BUREAU OF AGRICULTURAL ECONOMICS

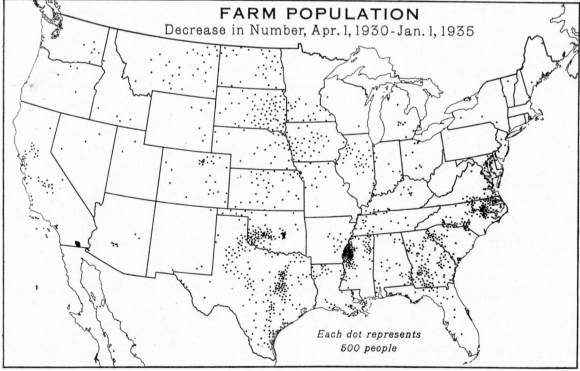

FARM POPULATION
Decrease in Number, Apr. 1, 1930 - Jan. 1, 1935

*Each dot represents
500 people*

U.S. DEPARTMENT OF AGRICULTURE   BUREAU OF AGRICULTURAL ECONOMICS

FIGURE 3.—Change in farm population, 1930–35.

hausted. Life in the country was less enjoy-
able in reality than in prospect to many who
had become accustomed to the electric lights,
running water, and movies of the city. Moreover, as the administration of relief was transferred from private to public agencies, distinct
disadvantages resulted from moving to the
country. Not only was the family relief allowance considerably smaller in rural areas,
but it was also more difficult for migrants to
obtain. Leaving the city also affected legal
residence, one of the primary requirements for
obtaining relief. In effect, the administration
of public relief placed a premium on length of
residence and stability. It is not surprising
that the first impulse to move to the country
was eventually stifled by the relative advantages of staying in the city, however meager
these might be. Moving to the outskirts of
the city did not involve all the disadvantages
of moving to the country, so that this movement assumed quite large proportions.

Changes in the farm population, 1930–35.—
One out of every 16 persons living on farms,
January 1, 1935, reported that he had lived in
nonfarm territory 5 years previously. The estimates of the Bureau of Agricultural Economics indicate that this is not an unusually
high proportion. One-third of these had settled around the urban centers extending from
southern New England westward to Lake
Michigan; another third were located in the
South, mainly in mining and industrial communities; and the remaining migrants were
scattered through northern New England, the
Northwest, and Far West. Many of these
migrants had settled on small farms seeking to
produce at least part of their own food, particularly vegetables, eggs, and milk.

The movement from farms was definitely restricted by the depression, but continued in
numbers more than sufficient to counterbalance
natural increase. (See table 1.) If there had
not been nearly 2 million people living on
farms in 1935 who were living in nonfarm territory in 1930, the farm population of the
Nation would have decreased by more than
500,000 persons during this 5-year period.

The partial checking of farm-to-city migration reversed the earlier trend toward a gradual decrease in the absolute number of people
living on farms. The farm population of
31,800,000 persons on January 1, 1935, was the
largest ever recorded. It exceeded that of
April 1, 1930, by more than 1⅓ million. Large
increases in the farm population occurred in
southern New England, eastern Ohio and
western Pennsylvania, the southern Appalachians, the Ozarks, northern Wisconsin, and eastern Minnesota, and in the Puget Sound and
Willamette Valleys. The increase was greatest
near industrial centers, in mining counties, and
in subsistence farming areas. (See fig. 3.)

There were decreases during the same period
in the number of persons living on farms in

TABLE 1.—*Estimated farm population, natural increase,
and number of persons moving to and from farms,
United States, 1930–34* [1]

[In thousands]

Year	Farm popu-lation, Janu-ary 1	Arriv-als from non-farm terri-tory	Depar-tures for non-farm terri-tory	Gain or loss due to migra-tion	Natural in-crease	Net change
1930	30,169	1,611	1,823	−212	398	186
1931	30,497	1,546	1,566	−20	407	387
1932	30,971	1,777	1,511	266	418	684
1933	31,693	944	1,225	−281	395	114
1934	31,770	700	1,051	−351	405	54
1930–34		6,578	7,176	−598	2,023	1,632 [2]
1925–29		7,770	10,735	−2,965	2,070	−895 [3]

[1] Prepared by the Bureau of Agricultural Economics. It should be
noted that the estimates of arrivals and departures represent gross movement in both directions. Many persons moved from farm to city and
back to farms, and vice versa, during this period. The number of persons over 5 years of age who had moved from nonfarm territory to farms
after Jan. 1, 1930, and who were still there on Jan. 1, 1935, was reported
to be 1,995,000 by the census of 1935. The number of persons leaving
farms and not returning between Jan. 1, 1930, and Jan. 1, 1935, is estimated to be at least 2,593,000.

[2] Gain in farm population, adjusted on basis of agricultural census
data for 1935. The adjusted figure includes an estimated increase of
207,000 persons "on farms" due to change to farming as an occupation
without change of residence, and to changes in the interpretation of a
"farm."

[3] Loss in farm population.

the drought area (extending from Montana
eastward to western Iowa), in northeastern
North Carolina, Georgia, the Yazoo Delta, the
Black Belt of Texas, and southwestern Oklahoma. The number of Negro farm residents
decreased by nearly 200,000.

Certain reservations must be made in interpreting these data. Although direct evidence
is lacking, it is reasonable to suppose that an
appreciable proportion of the apparent increase in farm population between 1930 and
1935 was due to differences in the interpretation of a "farm" and in methods of enumeration at these two dates. Reports from all parts
of the country indicate that many farms were
enumerated in 1935 that were not so classed in
1930. In 1930 many part-time farmers in industrial and mining areas were not producing
enough farm products to be classed as farmers
by the census. By 1935 many such persons
were unemployed and doing enough farming
to come within the census definition of a
farmer. A considerable part of the increase in
farm population near cities, especially in
southern New England, and in areas where
mining and forestry are predominant industries, may be attributed to this shift in occupation rather than to a change in residence. This
thesis is borne out by the decrease in the average size of farm between 1930 and 1935. The
average acreage per farm decreased in Connecticut by 23 acres, in Massachusetts by 15
acres, and in West Virginia by 17 acres. Undoubtedly, much of the apparent increase in
farm population from nonfarm territory in
northern Idaho and in eastern Ohio, western
Pennsylvania and West Virginia was due to
change in occupation from mining and forestry
to subsistence farming. It is quite possible
that the decrease in farm population in the

South resulted partly from the crop-reduction program. The decrease in cotton acreage led to the displacement of many farm laborers and tenants. A number of them occupied dwellings in the country and in villages, but were not classed as farmers by the census in 1935.[1]

Almost no information is available concerning the migration of the nonfarm population since 1930. It is apparent, however, that the Pacific Coast States no longer attracted large numbers of people from the East and Middle West, except casual laborers who were no longer welcome. The suburban movement already in evidence during the twenties apparently continued in most parts of the country.

The transients.—The number of transients undoubtedly increased rapidly during the early thirties. The Committee on Care of Transient and Homeless estimated that there were more than 1 million homeless transients in this country in the early months of 1933.[2] No exact comparison with earlier conditions is possible. It soon became apparent that local resources were inadequate to provide for the steadily increasing number of transient unemployed. The transient problem had become so serious by autumn of 1932 that the Federal Emergency Relief Act of May 1933 provided for Federal aid. These transients were mainly young people, two-thirds or more of the unattached individuals being less than 35 years of age. About 80 percent of the heads of transient family groups were under 45 years of age. Unattached transients came principally from east of the Mississippi River, particularly from New York, Pennsylvania, Ohio, Illinois, and Michigan. Massachusetts, Missouri, Oklahoma, Texas, and California were other important States of origin. Transient family groups, on the other hand, came mainly from the Southwest—Texas, Oklahoma, Arkansas, Missouri, and Kansas. California in the Far West and Illinois, New York, and Pennsylvania in the Northeast were the other principal areas of origin.

The depression transients traveled from city to city in search of employment. Usually they lacked a definite destination, drifting aimlessly from place to place. Their movements were governed by vague rumors of work and by unrest. There was a tendency for the Eastern States to lose, and for the States of the West and Southwest to gain transients; but the movement consisted chiefly of aimless crosscurrents of travel. In the words of a report of the Federal Emergency Relief Administration, "the migration of a considerable part of the transient relief population appears to have been a waste of effort. Much of the movement was away from urban areas that from the point of view of economic development were more likely to afford employment than were the areas which particularly attracted the transient. As business and industry recover, it may be expected that many of the depression transients will return to areas similar to the ones they left."[3]

In contrast to the migration of the predepression decade, which was primarily a migration of hope, the depression migration was a migration of despair. During the twenties people left their home communities in search of real or imaginary opportunities elsewhere. There were exceptions to this, such as the migration from Montana, but in general people were then attracted by the greater economic opportunity believed to exist in other areas, rather than expelled from their home communities by inability to make a living. Many of the depression migrants took to the road because there was no opportunity at home. The migration from the drought-stricken States of the Great Plains illustrates this. It is true that opportunities elsewhere were slight or even nonexistent, but this had not been demonstrated so clearly as the lack of opportunity at home.

The depression also witnessed a change in attitude toward migrants. As unemployment mounted and relief expenditures multiplied, migrants were no longer welcomed but were regarded as potential liabilities. Two States, California and Florida, refused admittance to persons unable to establish their financial independence. When employment opportunities vanished, welcome also disappeared.

Recent estimates by the Bureau of Agricultural Economics indicate increased migration from farms to cities, beginning in 1935. Other data indicate a resumption of urban population growth.[4] We will return to the consideration of the outlook for future mobility after a somewhat more detailed analysis of recent population movements, and a consideration of conditions controlling these changes.

2. Analysis of Net Population Changes in Different Areas

Factors in Population Change

The stork and the grim reaper are agents of population redistribution as well as the open road and the railway. Varying rates of births and deaths are reflected in natural population changes. At the same time local movements directly affect the growth and decline of different communities. The processes of natural change operate as slow, invisible, fairly constant forces, causing the gradual accumulation or decrease of population in dif-

[1] These statements are confirmed by Beck, P. G., and Forster, M. C., *Six Rural Problem Areas,* Federal Emergency Relief Administration, 1935.
[2] Webb, John. "The Transient Unemployed", *Monthly Report of the Federal Emergency Relief Administration,* Jan. 1 through Jan. 31, 1936

[3] *Ibid.*, p. 25.
[4] Data on the year-by-year movement of population in Cleveland, Ohio, collected by Howard Whipple Green, show a resumption of population increase in that city beginning with 1933, after an earlier decline from the 1930 level.

ferent areas. The shift of the people from place to place is conspicuous and often brings about rapid changes.

Sometimes the flow of migration merely tends to restore an equilibrium in the distribution of people that would otherwise be disturbed through differential rates of reproduction. In other cases, the effects of migration are more positive, resulting in a new pattern of population distribution. In either case, migratory movements may influence birth rates and death rates, through changes in the age and sex composition of different communities, and through more subtle changes in social attitudes and characteristics. Changes in the geographical location of people are constantly taking place through the interaction of these two factors: (1) Natural increase or decrease, and (2) migration. Again, these factors influence and are influenced by economic and social processes.

Areas of Population Increase, 1920–30

The relative importance of the component elements in population change in different parts of the United States during the decade 1920–30 is shown in figure 4. In this chart, "natural change" represents the immediate effects of crude birth rates and death rates during the period in question; "international migration" represents accessions to each area of immigrants entering the United States between 1920 and 1930; "internal migration" represents the net result of interchange of peo-

ple between States. The areas used here are selected by grouping States with similar demographic trends.

Wide geographic variations in population change are evident. The most rapid increases during the twenties occurred in three areas: (1) New York, Connecticut, and New Jersey; (2) the Great Lakes States; and (3) the Far West. In the first of these areas all three factors contributed substantially to the increase; in the second the increase consisted largely of natural change; in the third, of interstate migration. In some areas, notably in Georgia and South Carolina, out-movements nearly balanced natural increase, so that there was little net change.

During the decade 1920–30 urban areas absorbed more than 85 percent of the total increase in population. The remainder was distributed through rural nonfarm territory, chiefly that adjacent to metropolitan centers. The net movement from farms, involving from 5½ to 6 million persons, exceeded the natural increase by more than one-third. Consequently the farm population sustained a net loss of more than a million persons during the decade. On the other hand, natural increase accounted for only 45 percent of the reported increase in the urban population. The number of migrants to cities from rural areas and from foreign countries about equaled the excess of births over deaths. The rest of the apparent increase was due to change in classification.

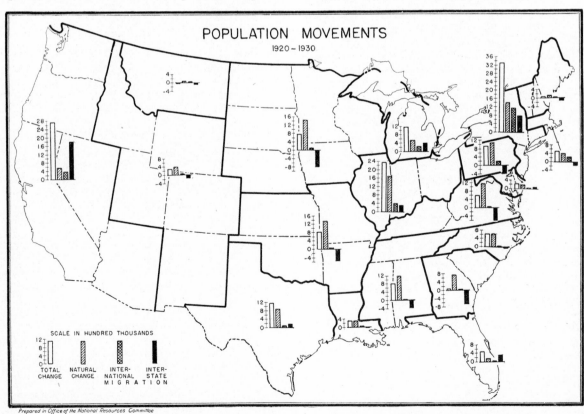

FIGURE 4.—Total population change by groups of States, 1920–30.

Only 14 States gained more people than they lost between 1920 and 1930. As already noted, these States comprise three main areas: (1) New York, Connecticut, and New Jersey; (2) three Great Lakes States—Ohio, Illinois, Michigan; and (3) five Far Western States—California, Oregon, Washington, Arizona, and Nevada. The latter States gained 2,100,000 persons. California alone attracted more people than New York, New Jersey, and Connecticut combined. The movement of population into California—nearly 2 million persons—was the largest ever recorded for any State in a single decade. Of this number, 1,650,000 came from other States, and about 300,000 of those coming from other countries to the United States during this period settled in California.

The population of New York, New Jersey, and Connecticut increased through migration to the extent of 1,900,000 persons, about 780,000 of whom were foreign-born immigrants arriving since 1920. This area also attracted more native American migrants from other States than any other east of California.

The Great Lakes States gained 1,300,000 persons, including about 600,000 foreign-born immigrants. The movement into Michigan was exceeded in volume only by that into California and New York. Nearly one-half of the migrants to the Great Lakes area went to Michigan, mainly to seek employment in the automobile and allied industries. In contrast to the other States in the area, Indiana sustained a net loss through migration of native-born; but this net out-movement of native-born persons was about counterbalanced by the arrival of foreign-born immigrants.

Texas, Florida, Maryland, and the District of Columbia were the other areas with a net gain in population through migration. Migrants to Texas were attracted mainly by the developing oil industry and the expansion of cotton cultivation. Florida's climate and expanding agriculture drew most of its migrants. The increase in Maryland and the District of Columbia reflects the growth of population in Baltimore and the National Capital.

Areas of Emigration, 1920–30

Every agricultural State, except Oregon, Texas, and Florida, lost by migration in this decade; but only two (Montana and Vermont[5]) lost more through net interstate movements than the number added through natural increase. Net out-migration to other States equaled two-thirds or more of the natural increase in nine other States—Maine, New Hampshire, Virginia, South Carolina, Georgia (where the net loss was equal to 95 percent of the natural increase), Arkansas, Iowa, North Dakota, and Idaho. The two main areas from which people were moving—the States south of

the Ohio and Potomac Rivers and east of the Mississippi River, except Florida; and the States between the Rocky Mountains and the Mississippi River, except Arizona and Texas—each lost about 1,700,000 persons. Northern New England and Pennsylvania lost about 115,000 and 390,000 persons, respectively, although these losses were partly offset by accessions of 45,000 and 200,000 foreign-born immigrants.

It is significant that all of the New England States except Connecticut were areas of emigration during the twenties. In Massachusetts and Rhode Island the net emigration characteristic of much of the nineteenth century had been reversed about 1900 as a result of new industrial developments. The reappearance in the twenties of a net population loss through migration reflects expansion of industrial areas outside New England. The arrival of 225,000 foreign-born immigrants between 1920 and 1930 more than offset the net migration of about 160,000 persons from Massachusetts and Rhode Island, but accessions of this sort cannot be expected in the future. By contrast, the migration in and out of North Carolina nearly balanced, undoubtedly as a result of the developing textile industry in the Piedmont area.

Louisiana had the smallest net out-migration of any of the Southern States. This State has long been characterized by an unusually stable population, neither receiving nor sending forth many migrants in exchange with other States. Since 1900 the average proportion of the native white population born in the State but living in other States has been smaller for Louisiana than for any other State except California. In 1930 Louisiana was still found among the States with relatively small losses to other States through emigration, along with California, Texas, New York, New Jersey, North Carolina, and Florida.

The Increasing Concentration of the Population

Two other important trends in population distribution between 1920 and 1930 should be noted. First, more cities and counties lost population than had ever done so during any previous intercensal period. More than 40 percent of the counties in the United States decreased in population during this decade. While the largest losses were in the farm population, nearly half the villages with less than 2,500 inhabitants and one-fifth of the cities with less than 100,000 inhabitants decreased in population. Increase was concentrated in a relatively few areas; the large cities and their metropolitan areas drew people not only from farms but also from smaller cities. Nearly all of the rapidly growing small cities were "satellites" of larger cities; that is, they were located within a metropolitan area. The population of these satellite cities increased 36 percent between 1920 and 1930, as compared with an increase of 19 percent for the nonsatellite cities.

---

[5] Net decrease of population in Vermont during the twenties was prevented by the relatively small accession of foreign-born, mostly from Canada.

The Centrifugal Trend of Metropolitan Populations

Secondly, within the areas where population was increasing rapidly, there was at the same time a general movement from the central city to the immediate environs. The population in the territory adjacent to the central cities of the metropolitan areas increased twice as rapidly as that in the central cities themselves. This was probably due in part to the actual movement of old residents who had formerly lived in the central cities, and in part to the settlement of incoming migrants in the environs rather than in the city proper. In general, within the metropolitan areas, the smaller the place the more rapid the rate of increase; the suburban country districts grew even faster than the satellite cities.

Available data indicate that this suburban trend continued during the 5 years following 1930. Unfortunately, these data do not make possible an analysis comparable to that shown for the years 1920–30. The contrast would be especially interesting, due to stoppage of net immigration from abroad, and to the tendency for people to leave many of the areas that had attracted them during the twenties.

3. The Migration Record of Different Areas

Migration History as Revealed by State-of-Birth and State-of-Residence Data

Although the relative attracting and holding power of States has varied from time to time during the past century, certain States have been consistently areas of absorption, and others have been areas of diffusion. A few have been areas of high interchange of population, both giving and receiving large numbers of people. Three States besides those of the Far West have been constant centers of attraction and absorption of native population, receiving more persons than they have lost: New Jersey in the Northeast, Michigan in the Great Lakes area, Florida in the Southeast. On the other hand, the northern New England States, Pennsylvania, and all of the Southern States east of the Mississippi and south of the Potomac and Ohio Rivers, except Florida, have continually lost more people than they have gained. More recently, areas of net emigration have appeared in Middle and Western States, which were previously areas of gain. By the close of the Civil War the Corn Belt States were losing more persons than they were gaining; by 1900 the area of loss had extended to Kansas, Nebraska, and Minnesota; by 1930 all the States west of the Mississippi River except the three Pacific Coast States and Arizona and Nevada were losing more people than they were gaining through migration.

New York, Ohio, and Illinois are representative of the States which have both received and sent out large numbers of people. In 1930, 1,500,000 persons born in New York were living in other States, compared with 1,400,000 born in other States but living in New York.

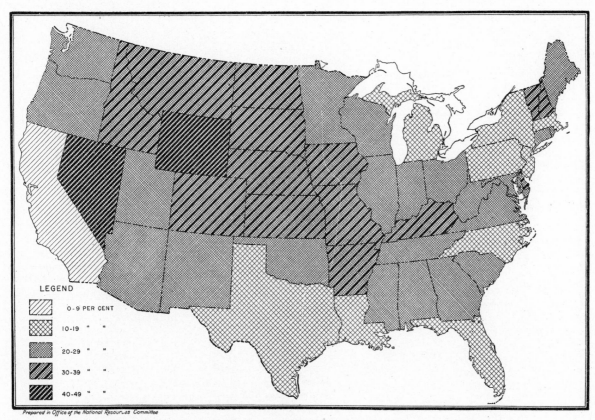

LEGEND

0 - 9 PER CENT
10-19 " "
20-29 " "
30-39 " "
40-49 " "

Prepared in Office of the National Resources Committee

FIGURE 5.—Percentage of the total population born in each State living in other States, 1930.

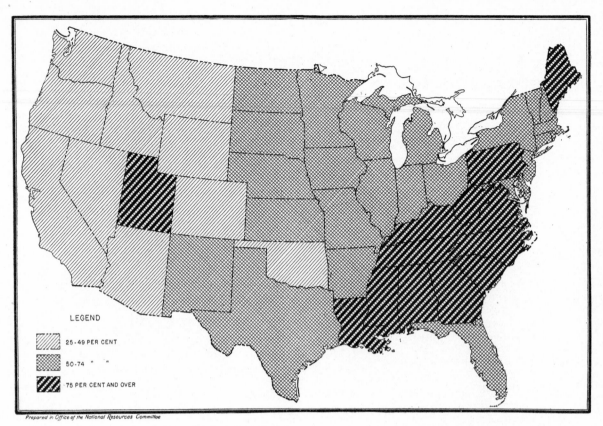

Prepared in Office of the National Resources Committee

FIGURE 6.—Percentage of the total population living in each State, 1930, which was born in that State.

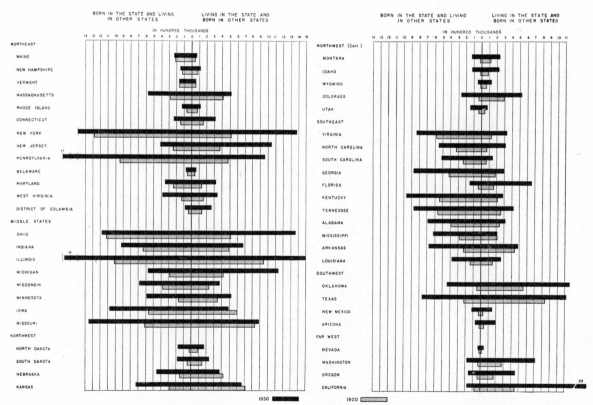

FIGURE 7.—Gain and loss through interstate migration, as indicated by State of birth and State of residence data from the census, 1900 and 1930.

At the same time the net loss in population of Ohio from migration was only 200,000, although more than 1,400,000 Ohio-born citizens were living elsewhere. In Illinois the gross movement in and out of the State was even larger, but the net gain was small. One million seven hundred thousand in-migrants were nearly balanced by 1,600,000 out-migrants.

Variation among States in the percentage of native sons and daughters living in other areas in 1930 is shown in figure 5. Variation in the extent to which the present population of each State is made up of persons born in that State is shown in figure 6. Gains and losses in population through interstate migration between 1900 and 1930 are indicated by figure 7. The areas in which the migrants to certain States were born, and the areas in which migrants from these States are located appear on a series of maps (figs. 8 a–f). They serve to illustrate variations in the migration record of different States as revealed by an analysis of census data on the State of birth and State of residence of the 1930 population.

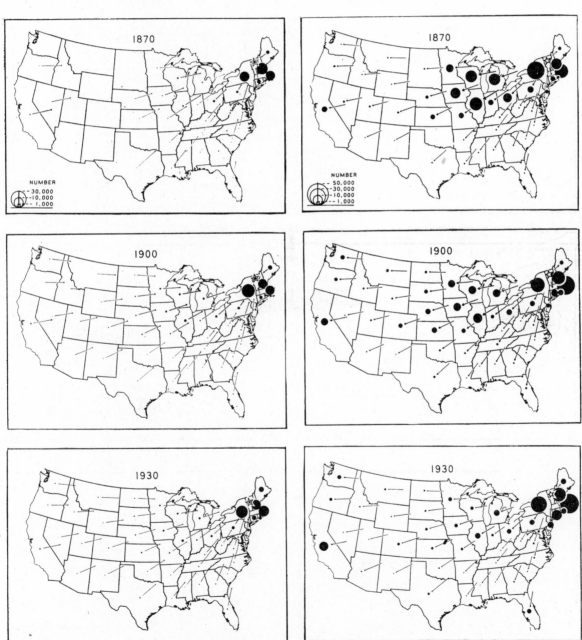

FIGURE 8a.—Migration of native whites to and from selected States. From Galpin and Manny, *Interstate Migration Among the Native White Population as Indicated by Differences Between State of Birth and State of Residence.* a Vermont.

Redirection of Emigration in Recent Decades: Vermont and Kentucky

The migration records of the native sons of Vermont and of Kentucky are closely parallel. During the last half of the nineteenth century, migration from Vermont was directed primarily to the agricultural States of the Middle West. In 1870 nearly one-half of the persons born in Vermont and living elsewhere resided in the North Central States, but in 1930 only one-tenth of the migrants from Vermont were

located in this area. Meanwhile the number of native Vermonters living in the other New England States more than doubled, indicating that the early agricultural migration has been replaced by a drift to urban industrial areas. Similarly, the early movement of native Kentuckians was primarily to the West and Northwest. About the turn of the century the filling up of Oklahoma and Texas attracted a considerable number, but by 1930 the industrial cities around the Great Lakes constituted the main centers of attraction.

TO   FROM

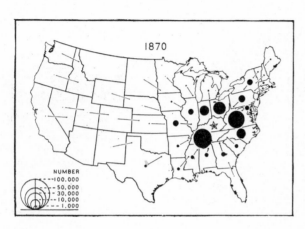
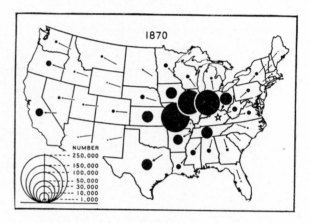

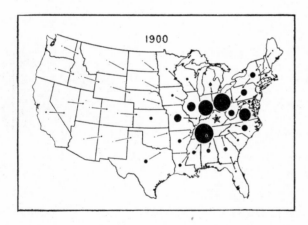
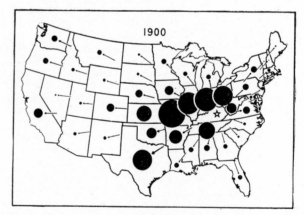

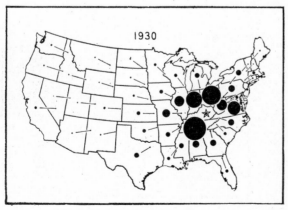
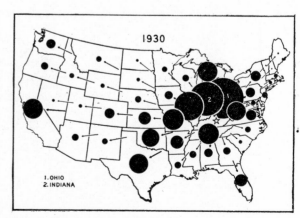

FIGURE 8b.—Kentucky.

Movements In and Out of New York

New York, New Jersey, and Pennsylvania present interesting contrasts in migration history. New York has always been an area of high mobility, both in and out; New Jersey has consistently attracted more people than it has lost. Pennsylvania has continually lost a large proportion of its native-born, but at the same time has attracted a large foreign-born population which has partially offset this loss.

About 40 percent of the people living in New York State in 1930 were born outside the State. Those born in the State numbered 7,800,000;

those born in other States, 1,400,000; and those born in foreign countries, 3,300,000. At the same time 1,500,000 persons born in New York State were living in other States. Most of the interstate migrants, both to and from New York State, were located in urban areas in 1930. This was in each case about 4 out of 5. Of those coming into New York, a fourth came from the South, a third from New Jersey and Pennsylvania, and a fifth each from New England and the Middle West. The migrants from New England and New Jersey came largely from urban communities, those

TO
FROM

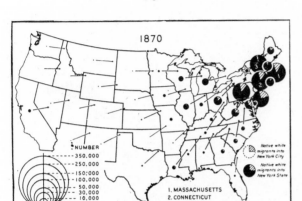
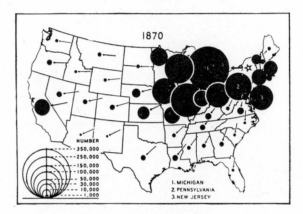
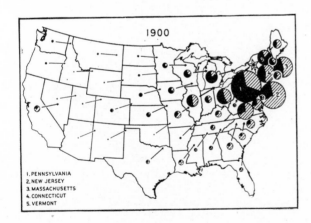
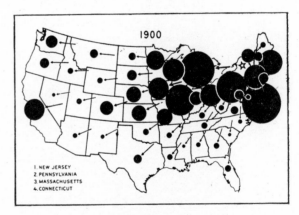
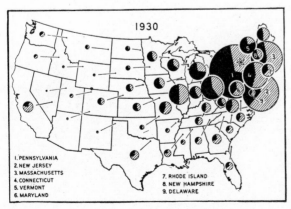
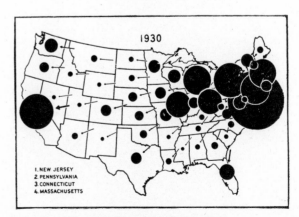

FIGURE 8c.—New York, with distinctions between sources of migration to New York City and the rest of the State.

from the South and Middle West came largely from farms. Thus about 1,200,000 native-born New Yorkers have moved to the urban areas of other States, while the cities and towns of New York have attracted an equivalent number from other States, many of whom have come from rural territory.

The composition of the population of New York City illustrates, even better than that of New York State as a whole, the tendency for urban populations to be recruited from rural areas. In this case, however, the migration has been in large part drawn from rural areas

in Europe. Nearly one-half of the 1930 population of New York City was born outside the State; 700,000 persons had been born in other States and 2,400,000 persons in foreign countries, as compared with 3,800,000 persons born in New York State. One-third of the native-born migrants to New York City were born in the South and about one-seventh were born in the Middle West. There is a tendency for those coming into the State from long distances, especially from the South, to settle in New York City, as is also the case with migrants from New Jersey. But those coming

TO

FROM

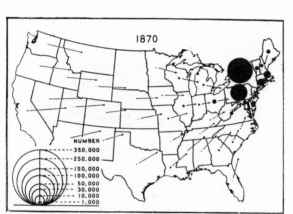

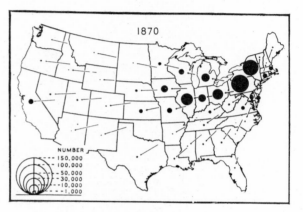

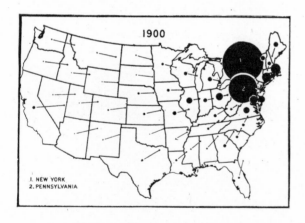

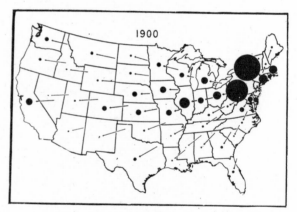

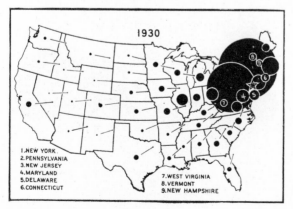

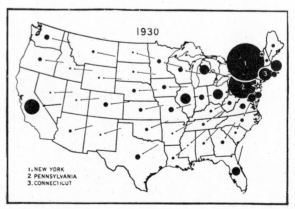

FIGURE 8d.—New Jersey.

from Pennsylvania and the Middle States are most frequently found in upstate communities.

New Jersey: Area of Absorption

New Jersey, in contrast to most eastern States, has continually attracted more people than it has lost through migration. Its interchange of population, however, has been largely with neighboring States. In 1930, only California and Texas showed a significantly higher proportion of those born in the State still living within its boundaries. At the same time, one-third of the native American population living in New Jersey had come from other States; this ratio was exceeded by no State east of the Mississippi except Florida. Emigrants from New Jersey, unlike those from many States, have moved short distances only; more than 60 percent of them were living in New York and Pennsylvania in 1930. Apparently the movement from New Jersey has always been chiefly to neighboring cities and towns rather than to agricultural areas. Similarly, those who have moved into New Jersey have come from nearby, chiefly from Pennsylvania and New York. No other State

TO

FROM

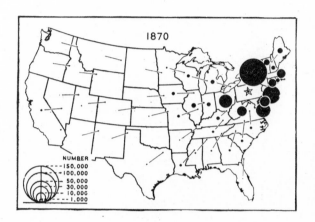

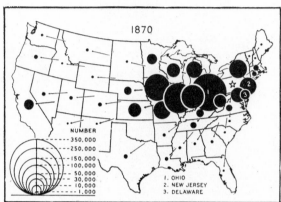

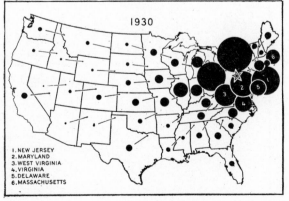

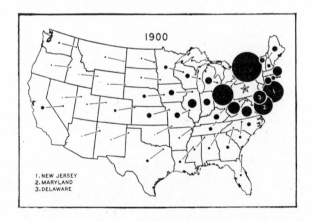

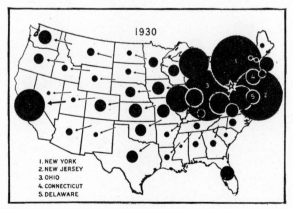

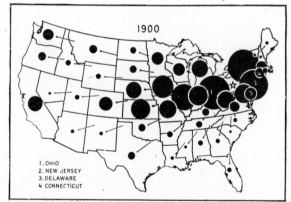

FIGURE 8e.—Pennsylvania.

except New Hampshire has drawn so large a proportion of its migrants from adjoining States. New Jersey's location, adjoining two States with relatively large populations, helps to account for this situation.

Pennsylvania: Area of Diffusion

Contrary to general opinion, Pennsylvania has always been an area of net loss in native population. No other State has contributed so large a number of people to the rest of the Nation, although the proportional emigration of those born in many States has been greater. Moreover, only in Maine, North and South Carolina, and Mississippi is the proportion of the resident native population born in other States lower than in Pennsylvania. The native migrants as well as foreign-born immigrants to Pennsylvania have settled mainly in industrial areas. In 1930, 42 percent of the native immigrants to this State were located in Philadelphia and Pittsburgh, although these two cities held only about one-fourth of the State's total population.

TO

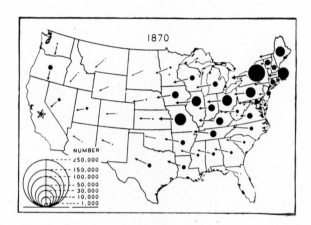

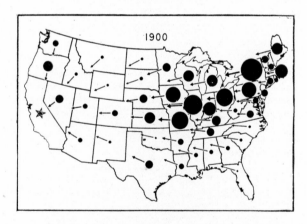

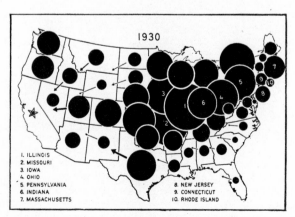

FROM

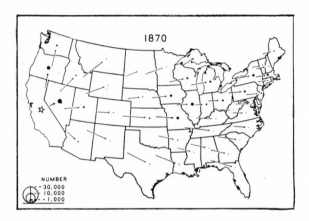

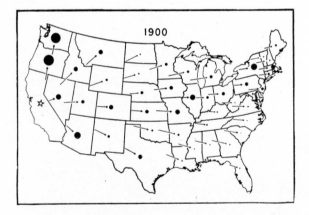

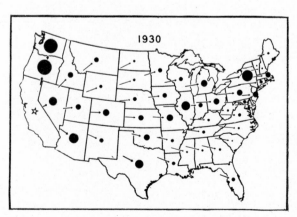

FIGURE 8f.—California.

The Attraction of California

The movement of native-born persons to California has been unequaled in volume by similar movements to any other State. In 1930 the number of residents in California who had been born in other States was more than 600,000 greater than the total population of Philadelphia, the third largest city of the Nation. The number of persons who were born elsewhere but were living in California in 1930 was about one-third the total population of Canada. Not only has California attracted large numbers of migrants, but it has also held a very high proportion of the persons born there. Only 8 percent of those born in California were living in other States in 1930. In contrast to the movement to and from other States, that for California has reached all corners of the Nation. Just as the migrants to this State have come from widely scattered places, so the migrants from this State have been distributed more evenly throughout the Nation than those from any other State.

Movements of the Negro Population

Negro migration constitutes a special aspect of the general movement from south to north. At the outbreak of the Civil War 92 percent of the Negro population of the United States lived in the South. The first important migratory movement after emancipation was across the Mississippi River to the newly developed lands of Arkansas, Oklahoma, and Texas. The proportion of the total Negro population living in the West South Central States increased from 14 percent in 1860 to 20 percent in 1910, but after 1910 these States began to lose more Negroes than they gained. The westward movement of the Negro never involved a large number of people. In 1900, when it had reached its peak, only 330,000 Negroes born east of the Mississippi were living to the west of that river. By 1930 this had decreased to 320,000, showing that not enough Negroes were moving westward to replace those who died or returned east.

After 1910 an important change occurred in the volume and direction of Negro migration. At this time the percentage of Negroes living in the South was only 3 units lower than the corresponding percentage in 1860. The shortage of labor in northern industrial cities during the World War attracted large numbers of Negroes. Once begun, the movement northward continued at an increasing rate until, in 1930, 20 percent of the total Negro population of the Nation was living north of the Mason-Dixon line. Contrary to the movement of the white population, however, very few Negroes have gone to the Far West. Only 1 percent of all Negroes were living there in 1930. Even California has had little attraction for them. Prior to 1900, Negroes were much less inclined to move than whites. In 1900 only one out of

every six Negroes resided outside his State of birth. The increase in mobility during the past 20 years is revealed by the fact that, in 1930, one out of every four Negroes had left his home State. At the present time the proportion of native-born citizens of the United States who are living outside their States of birth is about 2 percent higher among Negroes than among whites.

The northward movement, which was at first largely from Virginia and Kentucky, soon spread. By 1930 the largest movements were from the deep South—Alabama, Mississippi, and Georgia—although large numbers also came from Virginia and the Carolinas. During recent years the proportion of Negroes leaving the South has been larger than the corresponding proportion of whites.

Much of the Negro migration has been a State-to-State displacement. By 1930, for example, 72,000 Negroes had moved into North Carolina from South Carolina, but 47,000 had moved out of North Carolina to Virginia and Maryland. More than 50 percent of the Negroes leaving South Carolina, Georgia, Alabama, Mississippi, and Louisiana have settled in other southern States, while about 90 percent of those leaving Kentucky and 65 percent of those leaving Virginia and Tennessee have settled in the North. At the same time there has been considerable migration directly from the deep South to the North.

The northward migration of Negroes has been almost entirely to large urban centers. In 1930, 88 percent of the Negro population of the North lived in cities. The situation in the South presents a striking contrast to this; only 32 percent of all southern Negroes live in cities. The percentage of southern Negroes who are found in cities has been rising, but the proportion of the southern white population living in cities has been increasing still more rapidly, so that the proportion of Negroes in the population of most southern cities has been decreasing.

The Growth of Cities: Sources of Population Supply

Extensive migration has accelerated the rapid urbanization of the Nation. Seventy-five of the 93 cities with more than 100,000 population in 1930 had received at least one-third of their total population from foreign countries or from States other than that in which the city is located. An appreciable number even of those born in the same States came from outside these cities. It is safe to say that, with the exception of a few southern cities, a large share of the 1930 population of all large cities (ranging from 30 to 80 percent for the individual cities) was born elsewhere (see figs. 9 and 10a–b). The cities at either end of the scale afford interesting contrasts. In 26 large cities (9 of them southern) two-thirds or more of the population was born in the same State in which the cities are located.

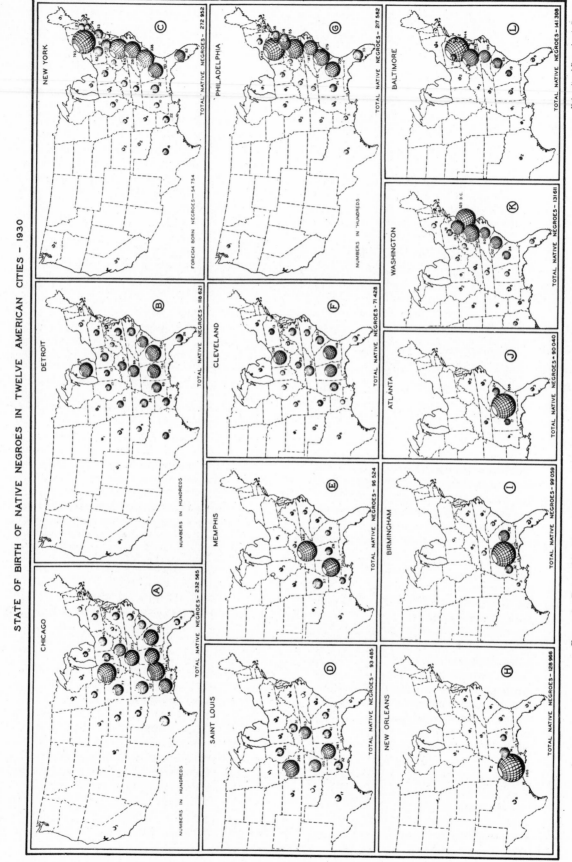

University of Pennsylvania Press.

FIGURE 9.—Prepared by Thornthwaite, from Goodrich and others, *Migration and Economic Opportunity*.

Population Problems

In 9 other large cities (6 of them on the Pacific coast) two-thirds or more of the total population was born in other States or in foreign countries.

In general, the cities east of the Mississippi have a large fraction of their population (usually at least half of the total) born in the State of residence. Many of the cities north of the Mason-Dixon Line have also large proportions of foreign-born immigrants. In most of the southeastern cities (except those in Florida) the population has grown chiefly by natural increase and by migration from within the State where the city is located. The population of the cities west of the Mississippi River, on the other hand, is largely native-born, but has been drawn from other States than the one in which the present city of residence is located. Without its population born outside California, Los Angeles would in 1930 have been a city of 250,000 people, instead of the fifth largest city in the United States with a total population of 1,238,000.

Many of the northeastern and north central cities have gained one-third or more of their native in-migrant population from the South, especially from Kentucky, Tennessee, Mississippi, Alabama, and Georgia. The native in-migrant population of the large cities of the Far West, with the exception of San Francisco, has been drawn largely from the agricultural States of the Middle West.

The foreign-born.—The rapid growth of large cities in the past has been due to a considerable extent to immigration from other countries, as shown by the fact that in 1910 more than 25 percent of the population was foreign-born in nearly one-half (41 out of 93) of the cities that in 1930 had more than 100,000 residents. In four large cities, New York, Fall River, Lowell, and New Bedford, the foreign-born constituted more than 40 percent of the total population at that time. Since then the foreign-born have formed a declining proportion of the population. In 1930 they comprised more than 25 percent of the total population in only 21 of the 93 large cities. Somerville, Mass., is the only city of more than 100,000 population in which the foreign-born were a larger proportion of the total population in 1930 than in 1910. The growth in population of all other large cities has been coming in increasing proportion from native-born persons.

Movements of native-born to cities.—The increase in population of the cities of New England, except for those in Connecticut, has come in an increasing proportion from the State in which the city is located.[6] Only Cam-

[6] The relative increase in the number of persons born in the State where the city is located of course includes the natural increase of the city, as well as migrants from other parts of the State. A city located near a State boundary might be expected to draw migrants from the neighboring State, due merely to its geographic location, but this factor is of major importance in only a few instances.

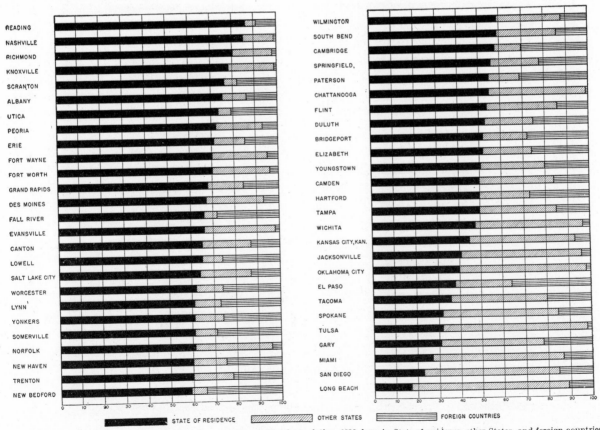

FIGURE 10a.—Cities of 100,000 to 200,000 population: percentage of total population, 1930, born in State of residence, other States, and foreign countries.

bridge, Mass., showed an increase between 1910 and 1930 in the proportion of its population born in other States, and this increase was negligible.

The cities of Connecticut, however, are similar to those of New York, New Jersey, and Pennsylvania. All of the 21 large cities in these four States, except Jersey City, drew a proportionately larger part of their increase in native population from outside the State between 1910 and 1930 than prior to 1910. Ten of these cities drew a larger share of their increase in population between 1910 and 1930 from other States than from the State where they are located.

Although the cities in the Great Lakes States obtained an increasing proportion of their population growth from other States, only in Ohio and Michigan was the number of such persons significantly larger than the number gained from the State in which the city is located. Akron received a larger proportion of its increase in population from outside the State than any other large city in the United States. From 1910 to 1930 the percentage of its total population born in other States increased from 17 to 40. Detroit, with an increase from 13 to 31 percent, was a close second.

Growth of the cities west of the Mississippi River, 1910–30, was of an entirely different character. Only 5 of the 20 large cities in this area drew a larger proportion of their increase in population from outside the State than from within. Four of these cities were in California; the other was St. Louis, Mo. In all the remaining large cities the proportion of out-of-State migrants decreased between 1910 and 1930. In general, except for the five cities mentioned, the large urban centers west of the Mississippi River did not have sufficient attractive power during these 20 years to draw migrants from long distances.

The pattern of growth of most large cities in the Southern States, except for Florida and North Carolina, was similar to that of the cities west of the Mississippi River. The growth of industry in the towns of the Piedmont area of North Carolina and the climatic attractiveness of Florida enabled the cities of those two States to draw a large proportion of their population increase from other States. Due mainly to the northward migration of Negroes, Richmond, Norfolk, and Baltimore obtained a larger share of their population increase from out of the State than from within. Washington, D. C., because it is the National Capital, has drawn an increasing proportion of its population from the rest of the country.

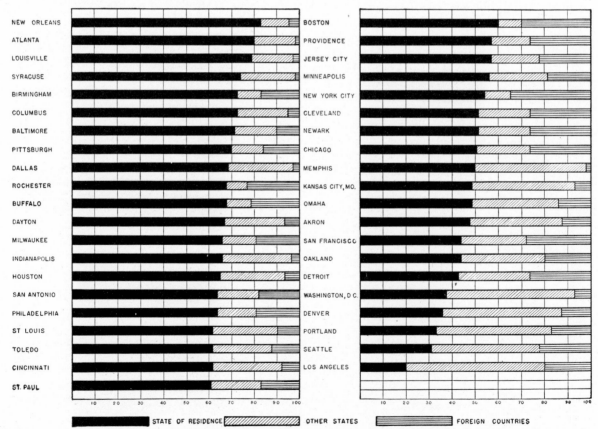

Figure 10b.—Cities of 200,000 population and over: percentage of total population, 1930, born in State of residence, other States and foreign countries.

Prospects for Future City Growth

It is obvious that the slowing down of population growth in the Nation as a whole will also involve a general slowing down of the increase of city population. Moreover, the trend toward urban concentration has already gone so far that it probably will not be projected at the same rate far into the future.

With the virtual cessation of immigration and the rapid decline in natural increase which is especially characteristic of urban communities, there will be much more competition among cities to attract the decreasing number of available migrants. During the past century, the number of migrants has been so large that an appreciable number have gone even to areas of meager opportunity, so that all parts of the Nation have shared in the increase in population. In the future this will not be the case unless immigration bars are let down, which is unlikely. Instead of a general scattering of the population, the movements of the future will probably be toward relatively few areas. Will the large metropolitan areas become more densely populated while the population of the smaller cities and rural areas remains nearly stationary, or will economic opportunities in the latter be sufficiently increased by the decentralization of industry to balance the pulling power of the large cities?

A satisfactory answer to this question would involve an analysis of the relative economic opportunities of different cities and is beyond the scope of this report. But, insofar as economic opportunities are reflected in the source and rate of increase of the urban population, and insofar as the economic trends prevailing from 1910 to 1930 continue without major alteration into the future, the probable rate of growth of large cities during the next few decades is indicated by the foregoing analysis. It should be understood that the following inferences apply only to the cities of each area considered as a group, and that the population changes of certain individual cities may be entirely different.

The large cities of the New York metropolitan area, including Pennsylvania, and those near the Great Lakes may be expected to attract a large proportion of the available migrants. It is possible, however, that a permanent decline in the relative importance of foreign commerce may change this. Growth of the large cities in California and Florida will depend to a considerable extent upon the level of per capita income in the Nation. With the return of prosperity the number of people moving to these two areas may once more increase. A continued increase in the urban population of North Carolina will depend largely upon the rapidity with which the textile industry develops in that area. In any case the cities in this section will probably not attract an appreciable number of migrants from outside the surrounding region.

If recent trends continue, the large cities of New England, except in Connecticut, the large cities west of the Mississippi River, with the possible exception of those in California, and the large cities of the South, with the exceptions noted above, will depend more and more upon their own natural increase and migration from other localities within the State for their growth in numbers. This means inevitably a slower rate of growth than in the past, and for some cities a decrease in population.

A marked decrease in the rate of growth of many cities, while necessitating certain economic adjustments and having a depressing effect on local pride, will provide an opportunity for the improvement of municipal administration. Slums can be cleared, health facilities improved, parks and playgrounds provided, traffic congestion eliminated by street and boulevard changes, so that cities will become more pleasant places in which to live. Perhaps cities will in the future take pride in the healthful and pleasing environment provided for their residents, rather than in the rapidity with which their population is increasing.

4. The Search for Greater Economic Opportunity or Security— Before and During the Depression

Did the migrants of the twenties move to communities that were, on the whole, better off economically toward the end of the decade than those from which they departed? Did this movement leave them in communities least subject to the effects of the depression? Important as the answers to these questions may be, they can be given only approximately and with considerable reservation, due to the lack of satisfactory measures of economic well-being. Also it is impossible to segregate the migrants from the rest of the population, so that comparisons must be made between communities and not between individuals.

Character of Migratory Movements During the Twenties

During the twenties migrants for the most part were finding their way to places of greater economic opportunity. With some exceptions, the less favorable lands lost population to the more favorable; the least prosperous communities, chiefly agricultural, lost persons to the most prosperous communities, largely urban and industrial. It is true that many people left the best agricultural counties of Iowa and Illinois, but these were areas of relatively high natural increase and fairly stabilized agriculture with very little opportunity for new developments. Moreover, mi-

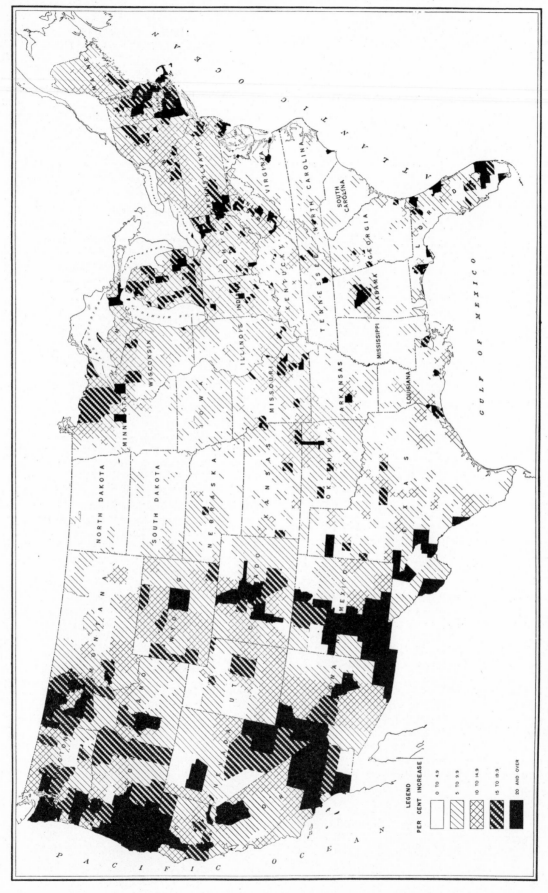

FIGURE 11.—Persons living on farms January 1, 1935, who were living in nonfarm territory in 1930; expressed as percentage of 1930 farm population in each county.

grants from these areas were attracted by the economic advantages of nearby large cities.

There is evidence of large population movements during the twenties away from areas of economic insecurity and low levels of living. The counties with the highest percentage of population on relief in 1933–34 were, as might be expected, in most cases counties with low levels of living in 1929–30, as measured either by gross agricultural income per rural-farm inhabitant or by the plane of living index already described. In these poor counties fertility is far in excess of that necessary to maintain the population permanently. In several of the counties the population would double within one generation if there were no emigration. Nevertheless, people were leaving these counties in such large numbers during the decade 1920–30 that their populations, with the single exception of Wayne County, W. Va., increased more slowly than that of the Nation as a whole, and in some cases actually decreased in number. This tendency to leave areas of meager opportunity in numbers large enough to offset the rapid natural increase appears to have been checked during the depression (see table 2).

TABLE 2.—*Characteristics of counties with highest percentage of their population on relief 1933–34* [1]

County	State	Average number of persons on relief 1933–34 as percent of 1930 population	Plane of living index	Gross farm income per rural-farm inhabitant 1929 (in dollars)	Index of net reproduction per generation (100=rate of permanent replacement)	Percentage change in population 1920–30	Percentage change in farm population 1930–35
United States		11.6	100	365	109	16.1	4.5
Schuylkill	Pa	50.9	63		135	8.2	10.7
Randolph	W. Va	36.0	35	167	172	-6.5	19.0
Upshur	W. Va	37.2	31	181	153	0.5	18.9
Wirt	W. Va	40.2	40	174	188	-15.6	14.7
Lincoln	W. Va	53.4	11	99	233	-1.1	17.7
Wayne	W. Va	59.0	15	104	200	20.0	21.7
Breathitt	Ky	45.1	6	71	250	2.6	9.2
Clay	Ky	48.7	4	93	247	-6.4	18.1
Jackson	Ky	54.2	3	110	232	-10.4	12.0
Leslie	Ky	51.6	2	95	277	6.6	10.9
Magoffin	Ky	51.5	7	89	227	1.5	16.2
Martin	Ky	52.8	2	66	251	12.2	35.1
Morgan	Ky	36.9	8	101	212	-8.4	14.0
Wolfe	Ky	39.3	4	82	233	-4.1	28.4
Owsley	Ky	37.6	7	93	225	-7.6	20.2
Whitley	Ky	36.2	26	95	176	7.1	42.9
Tyrrell	N. C	46.5	8	209	160	6.5	-0.8
Berkeley	S. C	40.1	4	81	175	-1.4	11.5
Gilchrist	Fla	36.3	8	206	163	(2)	-5.3
Lafayette	Fla	39.6	4	144	165	(2)	-21.8
St. Helena	La	36.5	1	177	177	0.8	10.5
Vernon	La	39.6	17	119	152	-2.2	23.6
Franklin	Ark	36.8	22	146	160	-18.6	13.9
Montmorency	Mich	38.3	39	252	171	-31.2	27.4
Kalkaska	Mich	62.9	48	282	172	-31.9	11.2
Lake	Mich	44.9	40	237	142	-8.4	11.2
Keweenaw	Mich	62.1	45		155	-19.7	182.5
Burke	N. D	39.9	66	565	166	5.1	-6.1
Huerfano	Colo	40.9	43		167	1.1	8.3

[1] Adapted in part from Goodrich, Carter; Allin, Bushrod W.; Hayes, Marion, *Migration and Planes of Living, 1920–1934*, pp. 44, 45.
[2] Not available because of change in county boundaries.

Analysis of the Depression Migration

There has been much speculation about the character and direction of migration move-
ments between farm and nonfarm territory from 1930 to 1935. Did those leaving cities during the depression years settle on fertile or infertile soil? Did people move in larger numbers from good farms or from poor farms during these years? The available data do not yield a direct answer to these questions, since the value and productivity of the land occupied by individual migrants to farms, or abandoned by migrants from farms, is unknown. It is possible, however, to compare changes in farm population in counties where all or most of the land is relatively infertile with changes in counties where most of the land is well adapted to farming.

Apparently there were large increases in farm population from 1930 to 1935 in certain rather poor farming areas—eastern Ohio, western Pennsylvania, the southern Appalachians, the Ozarks, eastern Oklahoma, and northern Wisconsin and Minnesota. On the whole, these are areas of subsistence farming, or, at best, regions where the income per farm is well below the national average. There were also large increases near industrial centers and in mining communities. An increase in farm population in these areas is not surprising. The persons who left farms between 1920 and 1930 would be expected to return to their home communities if they left the city during the depression. Since a large proportion of the farm-to-city migrants in the past decade came from the less fertile farming regions, the population of these regions would be increased by the return of former migrants. Moreover, the largest number of vacant farmhouses are in areas of previous emigration. Persons who had lived all or most of their lives in urban territory would be expected to move to the environs of a city. The increase in farm population near industrial centers and in the less fertile agricultural areas is evidence of those expected movements.

There is a different sort of movement which would tend to increase farm population in better areas in hard times. During a period of prosperity many farm owners rent their farms to tenants, or sell them subject to mortgages, and retire to villages or cities. But most farms cannot support two families in a period of low agricultural prices. The retired farmer is therefore likely to return to his farm, discharging the tenant or foreclosing the mortgage. Other farm owners in prosperous times rent additional acres from neighboring farms; in depression such farmers retrench by ceasing to rent. These depression changes tend to increase the number of owner-operated farms, particularly in the better farming areas. The Government's crop-reduction program tended to have a similar effect. Between 1930 and 1935 there was actually an increase of more than 300,000 in owner-operated farms.

The movement to farms from nonfarm territory.—Figure 11 shows the relative increase in the number of people living on farms, due to migration from nonfarm territory, from 1930 to 1935. The largest increases are found in the following areas: Southern New England, eastern Ohio, western Pennsylvania, a few counties in West Virginia, the lower peninsula in Michigan, the cut-over area of Minne-

sota and Wisconsin, the Rio Grande and San Juan River Valleys of Colorado and New Mexico, northern Idaho, northwestern Montana, and the Puget Sound and Willamette Valleys in Washington and Oregon. The migrants who went to northern Minnesota and Wisconsin, western Oregon, southern Nevada, northern Idaho, and northwestern Montana settled for the most part in poor agricultural areas. Many of the other areas showing a relatively large number of migrants to farms, however, are characterized by relatively fertile farm land. It should be remembered that only the relative number of migrants is shown in figure 11. The absolute number of persons settling in many of the western counties was small.

Among the agricultural counties of the Nation the increase in farm population due to migrants from nonfarm territory was only slightly greater in the "problem" counties [7] (7 percent) than in the "nonproblem" counties (6.4 percent). (See table 3, column 3.)

As would be expected from the previous discussion, the increases in the problem counties were greatest in the Northeast and Middle States. In the Far West and Northwest, on the other hand, the relative increase in farm population due to migrants from nonfarm territory was larger in the nonproblem than in the problem areas. In about one-half of the States the increases were larger in the problem areas. In the other States the increases were larger in the nonproblem areas. There

TABLE 3.—*Percent change in farm population in total, "problem" and "nonproblem" counties, by regions, 1930–35*

Region and area	Percent of farm population, 1930	Percent change in farm population, 1930-35		
		Total	By accession of migrants from nonfarm territory	Exclusive of migrants from nonfarm territory
United States	100.0	4.5	6.6	-2.1
Nonproblem	75.2	3.3	6.4	-3.1
Problem	24.8	8.1	7.0	1.1
Northeast	100.0	15.1	11.3	3.8
Nonproblem	66.8	13.4	10.8	2.5
Problem	33.2	18.5	12.2	6.3
Middle States	100.0	5.0	8.0	-3.0
Nonproblem	82.6	3.6	7.6	-4.0
Problem	17.4	11.4	9.8	1.6
Northwest	100.0	-1.1	5.9	-7.0
Nonproblem	84.5	-0.7	6.2	-6.9
Problem	15.5	-3.4	4.1	-7.5
Southeast	100.0	4.2	4.1	0.1
Nonproblem	65.7	3.1	3.7	-0.6
Problem	34.3	6.3	4.8	1.5
Southwest	100.0	0.1	6.0	-5.9
Nonproblem	93.8	-0.2	6.0	-6.2
Problem	6.2	4.9	6.4	-1.5
Far West	100.0	3.7	14.2	-10.5
Nonproblem	68.1	3.5	14.7	-11.2
Problem	31.9	4.2	13.1	-8.9

[7] Problem counties are those in which all or part of the farm land has been recommended for transfer from agriculture to forestry, stock grazing, or other conservational uses. These counties were selected by the Rural Resettlement Administration.

TABLE 4.—*Percent change in farm population in "problem" counties classified by the percentage of farms recommended for withdrawal from agriculture, 1930–35*

Region and percent of farms to be withdrawn from agriculture	Percent of total farm population in each region, 1930	Percent change in farm population 1930-35		
		Total	By accession of migrants from nonfarm territory	Exclusive of migrants from nonfarm territory
United States:				
Under 20	10.6	5.4	6.6	-1.2
20-59	12.1	9.4	7.3	2.1
60 and over	2.1	13.9	7.3	6.6
Northeast:				
Under 20	18.0	17.3	11.8	5.5
20-59	15.2	19.8	12.7	7.2
60 and over				
Middle States:				
Under 20	4.5	9.1	10.2	-1.1
20-59	9.7	12.8	9.6	3.2
60 and over	3.2	10.2	9.6	0.6
Northwest:				
Under 20	10.4	-4.0	4.0	-8.0
20-59	5.0	-2.3	4.7	-7.0
60 and over	0.1	2.0	4.9	-2.9
Southeast:				
Under 20	14.3	2.9	4.1	-1.2
20-59	17.1	7.3	5.3	2.0
60 and over	2.9	17.9	5.4	12.5
Southwest:				
Under 20	1.0	-6.9	3.4	-10.3
20-59	4.4	6.7	7.0	0.3
60 and over	0.8	9.3	6.1	3.2
Far West:				
Under 20	22.7	5.3	12.1	-6.8
20-59	7.6	4.0	15.4	-11.4
60 and over	1.6	-10.0	15.9	-25.9

TABLE 5.—*Change in farm population in all counties, industrial and agricultural types, 1930–35*

Region and type	Percent farm population, 1930	Percent change in farm population, 1930-35		
		Total	By accession of migrants from nonfarm territory	Exclusive of migrants from nonfarm territory
United States	100.0	4.5	6.6	-2.1
Industrial	21.5	13.3	11.5	1.9
Agricultural	78.5	2.0	5.2	-3.2
Northeast	100.0	15.1	11.3	3.8
Industrial	68.0	17.3	10.6	6.6
Agricultural	32.0	10.3	12.6	-2.3
Middle States	100.0	5.0	8.0	-3.0
Industrial	27.7	9.4	11.8	-2.4
Agricultural	72.3	3.3	6.5	-3.3
Northwest	100.0	-1.1	5.9	-7.0
Industrial	9.1	0.8	13.4	-12.6
Agricultural	90.9	-1.3	5.2	-6.5
Southeast	100.0	4.2	4.1	0.1
Industrial	10.7	16.9	9.2	7.7
Agricultural	89.3	2.7	3.5	-0.8
Southwest	100.0	0.1	6.0	-5.9
Industrial	10.5	9.0	11.9	-2.8
Agricultural	89.5	-0.9	5.3	-6.3
Far West	100.0	3.7	14.2	-10.5
Industrial	40.7	14.1	18.4	-4.4
Agricultural	59.3	-3.4	11.3	-14.7

TABLE 6.—*Change in farm population in "problem" counties,[1] industrial and agricultural types, 1930–35*

Problem areas, region and type	Percent of problem-county farm population, 1930	Percent change in farm population, 1930-35		
		Total	By accession of migrants from nonfarm territory	Exclusive of migrants from nonfarm territory
United States	100.0	8.1	7.0	1.1
Industrial	20.6	17.7	11.1	6.6
Agricultural	79.4	5.6	6.0	-0.4
Northeast	100.0	18.5	12.2	6.3
Industrial	58.9	21.0	13.6	7.4
Agricultural	41.1	14.9	10.1	4.8
Middle States	100.0	11.4	9.8	1.6
Industrial	24.1	17.1	11.6	5.5
Agricultural	75.9	10.0	9.2	0.4
Northwest	100.0	-3.4	4.1	-7.5
Industrial	0.9	29.6	19.4	10.2
Agricultural	99.1	-3.7	4.0	-7.7
Southeast	100.0	6.3	4.8	1.5
Industrial	10.5	22.3	8.4	13.9
Agricultural	89.5	4.4	4.3	0.0
Southwest	100.0	4.9	6.4	-1.5
Industrial				
Agricultural	100.0	4.9	6.4	-1.5
Far West	100.0	4.2	13.1	-8.9
Industrial	50.3	12.4	8.8	3.6
Agricultural	49.7	-4.0	17.4	-21.4

[1] The classification of counties as "problem" counties in these tables refers wholly to the *agricultural* situation in these counties, not to industrial enterprises. See text.

was some tendency for increases to be greatest in the poorest agricultural areas where more than 60 percent of the farms are recommended for withdrawal from agriculture. This was especially true in the Northeast, Northwest, Southwest, and far West (table 4, column 3).

Many of the areas of largest increase shown in figure 11 are industrial and mining counties. Before concluding that people were moving in relatively larger numbers to the less fertile farming areas, the increase in farm population in such areas should be compared with the increase in industrial and mining counties. The migrants from nonfarm territory to farms during the years 1930–35 are found in relatively greater numbers in industrial [8] than in agricultural areas, in all parts of the country except in the Northeast (see table 5, column 3). In the problem agricultural counties the larger accessions are again found in industrial rather than in typically agricultural areas, with the exception of the far West (see table 6, column 3). In both instances the percentage increase through migration from nonfarm territory to farms is approximately twice as great, for the country as a whole, in the industrial as in the agricultural counties. Although only 21 percent of the problem-county farm population in 1930 lived in industrial areas, 33 percent of the migrants from nonfarm territory to problem-county farms settled in those industrial areas (including mining counties). So

[8] Industrial counties are those in which there were more gainful workers in forestry, mining, and industry than in agriculture in 1930, excluding workers in professional, clerical, and service occupations, trade and transportation.

far as there was any depression "back-to-the-farm" movement, it was predominantly a movement to lands in the vicinity of industrial and mining enterprises.

The movement from farms.—Counterbalancing the movement to farms from nonfarm territory just described was a fairly large movement away from farms in most parts of the country (see fig. 12). This was especially true throughout the South, in Michigan, in the Great Plains States, and on the west coast. If there had been no migration to farms from nonfarm territory, the farm population of the Nation would have decreased by more than half a million persons between 1930 and 1935, due to excess of out-migration over natural increase.

Except in the southern Appalachians, a few counties of northeastern Minnesota, and northern Wisconsin, farm people were leaving poor as well as good agricultural areas (see fig. 12; see also column 4 in tables 3, 4, 5, and 6). However, after eliminating the migrants from nonfarm territory, the decrease of farm population was less in the poor farm areas than in the rest of the country. This was due in part to the higher rates of natural increase prevailing in these problem counties (see ch. IV). It may also have been due in part to somewhat lower percentages of out-migration from farms in these areas during the years 1930–35. The farm population in the nonproblem agricultural areas would have decreased by more than 700,000 persons if there had been no accessions from nonfarm territory. The number of out-migrants from farms in the problem counties was slightly smaller than the natural increase, so that the farm population in these counties would have increased slightly (1 percent) even if there had been no migrants from nonfarm territory (see table 3). However, in the case of those problem areas that are chiefly agricultural in character the out-migration more than balanced the natural increase for the country as a whole and in each region except the Northeast. There was a definite accumulation of farm population only in the industrial and mining counties (table 6, column 4). Meanwhile there continued to be large out-migration from the nonproblem agricultural counties. In these areas, the farm population would have decreased by nearly three-quarters of a million persons if it had received no migrants from nonfarm territory.

Summary.—The movements of farm population during the depression may be briefly summarized as follows: The increase in farm population from 1930 to 1935 was not due to any absolute blocking of movement from farms, which continued to exceed the rate of natural increase, although less than in the preceding decade. The increase of farm population must be attributed to movement from cities and villages to farms, although for the country as a whole this movement was over 15 percent less than during the preceding decade. There was a general slowing down in the interchange of population between farms and towns, along with a change in net effect from decrease to increase of farm population.

The people who moved to farms did not settle chiefly in isolated poor farming counties, as has often been assumed. Instead they settled on part-time or subsistence farms in or near industrial and mining communities. Migrants from farms came chiefly from agricultural areas, both of the poorer and of the better type. Little or no net movement of farm population from the industrial and mining counties appears after allowance is made for estimated natural increase. Therefore the large increases of population on farms in these counties were not offset in any way. As a result the big increases in farm population from 1930 to 1935 are concentrated in these counties. Although only 21 percent of the total farm population of the United States in 1930 lived in industrial counties, 64 percent of the total increase in farm population during the next 5 years took place in these counties.

Much of the cultivated land in some of the mining and industrial counties is infertile, poorly drained, or located on steep hillsides. If families settling there are forced by lack of industrial employment to make their entire living from these farms, it will be necessarily at or near the subsistence level. In some of the mining areas, and perhaps also in some of the industrial communities, opportunity for industrial employment may never come. Many people will eventually be forced either to move to other places or to continue as subsistence farmers. This is especially likely to be true for many of the middle-aged and elderly heads of families who may have difficulty in securing employment again even if new opportunities develop in the vicinity of their present residence. For many, however, subsistence farming is doubtless merely a stopgap to tide them over a period of unemployment. Others may find opportunity for combining part-time industrial or mining work with some farm work.

Moving to the country enabled many families to support themselves in depression fashion, and thus lessened urban relief expenditures, but the corollary was increased financial burdens in rural areas. Many of these families could not support themselves completely and were forced onto relief rolls. In nine rural counties in Tennessee it was found that 12 percent of the families receiving relief in 1935 and living in the open country had moved into the county since 1930.[9] In a study of nonfarming rural families in the four northwestern counties of Indiana, it was found that 27

percent of these families were receiving relief in 1933. The extra taxes levied on the rural nonfarming families covered only about one-fifth of the total additional expense for schooling and relief.[10] Many of these families were living on land where others failed to make a living even in prosperity. Hence it is doubtful whether they can become self-sufficient and pay their share of the costs of local government. Unless most of these persons can be reemployed in industry, the financial burden on the rural communities where they are now living will become too great for the local taxpayers to bear. Except as opportunities for industrial employment increase, little or no improvement can be expected in the material well-being of these families or of that of the other farm families in the same community.

The depression migration was not so much a search for greater economic opportunity as it was a search for security. This was undoubtedly found in some degree by many of the migrants to farms, even though it was at a low economic level. Whether those who left farms during the depression increased the ranks of the unemployed, either by failure to find a job or by forcing others to lose their jobs, is unknown. The continuation of these movements would tend inevitably to depress rather than to enhance the opportunities of the farm population. A more favorable distribution of the open country population in relation to economic resources depends on an increase in employment opportunities arising from a general revival of industry.

5. The Social Effects of Migration

The different rates of social change in various parts of the Nation are closely associated with the amount and rate of population interchange. California, with 2 million persons who were born within the State, 2½ million born elsewhere in the United States, and 1 million born in foreign countries, is a composite of widely divergent ways of life. The population of some North Atlantic States includes even larger proportions of foreign stocks. On the other hand, the population of South Carolina in 1930 was composed almost wholly of natives of that State. There were only 136,000 persons born elsewhere in the United States and only 5,000 from foreign countries, in a total population of 1,740,000 people. In the former situation different ideas and customs are continually introduced by incoming migrants. In the other, habits and customs are more likely to remain static, since the area loses many people but attracts few in return.

At present the most important movements of population both in magnitude and economic

[9] Allred, Charles E., Leubke, Benj. H., Tosch, Charles A., Mobility of Rural Relief Families in Tennessee. Cooperative plan of Rural Research of the Tennessee Agricultural Experiment Station and the Works Progress Administration. Report No. 14, 1936.

[10] Robertson, Lynn, The Economic Significance of the Nonfarming Rural Population in Northwestern Indiana, Purdue University, Agricultural Experiment Station, Bulletin 388, 1934.

consequence are between rural and urban areas. This will probably also be true in the future. The urban population of the Nation in 1930 numbered 69 million persons. Of these, 42 million were born in their State of residence, 16 million elsewhere in the United States, and 11 million in foreign countries. A large proportion of the 42 million city people born in the State of their 1930 residence, as well as the majority of the 16 million who had moved in from other States, were born and reared on farms. It is probable that the urban population of the Nation as a whole has produced less than 50 percent of its present members. On the other hand, of the 30 million persons on farms in 1930, 25 million were born in their State of residence, 4 million in other States, and only 1 million in foreign countries. Some of those born in any one State and living on farms in that State in 1930, and also some of the farm population moving in from other States, were born in urban territory; but it is probable that 80 to 90 percent of the farm people in 1930 were born in farm territory. Movements of this magnitude create striking differences in the composition of the population. Among such differences, those of age and sex are perhaps the most conspicuous.

It is well known that more males than females are born, but that males die at a more rapid rate than females. In a population undisturbed by migration, the sex ratio would decrease gradually until somewhere in the middle adult years; at the later ages women would outnumber men. If the urban and rural-farm population are compared, important exceptions to this generalization are noted. Some of these exceptions may be due to understatement of age by adults, but this should affect both populations in nearly the same proportion. It is certainly not important enough to account for the large dissimilarity in the relative proportions of the two sexes (see fig. 13).

Changed Proportions of Men and Women in Rural and Urban Areas

The farm population is on the whole definitely masculine. Two exceptions to this statement will be seen in figure 13. For the age-group 30–34 the two sexes are about equal in number, and in the numerically unimportant group over 85 years of age women predominate. Except for these two groups, there are from 103 to 146 farm men per 100 farm women in each age class.

Girls begin to migrate to the city several years earlier than boys, so that the relative number of males on farms increases in the first few years of life. By the age of 20, males leave the farm in larger numbers than females. This continues until about age 30, when there are actually more women than men on farms. The rapid rise in the proportion of men after the

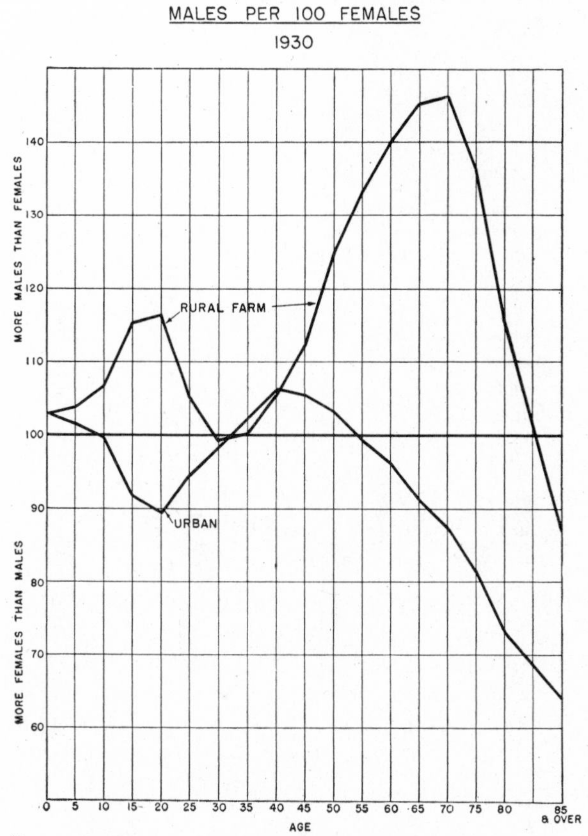

FIGURE 13.—Number of males per 100 females in the urban and rural-farm population, 1930.

115961°—38——8

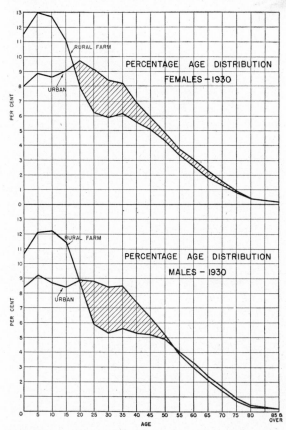

FIGURE 14.—Percentage age distribution by sex in the urban and rural-farm population, 1930.

age of 40 is undoubtedly due chiefly to the movement of single and widowed women to villages and cities, where employment opportunities are better.

The urban population, in spite of a foreign element that is predominantly male, is becoming more and more female in its composition. This is due largely to the fact that employment opportunities for women are better in cities than on farms. In the urban population women outnumber men, with two exceptions: in the first 10 years of life, and from 35 to 55 years of age. At no age are there more than 106 males per 100 females. After the age of 55, the relative number of females increases very rapidly. Among urban persons aged 75 there are nearly 25 percent more women than men. The sex ratio varies considerably, however, from city to city. In cities where a large proportion of the available jobs are in heavy industries—Detroit and Youngstown, for example—the relative number of men 25 to 55 years of age is large. In textile and light industry cities, on the other hand, there are relatively more women.

The Cityward Movement of Young Adults

Figures 14 and 15 reveal the importance of the farm population as the source of a large proportion of urban workers, especially in the

most economically productive ages (e. g., 20 to 50 years). Relative to the total population, the farm population has many more children but considerably fewer adults under 50 years of age than the urban population. This results from the large migration of rural young people to nonfarm territory. Approximately 40 percent of the farm boys and girls who were 10 to 20 years old in 1920 left the farm between 1920 and 1930. A smaller proportion of those 20 to 50 years of age migrate to the city. In late adult life, however, migration from farms is resumed and continues at a rapid rate, especially among elderly women (see fig. 15).[11]

The Economic Balance Sheet of Farms and Cities

Some of these persons settled in villages and small towns, but the majority of the young

[11] This index of migration is constructed by (1) computing the ratio of the number of native white persons of a given age in 1930 in each sized community to the number of such persons in that community 10 years younger in 1920, and (2) expressing the ratio for each sized community as a percentage of the corresponding ratio for the total native white population, in order to eliminate approximately the effect of deaths. The resulting index is affected somewhat by errors in the reporting of age, differences in mortality rates among communities, and misstatement of nativity by the foreign-born. The first error should affect the indexes for each sized community about equally. Differences in mortality would have little effect before age 30; for the older ages the rural indexes would be too high. The reporting of foreign-born immigrants as natives tends to increase the urban indexes. The rural nonfarm indexes are too low and the urban indexes are too high, due to the classification as urban in 1930 of a number of areas classed as rural nonfarm in 1920. However, the combined effect of these errors is unimportant, compared with the large variations in the indexes.

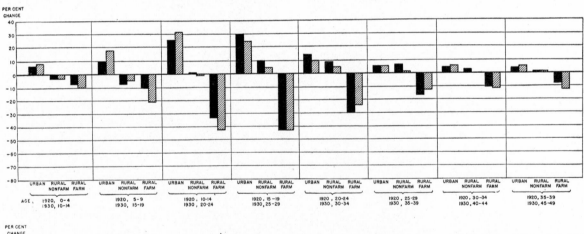

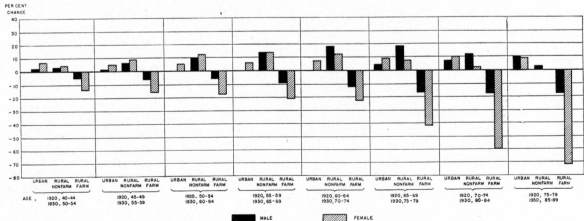

FIGURE 15.—Index of migration at specified ages for the urban, rural-nonfarm and rural-farm native white population, 1920-30.

migrants went to large cities. It is evident that the farm population bears the expense of rearing and educating a large number of children who move to the city just as they begin to be able to repay this cost. A large amount of wealth is transferred from rural to urban areas by this movement. During the past decade the farms have had to feed, clothe, and educate a large proportion of the young people who have joined the urban productive population. If an allowance of $150 per year is made for the cost of rearing a child (including community costs), the average farm youth 15 years of age represents an investment of from $2,000 to $2,500. At this rate the 6 million net migration of youths from farms between 1920 and 1930 would represent a contribution of about 14 billion dollars from the farming communities of the Nation to its cities.[12]

There are many other movements of wealth to cities, one of the most important of which is interest paid to persons other than farm operators. Baker has estimated that during the past decade the total movement of farm wealth to cities may have amounted to nearly one-third of the gross farm income. There is a large margin of error in estimates of this nature, but they suggest the magnitude of the problem. The consequences are reflected in inadequate health facilities, inferior schools, and the difficulties of maintaining essential community services.

Effects on Rural Institutions

In many places migration has intensified maladjustment in rural institutions and organizations. The reduced number of people and the transfer of wealth have made the support of local institutions possible only at an increased cost per person. Instead of abolishing unnecessary services, rural communities have usually retained all those inherited, adding to them the new services required by changing conditions. The general result has been maintenance at a lower standard of efficiency. For example, many features of county and township government in the Northeast were established in colonial times. Although unsuited to modern conditions, they are maintained intact. The outward movement of young people from farms has created a social problem for those remaining, who are frequently too few in number to maintain local organizations. The existing organizations are mainly for the two large age groups in the farm population—school children and elderly persons. The program of these organizations has little appeal for youths 16–29 years, which in turn encourages further migration.

Effects on Urban Institutions

There has been very little research on the effects of the inflow of young people and adults nurtured in rural areas on the characteristics and institutions of the city populations. It would be interesting to know how this movement affects religious associations, labor union activities, political alinements, and so forth. It would also be interesting to know the effects of this change in environment on individual and family adjustment. The topic will be treated briefly in relation to the problem of immigrant adjustments in the last chapter of this report. It is a subject that merits the critical attention of social scientists.

One very interesting analysis that, if substantiated by later investigations, may have an important bearing on this problem, has been reported by Malzberg.[13] He reports that the admission rate to hospitals for mental disease in New York State is significantly higher for the native population born in other States than for the population born in that State. In fact, he finds that among native whites the crude rates are about 3½ times as high for those born without as for those born within the State, both for all psychoses and for each of 5 major classes treated separately: (psychoses with cerebral arteriosclerosis, general paresis, alcoholic, manic-depressive, and dementia praecox). Among Negroes he finds the admission rate to be 4.7 times as high for the migratory group as for the indigenous group. Presumably these differences would be very appreciably lowered if corrected for the influence of differences in age distribution and differences in type of community occupied by those born within and by those coming from without the State. It seems unlikely, however, that such correction could wholly eliminate the significance of these figures unless they are affected by some unrecognized factors. If there is a real difference in the incidence of mental disease between those born within and those coming from without certain States in the industrial sections of this country, the effect might be attributed either to strains involved in the adaptation to new situations or to selective factors in rural migration or both.

Is Rural-Urban Migration Selective?

The debate concerning the selective influence of farm-to-city migration is of long standing, but it has produced almost no factual evidence. One group maintains that as a result of migration many communities, as E. A. Ross so graphically states, "remind one of fished-out ponds populated chiefly by bullheads and suckers." The opposite point of view is summarized by Sorokin and Zimmerman, who conclude that "There is no valid evidence that migration to the cities is selective in the sense that the cities attract in a much greater proportion those from the country who are better physically, vitally, mentally, morally, or so-

---

[12] Baker, O. E., "Rural-Urban Migration and the National Welfare," *Annals of the Association of American Geographers*, 23 : 87.

[13] Malzberg, Benjamin, "Rates of Mental Disease Among Certain Population Groups in New York State", *Journal of the American Statistical Association*, XXXI : 545–548 (September 1936).

cially, and leave in the country those who are poorer in all these respects." [14]

Before this argument can be settled satisfactorily, a considerable amount of careful research will be necessary. There is little or no valid evidence proving that rural-urban migration is depleting the biological stock of the country. Various studies demonstrate that those who leave have attended school more years than those who remain. Migration of the better trained undoubtedly has social effects which are probably much more important at present than deterioration of biological stock. There is the further consideration that unless the prospects of farm living are attractive, increase in communication and in freedom of movement may make rural-urban migration far more selective in character in the future than it has been in the past. If this is true, it points clearly to a need for improving both the economic and the social conditions of rural life, especially of farm life in areas where the outlook is now discouraging.

The Necessity of Continued Migration from Farms

One should not hastily conclude that the net rural-urban migration has been entirely harmful to rural areas. Great overpopulation would have arisen in many places if such a movement had not occurred. Estimates indicate that the present population of Maine would be about 40 percent larger, and that of Vermont 65 percent larger, if all the natural increase of the past 80 years had accumulated at home. An increase of 300,000 persons in the population of Maine and of 250,000 persons in the population of Vermont would undoubtedly have had a depressing effect on local living standards. Farms, already too small, would have been subdivided; infertile land would have been cultivated, and trees would have been cleared from hillsides that should be wooded. The net effect of the farm-to-city migration has undoubtedly been to increase the national welfare, but it has entailed some unfortunate consequences both for urban and for rural communities.

The importance of migration as a means of adjusting population and economic resources, especially in poor agricultural areas where the birth rate is high, can be seen from figure 16. This shows the percentage increases expected in the rural-farm population of each State, 1930 to 1960, on the arbitrary hypothesis of no migration between farms and cities and on certain likely hypotheses concerning fertility and mortality.

The total urban population of the Nation would be about the same size in 1960 as it was in 1930 if its growth depends entirely upon natural increase. The only States whose urban population would increase are those with a large number of foreign-born immigrants: The New England States, New Jersey, Pennsylvania, Michigan, and Wisconsin. Throughout the rest of the country the urban population would remain stationary or decrease in number.

With the single exception of Florida, the farm population of every State in the South from the Atlantic Ocean to California would increase more than 50 percent. The growth of farm population in the northwestern States (east of the Rocky Mountains and west of the Mississippi River) would be slightly less, averaging from 40 to 50 percent. In absolute figures, 10 million persons would be added to the farm population of the South and 1 million to the farm population of the Northwest. At the same time many cities and towns would decrease in population. It is not expected that these estimates of population distribution will come true, but they show vividly the interrelationship of migration and reproduction and the importance of migration as a means of adjustment.

The whole subject considered in this section, the social effects of migration within the United States, is one on which there is surprisingly little information. In the decade before 1930 the pressure of high fertility in rural sections and increasing opportunities in urban areas drew a large proportion of the rural-farm youth to seek city employment. Large migrations may be necessary in the future if a higher level of living is to be established in rural areas where living is now at the subsistence level. The social consequences to our national life of continued movements of such magnitude call for careful investigation.

6. The Outlook for Future Mobility

Past trends seem to show that Americans are becoming increasingly mobile. The proportion of the native population living outside the State of birth has increased steadily since 1890. Many others have moved from one community to another, especially from farms to cities, within States. But the history of migration also shows that Americans have adjusted themselves rapidly to changed conditions. It is impossible to forecast with certainty the magnitude and direction of future migratory movements without knowledge of the location of future economic opportunity. It is possible, however, to take account of certain problems that would arise if no migration occurred, and to discuss factors tending to increase or retard mobility.

The Continuing Pressure of Farm Population

The analysis of regional variations in economic opportunity gave evidence of great inequality in income and level of living, due in part to maldistribution of population in relation to resources. (See ch. II.) The most

---

[14] Sorokin, P., and Zimmerman, C. C., *Principles of Rural-Urban Sociology*, p. 582.

serious problems revealed by this analysis relate to the rural population of the Southeastern States—both as regards the numbers of people affected and as regards the consistency and degree of handicap shown by different economic and social indices. Perhaps the most striking result was obtained by experimenting with the hypothesis of a rise in the value of products per farmer in this region to the level of the average value of products per farmer in other parts of the country (using data for the middle of the decade 1920–30), without any change in the relative prices of different agricultural products. It was found that with such a change in average productivity per farmer, crops equal in value to those produced by the present farm population of the Southeast could be produced by less than half as many workers, thus releasing about 9 million people to seek other means of support.

Part of the workers thus released might be absorbed in meeting the consumer demands of those remaining in agriculture in the Southeast now made effective, on this hypothesis, by increased purchasing power, but this service might be performed for the most part by the present nonfarm population of the region. Of course, a large part of the increase in expenditure would go to purchase goods produced in other regions. With increased efficiency in farm operation, a larger share of the energies of the present farm population in the South might go into increasing self-sufficiency, enriching diet with more milk, fruits, and vegetables, improving farm buildings, and giving greater attention to study, recreation, and art. Again, it might be possible to increase the marketable volume of agricultural products in the Southeast by greater diversity of production—in competition with other sections, and in meeting an enlarged national demand if a rise in average income in other parts of the country accompanied the increase of average productivity in the Southeast. Furthermore, some of the workers released from southern agriculture by increased value-productivity per worker might be absorbed by an expansion of industries in certain localities in the South, for example the Piedmont area, the Birmingham area, and the Tennessee Valley. Finally, the poverty of the families of many rural laborers and tenants might be mitigated by a more equitable distribution of incomes in the South.

Nevertheless, after due allowance has been made for all these factors, we are forced to the conclusion that an effective alleviation of the chronic depression of the farm population in many parts of the Southeast must include as one fundamental condition extensive emigration to areas of greater economic opportunity. It is therefore highly probable that if the South is to enjoy prosperity equal to what can be achieved in other parts of the

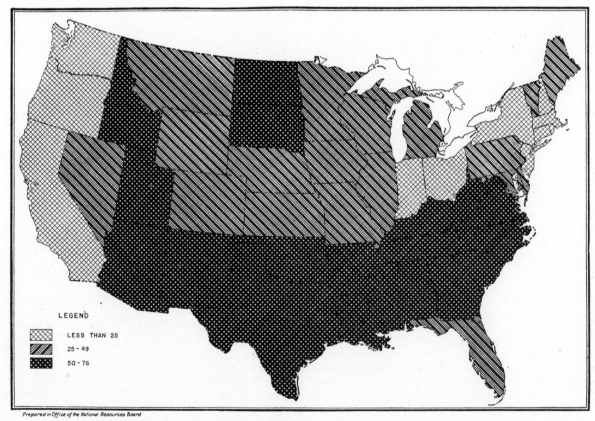

LEGEND

LESS THAN 25

25 – 49

50 – 76

Prepared in Office of the National Resources Board

FIGURE 16.—Estimated percentage increase in the rural-farm population, 1930–60, assuming no migration, by States.

United States, the proportion of the Nation's population living in the Southeast must be reduced.

The establishment of general rural prosperity would also involve considerable emigration from certain other areas, notably the Great Lakes cut-over region and the overcultivated portions of the Great Plains. Some emigration from certain mining areas is also indicated. Readjustments between different industrial areas will be inevitable, but there is no indication that these adjustments will result in any great change in the distribution of total population.

These conclusions are, in general, in line with those developed by the Social Science Research Council's Study of Population Redistribution, the Southern Regional Committee, and the findings of various governmental agencies. They afford a reasonable hypothesis regarding lines of population redistribution to be encouraged in the immediate future.

Interpreted in terms of broad divisions of industry, these conclusions imply the likelihood of a trend away from extractive industries toward manufacturing and mechanical pursuits, and still more toward professional, trade, and service occupations. Such a trend would be exactly in line with developments in this country during preceding decades. The basis of economic progress lies in the stable organization of industrial, commercial, and service enterprises, not in a reversion to greater reliance on the exploitation of natural resources, which in some areas would involve further exhaustion of the best resources, accompanied by diminishing returns.

The Future Demand for Agricultural Workers

This conclusion about agriculture can be checked by a consideration of the probable future demand for agricultural products, especially on the hypothesis of a possible increase in the general level of purchasing power among American families. By limiting our analysis at this point to a consideration of the proportion of total workers needed in agriculture to meet hypothetical consumer demand, we can eliminate the influence of changes in total population—assuming that a pair of hands for producing goods comes with each mouth to be fed.

A theoretical approach to this question can be made through an analysis of the manpower needed, under present conditions of production, to supply the food needed for the maintenance of various levels of nutrition in the general population. The present per-capita food consumption of a large proportion of the population is far below the level recommended by nutrition experts, especially as to quality. Workers in the Bureau of Home Economics

have prepared diets at four levels of adequacy, as follows: [15]

1. Restricted for emergency use; i. e., sufficient for the temporary maintenance of health over a short period but deficient in foods needed for body building.

2. Adequate at minimum cost.

3. Adequate at moderate cost.

4. Liberal; i. e., allowing for considerable variety.

Other workers in the Department of Agriculture have estimated the land and labor necessary to produce the food required to maintain the total population of the United States at each of these dietary levels. The manpower expended in the production of food for domestic consumption in the United States during the years 1928–33 would have been just about sufficient to supply the "adequate at minimum cost" diet for 125 million people, although some shifting of types of production would be necessary. An increase of 40 percent in manpower would be needed to supply the total population with the "adequate at moderate cost" diet, and an increase of 68 percent in manpower would be needed to make the "liberal" diet universal, together with considerable shifts in production.

Such a radical increase in domestic demand for food would be barely sufficient to afford general prosperity in the present farm population, since half of the Nation's farms produced 90 percent of all agricultural products sold or traded in 1929. Moreover, such an increase in effective demand for food would involve a great increase in the average purchasing power of every family. This could only be achieved if there were a great increase in the average value-productivity of each worker. Such a change would presumably be associated with technological improvements in agriculture as well as in other industries and would thereby reduce the number of workers needed to produce a given quantity of food. Furthermore, as is pointed out by the authors of *Migration and Economic Opportunity*, speculation concerning these diets can easily become unrealistic.

On the basis of a large number of studies of family budgets showing the relation between total expenditures and those for food, the home economists have estimated that at 1934 food prices (which were lower than present prices) a family of four must have an annual income of at least $2,000 in order to consume the "adequate at moderate cost" diet, and that the "liberal" diet would require an income of at least $4,000. In 1929 only 34.7 percent of all families and unattached individuals in the United States had incomes of $2,000 or more, and only 10.7 percent had $4,000 or more. To reduce food prices enough to enable the lowest-income groups to purchase either diet would require such enormous reductions in the cost of production as to be outside the realm of prac-

[15] Stiebeling, H. K., and Ward, M. M. Diets at 4 Levels of Nutritive Content and Cost, United States Department of Agriculture, Circular 296, November 1933.

tical consideration. And even if food were so cheap, it would be a long time before the consumption habits of the people could be changed sufficiently to induce a large proportion of them to purchase either diet. The inclinations of many would be to continue present food habits and use part of the income formerly spent for food for the purchase of other commodities. Both diets call for great increases in the consumption of fruit and vegetables, and reductions in the use of such staples as beans and wheat. It might prove as difficult to induce a large proportion of our people to make the required reductions in their consumption of these latter foods as it has been to discourage the use of alcohol and nicotine * * *. Perhaps there will be gradual tendencies toward both lower food prices and higher incomes, but such tendencies are likely to be fully as gradual as improvements in agricultural efficiency.[16]

Perhaps the most realistic approach to an analysis of the possible effect of increases in average family income on the demand for foods is that obtained by an examination of actual

[16] See Goodrich, *op. cit.*, pp. 403–404.

changes in expenditure for different types of goods and services at different levels of living. The data for such an analysis are supplied in table 7.

The families used in this analysis are classified according to total annual expenditures relative to the number of "consumption units" in the family.[17]

It should be noted that these data refer only to families of wage earners and lower salaried clerical workers in selected cities, and that ex-

[17] A "consumption unit" is a statistical unit, not an actual person. Food consumption was computed per adult male equivalent, with allowance for differences in age, sex, and occupation of the members of the family, based on actual expenditures as determined by field studies (using weights computed by the Bureau of Home Economics). Clothing consumption was computed on the base of actual expenditures per male of 21–35 years of age (as found in the field study made by the Bureau of Labor Statistics) taken as unity, with expenditures for other members of the family computed as relatives on this base. Other expenditures were computed per member of the family. The "consumption unit" is a composite of the special units for food and clothing, and of actual persons for other items of expenditure.

TABLE 7.—*Ratio of expenditures by families at higher economic level (total annual expenditure over $400 per consumption unit) to corresponding expenditures by families at lower economic level (total annual expenditures under $400 per consumption unit = 100)* [1]

[Expenditures of families at lower level used as base=100]

Type of expenditure	New Hampshire cities (classified by population)				Grand Rapids	Lansing	Marquette	Richmond
	Over 50,000 [2]	20,000–50,000 [3]	10,000–20,000 [4]	Under 10,000 [5]				
Average expenditure per family:								
Total	111	131	123	122	130	136	141	140
Food	91	95	99	92	99	105	107	98
Clothing	95	122	116	105	113	140	166	149
Housing and household operation	109	147	129	124	132	126	141	141
Transportation	250	284	261	251	215	294	235	241
Recreation	137	146	140	140	126	170	159	198
All other expenditures	135	158	136	155	176	159	199	181
Average expenditures per person:								
Total	177	220	203	214	200	213	233	231
Food	146	160	163	163	153	165	178	163
Clothing	152	205	192	185	175	219	273	247
Housing and household operation	175	247	213	218	204	198	232	233
Transportation	401	477	430	442	332	460	388	398
Recreation	219	245	231	246	195	267	262	327
All other expenditures	217	266	225	273	272	249	328	299
Expenditure for food per food-consumption unit	149	147	154	146				155

[1] Computed from data supplied by the Bureau of Labor Statistics. For data on size of sample, average size of family, and total annual expenditures, see the following articles in the *Monthly Labor Review*: Williams, Faith M., "Money Disbursements of Wage Earners and Clerical Workers in 11 New Hampshire Communities" (March 1936); and "Money Disbursements of Wage Earners and Clerical Workers in Richmond, Birmingham and New Orleans" (May 1936); also "Money Disbursements of Wage Earners and Clerical Workers in Four Michigan Cities" (June 1936); "Money Disbursements of Wage Earners and Clerical Workers in Boston and Springfield, Mass." (September 1936).
[2] Manchester.
[3] Nashua, Concord, Berlin.
[4] Portsmouth, Keene, Dover, Laconia, Claremont.
[5] Littleton, Conway.

Type of expenditure	Birmingham	New Orleans	Boston, Massachusetts—Expenditure classes per consumption unit				Detroit, Michigan—Expenditure classes per consumption unit			
			$400–499	$500–599	$600–699	$700 and over	$400–499	$500–599	$600–699	$700 and over
Average expenditure per family:										
Total	147	149	115	127	122	143	113	117	129	144
Food	113	115	104	105	92	102	98	92	99	92
Clothing	138	160	124	128	137	154	118	106	135	145
Housing and household operation	161	145	110	128	121	141	108	116	121	133
Transportation	220	247	136	152	214	297	158	184	218	346
Recreation	152	170	142	162	165	190	119	146	141	190
All other expenditures	180	215	156	204	195	247	144	163	189	211
Average expenditures per person:										
Total	225	226	156	194	231	319	157	190	230	314
Food	172	175	141	160	174	226	137	150	177	200
Clothing	211	244	169	195	258	343	164	173	242	317
Housing and household operation	246	220	149	195	228	313	151	189	217	292
Transportation	336	375	185	231	404	660	220	300	389	756
Recreation	231	259	193	246	312	424	165	238	251	415
All other expenditures	273	328	212	310	369	549	200	265	337	461
Expenditure for food per food-consumption unit	159	170	136	152	162	207	130	145	165	184

penditure per consumption unit is affected by both differences in total family income and differences in size of family. The relative expenditures at higher disbursement levels indicate the way in which a general increase in income might affect the demand for different types of goods and services. It will be seen that when total expenditure per capita doubles, expenditure for food usually rises about 65 percent, more or less; expenditures for clothing and housing rise about 100 percent (the ratios for clothing being higher in some communities, and the ratios for housing higher in others); expenditures for transportation (chiefly automobile purchase and maintenance) rise four to sixfold; expenditures for recreation and for other miscellaneous items also rise much more rapidly than total expenditure.

The implication of these findings, which are in line with well-known principles of consumption, is that a general increase in per capita income would increase the demand for agricultural products, but much less rapidly than it would increase the demand for nonagricultural goods and services. The rapid increase in expenditures for items other than food, clothing, and housing is reflected in occupational statistics showing rapid expansion in automobile production and in professional and service occupations and trades during the prosperous twenties.

Two factors have been neglected in this treatment of the effect of a rise in average level of living on the proportional distribution of workers in agriculture and in other industries (based on an analysis of data on family and per capita expenditures). They are (1) possible change in the foreign demand for agricultural products, and (2) the effect of future technological changes in causing an increase in average productivity of farm workers relative to an increase in the average productivity of nonfarm workers. There is, however, no reason to suppose that the net effect of these unknown factors would reverse our finding that an increase in average family income in the United States would tend to decrease the proportion of all workers needed in agriculture. And we have already seen that in comparison with present economic opportunities there are now too many workers in agriculture. It is possible that there may be some increase in the demand for agricultural raw materials for industrial purposes, but there is no evidence at present of any great impending developments along this line. If it were possible more nearly to equalize hours and conditions of work among different occupational groups, this process in itself would greatly increase the need for manpower in agriculture, which is now characterized by long hours per day as well as a 7-day week. Further decreases in the reproduction rates of farm groups would, of course, also tend to relieve the constant tendency toward population pressure in rural areas.

Differences in Reproduction Rates as a Factor in Migration

We have also seen that the large differences in reproduction rates between farm and nonfarm groups would force continued and extensive emigration from farms to cities and towns. This would be true even if there were now no excess of population dependent on agriculture for support, and even if there were no change in the consumer demand for farm products relative to that for other kinds of goods and services. If it were not for its favorable age distribution, more deaths than births would occur in urban population. In a few large cities we already find more deaths than births. The same will be true in many large cities within a few years. On the other hand, the farm population at present reproduction rates would increase about 60 percent in one generation if there were no migration. In a few areas, the largest of which is the southern Appalachians, it would double in 25 to 30 years. Without migration, and allowing for a greater decline in the farm than in the city birth rate, the urban population of the United States would be no larger in 1960 than it was in 1930. At the same time the farm population would have increased nearly 50 percent.[18] Altogether the evidence indicates clearly that there must be continued migration from farms to nonfarm areas, unless the present disparity in economic level of living between rural and urban communities is to be intensified, with further impoverishment of large sections of the farm population.

The Outlook

Continued emigration from farm areas thus seems desirable, at least from the economic standpoint. What is the likelihood that it will take place? The answer seems almost inevitable. It is significant that, beginning in 1933, there has again been a net movement from farms to cities, although so far this has been in smaller proportions than the predepression cityward march.

There is no clear evidence of major trends in the redistribution of industrial workers among the different regions, or of those engaged in trade, technical, professional, and service occupations. Some continuation of the movement into the Far West may be expected, but probably in greatly diminished numbers. There are definite indications of a retardation in the expansion of industry in southern New England, but there is no reason to expect any marked population changes in this region. Analysis of the gainfully occupied populations

[18] Estimates prepared for the National Resources Committee by the Scripps Foundation for Research in Population Problems.

of different States by social-economic classes reveals areas that have relatively few persons in trade, and in the professional and service occupations.[19] Whether or not economic changes will permit correspondingly greater increases in these fields is uncertain.

Therefore, except for areas from which emigration is indicated because of the unfavorable outlook for the extractive industries on which the people now there are dependent for support, the present pattern of population distribution in the United States is not likely to change greatly in its broad outlines in the immediate future. But while the regional pattern is likely to remain fairly fixed, there is every reason to expect a continuation of the spread of population out from the centers of metropolitan areas into surrounding satellite cities, suburban communities, and adjacent rural areas.

It is highly probable also that there will be an absolute increase in the number of individuals moving to and from different localities. Such a trend toward greater individual mobility is indicated by the analysis of past population changes, and may be expected to follow the rapid improvement of means of communication and transportation. Extensive movements of population are essential to the economic progress of areas of relative overpopulation, with high reproduction rates. Interchange of population between other areas will facilitate adjustments to technological changes. Interchange of people and ideas may tend indirectly to equalize birth rates in different parts of the country. It will have important effects on the social life of the Nation which it is difficult to analyze or evaluate. It is easy to draw an exaggerated picture of a Nation on wheels, but the sudden appearance of trailers on American highways is undoubtedly symptomatic of a current trend toward mobility of population. Perhaps after a time there may be a counter tendency toward greater permanence of residence, but this does not seem to be indicated for the immediate future.

Isolation can no longer be assumed to be a serious barrier against emigration from, or immigration to, any region in the United States. Extreme isolation is necessary to keep population increasing rapidly in an area of low opportunity. This condition was characteristic of the southern Appalachian area during the nineteenth century, but toward the end of the century the opening up of the coal mines in this region, through the extension of railway lines, attracted part of the excess natural increase from the adjacent farming counties. A continued increase in employment opportunities in coal mining is improbable, but lines of communication have been extended

into outlying industrial areas. The isolation of the mountain communities is rapidly disappearing. States that include large mountain populations now show a fairly high proportion of their native sons and daughters living in other States. In this respect, West Virginia (with 23 percent of those born in the State living in other States in 1930) was only slightly below the average for all States (23.5 percent). Kentucky and Tennessee were well above (nearly 30 percent). Although these States have a natural increase considerably greater than that for the Nation as a whole, their rate of growth for several decades has been definitely less than that for the rest of the country. The situation is similar in other rural States. From 1920 to 1930 Montana, Idaho, Arkansas, Georgia, South Carolina, Virginia, Maine, Vermont, New Hampshire, Iowa, and North Dakota grew less than one-third as rapidly as the rest of the country. Moreover, the cities of over 25,000 population in many of these States were growing more rapidly than the Nation as a whole, while their small towns and rural areas were growing very slowly, or actually declining in population.

Much the same impression is obtained from a study of changes in population by counties. The only areas in the southern Appalachians that increased in population more rapidly than the Nation during the past decade were mining counties in southern West Virginia and eastern Kentucky. Central Georgia was the most conspicuous area of decline. There were areas of considerable population decline in all the southern States, except Florida, as well as in most of Missouri and the Ouachita-Ozark region of Arkansas and Oklahoma. Relative lack of communication facilities is apparently more important in maintaining the fertility of the population than it is in restraining migration, but there is some evidence that even this differential is diminishing.

This should not be interpreted to mean that migration has brought about perfect adjustment of population and economic resources in all areas. In spite of much emigration, most of the less fertile agricultural counties have more people than can be maintained at a level of living similar to that in the better farming communities. Isolation, associated with high reproduction rates and meager educational facilities, produces a lag in the adjustment of population to economic opportunity and leaves those who do migrate ill equipped for the change to conditions of living in other areas.

A variety of conditions, some of which are subject to social control, tend to impede the adjustment of population to economic opportunity through migration. Success in choosing new locations depends on many factors beyond the migrants' control. A wrong de-

---

[19] See ch. II, tables 11a–b, and the Statistical Supplement.

cision has unfortunate consequences, both for the individual and for the community to which he goes. In many communities migrants are no longer welcome unless they are financially independent. They are regarded as potential liabilities rather than as assets.

Public administration of relief has in general tended to restrict mobility. Few communities are willing to support any but their own residents; hence a specified length of residence is prerequisite to receipt of relief. It is probable that the maintenance of legal residence will become increasingly important in the future as more and more States adopt social security laws, except insofar as this effect may be modified by Federal legislation or interstate agreements. Many of the unemployment insurance systems exclude certain occupations, including agriculture, from their benefits. The extent to which this will affect the mobility of labor cannot be foreseen at present.

Migration in the past has been largely spontaneous and undirected, although the direction has been influenced by the colonization schemes of railroad and land companies. The development of a comprehensive Nation-wide system of unemployment registration and exchange may do much to obviate the undesirable consequences of unguided migration, to discourage movements premised on false information, and to facilitate the location of real opportunities corresponding to individual interests and qualifications. The improvement of educational opportunities in areas from which emigration is to be expected may prove even more helpful.

It is important to recognize that internal migration may affect the life of receiving communities quite as profoundly as immigration from other countries. The interchange of people and of ideas from region to region is becoming more rapid. Progress or deterioration, cooperation or conflict, in any group affects the life of other groups. Furthermore, in view of the movement of people from area to area and the tendency toward increasing intermarriage among all groups except between the most distinct racial types, and even this exception may cease to hold, the biological trend of any group may be expected to affect generally the biological capacities of future generations in this country. These considerations raise important problems that will be explored in other sections of this report.

IV. REGIONAL AND
RACIAL DIFFERENCES
IN REPRODUCTION RATES

1. Geographic Variations in Reproductive Tendency

The Significance of Differential Reproduction

Variations in rates of reproduction are, as we have already seen, a fundamental factor in the redistribution of population. In short-time effects, migration appears to be far more important than reproduction. On further analysis, the former is found in many instances to be controlled by the latter, in the sense that continuous streams of internal migration of considerable magnitude are needed to offset the imbalance that would otherwise result from differential rates of reproduction.

Large variations in reproductive tendencies among different population groups may also have a profound effect, in the course of a few generations, on the composition and social characteristics of the national population. Differences in net rates of reproduction, commonly found today, are sufficient to give one of two equal groups twice as many descendants as the other in the next generation. At the present time the social effects of differential reproduction outweigh the apparent biological effects, since the greatest differences among large groups exist among people located in different areas and in different types of community.

Under modern conditions, differences in birth rates are far more important than differences in death rates in their influence on net reproduction trends. Thus the ratio of children under 5 years of age to women aged 20–44 years among native whites in North Carolina, West Virginia, New Mexico, and Utah is 98 percent, 103 percent, 96 percent, and 92 percent, respectively, higher than in New York State. In all these States the ratios are well over 100 percent higher than in California. On the other hand, the number of children required to replace a thousand white women of childbearing age, in the States with the highest mortality rates, is only 5 percent greater (using 1929–31 death rates) than the number required in the States with the lowest

mortality rates. Thus the range of variation in fertility among States is about 20 times as great as that of permanent replacement quotas which represent differences in mortality rates.

The Distinction Between Crude and Intrinsic Rates of Natural Increase

Natural population change is affected, not only by the fertility rates of women of child-bearing age and by the death rates at each age, but also by the proportion of persons living at different ages in any population. This fact must always be borne in mind in using crude rates of fertility, mortality, or natural increase. It is possible, however, to calculate the reproduction rates that would result from the continued operation of any set of specific birth and death rates for particular ages, in the absence of migration. Such a rate is usually referred to as a *net reproduction rate* or an *intrinsic* rate of natural increase. It indicates the rate at which the population would increase after the present irregularities in age distribution have disappeared, provided that the current birth and death rates remained unchanged. It measures the reproduction rate toward which any population is actually tending.

In the United States crude rates of natural increase are generally higher than the corresponding intrinsic rates. This is especially the case in cities where there have been large accessions of young adults. Although in 1930 the net reproduction rate of the white population of 12 States was less than that necessary to maintain the population permanently, there were actually more births than deaths in all of these States. But if present trends continue, the excess of births over deaths will decrease in many parts of the United States until the number of deaths becomes larger than the number of births.

We shall first take account of the present crude rates of natural increase in different regions of the United States. The intrinsic rates of natural increase will then be examined in order to discover the long-time trend that is indicated by present conditions.

Regional Variations in Crude Rates of Natural Increase

The natural increase resulting from excess of births over deaths has a regional distribution that is quite different from that of the present population. (See fig. 1.) Fifty-five percent of the natural increase of the United States comes from three regions—Southeast, Southwest, and Northwest—that contain altogether only about one-third of the total population. Conversely, the Northeast, Middle States, and Far West, with 66 percent of the total population in 1930, accounted for only 45 percent of the total excess of births over deaths during the ensuing 5 years.

Similar differences appear in comparing the distribution by States of increases through excess of births over deaths (1930–34) with the distribution of total population in 1930 (figs. 2a and 2b). For example, accession through natural increase is now taking place about as rapidly in North Carolina as in the combined areas of Massachusetts, Rhode Island, and Connecticut, although in 1930 the population of the latter States was more than twice as great as that of North Carolina. Without migration, such differentials in natural increase would change greatly the present distribution of population within one or two generations.

Regional Variation in Intrinsic Rates of Natural Increase

These differences will be increased if the present trends in birth and death rates con-
tinue.[1] According to the mortality and fertility conditions prevailing in 1930 in the white population of the United States, the survivors from 1,000 newborn females would be expected to give birth during their lifetime to 1,079 daughters. This reproductive rate, if continued, would result in a nearly stationary population, increasing at a rate of only 7.9 percent per generation (about 28.5 years), or about 0.3 percent per year.

The large disparity between the present crude rate and the intrinsic rate of increase of the population of the United States is due to the large immigration and high birth rates of the preceding 50 years, which have resulted in a temporary bunching of the population at the reproductive ages. The influence of these factors will soon vanish. It has already been pointed out that there were fewer children under 5 in 1930 than in 1920. After about 20 years, therefore, the number of women in the childbearing ages will decrease. Even if there

---

[1] As a demonstration of the method of measuring the net reproduction rate, we may follow the history of 1,000 white females who start life together. As they grow up, their number is gradually reduced by deaths. According to the mortality rates prevailing in 1929–31, 921 of these girls would be living on their fifteenth birthday, 882 on their thirtieth birthday, and 820 on their forty-fifth birthday. The birth statistics for 1930 show that 1,000 white females bore on the average about 120 infants during their twentieth year of life. At this rate the 910 survivors of the original 1,000 girls would during their twentieth year have 109 babies. The number of children can be computed similarly for each age of the mothers. By adding the number born at each age, the total number of children expected during the lifetime of these females can be computed. For simplicity, this index of net reproduction is based on the number of daughters expected per 1,000 females born alive.

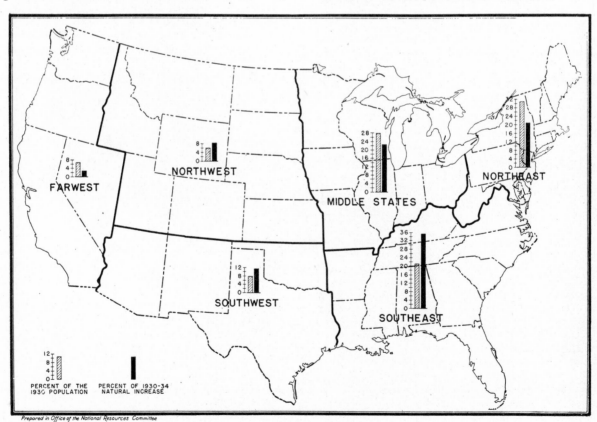

FIGURE 1.—Percentage of the total 1930 population and percentage of the total natural increase, 1930–34, by regions.

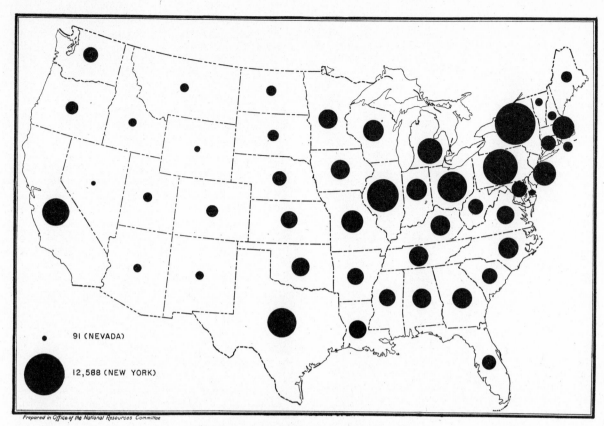

FIGURE 2a.—Population in thousands, by States, 1930.

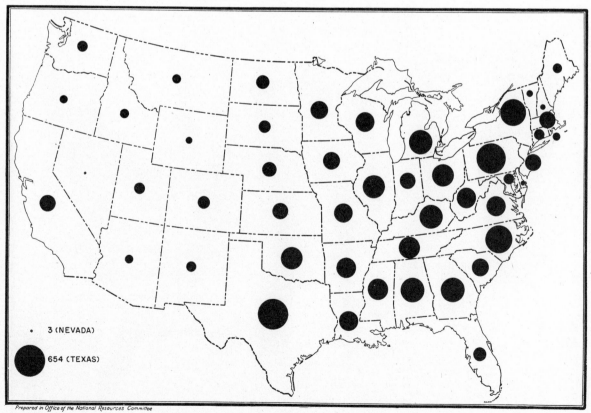

FIGURE 2b.—Average annual natural increase, by States, 1930–34.

is no further change in fertility, the total number of births will tend to decrease, due simply to the smaller number of women at the childbearing ages.

It is, therefore, important to examine the reproduction rates that would result from continuation of the present birth and death rates. On this hypothesis, in one-fourth of the States 1,000 white females would during their lifetime bear less than 1,000 daughters (fig. 3). In six States (Oregon, New York, California, Washington, New Jersey, and Illinois), the white population would fail to reproduce itself by as much as 10 to 20 percent. In six other States (Massachusetts, Rhode Island, Connecticut, Florida, Missouri, and Maryland) the deficit would be 10 percent or less. In another 10 States, extending in a belt south of the Great Lakes and north of the Ohio River, the white population barely replaces itself, the excess being less than 10 percent. In about half of the country, comprising more than 60 percent of the total population, as soon as the relatively large proportion of the population now in the childbearing ages passes into the older age groups, the number of daughters born will not be sufficient to maintain the parent generation, even if there is no further decline in fertility.

The group of States with low reproduction rates extends from southern New England westward through the States of the Middle West and north of the Ohio River, until it reaches Kansas, Nebraska, and Colorado. The Pacific Coast States and Florida complete the group. It should be noted that all the highly urban and industrial States except Michigan are included. On the other hand, the agricultural Southeast and Southwest (south of the Potomac and Ohio Rivers and westward to the Rocky Mountains) is a region of high fertility. Due partly to the presence of a relatively large Mexican population, many of whom are returned by census enumerators as "white", New Mexico leads the Nation in fertility. A thousand "white" females there would bear about 1,600 daughters during their lifetime, at present rates of fertility and mortality. Utah, North Dakota, Arizona, Arkansas, Kentucky, and West Virginia are also characterized by very high fertility.

The conclusions drawn from the analysis of trends in reproduction for entire States are borne out by a similar analysis on a county basis. (See fig. 4.) The highest fertility in the United States is found among the women of the southern Appalachians. If there were no emigration, the population of the counties of southern West Virginia, southwestern Virginia, western North Carolina, eastern Tennessee would double within one generation. In Breathitt, Knott, Leslie, and Martin Counties, Ky., and in Dickenson and Buchanan Counties, Va., the

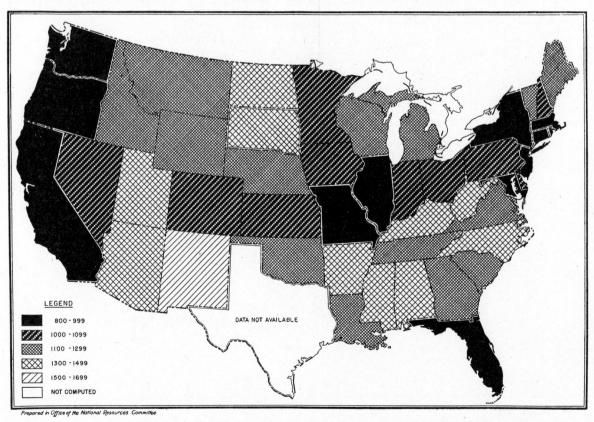

LEGEND

■	800 - 999
▨	1000 -1099
▥	1100 - 1299
▨	1300 - 1499
▨	1500 - 1699
☐	NOT COMPUTED

DATA NOT AVAILABLE

Prepared in Office of the National Resources Committee

FIGURE 3.—Expected number of daughters per 1,000 white females at birth and death rates of 1929–31.

population would increase two and one-half times in about 30 years without emigration. Only among the women of Garfield County, Utah, is fertility as high as this. Of the 113 counties in the United States where present fertility would double the population in one generation, 59 are in the Southeast and 34 are in the Northwest. All except three of these northwestern counties are located in North and South Dakota, southern Idaho, and Utah.

The areas of highest fertility extend in two belts along the northern and southern boundaries of the United States, and are connected in the west to form a huge horseshoe. Beginning in northern Maine, one area follows the Canadian boundary westward to the Continental Divide in western Montana. The northern limit of the southern area follows roughly the 39th parallel, from the Atlantic seacoast westward through southern Ohio, Indiana, Illinois, Missouri, and Kansas, to western Colorado. Florida, however, is not included in this group of States. A third area of high fertility extends north and south, east of the Rocky Mountains, between about 100° and 110° longitude, and connects the two east-west belts. Areas of low fertility lie between these belts and also along the Pacific coast.

Fertility is below that necessary to maintain the population permanently in 156 counties. In another 200 counties, the intrinsic birth and death rates practically balance. These counties, located mainly in the Northeast, Middle States, and on the Pacific coast, include more than one-half the total population of the United States. Eighty-one of the ninety-three cities of more than 100,000 population in 1930 are included. Almost without exception, areas of low fertility are adjacent to large cities. The birth rate of people living in large cities, even in areas of high fertility, is below replacement needs.

The Trend of Fertility Since 1800

The historical background of present variations in fertility in different parts of the country is shown in figure 5. Beginning in southern New England, shortly after the opening of the nineteenth century, the decline in fertility proceeded westward into the Middle Atlantic States with the development of industry and the growth of cities. By 1820 the ratio of children to women in the frontier States from Ohio to Mississippi, where agriculture was dominant, was nearly twice that in southern New England.

At the outbreak of the Civil War the ratio had decreased nearly 50 percent in the New England States. The area of high fertility had moved westward to the Mountain and Pacific States. In Utah, Oregon, and Washington the ratio was greater than 1,000. The agricultural South and the Middle West still had ratios nearly 50 percent higher than the Northeast.

During the years immediately following the Civil War, fertility declined rapidly among women on the Pacific coast (especially in California), in New England, the Middle Atlantic, and the States bordering on the Great Lakes. In the South, on the other hand, fertility decreased very slowly.

By 1880 the decline in fertility had practically ceased in New England, although it continued unabated in the remainder of the country, with the smallest changes occurring in the rural South. In 1930 the area of high fertility was definitely located south of the Potomac and Ohio Rivers, excluding Florida, and in Louisiana, Arkansas, Oklahoma, New Mexico, Utah, and the Dakotas. The fertility of New England was only slightly lower than 50 years previous.

The trend of net fertility (measured by ratios of children to women) among native white and Negro elements in different parts of the United States during the last 20 years is shown in figure 6. The maps reveal a new characteristic of the "solid South": rapid reduction in reproductive tendency among both whites and Negroes, with decreases in net fertility between 20 and 40 percent in most of the Southern States. This is clearly due (1) to the increase of urbanism and (2) to the spread through these groups of the lower birth rate pattern which was already widespread in most other parts of the United States.

These maps (fig. 6) show a slight actual increase from 1910 to 1930 in ratios of children to native white women in New England; but this ratio is affected by reduction in infant mortality and by internal migration. The fertility of the native white population of this region was fairly constant during the present century, up to the time of the depression. To what extent this may be affected by the infiltration of more fertile second-generation immigrant stocks into the native white group is a moot question to which it is impossible to give a definite answer at the present time.

The increase in net fertility among Negroes in most Northern States may be attributed in part to improvement in health conditions, especially the lowering of infant mortality rates, and in part to the introduction into northern cities of many Negro families with the background and traditions of the rural South.

These data show clearly a tendency toward the leveling off of birth rates in areas long influenced by the lower birth rate pattern. The decreasing rate of decline in fertility in the areas where the downward trend in the birth rate was first noticeable indicates that fertility rates may soon become stabilized in these areas, although at a level below that necessary to maintain the present population without migration. A continued decline in fertility may be expected where birth rates are still high; but large differentials between communities of

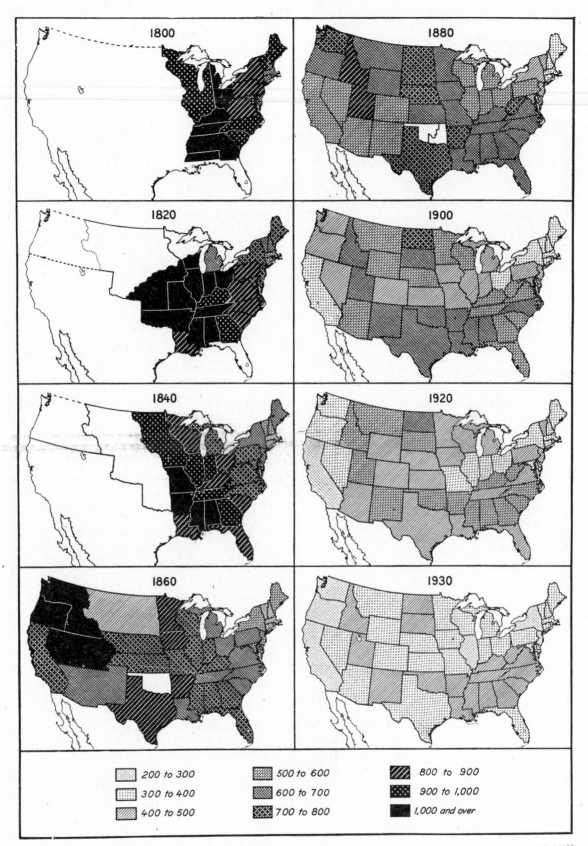

FIGURE 5.—Number of white children under 5 per 1,000 white women aged 15–49, 1800–1930.

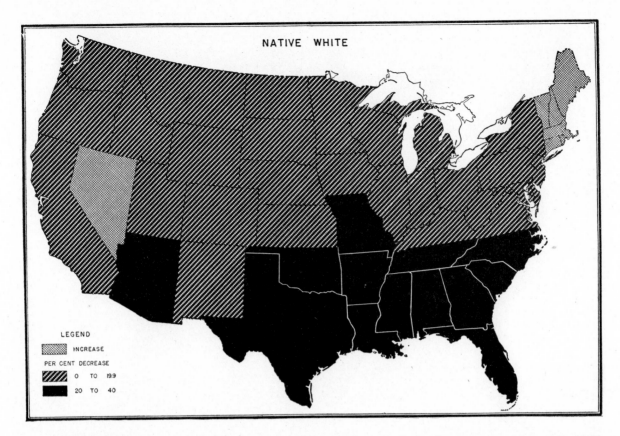

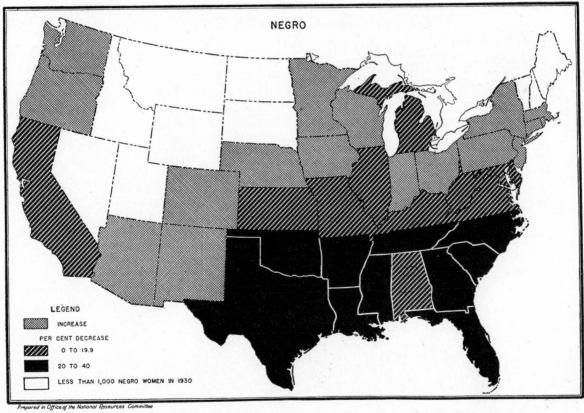

FIGURE 6.—Percentage change in number of children under 5 per 1,000 native white and Negro women aged 20–44, 1910–30.

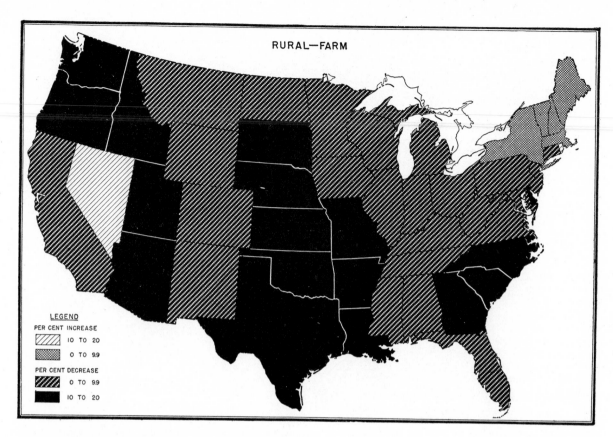

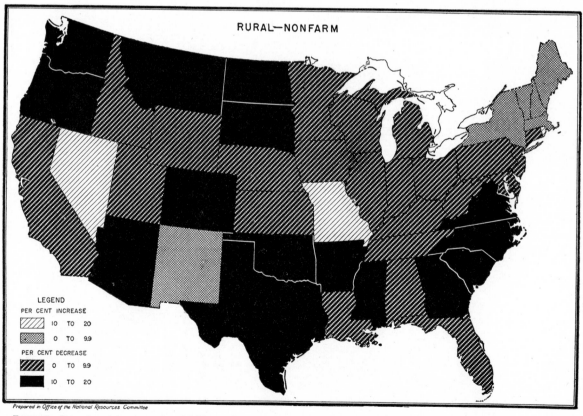

Prepared in Office of the National Resources Committee

FIGURE 7.—Percentage change in number of children under 5 per 1,000 native white women aged 20–44, rural-farm and rural-nonfarm, 1920–30.

various size and between regions are to be expected for several, perhaps many, decades.

Recent Changes in Fertility in Communities of Different Size

Fertility declined much more rapidly in the total population than in either urban or rural groups separately. This somewhat surprising result is due to the changing proportions of rural and urban groups in the total population. Since the fertility of the farm population is about twice that of the urban population, the increasing proportion of the population living in urban communities accelerates the decrease in the general birth rate.

Between 1910 and 1930 the net fertility of the urban white population (measured by ratios of children to women) declined more rapidly among women living in the large cities of more than 100,000 inhabitants and in the small towns of 2,500 to 10,000 inhabitants than in cities of moderate size. (See table 1.) The rapid decline of the birth rate in large cities during this period is due in large measure to the presence in these cities of large foreign-born elements, among whom the decline in fertility has been most pronounced. In the case of the Negro population there was rapid decrease of fertility in small cities of 2,500 to 10,000 inhabitants, but actual increase of net fertility in large cities.

TABLE 1.—*Percentage change in fertility by nativity and race in different sized communities, 1910–30* [1]

Size of community	Native white	Foreign-born white	Negro
Total	−16.0	−30.2	−24.7
Total rural	−12.3	−26.7	−3.6
Total urban	−4.8	−28.1	−2.7
100,000 or more population	−3.7	−29.6	12.8
25,000 to 100,000 population	−1.3	−24.3	5.0
10,000 to 25,000 population	−0.9	−20.0	−5.1
2,500 to 10,000 population	−4.9	−24.3	−17.1
Rural-nonfarm	−[2]5.3	−[2]34.8	−[2]0.3
Rural-farm	−[2]8.4	−[2]20.8	−[2]3.6

[1] Based on changes in the number of children under 5 per 1,000 women 20–44 years of age. The number of children under 5 reported by the census was increased by the following factors to adjust for estimated underenumeration: White 1.05 in all cases; Negro 1.13 for the total United States, 1.11 in the North, 1.135 in the South and 1.08 in the West. The ratios were standardized to the age distribution of women in the United States in 1930. Mexicans are not included with whites in 1930, but are included in 1920 and 1910, in accordance with census procedure. City and rural-urban groupings were made according to the population in the current census, except that the 1920 basis of rural-urban classification was used in 1910 for Maine, Vermont, and Connecticut.
[2] Change from 1920 to 1930.

In both the native white and the Negro populations, fertility declined more rapidly in the rural-farm than in the rural-nonfarm population. The geographic distribution of recent changes in the net fertility of the rural-farm and the rural-nonfarm population has been much the same since 1920 (see fig. 7). Net fertility declined only slightly or actually increased in the Northeast, especially in New England. In general the largest decreases occurred in areas where fertility was highest in

1920. The Pacific Coast States are a notable exception.

In communities of every size the smallest decreases in fertility occurred in the Northeast and in the States around the Great Lakes. This is the most highly urbanized part of the country and the area where the birth rate first started to decline. The most rapid decline in fertility took place in the South, in the Northwest, and on the Pacific coast. Except for the latter, these are the areas where the birth rate is still high.

The more rapid decline of the birth rate among native white women in rural areas, which first made greatest headway in cities, is now spreading rapidly throughout the rural population. How much this will reduce the present large differential between urban and rural women cannot be foretold at the present time.

2. Recent Changes in Fertility Among Native White, Foreign-born White, and Negro Women

The decrease in fertility of foreign-born white women was perhaps the outstanding feature of the decline in the birth rate during the twenties. From 1920 to 1929, the standardized birth rate of native white women decreased 20 percent, that of Negro women decreased 18 percent, and that of foreign-born white women decreased 32 percent (see fig. 8). The much greater decrease in the birth rate of foreign-born white women at all ages, especially at the

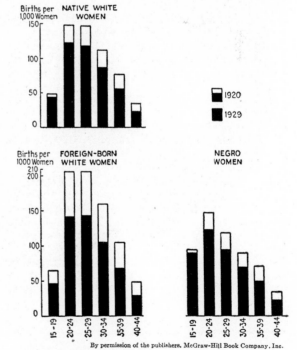

By permission of the publishers. McGraw-Hill Book Company, Inc.

FIGURE 8.—Birth rates by age, race, and nativity of women, United States, 1920 and 1929. From Thompson and Whelpton, *Population Trends in the United States.*

younger ages, is all the more striking since changes in the relative proportion of different national stocks might be expected to have had the opposite effect. Not only was there an increase in the proportion of foreign-born white women from the countries of high birth rates in southern and eastern Europe, but these women were younger on the average than those from the countries of low birth rates in northern and western Europe. A rapid decline in fertility of foreign-born women at all ages has been notable.

The decline in the general birth rate was accelerated by the rapid decline in fertility of women over 30 years of age, who bore only 70 to 80 percent as many children in 1929 as in 1920. The birth rate of women aged 40–44 decreased about twice as rapidly as that of women aged 20–24 between 1920 and 1929, among both native whites and Negroes. But among foreign-born white women, large decreases in fertility occurred at all ages, the decrease for young women being nearly as large as that for older women.

In 1929, according to the recorded birth statistics, the fertility of foreign-born white women was 20 percent greater than that of native white women, but the real differential is probably much less. Most of the foreign-born white women live in northern cities where birth registration is very nearly complete. A large proportion of native white women live in the South and West, where nonregistration is more frequent, with deficiency of 10 to 20 percent in some areas. The rates shown in figure 8 have not been corrected for nonregistration. The birth rate of foreign-born white women is now probably no more than 15 percent—possibly only 10 percent—higher than that of native white women. This conclusion is borne out by a study of the fertility of native and foreign-born white married women in New York State, exclusive of New York City.[2] The fertility of the foreign-born white women was found to be 45 percent greater than that for the native white women in 1920, but by 1934 this differential had been reduced to 8 percent.

The difference in fertility between native white and Negro women can be stated with much less confidence. Although the registration of Negro births is probably less complete than the registration of white births, the exact proportion of unregistered Negro births is unknown. The percentage underregistration of Negro births is estimated to be 5 to 10 points greater than that for white births. It may be concluded that the birth rates of foreign-born white and Negro women are approximately equal at the present time, but that the fertility of the former is decreasing at a more rapid rate.

It should not be concluded from this statement that the Negro population is increasing more rapidly than the white population. Although more children are born to Negro females during the childbearing ages, more of them die before maturity, so that the rate of natural increase is probably no greater than for the white population.

3. Racial Differences in Reproduction Rates

Fertility of Different Racial Groups

There are about twice as many children under 5 years per 1,000 women aged 20–44 years in the minor racial groups as in the white or Negro populations. (See table 2.) However, except for the Mexicans, the minor racial groups are numerically unimportant. The high fertility rates of these races arise in part from the fact that a large percentage of the women are married, but more especially from the low levels of living which prevail among these groups. Nevertheless, these rates are only slightly larger than those among farm women in the South, and are actually less in most cases than the corresponding ratios for women in the poorer farming areas of the Southeast.

So far as can be determined, urban residence has much the same effect upon the fertility of the minor racial groups as upon that of whites and Negroes, although rural-urban differences are usually smaller among the former. Contrary to the trend among whites and Negroes, the fertility of the minor races was about as high in 1930 as it was 10 years previous. To what extent this merely reflects a more complete enumeration of the population, especially children, in 1930 cannot be stated with certainty. It is well known that the statistics of the number of Indians are not only inaccurate but also incomparable, due to difficulties in census enumeration.[3]

TABLE 2.—*Number of children under 5 per 1,000 women aged 20–44 years, and per 1,000 persons aged 20–54 years, in different racial groups, United States, 1930*

Group	Number of children under 5 years	Children per 1,000 women aged 20–44 years	Children per 1,000 persons aged 20–54 years
White	9,927,396	481	186
Negro	1,230,206	497	210
Mexican	214,773	906	335
Indian	46,680	924	230
Japanese	17,696	824	262
Chinese	5,781	1,051	131
Filipino	1,423	1,090	37

[2] Kiser, Clyde V., "Recent Trends in Birth Rates among Foreign and Native-White Married Women in Up-State New York", *Milbank Memorial Fund Quarterly* XIV: 173–179, 1936.

[3] Indian Land Tenure, Economic Status and Population Lands, *Supplementary Report of the Land Planning Committee to the National Resources Board*, Pt. X. 35.

Except in the case of the American Indians, all of these minor racial groups have an abnormally high ratio of men to women, due to immigration. Accordingly, the ratios of children to adults have a markedly different distribution from that of the ratios of children to women of childbearing ages.

The Reproduction Rates of Native Whites and Negroes in Communities of Different Size [4]

It is a common observation that Negro families apparently have more children than white families. From this observation the belief has arisen that the number of Negroes in the country is increasing more rapidly than the number of whites, especially of native whites. But since the date of the first census in 1790 the Negro population has increased only about one-half to two-thirds as rapidly as the white population. As a result, the proportion of Negroes in the population has decreased from one-fifth in 1790 to less than one-tenth in 1930. Of course, this has resulted chiefly from the large immigration of foreign-born whites; hence, with the practical cessation of immigration resulting from quota restrictions, the decennial rates of increase of whites and Negroes may be approximately equal, for the immediate future at least.

According to fertility and mortality rates prevailing in 1930, 1,000 newborn white females would bear 1,079 daughters by the end of their reproductive period, whereas 1,000 Negro females would bear only about 1,034 daughters.[5] At these rates, after the present age distributions had become adjusted to present fertility and mortality conditions, about 540 years would be required for the Negro population to double in size, as compared with 250 years for the white population. Fertility and mortality will not remain unchanged; but these figures give an idea of the relative nearness of the Negro and white populations in 1930 to birth rates which just balance their death rates. Since 1930, birth rates have continued to decrease; the fertility of both whites and Negroes is now too low to maintain permanently their respective populations. A general improvement in health conditions would partly offset the decline in fertility. This possibility is much greater for Negro than for white females, since the latter now live about 13 years longer on the average and are nearer the upper limit of the improvement possible with present knowledge.

The long-time rate of increase of the Negro population depends upon many variable factors, any one of which may change sufficiently to invalidate forecasts of future trends. One of the most important of these is the influence of a continued Negro migration to northern cities. At present, Negro females living in the North, a large proportion of whom have migrated from Southern States, are only about two-thirds as fertile as those living in the South. According to fertility and mortality rates prevailing in 1920, 1,000 Negro females in the North would bear about 800 daughters during their lifetime; the conditions existing in 1930 give about the same result.[6] At this rate a population would decrease 20 percent in a generation (about 28 years).

The maintenance of net fertility by northern Negroes between 1920 and 1930 was made possible only by a decrease in mortality. If the 1920 mortality rates had remained constant, 1,000 Negro females would bear only 715 instead of 800 daughters at 1930 birth rates. In other words, the improvement in health conditions among northern Negroes has just about offset the decline in fertility.

Among Negro women in the South, improvement in health has not been sufficiently great to offset the decline in fertility. At 1920 birth and death rates, 1,000 Negro females in the South would bear about 1,435 daughters during their lifetime. In 1930, the corresponding number would be 1,130.[7] Had it not been for the improvement in mortality conditions, the 1930 figure would have been 1,055 instead of 1,130.

To what extent this difference in net reproductive tendency is due to selective migration and urban living conditions cannot be stated definitely. It is quite possible that it will diminish in the future because of the more rapid decrease in the fertility of southern Negroes. The net fertility of northern Negroes, which is already far below the level necessary for replacement, may remain relatively stationary for some time, provided they are able to adjust themselves to urban conditions. Unless there is a marked increase in the fertility of northern Negroes, it is obvious that a continuation of northward migration will result in a rate of natural increase for the total Negro population well below that necessary to maintain the population, quite apart from any decrease in the fertility of Negroes in each area.

Except in rural areas, fertility among native white and Negro women is already well below that necessary to maintain the population permanently. (See figs. 9 and 10.) In

---

[4] For detailed data on ratios of children to women, 1910, 1920, and 1930, by race and nativity, by States, and by classes of communities, see Statistical Supplement.

[5] This assumes about 9 percent underregistration of white births and 15 percent underregistration of Negro births. To raise the number of daughters born per 1,000 Negro females to a number comparable for the 1,000 white females would involve assuming an underregistration of Negro births of 20 percent.

[6] These figures are subject to some error because of the incompleteness in birth registration. The recorded birth statistics indicate 732 and 753 daughters, respectively. Eight percent underregistration in 1920 and 6 percent underregistration in 1930 give the above figures. If the increase in completeness of registration has been greater than this, the 1930 figure will be correspondingly smaller than the 1920.

[7] The recorded birth statistics give 1,176 and 927, respectively. These have been increased 18 percent at both periods. Due to the inclusion of additional States in 1930, it is doubtful if the completeness of birth registration improved during the decade.

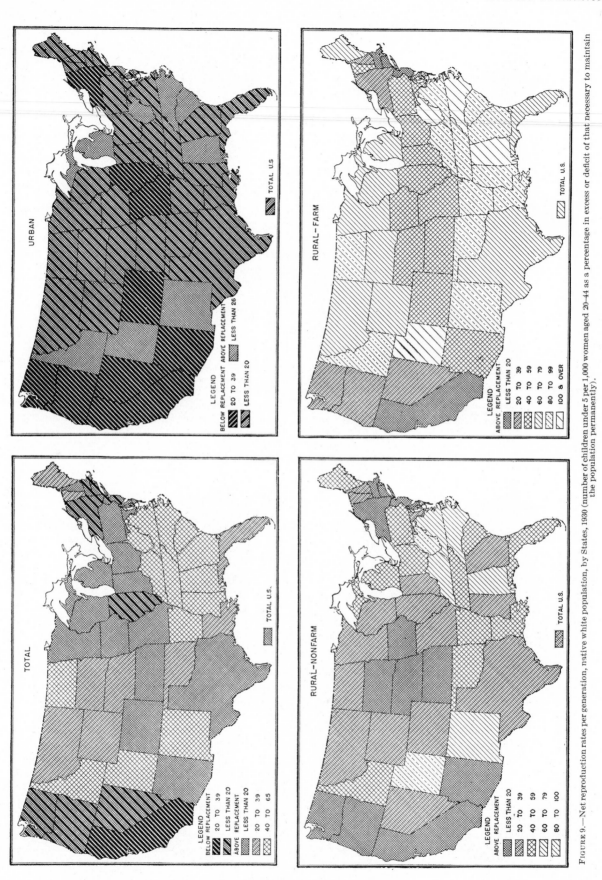

FIGURE 9.—Net reproduction rates per generation, native white population, by States, 1930 (number of children under 5 per 1,000 women aged 20–44 as a percentage in excess or deficit of that necessary to maintain the population permanently).

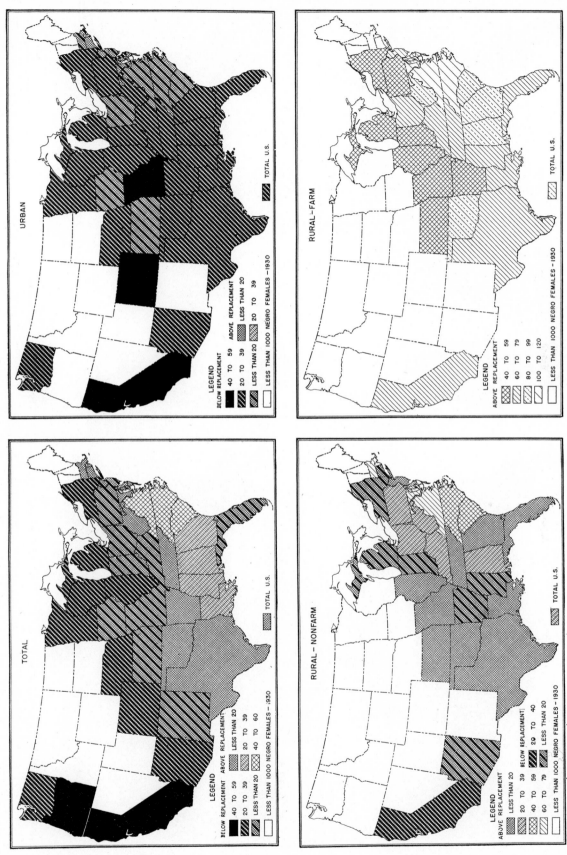

FIGURE 10.—Net reproduction rates per generation, Negro population, by States, 1930 (number of children under 5 per 1,000 women aged 20–44 as a percentage in excess or deficit of that necessary to maintain the population permanently).

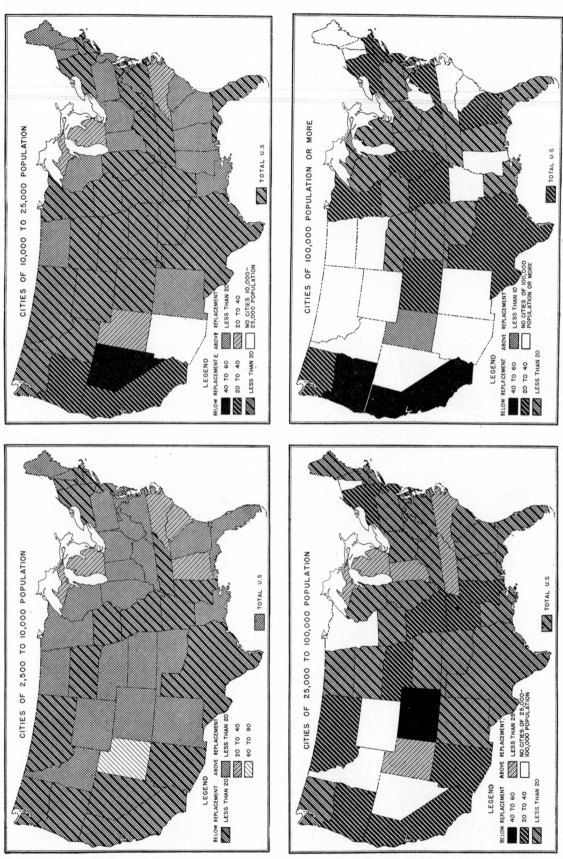

FIGURE 11.—Net reproduction rates per generation, in urban communities of different size, native white population, by States, 1930 (number of children under 5 per 1,000 women aged 20–44, as a percentage in excess or deficit of that necessary to maintain the population permanently).

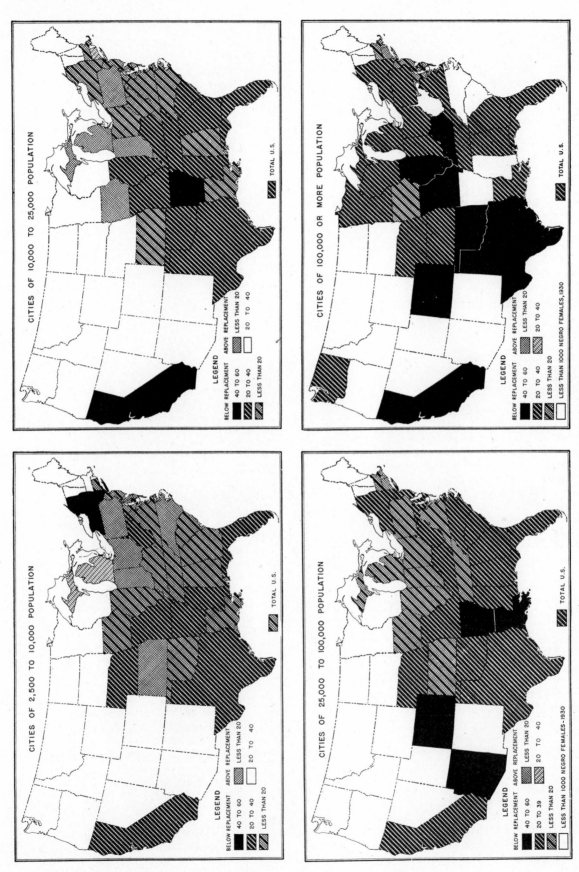

FIGURE 12.—Net reproduction rates per generation, in urban communities of different size, Negro population, by States, 1930 (number of children under 5 per 1,000 women aged 20–44, as a percentage in excess or deficit of that necessary to maintain the population permanently).

urban areas in 1925–29, the fertility of native white women was 14 percent below, and that of Negro women 28 percent below, the corresponding permanent replacement levels. (See table 3.) Fertility drops as the size of the community increases. It falls from rates of increase per generation of 69 percent for native white women and 80 percent for Negro women in the farm population to rates of decrease of 24 percent and 32 percent, respectively, for white and Negro populations in cities of 100,000 or more inhabitants. (See figs. 11 and 12.)

TABLE 3.—*Reproduction rates per generation among native white and Negro women, by size of community, 1930* [1]

Size of community	Native white	Negro
United States	1.12	1.13
Rural	1.54	1.61
Urban	.86	.72
100,000 or more population	.76	.68
25,000 to 100,000 population	.88	.72
10,000 to 25,000 population	.97	.80
2,500 to 10,000 population	1.04	.84
Rural—nonfarm	1.37	1.23
Rural—farm	1.69	1.80

[1] Number of children aged 0–4 per 1,000 women aged 20–44 as a ratio of the corresponding life table value. The life tables were computed by the Metropolitan Life Insurance Co.

Urban residence reduces the fertility of Negroes about 10 percent more than that of native whites. Whether this difference arises from selective migration or from the social and economic conditions of urban life cannot be stated positively at present. Even in the deep South the fertility of urban Negroes is from 20 to 30 percent below that necessary to maintain the population permanently. Only in Connecticut and Rhode Island (where there were altogether fewer than 40,000 Negroes in 1930) would the urban Negro population be able to replace itself permanently without immigration. The only southern Negro urban group with a reproduction rate per generation above unity is that living in towns of 2,500 to 10,000 population in North Carolina. With this exception, fertility is lower among urban Negroes in the South than among those in the North. The fertility of Negro women living in southern cities of more than 25,000 population is from 30 to 40 percent below that necessary to maintain the population permanently without immigration.

In general, both among whites and among Negroes, a lower birth rate is more directly associated with urban residence than with geographic region. The birth rate of women in Atlanta, Birmingham, or New Orleans is more like the birth rate of women living in New York, Chicago, or Denver than it is like that of rural southern women.

In the case of large cities over the 100,000 limit, 96 percent of the total native white and 97 percent of the total Negro population live in places for which the index of reproduction is below the replacement level. The remaining 4 percent of the native white population resides in Salt Lake City, Flint, Knoxville, and Gary; the remaining 3 percent of the Negro population is located in southern New England. Among northern cities, if we exclude consideration of cities of more than 100,000 inhabitants, the reproduction rate per generation is highest in the native white urban population of Indiana and Michigan. Only in Utah and North Carolina is the fertility of native white women above the permanent replacement level in all sizes of cities, as classified in this section.

The native white rural-farm populations in Utah, North Carolina, and West Virginia are characterized by a reproductive rate sufficient to double their numbers in about 30 years if there were no emigration. Only in Maryland, Virginia, and North Carolina is fertility as high as this among Negro women. Among rural-farm women of both races in all parts of the Nation, however, fertility is considerably above permanent replacement needs. The only exception is Connecticut, where the reproduction rate of the native white farm population is practically unity.

The reproduction rate of the rural-nonfarm population is appreciably lower than that of the rural-farm population, both for native whites and for Negroes, but it is only among Negro females that it falls below unity in any part of the country. Even in Arkansas and Mississippi the fertility of rural-nonfarm Negro women is below the permanent replacement level. A considerable proportion of the rural-nonfarm population lives within a short distance of large cities and is directly influenced by urban conditions.

Among both whites and Negroes, fertility is highest in the South and lowest on the Pacific coast and in Illinois, New York, New Jersey, and southern New England. Although fertility is also high among native white women living in the Northwest, it is low among Negro women in all parts of the Nation except in the coastal States from Virginia to Louisiana, excluding Florida. In all States where there is a sufficient number of Negro women to make fertility rates reliable, the net fertility of native white females exceeds that of Negro females. The fact that the reproduction rates of the native white and Negro populations are practically identical for the entire country is due to the geographical concentration of the latter in the rural areas of the South. If Negroes continue to leave the farm for the city, their net fertility may soon fall distinctly below that of the native white population. (See figs. 13 and 14.)

These differentials in fertility among communities classified by size would change radically the present distribution of population

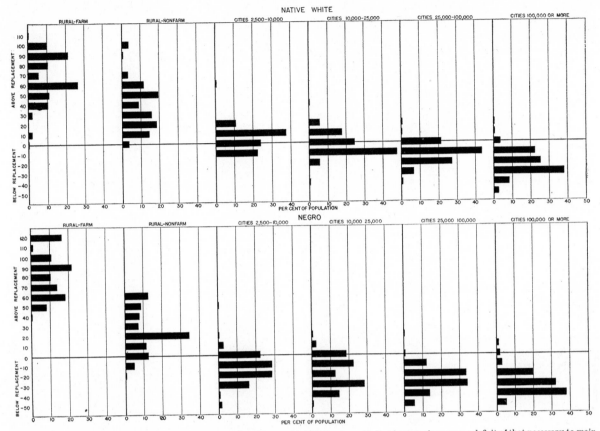

FIGURE 13.—Percentage of population in communities of different size with fertility at specified percentages in excess or deficit of that necessary to maintain the population permanently, 1930 (in determining the percentage of population in any fertility class, cities of 100,000 or more were taken as a unit; for other communities, each State was taken as a unit).

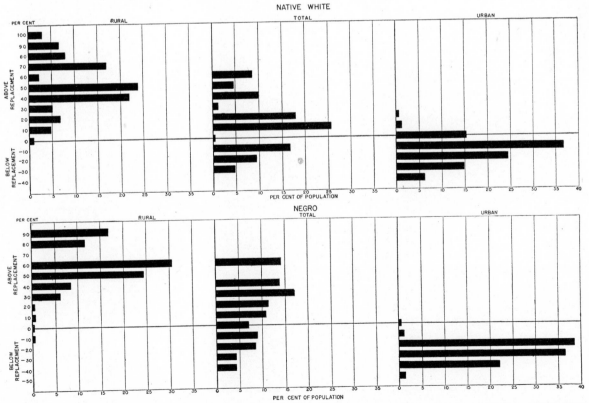

FIGURE 14.—Percentage of total population with fertility at specified percentages in excess or deficit of that necessary to maintain the population permanently, 1930 (in determining the percentage of population in any fertility class, each State was taken as a unit).

within the course of two or three generations, unless large numbers of people migrated from one community to another. Without migration, the population of the large cities would soon begin to decrease. It has been argued that this time is still in the future and that meanwhile the number of births far exceeds the number of deaths. But this is not entirely true. At the present time the number of recorded white deaths is about equal to the number of recorded white births in California and Nevada. In 1932 and 1933, the only years for which the requisite data are available at present, more deaths than births occurred in one-third of the counties of New York State, when nonresident deaths and births were allocated to place of residence. Even during the next generation a continued increase in the urban population is dependent upon migrants from rural territory.

4. Regional Variations in Fertility in Relation to Levels of Living

From foregoing sections in this chapter it is clear that regional differences in fertility are associated with variations in nativity, race, and urbanization. Another condition intimately related to regional differences in fertility is the general plane of living. The importance of economic status as a factor in the fertility of families is discussed in the following chapter. Comparisons will be made here only between regional variations in fertility and in level of living. These variations, especially as they affect the distribution of farm population, are of considerable importance in formulating and administering agricultural programs. At present the Government is trying to retire as rapidly as possible land which is not adapted to farming. But if the population in marginal farm lands is increasing more rapidly than families can be removed through resettlement, and if there is little spontaneous migration, governmental efforts will be ineffective.

In this analysis two indices of economic opportunity are employed. Each uses the county as a unit and is presented for the broad geographic areas used in the preceding chapters. The first is the plane-of-living index developed by the Study of Population Redistribution The second is based on the proportion of farms in each county that should no longer be used for crops, according to estimates prepared by the Resettlement Administration.

The Relation of Fertility to Plane of Living

Fertility declines rapidly as the level of living rises in all regions of the United States.[8] For the United States as a whole, fertility in

[8] Fertility is measured by the number of children under 5 per 1,000 women aged 20–44 in the total population, expressed as a percentage above or below the number necessary to maintain the population permanently. For a description of the index of economic level used here, see ch. II above.

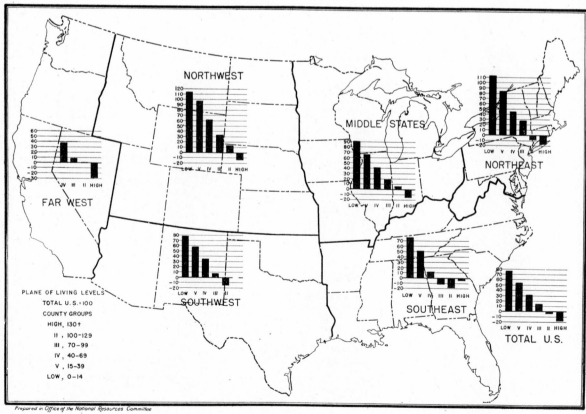

FIGURE 15.—Net reproduction rate per generation in groups of counties classified by plane of living (number of children under 5 per 1,000 women aged 20–44 as a percentage in excess or deficit of the number needed to maintain the population permanently).

the poorest areas is 77 percent in excess of that necessary to replace permanently the population in those areas (fig. 15). This stands in contrast to a deficit of 17 percent in the areas with the highest level of living.

In the entire Far West fertility is as low as it is in areas of the highest economic level for the entire country. This is due partly to the fact that a larger proportion of the population lives in cities than in any other region except the Northeast; but even in the rural parts of this region fertility is just at the replacement level. However, even though the general level of fertility is considerably lower than in the rest of the country, the same inverse relationship between fertility and economic level holds true. On the average, fertility is more than 25 percent above that necessary to maintain the population permanently throughout the Southeast and the Southwest, but even in these regions it is well below replacement needs in counties with higher levels of living.

Even when the counties are classified by density of population, in order to differentiate rural and urban areas, an inverse relationship between fertility and level of living prevails in the most sparsely settled as well as in the most densely populated sections, although the general level of fertility is higher in the former.

Fertility in Problem Farming Areas

The Resettlement Administration has compiled a list of counties in which all or a part of the land now in crops should be transferred to stock raising, forestry, recreation, or other conservational uses. These counties have been grouped into three classes on the basis of the percentage of farms which should be transferred from agricultural to other uses: (*a*) Less than 20 percent, (*b*) 20–59 percent, and (*c*) 60 percent and over.

Except in the Far West, fertility rises with increases in the percentage of farms which should be retired from agriculture. (See fig. 16.) The only exception to this general statement is found in the Far West; but here the data are inconclusive, since there is a very small population in those areas where 60 percent or more of the farms should be transferred from agriculture to other uses. The conclusion that fertility is highest among women living on the poorest farms is corroborated by a comparison of the ratio of children to women in problem areas with comparable ratios for the farm population living outside these areas, but in the same regions. Fertility is uniformly greater in the problem areas, again with the exception of the far West. The difference ranges from 6 percent in the South-

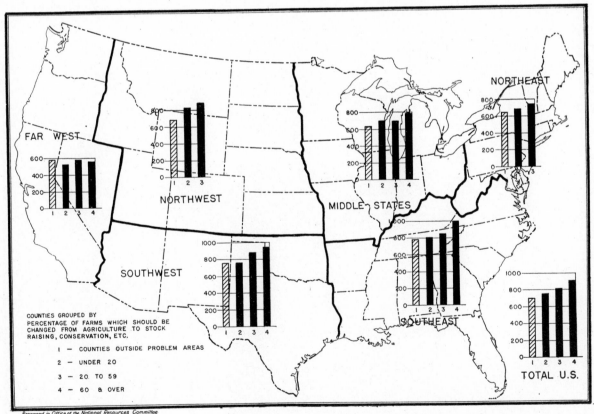

FIGURE 16.—Number of children under 5 per 1,000 rural-farm women aged 20–44 in agricultural problem areas, by regions, 1930.

east to 22 percent in the Northwest. In the far West the ratio of children to farm women is 8 percent less in problem areas than in better agricultural counties. This is probably due to the settlement of large families, especially Mexicans, on the fertile fruit and vegetable farms where there is need for a large amount of hand labor. For the country as a whole, the ratio of children to farm women is 10 percent higher in problem than in nonproblem areas. The difference is small (5 percent) in counties where less than 20 percent of the farms should be retired from agriculture, but it rises to 26 percent in counties where three-fifths or more of all farms are so listed.

For the period represented by these statistics (1925–29), the number of children in the entire problem area exceeds by 80 percent the number necessary to maintain the population permanently, as compared with an excess of 60 percent in the total farm population outside these problem areas. In the very poorest areas there are more than twice as many children as are necessary to maintain the present population. Some reduction in birth rates is expected in all areas, but without considerable emigration the farm population in problem areas will increase rapidly. Present reproductive tendencies would cause a doubling of the farm population in the poorest problem areas in each generation.

Summary

The data presented here, when related to the data on economic variables presented in chapter II, lead inevitably to the conclusion that that part of the Nation most able to support a large number of children has relatively few. On the other hand, the poorer rural areas, with low incomes and levels of living, and consequently with least ability to carry the burden of a large child population, are producing a disproportionate part of future generations. The continuation of present differentials in fertility will increase rather than decrease these economic inequalities.

These facts further emphasize the necessity of a large continuous migration from the less productive agricultural areas, unless the level of living—already far too low—is to be depressed still further. They suggest that, in the long run, changes in fertility may have a profound effect on the distribution and social characteristics of the people of the United States.

V. SOCIAL CONDITIONS AFFECTING BIRTH RATES[1]

KNOWLEDGE of the sources of our natural increase is quite as important as analysis of trends in its size and distribution. The rates at which various groups are contributing to its numbers may have an important bearing on the quality of the future population of the Nation. This statement is not dependent on any theory of biological determinism. For present purposes it is necessary only to admit, as everyone's experience teaches, that the characters and abilities of children are influenced by the social environments into which they are born and in which they are reared. It is therefore desirable to know the variations in reproduction among groups differing in economic status, occupation, education, and intelligence.

1. Economic Conditions and Fertility

Birth Rates of Families on Relief

Students of social welfare problems have long been aware of the frequency of large families among the poor. Popular interest in one aspect of this situation has recently been manifested in concern about the fertility of families supported by public relief. Factual investigations have been consistent in their indications that recipients of relief are more fertile than the general population.[2] These findings have often been misinterpreted as meaning that birth rates increase after families go on relief. Actually, no basis for such a conclusion is found in any studies thus far made on this subject, because they have supplied no comparisons of birth rates of the same families before and during the receipt of relief. There is little doubt that the apparently high fertility of those on relief is partly due to the readier extension of public support to large families

and to those with a newly born or expected child. Stouffer found, however, that the higher fertility of relief families persisted when the analysis was confined to births occurring 9 months or more after the receipt of relief, and when comparison with nonrelief families was carried out within the same broad occupational groups. It is quite possible that the higher fertility after receipt of relief is associated with higher fertility of these same families before application for relief. It is probable that these studies simply reveal, in accentuated form, the general relation between poverty and high fertility.

Birth Rates in Relation to Rental Value of Homes

That fertility rates are generally higher in the underprivileged groups than in the higher income groups has been found consistently, regardless of whether the index of economic status is income, rents paid by single families, or average rentals in given areas.[3] Expenditures for rent afford a generally satisfactory index of economic status and in certain large cities information on this subject can be secured from census tract data. That birth rates are higher in areas of low rental than in areas of high rental is illustrated by relevant data for the whole of Chicago in the year 1930.[4] For all Chicago there were 16.4 births per 1,000 population during the year 1930. The comparable

[1] Prepared by Clyde V. Kiser through cooperation of the Milbank Memorial Fund.

[2] See Sydenstriker, E., and Perrott, G. St. J., Sickness, Unemployment, and Differential Fertility, *The Milbank Memorial Fund Quarterly*, XII : 126–133 (April 1934).

Stouffer, Samuel A., Fertility of Families on Relief, *Journal of The American Statistical Association*, XXIX : 295–300 (September 1934).

See Notestein, Frank, The Fertility of Populations Supported by Public Relief, *Milbank Memorial Fund Quarterly*, XIV : 37–49 (January 1936).

[3] See Pearl, Raymond, "Some Data on Fertility and Economic Status", *Human Biology*, IV : 525–553 (December 1932).

Sydenstricker, E., and Perrott, G. St. J.: "Sickness, Unemployment, and Differential Fertility", *op. cit.*, 126–133.

Ogburn, William F.: "The Family and its Functions", *Recent Social Trends*, Vol. I (1933), 661–708.

Green, Howard Whipple, *Population Characteristics by Census Tracts. Cleveland, Ohio, 1930*, Plain Dealer, Cleveland.

Whelpton, P. K., "Geographic and Economic Differentials in Fertility", *Annals of the American Academy of Political and Social Science*, 188 : 37–55 (November 1936).

[4] Hitherto unpublished material concerning 1930 birth rates in Chicago according to nativity, color, and median rentals by census tracts is available through the courtesy of Philip M. Hauser, of the Department of Sociology and the Social Science Research Committee of the University of Chicago and the Julius Rosenwald Fund. The National Resources Committee wishes to acknowledge its indebtedness to Mr. Hauser, to members of the Committee, and to the Julius Rosenwald Fund for their generous cooperation in releasing unpublished data. The data were derived from a complete analysis of Chicago birth certificates for the year 1930. Census tract data for 1930 were used for grouping of tracts according to median rentals and for population basis.

rate was 19.7 in tracts with median rentals under $30 and 11.3 in tracts with median rentals of $75 and over. Furthermore, among native whites, foreign whites, and Negroes, considered separately, there was a marked and consistent lowering of fertility with increase of rentals. These contrasts are shown, in more refined form, in figure 1. The values in this diagram represent birth rates per 1,000 women 15–44 years of age, with further standardization to eliminate the influence of varying proportions of older and younger women in different groups. (See also table 1.)

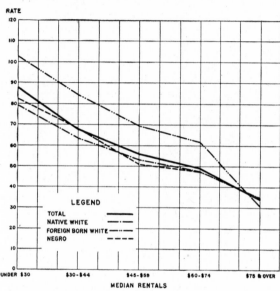

FIGURE 1.—Standardized birth rates per 1,000 women aged 15–44 by nativity, race, and economic status, Chicago, 1930. Data through the courtesy of Mr. Philip M. Hauser, Department of Sociology, University of Chicago.

TABLE 1.—*Standardized birth rates per 1,000 women aged 15–44 by nativity, race, and economic status, Chicago, Ill., 1930* [1]

	City as a whole	Under $30	$30–$44	$45–$59	$60–$74	$75 and over
Total population	60.3	87.8	67.8	56.0	49.1	34.1
Native white	54.9	79.3	63.6	53.0	47.2	34.8
Foreign-born white	75.6	102.8	84.1	69.2	61.4	30.7
Negro	63.0	82.5	68.0	50.8	47.1	(2)

[1] By Philip M. Hauser, Department of Sociology, University of Chicago. The population of Chicago in 1930 used as base for standardization.
[2] Only 5 births were reported to Negroes in census tracts with a median rental of $75 and over.

These materials, supported by studies in other cities, show clearly the negative association between fertility and economic status in American cities at the present time, both for the total population and for each of the main race-nativity groups considered separately. In fact, in spite of the generally higher level of fertility found among the foreign-born, the proportional decline in the fertility of the group with advancing economic status is almost exactly parallel to that of the native groups, except at the top rental classes, where the drop in the fertility of the foreign-born is even more pronounced. The rates for Negroes

are almost the same in each rental area as those for native whites. The standardized birth rate for native whites in low rental areas (less than $30 per month) is slightly higher than that for the foreign-born group as a whole; it is more than twice as high as the corresponding rates for either native or foreign-born whites in areas with average rentals above $75 per month.

2. Occupational Differences in Fertility

Recent Data

It is a well-established fact that in this country, as in other western countries, birth rates in the so-called upper occupational groups are

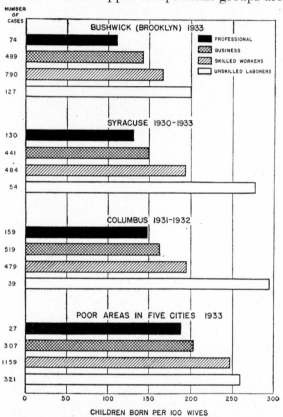

FIGURE 2.—Children born per 100 wives under 45 years of age, according to usual occupation of husband. The rates have been standardized for age; data relate to unbroken unions in which the husbands and wives were native born. The "poor areas" in five cities are the sections covered by the "Health and Depression Survey" in Baltimore, Cleveland, Detroit, Pittsburgh, and Syracuse

lower than those among the laboring classes. Evidence on this point from several surveys carried on since 1930 is presented in figure 2.[5]

[5] The Columbus survey, embracing a total of approximately 3,000 families, was conducted in 1931 by the Milbank Memorial Fund with the help of the department of sociology of the Ohio State University. The Syracuse survey also covered about 3,000 families and was carried on during 1930–33 by the Milbank Memorial Fund, the United States Public Health Service, and the Syracuse Department of Health. The Bushwick survey included a little over 5,000 families and was made in 1933 by the Milbank Memorial Fund with the aid of "white-collar" workers from the New York City Emergency Work and Relief Bureau. The Health and Depression Survey was undertaken in 1933 by the United States Public Health Service with the assistance of the Milbank Memorial Fund. Approximately 1,000 families were visited in each of the five cities represented here.
The rates were standardized by applying the age distribution of samples of 65,070 native white married women under 45 years of age drawn from the 1910 census.
A slightly revised form of the 1920 census occupational manual was used for coding occupations.

In these investigations, the information solicited from each family included basic items such as occupation, nativity, present ages, ages at marriage, and total number of children ever born. On the basis of the husband's usual occupation, the families were classified into four broad occupational groups: (1) Professional, (2) business, (3) skilled, and (4) unskilled. The data are restricted to unbroken unions in which both the husband and wife were native-born whites and in which the wife was under 45 years of age.

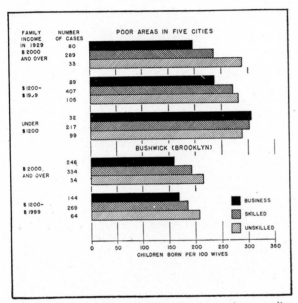

FIGURE 3.—Children born per 100 wives under 45 years of age, according to income of family and occupation of husband. The rates have been standardized for age; data relate to unbroken unions in which the husbands and wives were native-born whites. Incomes relate to 1929.

The numbers in some of the classes are small, but the data are internally consistent and in accord with other investigations. They indicate that urban fertility rises with "lowering" occupational status. In the four surveys the birth rates among unskilled laborers ranged from 38 to 113 percent higher than those of the professional class. The business class and the skilled workers fell between the extremes in a manner consistent with the principle of inverse association between occupational status and fertility.

The largest differences between birth rates of families of professional and manual workers were observed in Syracuse and Columbus. These differences may be somewhat exaggerated due to the small numbers of unskilled laborers involved, but it is noteworthy that in each of these surveys, enumerations included selected areas ranging from university neighborhoods to very poor districts.[6] The differences found in other samples are smaller, but these samples did not include areas of such diverse character. In all of the samples, birth rates were found to vary inversely with occupational status (fig. 2.)

Occupational Differences in Fertility at the Same Income Levels

Within certain limits, at least, there appears to be a persistence of occupational differences in fertility when incomes are virtually the same. This is indicated in figure 3, which presents the birth rates for specified occupational and income groups included in the Bushwick and "Health and Depression" surveys. The similarity in the birth rates among families earning under $1,200 in 1929 suggests the disappearance of occupational differences in fertility when standards of living are uniformly low; however, the numbers involved in these groups are too small for close interpretation. It is also conceivable that occupational differences may decrease among families enjoying very lucrative incomes, but the surveys yielded too few of these families for separate analysis. Due also to small numbers it was necessary to use income groups that are really too broad for sufficient control of the factor of income. In spite of these deficiencies, however, the data at least provide good indications that occupational differences in fertility cannot be resolved entirely into differences in economic status.

Variations in Net Reproduction Rates

While infant and childhood deaths are relatively less frequent in the upper than in the lower urban income groups, these differences are not sufficient to offset the difference in birth rates between these groups. Evidence on this point is available from an analysis of *Birth, Stillbirth, and Infant Mortality Statistics* of 1928 for the United States registration area. This analysis is based on average numbers of children born and average numbers of children living among women who bore children in 1928, grouped according to age of wife and occupation of husband. Since other data indicated that the total nonagricultural workers were just about maintaining their numbers in the years covered by these reports, the estimated net reproduction rate of this group was used as a base, expressed as 1.00.[7] With this system, an index of less than 1.00 for a specific occupational class indicates that the group was not replacing itself under the conditions of its birth and death rates. The results for five nonagricultural classes and for the agricultural class are presented in figure 4, adapted from the data. As expected, the agricultural workers constituted the chief population reservoir. It also appears that urban laborers, especially

---

[6] See Notestein, Frank W., and Kiser, Clyde V., Fertility of the Social Classes in the Native White Population of Columbus and Syracuse, *Human Biology*, 6 : 595–611 (December 1934).

[7] The net reproduction rate was estimated for different occupational groups "on the hypothesis that the difference between the means for numbers of children ever born and for numbers of children living at certain ages of mothers (i. e., 30–39) represents about one-half of the total reproductive loss resulting in each group from deaths of females between birth and completion of the reproductive period." See Lorimer, Frank and Osborn, Frederick, *Dynamics of Population*, New York (1934), 66–75.

the unskilled, were contributing more births than were necessary for replacement even after adjustments were made for losses of offspring through death. It should be remembered that these rates are based upon married women reporting births in a given year, so the rates take into account neither differences in proportions married nor differences in proportions of childless women. Other data based upon all females of childbearing age show the reproduction index of agricultural workers as about 1.62. The reproductive rates of both white-collar groups were below replacement needs. The professional classes were replacing their numbers only to the extent of approximately 75 percent.

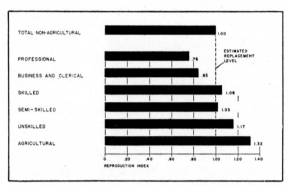

FIGURE 4.—Estimated net reproduction rates per generation of broad occupational classes. Adapted from Lorimer and Osborn, *Dynamics of Population.*

Analysis of Fertility by Occupation and by Type of Community

That differences in birth rates by occupational classes have been of long-standing duration is indicated by the Milbank Memorial Fund's analyses of large samples of relevant data drawn from the original enumeration schedules of the 1910 and 1900 censuses.[8] The sample extracted from the 1910 census consisted of fertility records and other data for approximately 100,000 married women, of whom approximately 60,000 were urban residents and 40,000 were dwellers in rural areas.[9] The records selected were limited to those for unbroken unions in which both the husband and wife were native white of native parentage. The sample was further restricted to northern and western areas, the urban women being secured from 33 selected cities of 100,-

[8] In the enumerations of 1900 and 1910, but not in later censuses, the enumerators asked of each married woman the total number of children she had ever borne. Occupations of husbands and other relevant facts were also available, so these data were excellent for the analysis of differences in birth rates by occupational classes. Since the Bureau of the Census never tabulated these data for such purposes, the Milbank Memorial Fund transcribed and analyzed a large sample from the 1910 census records. Later the same organization assisted in securing similar data from the 1900 census returns.

[9] See Sydenstricker, Edgar, and Notestein, Frank W., "Differential Fertility According to Social Class," *Journal of the American Statistical Association* XXV; 9–32 (March 1930).

000 to 500,000 population and the rural women from districts surrounding these cities.

As seen in figure 5, the rural women were considerably more fertile than the urban women, but there were marked internal differences within each group. The total rural rate of 260 children born per 100 wives of child-bearing age was 63 percent higher than the urban rate. Within the rural sample the farm laborers were most fertile. The rate observed among them was 299 children per 100 wives, a rate which was 21 percent higher than that exhibited by farm owners, the least fertile rural class.

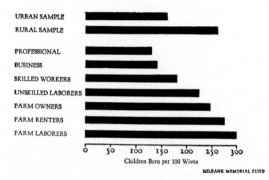

FIGURE 5.—Children born per 100 rural and urban wives under 45 years of age according to occupational status of husband. Data drawn from the 1910 Census. From Notestein, F. W., "The Relation of Social Status to Fertility of Native-Born Married Women in the United States," *Problems of Population,* edited by Pitt-Rivers, London, 1932, p. 153.

Within the urban sample the rate for the unskilled laborers was 73 percent higher than that for the least fertile, the professional class. Birth rates for the business and skilled classes fell in intermediate positions. In 1910, therefore, the order was the same as that revealed in the more recent data discussed above. Unfortunately, there is no decisive evidence as to whether these differentials have been diminishing or increasing in recent decades.

Since birth rates are generally lower in large cities than in small urban communities, a question arises about the relative extent of occupational differences in fertility in communities of varying size. A fairly precise comparison, by size of community, of the order and spread of occupational classes with respect to fertility is afforded by 1900 census data. These data relate to 42,000 native white married women living in communities of varying size in the East North Central States. In figure 6 the number of children born per 100 wives of childbearing age is shown according to occupation in metropolitan, moderately urban, village, and rural communities. Despite the decrease in the fertility of each occupational group with increase in size of community, the relative differences between the classes are fairly constant. This similarity in the order and spread of the rates in the three types of communities is better illustrated by figure 7, which reveals proportionate rather than absolute differences in the fertility of specific occupational groups.

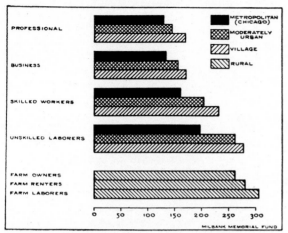

FIGURE 6.—Children born per 100 wives under 45 years of age, by type of community and occupation of husband. Rates are standardized for age; data relate to samples drawn from the 1900 Census; unbroken unions in which the husbands and wives were native whites of native parentage. From Kiser, "Fertility of Social Classes in Various Types of Communities of the East North Central States in 1900", *Journal of the American Statistical Association*, December 1932.

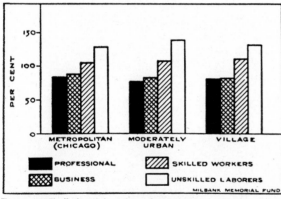

FIGURE 7.—Similarity of the order and spread of birth rates for occupational classes in different types of communities. The standardized birth rate for native white wives under 45 years of age in each occupational class is shown as a percentage of that for all classes combined in the same communities. See Kiser, *op. cit.*

Variations in the Frequency of Childless and of Very Large Families

Variations in proportions of childless and of very large families are of particular interest in a discussion of occupational differences in fertility. Notestein ascertained such variations for approximately 19,000 native white married women who were 40–49 years of age at the time of the 1910 census.[10] In these virtually completed families approximately 16 percent of the urban wives, as compared with only 9 percent of the rural wives, had borne no child. (See fig. 8.) Within the urban class the proportion of childlessness extended from about 18 percent in the professional class

---

[10] Notestein, Frank W., "The Differential Rate of Increase Among the Social Classes of the American Population," *Social Forces*, XII : 20, 21 (October 1933).

to 14 percent among unskilled laborers. In the rural sample 10 percent of the wives of farm owners and 7 percent of the wives of farm laborers were without children. However, rural-urban and occupational differences in fertility are due not so much to variations in proportions of childlessness as to differences in proportions of large families. Mothers of five or more children constituted 39 percent of the rural wives 40–49 years of age and only 17 percent of the city-dwelling women of these ages. Families prolific to the extent of five or more children were observed among half of the farm laborers, among about one-third of the farm owners and urban unskilled laborers, but among only one-tenth of the professional families.

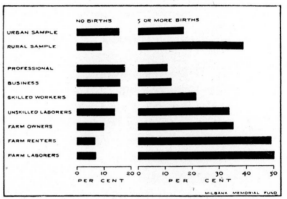

FIGURE 8.—Percentage of wives 40–49 years of age who have borne no child and percentage having borne five or more children, by rural-urban residence and occupation of husband. Data from 1910 Census; unbroken unions in which the husbands and wives were native whites of native parentage. See Notestein, "The Differential Rate of Increase among the Social Classes of the American Population", *Social Forces*, October 1933.

Significance of Differences in Age at Marriage

Differences in age at marriage account for part, but by no means all, of the occupational differences in total number of children born. Figure 9 shows the most frequent ages at marriage, based on the 1910 census material, for women who were under 40 years of age and had been married 5 to 10 years at the time of the census. In general, the urban women married later in life than the rural women, but wives of urban skilled and unskilled laborers married somewhat earlier than did those of farm owners. It is possible that there are some differences between occupational classes in the proportion who never marry, but there is no adequate information on this point. Nevertheless, it is significant that within both the urban and rural classes the age at marriage advances with rising occupational status.

The bearing of these differences in age at marriage on occupational differences in fertility is indicated in figure 10. In this chart is shown the number of children ever born per 100 wives of specified occupation by age at marriage. The inverse association between occupational status and birth rates was most marked among women who married at the youngest ages. When representatives of each occupational class were restricted to those who married at 25 or later, differences in the fertility of the urban classes disappeared. There is even the suggestion that women of the professional and business class who married at the age of 25 or later were more fertile than wives of laborers who married at the same ages. This reversal of occupational differences in fertility as one proceeds from early to late ages at marriage appears to indicate that even prior to 1910 there was deliberate and effective control of fertility in the young marriages in the higher income groups. At all events it is clear that the higher fertility in the laboring classes was due only in part to younger ages at marriage. Early marriages in the higher income brackets were considerably less fertile than early marriages among the laboring classes.

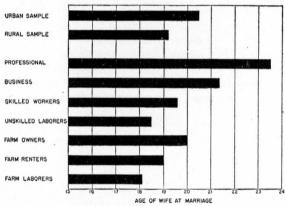

FIGURE 9.—Most frequent (modal) age at marriage of women in urban and rural areas, by occupational status of husbands. Data from 1910 Census relating to women under 40 years of age at marriage who had been married 5–10 years at the time of the 1910 enumeration. Unbroken unions in which the husbands and wives were native born of native parentage. See Notestein, "The Relation of Social Status to Fertility in the United States of America", in *Problems of Population*, 1932.

Summary

In summary, the chief points to be emphasized in this section are as follows:

1. As a class the total farm population is supplying about 60 percent more births than are necessary for replacement. As shown in the previous chapter, this excess is not uniformly distributed in all sections of the farm population, but the highest fertility rates are found in areas with low farm values. The occupational analysis shows that, as a class, the farm owners are less fertile than farm renters and considerably less fertile than farm laborers.

2. Although the total nonfarm population may be just about reproducing itself, there are marked internal differences in urban fertility levels. The rates of the professional class are lowest; those of unskilled laborers are highest. According to data drawn from 1928 birth registration reports, the professional and business

class rates ranged from 15 to 25 percent lower than the requirements for population replacement of these groups.

3. The relatively low fertility of urban "white-collar" workers is due in part to later ages at marriage. However, the fact that maximum occupational differences in fertility appear among those who married at the youngest ages would seem to indicate deliberate and effective postponement and limitation of births among younger couples in the higher income groups.

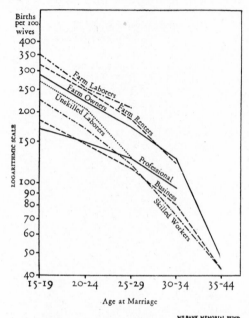

FIGURE 10.—Number of children born per 100 wives under 45 years of age, by age of wife at marriage for each urban and rural occupational class. Data from 1910 Census; unbroken unions in which the husbands and wives were native whites of native parentage. Rates calculated on the assumption of a standard duration-of-marriage distribution for each age-at-marriage group. From Notestein, *op. cit.*

3. Education and Fertility

There is evidence that in the United States, as in other western countries, married couples with little or no schooling have more children, on the average, than those with a moderate or considerable amount of education. On the other hand, the inverse association between education and fertility is not a rigid one. There are indications that, after certain levels of formal education are attained, further schooling has little effect upon fertility when other social factors are held constant.

The average birth rates of illiterates generally appear to be higher than those of literates. The Canadian census, with data bearing on this point, shows that in 1921 the average number of children (not births) per family was slightly higher among illiterates than among literates in seven of the nine provinces of the Dominion.[11] Quebec and Prince Edward Is-

---

[11] *Sixth Census of Canada*, 1921, III: 94–102, Population. For further discussion of these data, see Lorimer and Osborn, *op. cit.*, 315–316.

land were the only two separate areas failing to indicate this type of relation.

An analysis of 1920 census figures for the United States on percentages of illiteracy, number of children under 15, and number of women 15–54 years of age, by States, who had been married or were married, led to the following conclusion:

"The correlation between fertility, as measured here, and illiteracy is +0.62±0.06, the relationship being linear. This is interpreted as meaning that illiterates have larger families, on the average, than do the literate." [12]

A study of the census tract data for Chicago in 1934 shows a high negative correlation ($r=-0.73$) between education (as indicated by average grade completed by persons in each neighborhood) and fertility (as measured by ratio of children to women). The negative correlation between education and fertility thus obtained was higher than that between rental value of homes and fertility, according to a recent paper by Richard O. Lang on "Population Characteristics Associated with Educational Levels and Economic Status in Chicago" (read at a joint meeting of the American Statistical Association and the American Sociological Society in Chicago, Dec. 29, 1936).

A comparison of fertility rates for families classified according to the education of the husband is shown in table 2 and figure 11 for sample populations of native-born white married couples in certain occupational classes. The rates presented here have been standardized for age. Two points are worth noting: (1) The groups with common school or less education were consistently and conspicuously more fertile than the high school and college groups in each area and within each occupational group; (2) within each occupational group there was little difference between the

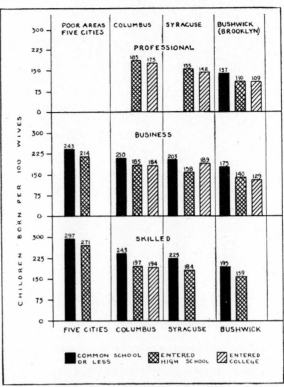

FIGURE 11.—Number of children ever born per 100 wives of all ages, by occupational and educational status of husbands; selected areas of several cities. Data drawn from field surveys conducted between 1930 and 1933; unbroken unions in which the husbands and wives were native-born whites. The "poor areas" were those referred to in Figure 2.

high school and college groups with respect to fertility.[13] It may be that, under our present systems of education and economy, high school education is sufficient to inculcate desires for those standards of living that are more likely to be attained with a limited family.

Other investigations confirm the foregoing indications that after high school the factor of continued education, in itself, has little influ-

[12] Winston, Sanford R., "The Relation of Certain Social Factors to Fertility," *American Journal of Sociology*, XXXV, 758 (March 1930). Strictly, the data indicate that birth rates of native whites are higher in States having high percentages of illiteracy among native white women 15–54 years of age. However, the conclusion as stated is in accord with results of other investigations.

[13] While not shown on the chart, the differences between the high school and college groups, when all occupational classes are combined, appear to be relatively insignificant compared with those between the high school and common school groups. See Notestein, Frank W., and Kiser, Clyde V., "Factors Affecting Variations in Human Fertility," *Social Forces*, XIV: 34–35 (October 1935).

TABLE 2.—*Birthrates by occupational and educational status of husbands among native whites in Columbus, Syracuse, Bushwick (Brooklyn), and in poor areas of 5 cities* [1]

Social class	Columbus			Syracuse			Bushwick (Brooklyn)			5 public health cities [2]		
	Common school or less	Entered high school	Entered college	Common school or less	Entered high school	Entered college	Common school or less	Entered high school	Entered college	Common school or less	Entered high school	Entered college
Births per 100 wives standardized for age:												
Professional	(3)	185	175	(3)	155	142	137	110	109	(3)	(3)	(3)
Business	210	185	184	203	158	189	175	140	129	243	214	(3)
Skilled	243	197	194	225	184	(3)	195	159	(3)	297	271	(3)
Number of wives:												
Professional	(3)	56	195	(3)	56	136	43	32	37	(3)	(3)	(3)
Business	274	440	186	184	354	100	539	198	44	208	160	(3)
Skilled	444	281	34	419	256	(3)	1,107	147	(3)	1,192	275	(3)

[1] The data relate to marriages in which husbands and wives were native whites.
[2] The 5 public health cities are Baltimore, Cleveland, Detroit, Pittsburgh, and Syracuse.
[3] Insufficient data.

ence on marital fertility. A recent study of questionnaires supplying information concerning 475 college women and 461 noncollege women "of the same walk of life" indicated that the average numbers of children per marriage for the two groups were 1.56 and 1.72, respectively, for college and noncollege groups.[14] The small difference observed appeared to be due entirely to somewhat later marriages of the college group. In fact, slightly higher rates were observed among the college group when the comparison was based upon average number of births per year of married life. That these findings do not represent a new situation is indicated by the fact that approximately the same results were secured from a similar type of investigation conducted in 1900.[15]

On the other hand, it should be emphasized that while college education appears to have little direct influence on marital fertility, the marriage frequencies of college women are well below the general average. The 1930 Census shows that 90.4 percent of all women 40–44 years of age were, or had been, married. Reliable studies of graduates of several well-known colleges indicate that the proportion of college women who eventually marry ranges from only 50 to 75 percent. In their analysis of this problem, however, Lorimer and Osborn cite evidence indicating that recent women graduates are marrying more frequently than their predecessors. Among 151 Vassar alumnae who graduated in 1876 and supplied family records in 1919 (when their average age was about 65), only 56 percent had ever been married. Among 951 who graduated in 1916 and supplied information in 1929 (when the average age was about 35), almost three-fourths reported themselves as having been married.[16] It is possible that this increase arises in part from the widening appeal of women's colleges, whereas a generation or two ago college attendance by women was more restricted to aspirants for academic careers. In contrast to those of college women, the marriage frequencies of college men appear to be almost as high as those in the general male population.

In summary, the question of the association between education and reproduction should be considered from the standpoint of marital fertility and frequency of marriage. Marital fertility rates seem to be generally higher among illiterates than among literates in this country, and higher among common school groups than among high school groups. However, the birth-rate differences between high school and college groups appear to be very slight. In one investigation the slightly lower average number of children born to married graduates

of women's colleges as compared with noncollege wives of similar social status was found to be due entirely to somewhat later age at marriage among the college women. This smaller difference is considerably increased by the tendency toward somewhat less frequent marriages of college women, but the difference between marriage rates of college and noncollege women has been decreasing.

4. Intelligence and Fertility

Statement of Problem

Popular interest in the question of the relation between birth rates and intelligence arises from the fact that intelligence, like health, is universally accepted as a desirable individual and social goal. There is, however, much disagreement about the manner in which mental ability is transmitted from one generation to another. This disagreement arises in large part from a lack of knowledge concerning the nature of mental ability and the conditions that influence its development. Recent research, however, has contributed toward greater precision of knowledge concerning component parts of mental abilities and aptitudes.[17] For present purposes, it is unnecessary to assess the relative roles of environment and heredity to recognize that the rate of reproduction according to intelligence has bearing on the social and cultural complexion of our population. The influence of home environment on the intellectual development of children affords a sufficient reason for attention to the sources of population replacement, apart from the consideration of possible hereditary influences.

Recent attempts to provide unbiased data on the question of the association between intelligence and birth rates have usually proceeded by correlating intelligence test scores of school children with sizes of families from which those children come. The justification of this method hinges upon the adequacy of tests as measures of intelligence and upon the relation between the intelligence of parents and that of their children. Apart from assumptions about the relative importance of biological and cultural factors in the ability to score high in an intelligence test, it is reasonable to accept the supposition that the standard tests do provide gages of "cultural-intellectual" status if they are administered and interpreted with care. This position is confirmed by their usefulness in educational and occupational placement.

The value of studies of the relation between intelligence and fertility would be considerably enhanced if extensive data were available on intelligence ratings of the adult population supplemented by records of fertility. For obvious reasons, however, it has been more feas-

[14] Goodsell, Willystine, "The Size of Families of College and Non-College Women," *American Journal of Sociology,* XLI: 585–597 (March 1936).
[15] Smith, Mary Roberts, "Statistics of College and Non-college Women," *Quarterly Publications of the American Statistical Association* (1900), 7: 1–26.
[16] See Lorimer and Osborn, *op. cit.,* 321–322.

[17] See following chapter.

ible to administer tests to large numbers of school children than to a random sample of adults in the general population. Some justification for relating fertility of parents to intelligence ratings of children is afforded by studies of parent-child resemblance in intelligence. While these studies do not usually show strikingly high correlations, they are consistent in their indication of significant positive association. Such findings are in line with common observation that, despite numerous individual exceptions, mental characteristics tend to cluster in families, whether the basis of intelligence is hereditary, cultural, or both.

Available Evidence

There is much evidence that children making high scores in intelligence tests come on the average from smaller families than do children with low ratings. Figure 12 portrays the results secured by Lentz in an analysis of clinical records, 4,330 children in New York City, St. Louis, and other localities in Connecticut, New Jersey, and Missouri.[18] Children scoring highest, 150 and up, came from families averaging 2.2 children, while those scoring lowest, under 60, came from families averaging a little more than 5.5 children. Since Lentz's data were drawn from widely different areas, it is very likely that such extreme variations are due partly to local, racial, and general social factors. Chapman and Wiggins' analysis of school children from 650 completed families in one area, Meriden, Conn., yielded an average intelligence quotient of 118 among children from two-child families and averages of 106 among five- and six-child families considered separately.[19] These differences were due in part to the factor of nativity. Conrad and Jones reported an absence of association between the number of children born and intelli-

gence ratings of children in village and rural areas of Vermont.[20] It appears, therefore, that much of the relation between intelligence and fertility is associated with cultural conditions.

A further modification of the results shown in figure 12 should be noted. On the basis of a large clinic series studied in Chicago, Thurstone and Jenkins found that while children with moderately low intelligence (intelligence quotients between 50 and 80) came from families well above the average in size, the families with imbeciles or idiots (intelligence quotients less than 50) were no larger on the average than those with children of normal intelligence. (See fig. 13.) At the other end of the scale the results available suggest that among college graduates there is little association between intellectuality, as such, and number of offspring.[21]

Results obtained by the study of variations in intelligence test scores among individuals in different occupational groups are consistent with the major results of the above types of studies already reviewed. We have already noted that birth rates are usually higher in the less privileged groups than in the occupational levels with high educational requirements and larger incomes. Studies of intelligence among adults and among children from different occupational levels usually show that representatives from the higher ranks achieve higher average intelligence scores than those from the lower ranks.[22] Illustrative of the results are those secured by Haggerty and Nash in a study of 6,688 pupils in New York village

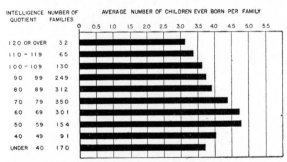

FIGURE 13.—Average size of families classified according to intelligence quotients of children examined at the Institute for Juvenile Research, Chicago. Adapted from data in Thurstone and Jenkins, *Order of Birth, Parent-Age and Intelligence* (University of Chicago Press).

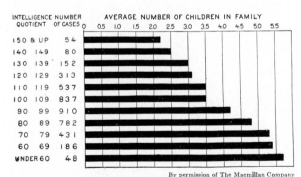

By permission of The Macmillan Company

FIGURE 12.—Distribution of families by size in relation to intelligence quotients of children. School and clinic data for 4,330 cases collected by Lentz. From Lorimer and Osborn, *Dynamics of Population.*

[18] Lentz, Theodore, Jr., Relation of I. Q. to Size of Family, *Journal of Educational Psychology*, 18: 486–496 (October 1927).

[19] Chapman, J. Crosby, and Wiggins, D. M., Relation of Family Size to Intelligence of Offspring and Socio-Economic Status of Family. *Pedagogical Seminary*, 32: 414–421 (September 1925). The negative correlation between parental fertility and intelligence ratings of children dropped from r −.33 for the whole series to r −.22 for variations among the native American families and to r −.24 among the foreign families.

[20] Conrad, H. S., and Jones, Harold E., A Field Study of the Differential Birth Rate, *Journal of the American Statistical Association*, XXVII: 153–159 (June 1932).

[21] For an account of these studies, see Lorimer and Osborn, *op. cit.*, 197.

[22] Haggerty, M. E., and Nash, H. B., "Mental Capacity of Children and Parental Occupation," *Journal of Educational Psychology*, 15: 558–572 (December 1924).

Collins, J. E., "The Intelligence of School Children and Parental Occupation," *Journal of Educational Research*, XVII: 157–169 (March 1928).

Dexter, Emily S., "The Relation Between Occupation of Parent and Intelligence of Children," *School and Society*, XVII; 612–614 (June 2, 1923). The army intelligence scores, though laden with many imperfections, offer a comprehensive body of material concerning intelligence ratings of male adults according to civilian occupations. Intelligence ratings of children in relation to occupation of fathers have frequently been studied. In addition to the Haggerty and Nash study, see, for example, Collins' study of 4,727 urban children in Ohio and Dexter's survey of 2,782 children in Madison, Wis.

and country schools, in which the median intelligence score of professional parents was 116 and that of unskilled laborers was 89.

The measures of mental development used in this section do not refer to hereditary capacity for intellectual development but rather to cultural-intellectual status, which is assumed to be influenced both by genetic factors and by environmental conditions. Evidence as to whether or not intelligence has a bearing on size of family when other factors are held constant is inconclusive. In general it appears that, insofar as intelligence is related to fertility, this factor is intimately merged with cultural conditions. The studies cited show that there is a general tendency for children with inferior cultural-intellectual development to come from larger families than those with superior development as measured by tests. This tendency carries social implications of such importance that they cannot safely be ignored.

5. Factors Underlying Group Differences in Fertility*

Recognition of the existence of differences in fertility among groups leads directly to an appreciation of the importance of understanding the causal conditions underlying these differences. Emphasis upon biological factors [23] had fairly wide currency until recently, and such factors cannot be ignored altogether in accounting for variations in birth rates. There is some evidence, for instance, that stillbirths are more frequent among economically underprivileged classes.[24] The extent of actual sterility in different groups needs investigation and there is need for study of the effect of certain diseases upon reproductive powers in various elements of the population.

Recent investigations, however, have provided conclusive evidence of the major importance of deliberate family limitation and hence of the inadequacy of the biological interpretation of group differences in fertility. Outstanding in this connection is Pearl's investigation of pregnancy histories and reproductive practices of 30,000 women interviewed after confinement in urban hospitals. The records were collected during 1931 and 1932 by physicians and internes. In broad terms the outstanding findings

from a progress report [25] may be briefly stated as follows: (1) The proportion of white women reporting any deliberate efforts at family limitation since marriage extended from only one-third among the "very poor" to over three-fourths among the "well-to-do and rich". (2) Women practicing family limitation most intelligently and consistently had pregnancy rates from 50 to 75 percent below those who reported no such efforts whatsoever. (3) Women who limited their families by similar methods had pregnancy rates of about the same order, regardless of economic status. Among the women who reported no attempts to limit their families since marriage there appeared to be no significant differences in pregnancy rates. This and other bodies of data strongly suggest that voluntary control of family size has been the principal factor in trends and differentials of population change.

Lest the causes for variations in birth rates appear too simple it must be remembered that the deliberate effort to restrict size of family is only a manifestation of underlying attitudes and customs. Back of the means employed to limit births, are the intricate cultural factors which lead some groups, more than others, to adopt such methods. Increasing urbanization has been accompanied by changing attitudes towards the family, and the rise of the small-family pattern has been predominantly an urban phenomenon, closely associated with such factors as urban standards of living, postponement of marriage among certain groups, the gainful employment of women outside of the home, and the diminishing social and economic unity of urban family life. The very prevalence of small families among certain groups may serve to set the "norm" of family size through the crystallization of attitudes that two or three children are enough. Improvement of educational opportunities and standards of living in poorer regions and among handicapped classes would probably be accompanied by more general family limitation, and by gradual reduction in the disparity between birth rates of different classes. On the other hand, there is little evidence of any forces now at work that seem likely to increase measurably the low birth rates of the more privileged classes in urban centers. Any considerable increase in reproduction in these groups will probably depend on quite profound changes in economic and social relations, and on changes in social philosophy, outlook and interests.

---

*This section has been put in at the request of the author in substitution for what appeared in the first printing.

[23] For a strictly biological point of view, see: Gini, Corrado, "The Cyclical Rise and Fall of Population." *Population* (Lectures on the Harris Foundation). Chicago (1929), 3–140. For a modified biological interpretation, see: Hankins, F. H., "Has the Reproductive Power of Western Peoples Declined?" Pitt-Rivers, G. H. L. F. (Ed.) *Problems of Population*, London (1932), 181–188.

[24] Woodbury, Robert Morse, "Causal Factors in Infant Mortality." United States Department of Labor, Children's Bureau Publication No. 142, Washington, D. C. (1925), 173.

[25] Pearl, Raymond, "Contraception and Fertility in 4,945 Married Women. A Second Report on a Study of Family Limitation," *Human Biology*, VI, 355–401 (May 1934). For related studies see Stix, R. K., and Notestein, F. W., "Effectiveness of Birth Control," *Milbank Memorial Fund Quarterly*, XIII; 162–178 (April 1935) and Stix, R. K., and Wiehl, Dorothy G., "Abortion and the Public Health." *American Journal of Public Health*, XXVIII; 621–628 (May 1938).

VI. PHYSICAL CHARACTERISTICS
AND BIOLOGICAL INHERITANCE

1. Introduction

In the earlier chapters attention has been directed to the numerical aspects of population change and the relation of numbers to economic resources. In passing from the consideration of mere numerical changes in total population to consideration of the potentialities of and opportunities for the human resources of the United States, we enter a field of greater difficulty, though perhaps of greater importance.

Biological and Environmental Factors Always Operate in Conjunction

In considering the qualitative effects of population changes, it is important to bear in mind that the characteristics of groups, as well as those of individuals, are affected at all points both by biological inheritance and by environmental influences. It has been shown by physical anthropologists that the physical traits usually considered most fixed, and therefore the best indexes of race, may be considerably modified by environmental influences. Boas has demonstrated that Americans derived from different immigrant stocks differ significantly in bodily form from the parent stocks from which they are derived. Bowles has shown that young men graduating from Harvard in recent years are 2 inches taller on the average than those graduating 60 years ago, and that corresponding differences appear in other bodily dimensions. Such changes are also found when the measurements of individual students are compared with the measurements of their fathers. Similar changes in stature have been revealed in other studies of college students in America, and in studies of army conscripts in several countries. Since it is possible that these changes may be due in part to unrecognized hereditary factors, Bowles is careful to avoid a dogmatic limitation to environmental causes. Nevertheless, such studies strongly suggest the influence of environmental factors on traits that might be supposed to be most fixed by inheritance.

The extensive influence of social heritage in the determination of intelligence and personality traits has been even more clearly established. It is important to recognize that no direct measurements of capacity for intellectual development or of biological factors in personality development have yet been devised. Intelligence tests and personality inventories measure developed traits. Studies of the influence of heredity and environment on intelligence and character must proceed through inferences based on the relation of variations in developed traits to degrees of kinship and environmental conditions.

Caution Necessary in Discussing Relative Importance of These Factors

It is impossible to overstate the need for caution in forming conclusions about the relative influence of genetic and social factors in human development. It is, however, clear that family influences bulk very large among the environmental factors, so that where scientific analysis points to the importance of cultural influences in producing effects formerly ascribed to heredity, it sometimes merely shifts attention from the biological influence of families to social heritage transmitted through families. The caution against hasty generalization applies equally to broad assumptions regarding the importance of environmental factors and to assumptions regarding the force of heredity.

The influence of hereditary and environmental factors on health and on physical development will receive some attention in this and the following chapters. It would be impossible in so brief an account to give a definitive statement of so complex a problem, but an attempt will be made to sketch in broad outlines some of the principles established through biological and medical research, and to gain some insight into the possibilities for improving the health and longevity of the people of the United States. A general survey of the principles of genetics will be introduced as providing an essential basis for the scientific treatment of this topic.

It may be stated in advance that hereditary influences are often concealed in their operation, for reasons that will be discussed below. Furthermore, the interrelations of hereditary and environmental factors are very complex. Experimental studies with animals within the same species have demonstrated hereditary differences in resistance to diseases that are known to be due to bacterial or parasitic infections. Similarly, considerable evidence has been accumulated to show differences in hereditary susceptibility to tuberculosis in man, although it is well known that the primary cause of this disease is bacterial infection and that the control of the milk supply and sanitary conditions results in spectacular decreases in its frequency. It is probable that both hereditary and environmental factors may be involved in many common diseases, such as cancer and various mental disorders, but the exact role of different causes is still obscure in most cases.

The improved control of disease and the elimination of disabling defects depends upon increased knowledge of causes. The practical significance of results to be expected from biological and medical research concerning the relative effects of heredity and enviroment on health is likely to be broader than might at first appear. In some instances, serious defects or diseases may be found to be due to hereditary factors for which no environmental alleviation or control is possible. In other instances, as in the case of hemophilia (failure of the blood to clot, leading to excessive bleeding), some alleviation is possible, but the known hereditary character of this defect and its serious consequences strongly suggest the desirability of attempts to eradicate it by control of inheritance. In the case of many diseases, hereditary factors are of wholly negligible importance in comparison with environmental causes. In still other cases, and the number of these cases is probably far greater than is generally supposed, an exact knowledge of hereditary factors may be of great importance in directing medical attention to the prevention of diseases in the individuals most susceptible to their attack.

2. Physical Characteristics of Racial Stocks and Geographic Groups

The range of variations in physical traits among American groups is illustrated by data on height, weight, and chest circumference. Such indices are available for the total male population of army age at the time of the World War. The variations among various racial and nationality groups in stature, chest

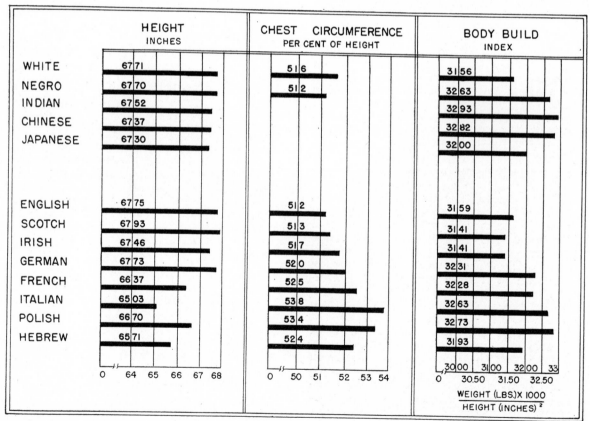

FIGURE 1.—Comparison of height, relative chest circumference and body build index of World War recruits at demobilization, by racial and national groups. From Lorimer and Osborn, *Dynamics of Population.*

circumference relative to height, and bodily build (weight in pounds relative to the scale of height in inches) are shown in figure 1. The variations in stature of drafted men from different States are shown in figure 2. The variation in height among several of the European groups, classified by national origin or religion, is greater than among the major racial groups in the United States. Thus the Italian and Jewish drafted recruits were, on the average, 2 inches shorter than the English, Scotch, or German recruits, whereas the Japanese in this series were on the average only four-tenths of an inch shorter than the whites and Negroes. The latter two races happen to be almost identical in average height.

Physical variations among State populations are strongly influenced by racial composition. This accounts for the grouping of New Jersey, Massachusetts, New York, Pennsylvania, Connecticut, and Rhode Island at one extreme. Inasmuch as Negroes are approximately equal in average stature to whites, the presence of Negro elements in any State population does not cause the average for the total population to differ much from that of the white population alone. The presence of Negroes, however, may lower the average somewhat in the case of a State population composed of old American stock and Negroes, because old Americans—like the English, Scotch, and Germans from whom they are for the most part derived, and like the Scandinavians—are distinctly taller than most of the southern and eastern European peoples.

More detailed studies of particular anatomical and physiological traits have been made in various sample populations representing different racial and regional groups in this country. Some of the most interesting studies are those of Old Americans by Hrdlička, and more recently by Hooton and others. These studies point to a high degree of variability in the so-called Anglo-Saxon stocks. They also afford evidence of the emergence of regional types, capable of being differentiated statistically with regard to average measurements and variability of specific traits. In view of the high mobility of the American population, however, such differentiation of regional types is not likely to have much importance in the visible future.

There is no clear evidence of any important differences between races in "vitality", as defined by Sydenstricker, namely, hereditary capacity for health and longevity, although there is evidence of racial differences in susceptibility to specific diseases. The existence of conspicuous differences between races in sickness case rates and in death rates cannot, of course, be assumed to show differences in hereditary traits—because of the influence of environmental factors, differences in diagnosis and reportage and so forth—except where such influences can be controlled or accurately taken into account.

Studies of the effects on health and mental traits of intermarriage between widely different races are quite inconclusive. There seems to be no substantial evidence that racial intermarriage, as such, between healthy individuals causes any serious biological handicaps, however disturbing the social effects of such marriages may be under present conditions.

Physical anthropology is still a relatively undeveloped science. It is possible that in the future important contributions to population theory may be made by physical anthropologists, in collaboration with students of physiology, genetics, and other fields of biological and social research.

3. Survey of Human Genetics [1]

Since the rediscovery of Mendel's laws at the beginning of the present century, amazing progress has been made in the study of the physical mechanism by which the determiners for hereditary characters are transmitted from one generation to the next in both plants and animals, including man.

The Physical Mechanism of Heredity

The genes, or physical unit-determiners underlying hereditary characters, are linearly ar-

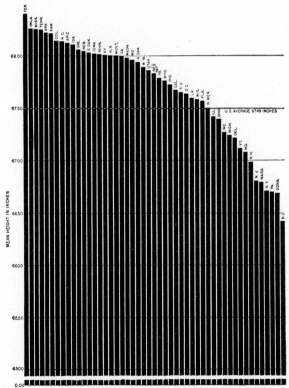

FIGURE 2.—Comparison of mean height of men drafted for the World War, by States.

[1] By Clyde Keeler of Harvard University.

ranged within the chromosomes. The chromosomes themselves are tiny bodies that, when stained, are visible in the nucleus of a cell at the time of cell division. (See fig. 3.) The physical location of genes within the chromosome has been observed in one type of cells, those of the salivary gland of the fruit fly, Drosophila. In this case, detailed predictions, as to physical conditions in a particular region of a particular chromosome, have been confirmed by microscopic examination of chromosome structures.

The chemical formulas of genes are unknown, but they are probably protein in nature. Their size has been calculated to be slightly larger than the estimated size of the hemoglobin molecule. The genes vary structurally. Each brings about a different end-product in the growth or structure of the developing organism. Certain genes are quite stable in chemical constitution, whereas others are relatively mutable. When a particular gene mutates, it usually changes to one of a series of definite physicochemical states called multiple allelomorphs or allels. Rates of mutation for specific genes are fairly constant under a given set of conditions, but the rate of mutation may be increased by subjecting maturing germ cells to treatment with heat, cold, X-rays, or radium.

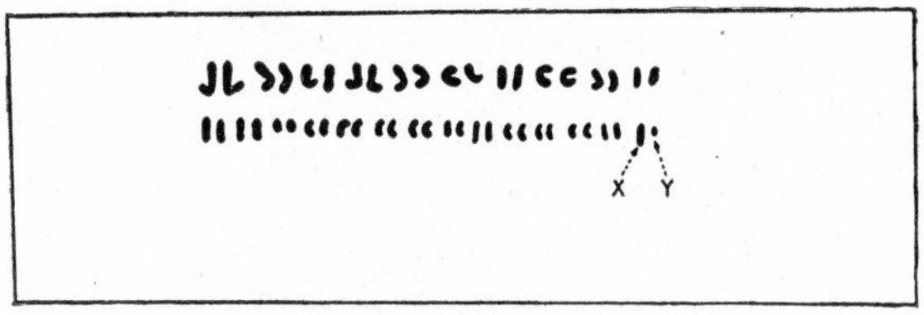

FIGURE 3.—The chromosomes of man.

Two genes residing in the same chromosome are said to be "linked" because they are normally inherited together, but may be separated in case the chromosome breaks between the two genes. In this case a breakage and exchange of parts ("crossing-over") takes place between the chromosome and its mate. The rate of crossing over at given regions in corresponding chromosomes is usually fairly constant, although it may be altered by X-ray radiation, and perhaps by other physical conditions. These discoveries reveal the extreme complexity and the variability of the mechanism of biological inheritance.

Genes are known to affect the development of different kinds of tissues in all parts of the body. The reaction of the same gene in different individuals is constant in that it produces identical effects upon particular types of development at a definite point in the life history of the individual, and in a particular group of cells, except as its effect is modified by the external environment, or by the presence of other particular genes.

We may detect the presence and effects of a gene only when, as a result of mutation, it is present in at least two alternative forms (allels) whose existence is manifested through producing contrasted characteristics in surviving individuals receiving them. There may always remain a great mass of germplasm that cannot be analyzed into its component genes, because the mutation of any gene within this residuum destroys some necessary cellular life process, and all cells bearing such mutations promptly die.

Müller in 1922 estimated the total number of genes in the fruit fly to be about 4,000 on the basis of number and arrangement of mutated loci. Employing the recently developed technique for studying giant salivary gland chromosomes in Drosophila, Bridges in 1935 enumerated the bands which are thought to correspond to the genes. His count places the number at 5,000 genes, carried in four pairs of chromosomes. Man has 24 pairs of chromosomes, and since gene bands have not been counted in human chromosomes it would be rash to venture a numerical estimate of the myriads of genes which underlie human heritage.

There are normally two of each kind of chromosomes in every cell of which our bodies are made up. One of each pair of chromosomes is contributed by the paternal sperm cell, one by the maternal egg cell. Accordingly, each gene is represented twice in every somatic cell.[2] The individual genes are arranged linearly in the chromosomes, somewhat like beads on a string. When the cells divide, each chromosomal "gene-string" divides by splitting longitudinally, one split half going to each of the two daughter cells, so that the number of genes and chromosomes remains constant. The precise mechanism of egg and sperm maturation[3] provides that but one of each of the chromosome pairs (and hence but one representation of every gene) gets into each germ cell. Each chromosome pair is segregated haphazardly in the maturation of germ cells, so that in any given mating a parent can pass on to his offspring only half of his genetic constitution. This random selection of genes in the formation of germ cells, and the re-pairing of the chromosomes and genes at fertilization, is the basis of Mendelian ratios.

Dominant and Recessive Traits

A few basic Mendelian ratios describe the transmission of simple traits, according to whether the gene determining the character in question is "recessive" or "dominant", and

[2] Referring to body tissues; having 2 sets of chromosomes, 1 set normally coming from the female parent and 1 from the male; as contrasted with germ cells having a single set of chromosomes. *Journal of Heredity Glossary.*
[3] A process which germ cells undergo before they become functional, consisting usually of 2 cell divisions, during which the number of chromosomes is reduced to one-half that of the body cells (*ibid.*).

whether or not it is "sex-linked." [4] Equally specific ratios characterize the expression of characters which are determined by two, three, or many pairs of genes. Thus a ratio of 15 dominants to one recessive is obtained in the second generation of a cross in which the parents differed in a character determined by two recessive genes (two sets of alleles). These multifactorial Mendelian ratios can rarely be demonstrated in the study of human heredity, because they can be detected only in the progeny of controlled matings, where large numbers of progeny may be observed. Nevertheless, such complicated hereditary influences may have major weight in the transmission of the most important human characteristics.

When a normal gene has been received from one parent and its mutated allele from the other, the result may fall into any one of several categories, depending upon the particular pair of allels involved. Frequently the mutant gene appears to rest and do nothing. In this event, should the normal allel be capable of doing the required job alone, an organism that is hybrid for these two allels will develop normally. In this case the mutant gene is said to be recessive to the normal allel.

When germ cells (eggs or sperm) are formed in such a hybrid individual, half of them will contain a representative of the normal gene and half will contain a representative of the recessive mutant gene. So long as this person marries a normal individual producing germ cells all of which contain the normal allel, no one could suspect that lurking in the germ-plasm of half their children is an inactive copy of the mutant gene. This hidden transmission may go on indefinitely, generation after generation. But should two individuals marry, both of whom harbor a copy of the recessive mutant allel, on the average one child, regardless of sex, will receive two normal genes and develop normally, two children will receive a normal gene and a mutant gene and will also develop normally, but a fourth child will receive two mutant genes. In this last child, because both mutant genes loaf on the job, and because there is no normal allel to do their work, their specific task remains undone, and an abnormal characteristic results. (See fig. 4).

Where blood relatives marry, there is more opportunity for such unsuspected recessive characters to come to the surface, the mutant gene having been received latently by both parents from a common ancestral source. This explains the fact that certain hereditary defects may appear more frequently in inbred strains. But, except where such lurking hereditary defects exist, inbreeding does not cause any harmful effects.

A large proportion of the genetic factors which condition the development of common pathological characteristics are of this type. Pedigrees of families with albinism illustrate the nature of the simple recessive transmission of a definite trait.

Often, however, a mutant gene is of such a nature that it does not remain inactive but produces harmful effects, in which case nothing that the normal gene can do by working along its prescribed lines can correct the damage. Since the presence of such an active abnormal gene cannot be hidden, it is said to be dominant to its normal allel.

Persons hybrid for a dominant gene (see fig. 5) form germ cells, half of which contain the mutant gene and half the normal allel. If such a person marries a normal individual, as is usually the case, half of the children, regardless of sex, will receive a normal gene from both parents and develop normally, whereas the other half will receive a normal gene from the normal parent and the dominant mutant gene from the abnormal parent, and hence will develop the latter's abnormality. Hereditary cataract, cause of the greatest proportion of hereditary blindness, otosclerosis, which brings about most hereditary deafness, and achondroplasia (which produces dwarves with relatively normal-sized bodies but with very short arms and legs) are, in many instances at least, transmitted through dominant genes.

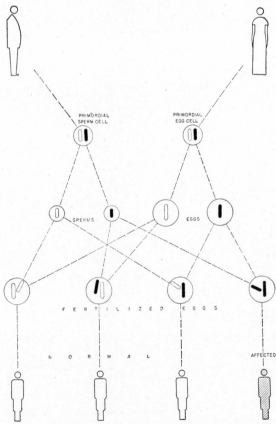

FIGURE 4.—Inheritance of a recessive character (erythroblastic anemia).

[4] These terms will be defined and illustrated in the following paragraphs.

Sex-Linked Traits

Sex is determined in a fashion similar to that by which other dominant characters are inherited. (See fig. 6.) Males and females are presumably initially determined in equal numbers. In the early stages of the development of fertilized eggs, those destined to be males appear to survive in larger numbers, but in the later stages of embryo development and in early infancy males are lost in larger numbers than females. The ratio of males to females at birth varies from country to country. In countries with advanced maternal care there are about 106 males per 100 females born alive.

All the body cells of the female bear two sex-chromosomes, or "x-chromosomes", whereas the cells of the male bear only one x-chromosome and a small mate, the "y-chromosome." Hence the female sex-chromosomes have a pair of normal allels for all the sex-determining factors borne in them, while the y-chromosome of the male lacks most of these allels, including the x-chromosomal sex-factors. After the process of cell-division which prepares the reproductive cells for mating, each of the mature egg cells bears an x-chromosome, whereas half the sperm cells bear an x-chromosome, and half carry only the inert y-chromosome. Hence, by the random union of eggs and sperm, two kinds of children are formed in equal numbers with regard to sex. Those receiving an x-chromosome from the mother and another x-chromosome from the father develop into girls; those receiving an x-chromosome from their mother and a y-chromosome from their father are boys. When a recessive gene for a character other than sex is present in one of the x-chromosomes of a female, it is latent like any other recessive gene, the normal job being done by its normal allel in the other x-chromosome. But when an x-chromosome containing such a recessive gene is bequeathed to the woman's son, the abnormal character develops in him, since there is no normal allel of that gene in the y-chromosome received from the father. Should the affected son marry a normal woman, he will transmit the abnormal x-chromosome to all his daughters, who will be normal because of the normal allel in the x-chromosome received from their mother. His sons will receive a y-chromosome from their father and a normal x-chromosome from their mother, and they and their children will be free from that character forever. The daughters, however, will carry the character latently, and will transmit it to half their sons, as their paternal grandmother did. Such recessive characters, transmitted by both males and females but usually appearing only in males, are called sex-linked characters. They are usually transmitted by an affected man through his unaffected daughters to half of the sons of each of his daughters (see fig. 7). The best known sex-linked characters in man are hemophilia and color-blindness.

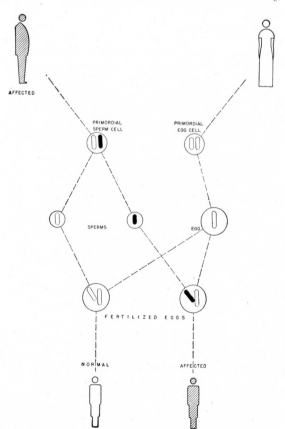

FIGURE 5.—Inheritance of a dominant character (achondroplasia).

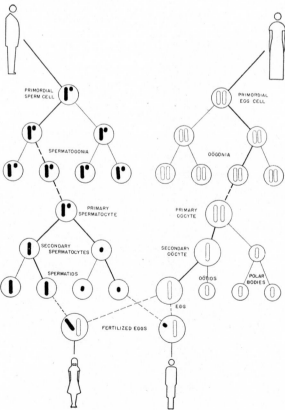

FIGURE 6.—Inheritance of sex.

In the case of most genes studied in the laboratory, an individual gene once dominant is always dominant, and a gene once found to be recessive also behaves with constancy. However, a number of genes are known whose dominance is subject to fluctuations, dependent on conditions in the environment or on the effects of other genes.

In man this fluctuation in dominance is exemplified by a pedigree of diabetes mellitus. (See fig. 8.) There are two portions of this pedigree to be considered, both having received the same gene for diabetes from a common ancestral source. In one part of the pedigree (*A*) outcrosses were made to normal individuals, and the disability disappeared in the children. It reappeared, however, as a recessive when the normal progeny of these outcrosses married each other and reproduced.[5] In the other part of the family (*B*) outcrosses were made to stocks free from diabetes, and half the offspring were diabetic or had questionable glucose tolerance in the following generations, as expected of a dominant character. Other examples of characters with fluctuating dominance are harelip, and allergies such as hay fever, eczema, and asthma.

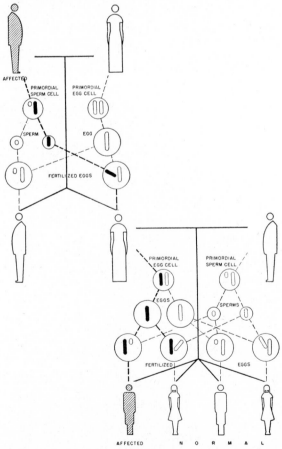

FIGURE 7.—Inheritance of a sex-linked character (haemophilia).

[5] In this pedigree the defect in the third generation was confined to the males, but this was a chance result, and not because the character was sex-linked.

The Problem of Mutation

Heritable characters may be produced in various ways, such as gene mutation, translocation of sections of chromosomes, reduplication or loss of chromosome parts. Little is known of the actual frequency of natural mutation in man.

It should, of course, also be pointed out that mutations may sometimes produce variations that have survival value or, in human development, are otherwise desirable. Far more frequently, however, mutations cause unfavorable aberrations. The continual mutability of gene structures introduces a slight element of unpredictability even in the case of traits for which the normal inheritance is known.

Although we have no significant figures on the subject, visible mutations in man do occur continually, and when dominant they may be detected at once. Probably the most common type of visible dominant mutation is that producing "crab-claws", which is a definite physical handicap. Achondroplasia is another character which frequently arises de novo. Various dominant types of blindness have been known to arise by mutation. Once such a hereditary character arises by mutation, it is transmitted according to Mendel's laws. If the mutated gene is dominant, the characteristic produced may be observed in all generations following the original variation. Mutation in man cannot be neglected as a source of handicapping characters.

Multifactorial Traits

Quantitative characters which fluctuate by numerous degrees are dependent upon many pairs of Mendelian factors, the effect of any one pair of which is too slight to be detected alone. Some multifactorial characters in humans are size, height, weight, amount of various glandular secretions, skin-pigmentation, and the hereditary factors in intelligence. When individuals differing radically in such quantitative characters are mated, the offspring are usually a blend between the two extremes. If two such hybrids are mated most of the grandchildren are intermediate, but others cover the range between the qualities of the two grandparents. For example, if a white man mates with a black woman, their immediate offspring will be brown, but if two such hybrid browns marry and have many children, they may vary widely in color, although they will be predominantly brown.

Hereditary Defects and Diseases

The importance of human heredity in the production of handicapping characters is attested by the fact that more than 120 types of hereditary variations of the eye and its accessories, most of them pathological, are listed by Waardenburg. Baur, Fischer, and Lenz list about 275 apparently hereditary human conditions. The field is extensive and has great bearing upon sociology and medicine, but the field of human genetics still awaits extensive, systematic, and critical investigation.

Contrary to popular belief, hereditary diseases may have their onset at any time from fertilization to senility. In the mouse, for example, one gene known as "lethal yellow", when present together with its normal allel, stops the pigment-forming reaction in the hair coat at the yellow stage and predisposes the owner to obesity in old age. But if present in two doses, the pair of "yellow" genes cause the death of their owner five or six days after fertilization.

Many human diseases and anomalies are congenital, that is, developed prior to and recognizable at birth. Some of these are erythroblastic anemia, harelip, clubfoot, some types of cataract, amaurotic idiocy, and albinism. Some disabilities, including other types of cataract and muscular atrophy, usually have their onset during youth. Still other hereditary disabilities, including other types of cataract, usually make their appearance in middle life. Other characters strike in old age. There is no connection between the time in the life cycle at which a character makes its appearance, and its dominance or recessiveness. Thus Huntington's chorea (a dominant) appears between the ages of 15 and 45. Diabetes mellitus, usually

transmitted as a recessive, also becomes manifest most often in this same age bracket.

Little study has yet been made of the earliest manifestations of specific hereditary diseases relative to the time of onset in particular families. Such procedure is of great clinical importance. As hereditary diseases are recognized, it becomes possible to keep vigilant watch over normal members of affected families, so as to recognize the earliest symptoms and develop preventive measures.

There are no statistics from which we may determine accurately what percentage of physical handicaps are hereditary. Many persons bear various types of hereditary characters, such as short fingers, color blindness, faulty taste buds, and some of the allergies, which constitute partial handicaps. Persons inheriting hemophilia, multiple scleroses, crab-claws, and deafness are more highly limited, while persons inheriting such characters as fragile bones, various types of blindness, and hereditary disorders of the central nervous system are seriously restricted and often completely incapacitated for work.

Many of the pathological traits for which knowledge about heredity is most exact are relatively rare. In spite of extensive research already directed to studies of hereditary and environmental factors affecting many of the major diseases, such as cancer, nephritis, tuber-

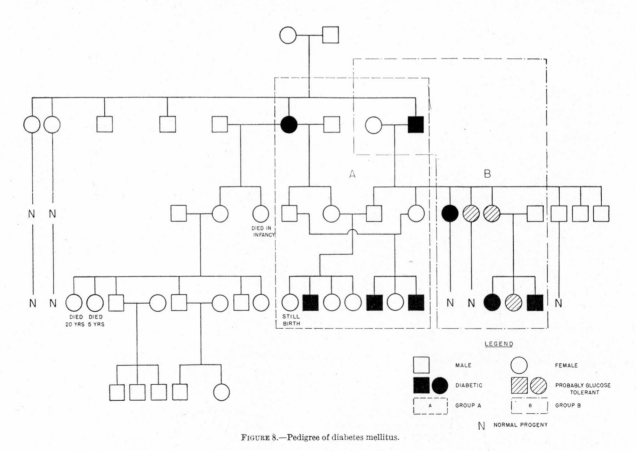

FIGURE 8.—Pedigree of diabetes mellitus.

culosis, and dementia praecox, the problems of causation are still obscure.[6]

4. Hereditary Factors in Mental Disease [7]

Mental disease is one of the most serious problems of modern civilization. At the end of 1933, there were over 400,000 persons in hospitals for the mentally diseased in the United States, and in addition probably over a million more persons were suffering from serious mental illness. Despite this incredible toll of human misery, comparatively little is known as to the causes of most of the major mental diseases. Unfounded speculations, even beliefs approaching the ancient superstitions of demoniacal possession, are prevalent. Enlightened public policy must be based on the most accurate knowledge possible as to causal factors involved in specific mental diseases.

The Relative Force of Hereditary and Environmental Factors

The attempt to oppose hereditary and environmental forces and determine in any exact form the proportionate influence of each is logically indefensible. The neural mechanisms and reaction patterns of an individual who develops a mental disease at the age of twenty-five are the result of long years of constant interplay between his fairly stable hereditary potentialities and his constantly changing environment. The environment may destroy, inhibit, or advance inborn potentialities. Perhaps certain types of hereditary equipment may doom individuals to partial or complete mental disintegration, regardless of the type of environment. In any event, it is not heredity or environment, but heredity and environment in their developmental inter-relationships which must be studied.[8]

Specific research on the causes of mental diseases substantiates this theoretical position. Bowman and Kasinin concluded, on the basis of an intensive 2-year study of 151 cases of schizophrenia, that this particular psychosis usually arises on the basis of multiple causation. They found heredity as a definite factor in 64 percent of the cases, environmental stress in 81 percent, and constitutional anomalies in 40 percent.[9]

There is some evidence that a hereditary mental instability may be involved in the development of at least some of the organic psychoses. The immediate cause of general paresis is syphilitic infection of the brain, but some studies indicate that there may be a familial incidence in susceptibility to brain infection by the spirochaete which produces syphilis. A recent study of 100 manic-depressive patients and 100 general paresis patients showed that the percentage of psychopathic conditions in the ancestry of the paresis patients was as high as in that of the manic-depressive patients.[10] The so-called alcoholic psychoses constitute another group in which it appears that environmental factors often precipitate a mental disorder in persons with inherited mental instability. There is also evidence that traumas of apparently equal severity result in epilepsy in some cases and not in others.

Studies of the Familial Basis of Mental Disease

Many of the earlier studies of the inheritance of mental disease were concerned with the prevalence of "taints" in the ancestry and descendants of "the insane" or "the mentally diseased." The definition of what constituted a taint differed from study to study, but might include nervousness, temper tantrums, suicide, alcoholism, immorality, criminality, shiftlessness, vagrancy, and so forth. Such studies, especially if no control population was used and if they were based on hearsay evidence, or on investigations by untrained persons, are practically valueless as scientific studies of the comparative importance of hereditary and environmental factors. At best, they suffer from the fundamental defect of being statistical compilations of physical, mental, social, and moral traits, with no medical or psychiatric information as to the significance for mental disease either of their relationship to each other or of their appearance as single traits, either in individuals or in the mass.

Studies of "tainting" in the families of the psychopathic have some value if a normal group is used as a control on the significance of the results. For instance, Koller and Diem, working in the same district of Zürich some fifteen years apart, used family histories to compare the total and specific "tainting" of various degrees of relationships of an "insane"

---

[6] For a brief statement of the relation of heredity to disease, see Lewis, Paul A., "The Inheritance of Disease," in *Human Biology and Racial Welfare* (1930). For a critical treatment of the possibilities and difficulties of eugenic selection, see Holmes, Samuel J., *The Eugenic Predicament* (1933), and Hogben, Lancelot T., *Nature and Nurture* (1933). For consideration of eugenic selection in relation to problems of hearing and sight, by medical and social workers in these fields, see National Research Council, Committee on the Physical Causes of Deafness, "The Physical Causes of Deafness" (1928) ; White House Conference on Child Health and Protection, Committee on Physically and Mentally Handicapped, "The Deaf and Hard of Hearing", in *The Handicapped Child* (1933) ; Union of Counties Associations for the Blind (England), Prevention of Blindness Committee, *Report*, 1933 ; and Best, Harry, "Blindness and Heredity", in *Blindness and the Blind in the United States* (1934). See also Blacker, C. P., editor, *The Chances of Morbid Inheritance* (1934).

[7] By Irene Barnes Taeuber of the Population Association of America, in consultation with the psychiatric staff of Sheppard and Enoch Pratt Hospital, Towson, Md.

[8] See statement by Abraham Myerson in *American Journal of Psychiatry* 92 : 615–625 (November 1935).

"* * * it may be definitely stated on the basis of present day genetics that any separation of the environment and the germplasm as independent forces belongs to a past scientific viewpoint. * * * This concept of the interdependence of the environment by no means minimizes the importance of the latter. * * * It merely means that for the present, at any rate, no thorough-going application of the laws of genetics to human life, and especially to the mental and personality diseases is possible."

[9] Bowman, Karl M., and Kasinin, Jacob, Constitutional Schizophrenia, *American Journal of Psychiatry*, 13 : 645–658 (November 1935).

[10] Farr, Clifford B., Schwartz, L. A., and Smith, Lauren H., The Relative Importance of Hereditary Factors in Constitutional and Organic Psychoses, *Journal of Nervous and Mental Diseases*, 71 : 36–44 (January 1930).

and a normal group. The proportion of "insane" and neuropathic relatives among the general population was used as a control to determine the significance of "insanity" and neuropathic conditions in the relatives of the "insane."[11]

More reliable results can often be obtained by comparing the rates of specific mental diseases in selected family groups with normal rates for the same diseases in the general population. Ernst Rüdin and his coworkers in the Deutsche Forschungs-Anstalt für Psychiatrie in Munich have contrasted the proportion of dementia praecox and other psychoses in the ancestry of over 700 dementia praecox patients with the normal expectation for Munich at the same period. The rate of dementia praecox among the brothers and sisters of individuals classified as having this disease was far higher than the normal frequency of this disease in the general population. It is perhaps even more significant that the ratios of actual cases to normal expectation were much higher for dementia praecox than for all psychoses. This suggests that dementia praecox (schizophrenia) involves a more definite familial basis than "psychotic condition" in general (see table 1).

TABLE 1.—*Prevalence of dementia praecox and other psychoses among siblings of dementia praecox patients, Rüdin's data for Munich clinic* [1]

Type of parents of dementia praecox patients	Psychoses in siblings of probands [2]			
	Dementia praecox		Total psychoses	
	Percent	Ratio to normal expectation [3]	Percent	Ratio to normal expectation [3]
Both "sound"	4.48	5.3	8.60	1.9
One dementia praecox, one "sound"	6.18	7.3	16.48	3.7
One other psychosis, one "sound"	8.21	9.6	16.42	3.7
Both alcoholic, not psychotic	7.80	9.2	13.00	3.0
One psychotic, either alcoholic	15.78	18.6	23.67	5.4
One or both psychotic, one or both also alcoholic	14.81	17.4	22.21	5.1
Both mentally diseased	22.72	26.7		

[1] Adapted from summary by Pollock, Malzberg, and Fuller of Rüdin, Ernst, *Studien über Vererbung und Entstehung geistiger Störungen. I. Zur Vererbung and Neuentstehung der Dementia Praecox.* Berlin, Julius Springer (1916). Schulz showed that similar comparisons held for all the clinical varieties of dementia praecox in Rüdin's material. (Schulz, Bruno, "Zur Erbpathologie der Schizophrenie," *Zeitschrift für die gesamte Neurologie und Psychiatrie,* 143:175–293 (1932). Also Rüdin, Ernst, "Über die Vorhersage von Geistesstörung in der Nachkommenschaft", *Archiv für Rassen und Gesellschafts-Biologie,* 20:394–407 (September 1928).
[2] "Proband" designates the patient as contrasted with other siblings.
[3] "Normal expectation" for Munich is estimated by Rüdin as 8.5 per 1,000 population for dementia praecox and 4.39 for all psychoses.

Pollock, Malzberg, and Fuller, of the New York State Department of Mental Hygiene, recently completed a study of hereditary and environmental factors in the causation of dementia praecox (schizophrenia) and manic-depressive psychoses, based on an analysis of

the family stock of all first admissions to the Utica State Hospital for 1928, 1929, and 1930.[12] They compared the incidence of mental diseases in the several degrees of relationship with the expected incidence for such a group if the latter were selected at random from New York State. (See table 2 and fig. 9.)

TABLE 2.—*Ratio of mental disease among relatives of mentally diseased persons to normal expectation of mental disease in the general population of New York State* [1]

Relationship	Number with known histories	Number of cases of mental disease		Ratio of "corrected" actual to expected
		Expected [2]	"Corrected," actual [3]	
Manic-depressive (155 cases):				
Brothers	369	14.8	24.8	1.7
Sisters	376	13.2	25.2	1.9
Father	154	6.2	4.6	0.7
Mother	154	5.4	7.8	1.4
Other relatives	1,324	49.6	30.3	0.6
Total	2,377	89.2	92.7	1.0
Dementia praecox (175 cases):				
Brothers	374	15.0	23.7	1.6
Sisters	342	12.0	22.4	1.9
Father	174	7.0	6.4	0.9
Mother	174	6.1	15.8	2.6
Other relatives	1,451	54.5	53.2	1.0
Total	2,515	94.6	121.5	1.3

[1] Adapted from Pollock, Malzberg, and Fuller, *op. cit.,* 8:87 (January 1934); and 8:560 (July 1934).
[2] Expectation based on general population of New York State, and defined as "the chance of an individual being treated in a hospital for mental disorder in the course of a lifetime." See *Psychiatric Quarterly,* 2:549–579 (January 1928).
[3] Actual number of cases, plus cases anticipated (expected to develop in future among persons still living, based on expectations for general population of New York State at specific ages).

The most significant findings are those for the brothers and sisters of the patients, since there was admittedly underenumeration of psychoses in the "other relatives" (paternal and maternal aunts, uncles, grandfathers, and grandmothers) and probably also in the case of parents. It could hardly be supposed that mental break-down in one individual is positively related to mental health in the fathers, grandparents, and uncles of the patient. In many cases the parents and some other relatives were born and died abroad, so that accurate information about their mental condition was not available. The higher ratios ("corrected") of actual cases to expected cases for mothers as compared to fathers appears to indicate the operation of environmental factors, especially since there is little specific evidence of genetic sex linkage.[13]

The general conclusion of Pollock, Malzberg, and Fuller, based on their own data and a de-

[12] Pollock, Horatio M., Malzberg, Benjamin, and Fuller, Raymond G., Hereditary and Environmental Factors in the Causation of Dementia Praecox and Manic-Depressive Psychoses, *Psychiatric Quarterly,* 7:450–479; 8:77–97, 337–371, 553–599; 9:129–142, 287–296 (July 1933; January, April, July, 1934; January, 1935).
[13] In manic-depressive psychoses, the female siblings showed a higher incidence than male siblings. This held true for both male and female patients. This is contrary to the hypothesis for sex-linked inheritance. (See sec. 3 above.)

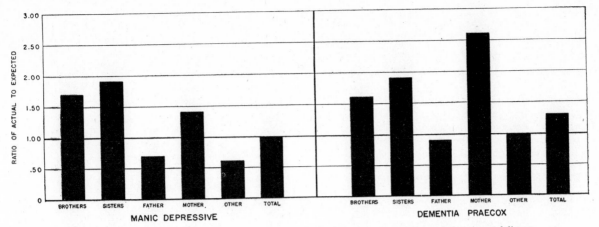

FIGURE 9.—Ratio of mental disease among relatives of mentally diseased persons to normal expectation of mental disease.

tailed review of the literature, is that "the frequency of mental disease among the close relatives of patients with mental disease exceeds that of the general population. * * * The frequency of mental disease within a family stock increases with the severity of tainting among the ancestors, and the closer the degree of relationship to the proband, the greater is the frequency of mental disease. The conclusion from such data appears inescapable, that there is a familial basis for certain forms of mental disease, especially in the case of dementia praecox and the manic-depressive psychoses."[14]

These data were also analyzed to determine whether or not they could be fitted into the Mendelian expectations if the psychoses were inherited as single-factor recessives. In no type of mating in the families of either the manic-depressive or the dementia-praecox patients did the frequencies of mental disease among the offspring conform to formulas for simple Mendelian inheritance. Such conformity could hardly be expected for several reasons. There are few clear-cut clinical entities with respect to the several types of mental disease. "Schizophrenia", for instance, is a loose grouping of many types of abnormal reaction, which may result from various factors interacting in different relations. It may be expected that further classification of different types of psychopathic reactions and the study of associated physical conditions will supply the basis for more refined genetic research.

Research on Twins

A very significant study of the incidence of specific psychoses in twins of different types (identical, dissimilar same sex, and dissimilar opposite sex) has been carried on under the

direction of Aaron Rosanoff.[15] Data were collected on 1,014 pairs of twins, at least one of whom was mentally diseased or defective. Since identical twins presumably have exactly the same heredity, any psychosis absolutely determined by genetic factors would have to be present in both or neither. Furthermore, since other twins have no greater similarity of heredity than ordinary siblings, insofar as genetic factors are operative, one would expect that the frequency of psychoses among the brothers or sisters of dissimilar twins who were psychotic would be the same as that of all siblings. Any deviation would indicate the action of environmental factors, in utero, at birth, or in later life. Thus a much greater prevalence of mental disease in the other members of pairs of identical twins, one of whom is affected, than among pairs of dissimilar twins would point toward the existence of hereditary factors.

The series included 142 pairs, 1 or both of whom was classified as schizophrenic. (See fig. 10, also table 3.) Among these, 41 pairs were classified as identical, 101 pairs as dissimilar twins. Both were affected with some psychosis (not necessarily schizophrenia) in 68 percent of the pairs of identical twins and in 15 percent of the pairs of dissimilar twins. Despite the fact that the so-called schizophrenic psychoses probably constitute a heterogeneous group, specific heredity seems to play an important part. The identical twin brothers and sisters of schizophrenic patients were affected with schizophrenia in 61 percent of the cases, whereas the corresponding figure for dissimilar twins was 10 percent and for other

---

[14] *Ibid.*, 292. The term "familial" is used as synonymous with "hereditary." The authors state that, though logically the existence of several cases of a disease within a family is not conclusive proof of heredity, "the absence of exceptional frequencies of mental disease within a family stock must be interpreted as proof of the lack of a hereditary basis" (p. 552).

[15] Rosanoff, Aaron., *et al.*, The Etiology of the So-Called Schizophrenic Psychoses with Special Reference to Their Occurrence in Twins, *The American Journal of Psychiatry*, 91 : 247–286 (September 1934).

———, The Etiology of Manic-Depressive Syndromes with Special Reference to Their Occurrence in Twins, *loc. cit.*, 91 : 725–762 (January 1935).

———, Etiology of Epilepsy with Special Reference to Its Occurrence in Twins, *Archives of Neurology and Psychiatry*, 31 : 1165–1192 (June 1934).

——— Some Clinical Manifestations of Traumatic Decerebration, *Psychiatric Quarterly*, 9 : 116–128 (January 1935).

The term identical is used here for monozygotic twins, and dissimilar for dizygotic twins.

siblings 3 percent.[16] However, the indications of the presence of specific heredity can easily be overemphasized. In the 61 percent of the cases in which both members of pairs of identical twins were affected with similar psychoses there were differences in time of onset, symptoms, duration, and so forth. In 7 percent of the cases both were affected, but with qualitatively dissimilar psychoses (i. e., in another diagnostic group). In 32 percent of the cases only one was affected. This last figure is highly significant, since if heredity were the sole determining factor both members of a pair of identical twins would have to be affected if one were. The fact that the

---

[16] Humm, D. G., Mental Disorders in Siblings, *American Journal of Psychiatry*, 12 : 239–283 (September 1932).

TABLE 3.—*Percentage of mental disease in twin brothers and sisters of individuals suffering from mental disease* [1]

Mental disease and type of twin	Number of pairs of twins			Percent with both affected
	Both affected [2]	One affected	Total	
Schizophrenia:				
Identical [3]	28	13	41	68
Dissimilar:				
Same sex	10	43	53	19
Opposite sex	5	43	48	10
Total	43	99	142	30
Manic-depressive:				
Identical	16	7	23	70
Dissimilar:				
Same sex	8	27	35	23
Opposite sex	3	29	32	9
Total	27	63	90	30
Epilepsy:				
Identical	14	9	23	61
Dissimilar:				
Same sex	7	32	39	18
Opposite sex	13	32	45	38
Total	34	73	107	32

[1] Compiled from articles by Aaron J. Rosanoff *et al.*: The Etiology of So-Called Schizophrenic Psychoses with Special Reference to Their Occurrence in Twins, *The American Journal of Psychiatry*, 91 : 247–286 (September 1934); The Etiology of Manic-Depressive Syndromes with Special Reference to Their Occurrence in Twins, *loc. cit.*, 91 : 725–762 (January 1935); Etiology of Epilepsy with Special Reference to Its Occurrence in Twins, *Archives of Neurology and Psychiatry*, 31 : 1165–1192 (June 1934).

[2] Both twins affected with a mental disease, though the other twin need not necessarily be suffering from the same disease; i. e., the twin of a schizophrenic individual may be epileptic, etc.

[3] Author uses word "probably" with both identical twins and dissimilar twins of same sex. Twins of opposite sex are by definition dissimilar.

---

other member of one pair was not affected with any psychosis in approximately one-third of the cases indicates that, if hereditary factors were present, they were not solely responsible for the development of mental diseases in the individuals so affected. Rosanoff's data on 90 pairs of twins of whom one or both were manic-depressive point to similar conclusions with reference to the role of hereditary factors. Data on 107 pairs of twins, at least 1 of whom was epileptic, show somewhat less apparent influence of hereditary factors.

Many criticisms of this study of psychoses in twins might be made, especially in view of the similarity of environment and tendency toward personality identification of identical twins. Since the biological relationship of ordinary siblings and dissimilar twins is the same, the progressively increasing incidence, in both manic-depressive syndromes and schizophrenia, from ordinary siblings to opposite-sex twins to same-sex dissimilar twins clearly shows the action of environmental factors. It is impossible to determine how much of the additional incidence in identical twins is due to environment, and how much to their identical heredity.

Rosanoff's studies furnish no indication of the mechanism or even the proportional influence of hereditary factors. His data on identical twins prove definitely that heredity is not the absolutely determining causal factor in many cases of schizophrenia, manic-depressive syndromes, and epilepsy. However, the incidence of mental disease in both members of pairs of identical twins is so much greater than in dissimilar twins as to make the action of a hereditary factor or factors appear the most probable explanation.

Summary of Findings

Present knowledge on the subject of the role of heredity in mental diseases is well summarized in the following excerpt from the report of a special committee appointed to investigate the subject under the British Department of Health: [17]

---

[17] Report of the Departmental Committee on Sterilisation, Presented by the Minister of Health to Parliament by Command of His Majesty, December 1933, London, H. M. Stationery Office (1934), 27–28, par. 47.

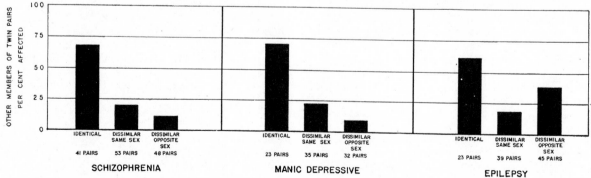

FIGURE 10.—Percentage of mental disease in twin brothers and sisters of individuals with mental disease.

1. Heredity plays a large part in the causation of mental disorders, though except in the case of Huntington's chorea and myoclonus epilepsy, which are both rare types, there is no conclusive evidence that the transmission follows Mendelian ratios.

2. In many mental disorders other than Huntington's chorea and myoclonus epilepsy the part played by heredity varies widely between different types.

3. Manic-depressive insanity and schizophrenia appear to show a markedly higher familial incidence than other types of mental disorder which are of frequent occurrence.

4. While psychopathic parents tend to have psychopathic children, the view that familial mental instability is usually progressive and tends to become more severe in each succeeding generation is not established. The familial incidence in such cases is not necessarily entirely genetic in origin, since the environmental conditions in which children of psychopathic parents are brought up may tend to aggravate any inherited instability.

5. Familial mental disorder is not necessarily transmitted in the same form, and in many cases what appears to be transmitted is not a specific character but a generalized predisposition.

6. Where such a predisposition exists the immediate or exciting cause of the break-down may be of an apparently trivial nature.

7. In a proportion of cases of mental disorder an environmental factor, such as a toxic condition, syphilis, or arteriosclerosis, is the immediate cause and often the only discoverable cause. In some of these cases there is evidence that these environmental factors are associated with an inherited predisposition.

8. There is little evidence that alcoholism is a frequent cause of mental disorder, and in many cases which at present are classed as alcoholic the alcoholism appears to be a symptom of mental abnormality rather than its cause.

Much more accurate information is required before precise statements can be made as to the role of hereditary factors in producing mental disease. At the present time it is impossible to classify the major mental diseases as hereditary or as purely environmental. Research already carried out strongly indicates the presence of hereditary factors in some mental disorders. It is possible that a more complete understanding of the physiological conditions associated with various types of psychoses may reveal the mechanisms by which hereditary factors operate where they exist, including conditions of the central nervous system and conditions affecting glandular functions. The progress that has already been made in the purely psychological treatment of many persons suffering from mental disease, although it does not conclusively establish the primary importance of mental situations in the development of these diseases, does strongly point in that direction.

Psychiatrists are well aware of a wide variety of research approaches in the study of causes of mental disease. Genetic research with regard to mental disease may be expected to proceed along with other lines of research, including refinement in diagnosis and experiments with various types of therapy. Additional and more carefully controlled data on the incidence of various mental diseases in the general population are urgently needed.

Most data at present concern institutional populations, and hence do not afford accurate insight into the comparative prevalence of various psychoses in different groups, under different conditions, in different places, and at different periods of time. In view of the tremendous cost and suffering caused by mental disease, and in view of the research outlook in this field at the present time, it is hardly too much to say that no line of scientific investigation is likely to contribute so much to the relief of human suffering as the systematic development of this field during the next few decades.

5. Hereditary Factors in Intelligence

Recent psychological research on the relative importance of nature and nurture in the development of intelligence has established the importance of both sets of factors in the development of human personality. Discussion of this topic among scientists no longer moves between such extremes of contrary opinion as were advanced earlier. Nevertheless, very little is known about the exact relations of heredity and environment in determining differences in intellectual development found among different groups and under different conditions.[18]

Individual Differences

The simplest problem relates to the interpretation of *individual differences* between persons in similar environments, i. e., within the same broad social-economic class, in the same or similar communities with similar racial-cultural background. Extensive studies of differences between identical twins, nonidentical twins, other brothers and sisters, and persons of other degrees and types of relationship, as well as studies of specific environmental influences, bear directly on this problem.[19] Here both environmental influences (effects of different patterns of family life, schooling, occupational choice, health, and "chance" factors) and genetic factors must be taken into account, but *within* groups that are similar with regard to geographical location and social status hereditary factors apparently outweigh the

[18] See surveys of the literature on this subject by Freeman, F. N., Holzinger, K. T., and Mitchell, B. C., in *National Society for the Study of Education, 27th Yearbook* (1928), Part I: 103–217; Hogben, Lancelot T., *Nature and Nurture* (1933); Lorimer, Frank, and Osborn, Frederick, *Dynamics of Population* (1934); Murphy, Gardner, and Murphy, Lois B., *Experimental Social Psychology* (1931); Schwesinger, Gladys C., *Heredity and Environment* (1933).

[19] For research on twins see Hogben, *op. cit.*; Schwesinger, *op. cit.*; Holzinger, K. T., The Relative Effect of Nature and Nurture Influences on Twin Differences, *Journal of Educational Psychology*, 20 : 241–248 (April 1929); *Eugenical Sterilization* (1936); Verschuer, O. von, Ergebnisse der Zwillingsforschung, *Verhandlungen der Gesellschaft für physische Anthropologic*, 6 : 1–65 (1932); Jones, Harold E., and Wilson, P. T., Reputation Differences in Like-Sex Twins, *Journal of Experimental Education*, 1 : 86–91 (December 1932); the study by Newman, Horatio H., to be published by the University of Chicago Press; and *Proceedings of the Maxim Gorky Medico-Biological Research Institute*, vol. 3, Moscow-Leningrad (1934), containing 20 articles of the work of the Institute on twin likenesses and differences.

environmental in determining differences in individual ability. This conclusion holds good for extreme deviations either toward genius or toward mental deficiency, as well as for less extreme variations in ability.[20]

Studies of factors affecting apparent variations in intellectual development among people of similar racial origin living in very dissimilar environments indicate that in most cases the environmental factors outweigh the genetic factors in causing the variations commonly indicated by intelligence tests and other criteria of "cultural-intellectual ability." On the other hand it is possible that hereditary variations, resulting from selective migration, may in some cases significantly affect these results.[21]

Racial Differences

The conclusion is similar with reference to apparent differences in intellectual development of racial groups. In this case it has been shown that group differences persist to a significant degree for several generations among groups living in physical proximity in American communities, but this in itself might be attributed to the persistent influence of cultural patterns affecting child development and later interests and activities. On the other hand it has been shown that regional contrasts among people of the same race are greater in some cases than contrasts between different races living in the same environment. For example, the median rating on the Army intelligence tests of Negroes from some Northern States was as high as, or higher than, the median rating of whites from some of the Gulf States; and a high correlation has been found between intelligence ratings and length of residence of Negroes in some northern cities. These results may possibly in some cases be influenced by selective migration, but in the main must be attributed to the influence of variations in environment on intelligence test performance.

It is obvious that there is great overlapping in individual abilities among all racial groups, many individuals in groups that are now retarded being intellectually superior to many individuals in more advanced groups. There may be differences between races in average hereditary capacity for intellectual development and in the distribution of capacities, but whether or not this is the case to any important degree has not yet been either proved or disproved.

Differences Between Social-Economic Groups

Several studies have been reported which throw light directly on the relative importance of heredity and environment in determining differences in intellectual development between broad social-economic classes, through the study of foster children classified with reference to (1) the occupations of their original fathers (blood relatives) and (2) the occupations or social characteristics of their foster parents.[22] Although the number of cases is small in each of these studies, the differences indicated appear to be statistically significant, at least in some cases, and the results are in substantial agreement. These studies show that surrounding child development) are a considerable factor in creating the differences found in school grades, intelligence test performance, and the adjustments of later life. They also suggest the hereditary influence of selective factors in occupational status along with chance variations in opportunity and differences in taste and temperament. The meager evidence at hand indicates that a large part of the differences in average scholastic ability found between children in the same community classified with reference to the social-economic status of their parents may be due to genetic factors, the remainder being attributable to differences in environmental opportunity. It cannot be too strongly emphasized that hereditary ability varies widely among individuals in all social groups, ranging from low mentality to genius in all groups and that these individual variations are far more important in most respects than the smaller average differences between groups. However, the existence of large differences in reproduction rates between different social groups may give group differences in average hereditary ability a long-time significance that they would not otherwise have.

[20] For reports of research on factors in mental deficiency see Doll, Edgar A., Phelps, Winthrop M., and Taylor, Ruth, *Mental Deficiency Due to Birth Injuries* (1932); Lokay, A., Über die hereditären Beziehungen der Imbezillität, *Zeitschrift für die gesamte Neurologie und Psychiatrie*, 122:90–142 (1929); Pleger, W., Erblichkeitsuntersuchungen an schwachsinnigen Kindern, *ibid.*, 135:225–252 (1931); Moorrees, V., The Immediate Heredity of Primary Aments Committed to a Public Institution, *Journal of Applied Psychology*, 8:89–127 (March 1924); Ordahl, George, Heredity in Feeble-Mindedness, *Training School Bulletin*, 16:2–16 (March and April 1919); Penrose, Lionel S., *Mental Defect* (1933); Pintner, Rudolf, The Feebleminded Child, *A Handbook of Child Psychology*, edited by Carl Murchison, revised edition (1933), 20:802–841; Sjögren, T., *Klinische und vererbungsmedizinische Untersuchungen über Oliogophrenie in einer nordschwedischen Bauernpopulation* (1932); Wildenskov, H. O., *Investigations into the Causes of Mental Deficiency* (1934).

[21] See Baldwin, Bird T., Fillmore, Eva A., and Hadley, Lora, *Farm Children, An Investigation of Rural Child Life in Selected Areas of Iowa* (1930); Jones, Harold E., Conrad, H. S., and Blanchard, M. B., Environmental Handicap in Mental Test Performance, *University of California Publications in Psychology*, 5:63–99 (1932). For review of earlier literature on this topic, see Sorokin, Pitirim, and Zimmerman, Carle C., *Principles of Rural-Urban Sociology* (1929).

[22] See studies by Burks, Barbara S., in *National Society for the Study of Education*, 27th Yearbook (1928), Part I:219–316; Freeman, Holzinger, and Mitchell, *op. cit.*; Lawrence, Evelyn M., An Investigation Into the Relation Between Intelligence and Inheritance, *British Journal of Psychology*, Monograph Supplement, No. 16, London (1931); Leahy, Alice M., *Nature-Nurture and Intelligence*, Genetic Psychology Monographs, 17:235–308 (1935). Sewall Wright, *Journal of the American Statistical Society*: 26, 155–163 (1931), estimates that between 50% and 90% of the variance of I. Q. is due to heredity and between 10% and 50% to environment.

6. Significance of Genetic Research for Population Theory

Genetic research has given the popular concept of inheritance an exact content through the development of definite formulas describing the transmission of particular traits in plants and animals. These formulas have been related to the visible physical units of cell structure. It is well established that the same mechanisms underlie the transmission of qualities affecting human health, intelligence, and personality; but these traits are affected by a great number of genetic factors and are subject in their effects to environmental modification, so that it is impossible to make any exact prediction regarding offspring from knowledge of parents. On the other hand, measurable degrees of correlation between individuals and parents, brothers and sisters, and other relatives have been established for various traits. Such correlation in traits has been demonstrated with considerable exactness in the case of stature and other physical measurements. It presumably holds with regard to capacity for intellectual development and the basic constitutional factors that underlie personality development. Thus, although no definite predictions can be made regarding the musical talent of the child born of gifted musicians, the probability of musical aptitude for such a child is far above that for the general population.

At the same time the cultural anthropologists and sociologists have shown the far-reaching influence of ways of living, or culture patterns, handed down through family and community associations.

The combined influence of genetic inheritance and social inheritance must be taken into account in all attempts to effect social changes through formal education. Education may channelize and redirect social inheritance; but it would be hazardous to assume that the formal institutions consciously established by society can easily outweigh or reverse the effects of differential reproduction where the combined influence of biological inheritance and social heritage runs directly counter to their objectives.

The net effect of biological and social studies in factors operating in the formation of personality is to indicate the undoubted importance of family background, biological constitution, and conditions affecting child development. At the same time the relative importance of biological and social factors is so obscure, and there is such great overlapping in the developed abilities of individuals making up different racial groups, that there is no scientific basis for a program of racial selection on biological grounds. There may, however, be some justification for giving consideration to possible differences in the capacity of diverse racial groups, in the formulation of immigration policy, even where there is lack of evidence sufficient to warrant any radical policy of racial selection applied to groups already included in the composition of the Nation.

Provision for the sterilization of certain groups of diseased or defective persons represents one important line of direct attack on the problems of hereditary disability. The sterilization of defective individuals was recommended, under certain conditions, by the Committee on Physically and Mentally Handicapped of the White House Conference on Child Health and Protection. Sterilization laws have been passed by more than one-half of the States, and over 1,000 operations under these statutes have been performed in each of three States—California, Michigan, and Virginia. A special committee for the investigation of eugenical sterilization, appointed by the American Neurological Association, made the following recommendations on this subject.

This Committee has studied the principal literature of the world on the subject which was assigned to it by the Association. In many respects the survey has been disappointing in that it appears that not much scientifically valid work has been done on the subject of inheritance of the diseases and conditions which have been considered. This might have been anticipated for neither psychiatry nor human genetics approach at present the status of exact sciences. It appears that most of the legislation which has been enacted so far is based more upon a desire to elevate the human race than upon proven facts.

We believe that certain definite, though in a sense negative, recommendations should first be made.

First. Our knowledge of human genetics has not the precision nor amplitude which would warrant the sterilization of people *who themselves are normal* in order to prevent the appearance, in their descendants, of manic-depressive psychosis, dementia praecox, feeble-mindedness, epilepsy, criminal conduct, or any of the conditions which we have had under consideration. An exception may exist in the case of normal parents of one or more children suffering from certain familial diseases, such as Tay-Sachs' amaurotic idiocy.

Second. Particularly do we wish to emphasize that there is at present no sound scientific basis for sterilization on account of immorality or character defect. Human conduct and character are matters of too complex a nature, too interwoven with social conditions, such as traditions, economics, education, training, opportunity, and even prejudice, especially when these factors operate in the earlier years of life, to permit any definite conclusions to be drawn concerning the part which heredity plays in their genesis. Until and unless heredity can be shown to have an overwhelming importance in the causation of dangerous antisocial behavior, sterilization merely on the basis of conduct must continue to be regarded as a "cruel and unusual punishment."

Third. Nothing in the acceptance of heredity as a factor in the genesis of any condition considered by this report excludes the environmental agencies of life as equally potent and, in many instances, as even more effective. That scientific day is passed when the germplasm and the environment are to be considered as separate agencies or as opposing forces. Both operate in the production of any character, though in different degrees, but the degree in which each operates is, at present, mostly in the field of the unknown. Neurology and psychiatry still have as their duty the laborious task of discovering pathology, pathogenesis, and therapeutics even for those conditions in which heredity undoubtedly plays a role.

Thus modern research has uncovered the fact that diabetes has a constitutional heredity basis. Yet the establishment of its relationship to the pancreas and the introduction of insulin are, none the less, triumphs of medicine.

We present the following recommendations concerning sterilization to the Association for its consideration:

1. Any law concerning sterilization passed in the United States under the present state of knowledge should be voluntary and regulatory rather than compulsory. The present survey clearly shows that the compulsory features of the laws which have been passed in this country have, with rare exceptions, remained unused. Either the custom of obtaining the consent of the patient has become established or the law has remained practically unenforced.

2. Any law concerning sterilization should be applicable not only to patients in State institutions but also to those in private institutions and those at large in the community. We see no reason for group or class discrimination.

3. The essential machinery for administering any law in regard to sterilization should be one or several boards composed chiefly of persons who have had especial training and experience in the problems involved, which should study each case on its individual merits, and should strongly urge, suggest, or recommend against, sterilization according to its findings. Cases could be brought before such a board by superintendents of institutions, private physicians, parents or guardians, or by the patients themselves. This arrangement would promote elasticity in the application of the law, and permit the utilization of future advances in knowledge.

4. Adequate legal protection for the members of such a board, and for the surgeons carrying out the recommendations, should be secured by statute.

Your Committee feels, in short, that it can only recommend sterilization in selected cases of certain diseases and with the consent of the patient or those responsible for him. We recommend that such selective sterilization be considered in cases of the following diseases (arranged roughly in the order in which sterilization would appear to be indicated):

1. Huntington's chorea, hereditary optic atrophy, familial cases of Friedreich's ataxia, and certain other disabling degenerative diseases recognized to be hereditary.

2. Feeblemindedness of familial type.

3. Dementia praecox (schizophrenia).

4. Manic-depressive psychosis.

5. Epilepsy.

Each of these categories carries its own special implications:

1. Definitely hereditary and familial neurologic conditions are rare, but the indications for sterilization are usually obvious to the physician and should be so to the patient. The services of an expert board should be of value in doubtful cases.

2. There need be no hesitation in recommending sterilization in the case of feeblemindedness, though it need not, of course, be urged in the case of those conditions which are definitely of environmental origin. Though we hesitate to stress any purely social necessity for sterilization, it is obvious that in the case of the feebleminded there may be a social as well as a biological situation of importance. Certain of the feeble-minded can only, under the most favorable circumstances, care for themselves, and a family of children may prove an overwhelming burden. However, in a world which has much low grade work to be done, there is still room for the people of low grade mentality of good character.

3. Dementia praecox will need, we believe, but little attention from the surgeon. Most cases which are recognized in time to prevent procreation spend their days in hospitals. Moreover, the sexual urge in dementia praecox is low and the marriage and birth rate correspondingly low. Those who come in contact with cases in the community or prior to their discharge from a hospital need not, however, in most

cases hesitate to recommend sterilization since desirable qualities of other kinds are only incidental to dementia praecox and not part of its make-up.

4. The problem of the manic-depressive psychoses presents complications which will tax the judgment of the wisest board, and it must be met with conservatism and caution. The cyclothymic temperament is frequently the source of the highest achievement and ability of which mankind can boast. Decision in any case must take into account the total assets of the individual character as well as the liabilities incident to the psychosis.

5. The inclusion of epilepsy, in most instances, is mainly on the ground of the social situation rather than on its biology. If the epileptic attacks from which the individual suffers are infrequent and if the qualities of the personality are intact, we see no reason in our present knowledge for recommending sterilization. If the contrary holds true, then sterilization is desirable.

FURTHER RESEARCH

The Committee believes that its most important recommendations are those looking toward a concerted, coordinated, and planned long-time research. It is obvious to us that investigation of the problem of inheritance, especially of the psychiatric conditions, has been haphazard and often inexact. This is no criticism of the able men who have devotedly studied these most difficult problems and it well may be that no complete scientific approach is possible in the present state of our knowledge or rather of our ignorance, but it is time that a prolonged research be undertaken in which psychiatrists, statisticians, and geneticists will collaborate.[23]

The final recommendation of the American Neurological Association's committee includes a series of specific research proposals. Among these first place is given to the need for controlled studies of the incidence of nervous and mental diseases and mental deficiency in the general population. It would seem that the primary responsibility for the development of such surveys, with uniform procedures in different localities, rests with the United States Public Health Service.

The report concludes with a warning against hysterical procedure in this field. "It is emphasized that no great or radical change in the complexion of society can be expected from any such sterilization program as we recommend, nor from any justifiable legislation. * * * Although the problem of mental disease and defectiveness is enormous, there is no new social or biological emergency."

Sterilization, even when drastically applied, may not be so effective as is sometimes supposed. The widely proclaimed German sterilization program resulted in 84,256 court decisions during 1934, affecting 0.13 per 1,000 inhabitants.[24] No information regarding the actual number of sterilizations performed is available, but at the end of the year it appears to have been 20 to 40 percent of the total actions disposed of by the courts. During this

[23] *Eugenical Sterilization: a Reorientation of the Problem,* report of the Committee of the American Neurological Association for the Investigation of Eugenical Sterilization, New York (1936), 177–181. The following persons served on the committee: Abraham Myerson, James B. Ayer, Tracy J. Putnam, Clyde E. Keeler, Leo Alexander.

[24] Cook, Robert, A Year of German Sterilization, *Journal of Heredity,* 26: 485–489 (1935).

year about 75 percent of the cases brought before the court were disposed of. "This high percentage is to be accounted for largely by the fact that during the early months the unquestionable, institutionalized cases were brought to decision." Thus during the first year of this program the ratio of persons legally selected for sterilization to births amounted to nearly 1 sterilization action to each 100 births. However, it seems unlikely that so high a rate of actions will be maintained in future years or that such a rate is likely to be established in other countries. We may then infer that a fairly strict legal sterilization program is likely to result in a sterilization case rate somewhere between 1 per 100 and 1 per 1,000 births. It must be noted, however, that a considerable proportion of the persons sterilized are likely to be institutionalized in any case, and that the fertility of both the insane and the extreme feeble-minded is usually below the average for the general population. This consideration and recognition of the genetic principle that recessive factors carried by individuals who show no symptoms of their presence are responsible for a large proportion of the major hereditary defects add weight to the conclusion of the American Neurological Association's committee that a properly safeguarded sterilization program, though sound, is not likely to bring about any "great or radical change in the complexion of society."

In fact, from the strictly biological viewpoint it must be recognized that large differentials in the voluntary reproduction rates of numerous population groups, if negatively selective with reference to hereditary capacities, might easily result in a definite trend toward racial deterioration in the face of a well-enforced and fairly drastic sterilization program. Insofar as the conservation of biological qualities making for health and intelligence is an objective of population policy, primary attention must be directed to mass differences in family reproduction rates. If emphasis is placed on conservation of the most highly developed cultural traditions, the same conclusion follows even more directly.

The statistical implications of our knowledge of the physical mechanism of inheritance make possible certain general conclusions.

While some important human characteristics are controlled in their development by a single gene, most of them depend on several "key genes" for their expression. Thus the genetic basis of stature is dependent on several genes. The same multifactorial type of inheritance undoubtedly underlies the biological basis of intelligence, personality, or such complex special traits as musical ability. The mathematical difficulties of selection for a considerable number of independently inherited genes are so great that in a slowly reproducing organism

like man any attempt to bring together all the desirable human characteristics in a single ideal type appears to be quite fantastic. Fortunately human society is so diverse that it needs a large variety of abilities. The problem of conserving the biological basis of human culture is not dependent on the formulation of any such perfect human type, or devising unworkable means of breeding what is statistically an impossibility. It is rather a problem of recognizing that healthy, intelligent human personality is dependent on a complex biological substratum, and that the same Mendelian mechanism that makes it impossible to breed a strain of superhumans may cause a deterioration of this essential biological heritage. In the history of the race various natural conditions have performed this selective function. Many of these have ceased to operate in civilized society. The logical answer of an enlightened society to this situation would seem to be the development of a "human conservation" policy.

In the past we have as a Nation considered our natural resources and our human resources alike to be virtually inexhaustible. It has come as rather a shock in recent years to learn that the acreage of formerly fine farm land that has been permanently destroyed runs into a staggering number of millions. In exactly the same way our human heritage is not inexhaustible. Millions of years have gone into building it up, just as in the case of the soil. The possibility of the wastage of genes favorable to human development through social conditions causing adverse selection suggests a more serious national problem than any amount of soil erosion. Sociological considerations would suggest that a policy calculated to conserve the desirable biological heritage of the race generally would not conflict with measures to foster social progress in other directions. It would appear to be highly important that there should be serious, deliberate recognition of the basic factor of biological heritage in individual and national development.

We may conclude that an informed appreciation of the nature and complexities of biological inheritance and of the operation of social inheritance tends to focus attention on variations in reproduction rates among large population groups and among individuals distinguished with reference to health, character, and present intellectual attainments. The best guarantee of sound biological and social national development would appear to be a situation in which the determining factors in size of family would be not ignorance, isolation, or indifference as contrasted with ambition and anxiety, but interest in child life and ability to provide favorable environment for child development.

VII. HEALTH AND PHYSICAL DEVELOPMENT

1. The Appraisal of Health

A review of the health and physical condition of the people of the United States is fundamental to any consideration of their development and opportunities. What is the present state of the Nation's health? What are the possibilities of future improvement? How can existing facilities be modified and extended so as to provide more adequate health protection?

An appraisal of the health of the Nation is a difficult undertaking. Lapses from perfect health are caused by illnesses, whether or not wholly disabling, by physical defects, and by other conditions that impair health and vigor. Information on the prevalence in this country even of disabling defects and diseases has until recently been quite lacking and is still incomplete. A miscellany of data must be used to throw some light on this important subject.

The Age Curve of Good Health

An "age curve of good health" was made by Edgar Sydenstricker on the basis of studies in Hagerstown, Md., and later by experts of the Committee on the Costs of Medical Care.[1] This latter curve, based on data from over 8,500 white families in different parts of the United States, shows the proportion of persons of each age for whom no illness was reported for an entire year. The peak of freedom from illness as shown here comes in the late 'teens for women and in the early twenties for men. The curve of good health for men is higher than that for women. The findings of this survey agree with Sydenstricker's data on these points. It is not surprising to find the least illness at about 20 years of age, when athletic prowess is greatest, although the lowest death rates are found 10 years earlier, at about 10–13 years of age. The fact that

women are reported as being less healthy than men is perhaps more surprising, particularly in view of the fact that, under modern conditions, death rates are consistently higher for adult males than for adult females. Records of days lost through disabling illness by industrial workers, as reported by the Metropolitan Life Insurance Co. and in several European studies, show a somewhat different relationship between the sexes, with higher illness rates for women than for men between the ages of 15 and 44, but with lower illness rates for women after this period. (See table 1.)

The curves of good health shown here are presented as interesting approximations to the actual situation, but the data on which they are based are open to question. For example, it is quite possible that the illness records obtained from home interviews are more complete for women than for men. At most ages between 5 and 65 years, the proportion of persons who pass a whole year without illness ranges between 40 and 60 percent.[2] Roughly

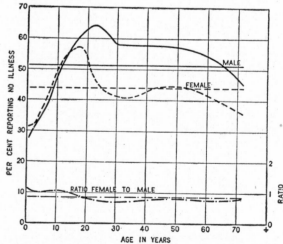

FIGURE 1.—The age curves of "good health." From Falk, Klem, Sinai, *The Incidence of Illness.*

---

[1] The curves are given in Falk, Isidore S., Klem, Margaret C., and Sinai, Nathan, *The Incidence of Illness and the Receipt and Costs of Medical Care*, Committee on the Costs of Medical Care, Publication No. 26 (1933), 67. See also Sydenstricker, Edgar, The Illness Rate Among Males and Females, *Public Health Reports*, 42: 1939–1951 (July 29, 1927).

[2] An illness was defined in this study as "any disorder which wholly or partly disables an individual for one or more days or any experience for which medical service of any kind is received. Any condition, symptom, or disorder for which drugs costing 50 cents or more are purchased is considered an illness." Falk, Klem, and Sinai, *op. cit.*, 8.

speaking, sickness now strikes about half of the population one or more times a year. Slightly over one-half of all illness as here defined causes some loss of time from school or work; about one-sixth of the cases involve an absence of 12 days or more.[3]

The Extent and Costs of Illness

Comparing total illnesses with total population, it is conservatively estimated that there is about one illness per person per year.[4] Each male worker, on the average, loses about 1 week each year, 7 to 9 days. The average loss for each female worker is somewhat greater, from 8 to 12 days.[5] The extent of disabling illness for male and females at different ages as revealed through a series of surveys is shown in table 1.[6] The rates shown here represent the proportion of persons ill at the time of the census. About 2 percent of the total population surveyed were found to be disabled through sickness at the time of the census.

[3] Falk, Klem, and Sinai, *op. cit.*, 275.
[4] Sydenstricker, *Health and Environment*, p. 35; Mills, Alden B., *The Extent of Illness and of Physical and Mental Defects Prevailing in the United States* (1929), 5.
[5] Mills, Alden B., *op. cit.*, 5.
[6] The communities studied were Rochester, N. Y.; Chelsea neighborhood of New York City; Trenton, N. J.; Boston; industrial villages of North Carolina; cities in Pennsylvania and West Virginia; and Kansas City, Mo.

Some idea of the major illnesses and impairments affecting the people of the United States today is conveyed by table 2. This table shows the Nation's need for medical care, in terms of the estimated number of cases of different kinds requiring diagnosis and treatment in any one year.

The daily productivity of American workers is apparently cut directly by about 2 percent through absences due to acute illness and accident. When additional losses in production resulting from delays, disorganization of rou-

TABLE 1.—*Prevalence of disabling illness by age and sex, Metropolitan Life Insurance Co. surveys, 1915–17* [1]

Age	Percentage of persons sick and unable to work		
	Both sexes	Male	Female
0–14	1.1	1.1	1.1
15–24	1.3	1.2	1.4
25–34	1.6	1.4	1.8
35–44	2.1	2.0	2.2
45–54	3.0	3.3	2.8
55–64	4.8	5.4	4.2
65+	9.5	10.6	8.7

[1] From Sydenstricker, Edgar, *Health and Environment* (1933), p. 33. Based on *Some Recent Morbidity Data* compiled by Margaret Loomis Stecker from the reports of the Community Sickness Surveys by Lee K. Frankel and Louis I. Dublin.

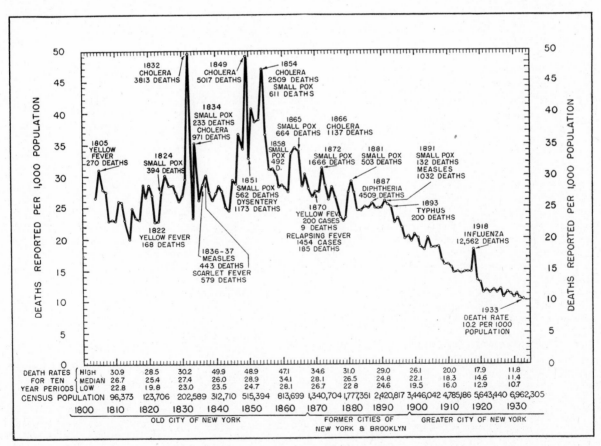

FIGURE 2.—Trend in mortality in New York City, 1804–1929. From Boldaun, "The Conquest of Pestilence", *Milbank Memorial Fund Quarterly*, vol. XIII, no. 3 (July 1935).

tine, time spent in training substitutes, and lowered efficiency resulting from acute disabilities are taken into account, it is probable that the total loss from such disabilities is at least 5 percent of the normal productivity of the Nation.[7] At the 1929 price level, this estimated waste of productive capacity represents an annual loss to the Nation of about 4 billion dollars. This is approximately equal to the ordinary expenses of the Federal Government in 1929.

TABLE 2.—*Estimate of cases of disease and conditions requiring medical diagnosis and treatment* [1]

Disease	Expectancy rates per 1,000 persons, all ages	Estimated cases, United States, 1930
Total	936. 30	114, 954, 000
Respiratory system	459. 00	56, 354, 000
Digestive system	117. 00	14, 365, 000
Acute communicable diseases	92. 50	11, 357, 000
Injuries from external causes	54. 00	6, 630, 000
Puerperal state	23. 56	2, 893, 000
Syphilis and gonorrhea	23. 00	2, 824, 000
General diseases	21. 00	2, 578, 000
Diseases of the skin and cellular tissue	19. 90	2, 443, 000
Nervous and mental conditions	16. 29	2, 000, 000
Nonvenereal diseases of the female genital organs	16. 00	1, 964, 000
Diseases of the ear and mastoid process	15. 00	1, 842, 000
Neuralgia, neuritis, and sciatica	13. 10	1, 608, 000
Neurasthenia and nervous exhaustion	13. 10	1, 608, 000
Diseases of the muscles, bones and joints	13. 00	1, 596, 000
Diseases of the kidneys and adnexa	12. 10	1, 486, 000
Diseases of the heart, arteriosclerosis and high blood pressure	11. 70	1, 436, 000
Diseases of the eye and adnexa	8. 50	1, 044, 000
Other diseases of the circulatory system	6. 80	835, 000
Nonvenereal diseases of the male genital organs	0. 75	92, 000

[1] Expectancy rates from Lee, Roger I., and Jones, Lewis W., *The Fundamentals of Good Medical Care*, Committee on the Costs of Medical Care, Publication No. 22 (1933), 97–100.

The estimate given above does not include the costs of medical care, chronic disability, or the destruction of life through death. Nearly as great an amount was also spent directly for medical services, including the minor outlay for preventive services. (See table 3.)

The loss through death, before they reach the age of 18 years, of 10 out of every 100 children born in this country, and the additional loss of 10 out of every 100 possible years of life between 18 and 60, is appalling. Many of these lives might be saved through the application of measures already known; others may be saved by future advances of science. It is easy to derive fictitious estimates of the economic loss to the Nation from deaths, by reckoning the reduction in capacity for production and ignoring the reduction in con-

[7] Brundage estimates that the average cost to the employer for illnesses among industrial workers is equal to 1½ times the wage loss of employees. This estimate does not cover loss in productive capacity resulting from chronic unemployment due to ill health. On the other hand, the costs of disability are probably higher in industry than in agriculture. No exact estimate of any of these items is possible. See Brundage, Dean K., "An Estimate of the Monetary Value to Industry of Plant Medical and Safety Services", *Public Health Reports*, 51: 1145–1159 (Aug. 21, 1936).

TABLE 3.—*Total expenditures for medical care* [1]

[In thousands of dollars]

Service	Total	Sources of funds			
		Patients	Governments	Philanthropy	Industry
Physicians in private practice	1, 090, 000	1, 040, 000			50, 000
Dentists in private practice	445, 000	445, 000			
Secondary and sectarian practitioners	193, 000	193, 000			
Graduate nurses, private duty	142, 000	142, 000			
Practical nurses, private duty	60, 000	60, 000			
Hospitals, operating expenses	656, 000	278, 000	300, 000	54, 000	24, 000
Hospitals, new construction	200, 000		100, 000	100, 000	
Public health	121, 000		93, 500	27, 500	
Private laboratories [2]	3, 000	3, 000			
Orthopedic and other supplies [2]	2, 000	2, 000			
Glasses [2]	50, 000	50, 000			
Drugs [2]	665, 000	665, 000			
Organized medical services	29, 000	7, 790	16, 000	210	5, 000
Total	3, 656, 000	2, 885, 790	509, 500	181, 710	79, 000

[1] Source: *Medical Care for the American People; the Final Report of the Committee on the Costs of Medical Care* (1932), p. 14. The data, with a few minor exceptions, apply to the year 1929.
[2] Includes only those expenditures not included in other items.

sumption needs, or by reckoning the costs of supporting children and ignoring the costs of supporting aged people. From the economic and social standpoint, the loss sustained by individual families suddenly deprived of breadwinners is very great. But these losses must be measured chiefly in terms of human suffering, defeated hopes, and disrupted homes.

It is impossible to estimate accurately the economic cost, to say nothing of the immediate personal losses, caused by lowered vitality resulting from malnutrition, indigestion, allergies, colds, malaria, organic impairments of various kinds, mental deficiency, and mental disease.

2. Trends of Death and Health in the United States

In assessing the progress made in overcoming disease, it is necessary to rely at many points on fragmentary data. It is especially difficult to get reliable data on trends in diseases and impairments; here we must rely largely on death rates. This is unsatisfactory, since disease rates are often far from proportional to death rates from the corresponding disorders. Accurate data on the health and physical condition of the population depend on standardized examination procedures, and on recording systems that have not yet been applied extensively. The collection of data on births and deaths for the total United States has just begun, and in some areas even this information is sadly deficient. The efforts made by the Committee on the Handicapped Child of the White House Conference on Child

Health and Protection to assemble information on physical and mental handicaps in childhood reveal the gaps in knowledge in this field. The development and correlation of knowledge in the fields of human biology, including anthropology, physiology, genetics, psychology, and medicine, is a task that will tax the resources of scientific workers for many decades. At present it is possible to sketch the story of progress in health and of group variations in disease and impairment only in broad and sometimes uncertain outlines.

Three points stand out in a summary review of the health record of the past 100 years:

1. The prevention of severe epidemics of smallpox, cholera, and yellow fever has eliminated violent fluctuations in mortality from these diseases.

2. Beginning about 1875, many communicable diseases have shown steady decreases, following a decline in tuberculosis which had begun before that time.

3. The record is ambiguous as to many other diseases; in many cases the trend of age-specific death rates has been clearly downward, but in other cases it has been stationary or even upward.

These changes reflect, in large part, the influence of the public health movement in applying systematically the findings of medical research. At first the emphasis was placed upon sanitation and provision of pure water supplies. Measures of control over communicable diseases, such as diphtheria, were developed later. Now the stage of a general attack on all diseases, with attention to basic factors in health, such as industrial conditions, nutrition, and recreation, has been reached.

Control of Epidemic Diseases

The great epidemics of cholera and yellow fever that visited this country periodically during the nineteenth century no longer exist. Smallpox, which used to be regarded as a common disease of childhood and which also attacked many older people, is now quite rare. In 1902 there were 2,000 deaths from smallpox within the death-registration area, which then included only two-fifths of the population of the country; in 1934, there were only 24 deaths from this disease in the whole United States. Continued vigilance—vaccination, notification of cases, and segregation of the sick—will maintain the good record in meeting this disease.

The partial conquest of typhoid fever is another outstanding achievement in the public-health field. In the 1900's typhoid fever caused more than 10,000 deaths each year in the death-registration area as defined in 1900. For the entire country there were perhaps 25,000 deaths annually, with 250,000 cases a year. Control of typhoid has come through improvement of sanitation, better water and milk supplies, especially in cities, methods of tracing each case to its point of origin, and identification and control of typhoid carriers. As a result, typhoid fever has been virtually eliminated in the larger cities with good water and milk supplies. The rate in such cities is 1 or less per 100,000. At the rate prevailing in 1900 (35.9 per 100,000 population) there would have been 44,035 deaths from typhoid and nearly half a million cases in 1930; actually there were only 4,300 deaths and 40,000 cases. Figure 3 pictures the control of typhoid fever in one large city, Philadelphia.

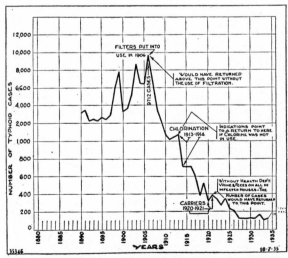

FIGURE 3.—Decrease in typhoid fever, Philadelphia, 1880–1935. From Johnson, "Epidemiological Features of a Typhoid Fever Outbreak after a Supper", *American Journal of Public Health*, vol. XXVI (September 1936).

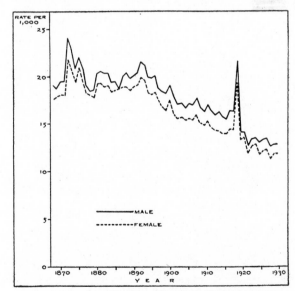

By permission of the publishers, McGraw-Hill Book Company, Inc.

FIGURE 4.—Decline in mortality for males and females, Massachusetts, 1868–1930. From Sydenstricker, *Health and Environment*.

The Decline in the Death Rate

The trend in the general death rate, representing chiefly the gains made in the control of communicable diseases, is shown in Figure 4 for one State (Massachusetts) in which good records are available for the past 50 years. Prior to 1875 the records may be incomplete; after that date a consistent downward trend appears, save for the sharp rise caused by the influenza epidemic of 1918. The greatest advances in lowering mortality have been made at the first years of life, since children are especially susceptible to infectious diseases.

The progress made in control of some dread diseases, especially tuberculosis, that attack people of all ages is shown by lowered death rates at all ages between 15 and 55 years (see Figure 5). On the other hand, there has been little net change in death rates above age 55. Here death results most frequently from degenerative diseases, such as heart disease, nephritis, cancer, the causes of which have proved extremely baffling. In order to understand trends in death rates and the outlook for longevity and health, therefore, it is necessary to take account of the very different incidence of death from particular diseases at different ages, as illustrated in Figures 6 and 7.

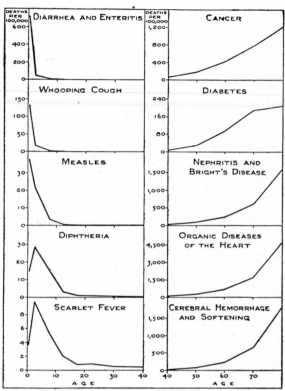

By permission of the publishers. McGraw-Hill Book Company, Inc.

FIGURE 6.—Age incidence of mortality from selected diseases, 1930, United States death registration area of 1900. From Sydenstricker, *op. cit.*

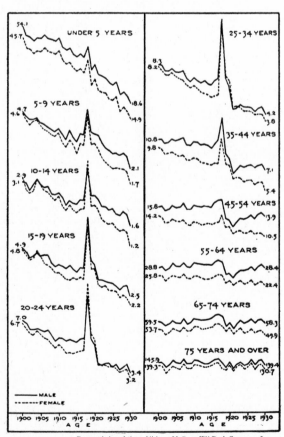

By permission of the publishers. McGraw-Hill Book Company, Inc.

FIGURE 5.—Trends in mortality by age and sex, United States death registration area of 1900. From Sydenstricker, *op. cit.*

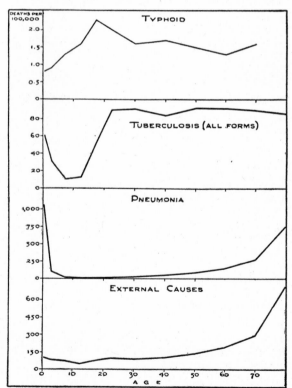

By permission of the publishers. McGraw-Hill Book Company, Inc.

FIGURE 7.—Age incidence of mortality from certain important causes of death, 1930, United States death registration area of 1900. From Sydenstricker, *op. cit.*

Conditions Relating to Birth and Infancy

There is a fundamental distinction between the problems encountered in the control of infectious diseases and those relating to organic impairments. This is important in understanding the progress made in overcoming infant mortality. In this field, the decline in the death rate has been least during the first weeks of life. This situation is found in all countries.[8] In New Zealand, where infant mortality has reached the lowest figure achieved anywhere, the death rate for infants during the last 11 months of the first year of life fell from 60 per 1,000 live births in 1881–85 to 10 per 1,000 in 1931–32. On the other hand, the death rate during the first month of life remained fixed around 30 per 1,000 live births from 1881–85 until 1911–15. Although it has declined since then, it has not yet reached the level of 20 per 1,000. Detailed analysis of causes of death and related conditions shows that the great gains in this field have come through reduction of diarrhea and enteritis and other infectious diseases, whereas the early infant deaths that are due in large part to congenital conditions and accidents of birth are far more difficult to control.

Waste of life through miscarriage and stillbirths and associated problems of maternal mortality still present a challenging field for medical research and organization. In Maryland, where all reported losses of "products of gestation" are classified as "stillbirths", the number of such losses is now about equal to the loss through death during the first year of life. Even this is an understatement of the total loss, as most spontaneous abortions, as well as most induced abortions, escape report.

The loss of 6 lives out of every 1,000 maternity cases in the United States should command earnest attention. It has been shown by a special study in Boston that these losses are largely concentrated among women with complications before childbirth. For them the risk of pregnancy appears to be six times as great as in the case of pregnancies without such complications.[9] This points to the possibility of great improvement in maternal health through diagnosis and treatment of complicating conditions, chiefly conditions of the kidneys, and the avoidance of pregnancy in cases where health hazards are likely to develop.

Advances in Child Health

There have been great advances in the whole field of child health during the last 50 years, chiefly through control of communicable diseases, but more recently in nutrition and in other aspects of general health.[10] The control of diphtheria shows the most striking results, due to the discovery of antitoxin, and methods of immunization by toxin-antitoxin or toxoid. The annual death rate for this disease has dropped from 43.3 per 100,000 population in 1900 to 3.3 in 1934. It appears in the latter year in third place among the common diseases of childhood as a cause of death, below whooping cough and measles. Each of these latter diseases, however, still afflicts more than a million children and causes from 4,000 to 8,000 deaths in the United States each year (see table 4). The number of deaths from whooping cough and measles has also decreased greatly. Between 1909 and 1933 the death rate for measles decreased from 9.6 to 2.2 per 1,000, though in 1934 it rose to 5.5. No comparable evidence is available as to whether the number of cases of measles has diminished, if at all, during the same period. Whooping cough here appears as the most serious of the diseases of childhood. It should be noted, however, that the frequencies of contagious diseases vary greatly from year to year.

TABLE 4.—*Deaths and estimated number of cases of certain common diseases of childhood, United States, 1934*[1]

Disease	Estimated cases	Deaths
Whooping cough	1,500,000	7,518
Measles	1,800,000	6,986
Diphtheria	46,000	4,159
Scarlet fever	300,000	2,524
Mumps	1,440,000	----------
Chickenpox	1,000,000	----------

[1] For case-rate estimates, see Sydenstricker, Edgar, and Wheeler, Ralph E., Whooping Cough in Surveyed Communities, *American Journal of Public Health*, 26: 582 (June 1936). Also Collins, Selwyn D., Age Incidence of the Common Communicable Diseases of Children, *Public Health Reports*, 44: 763–826 (April 5, 1929). *Public Health in New York State*, State of New York, Department of Health (1932), 404.

Some Outstanding Achievements and Problems in the Control of Disease

Malaria.—Progress in the control of tuberculosis and typhoid fever has made possible the greatest gains yet achieved in the saving of adult life, although much remains to be done about both diseases. Less has been accomplished as yet toward the control of malaria, which is one of the major debilitating diseases in this country. Although its fatality rate is low, it is now comparable to typhoid fever as a cause of death in the United States. It is confined largely to certain areas in the Southern States, although it may appear sporadically elsewhere. In 1932, when the prevalence of malaria was at a low ebb, the number of cases was estimated at one and a half million. In 1934 its prevalence was higher than it had been for years; estimates of cases ran as high as five and six millions, but the figure presented here is 2,700,000 cases. (See table 5.)

Tuberculosis.—Tuberculosis is still a major cause of death, although the control of milk supply, improved care of patients, public

[8] Stouman, K., The Perilous Threshold of Life, *League of Nations, Quarterly Bulletin of the Health Organisation*, 3 : 531–612 (December 1934).
[9] The Hazards of Complications in Pregnancy, *Statistical Bulletin, Metropolitan Life Insurance Co.* (September 1932), 6.
[10] See sec. 4 below.

TABLE 5.—*Deaths and estimated number of cases of tuberculosis, malaria, and typhoid fever in the United States, 1934*

Disease	Deaths	Estimated cases [1]
Tuberculosis	71,609	644,000
Malaria	4,520	2,700,000
Typhoid and paratyphoid fever	4,237	42,000

[1] Basis for estimates supplied by L. L. Williams, Jr., M. D., of the United States Public Health Service.

health education, and general rise in level of living has reduced its annual toll per 100,000 population from 201 deaths in 1900 to 57 deaths in 1934. In view of the fact that there is a high incidence of tuberculosis among young adults, reduction of that disease means an enormous saving of years of human life. In the white population, for which tuberculosis death rates are much lower than for the colored population, this disease in 1930 still cut about 1 year from the expectation of life of each child at birth.[11] The reduction in tuberculosis death rates at specific ages for white and colored males and females is shown in figure 8. It will be noted that a distinct peak appears at about 20 years of age in the graphs for females, both white and colored, and for colored males. Effective attack, therefore, is especially directed toward conditions affecting susceptibility to the disease in the late 'teens and early twenties.

The respiratory diseases.—Pneumonia and influenza together constituted the third most important cause of death in the United States in 1934—122,441 deaths, or 96.9 per 100,000 population. Slightly more than 100,000 of these deaths were from pneumonia. On this basis (with an average fatality rate of about 20 percent) it can be estimated that there were 500,000 cases of pneumonia in the United States in 1934.[12]

The minor respiratory diseases bulk very large in morbidity rates. Recent studies of the prevalence of the common cold suggest that each individual has on the average three and one-third colds a year.[13] Some lucky ones get through a season with none at all, while others suffer repeated attacks. With a total population of 128,000,000 this means the staggering total of 425,000,000 colds a year; a vivid picture of the amount of discomfort and minor disability that this ailment causes. A small proportion, perhaps one-tenth, of these cases involve actual absence from work or school. The common cold is more sinister than is ordinarily assumed, since it may result in pneumonia. There is much interest at present

in research on the respiratory diseases, many of which result from virus infections. Some scientific experiments already in progress afford hope that considerable advance may be made without too much delay.

Syphilis.—Syphilis is coming to be recognized as a major problem in the public health field. This dread disease shows, in a series of surveys covering communities with a total of 29,000,000 population, 4.3 cases actually under treatment per 1,000 persons.[14] This indicates the probable presence in this country of some 5,000,000 people, either being treated or in need of being treated for syphilis. Though the disease does not figure largely in the death rates, it is a factor in many deaths attributed to other causes. The problem is one of control over sources of infection and of requiring treatment of all those infected. Methods of public-health control developed in Sweden and Denmark have produced great reductions in this disease. Trends in the number of known cases in several Scandinavian cities are shown in figure 9. (The apparent peak in 1920 may be due to the new registration of old cases at that time.) The introduction of similar measures in this country would undoubtedly produce similar results. The control and eradi-

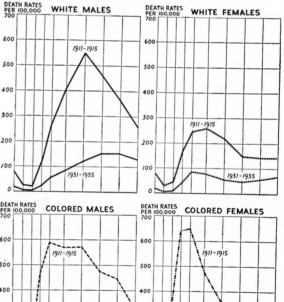

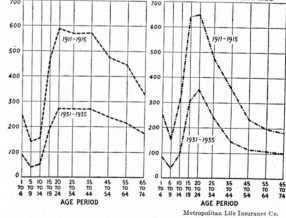

Metropolitan Life Insurance Co.

FIGURE 8.—Trends in age incidence of mortality from tuberculosis by sex and color. From *The Mortality from Tuberculosis.*

[11] For comparisons see Dublin, Louis I., and Lotka, Alfred J., *Length of Life* (1936), 127–128.
[12] Green, Howard W., and Moorehouse, George W., "Corrected Fatality Rates in Public Health Practice", *Public Health Reports*, 45: 169–177 (January 24, 1930).
[13] Collins, Selwyn D., and Gover, Mary, "Incidence and Clinical Symptoms of Minor Respiratory Attacks with Special Reference to Variation with Age, Sex, and Season". *Public Health Reports*, 48: 1155–1178 (September 22, 1933).

[14] Usilton, Lida J., "Trend of Syphilis and Gonorrhea in the United States based on Treated Cases", Reprint No. 51 from *Venereal Disease Information*, 16: 15 (May 1935).

cation of syphilis is not a question of medical knowledge but simply one of public willingness to bring about legislation which will make this knowledge effective.

The degenerative diseases.—The most baffling problems in medicine today relate to cancer and the degenerative diseases. Human life, unless ended voluntarily, must end through accident or disease. A better understanding of physiology and conditions affecting the structure and functioning of various bodily organs may increase the span of life considerably, but it cannot obviate the expectation of an eventual breakdown in some organic systems in the years preceding death. In many cases the impairment of vital organs results from infections, and the control of such infections may prevent or delay the illness that would otherwise result.

The situation with regard to heart diseases illustrates this possibility. Although this group of diseases is now the leading cause of death, there has been very appreciable lowering of the death rate from heart disease among young adults.[15] This has been brought about chiefly through decreasing deaths from valvular heart diseases by reduction in rheumatic

and other types of infection affecting the heart. The control of syphilis affords one important avenue of further progress in this field.

Industrial Hygiene and Control of Accidents

In the last 20 years considerable progress has been made in the field of industrial hygiene; benefits in many cases have accrued, not only to employees, but also to their families and the communities where they live. The possibilities of such developments, however, are by no means exhausted, and still affect only a small minority of the industrial population.[16] This will probably continue to be true until there is more general understanding of the fact that the largest dividends from proper industrial medical service are realized by employers. Safeguarding employees from accident and sickness has an economic as well as a humanitarian motive. A recent estimate of possible savings to employers from accident- and sickness-prevention campaigns sets an annual figure of $8,600 per 1,000 employees from reduction in accidents and $4,000 per 1,000 employees from a decrease in the sickness time-lost rate. These figures were computed for industries in which there were no extraordinary occupational hazards.[17] Great progress in decreasing accidents of all kinds has been made as a result of workmen's compensation laws.[18]

Much has already been accomplished through safety devices, designing of machinery and tools, educational campaigns, reorganization of plants, and so on. Some methods are designed to eliminate unnecessary hazards, others to protect the worker from hazards that cannot be eliminated. An example of the first type is the provision for rock-dusting of gaseous coal mines to prevent explosions and mass accidents in unprotected mines; an example of the second is the requirement that workers exposed to flying particles wear glasses. Examinations that test the susceptibility of individual employees to certain poisons and other hazards to health are also important. Another method is the identification and elimination of employees who are prone to accident. The chief industrial hazards, aside from exposure to accidents, are the inhalation of harmful dusts of various kinds, the absorption of pow-

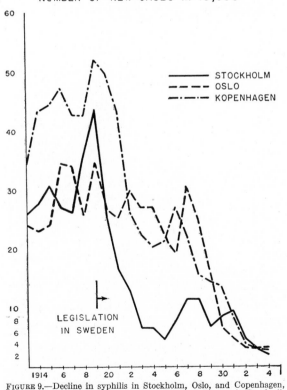

SYPHILIS IN STOCKHOLM, OSLO AND COPENHAGEN
NUMBER OF NEW CASES IN 10,000

—— STOCKHOLM
----- OSLO
—·—·— KOPENHAGEN

LEGISLATION IN SWEDEN

FIGURE 9.—Decline in syphilis in Stockholm, Oslo, and Copenhagen, 1914–24. From Rietz, "Prevention of Venereal Disease in Sweden", *American Journal of Public Health*, vol. XXXVI (April 1936).

[15] See Dublin, Louis I., and Armstrong, Donald B., *Favorable Aspects of Heart Disease*, Metropolitan Life Insurance Co., Industrial Department (October 9, 1933).

[16] A study of plans for health services in industrial establishments was made by the United States Bureau of Labor Statistics in 1926. Whitney, Anice L., *Health and Recreation Activities in Industrial Establishments, 1926*, U. S. Bureau of Labor Statistics, Bulletin No. 458 (1928), summarized the plans in effect in leading companies, but did not give any comprehensive picture of the scope and extent of such plans. The Committee on the Costs of Medical Care made studies of the health services given in the Endicott-Johnson Company and in two or three communities where plants with industrial health services were located, but it made no comprehensive study of the extent and scope of such plans. For a summary of their findings on this subject see *Medical Care for the American People*, Final Report, Committee on the Costs of Medical Care, Publication No. 28 (1932), 79–83, also publications 5, 18, and 20.
[17] Brundage, *op. cit.*, 1158.
[18] See Woodbury, Robert M., *Social Insurance, An Economic Analysis* (1917).

erful poisons, and excessive heat, cold, or humidity. The effects of these conditions have been studied and many important practical improvements have been introduced. But important advances may still be expected from research in this field. Hazards are often discovered only after the adoption of new processes. With greater care, and cooperation between medical and production departments, the development of some of these risks could be prevented.

Public accidents take an enormous toll of life, owing to the rapid increase in automobile traffic and the increasing speed of travel. The primary responsibility rests with public officials in charge of traffic control and of motor-vehicle registration. There is need for further study both of physical conditions affecting highway accidents, and of the relative importance and means of controlling the human factors involved, such as fatigue, drunkenness, eye-strain, and so forth.

Conclusion

Insight into the practical possibility of the improvement of health in the United States of a sort that would be reflected in increased longevity can be obtained from a comparison of death rates for specific diseases in this country with those now prevailing in New Zealand, where public health activities are more advanced and other conditions are more favorable to health. The expectation of life in New Zealand in 1931 was 65.04 for males and 67.88 for females—on the average about six years in excess of ours. This is an attainable goal for this country, provided the conditions that produce it can be equaled. Between 1906 and 1910 New Zealand's life expectancy was a little over 60 years, approximately the same as that of the United States in 1930.[19] Some of the outstanding possibilities of reduction of mortality in this country, merely through the more effective use of methods already known to medical science, are suggested by noting differences in favor of New Zealand in the death rates for certain groups of diseases. Expectation of life at birth is also significantly higher in Denmark, Holland, Norway, and Sweden than in the white population of the United States. The technical knowledge for further progress in health and longevity is already waiting to be applied.

3. The Prevalence of Common Mental and Physical Handicaps

We turn from diseases that are important causes of death to consider handicaps and impairments that lower efficiency, prove a lifelong thorn in the flesh, or, in the case of

mental deficiency and insanity, entail the loss of individual freedom and tragic social consequences. It is usually impossible to get any reliable evidence as to whether these conditions are increasing or decreasing and often difficult to estimate their actual prevalence.

The Prevalence of Mental Defects

The most comprehensive data on mental defects are those for drafted men, supplemented by subsequent mental examinations by Army psychiatrists. According to these figures the relative frequency of mental defect may be estimated at 12 per 1,000 for males aged 18 to 30.[20] Applying this percentage to the total population, there appear to be about 1,500,000 mental defectives in the United States. Because of the high death rates characteristic of the mentally deficient, the proportion of children who are so handicapped must be about 2 percent. A small proportion only of the feeble-minded are institutionalized, a total of about 100,000 persons.[21] Hereditary factors are probably the main cause of mental defect, although mental deficiency ratings are considerably influenced by environmental conditions; but some cases of feeble-mindedness are due to glandular diseases, birth injuries, and infections which involve the central nervous system.[22]

The Prevalence of Mental Disease

The problems of mental disease are in many respects more poignant and baffling than those relating to mental deficiency. There has been a large increase in recent years in the number of persons diagnosed as mentally diseased. This is due in part to improved facilities and greater attention to the needs of mental patients, and in part to the larger proportion of aged people in the population. It also reflects the difficulty of adjustment to urban conditions of persons who might get along fairly well and be accepted merely as "a little queer" in rural communities. Much insight into factors affecting the development of mental disease may be gained through studying variations in incidence among different groups and under different conditions, for example, by comparing rates of first admission to hospitals for mental

---

[19] See Thompson, Warren S., and Whelpton, P. K., *Population Trends in the United States* (1933), 258. Also Dublin and Lotka, *Length of Life* (1936), 346, 354, 372–373.

[20] For a compilation of the Army data on this subject see Lorimer, Frank, and Osborn, Frederick, *Dynamics of Population* (1934), 148–150.

"In the consideration of mental deficiency the standard for rejection was not always uniform, although generally understood to be a mentality of or below that of a child of 8 years." *Neuropsychiatry in the United States*, The Medical Department of the United States Army in the World War, X: 69.

[21] The United States census of 1933 reported 76,292 mental defectives in State institutions for mental defectives and epileptics (*Mental Defectives and Epileptics in Institutions, 1933*, p. 16), besides some 12,000 reported feeble-minded persons in almshouses (the latter figure is for 1923, as later figures on almshouses are not available). In State hospitals for mental diseases there were 24,388 patients diagnosed as mentally deficient (*Patients in Hospitals for Mental Disease, 1933*, p. 119). This gives a total of well over 100,000 mental defectives in institutions, or 0.81 per 1,000.

[22] See previous chapter for references and more extended discussion.

disease among those born within any state or community with rates for in-migrants from other areas (see ch. III, sec. 5, "The Social Effects of Migration"). Whether or not there has also been a real increase in the tendency to mental disease is one of the important problems in qualitative population study to which no definite answer can be given at the present time.

It is, in fact, extremely difficult to estimate the number of the mentally ill in this country at the present time, according to any given criterion. At the close of the year covered by the 1933 report on patients in hospitals for mental diseases, there were 435,571 persons in State institutions, institutions of the Veterans' Administration, and in county, city, and private hospitals.[23] This gives a rate for mental illness of 3.5 per 1,000 persons of all ages. This rate, of course, reveals the prevalence of mental illness only so far as provision is made for the care of mental disease and only so far as such provision is accepted. New York and Massachusetts, which have the best provisions for hospital care of mental patients, had a rate of 4.4 patients accepted for care per 1,000 population at the beginning of 1933, in comparison with the average for the country at that time of 2.6 per 1,000.[24]

Some light is thrown on the probable prevalence of mental disease in the general population by data on the frequency of mental disease among men drafted during the World War, reported prior to their transfer to France or actual participation in warfare. It must be noted, however, that the army experience even in this country involved unusual strain and may have led in some cases to the appearance of mental disorders that would never have developed or would have passed unnoticed in the men's home communities. The draft data related to men from 21 to 30 years of age, not including any who were actually in the hospitals. In New York State the number rejected by local boards for "mental alienation" (excluding mental deficiency) was 3.0 per 1,000 men of draft ages.[25] An additional 5 per 1,000 men, accepted by the local boards and sent to camps, were diagnosed in camp as having psychoneuroses, as being constitutionally psychopathic or as having psychoses.[26] Practically all these cases were recommended for discharge, and most of these recommendations were carried out. The rate for the age class 20 to 30 years in mental

hospitals in New York State at that time was 2.9 per 1,000.[27] Thus there were about 2¾ cases of diagnosed mental illness outside the hospitals for each person of this age group in the hospitals. A similar computation for Massachusetts indicates about 2½ times as many persons aged 20–30 years outside of hospitals in that State who were diagnosed as psychopathic under Army conditions as there were persons of this age group in mental hospitals in that State per 1,000 persons of the same age. These figures agree tolerably well, indicating a total frequency of about 10 cases of mental disturbance per 1,000 young adults in their twenties. Still others (0.8 per 1,000 recruits) were diagnosed by the Army psychiatrists as showing milder types of mental defect, such as neuroses, hysteria, and neurasthenia. In view of the fact that hospital provisions are unusually adequate in these States, the number of the mentally ill in the United States must be three or four times the number of mental patients. This would indicate a total of 1½ to 2 million persons for the whole country.

Aside from the suffering and costs resulting from mental disorder among persons not in hospitals, the fact that more hospital beds are occupied by mental patients than by all other patients combined reveals the enormous personal and public problems raised by these disorders. A great body of knowledge is being accumulated relating to conditions affecting mental disease, but the main causal factors in most cases are still obscure. This situation clearly presents a challenge of the first order to modern science. National interest demands that every promising lead for research in this field be explored as rapidly and completely as possible.

The Blind

According to the census of 1930, there were 65,000 blind persons (including nearly 2,000 blind deaf-mutes), in a total population of 123,000,000, a rate of 52.8 per 100,000. Experts agree, however, that the census enumeration of the blind tends to understate the true number, because of the difficulties in locating all persons who belong in this category. The application of the definition of blindness by untrained census takers to borderline cases leads to uncertainties in enumeration.[28] A method of setting up and maintaining a register of the blind has been tried in a number of States. In connection with the census of 1930, a special check was made in two areas to determine the adequacy of these registers and to furnish a basis for an estimate of the true prevalence of blindness. The results of the

[23] United States Bureau of the Census, *Patients in Hospitals for Mental Disease, 1933*, p. 13. This number includes 42,304 persons who were on parole or otherwise absent from the State hospitals (p. 2).

[24] The difference between this rate (2.6) and that given above (3.5) represents patients on parole, those in local and private hospitals and in the hospitals of the Veterans' Administration, together with the increase in the number of patients during the year.

[25] *Defects Found in Drafted Men*, 626 ff.

[26] *Neuropsychiatry in the United States*, the Medical Department of the United States Army in the World War, X, p. 203. To form rates the numbers diagnosed by the psychiatrists are divided by figures for total strength furnished by the War Department.

[27] Ogburn, William F., and Winston, Ellen, The Frequency and Probability of Insanity, *American Journal of Sociology*, 34: 822–831 (March 1929).

[28] The instruction in 1930 was "Include as *blind* any person who cannot see well enough to read, even with the aid of glasses." *The Blind and Deaf Mutes in the United States 1930*, p. 2.

tests indicated that the rate of blindness was as high as 92 per 100,000.[29] This is considerably in excess of the census figure; it agrees closely with the results of an unpublished study made by the American Foundation for the Blind, in which the blind in 17 States with approximately half of the population of the country were estimated at 56,566, at which rate the blind in the whole country would number 114,000.[30]

About three-fourths of all blindness is caused by disease, one-fourth by external causes. Of the diseases, cataract, glaucoma, atrophy of the optic nerve, trachoma, and ophthalmia neonatorum cause the largest loss. Some of these are rapidly being brought under control; others involve hereditary conditions, of which only a part can be remedied by known medical or surgical methods. In this, as in many other health fields, progress can be most rapid in combating infectious diseases or other environmental factors. Industrial accidents are the most important in the latter category.

Although blindness handicaps a considerable number of children, total blindness is in the main an affliction of the aged. (See table 6.) The number of persons with seriously defective vision is, of course, far greater than that of the totally blind. Their needs, although less acute, are far more extensive.

Impaired Hearing

The census of 1930 revealed a total of 59,000 deaf-mutes (including 1,942 who were both blind and deaf-mute). An estimate by the Committee on Handicapped Children of the White House Conference places the number of children under 20 years of age with impaired hearing at 2 million.[31] This figure includes, of course, all degrees of impaired hearing; of the total, 17,000 are described as entirely "deaf." The committee estimated further that, on the basis of group tests for school children and for drafted men, 10 million persons in the United States suffer from impaired hearing to such a degree as to "seriously interfere with their educational and vocational progress, and with proper social adaptation."

The Crippled

The number of crippled children under 18 is estimated to be 300,000, one-third of whom need special education.[32] The estimated total

TABLE 6.—*Number of blind in the United States, distributed by age*

Age groups	Estimated number [1]	Estimated rate per 100,000 persons
Total	114,000	92.1
Under 5	912	8.1
5 to 9	2,052	16.3
10 to 14	3,306	27.5
15 to 19	3,648	31.6
20 to 24	3,534	32.5
25 to 44	18,012	49.8
45 to 64	32,034	149.5
65 and over	50,502	761.3

[1] The total in 1930, 114,000, as estimated in *The Handicapped Child*, p. 47, is distributed by age in the same proportions as the number of blind enumerated in the Census of 1930. The percentage distribution by age is: Under 5, 0.8; 5–9, 1.8; 10–14, 2.9; 15–19, 3.2; 20–24, 3.1; 25–44, 15.8 45–64, 28.1; 65 and over, 44.3.

number of crippled persons of all ages is 700,-000.[33] Adult cripples who were not crippled during childhood are in large part survivors of industrial accidents and war injuries. According to the standard million accident table, for every 932 fatal industrial accidents there are some 1,305 dismemberments involving more or less serious crippling.[34] On the basis of 22,500 fatal industrial accidents a year (estimate for 1918), Rubinow estimated that approximately 28,000 cases of dismemberments involving more or less crippling were being added each year to the adult population. More recently the number of fatal industrial accidents has been reduced to about 16,500 each year.[35]

Defects and Diseases Among Drafted Men

The Army draft data supply the most comprehensive information regarding the prevalence of diseases and defects among young men at the period of maximum physical vigor. (See table 7.) The conditions of the Army medical examinations were far from ideal for scientific purposes. However, the tabulation of these results gives some insight into the prevalence of handicaps of various sorts that afflict the young men of this Nation, at the ages when they are beginning their life work and undertaking family responsibilities.

[29] McKay, Evelyn C., Problems in Determining the Extent of Blindness, *Journal of the American Statistical Association*, 27: 47–52. *Proceedings* (March 1932).
[30] *The Handicapped Child.* Report of the Committee on Physically and Mentally Handicapped, White House Conference on Child Health and Protection (1933), 46–47.
[31] *The Handicapped Child*, 4.
[32] The estimate given by the Committee on Handicapped Children is made by using a standard ratio, based on a number of local surveys, of 2.5 crippled children per 1,000 population of all ages. (*Ibid.*, 132–133.) An alternative ratio of 3 per 1,000 gives 368,325 crippled children (pp. 133–134, 145).

[33] The estimate of 700,000 is secured by applying to the United States population the ratios of crippled to total population found in Massachusetts in 1905. The definition of crippled comprised the "lame, maimed, and deformed—the word maimed including the loss of an eye and other minor defects" (*Ibid.*, 127). An alternative method is to apply to the estimate of crippled children (300,000 under 18) the ratio of adult to child cripples found for Birmingham (1,001 adult to 728 child cripples under 16, or an estimated 961 adults to 768 child cripples under 18). This yields an estimated total of 687,000 cripples for all ages. If the larger figure of 368,000 child cripples under 18 is used, the cripples of all ages are estimated at 830,000. Rubinow, I. M., "A Statistical Consideration of the Number of Men Crippled in the War and Disabled in Industry", *American Journal of Care for Cripples*, 6: 84–98 (March 1918).
[34] Exclusive of eye cases and minor losses, e. g., one phalanx. *Ibid.*
[35] Letter from R. L. Forney, National Safety Council, dated May 23, 1936.

TABLE 7.—*Prevalence of diseases and defects among drafted men, 21 to 30 years of age inclusive, 1917–18, United States Army*

	Rate per 1,000 men [1]
Tuberculosis (total)	[2] 24. 86
Tuberculosis (pulmonary, plus suspected)	[2] 22. 02
Total venereal diseases	[3] 56. 69
Syphilis	[3] 10. 47
Chancroid	[3] 1. 50
Gonococcus infection	[3] 44. 72
Alcoholism	. 31
Drug addiction	. 54
Curvature of the spine	5. 53
Diabetes mellitus	. 27
Pellagra	. 09
Goiter, exophthalmic	3. 14
Goiter, simple	4. 35
Obesity	1. 80
Combined paralyses, hemiplegia, apoplexy, facial paralysis, paraplegia, monoplegia	2. 55
Epilepsy	5. 15
Chorea	. 22
Total, neurasthenia and neurosis, hysteria	. 89
Neurasthenia	. 54
Neurosis	. 12
Hysteria	. 23
Speech defective	1. 08
Total, deaf and dumb, mute; deaf, defective hearing	7. 69
Deaf and dumb mute	1. 00
Deafness	1. 22
Defective hearing	5. 47
Mental deficiency	[2] 12. 06
Mental alienation, all types	[2] 3. 02
Constitutional psychopathic status	[2] 0. 44
Dementia praecox	[2] 0. 65
Psychasthenia and psychoneurosis	[2] 0. 53
Psychosis, manic-depressive	[2] 0. 18
General paralysis of the insane	[2] 0. 08
Other	[2] 1. 14
Total eye defects	40. 74
Myopia	2. 85
Defective vision (cause not stated), astigmatism, hyperopia	30. 07
Trachoma	1. 37
Amblyopia	1. 07
Eye, enucleation of, blindness in one or both eyes	7. 81
Otitis media, perforated eardrum	8. 57
Deviation of nasal septum, hypertrophy of the turbinates	. 28
Sinusitis	. 52
Tonsillitis, hypertrophic	23. 09
Endocarditis, valvular diseases of the heart, etc	[2] 26. 26
Cardiac hypertrophy, cardiac dilation	4. 65
Myocarditis, myocardial insufficiency	. 72
All organic diseases of the heart	[2] 30. 74
Arterioclerosis and hypertension	. 37
Cardiac arrhythmias	1. 80
Tachycardia	4. 45
Total, hemorrhoids, varicocele, and varicose veins	8. 59
Hemorrhoids	1. 20
Varicocele	3. 25
Varicose veins	4. 14
Bronchitis	. 73
Asthma	2. 45
Defective and deficient teeth, with dental caries	13. 54
Total, hernia, and enlargement of inguinal rings	39. 82
Hernia	20. 83
Enlargement of inguinal rings	18. 99
Nephritis	. 80
Hydrocele	1. 14
Fracture, malunion of upper and lower extremity, shortening of lower extremity	7. 75
Upper extremity, loss of whole or part of	1. 93
Lower extremity, loss of whole or part of	3. 19
Total arthritis and ankylosis, bony and fibrous	9. 06
Arthritis	2. 31
Ankylosis, bony or fibrous	6. 75
Total, deformities and defects of the foot	128. 72
Hammer toe and hallux valgus	6. 79
Flatfoot, pes planus	109. 35
Pronated foot	6. 31
Foot deformity not specified, pes cavus	4. 03
Metatarsalgia	2. 24
Deformities of the hand, injury or infection	7. 50
Deformities, other	9. 34
Atrophy of muscle of upper or lower extremity	2. 59
Total, defective physical development, underweight and underheight	32. 93
Deficient chest measurement	. 87
Underweight	26. 50
Underheight	2. 91
Anorchism, cryptorchism, monorchism	3. 10
Cleft palate and harelip	. 53
Bullet or other recent wounds	. 51
Total, mechanical defects	215. 43

Source: Compiled from Love, Albert G., and Davenport, Charles B. *Defects Found in Drafted Men* (United States Surgeon General's Office) (1920), 101–168. See also pp. 53–58 for discussion of the bases used to derive ratios of defects.

[1] Ratios, unless otherwise specified, are total defects found by local boards and at camps, both among rejected and accepted men.
[2] Total rejections by local boards and at camps.
[3] Defects in second million men.

4. Diet and Nutrition

Nutrition and Health

In addition to the obviously crippled and defective, a considerable proportion of the population suffers from ill health and lowered energy and vitality due to improper nutrition. No single satisfactory index of physical well-being has been developed; no one criterion for judging a person's physical condition is universally applicable. Weight, color, endurance, poise, and sense of well-being all give evidence, but except for weight these are difficult to measure. The weight-height relationship and the adequacy of diets have been used frequently and are still probably the most satisfactory indices available.

The relation of height to weight has for a long time been used as a criterion for the selection of policyholders by life insurance companies. Their experience shows that before the age of 30, underweight of 10 percent or more is associated with higher than average mortality, especially from tuberculosis. After 30, overweight of 10 to 20 percent or more is associated with excess mortality, especially from heart disease, diabetes, and cancer, while underweight is associated with lower than average mortality.

The use of these relationships as general indices of health is practically impossible, since comprehensive information concerning the prevalence of underweight and overweight in the entire population is not available. There is ample evidence that average weight increases with age. This suggests that an increasing proportion of the population over 30 is tending away from the most desirable relation between weight and height. But there are no data showing whether this increase in average weight is sufficient to impair the health of an appreciable proportion of the population. Nevertheless, the weight-height relationship has value for each individual as a measure of his physical condition, quite apart from its value in the statistical appraisal of the entire population.[36]

There is ample proof that physical well-being is profoundly affected by diet. Experimental biology has shown that an animal's life processes may be disrupted by the omission from its food of any one of a number of food substances. In addition to the discovery of the influence of the various food elements upon amount and rate of growth, it has been demonstrated that conditions previously considered "normal" or as indicating a state of good health may be markedly improved with proper changes in diet. At the present time, however, much more is known about the kind of nutrients that should be included in the diet than about the exact amount of each essential element required for the best possible physical development.

Numerous studies indicate that relationships between nutrition and health which have been observed in animals also hold true among humans. Children of the poorer economic classes grow less rapidly and reach lower maximum height, on the average, than children in the better economic classes.[37] Increases in the average stature of college students and of children of immigrants indicate the influence of diet, medical attention, rest, and other environmental conditions subject to control.

Effects of Malnutrition

Gross diet deficiencies are revealed by the prevalence of certain diseases such as pellagra, rickets, scurvy, and beriberi. The last two diseases have practically disappeared as causes of death in this country, although they were common no longer than a generation ago.

Pellagra.—The most prevalent of the diet deficiency diseases in the United States is pellagra, which caused 3,602 deaths in 1934. This disease is relatively much more prevalent in the South, particularly the Southeast, than elsewhere, and is associated with diet deficiencies of certain groups in the population. (See fig. 10.) In some of these States a much

higher rate is found among the colored than among the white population. The mere number of deaths completely understates the extent of ill health due to pellagra. In Mississippi, where the system of reporting is best, there are approximately 20 reported cases for every death.[38] Even this figure is an understatement of its prevalence.

Rickets.—Rickets, a deficiency disease of young children, especially of those under 2 years of age, is characterized by lack of proper bone formation. In severe cases it may produce knock-knees, bowlegs, scoliosis, lordosis, and defective formation of teeth. Although it does not take a large toll in deaths, its effects are frequently visible throughout the lifetime of the individual affected. It was recently estimated that in urban areas "at least 50 percent of the child population under 2 years of age" have rickets.[39] The disease is less prevalent in rural districts, where more sunshine and less smoke give greater protection against rickets. The emphasis in recent years on proper diet for infants and young children has undoubtedly decreased the number of severe cases. Rickets shows a decided decrease in records of Chicago infant welfare stations from 1926 to 1935.

Other results of malnutrition.—The sharp rise of tuberculosis in Germany during the war years of food deprivation is evidence of the close relationship between nutrition and this disease. Anemia among children is also ascribed to faulty nutrition. The seriousness of the infectious diseases of childhood depends upon the state of health of those attacked. Children with rickets show a higher incidence of complications and a higher death rate than those in the same environment without rickets.[40]

The importance of nutrition in certain of these conditions is shown indirectly by tracing the effect of an extra supply of milk upon the rate of growth and health of school children. Orr cites the experiment of giving supplementary milk to 1,500 school children in Scotland during a period of 7 months. The rate of growth of those getting the extra milk was 20 percent greater than for those not receiving this addition to their food supply.[41]

Diet deficiencies resulting in obvious diseases or defects are serious enough in their social costs. Perhaps even more important, in view of the larger number of persons affected, is the lowered vitality caused by diets that are not sufficiently nutritious to promote the best possible health. Much more careful research is necessary before all of the nutritional requirements of human beings can be stated with a high degree of precision, but it is instructive

[36] The weight-height relationship formerly had a considerable vogue as an index of "nutrition" in children. But studies of Dublin and Gebhart and others showed the unscientific nature of such a test and the need for direct observation of clinical data on nutrition. It is nevertheless probably true that the proportion of underweight children, especially those more than 10 percent below average weight for height, who are undernourished or have defects is larger than the proportion among children who are of normal or average weight for height.

[37] For a summary of this evidence see McLester, James S., Nutrition and the Future of Man, *Journal of the American Medical Association,* 104 : 2144–2147 (June 1935).

[38] *The Notifiable Diseases. Prevalence in States* (1934). Supplement No. 117 to *Public Health Reports,* p. 12.
[39] Tonney, Fred O., "Vitamin D in Child Health", *American Journal of Public Health,* 26 : 665–671, esp. 668 (July 1936).
[40] Orr, John B., *Food, Health, and Income* (1936), 43.
[41] *Ibid.,* 48.

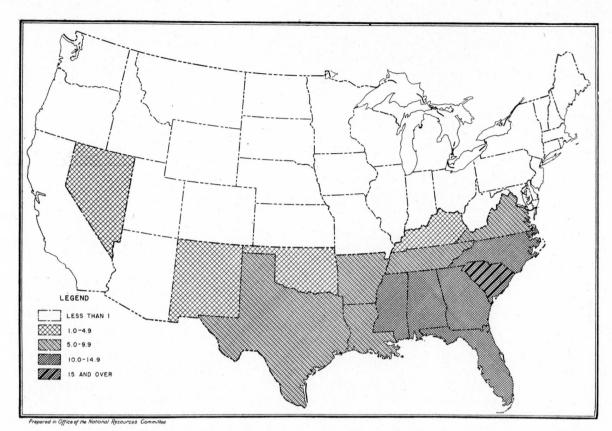

Prepared in Office of the National Resources Committee

FIGURE 10.—Mortality rate from pellagra (deaths per 100,000 population), by States, 1934.

to appraise everyday diets with reference to some of the more significant and well-recognized dietary factors.

Studies of Adequacy of the Diet of American Families

The nutritive value of the diets of a number of farm families is shown in figure 11. Although the number of cases is small, the main indications are borne out by supplementary data on family expenditures. Only when the average annual per-capita expenditure for food amounts to more than $100 do as many as one-

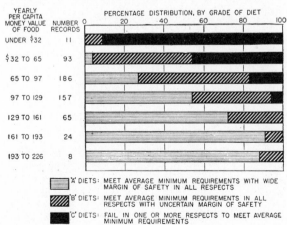

FIGURE 11.—Adequacy of farm family diets, 1917–32.

half of the families have diets that meet average minimum health requirements with a sufficient margin of safety. The significance of these data become more apparent when it is realized that in 1929 the gross agricultural income per rural-farm inhabitant throughout the South did not exceed $300 except in a very few counties. In extensive areas it was less than $150. The average yearly per-capita money value of the food consumed by a majority of the farm families in this area is undoubtedly far below $100. Moreover, since the nutritive value of foods, especially of the fats, minerals, and vitamins, may be greatly reduced in the process of cooking, the diets of these families are often more deficient than the per-capita value of food indicates. These dietary deficiencies may be reflected in listlessness, lack of energy, and low morale.

Even less is known about the adequacy of the diet of urban families than of farm families. There is reason for believing, however, that the diets of wage earners and lower-salaried clerical workers are perhaps more deficient nutritionally than the diets for farm families.[42]

The provision of more adequate diets throughout the population depends upon a more even distribution of income. It is pos-

[42] Stiebeling, Hazel K., "Nutritive Value of Diets of Families of Wage Earners and Clerical Workers in North Atlantic Cities 1934–35", *Monthly Labor Review* (July 1936), 43 : 14–23.

sible, however, through application of knowledge of foods and nutrition in food selection and preparation, for low income groups to obtain better diets and improve their nutrition and health, without necessarily increasing their total expense for food. For example, the diets of low income groups frequently include large proportions of flour and cereals and fats and fatty foods, but are deficient in calcium, iron, and vitamins B and G. Such families could improve the nutritive values of their diets if, at the expense of some of the foods which give rather small returns nutritionally for the expenditure, they would increase their consumption of milk, potatoes, and the leafy, green, and yellow vegetables. Such a shift in consumption habits depends on a much wider dissemination of the present knowledge of nutrition, as well as on more extensive investigation of the exact amount of the essential food elements necessary for proper nutrition. Changes in this direction would produce large social dividends, by increasing the general health and strength of the population. It would incidentally bring about an increased demand for new types of agricultural products.[43]

5. Variations in Health Among American Groups

Large variations in mortality and morbidity are found among groups in the same locality and in different sections of the country. Geographic variations in death rates and the prevalence of disease should not be regarded as in any sense permanent or unchangeable, or as arising either from unalterable climatic factors or from the biological heritage of the persons concerned. Such variations, as well as those between different economic and occupational groups, may more properly be ascribed to differences in local customs, knowledge of health provisions, and ability to provide for adequate medical facilities.

For diseases where morbidity bears little or no relation to mortality, regional comparisons are limited to the results of sampling surveys. Information of this sort is still meager, but has been extended considerably in recent years. Studies by the United States Public Health Service of the prevalence of such illnesses as pneumonia, colds, sore throat, and bronchitis do not reveal marked differences between broad geographic divisions.

In the case of diseases that are closely related to mortality, such as tuberculosis, malaria, typhoid fever, diphtheria, and others, death statistics afford some basis, even though an imperfect basis, for estimates of prevalence.

Geographic Differentials

Geographic differentials in mortality from all causes in the white population for the years 1929–31 are exhibited in figure 12. Since State populations vary considerably by sex and age, the standardized rates give a fairer idea of their relative positions. The standardized rates vary from 7.6 in South Dakota to 15.6 in New Mexico. The eastern seaboard has mortality rates slightly above the average, the West Central States have rates considerably less than the average. The four States of Colorado, Nevada, Arizona, and New Mexico had the highest mortality rates in the whole country, although the other States in the Mountain and far West divisions had lower than average mortality rates. The lowest apparent rates were found in North and South Dakota. In some cases these rates may be affected by incompleteness of registration.

Geographic differences in length of life vary inversely with mortality rates; the States with lowest mortality have the longest life expectancies. The latter range from a maximum of 64.4 years for white males and 66.8 years for white females for South Dakota, to a minimum of 48.1 years and 55.2 years, respectively, for Arizona, and 49.5 years and 52.2 years, respectively, for New Mexico. In the average expectation of life, there is a difference of nearly 15 years between the best and the worst States.[44] This figure is comparable to the gain of 15 years in life expectancy in Massachusetts between 1893–97 and 1930.

Rural-Urban Differences

States with the lowest mortality rates, and consequently the longest expectation of life, are States with a relatively large rural population. The greater average longevity of the rural population is well known; it undoubtedly arises from the more healthful environment and work in the open country. Within recent years, however, the provision of medical and hospital facilities and services, inspection of food and water supplies, protection against communicable diseases, and health education have progressed much more rapidly in urban than in rural communities. These things now largely offset the more healthy environmental conditions of the latter. Although comprehensive data are not available, the rural-urban differential in expectation of life at birth has probably been cut by more than one-half during the past 30 years.

A comparison of the mortality from specific diseases in urban and rural communities is largely vitiated by the fact that the deaths of

[43] See Waite, Warren C., and Black, John D., "Nutrition and Agricultural Policy", *Annals of the American Academy of Political and Social Science*, 188: 218–229 (November 1936).

[44] These differences may be somewhat overstated if the low mortality in South Dakota is due in part to inadequate registration of deaths, and if the high mortality of Arizona, New Mexico, Nevada, and Colorado is due in part to nonresident deaths—for example, deaths from tuberculosis of persons who have gone there from other States to avail themselves of climatic advantages.

rural residents who die in city hospitals have been (until 1935) recorded and tabulated according to the place of death rather than according to residence. For certain causes, such as appendicitis, urban rates are higher; for other causes, such as tuberculosis, rural rates are higher. A special tabulation in Ohio of mortality statistics for 1930 by residence of the deceased shows that there is little or no difference between urban and rural mortality rates during childhood and early adolescence. For the entire country, the infant mortality rate in urban areas is probably less than the rate in rural areas, although the reverse was true when the birth registration area was established in 1915. In Ohio in 1930 the death rate for the age class 20–30 years was significantly higher in the rural than in the urban native white population. After 30, however, urban rates become definitely higher, especially for males. (See fig. 13.)

It seems evident that these differences are influenced both by environmental conditions and by differences in health facilities. Rural people die in relatively greater numbers from the diseases of childhood—measles, scarlet fever, whooping cough, diphtheria—and from certain of the diseases of adolescence and young adult life such as tuberculosis. These are the diseases toward the control of which medical science has made the greatest progress. But the effort to control the diseases of adult life— heart disease, cancer, nephritis, cerebral hemorrhage, diabetes mellitus—has met with far less success, and these afflictions take a relatively smaller toll in rural than in urban communities.

It would not be surprising if illness rates were greater in rural than in urban areas, but almost no reliable data on this point are now available. The investigations of the Committee on the Costs of Medical Care suggest such a difference in favor of urban communities, but their data on this subject are inconclusive. The inequality of health services and information for rural areas is, however, clearly evident from the fragmentary information at hand.

Variations in the Incidence of Specific Diseases

Tuberculosis.—The same inequality explains much of the geographic variation in the incidence of different diseases. This is especially true for tuberculosis. It is true that the heaviest incidence is found in Arizona, New Mexico, Tennessee, and Colorado (see fig. 14), and the high rates in some Rocky Mountain and Southwestern States are due in large part to the migration of persons seeking the more health-

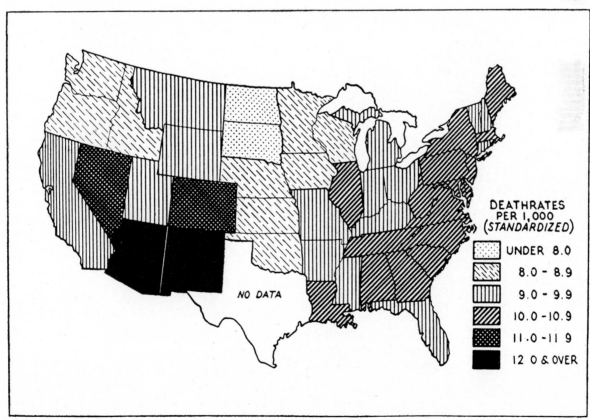

FIGURE 12.—Standardized death rates from all causes, white persons in the United States, 1929–31. ("White persons" includes Mexicans. Death rates are standardized on the basis of the Standard Million of England and Wales, 1901. The mortality for South Dakota is based on deaths for 1930 only.) From Dublin and Lotka, *Length of Life.*

DEATHRATES PER 1,000 (STANDARDIZED)

UNDER 8.0
8.0 - 8.9
9.0 - 9.9
10.0 - 10.9
11.0 - 11.9
12.0 & OVER

NO DATA

ful climate of these regions. A correction to eliminate the effect of such migration would give an entirely different idea of the incidence of the disease in these States. No such explanation seems to apply to the high rates of Tennessee (111 deaths per 100,000 population, yearly average for 1929–33) nor to the relatively high rates of Maryland (95), Kentucky (92), and Virginia (92). In these States the

rates for the entire population and for the white population alone are both much higher than in the surrounding States. Regions of low incidence are found in the Middle and Western States (Iowa, North Dakota, Nebraska, Kansas, Wyoming, Utah, and Idaho).

The situation of Tennessee and Kentucky and other States of the southeastern region has been further analyzed by Lumsden and

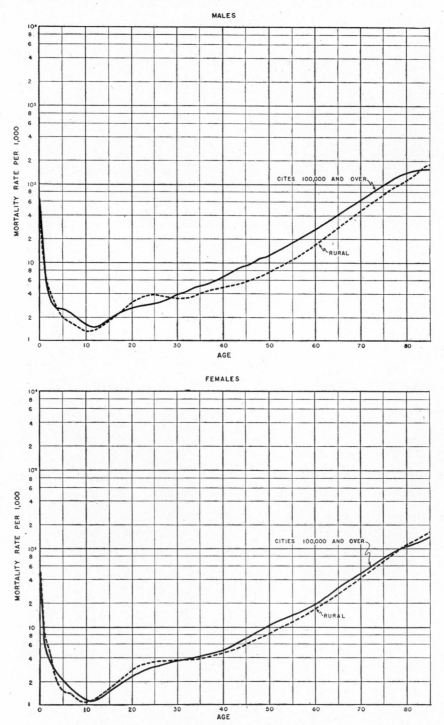

FIGURE 13.—Mortality rates per 1,000 native white persons, by age and sex, rural areas and cities of 100,000 or more population, Ohio, 1930.

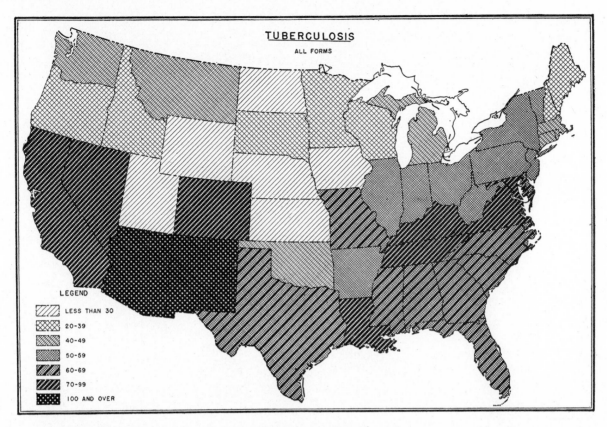

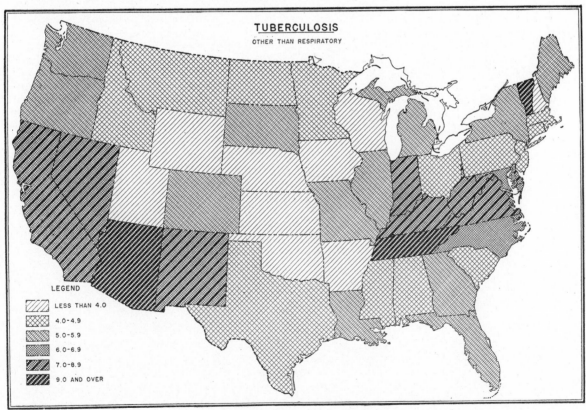

FIGURE 14.—Mortality rates from tuberculosis per 100,000 population, by States, 1934.

Dauer, who have prepared maps showing the distribution of tuberculosis by counties.[45] (See fig. 15.) These maps show a definite concentration of high mortality from tuberculosis for the white population in parts of Kentucky and Tennessee, with regions of relatively high rates in a surrounding belt covering the northern parts of Arkansas, Mississippi, Alabama, Georgia, North and South Carolina, and the whole of Virginia and Maryland. This area does not appear to correspond with any geographic characteristic, such as climate or temperature, that might help to explain the high incidence of tuberculosis. The fact that it is a region of high mortality is probably to be explained largely by such social conditions as low economic status, poor diets, and perhaps general ignorance of the best methods of combating the disease. In any case, these maps show areas where more intensive public health work against tuberculosis may be expected to yield large dividends.

The differences in regional distribution of tuberculosis among white and colored populations are of particular interest. Though there is some racial correspondence between regions of heavy incidence in Kentucky and Tennessee, there are many areas where high incidence of tuberculosis among colored is not associated with high incidence among the whites. The explanation for this may lie in the sharp differences between white and colored populations in the same districts as to habits, customs, and living quarters.

The sharp geographic differentials in tuberculosis rates clearly indicate possibilities for general reduction of this disease. Between 1900 and 1934 the mortality rate for this disease was reduced from 201.2 to 56.6, a reduction of 72 percent. But the rate for the country as a whole in 1934 was three times as high as that of Wyoming, the State with the lowest rate (18.5), and, as we have seen, much higher than average rates occur in some regions. The analysis of the country incidence of tuberculosis indicates that in some areas the mortality from tuberculosis has already been reduced nearly to the vanishing point. This suggests that by gradual extension of the areas that are practically free from the disease, tuberculosis can in large part be eliminated from the list of causes of death.

Malaria.—In contrast to tuberculosis, malaria is a relatively nonfatal disease; there are many cases of illness but a limited geographical range. This disease, formerly distributed throughout the country as far north as the Canadian border and west to the line of North

Dakota and Texas, is now limited to the States of the Southeast and Southwest—except that periodically, when the disease seems to take on increased virulence, it may appear sporadically in other States. A long downward trend of incidence, culminating in 1932, was followed by an increase of the rate and by an expansion of the area in 1934 and 1935, with a slight recession in 1936.

The range of difference between the rates is striking. Thirty-four States and the District of Columbia have either no deaths at all or less than 1 per 100,000 population. Among the remaining States, 4 have rates of less than 5 per 100,000, while 10 States (Missouri 5, Georgia 14, Florida 29, Tennessee 10, Alabama 11, Mississippi 33, Arkansas 32, Louisiana 17, Oklahoma 6, and Texas 5) constitute the present malaria belt. (See fig. 16).

Race differentials are considerable. Within any one State, the average rates for the colored are usually higher than those for whites. In 1933, for example, the rates for colored and white in Mississippi were 48 and 31, in Arkansas 59 and 42, in Florida 37 and 20, in Georgia 17 and 10, while in South Carolina the rates were 24 and 6, and in Tennessee 14 and 8. The high frequency of malaria among Negroes in some areas may be attributed to its prevalence in certain lowland areas inhabited largely by Negroes.

Cases of malaria are estimated variously at between 400 and 1,000 cases for every death, with an intermediate figure of 600 cases adopted by L. L. Williams, Jr., M. D., of the Public Health Service, as a reasonable estimate of the ratio of cases to deaths. There are 5 or 6 million cases of this debilitating illness annually, many of them lasting weeks and temporarily incapacitating the sufferers. Both the statistical data on local variations in the incidence of malaria and our knowledge of causes and means of control reveal the possibility of tremendous gains in combating this disease, and perhaps its eventual elimination.

Hookworm.—A survey of school children in Alabama in 1929 showed wide variations in the proportion affected by hookworm. In eight counties more than 60 percent of the school children examined had hookworm, but mild cases prevailed in some areas. A supplementary study of the intensity of the disease showed that four of these counties had a serious hookworm problem. Such surveys are of great value in indicating the area where specific public health measures need to be taken.

Similar variations exist for a number of other diseases for which prophylactics are known, such as typhoid, diphtheria, and syphilis. All emphasize the health handicaps of certain areas and the opportunity for improving the general level of well-being by a more equal distribution of health services.

---

[45] Lumsden, L. L., and Dauer, C. C., *Some Features of Tuberculosis Mortality Distribution in the United States.* Public Health Bulletin No. 225. The treatment of the Mexicans is not commented on in the bulletin. Mexicans, who were formerly classed as white, were included in the 1930 Census of Population as colored; in the registration of births and deaths a corresponding change has been attempted, but with varying success, since uniform reporting depends upon the local registrars.

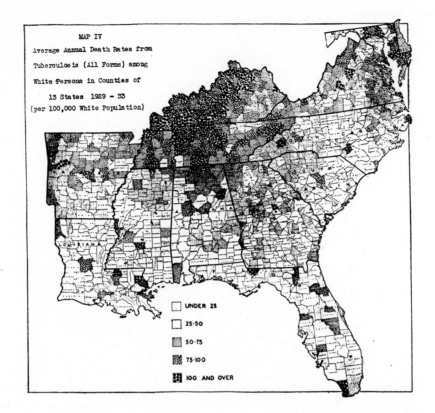

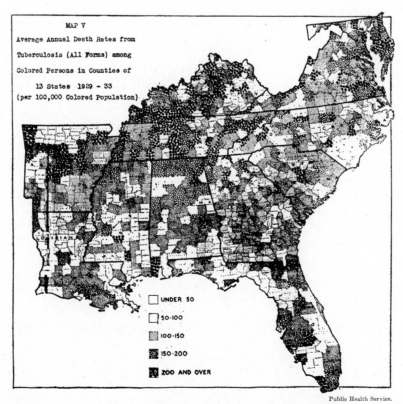

Public Health Service.

FIGURE 15.—Average annual death rates from tuberculosis in counties of 13 States, 1929–33. From Lumsden and Dauer, *Some Features of Tuberculosis Mortality Distribution in the United States.*

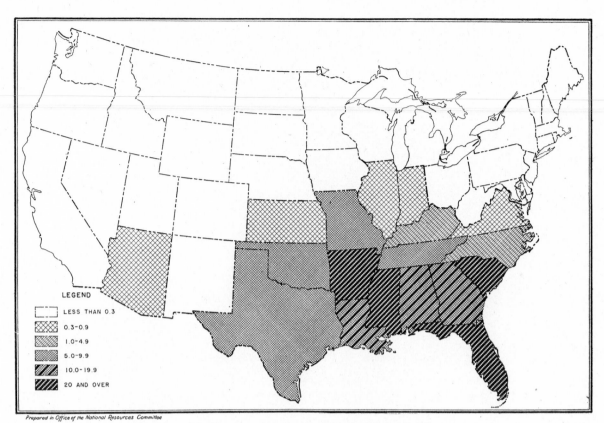

FIGURE 16.—Mortality from malaria (deaths per 100,000 population), by States, 1934.

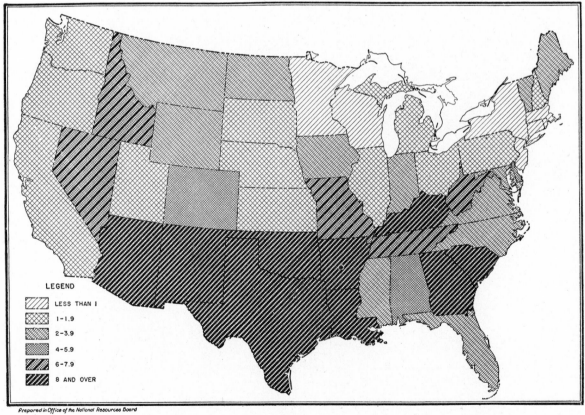

FIGURE 17.—Mortality from typhoid and paratyphoid fever (deaths per 100,000 population), by States, 1934.

Economic Differentials

As would be expected, the amount of ill health varies inversely with economic status.[46] In general, the lower economic classes have higher mortality rates. Collins summarizes the evidence as follows:

> Crude morbidity and mortality rates from all causes vary with economic status. The age curves show that the variations are still found when comparisons are made of similar ages in the different classes. Examination of the age curves, especially those carried into childhood, shows that the relative differences in death rates are generally greater in infancy than in the adult ages.

Economic differentials are especially evident in the case of infant mortality. Data from Cleveland, Chicago, and New York indicate that relative to population more than twice as many infants die in poor districts as in the more well-to-do areas. Data for Cleveland are presented in figure 18.

Much the same conclusions arise from studies of the general relation of illness to income level. In Hagerstown, Md., the annual illness rates per 1,000 persons in three economic classes were as follows: 991 for the well-to-do, 1,068 for the moderate, and 1,113 for the poor. (See fig. 19.)

The study made for the Committee on the Costs of Medical Care, on the other hand, indicates a larger amount of sickness in the higher economic groups. This is attributed by the authors as due to the definition of "illness" used in this study, and accompanying instructions.[47] However, when days of disability per person or per case are taken as the index of ill health, a marked relationship between disability and income is evident. Although the average annual disabling cases of illness per person were approximately the same in all income groups, the total days of disability in the lowest income group were more than twice those in the highest. (See table 8.) Thus persons in the upper income groups recover from illnesses more than twice as rapidly as the very poor. This undoubtedly reflects the differences in ability to obtain medical attention and services.

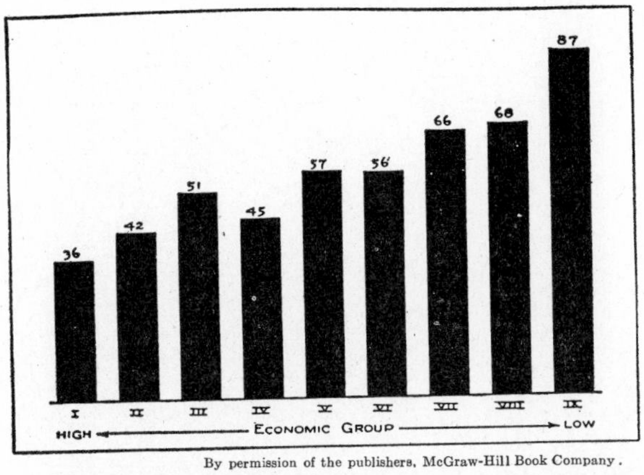

TABLE 8.—*Relationship between disability and income*

Annual family income	Annual rate		
	Disabling cases per person [1]	Days of disability	
		Per person	Per disabling case
Under $1,200	0.36	8.9	24.7
$1,200 to $1,999	.37	5.7	15.4
$2,000 to $2,999	.36	5.0	13.9
$3,000 and over	.34	3.8	11.2

[1] Wage earners, ages 15-64, both sexes, exclusive of farmers and farm laborers, professional persons, proprietors, managers, and officials.

Since the depression began, special surveys have been made of the effect of loss of income upon the incidence of illness in wage-earning families. A study of nearly 12,000 wage-earning families, including 49,156 individuals in 10 localities, showed a somewhat higher case rate of illness in families without employed workers than in families with one or more full-time workers.[48] This was true both as to illness beginning within the preceding 3 months—the period for reporting illness—and as to illness

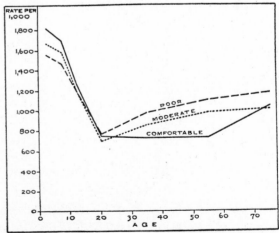

By permission of the publishers, McGraw-Hill Book Company.

FIGURE 18.—Infant mortality and economic status in Cleveland, 1928. (Figures over bars are infant death rates per 1,000 live births. Economic groups are differentiated according to rental and market value of dwellings.) From Sydenstricker, *op. cit.*

By permission of the publishers, McGraw-Hill Book Company.

FIGURE 19.—Annual incidence of illness from all causes among persons of different family economic status, Hagerstown, Maryland, December 1, 1921–March 31, 1924. From Sydenstricker, *op. cit.*

[46] See, for example, Collins, Selwyn D., *Economic Status and Health*, Public Health Bulletin No. 165 (1927); Sydenstricker, *Health and Environment*, 84–146; Prinzing, Friedrich, *Handbuch der medizinischen Statistik*, 2d Edition (1930–31), 580–632.

[47] Services received or expenditure of money for medical care were all included as illnesses. Even apart from these elements, the emphasis given in the definition of illness to costs of medical attention and to the calling in of a physician might have meant that the illnesses reported by the better situated families included many illnesses of a character that would not have been reported as illnesses in the poorer families. The frequency of illness attended by a physician does not necessarily correspond to the frequency of illness. Families with larger incomes are more likely to call physicians for minor ailments than families with low income. On this point see also Sydenstricker, *Health and Environment*, 89, footnote.

[48] Baltimore, Md.; Birmingham, Ala.; Brooklyn, N. Y.; Cleveland, Ohio; Detroit, Mich.; New York, N. Y.; Pittsburgh, Pa.; Syracuse, N. Y.; Greenville, S. C.; and Morgantown, W. Va. See Perrott, G. St. J., and Collins, Selwyn D., *Relation of Sickness to Income and Income Change in Ten Surveyed Communities*, Public Health Reports, 50: 595–622 (May 3, 1935).

beginning prior to these months but continuing into the period. The group of families without full-time workers, but with one or more part-time workers, occupied in general an intermediate position between the two extremes. For the cases of illness beginning within the period, however, the rates for minor illness were slightly higher than those for families with no employed workers.

When the data are examined further and classified by income, the illness case rates were higher in families with poor economic status than in families in comfortable or moderate circumstances. In families to whom the depression had brought a change in the classification of their economic status, as defined for this study, the illness rate showed marked increases as the economic status of the family grew worse. The authors point out that "the highest illness rate is exhibited by the group hardest hit by the depression, namely, the group 'comfortable in 1929 and poor in 1932' * * *. This group, with a rate of 174 cases per 1,000 persons showed an incidence of illness that was 45 percent higher than the rate (120 per 1,000) for their more fortunate neighbors who were equal in status in 1929 but suffered no drop in income by 1932."[49] Other comparisons show that the morbidity rates of families on relief tended to be highest of all the groups. The authors conclude:

The facts that the excess in illness rates appears among children as well as adults and that the highest illness rates are exhibited by families that dropped from the highest level in 1929 appear to point to a definite causal relation between lowered standards of

living and high illness rate * * *. The result of the depression has been to present to society for support a group of some 20,000,000 persons in the United States who are on relief rolls and among whom sickness is probably more prevalent than in the rest of the population.[50]

Occupational Differentials

Practically the only analysis of occupational mortality in this country is that published by the National Tuberculosis Association, edited by Jessamine S. Whitney, based on census data for 10 States. Rates for England and Wales are shown in figure 20. In America, mortality rates are lowest among agricultural workers, and increase among other groups in the following order: professional men, clerks and kindred workers, proprietors, managers, and officials, skilled workers and foremen, semiskilled workers, and unskilled workers. The unskilled workers had a standardized mortality 2.3 times that of the agricultural workers, but it must be borne in mind that any tendency to report occupation simply as "laborer" more frequently on death certificates than on census schedules would tend to exaggerate this differential. Factory and building construction workers had a standardized mortality 2.8 times that of agricultural workers, while the mortality among steam railroad laborers appeared only slightly greater than that of agricultural workers. Although there is serious doubt concerning the comparability of occupational statistics from mortality records with those in the census of population, the results obtained agree fairly well at many

---

[49] *Ibid.*, 611–612.

[50] *Ibid.*, 621.

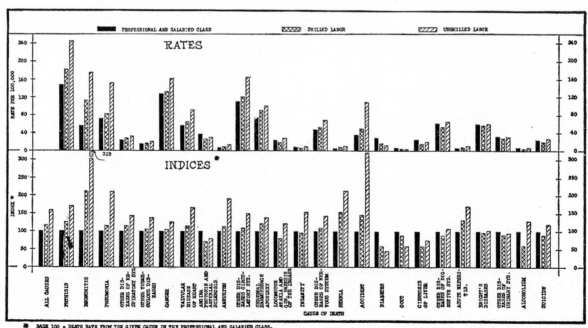

FIGURE 20.—Adjusted death rates by cause and occupational class, England and Wales, 1910–12. From Collins, *Economic Status and Health.*

points with similar data for England and Wales.

Marked variations appear in the incidence of diseases and defects in the different industries. For example, death rates from respiratory diseases are relatively low for workers in glass and pottery and in the post office, but high for those in cigar manufacturing, in the garment industry, and in foundry work.[51] Occupational differentials within the same industry appear to be less pronounced than differences between industries. However, there are many exceptions to this general statement. "In respiratory diseases, pressers and finishers of the garment industry have rates of 18 and 23, respectively, per 100 workers, well above the average for the industry. Nose and throat conditions are found to be prominent in the dust group of the glass industry. In the heart diseases and defects, the meter men in the gas industry stand out very clearly, having a rate of 33 per 100 or almost double that found in other occupations." [52]

In certain occupations, special poisons, dusts, or other environmental conditions increase the chances of workers becoming disabled by specific illnesses. One of the most serious of these is now a matter of past history. Phosphorus poisoning was found in the making of matches with phosphorus, but with the substitution of a different form of phosphorus compound, the danger from this disease has been wiped out. Lead poisoning is still a considerable hazard in many industries; for example, paint manufacturing, manufacturing of ethyl lead, manufacturing of storage batteries, pottery, ceramics, and corresponding occupations, such as house painting, that make use of lead paints. Processes using new chemical compounds often open up new industrial hazards. More or less familiar hazards include radium poisoning, X-ray burns, carbon-monoxide poisoning, benzene poisoning, and silicosis. The problems of occupational diseases and industrial hazards form an extremely important and complex field of medical research.

6. Prospects for Improvement of Health: Agencies, Methods, Policies

Changes in Expectation of Life

The progress already made in the saving of life and in the improvement of health is encouraging; but it must be recognized that future progress in physical well-being will prove more difficult than past achievements and will require greater expenditures and more effective organization.

The earliest life table for any area or population within the present United States was that of Wigglesworth for Massachusetts and New Hampshire for the year 1789. According to his computations the expectation of life at birth was then 34.5 years for males and 36.5 years for females. The data and methods used in the construction of this early table make the reliability of its results very dubious. If the results be accepted at face value and compared with later life tables, a saving of about 8 years in the average expectation of life at birth is indicated as the result of medical progress during the 100 years following, raising the corresponding figure for the total population of Massachusetts to 43.5 years in 1890. More than twice as great a saving of life was effected in the next 40 years, bringing the expectation of life at birth for the white population of Massachusetts to 60.9 years in 1929–30. The expectation for the white population of the United States for these years is about the same—59.3 years for males and 62.6 for females.[53]

The trend toward increased longevity can be continued, but not indefinitely. Causes of premature death can be eliminated, but senescence brings about destructive forces of an entirely different order. The immediate possibilities of materially increasing the average expectation of life in this Nation are revealed by existing variations among different groups. The average expectation of life at birth in South Dakota, as computed from death and enumeration statistics for 1930 (males, 64.4 years; females, 66.8 years) is 5 years higher for males and 4 years higher for females than the corresponding figures for the total white population of the United States; and the differences in favor of Kansas are almost as great.[54] Average length of life in this area of most favorable mortality now approaches but still does not equal that in New Zealand, where the expectation of life at birth in 1931 was 65 years for males and 68 years for females. It must also be borne in mind, however, that deficiency in registration of deaths would tend to raise apparent values for expectation of life; it is quite possible that the values for South Dakota may be somewhat exaggerated by such a fictitious factor. The average expectation for the white population of the United States, as a whole, is about the same as that for New Zealand 30 years ago; that for the Negro population is about 12 years less.[55] The more favorable health conditions prevailing in New Zealand may be attributed in part to conditions comparable to those prevailing in our Northwestern States and in part to the more adequate provisions for making medical services generally available to the

---

[51] See Britten, Rollo H., and Thompson, L. R., *A Health Study of Ten Thousand Male Industrial Workers*, Public Health Bulletin No. 162 (1926), 100. It is stated that since the survey in the pottery industry was made primarily to determine the prevalence of lead poisoning, no adequate record of other defects and diseases was obtained (*ibid.*, 138).
[52] *Ibid.*, 101.

[53] See *A Historical Retrospect on Expectation of Life, Statistical Bulletin, Metropolitan Life Insurance Co.*, 9: 5–8 (March 1928). Also Sydenstricker, *Health and Environment*, 163–164.
[54] See Dublin and Lotka, *op. cit.*, 346–357.
[55] *Ibid.*, 362–373.

whole population in that country. The most striking feature of the health situation in New Zealand, already commented on, is the very low infant mortality prevailing there. This can be attributed definitely, in a very large part, to the remarkable public health services in this field. Estimates of further increases in the expectation of life were discussed in connection with population estimates in chapter I. The actual trend of life in the future will depend in part on general economic and social conditions in this country and in part on specific measures for the control of disease and the improvement of the health and physical well-being of the people of the United States.

Means of Advancing the Health of the Nation

The progress already made in control of disease is perhaps the proudest achievement of modern civilization. Back of this progress in physical well-being are the forces of biological, chemical, and medical research; hospital equipment; the services of physicians, dentists, and nurses; the manufacture and distribution of surgical instruments, appliances, and medicines; public health control; education in nutrition; standards of living; and provisions for recreation. The possibility of further progress in health is dependent on (1) the quality of scientific research, (2) efficiency in the organization and administration of health services, and (3) adequacy of economic support for those services. Progress must be sought along all these lines.

Research

Expenditure and effort in medical research have yielded tremendous dividends in public welfare, and there is every reason to expect a continuance of large returns from large investments in this field. A half century ago the most important methods of attack in the control of disease were just becoming known; within this half century more has been done for the physical well-being of humankind than in all previous history. New methods of research and of medical practice are coming forward constantly. There is the reasonable prospect of much further progress in the near future, especially in the control of diseases that lower vitality and efficiency. It must necessarily be, in large part, along still more abstract and complex lines and thus more dependent upon basic chemical, physical, biological, and psychological research. More extensive and exact knowledge of the social and economic aspects of health and disease will assist greatly in furthering progress in these fields. A few of the most interesting fields of medical research have been mentioned in this brief survey, but these give no conception of the variety and complexity of problems on which research is actively going forward at the present time.

Organization of Medical Services

It may be that for the country as a whole the supply of physicians is fairly adequate. Any judgment on the matter is complicated by problems relating to professional standards and the organization of medical services. In any case it is obvious that there is great disparity in the distribution of physicians. The provision of hospital beds likewise shows striking variations in different States. (See figs. 21 and 22.) The number of beds per 100,000 population ranges from 142 in Mississippi to 654 in Colorado, the high figure for the latter State being due in part to the needs of tuberculosis patients sent there for climatic advantages. Eight States had less than 200 beds per 100,000 population. But even in Mississippi not all the hospital facilities are in full use; the average occupancy of beds in general hospitals in that State was only 49 percent. This must be attributed chiefly to the economic handicaps of the population in this region.

Improvement in the organization of public and private health agencies affords a great opportunity for widespread and rapid advance in health in this country in the near future. Progress in this field will make possible further concerted attack on specific health problems of

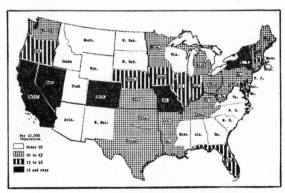

By permission of University of North Carolina Press.

FIGURE 21.—Supply of physicians per 10,000 population, by States, 1930.

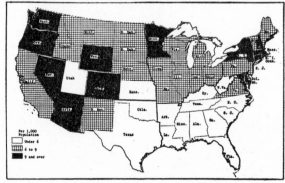

By permission of University of North Carolina Press.

FIGURE 22.—Hospital beds per 1,000 population, by States, 1930.

major importance, such as the control of venereal disease, the prompt diagnosis and treatment of cancer, special attention to the control of diseases that frequently result in organic heart disorders, continued attack on tuberculosis directed especially to those groups where the need is greatest, and the effective application in many other fields of the results of scientific research that are already well established.

As concerns the technical question of providing better medical care, the Committee on the Costs of Medical Care recommended that medical services should be furnished largely by recognized groups of physicians and associated personnel:

The Committee recommends that medical services, both preventive and therapeutic, should be furnished largely by organized groups of physicians, dentists, nurses, pharmacists, and other associated personnel. Such groups should be organized, preferably around a hospital, for rendering complete home, office, and hospital care. The form of organization should encourage the maintenance of high standards and the development or preservation of a personal relation between patient and physician.[56]

The theory of the family physician who advises all the members of a family regarding their health and directs them to specialists in case of need becomes increasingly difficult of application in the face of a greater use of expensive equipment in diagnosing physical conditions, the necessary division of responsibility for different types of medical service, and the greater mobility of urban populations. The fact is that there are millions of individuals in American cities, especially among those coming from other localities, who know of no way, except reliance on hearsay advice, to select a physician in time of need. In many instances they would prefer to accept the services or follow the recommendation of a hospital or clinic. It seems inevitable that some effective means should be established for meeting this widespread demand.

The Economic Support of Adequate Medical Services

Many problems relating to the organization and support of medical services are both tremendously important and extremely complex. The subject has been presented to the attention of the Nation by the report of the Committee on the Costs of Medical Care. The recommendations of this committee have been criticized in some quarters as extreme and in other quarters as inadequate. The mass of objective material assembled by this committee and its formulation of problems make its report inevitably the point of departure for discussions of this subject. The Committee on Population Problems cannot attempt to do more than summarize these results, leaving the solution of

the problems raised to experts in this field and to the forum of public discussion and to experimental trial:

The Committee recommends that the costs of medical care be placed on a group-payment basis, through the use of insurance, through the use of taxation, or through the use of both these methods. This is not meant to preclude the continuation of medical service provided on an individual fee basis for those who prefer the present method. Cash benefits, *i. e.*, compensation for wage loss due to illness, should be separate and distinct from medical services.[57]

When different income levels are considered, the poor receive inadequate medical service as compared with that received by the better-situated classes, though the differences are not so wide as would be expected from the differences in the ability to pay of these groups. A considerable amount of medical work for the poor is done on a charity basis, is never paid for, or is performed at public expense. The heavy burden that such charitable work places upon the medical profession, unequally upon different physicians, must be recognized. The present plan, or lack of plan, for carrying the burden of the medical care of those in straitened circumstances places too great a load upon certain physicians, and furthermore is not a satisfactory solution to the urgent problem of making adequate medical care available to all classes in the population. The situation of those with moderate incomes who hesitate to accept charity services and yet cannot meet the payments for adequate medical care in case of protracted illness, and who delay necessary dental work for lack of funds, is sometimes even more desperate.

A minority of the committee favored a specific recommendation for the principle of compulsory health insurance. In a separate comment on the report Walton Hamilton of the committee, explained his refusal to sign the final report because it did not, in his opinion, go far enough. In his view, compulsory health insurance was a minimum recommendation. Edgar Sydenstricker, who also refused to sign the report, expressed his disappointment at the committee's failure to consider the economic problem of meeting the cost of medical care—"the recommendations do not, in my opinion, deal adequately with the fundamental economic question which the committee was formed primarily to study and consider."[58]

The extension and improvement of public health services offers great possibilities. The Committee on the Costs of Medical Care recommends "the extension of all public health services—whether provided by governmental or nongovernmental agencies—so that they will be available to the entire population according to its needs."[59] The Committee recognized the

[56] *Medical Care for the American People,* 109.

[57] *Ibid.,* recommendation 3, 120.
[58] *Ibid.,* 201.
[59] *Medical Care for the American People,* 118.

inequalities of geographic distribution. In addition to geographic extension, the public health services should be expanded to include all "proper public-health functions" unless these are already performed by a non-governmental agency. Recognized public-health functions include—

(a) The collection and analysis of vital statistics; (b) the control of water, milk, and food supplies; (c) the control of sanitation; (d) the control, through quarantine and supervision, of communicable diseases; and (e) the provision of laboratory services. In addition to these, the Committee believes that the following activities are also proper public health activities: (f) the promotion of maternal, infant, and child hygiene, including medical and dental inspection and supervision of school children; (g) popular health instruction; (h) the provision of preventive dental care of children, and (i) the provisions of special services for the prevention, diagnosis, and treatment of patients with tuberculosis, venereal diseases, malaria, hookworm, or any other disease which constitutes a special health problem in the community that cannot be solved adequately and effectively by the other available medical and health agencies.[60]

The committee included such health problems as those of tuberculosis and venereal dis-

---

[60] *Ibid.*, 119.

ease as matters of public rather than of purely private concern. The well-being of the community is vitally affected by the sources and extent of infection. Not only is the community concerned, but effective measures of control will in general not be successfully initiated without definite assumption by the community of its responsibilities.

This committee does not put forward the recommendations of the Committee on the Costs of Medical Care as a final solution of so difficult a matter as the organization of medical services and public health services. But it feels definitely that the suggestions advanced by that committee and by other qualified workers in this field now afford a sufficient basis for trial and experiment, and that out of such experiments will come closer approaches to practicable and effective methods of meeting a very pressing public problem. Thus far this subject has been chiefly a matter of discussion which has not infrequently been acrimonious. It appears to be time for trial of promising methods rather than further debate, but with readiness to modify any approach as experience indicates desirable alterations.

VIII. SOCIAL DEVELOPMENT AND EDUCATION[1]

1. The Function of Education in American Society

The American Tradition in Education

Aims.—The American people have for a long time regarded their educational system as one of the means of carrying into effective operation the basic principles of their experiment in democracy. It has been fundamental to American theory that the school provide for each individual, regardless of economic status or social class, free opportunity for intellectual growth and cultural development. In this way, and in no other, it has been felt, the school could be made to contribute to the maintenance of equality of opportunity. Nearly a century ago, Horace Mann voiced a deep-seated and continuing conviction of the common man in America when he insisted that above all other devices of human origin, education, properly organized, is the great equalizer of the condition of men.

More than four decades ago, Charles W. Eliot gave vigorous expression to the ideal of individualized education in the following significant statement:

To discriminate between pupils of different capacity, to select the competent for suitable instruction, and to advance each pupil with appropriate rapidity, will ultimately become, I believe, the most important functions of the public-school administrator—those functions in which he or she will be most serviceable to families and to the state. * * *

Every child is a unique personality. It follows, of course, that uniform programmes and uniform methods of instruction, applied simultaneously to large numbers of children, must be unwise and injurious, an evil always to be struggled against and reformed, so far as the material resources of democratic society will permit. * * *

In the public schools of a democracy the aim should be to give the utmost possible amount of individual instruction, to grade according to capacity just as far as the number of teachers and their strength and skill will permit, and to promote pupils, not by battalions, but in the most irregular and individual way possible * * *.

Selection of studies for the individual, instruction addressed to the individual, irregular promotion, grading by natural capacity and rapidity of attainment, and diversity of product as regards age and acquisitions, must come to characterize the American public school, if it is to answer the purposes of a democratic society.[2]

In the American tradition, however, it has not been the exclusive function of the school to confer benefits upon the individual. The interests of society have been deemed of no less importance. As a people we have exhibited a profound confidence in our educational system as a means of safeguarding free, representative political institutions. In the early years of the nineteenth century, men were generally afraid that their experiment in social and political democracy would fail, and they had no doubt that it would fail if society neglected to cultivate in youth that degree of social intelligence necessary to enable them to make impartial analysis of public issues. More than a century ago it was recognized that the success of democracy as a form of political and social organization depends upon a citizenry having a critical understanding of the workings of their social and economic institutions.

Nowhere has the civic purpose of American education been more clearly defined than in the decisions of the courts. The following quotation from an opinion of the Supreme Court of New Hampshire could be paralleled in the decisions of the courts of practically every State in the Union.

The primary purpose of the maintenance of the common-school system is the promotion of the general intelligence of the people constituting the body politic and thereby to increase the usefulness and efficiency of the citizens, upon which the government of society depends. Free schooling furnished by the state is not so much a right granted to pupils as a duty imposed upon them for the public good. If they do not voluntarily attend the schools provided for them, they may be compelled to do so. . . . While most people regard the public schools as the means of great personal advantage to the pupils, the fact is too often overlooked that they are governmental means of protecting the state from the consequences of an ignorant and incompetent citizenship.[3]

The American States have established and maintained systems of public education not only to confer benefits upon the individual as such, but also to provide a type of civic education that would prepare for wise participation

[1] Prepared by Newton Edwards of the University of Chicago, assisted by Mabel Waltz, through the cooperation of the Commission on Youth of the American Council on Education.

[2] Eliot, Charles W., Shortening and Enriching the Grammar-School Course, *Educational Reform* (1898), 261–265, D. Appleton-Century Co.
[3] *Fogg* v. *Board of Education of Littleton*, 76 N. H. 299.

in the determination of public policy and that would, in numerous ways, contribute to the promotion of the general welfare.

Accomplishments.—It is obvious that the American educational system has succeeded only in part in accomplishing the high purposes assigned it in theory. It has in many respects failed to provide adequate training in citizenship. Because of an overemphasis on the personal and private values of education, we have entertained an undue respect for a curriculum that contributes much to personal prestige but far too little to social understanding. We have regarded the fruits of education as essentially personal and private rather than as public and social; in consequence, we have failed to develop a program that subjects our social and economic life to rigorous and critical analysis.

Perhaps the most serious indictment that can be brought against the American school system is its failure to provide equality of educational opportunity. In a country of such vast extent and of great regional differences in economic and cultural patterns, absolute equality of educational opportunity is not to be expected. But the existing differences in opportunity are not slight; they are so great as to constitute a threat to the whole fabric of American democratic institutions.

The comparatively meager educational opportunities afforded in many American communities constitute a challenge to educational statesmanship. Education may be the means of building up and perpetuating class, race, and regional distinctions that spell differences in opportunity. If formal educational attainments condition entrance to some economic and social spheres, and if great opportunities for educational advance are open to some groups while the educational facilities for others remain meager, it is obvious that education becomes an instrument of social stratification and of regional and racial inequality. Such differentiation of class through education may take place in a subtle way, even where free public education appears open to all equally. If, in some settings, education becomes a vital, stimulating intellectual process, while in other situations it remains formal, routine, and dissociated from daily life—with teachers holding "jobs", and pupils attending merely by grace of the truancy officer—the schools may function as a mechanism of social differentiation.

If the American educational system is to be made to serve the interests and needs of the people, some means must be found to extend its advantages more uniformly to the children of the Nation. But a mere extension of the system is not enough; it is no less important that the program of instruction be so reorganized as to provide for the individual pupil a type of experience that will meet his peculiar needs and stimulate his interest.

2. Social Forces and the Expansion of American Education

The changing conditions of American life have placed youth, and the schools that serve youth, in a perplexing situation. For a long time there has been a narrowing of opportunity for the kind of activity, such as that of the boy helping his father on the farm or an apprentice in a craft or small shop, that is at the same time economically productive and educational. The concentration of population in large cities and the specialization and standardization of industrial processes have for the most part forced youth to choose between gainful employment in a routine occupation, formal education, and idleness. During the last few decades there has been a tendency, suddenly intensified in recent years, toward the elimination of the first of these alternatives, so that the choice lies only between formal education and idleness.

Declining Employment of Young People

The expansion of industry during the nineteenth century, especially toward the end of the century, was accompanied by the employment of a considerable percentage of children between the ages of 10 and 15. A sharp reversal of this trend began about 1910. At that time approximately one-fourth of the boys and one-eighth of the girls 10 to 15 years of age were in gainful occupations, but by 1930 the gainfully occupied had dropped to 6 percent among boys and less than 3 percent among girls. (See fig. 1.) Although the total population at these ages increased from 5,600,000 in 1870 to over 14,000,000 in 1930, there were fewer such persons gainfully employed in 1930 than in 1870. By 1920 less than 1 percent of the gainfully employed in all the major occupational groups except agriculture were persons under 16 years of age.

There has also been a marked decline in recent years in the employment of older young people. Among those 16 years of age the proportion gainfully employed decreased from 40

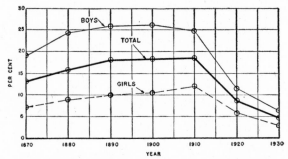

FIGURE 1.—Percentage of children 10–15 years of age gainfully occupied, 1870–1930.

percent in 1920 to 25 percent in 1930. Among the 17-year-olds, employment decreased during the same period from 50 to 39 percent; even in the case of those 18 and 19 years of age, the figure declined from 60 to 55 percent. Thus, even before the severe onset of the depression, less than half of all youths aged 16 to 19 years were gainfully employed. Opportunities for employment during the depression years have been especially curtailed for these young people as they have passed into their early twenties and for their oncoming brothers and sisters.

The trend toward the exclusion of children and youth from industry and toward the expansion of educational opportunities has been influenced by many different conditions and motives. Opinions differ as to the relative importance and priority of these influences. The finest impulse in this direction has been the humanitarian interest in freeing children from confining employment in mills and sweatshops, often at low wages, in order to open a door for them to sunlight, play, and education. This ideal has undoubtedly been uppermost in the minds of associations and legislators sponsoring this movement. There is a growing conviction that society cannot permit its youthful members to grow up under conditions that jeopardize their physical and mental health.

The possibility of increasing facilities for the formal education of individual children has been enhanced by the decreasing number of children to be supported per 1,000 adults. (See fig. 2.) In fact, the absolute number of children of elementary school age (6–14 years) has already begun to decline. (See fig. 3.) By 1940 there will be about 5 percent fewer children 6–9 years of age than in 1920. The total number aged 6–13 will be about equal to that in 1920 and 1½ million less than in 1930. The decrease in elementary school enrollment which became noticeable in 1930 will thus continue. The number of children of high school age (14–17 years) will continue to increase until about 1940, after which the downward trend will begin for that age group as well.

It is obvious that society's burden in caring for its young dependents, merely as to numbers, is being materially reduced. Since it has proportionately fewer young dependents to care for, society is enabled to take a new attitude toward youth, to lengthen the period of dependency, to delay entrance into gainful occupations, and to provide extended and enriched educational opportunities.

The introduction of machinery has also made the labor of children and youths less necessary and in many cases disadvantageous. The manning of machines requires steady application, reliability of performance, and frequently manual skill and judgment in considerable degrees. The most highly mechanized industries have least place for children and immature young people. At the same time, the introduction of machinery releases workers and creates, at least temporarily, a surplus of adults in need of employment. Thus in many cases industrial-management groups have been ready to dispense with child labor and have sometimes urged uniform legislation in this matter in order to reduce the competitive advantage of concerns so situated as to profit from child labor. Organized labor has been almost unanimously in favor of restrictions in this field, in part because child labor reduces the demand for adult laborers and tends to depress general wage levels.

Finally, the complexity of modern economic life makes the advantages of prolonged education seem more important to young persons themselves and to those concerned with financial and social administration. Corresponding to the tendency for an increasing proportion of young people to remain in school beyond the elementary grades, there is a tendency on the part of industrial and commercial organizations to require more extended training as a condition of employment. An investigation of the employment policies in this regard of selected industrial and commercial concerns in the Chicago area is summarized as follows:

In order to secure * * * evidence regarding the extent to which modern conditions demand training on the part of individuals, a canvass was made in 1930 of 51 industrial and commercial concerns in the Chicago area which employed boys and girls to whom work certificates had been issued by the authorities of the public schools. It was found that these concerns employed workers in 190 different classes of positions, ranging from those of messengers to those of expert mechanics and accountants. In 148 of these classes of positions the educational requirements had been distinctly raised since 1920. Sixty-five classes of employees were required to be high-school graduates or to have attended institutions of higher education; thirty-four were required to have had at least 2 years of high-school training; and

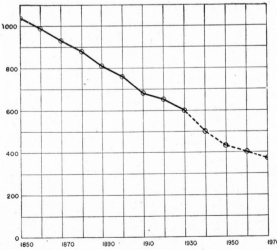

FIGURE 2.—Children under 18 years of age per 1,000 adults aged 20–69 years, 1850–1970.

forty-nine were required to show that they had completed the eighth grade. Only 42 classes of employees were accepted without regard to their educational qualifications, and even in these cases preference was often given to those who had longer school records. Thus, it is shown that industry and commerce not only restrict the entrance of children on occupations but even go so far as to impose explicit educational requirements as conditions of admission.[4]

All of these considerations have influenced the enactment of child-labor legislation, extension of educational facilities, and laws requiring school attendance. About the middle of the last century some of the States began to prohibit the employment of children under certain ages in manufacturing industries, but it was not until the eighties or nineties that there emerged any real social consciousness of the problems of child labor. Recent policy regarding the employment of young dependents is reflected in legislation on the subject. (See table 1.) In 1907 only 29 States restricted the employment of children 14 years of age or over; by 1936 all but two States had enacted some legislation in this field, and the authority to establish a uniform standard is now before the Nation in the pending child-labor

[4] Judd, Charles H., *Problems of Education in the United States* (1933). By permission of the publishers, McGraw-Hill Book Company, Inc.

amendment to the Constitution of the United States.

TABLE 1.—*Lowest ages mentioned in the laws of the 48 States restricting employment of children, vacations excluded, 1907–36* [1]

Age	Number of States		
	1907 [2]	1915 [2]	1936 [3]
No age mentioned	6	0	1
8	1	0	0
10	1	0	0
12	11	7	1
13	0	1	0
14	29	36	38
15	0	4	4
16	0	0	4
Total	48	48	48

[1] Employment in agriculture, domestic service, street trades, theatrical or other performances, and poverty permits not considered.
[2] From Judd, *op. cit.*, 26.
[3] "State Compulsory School Attendance Standards Affecting the Employment of Minors." U. S. Office of Education (1935), 54 pp. mimeographed), with revisions as of Jan. 1, 1936.

Meanwhile, school attendance requirements have been advanced progressively. Between 1852 and 1918 all the States enacted compulsory school attendance legislation.[5] There are,

[5] Deffenbaugh, Walter S., and Keesecker, Ward W., *Compulsory School Attendance Laws and Their Administration*, 8. United States Office of Education Bulletin, 1935, No. 4.

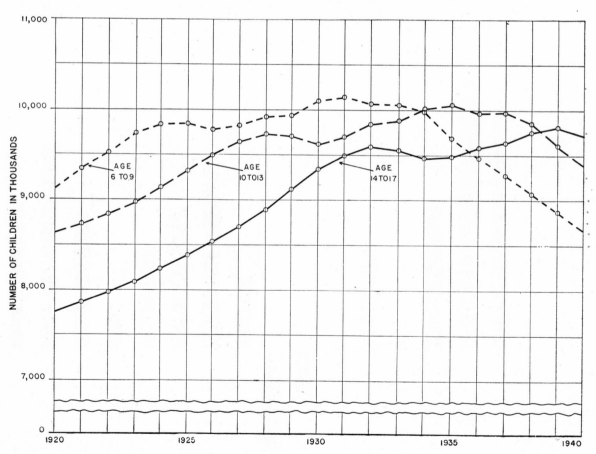

FIGURE 3.—Estimated number of children aged 6–9, 10–13, and 14–17 years, United States, 1920–40.

however, wide variations in State laws on that subject. The early laws were meager in their requirements and some of them were poorly enforced, as, indeed, some school attendance statutes are today. It would be a mistake to regard the establishment of effective legislation of this kind as a simple matter. Compulsory school attendance marked the modification of a fundamental English and American social policy. Under the English common law, both in England and colonial America, education was wholly a parental concern; there was a total lack of recognition of the obligation of society. The enactment of compulsory school attendance legislation is a more significant indication of society's growing sense of responsibility for youth than is generally realized. (See table 2.)

Increasing School Attendance

The social forces to which attention has already been directed have resulted in a remarkable expansion of the American educational system. The most striking increase has come at the upper grade levels. Between 1920 and 1930 there was an increase of 28 percent in the number of pupils attending the eighth grade. The changes in elementary and high school enrollments during the past 15 years are shown in absolute numbers in figure 4. The recent decreases in the lower grades are due to the decrease, already commented on, in child population of elementary school age.

During the past four decades the expansion and popularization of secondary education in this country have been little short of amazing. Figure 5 shows the rapidity of the increase in attendance at the secondary level during the past four decades. Figure 6 shows the proportions of children and young people of different ages who were attending school in 1910, 1920, and 1930. The United States Office of

TABLE 2.—*Regular school attendance required by the 48 States, 1907–36*

Ages	Number of years	Number of States		
		1907 [1]	1915 [1]	1936 [2]
No requirement		9	4	0
8–12 years	4	0	2	0
8–14 years	6	9	3	2
9–15 years	6	0	1	0
7–14 years	7	7	3	2
8–15 years	7	3	3	0
9–16 years	7	1	0	0
7–15 years	8	3	3	1
8–16 years	8	11	16	9
7–16 years	9	5	10	22
8–17 years	9	0	0	1
6–16 years	10	0	0	1
7–17 years	10	0	1	5
8–18 years	10	0	1	3
7–18 years	11	0	0	1
6–18 years	12	0	0	1
8–20 years	12	0	1	0
Total		48	48	48

[1] From Judd, *op. cit.*, 24.
[2] Deffenbaugh and Keesecker, *op. cit.*, 12, with revisions as of Jan. 1, 1936, supplied by the Children's Bureau of the U. S. Department of Labor.

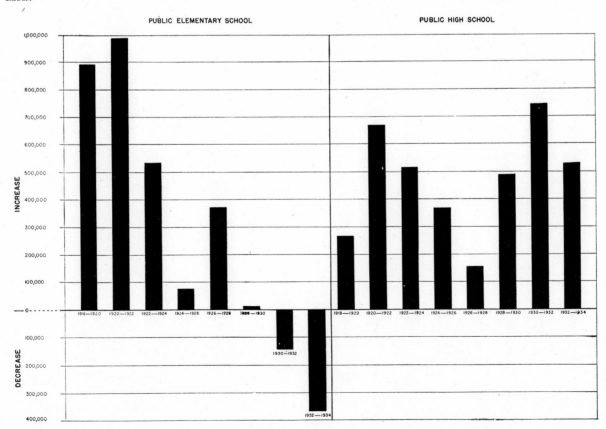

FIGURE 4.—Increase and decrease in elementary and high school enrollment (in thousands), 1918–34.

Education estimates that in 1936 the reporting secondary schools enrolled 62 percent of all children 14 to 17 years of age and that secondary school pupils in schools not reporting would easily bring the total up to 65 percent. Thus we have reached the stage where about two-thirds of all the children in the United States are attending high school. It should be noted that although the depression may have accelerated the swing toward secondary school attendance, the long-time movement in this direction is due to the sweep of social forces in American life.

Increase in enrollment at the college and university level has also been striking, though perhaps less phenomenal than in the secondary schools. In 1910, less than 5 percent of the population of college age was in attendance at the regular session of some institution of higher learning, but this was true of almost 13 percent of this age group in 1932. (See table 3.)

TABLE 3.—*Percentage of young persons of college age enrolled in the regular session of higher educational institutions* [1]

Year	Population 19 to 22 years of age, inclusive [1]	Enrollment, regular session [1]	Percent of population
1910	7,242,100	355,200	4.9
1920	7,321,000	597,600	8.2
1930	8,871,400	1,085,800	12.2
1932	9,081,500	1,154,100	12.7

[1] Based on data from the Bureau of the Census and the United States Office of Education.

The high school now attracts a larger proportion of the children of parents in occupations not requiring advanced education as a requisite. Counts in 1920 investigated the social composition of high school groups in four urban communities, Seattle, St. Louis, Bridgeport, and Mount Vernon, N. Y. A repetition of the study in Seattle and Bridgeport 10 years later showed a striking increase in the representation in high school of all occupational levels in the total population.[6] (See table 4.)

TABLE 4.—*Number of high school pupils from different occupational groups per 1,000 men over 45 in the same groups, Seattle and Bridgeport, 1920 and 1930* [1]

Occupational group	Seattle			Bridgeport		
	Ratio 1920	Ratio 1930	Percent change in ratio, 1929–30	Ratio 1920	Ratio 1930	Percent change in ratio, 1920–30
All occupations	166	322	94	171	308	80
Self-employed, managerial, commercial and clerical groups	303	452	49	375	485	29
Skilled, semiskilled, and common labor, transportation, public and personal service groups	91	215	136	93	232	149

[1] Adapted from Kefauver, Grayson N., Noll, Victor H., and Drake, Clarence E., *The Secondary-School Population*, 13. National Survey of Secondary Education, Monograph No. 4 (1933).

[6] Koos, Leonard V., and others, *National Survey of Secondary Education*, Monograph No. 1, "Summary" (1934), pp. 49–50.

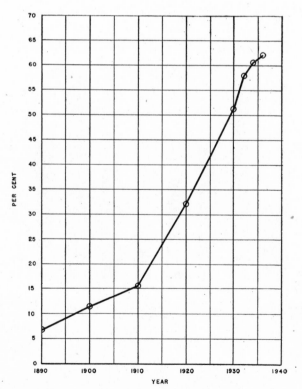

FIGURE 5.—Percentage of children of high school age (14–17) enrolled in public and private high schools, 1890–1936.

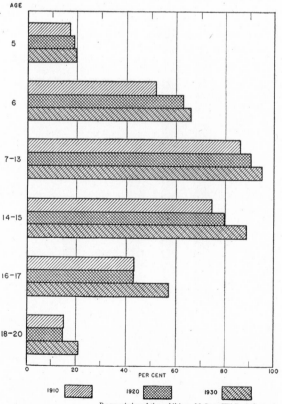

FIGURE 6.—School attendance of young persons of various age groups. From Judd, *Problems of Education in the United States.*

New Social Responsibilities of the Educational System

The democratization of secondary school education requires adaptation to the needs of young people, most of whom will not attend college and many of whom have little interest in the traditional academic courses. The situation is aggravated by the sense of economic uncertainty that now surrounds them. Some of those attending high school or taking more advanced studies would prefer to be employed but can find no opportunity.

This situation has been acute in recent years, as is well known. The necessary data are lacking to describe precisely the effects of the depression on the situation of youth in this country. The Youth Commission of the American Council on Education has estimated that there were in 1935 approximately 20,000,-000 persons aged 16–24 years, distributed as follows: 4,000,000 in schools and colleges; 7,600,000 employed full or part time; 500,000 unemployed and attending school part time; 400,000 in the Civilian Conservation Corps; 4,200,000 unemployed (including an indeterminate number in work relief other than the Civilian Conservation Corps) not in school, and seeking work; 2,800,000 married women not employed and not in school; and 300,000 others not employed, not in school, but for various reasons not seeking work.[7] It cannot be doubted that many young people turn to the schools, motivated not so much by high faith in the value of education or by a driving intellectual interest as by a sense of bewilderment, and a vague notion that going to school is at least better than just "hanging around." The situation is not altogether a happy one, either for the young people or for their teachers.

The social changes that have led to increased enrollment in elementary and secondary schools and in colleges and universities has also led to an expansion of the field of adult education. Morse Cartwright, president of the American Association for Adult Education, has estimated that during the 10 years from 1924 to 1934 there was an increase of 4½ million in the number giving attention to radio educational programs—partially balanced by a decrease of some 2 million in the number attending chatauquas and lyceums—and that at the later date over 2 million were attending special classes arranged as part of the unemployment relief program. Even apart from these items, he estimates that during this 10-year period the number of adults enrolled as participating in some sort of organized educational activity increased from about 11 to about 14 million.[8] He estimates that there was a marked decline in the enrollment in private correspondence schools (from 2,000,000 to 1,000,000), and in the number of those receiving training by corporations (from 100,000 to 50,000), but increases in enrollment in university extension (from 200,000 to 300,000), in vocational education courses of various sorts (from 300,000 to 400,000), in miscellaneous public school courses for adults (from 1,000,000 to 1,500,000), and in agricultural extension (from 5,000,000 to 6,000,000). Much of the educational work of adults has a vocational motive. This type of work has special importance in view of dislocations in employment caused by technological change—apart from cyclical unemployment. There has also been an apparent increase in recent years in organized recreation, art groups, museum attendance, and public library study courses.

It is clear that education has become a major American industry, for which the demand appears to be still increasing. There are great differences in the quantity and quality of educational opportunities in different areas; and this inequality presents some serious problems, as we shall see, when viewed in relation to reproductive and migratory trends in the population of the United States. But even where the educational system is best developed there are serious problems about its direction and significance.

The necessity of doubling the number of high school teachers each decade has placed a severe strain on existing teacher-training facilities. Teachers who instruct classes of 30 to 50 pupils during the year may spend their summers in teacher-training classes with 50 to 500 students. All this has, of course, traveled a long way from Mark Hopkins on one end of a log and a boy on the other.

New Problems in Secondary Education

A generation or two ago the primary function of the high school was to prepare a selected and relatively homogeneous group for further study at the college or university level. The obligations of the high school today, however, are not confined to the select few; they extend rather to all the youth of the community. Many of the pupils who enter high school at the present time have little or no interest in the older curriculum offerings. The curriculum of high school must be subjected to a thorough reorganization in order that it may be made to serve the interests of its new constituency.

Within recent years sharp differences of opinion have developed with regard to the procedures to be followed in adjusting American secondary education to its new and enlarged responsibilities. There are some who would resolve the difficulty by taking the downright position that society has no obligation to provide free secondary education for the masses of

---

[7] "Preliminary Inquiry on What Is The Youth Problem", Washington American Youth Commission of the American Council on Education, 1936 (mimeographed).
[8] Cartwright, Borse H., *Ten Years of Adult Education* (1935), 60.

youth. They regard the more recent curriculum offerings as "fads" and "frills"; they urge a return to the curriculum of a generation ago. The essential function of the secondary school, so they hold, is the preparation of an intellectual elite. These critics of the American school system seem to be wholly unaware of the social forces playing upon the school from without and equally unaware of the spirit of American democracy. The popularization of American education, the upthrust of an ever increasing stream of youth into high school and college, is the consequence of fundamental social change. The training of leaders, to be sure, is a major obligation of the educational system; it is an obligation which has not been fully met. It is equally true, however, that the American people, having experienced the benefits of popular education, are wholly unwilling to restrict the educational opportunities offered the masses of children.

Among those who welcome the extension of the sphere of secondary education there are still sharp differences of opinion. In some quarters there is a disposition to abandon the literary curriculum and to substitute for it courses specifically vocational in character. Some urge the establishment of trade schools distinctly separate from the traditional high school. Others see little value in the cultivation of the manual skills in school; they maintain that the secondary-school curriculum should consist of courses related to the interests of youth but essentially intellectual in nature, leaving industry responsible for specific vocational training.

Experience indicates the necessity of reconciling these two views. Where separate technical high schools have been established, it has usually proved impossible to divorce technical and academic education for any length of time. Pupils have been so insistent on an opportunity for a broader training that concessions have been made to their demands. It seems safe to assert that the American public will not consent to the segregation of youth into separate trade and technical schools where they will be denied the opportunity of a general education. On the other hand, it is equally clear that the secondary curriculum cannot be wholly academic in character. The great majority of secondary pupils do not continue their education beyond the high school, and many do not finish that. Some preparation must be afforded for effective participation in occupational life. The secondary school must provide for the individual a curriculum that will insure a satisfactory general training and at the same time make provision for the cultivation of professional and vocational efficiency.

Unemployed youth.—American society has a special responsibility for young people who finish or leave school but who are unable to find gainful employment. As yet our educational system has made no institutional arrangement for their further education or guidance. Many who are unable to find work stay in high school or return to it, even though the school has no program adequate for their needs. For these boys and girls the high school necessarily becomes little more than a custodial institution. For many of them, no doubt, gainful employment would afford a more educative environment than they now find in school. The Civilian Conservation Corps has recently provided a valuable experience for some, and it may be that it points the way toward a significant educational development. It is certain that society is faced with the problem of making some kind of institutional arrangement for the better care and direction of unemployed youth. It is possible that the secondary schools and colleges may assume this responsibility. It may be, on the other hand, that the best means of dealing with the problem is to establish a special agency, apart from the existing institutions but integrated with the whole educational system.

Cultivation of social judgment.—The educational institutions of this country have never been a particularly vital force in the creation of social intelligence. If the school is to be an instrument for the cultivation of an understanding of society, teachers must be accorded freedom to discuss with their pupils all issues and all institutions, with proper consideration of the social and intellectual immaturity of the students. Social studies should be introduced into the curriculum in such a way as to train pupils to gather evidence, to balance arguments, to arrive at critical understandings—in short, to be objective and experimental in their attitudes. It is the function of the school to make the pupil as intelligent as possible with respect to the social order in which he is to live, but this is not to say that the school should press upon the pupil the acceptance of specific formulas for the solution of social problems. No greater need exists in American education than the need for a vital teaching of the social studies.

Vocational needs.—It is natural that many young people, haunted by fear and uncertainty, seek to establish a basis for economic security, through education, yet it is just in this respect that school experience often proves least satisfactory. The nature of American enterprise makes the value of training for specific jobs, apart from actual employment opportunities, extremely dubious.

Vocational programs in the secondary schools should accordingly be so constructed as to give training in and thorough understanding of the basic machines, tools, and processes common to an occupational field and in habits of work and the standards of competency of that industry, so that those receiving the training will have initial employment assets for a number of specifit jobs in that occupational field. The probability of transfer from one job to another makes a high degree of general competence and adaptability most important, but these are qualities that cannot be developed in short order by standardized educational procedures.[9]

Curriculum.—The specialization of modern life and the increase of those seeking formal education but lacking interest in traditional school disciplines have led to a great diversification of educational offerings. Koos compares the courses listed in 35 high schools in the Middle States that were surveyed early in the present century and again after a lapse of nearly 25 years.[10] The median number of curriculums was found to have doubled, increasing from 2.5 to 5.2. During the interval, too, college preparatory courses decreased from more than half to about a third of the whole number of courses offered.

> Correspondingly, during the period general curriculums and commercial, industrial arts, household arts, fine arts, and other curriculums shifted to a position of numerical dominance.

At the opening of the period there were on the average 24 courses offered in each school; at its close the average number was 48. The evidence indicates an expansion of the offerings in all the subject groups, but the fields having the largest proportional increases were English, the social studies, commercial subjects, industrial arts, household arts, fine arts, and physical education. At the university level there has been a far greater multiplication of courses. This increase is doubtless due to a number of causes, but to some extent it certainly represents an effort to adjust instructional content to the varying needs of present-day citizens of the United States. It is well to emphasize the idea that the curriculum in school and college is not something fixed or absolute, or arbitrarily devised by educational experts. In the long run it is determined by the demands of society.

The attempt to democratize the secondary school by offering new types of curriculum has resulted in leaving these curriculums in many cases fragmentary and poorly integrated. Specific course offerings have been multiplied to the point that it is extremely difficult for the pupil to get an integrated view of any large area of human life, either past or present. Some critics of the school system have suggested a return to the curriculum of a generation ago as an escape from the confusion that has arisen from the multiplication of courses. A far better suggestion, and one which happily is being put into effect in some schools, is that the schools proceed to develop integrated curriculums. What has been said with regard to the need of integrated curriculums is as applicable to the college as to the secondary

school and it is applicable, in a measure, to the elementary school as well.

The democratization of secondary education has also led to a modification of the structural organization of the education system. As larger numbers attempted to ascend the educational ladder, lack of proper coordination between the different units of the educational system became apparent. The establishment of junior high schools and junior colleges, together with modifications of college entrance requirements, represent an attempt to secure a better articulation between the various units of the educational system. In the process of reorganization, the secondary school is being extended downward to include the last 2 years of the elementary school and upward to include the first 2 years of college. This general tendency is in conformity with the enlarged purpose of secondary education to provide a general education for the youth of the community.

The rapidity with which education has expanded in response to changing modern conditions, the experimentation with content and method, and the gradual reorganization of the whole structure of formal education in the United States are raising questions of great importance and complexity.

3. Education in Relation to Population Growth

Regional differences in reproduction rates cause great inequality in the distribution of child population relative to the supporting adult population and the economic resources of different areas.

Regional Variations in the Ratio of Children to Adults

Differences in the ratio of children of elementary and high school age to adults in the productive age-groups are shown for regions in table 5, and for States in figure 7. Ratios of children of elementary school age per 1,000 adults 20–64 years of age vary from 523 in South Carolina, 491 in North Carolina, and 438, 441, 445, and 438, respectively, in West Virginia, Alabama, New Mexico, and Utah, at one end of the scale, to 225 in California, 254 in New York, and 270 in Illinois. Thus the relative load as regards child population in need of care and education is from 70 to 100 percent higher in the six States first mentioned than it is in New York.

TABLE 5.—*Children of school ages per 1,000 persons aged 20–64 years, by regions, 1930*

Region	Ages 5–13 years	Ages 14–17 years	Ages 5–17 years
Northeast	295	125	420
Middle States	297	126	423
Northwest	350	146	496
Southeast	426	177	603
Southwest	380	157	537
Far West	236	100	336

---

[9] See sec. 5 of this chapter for a discussion of this problem.
[10] Koos, *op. cit.*, 168–170.

It might be supposed that the high ratios of children to adults in the Southern States are due chiefly to the high fertility of the Negro population. This is not generally the case; but it does help to account for the unusually high ratio found in South Carolina. For the Southeast as a whole there were 420 children in the white population and 441 children in the Negro population per 1,000 adults; the average ratio for the region was 426. The State variations for white and Negro populations in this region are shown in table 6. These ratios may be

somewhat affected by irregularities in census enumeration or in statements of age, but possible errors of this sort cannot have a large influence on the regional results.

Analysis of the distribution of child population, relative to adult population, with respect to type of community shows even more striking variations. (See fig. 8.) The ratio of children of school age to the supporting adult group in general increases in large steps with decreases in size of community. The number of children of school age is relatively low in all cities of 100,000 or more. This is true of children both at elementary and at high school level, and it is true regardless of the geographic region in which the city is located. There is, in fact, a surprising uniformity in the ratio of children to the supporting adult group in cities of this class. The larger cities in the Southeast and Southwest carry a school population no larger than cities in the rest of the country, except in the far West. The situation is similar in the case of the total urban population, including cities of all sizes. In communities classified as rural-nonfarm, the ratio of children of school age to adults is markedly greater than in urban communities, and very much greater than in the larger cities. This is particularly true in the Southeast, and to a lesser extent in the Southwest. It is, however, the rural-farm population that is

TABLE 6.—*Ratios of white and Negro children, 5–13 years of age, to white and Negro adults, 20–64 years of age, southeastern States, 1930*

State	Number of white children 5–13 per 1,000 white adults, 20–64	Number of Negro children 5–13 per 1,000 Negro adults, 20–64
Virginia	394	469
North Carolina	472	541
South Carolina	466	600
Georgia	416	459
Florida	328	317
Kentucky	421	287
Tennessee	408	336
Alabama	444	434
Mississippi	426	441
Arkansas	440	386
Louisiana	390	395
Total region	420	441

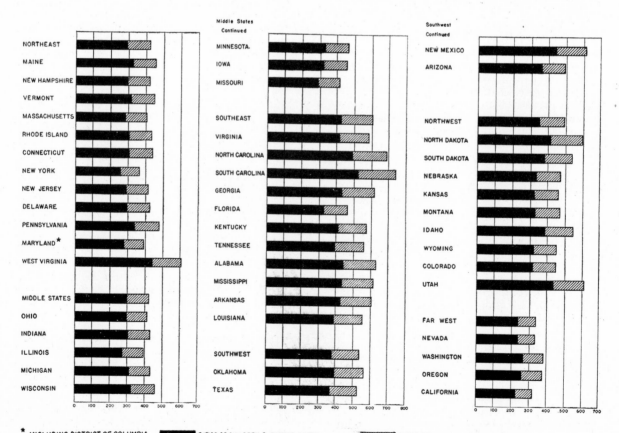

* INCLUDING DISTRICT OF COLUMBIA   ■ RATIOS OF CHILDREN 5-13 YEARS OF AGE   ▨ RATIOS OF CHILDREN 14-17 YEARS OF AGE

FIGURE 7.—Number of children 5–13 and 14–17 years per 1,000 adults aged 20–64, by regions and States, 1930.

carrying a burden of children of school age out of all proportion to that in other types of communities. The relative child load in communities of different sizes within each region is shown in table 7.

TABLE 7.—*Index of ratios of children 5–17 per 1,000 adults in rural-farm, rural-nonfarm, and urban communities, using ratios in cities of 100,000 and over as a base*

Region	Rural-farm	Rural-nonfarm	Total, urban
Northeast	162	137	107
Middle States	167	133	106
Northwest	168	132	109
Southeast	219	154	113
Southwest	206	148	113
Far West	185	145	112

It is evident that in some parts of the country the supporting group carries a burden of young dependents that is more than twice as great as that in other areas. These local variations are revealed on the accompanying map (fig. 9), based on census data for numbers of children (aged 7 to 13 years) related to the adult base (persons aged 20 to 64 years). The map shows an area extending from Maine to Maryland in which the ratio of children to adults is unusually low, although some counties both in Maine and in Maryland are exceptions to this general statement. The area of relatively few children extends westward from

New England and New York, getting broader as it reaches the Middle States and the prairies, and ending in the eastern parts of South Dakota and Nebraska and the central part of Kansas. From here to the Pacific coast the map shows a good deal of variation. In Nevada and along the entire Pacific coast the ratio of children to adults is unusually low. Low ratios also appear in parts of Florida and in a number of urban counties located in the southeastern and southwestern States.

Border regions of moderate ratios skirt the great area of low ratios. One of the border regions extends from southwestern Pennsylvania through southeastern Ohio, southern Indiana and Illinois, northern and western Kentucky, to southeastern Missouri. Another area of intermediate ratios runs north of the main low-ratio area, including the cut-over lands of the Great Lakes region. In the Southwest large portions of Oklahoma, Texas, and New Mexico and part of Arizona fall into this general classification, as do also many counties in the Great Plains area stretching from Texas northward.

Counties having an extremely high ratio of children to adults are located, in the main, in the Southeastern States, predominantly in the southern Appalachians and the old Cotton Belt. It is in these two areas that the adult group in the population is bearing the heaviest burden of responsibility for child care. There were,

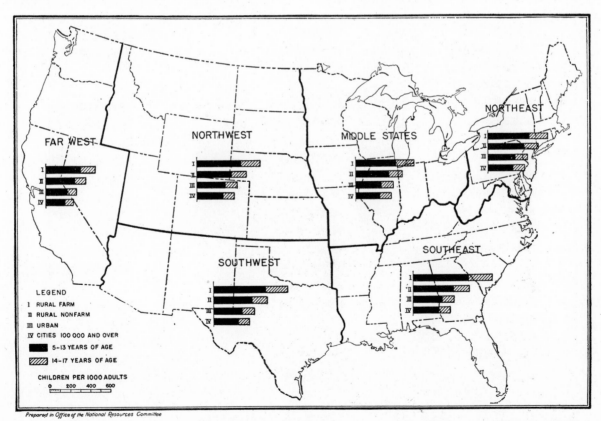

LEGEND
I RURAL FARM
II RURAL NONFARM
III URBAN
IV CITIES 100 000 AND OVER
▰ 5–13 YEARS OF AGE
▨ 14–17 YEARS OF AGE

CHILDREN PER 1000 ADULTS
0 200 400 600

Prepared in Office of the National Resources Committee

FIGURE 8.—Number of children 5–13 and 14–17 per 1,000 adults in rural-farm, rural-nonfarm and urban communities and in cities of 100,000 population and over, by regions, 1930.

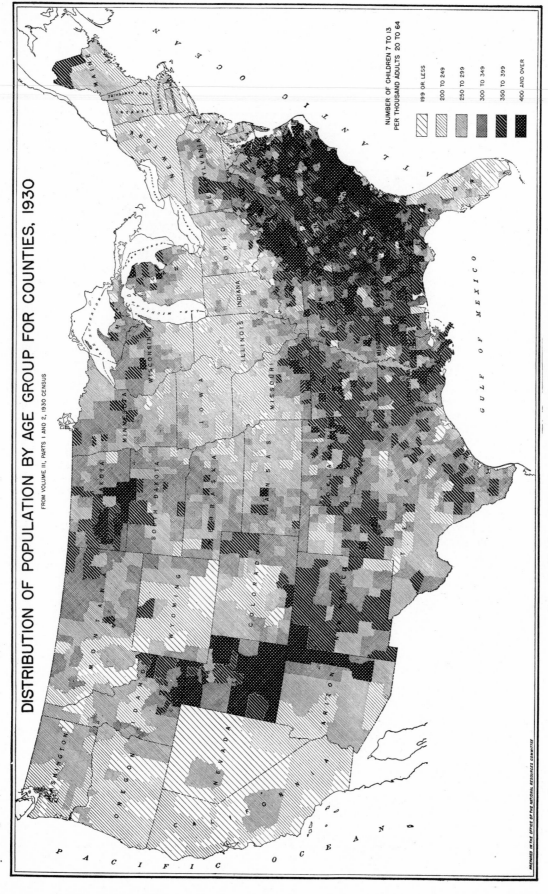

DISTRIBUTION OF POPULATION BY AGE GROUP FOR COUNTIES, 1930

FROM VOLUME III, PARTS I AND 2, 1930 CENSUS

NUMBER OF CHILDREN 7 TO 13
PER THOUSAND ADULTS 20 TO 64

199 OR LESS
200 TO 249
250 TO 299
300 TO 349
350 TO 399
400 AND OVER

FIGURE 9.—Number of children 7–13 per 1,000 adults aged 20–64, by counties, 1930.

PREPARED IN THE OFFICE OF THE NATIONAL RESOURCES COMMITTEE

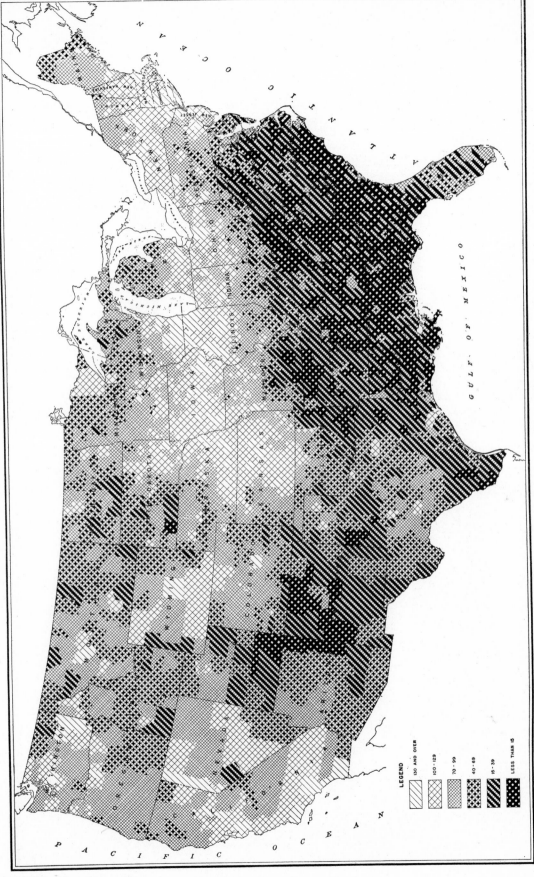

LEGEND

130 AND OVER
100 - 129
70 - 99
40 - 69
15 - 39
LESS THAN 15

FIGURE 10.—Plane of living, by counties, 1928–29. Adapted from Goodrich and others, *Migration and Economic Opportunity* (University of Pennsylvania Press).

206   *National Resources Committee*

for instance, less than 200 children per 1,000 adults (in the age classes described above) in 126 counties in the United States, but only 12 of these counties are located in the Southeast, including 5 counties in Florida. On the other hand, out of 365 counties with ratios of 400 or over, 298 are in the Southeast.

There are some counties outside the Southeastern States in which the ratio of children to adults is extremely high. A considerable number of such counties is to be found in Arizona, Utah, Idaho, and North Dakota, and a smaller number in Michigan, Missouri, Oklahoma, and Maryland. Counties with high, but not the highest, ratios of children to adults are found in large numbers in Texas, Oklahoma, New Mexico, Missouri, Montana, Idaho, Colorado, North and South Carolina, Minnesota, Wisconsin, Michigan, and Pennsylvania.

Variations in per Capita Incomes and in Levels of Living

The unequal distribution of pupil load assumes serious proportions when it is examined in relation to economic resources and income levels. The plane of living map, prepared by the Study of Population Redistribution to show county distribution of average levels of living in the United States, has already been introduced (ch. II). This map is reproduced here in juxtaposition with the map showing ratios of children of school age to the supporting adult population. The correspondence be-

tween areas with great child-population load and areas with low levels of living is very impressive (fig. 10). It is apparent that for the most part the areas with the lowest levels have the greatest responsibility for child nurture and education.

The comparison between total farm and total nonfarm population, with regard to distribution of child population and distribution of income, tells a similar story. (See fig. 11.) It appears that for the Nation as a whole, 31 percent of the children 5 to 17 years of age are located on farms, but only 9 percent of the national income (estimate of Brookings Institution for 1929) goes to the farm population. In every region in the United States, except the far West, the farm population has a percentage of children of school age far in excess of its percentage of the national income. It is, however, in the farm population of the southeastern States that the disparity between child population and income assumes startling proportions. The farm population of the southeastern States includes 13 percent of the Nation's children of school age (5 to 17 years); but it receives only 2 percent of the Nation's income. There are approximately 4¼ million children 5 to 17 years of age living on farms in the Southeast; there are approximately 8½ million children of school age in the nonfarm population of the Northeast. But, in dividing up the total national income, the southeastern farmers receive 2 percent, the nonfarm popu-

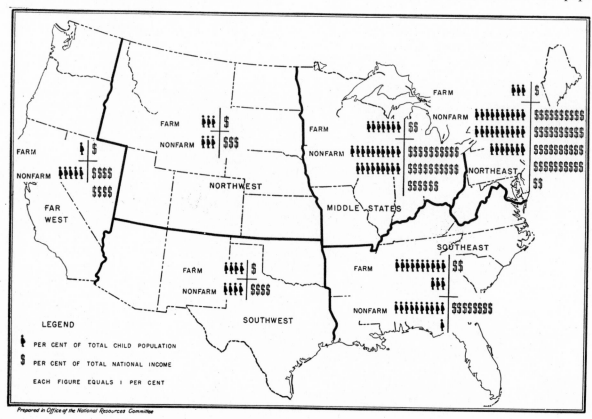

FIGURE 11.—Regional percentages of the child population and of the nation's income, farm and nonfarm communities.

TABLE 8.—*Percentage of child population aged 5 to 17, 1930, and percentage of Nation's income, farm and nonfarm communities, in the 48 States* [1]

| State | Percent of national total | | | | | |
| | Children | Income | Farm— | | Nonfarm | |
			Children	Income	Children	Income
Total	100.00	100.00	30.63	9.03	69.37	90.97
Northeast	29.66	42.93	2.70	1.24	26.96	41.69
Maine	.62	.56	.14	.08	.48	.48
New Hampshire	.34	.33	.04	.02	.30	.31
Vermont	.28	.25	.10	.04	.18	.21
Massachusetts	3.17	4.51	.07	.08	3.10	4.43
Rhode Island	.54	.66	.01	.01	.53	.65
Connecticut	1.28	1.76	.07	.06	1.21	1.70
New York	8.85	18.61	.59	.39	8.26	18.22
New Jersey	3.12	4.37	.10	.09	3.02	4.28
Delaware	.18	.34	.04	.02	.14	.32
Pennsylvania	8.08	8.56	.83	.29	7.25	8.27
Maryland and District of Columbia	1.55	2.07	.23	.08	1.32	1.99
West Virginia	1.65	.91	.48	.08	1.17	.83
Middle States	26.06	28.38	6.91	2.11	19.15	26.27
Ohio	5.07	5.74	.92	.28	4.15	5.46
Indiana	2.48	2.17	.73	.20	1.75	1.97
Illinois	5.61	8.17	.91	.33	4.70	7.84
Michigan	3.79	4.53	.74	.24	3.05	4.29
Wisconsin	2.36	2.18	.85	.37	1.51	1.81
Minnesota	2.08	1.71	.85	.24	1.23	1.47
Iowa	1.95	1.31	.89	.22	1.06	1.09
Missouri	2.72	2.57	1.02	.23	1.70	2.34
Northwest	6.26	4.59	2.83	1.19	3.43	3.40
North Dakota	.65	.31	.41	.13	.24	.18
South Dakota	.62	.32	.38	.12	.24	.20
Nebraska	1.13	.78	.55	.18	.58	.60
Kansas	1.51	1.17	.65	.29	.86	.88
Montana	.45	.41	.19	.10	.26	.31
Idaho	.40	.30	.19	.12	.21	.18
Wyoming	.18	.19	.06	.05	.12	.14
Colorado	.83	.78	.28	.14	.55	.64
Utah	.49	.33	.12	.06	.37	.27
Southeast	24.41	10.01	13.42	2.21	10.99	7.80
Virginia	2.27	1.14	1.04	.19	1.23	.95
North Carolina	3.26	1.09	1.85	.29	1.41	.80
South Carolina	1.86	.50	1.10	.13	.76	.37
Georgia	2.83	1.09	1.61	.23	1.23	.86
Florida	1.20	.86	.29	.13	.91	.73
Kentucky	2.39	1.13	1.23	.19	1.16	.94
Tennessee	2.38	.99	1.27	.19	1.11	.80
Alabama	2.59	.95	1.50	.20	1.08	.75
Mississippi	1.94	.63	1.45	.26	.49	.37
Arkansas	1.77	.63	1.18	.23	.59	.40
Louisiana	1.92	1.00	.90	.17	1.02	.83
Southwest	8.13	5.22	3.82	1.15	4.31	4.07
Oklahoma	2.20	1.31	1.10	.27	1.10	1.04
Texas	5.16	3.34	2.46	.76	2.70	2.58
New Mexico	.40	.22	.16	.06	.24	.16
Arizona	.37	.35	.10	.06	.27	.29
Far West	5.48	8.87	.95	1.13	4.53	7.74
Nevada	.06	.10	.01	.01	.05	.09
Washington	1.13	1.43	.27	.21	.86	1.22
Oregon	.68	.78	.19	.13	.49	.65
California	3.61	6.56	.48	.78	3.13	5.78

[1] Income estimates from *America's Capacity to Consume* (1934), 172–173

lation of the Northeast receives 42 percent. The percentage distributions of child population and of income for farm and nonfarm population by States are shown in table 8.

Variations in Educational Opportunity

Such disparity in levels of living and in income are inevitably reflected in wide regional and community differences in school efficiency and educational opportunity. It is difficult to measure accurately the efficiency of schools in rural and urban communities or in communities in different regions. It is possible, nevertheless, to indicate to some extent the differences in the educational opportunity provided for the youth of the Nation. The measures we shall use are (1) the qualification of teachers in the terms of the amount of training they have received, (2) the percentage of children of school age attending school, (3) the amount of school attendance, and (4) school expenditures per pupil.

Differences in teacher training.—Data from the National Survey of the Education of Teachers indicate clearly that teachers in the rural schools of the country are far less adequately trained than those in villages and urban communities. Table 9 shows that, for the country as a whole, the smaller the community, the less adequate has been the training of teachers responsible for the education of children there. If 2 years of college education be accepted as a standard of training for elementary school teachers, the proportions of these teachers in different sized communities falling below the standard are as follows: Open-country, one- and two-teacher schools, 62 percent; open-country, three- or more-teacher schools, 28 percent; villages of less than 2,500 population, 21 percent; cities of 2,500 to 9,999 population, 12.6 percent; cities of 10,000 to 99,999 population, 10.5 percent; and cities of more than 100,000 population, 9 percent.[11]

[11] Evenden, Edward S., Gamble, Guy C., and Blue, Harold G., "Teacher Personnel in the United States". *National Survey of the Education of Teachers*, II: 42 (1935).

TABLE 9.—*Percentage distribution, by highest level of training, of elementary and high school teachers in different types of location, school year 1930–31* [1]

| Location | Level of training | | | | | | | |
	Elementary school	High school, 1-3 years	High school, 4 years	College, 1 year or less	College, 2 years	College, 3 years	College, 4 years	Graduate work
Elementary teachers:								
1- and 2-teacher schools, open country	0.7	2.5	9.0	49.5	28.7	6.0	3.0	0.7
3- or more-teacher schools, open country	.3	1.4	2.7	23.9	47.0	13.4	10.2	1.2
Villages of less than 2,500 population	.4	1.2	2.5	16.9	54.0	15.7	8.4	1.1
Cities of 2,500 to 9,999 population	.2	.9	2.3	9.3	55.1	18.8	12.1	1.6
Cities of 10,000 to 99,999 population	.3	.8	2.5	7.0	55.1	19.7	13.0	1.8
Cities of more than 100,000 population	.2	.8	2.1	6.2	47.0	21.8	16.9	5.1
Total elementary	.4	1.4	4.0	20.5	46.2	15.5	10.2	1.9
Junior high school	.3	.6	1.1	4.2	17.5	16.0	43.7	16.7
Senior high school	.2	.3	.5	1.5	4.4	6.1	58.1	29.0

[1] Adapted from Evenden, Edward S., Gamble, Guy C., and Blue, Harold G., "Teacher Personnel in the United States", *National Survey of the Education of Teachers*, II: 43 (1935).

208

National Resources Committee

Differences in school attendance.—Data on the number of children of different ages reported as attending some kind of school for any length of time during the period from September 1929 to April 1930 are given in the 1930 census. Table 10 shows for each region, and for the types of communities within each region, the percentage of those 5 to 13 years of age who were so reported. For the Southeast and Southwest this percentage was notably less than in other regions. One notes, too, that throughout the country the school attendance rate among farm children of elementary school age is consistently lower than the attendance rate in urban communities.[12]

TABLE 10.—*Percentage of children 5–13 attending school, by regions and types of community, 1930*

	Total	Urban	Cities of 100,000 and over	Rural—non-farm	Rural—farm
Northeast	87	88	89	84	84
Middle States	88	89	89	86	86
Northwest	87	89	91	85	85
Southeast	76	82	84	75	74
Southwest	75	79	81	75	72
Far West	88	89	90	85	85

[12] There are similar regional differences in the percentage of children of high school age attending school, although the differences are not so great as might have been expected. These percentages for the six regions run as follows: Northeast 72, Middle States 77, Northwest 79, Southeast 66, Southwest 72, far West 88. But these figures may be misleading. They do not, it must be borne in mind, show the percentage of youth of high school age actually attending high school.

The number of pupils attending public or private high schools in any area, expressed as a percentage of the total population in that area aged 14 to 17 years, shows wide regional variations. These percentages run as follows: Far West, 75; Northwest, 65; Middle States, 59; Northeast, 52; Southwest, 50; Southeast, 34. State variations in these proportions are shown in figure 12.

The effectiveness of a school system is determined, in part, by the length of the school term and by the use that children make of their opportunity to attend school. Figures 12, 13, and 14 show great variations among States, with respect to the average number of days attended by each pupil and the percentage of the school term that is used.

Differences in school expenditures per pupil.—Data on expenditures for schools reveal that in general, in those areas in which fertility is low and the number of pupils relatively small, the expenditure per pupil is high. Conversely, in those areas in which fertility is high and the number of pupils relatively large, per pupil expenditure is low. The coincidence of a high fertility rate and a low per-pupil expenditure is brought out forcibly by comparing the reproduction index of the various States with their annual expenditure

They indicate, rather, the percentage of persons of high school age attending some kind of school—elementary, high school, college, business school, part time, or full time.

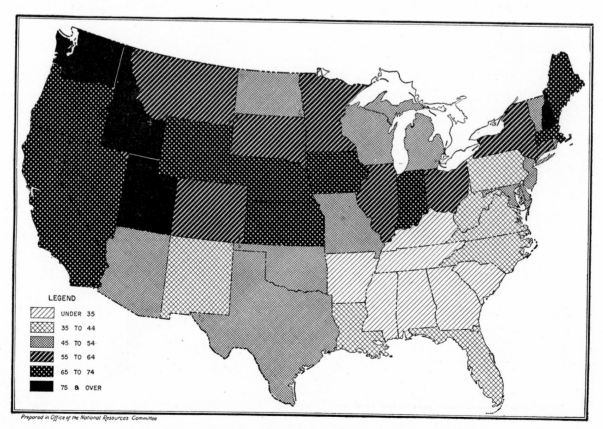

LEGEND
- UNDER 35
- 35 TO 44
- 45 TO 54
- 55 TO 64
- 65 TO 74
- 75 & OVER

Prepared in Office of the National Resources Committee

FIGURE 12.—Persons in high school per 100 persons aged 14–17 years, by States, 1930.

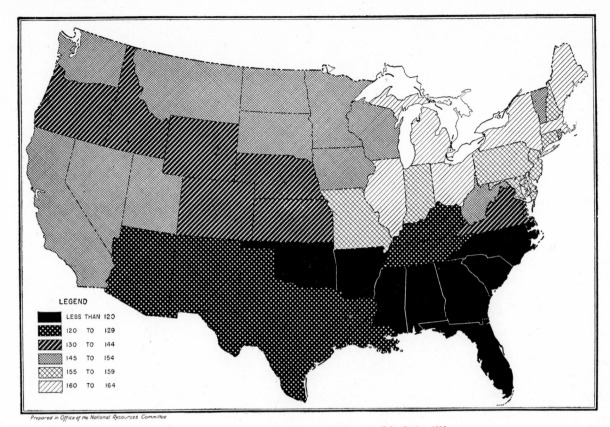

FIGURE 13.—Average number of days in school per pupil, by States, 1930.

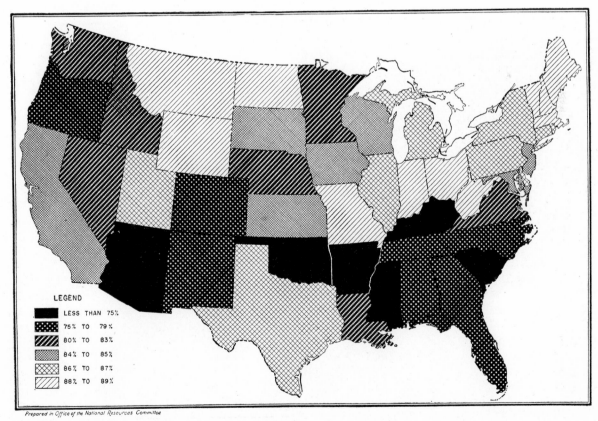

FIGURE 14.—Average attendance per pupil as percentage of school term, by States, 1930.

per pupil for education. (See fig. 15.) Almost without exception per-pupil expenditure is high in those States having an insufficient number of children to replace their present population, and, with few exceptions, expenditure per pupil is low in those States having children markedly in excess of their replacement quota. By way of illustration, the reproduction index for Alabama in 1930 was 1.41 and its per-pupil expenditure was $37.91; the reproduction index for New York was 0.84 and its per-pupil expenditure was $149.84. This situation is summed up in the following quotation from Osborn:

> Education is being concentrated on groups where there are the fewest children, and on children who in turn will have the fewest children. The least formal schooling is being expended on those children who undoubtedly are going to rear the largest families.[13]

Another aspect of education in relation to reproduction is equally important but more elusive. Data presented above (see ch. V) showed that urban populations with high school or more advanced education are, on the whole, having fewer children than the number needed for family replacement. The adults in American society with superior education are failing to reproduce themselves. This leads to the question as to whether the interests and

[13] Osborn, Frederick, Significance of Differential Reproduction for American Educational Policy, *Social Forces*, XIV: 23–32 (October 1935).

outlook on life inculcated by American institutions and American education are lacking some of the most vital considerations. This question is raised in the conclusion of the article by Osborn, cited above:

> A further possibility deserves serious consideration. Is American education today placing the proper emphasis on values? We have seen the change in emphasis from the classics to the physical sciences, and we are now witnessing an increasing emphasis on the sciences having to do with man. We may hope that this shift will continue. But this is not the emphasis we mean. We have in mind the redirection of education so as to inculcate the highest human values, which are associated not alone with learning, nor even alone with service to humanity, but with the basic processes of normal human life, and with the sacrifies, and responsibilities and the happiness which go with them. It is a question whether the education of young people in our high schools and colleges is preparing them for the self-denial and patient effort required of responsible parents. * * *
>
> It is possible that the most significant changes to be made in educational policy in the next decade will have to do with a reorientation as to what is worth while in life, both for the individual and for the Nation.

4. Education in Relation to Migration

The Prevailing Migration Movement Is Farm-to-City

We have seen that internal migration is playing a large role in the redistribution of population in the United States; in view of big differences in reproduction rates and in economic

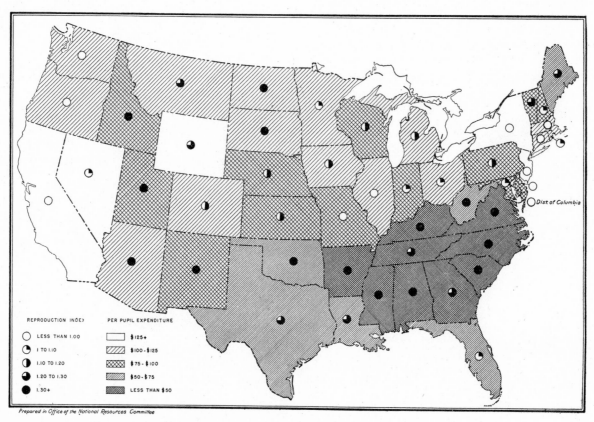

FIGURE 15.—Annual cost of education (expenditure per pupil) in relation to reproduction index, by States.

opportunity in various parts of the United States we must expect future movements of considerable volume. The trend from farm to town is the outstanding feature of this reshuffling of population in the United States. During the 10-year period 1920–30 there was a net movement from farms of nearly 6,000,000 people. The South was the principal area of emigration; about 60 percent of all migrants from farms came from that area.

The emigration of young people, nurtured in rural communities but seeking livelihood in industrial and commercial centers as they enter the period of economic productivity, predominates in this whole movement. We found that about 25 percent of the boys aged 10–14 years who were living on farms in 1920 had moved to villages and cities before 1930, and over 30 percent of the farm girls of the same ages had done so. Similarly, 30 percent of farm boys and 25 percent of farm girls in the next age class (those entering the decade as youths aged 15–19 years) had followed the same course.

Although the movement from farms to cities was considerably retarded during the early depression years, a critical analysis of available data for the years 1930–35 shows that this trend gathered momentum again in 1935. Continued movement of young people from farms to cities must be expected, and we have seen that there are sound economic reasons for encouraging this trend, especially movement from rural communities in the Southeast. The effect of the absence of such movement in intensifying overpopulation in the Southeastern States is shown by the hypothetical figures given in table 11, based on a realistic analysis of actual reproductive tendencies.

TABLE 11.—*Estimated increase in population of Southern States, 1930–1960* [1]

	Assuming no rural-urban migration	Assuming rural-urban migration in ratio of 1920–30
Total Cotton Belt [2]	10,618,000	1,890,000
Southeast [3]	7,820,000	1,135,000
Cotton States of the Southeast [4]	5,393,000	1,070,000
South Carolina, Georgia, Alabama	3,060,000	625,000

[1] From Goodrich, Carter, and others, *Migration and Economic Opportunity*, 134.
[2] North Carolina, South Carolina, Tennessee, Georgia, Alabama, Mississippi, Louisiana, Arkansas, Texas, and Oklahoma.
[3] Except Texas and Oklahoma.
[4] South Carolina, Georgia, Alabama, Mississippi, Arkansas, Louisiana.

Similarly, continued emigration must be expected from many other rural areas, notably from the Rocky Mountain States because of the high birth rates in that region, from the Great Lakes cut-over area because of declining economic resources, and from the Great Plains area because of recurrent drought. Numerous submarginal and problem areas are scattered through other parts of the United States.[14]

[14] The preceding paragraphs are based on evidence presented above. See chs. II, III, and IV.

Inequality of Educational Opportunity: A National Problem

The educational implications of the mobility of population have too often been ignored. In common practice, education in this country has been regarded as a purely local affair. However sound such a policy may have been in a pioneer society, it takes no great insight to discover its weakness today. With the degree of mobility that has characterized the American people in the past and is likely to continue in the future, the cultural and intellectual level of any region has its influence on the development of every other region. For good or ill, migrants enter into the social, economic, and political life of the communities in which they spend their mature years. They carry with them their knowledge or ignorance, their occupational adjustability or lack of it, their ability or inability to participate wisely in the determination of social policy.

Actually we find that the educational and cultural opportunities afforded youth in the very areas that constitute the principal sources of future internal migration are markedly below the national norm. The school term is shorter. Teachers are less adequately prepared. The percentage of children of school age attending school is conspicuously less. Per pupil expenditures for education are often less than half as great as in more favored areas. The curriculum is inferior.

The need for change is perhaps even more urgent when considered from the standpoint of the immediate interests of individuals. Young people now provided with the most meager educational advantages are the ones who, in largest numbers, will find it necessary to seek occupational opportunity outside the communities in which they were born. Under the most favorable conditions, transfer from one sort of cultural milieu to another requires a high degree of adjustment and adaptability. Those who have been denied the opportunity of anything more than the most restricted intellectual growth in home, community, and school will without doubt find the venture particularly hazardous.

The Need for a Reorientation of Rural Education

There is need, not only for an extension of educational opportunity for a large part of the rural youth of the Nation, but also for a reorientation of rural education to meet the intellectual needs both of those who will take up their residence in towns and cities and of those who will remain in the open country. An educational program of the right kind can be made an effective instrument for the facilitation of migration and for the better adjustment of those who do not leave their home communities. This statement does not carry any implication that the curriculum in city schools is usually best fitted to equip young people for urban living under contemporary conditions. Much of the content of school work both in cities and in country places is traditional and hackneyed and fails to provide vital stimulus for intellectual development. But there has been in recent years more significant experimentation in relating schoolroom activities to community needs in urban than in rural schools. And the problem of the relation of education to migratory trends centers very largely in this country at the present time in the situation of rural youth.

The discussion here is not primarily in terms of what is commonly known as "vocational education." There is an even more fundamental need in rural, as in urban, communities for education in the social institutions basic to civilized life, such as language, number, logical habits of thinking, social participation, literature, art, and government. Youth everywhere shares the common need of historical perspective, social insight, critical judgment, and an understanding of the workings of present social, economic, and political arrangements. Finally, it is suggested that the cultivation of general intelligence is the best guaranty of social and occupational adaptability.

This is not to say that rural youth has no need for special vocational guidance and education. On the contrary, there is no group in American life so much in need of training for occupational adjustability as young persons living in overpopulated rural areas. An adequate program involves exploration of the opportunities for vocational adjustment within the community, both with respect to the existing occupations and with respect to new economic enterprises that might profitably be developed. It also implies examination of the values that rural life has to offer, avenues of possible leadership in the community, and an attempt to develop a greater degree of cultural and economic self-sufficiency. Perhaps more important still, it should provide detailed and reliable information with respect to occupational opportunity in all parts of the country and thereby relieve youth from the necessity of relying wholly upon information provided by company agents, newspaper accounts, or the observations of imperfectly informed relatives and friends. A realistic program of vocational education would seek to prepare youth for work in the immediate community, but quite as much for work in industrial and commercial centers. It would avoid the too common tendency to limit vocational training to agricultural and industrial occupations to the neglect of the growing field of clerical, service, and professional occupations. Above all, it would avoid narrow specialization, aiming primarily at laying the foundations for vocational adaptability in a variety of related fields.

An imaginative approach to the needs of children in rural communities is set forth in a quotation from Edwin R. Embree in a recent review of the program of the Julius Rosenwald Fund. It was framed with special reference to the rural South, but it is equally applicable to other regions.

The first and great reform in rural schools * * * is that education shall direct itself to the peculiar needs of country children with a view to making them happy and useful citizens of country life. Let us look for a moment at the kind of preparation children need for rural living. Five items stand out— (1) the ability to read (and write) clearly and understandingly; (2) some skill in the use of figures; (3) knowledge of farming, including some general understanding of biological processes and an appreciation of nature; (4) manual dexterity, especially in the handling of wood, fabrics, and other materials, and in simple mechanics; (5) health. These are self-evident necessities for any successful life in the country. It seems naive to argue the need of education in such obvious items. But the simple fact is that rural children are not getting from their schools anything approaching adequate preparation in these fundamentals.

Reading is, of course, the first commandment even among the basic three R's. If a child can and does read, he can care for the rest of his education by his own efforts * * *.

In spite of its basic position in education, failure in ability to read is one of the commonest faults of American pupils. Any visitor to schools is shocked by the number of children who are almost completely deficient in the use of this elemental tool of knowledge. Many pupils even in the middle grades of elementary school cannot succeed in the guessing game of calling off words from the printed page. But much more serious is the great mass of pupils who, although they can glibly call individual words, have no comprehension of what they are reading; in fact, have no realization that reading is a means of acquiring information and inspiration, not merely a school exercise * * *.

Expression in written and oral language is the obverse of reading. It is a part of the process of gaining acquaintance and competence in the use of that amazing social tool—one of the most important inventions man has ever made—the communication of ideas by words. Penmanship and spelling are among the mechanics of writing; the ability to express oneself clearly and effectively is a higher aspect of the same process.

Ability to deal with numbers and figures is another of the essentials of modern life. The place of arithmetic in the school program needs no argument. It may be pointed out, however, that the goal is not knowledge of special traditional tricks of formal mathematics but a general understanding of the concept of number as a tool, together with skill in handling the usually very simple problems of everyday life. The task of arithmetic is really very easy if teachers would only set themselves to it. It is also very important, but this importance has to do with real life, not with a lot of crossword puzzle work, however hallowed these puzzles may be by history and tradition. * * *

We are not urging farming and manual training as vocational subjects. The education here should be just as general as that in reading or arithmetic, or other present school subjects. An understanding of farming carries one as far as he cares to go in the study of Nature and of biology, yet it has all the interest of life and the making of a living, all the definiteness and concreteness of specific tasks in planting, breeding, cultivating, and harvesting. There is variety of interest, for the harvest may be cotton or oats from a plant crop, eggs or milk from domestic animals, or honey from an intricately organized colony of insects. * * *

With all due modesty we suggest that an exact knowledge of how to manipulate corn and cows, and honey bees is even more enlightening (as well as more useful) than intimate acquaintance with the vagaries of least common denominators, lists of the kings of England, or other traditional tricks of the schoolmaster's trade.

Manual dexterity is equally necessary to the country boy. It is not merely that he be enabled to mend a broken chair or tinker with an automobile—important as these are—but also that he be given an outlet for creative work in making objects both useful and beautiful. This is not a suggestion that we repudiate machine production and return to a handcraft economy. But machines and hand skill should supplement each other. Much furniture, building, decoration, and clothing can be made more beautifully by hand than by any machine, and much more cheaply for the man who makes them. The person who can use his hands with a master's skill in building a house, painting a picture, playing the violin, or weaving cloth has a means of expression that is about as nearly godlike as a human being can achieve. He also has a pretty sure foundation for making a living. * * *

In connection with these arts of living, of course, attention will be given to the home as well as to the farm. Cooking, dressmaking, and housekeeping are natural partners of carpentry and planting.

Health is a more difficult subject for the school. The laws of bacteriology and physiology which underlie disease and the protection of health are so intricate as to be beyond the grasp of children. Furthermore, protection against the great contagions often requires public rather than private action.

Yet health is so important to any sort of robust living that every child should have some knowledge of its basic laws, some competence in protecting himself and his companions from the commoner diseases. This is especially true in the country, where public sanitation is apt to be less developed than in cities and where the struggle against disease is more nearly an individual or family matter. Some acquaintance with proper balance in diet is also essential, for, in spite of the supposed presence of nourishing and wholesome foods on the farm, rural eating is apt to fall into meager and ill-balanced patterns. Since poor country diet often results from the absence of diversity of crops, health and gardening become supplementary subjects. * * *

These five subjects we submit as the essentials of the elementary school in a rural district. If children gain competence in these, they may live happily and successfully. Surely the learning of five broad topics is not too much to expect from the 6 to 8 years of the common school. The reason these, or any other subjects, are not mastered is that the school attempts to cram a great multitude of lessons into the brief days. * * * It is not surprising that teachers driven by these fantastic schedules of rote lessons fail to offer real education in any subject, or that children hurried from class to class come to regard school as a place for reciting rather than for learning.[15]

5. Education in Relation to Occupational Trends

The quality of individual living, as well as the successful operation of the national economy, depends in large measure on a proper occupational distribution of the people. For those who earn their livelihood by work of hand or head the job is an important consideration. It is one's daily tasks that give life its tone and color; both for the worker and for his family many of the satisfactions of life grow out of the attractiveness of his occupation. Furthermore, the orderly operation of the economic system requires, among other factors, a balanced distribution of workers in the various occupational groups. It is enormously important, both from the individual and the social point of view, that the right persons with the proper training be appropriately distributed among the various occupations. Herein lies one of the major social obligations of the American educational system.

Any well-planned program that looks toward a more adequate adjustment of the population to occupational opportunity must be based on careful and detailed analysis of occupational trends and of the changing demands that the various occupations are making upon the skill, the intelligence, and the social qualities of the worker. Such an analysis has yet to be made, but there is enough evidence to enable one to see at least the general outlines of the picture.

Main Occupational Trends

One thing is certain: We have been developing a rapidly shifting occupational pattern. Perhaps the most characteristic feature of contemporary occupational life is the instability of employment opportunity. Within the span of a few years century-old occupations and trades are reduced to minor importance or disappear altogether and new ones take their places. The wheelwright, the glass blower, and the bookkeeper give place to the automobile mechanic, the factory operative, and the statistical clerk. Both the range and the quality of occupational opportunity are subject to sudden shifts due to such factors as advances in technology, changes in the consumption habits of the people, expansion or contraction of purchasing power, or fluctuations in prices and wages.

An analysis was made in chapter II of the trends in the three major occupational groups—extractive (agriculture, mining, forestry, and fishing), manufacturing and mechanical, and distributive and service. It was noted there that the proportion of the total gainfully employed engaged in the extractive industries has declined steadily since 1880. The proportion engaged in manufacturing increased about 10 percent between 1880 and 1920 but decreased almost 2 percent between 1920 and 1930. The relative losses in these two groups have, of course, been matched by a corresponding gain in the third group. This gain has been particularly marked in trade and transportation and in clerical service.

Something as to the shifts that have taken place recently in specific occupations is revealed in table 12, which indicates, for selected occupations, the number of employees per 1,000 of the total population in 1920 and in 1930. It will be noted that the chief losses during the decade occurred in agriculture, mining, iron and steel workers, and machinists. The chief gains occurred in such occupations as domestic service, the clerical occupations, and chauffeurs.

[15] Embree, Edwin R., *Julius Rosenwald Fund. Review for the Two-Year Period 1933–35* (1935), 5–10.

TABLE 12.—*Number of employees in selected occupations per thousand of the population, as shown by Census of Occupations, 1920, 1930* [1]

Occupation	1920	1930
Agriculture	100.9	85.3
Extraction of minerals:		
Miners, coal and metalliferous	8.4	6.1
Oil and gas well operatives	.8	.9
Manufacturing and mechanical industries:		
Blacksmiths	1.8	1.0
Boot and shoe workers	2.9	2.5
Carpenters and joiners	8.4	7.6
Electricians	2.0	2.3
Iron and steel workers, including blast-furnace, rolling-mill, foundry, etc., employees	8.0	6.7
Machinists	7.6	5.2
Painters, glaziers, and varnishers	3.0	4.3
Printers, compositors, pressmen, lithographers, bookbinders, etc	2.3	2.6
Rubber factory operatives	1.3	.9
Steam engineers and firemen (stationary)	3.7	3.1
Tailors, tailoresses, seamstresses, dressmakers, milliners, etc	6.7	4.4
Textile workers	9.1	7.8
Tobacco and cigar factory operatives	1.7	1.0
Transportation:		
Chauffeurs	2.7	7.9
Draymen, hackmen, teamsters, drivers, etc	4.0	1.2
Conductors, brakemen, and other railroad employees (not clerks)	10.9	7.7
Domestic and personal service:		
Barbers, hairdressers, and manicurists	2.0	3.0
Servants, housekeepers, stewards, stewardesses, etc	16.3	21.6
Clerical occupations:		
Clerks, stenographers, typewriters, bookkeepers, accountants, etc	26.7	30.3
Clerks and salesmen and saleswomen in stores	14.6	19.5

[1] Occupational Changes Since 1850, as Shown by Census Reports, *Monthly Labor Review*, XXXVII: 1019–1020 (November 1933).

An analysis from a somewhat different point of view of the changes that have been taking place in the occupational patterns has been made by Walter V. Bingham.[16] He classifies six major functions in the economic system and finds that during the 20 years 1910–30, while the population of the United States increased 33 percent, the number of persons employed in primary production of raw materials, the processing of goods, and the transportation of raw and finished goods increased approximately 6 percent; the number engaged in trading or merchandising, and in the financing and administration of exchange of goods increased by 80 percent; and the number engaged in professional and personal service by 50 percent.

Classifying occupations on the basis of the amount of education, special training, or talent required, Bingham found that between 1920 and 1930, while the total population increased 16 percent, persons engaged in the professions and other occupations requiring special abilities or advanced training increased by a slightly greater proportion (17 percent), while the number engaged in occupations involving little or no training increased by less than 12 percent.

The distribution of workers by social-economic classes, as analyzed by Edwards, has also shown significant trends in the past few decades.[17] Clerical and kindred occupations

have shown the most rapid percentage increase, followed by professional occupations, semiskilled workers, and wholesale and retail dealers. Actual percentage decreases have occurred since 1910 in the number of farm owners and tenants and of unskilled workers. Bradford F. Kimball, in his analysis of changes in the occupational pattern of New York State, found trends there substantially similar to those pointed out by Edwards for the United States as a whole.[18]

A detailed job analysis of manufacturing plants in Minnesota, made by Koepke for the Employment Stabilization Research Institute, throws considerable light on the amount of skill and training required of factory workers.[19] Workers were grouped into five classes on the basis of the skills required in the operation performed. Classes A and B include skilled mechanics; classes C and D, semiskilled operators; class E, unskilled workers. The proportions of workers having jobs in these five classes were as follows: A, 2 percent; B, 8 percent; C, 34 percent; D, 45 percent; and E, 11 percent. Thus the semiskilled group, according to this classification scheme, included almost 80 percent of persons in manufacturing establishments covered by this study. Persons in class C were machine operators performing highly repetitive operations; the operations grouped under class D were even more simple and could be learned in a short period of training.

Analyses of the changing occupational pattern of the Nation, incomplete as they are, lead to certain fundamental generalizations with respect to the type of vocational education needed. Recent years have been marked by a considerable relative increase in occupational opportunity in trade, communication, and transportation, in clerical and personal service, and in professional and public service. There has been a pronounced trend away from the productive and processing to the distributive and service occupations. Within industry the trend has been toward increase in the percentage of semiskilled operatives. Viewing the occupational field as a whole, one may expect in the future somewhat less opportunity for unskilled, the strictly "brawn workers", and increased opportunity for those who tend machines, while the opportunity for skilled workers and foremen may not alter substantially. Occupational opportunity for clerical and professional workers will perhaps for some time continue to show the largest gain.

[16] Bingham, Walter V., Abilities and Opportunities, *Occupations*, XII: 6–17 (February 1934).
[17] Edwards, Alba M., A Social-Economic Grouping of the Gainful Workers of the United States, *Journal of the American Statistical Association*, XXVIII: 377–387 (December 1933).

[18] Kimball, Bradford F., *Summary of Changes in the Occupational Pattern of New York State*, Educational Research Division, New York State Education Department (Albany, New York), 1935 (mimeographed).
[19] Koepke, Charles A., *A Job Analysis of Manufacturing Plants in Minnesota*, Employment Stabilization Research Institute Bulletins, vol. II, no. 8 (June 1934).

Education for Adaptation
Versus Training in Special Skills

Obviously the old trades requiring highly specialized skill and long periods of training are disappearing. The craftsman is giving place to the machine tender; he is surrendering his special knowledge to the specialist and his skill to the machine. For the great majority of productive workers the extreme division of labor has resulted in a drastic reduction of the time required to learn the requisite skills. In the Minnesota study by Koepke it was found that of the operations surveyed "22 percent required a training time of less than half a month for their satisfactory performance, 33 percent required from half a month to 2 months, 17 percent from 3 to 9 months, 16 percent from 10 months to 2 years, 8 percent from 2 to 4 years, and 4 percent more than 4 years."[20] Fifty-five percent of the operations required a training time of 2 months or less and 72 percent could be learned in less than 9 months.

The modern worker must be prepared to shift from job to job, from occupation to occupation, and even from industry to industry. The job analysis of manufacturing plants in Minnesota revealed that 54 percent of the operations were being performed by workers who had shifted from one industry to another.

These shifts in the skills and technical training required of the workers, based on technological advance and changes in the relative importance of different industries, emphasize the necessity of adaptability on the part of the present-day worker, with corresponding implications for vocational guidance and training. Such training, whether carried on in the school or the factory, should seek to develop in the worker the essential quality of adjustability to the variety of situations which he is almost certain to meet.

In the face of these changes, it is a mistake for the schools to teach the separate trades to any large number of pupils or to insist upon a narrow specialization. Factory workers today need fundamentally not so much a training in the handling of a particular machine as a knowledge of the skills and operations basic to industry as a whole. Instead of training for specific jobs or even for specific occupations or industries, emphasis should be placed on those operations and processes common to a number of occupations and industries. As Koepke points out, jobs involved in the production of such different types of products as milk and cast iron often have common denominators. A realistic program of vocational education will seek out the common denominators of industrial operations and processes and concentrate attention upon them.

The problem of vocational adjustment is not, however, wholly one of the proper distribution of human talent among the various occupations or of giving the worker command of the requisite skills. The worker's world is one of complex social relationships: he works for and with people, cooperates with them, directs them, serves their needs. It is a world requiring healthy personality, intelligence, and an understanding of current social and economic problems. A program of education that fails to cultivate these qualities will fall short of what it might or should accomplish.

Special problem of technological change.—The problems of occupational adjustment are particularly serious for older workers forced by technological changes to seek new types of employment. This problem will probably be acute for some time to come. The proportion of older workers will necessarily increase steadily, due to changes in the age structure of the population. (See ch. I.) Such a shift has been taking place for several decades and will continue into the future. There were less than 8,000,000 employed persons aged 45 years and over in 1920; but in 1930 more than 10,000,000 of the gainfully occupied were in this age group. Moreover, the median age of both male and female workers from 16 to 64 years has been increasing for some decades, and this tendency will continue during the next 50 years. In some way, in school or in factory, provision is needed for the more advanced training and retraining of these older workers.

Meanwhile, about a million and a half new recruits become eligible to enter the occupational lists each year, to replace older workers and women leaving employment for home duties, and to augment the number of those available for productive activity in the United States. Some of these potential new workers may delay search for employment while seeking further education, but most of them join the ranks of those seeking work. Increased accessions of young workers will continue during the next decade.

Finally, it should be pointed out that a large percentage of the available labor supply today is untrained or is equipped to meet opportunities that no longer exist. A large fraction of available labor is unprepared to respond to such employment opportunities as industry may offer. To enable this group to carry their own economic weight, an expanded program of vocational education and guidance seems essential.

The task of the secondary school.—The secondary school has two major social responsibilities: (1) It must organize into integrated curriculums whatever materials are necessary for a general education; and (2) it must make provision for specialized training for those who will and for those who will not pursue their education beyond high school. The latter courses should stress vocational training of a broad rather than a narrow and technical

[20] *Ibid.*, p. 14.

type. The courses should give emphasis to the general scientific and technical principles basic to industry and commerce. There are many principles and processes common to a number of occupations and industries. The program of vocational education should seek out these common denominators of industrial and commercial operations and processes and concentrate attention on them. Many, perhaps most, of the general principles applicable to industrial operations can be derived from a study of the sciences. For those pupils who will enter the industrial field upon completion of their high school course, a large part of the work in science might well be devoted to a discovery of these principles.

The cultivation of specific skills necessary for specific jobs should be regarded as the responsibility of the industries requiring such training. This division of responsibility between the school and industry is being increasingly attained in the development in an ever-enlarging number of high schools of the cooperative part-time type of organization, whereby pupils divide their time between receiving technical and general instruction in the school and actual work experience on the job in the occupation for which they are preparing. This type of organization saves the expense of keeping the school shops equipped with expensive machines and it makes possible a more effective type of vocational education in small high schools. In such a plan the school's responsibility for the education of the pupil does not end with the pupil's completion of his high school course. The school shares with industry the control and direction of the pupil's education until the pupil has acquired the skill necessary for regular employment.

6. Tax Resources and the Costs of Education

The maintenance of schools in this country has commonly been regarded as solely a matter of local or State concern. This traditional policy may be called into question for a number of reasons, most particularly with reference to current population trends. As already pointed out, there are gross inequalities in the educational opportunities open to young people in different parts of the United States. For millions of children the opportunity for anything more than a modicum of meager, formal education is largely conditioned by place of birth. Furthermore, there is in general little educational opportunity in the very areas where natural increase is so great that these regions are constantly sending forth migrants to other parts of the country. This situation strains the fabric of American social life. It challenges serious attention and calls for thorough investigation.

Further analysis shows that inadequacy of financial resources available for education in rural areas, and especially in rural areas of restricted economic opportunity, is a major factor in this unfortunate situation.

Regional Differences in Income per Child in Farm and Nonfarm Population

Data already referred to give a first index of variations in economic resources relative to numbers of children in different regions. Figures 16 and 17 present comparisons of the distribution of estimated total income in 1929 with numbers of children aged 5 to 17 years enumerated in 1930, in the total farm and nonfarm population of each major region and among the several States. The income of all families, divided by the number of children of school age, amounts to over $3,000 per child in 16 States. The corresponding amount is less than $1,500 in 11 other States. The total income of the farm population in the Northeast, if divided among the children of school age in that region, would yield $1,326 per child; that of the farm population in the Middle States and Southwest would yield about $900; the figure in the far West is much higher, while in the Southeast it is only $474. The relative position of the farm population as a whole is revealed by the fact that the farm population, with only about 9 percent of the Nation's income, was responsible, except as aided from other sources such as taxes from railroads and other public utilities, for the education of 31 percent of the Nation's children.

Regional Differences in Tax Resources per Child

A more specific measure of the relative ability of different States to support education is afforded by estimates of "tax resources"; that is, the revenue that would be supplied if a given model tax plan were applied uniformly in all States. Two studies of the taxpaying ability of the States are available for this purpose. That by Newcomer represents an index (based on 10 statistical series) of the ability of the different States to pay taxes under as nearly an ideal tax system as in her judgment could practically be devised.[21] The estimates by Chism are on the basis of a model tax plan developed by a committee of the National Tax Association.[22] The two plans do not employ precisely the same tax structure nor the same rates of taxation. The average yield per State is higher in Chism's estimates than it is on the basis of Newcomer's procedure. There are some striking differences between the two plans in the ranking of individual States. These measures are obviously not infallible; but they do reveal significant differences in the per-capita tax resources of different States.

[21] Newcomer, Mabel, *An Index of the Taxpaying Ability of State and Local Governments* (1935); for her revised data see Mort, Paul R., *Federal Support for Public Education* (1936).

[22] Chism, Leslie L., *The Economic Ability of the States to Finance Public Schools*. Teachers College, Columbia University, Contributions to Education, No. 669 (1936).

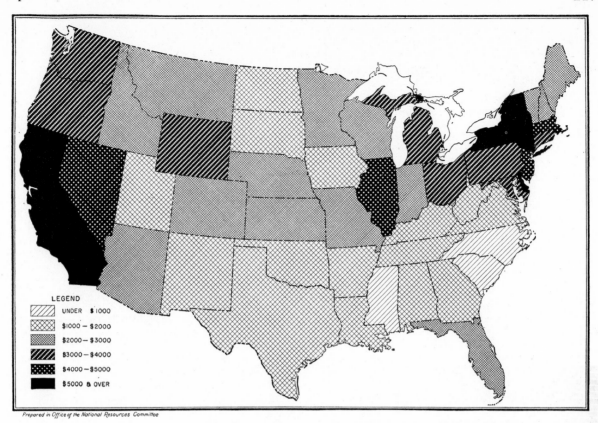

FIGURE 16.—Income of total, farm and nonfarm population per child aged 5–17, by regions, 1929.

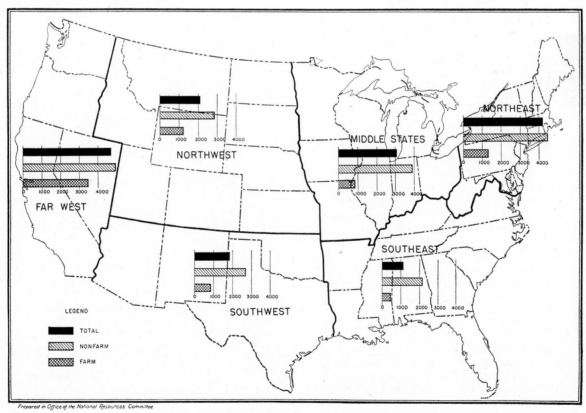

FIGURE 17.—Income of total population per child aged 5–17, by States, 1929.

An index of the relative ability of different States to support education is obtained, for present purposes, by relating the total expected revenue in any State to the number of children of school age in that State.

$$\text{Ability} = \frac{\text{Tax resources available under model tax plan}}{\text{Number of children aged 5 to 17 years}}$$

By applying this formula one is able to show the amount of taxes that would be raised per child of school age if the State should apply either the Newcomer or the Chism tax plan. It is not to be assumed, of course, that all the taxes available per child could be spent for education. The other costs of State and local government would have to be met from the same tax resources; and these costs vary from State to State. But if a tax plan in one State yields annually only $75 per child of school age, and the same plan in another State yields $150 per child, it is obvious that the two States are very unequally situated with reference to their ability to support education. On the Newcomer formula the average yield per child of school age for all States is $155; the result is nearly 40 percent higher on the Chism formula. The results for individual States on the former basis range from $50 or less in North and South Carolina, Georgia, Alabama, Mississippi, and Arkansas ($51 in Louisiana) to $200 or over in Massachusetts, Connecticut, New York, New Jersey, Delaware, Illinois, Nevada, and California. On the Chism formula all of the States in the first series show values under $90, and all of the States in the second series show values over $280, except Delaware, which receives a very different rating in the two series.[23] (See table 13.)

The striking differences in the ability of the States to support their school systems may be brought out in another way. For the country as a whole, the expenditure for education in 1930 was $58 per person aged 5 to 17 years.[24] Figure 18 shows the distribution of States classified according to the percentage of the total tax resources that would have been required on the Newcomer tax plan to provide an amount equal to the national average for the education of each child 5 to 17. In eight States more than 100 percent of the available tax resources would have been required; in eight other

States less than 30 percent would have been sufficient.

Differences in Adequacy of Financial Support of Schools Compared to Effort Expended

Perhaps the most striking result of this inquiry is that there is in general no significant correlation on either index between the adequacy of financial support for education in different States, as measured by expenditure for education per child of school age, and financial effort, as measured by the ratio of total expenditure for education to total tax resources. In figure 19 the symbols representing effort appear to be scattered at random, in relation to degrees of adequacy. (See also table 13.)

Among those States that rank high in adequacy of financial support, some, such as Wyoming, Montana, Colorado, and North Dakota, also rank high in relative effort; and others, among them New York, Massachusetts, Con-

TABLE 13.—*Expenditure for education per child, by States, compared with total expenditures for education as percent of tax resources of State*[1]

States	Yearly expenditure for education per child	Expenditure for education as percent of tax resources		Tax resources per child aged 5 to 17 years	
		According to Newcomer	According to Chism	According to Newcomer	According to Chism
All states	$58	38	27	$155	$215
Maine	49	39	22	127	229
New Hampshire	56	43	22	134	256
Vermont	56	50	29	112	191
Massachusetts	74	34	25	215	299
Rhode Island	58	32	23	182	253
Connecticut	71	32	23	220	302
New York	92	25	27	372	338
New Jersey	84	35	30	241	283
Delaware	60	4	23	1,625	257
Pennsylvania	57	39	23	148	244
Maryland	47	27	22	175	214
West Virginia	49	51	27	96	182
Ohio	68	42	27	161	257
Indiana	70	57	30	122	231
Illinois	69	35	25	200	280
Michigan	81	50	37	164	218
Wisconsin	60	44	28	137	215
Minnesota	70	51	28	138	254
Iowa	73	46	23	158	323
Missouri	47	32	20	148	231
North Dakota	73	80	34	91	214
South Dakota	68	58	25	117	272
Nebraska	67	46	23	147	289
Kansas	71	51	27	139	262
Montana	82	54	31	153	267
Idaho	68	56	34	120	200
Wyoming	106	55	46	196	232
Colorado	81	56	34	146	237
Utah	59	53	33	111	178
Virginia	28	38	21	73	132
North Carolina	28	56	33	50	85
South Carolina	23	77	32	30	74
Georgia	19	49	23	39	85
Florida	35	31	24	113	151
Kentucky	26	47	29	56	92
Tennessee	27	40	24	68	112
Alabama	22	61	31	36	70
Mississippi	25	78	38	33	67
Arkansas	20	46	22	43	88
Louisiana	28	55	26	51	107
Oklahoma	44	54	36	83	123
Texas	36	42	27	85	133
New Mexico	46	66	36	71	127
Arizona	71	53	33	133	214
Nevada	109	16	19	673	561
California	106	39	34	272	316
Washington	78	44	26	179	304
Oregon	75	41	25	183	305

[1] See text for sources.

[23] The high figure for the tax resources of Delaware given in the Newcomer index is due chiefly to the corporation organization tax of 0.5 percent proposed in the plan on which the Newcomer index is based. This one source of revenue accounts for four-fifths of the hypothetical tax resources of Delaware as shown by the Newcomer index. At present, of course, many corporations are organized in Delaware for the very reason that the legal requirements there are more liberal than in most States. The application of uniform regulations and a uniform tax plan would reduce the number of firms incorporated in Delaware and thereby lower the yield below the figure shown on this index. However, the low corporation organization tax and the annual franchise tax on authorized capital stock now in force in Delaware yielded in 1930 approximately $30 revenue per capita, a larger per-capita yield than that obtained from all taxes combined in any other State.

[24] Ashby, Lyle W., *The Efforts of the States to Support Education* (1936), 60.

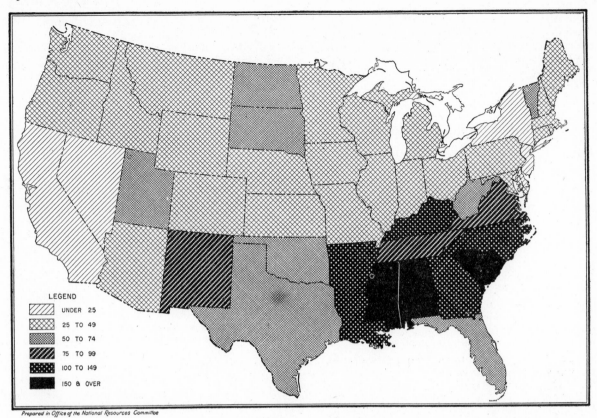

FIGURE 18.—Percentage of tax resources of each State (as estimated by Newcomer) needed to provide amount for education equal to the national average ($58 per pupil), by States, 1930.

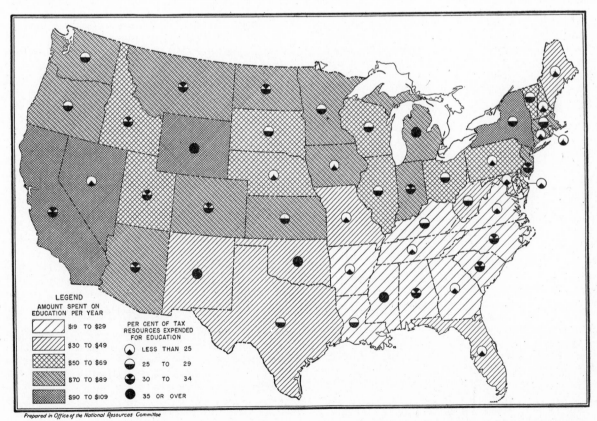

FIGURE 19.—Expenditure per pupil for education, by States, 1930, in absolute amounts, and as percentage of tax resources (as estimated by Chism).

necticut, Iowa, and Nevada, rank relatively high in adequacy and relatively low in effort. On the other hand, among the States that rank low in adequacy, a few, such as Mississippi, North and South Carolina, New Mexico, and Alabama, rank relatively high in effort.[25]

The evidence indicates clearly that some States provide relatively adequate support for education with relatively little financial effort involved; others support their schools equally well as the result of great financial effort; and in others education is supported only meagerly, in spite of the fact that a comparatively large percentage of total tax resources is expended for that purpose. States with great economic resources on the whole support their schools adequately and with relative ease; States with limited resources almost without exception rank low in adequacy of financial support even though, in general, they put forth greater effort than the richer States. In those States providing the least adequate support for education the fundamental difficulty lies in lack of financial assets. Even though a model tax plan were put into effect in the poorer States, they would not be able to support their schools adequately. In many of these States it would require all, or more than all, the taxes that could be raised under a model tax plan to provide an amount per child equal to the national average expenditure per child of school age.

Implications of This Analysis

This chapter opened on the note that it was a basic part of the American tradition in education that the public school should serve as an instrument for the maintenance of equality of opportunity. The very great inequalities in educational opportunity afforded American young people give rise to grave doubts that this end is in fact being accomplished. There is grave danger that the public school system, if present tendencies persist, may become a positive force in creating those very inequalities in the condition of men that it was designed to reduce. Such will certainly be the case if children who happen to be born in communities of culture and wealth are provided with rich and vitalizing educational experiences, while children in areas of limited economic resources are denied anything more than a meager schooling of the most formal type. Many of the American States, try as hard as they may, find it entirely impossible to offer their youth educational opportunities at all comparable to those provided in States of average wealth. If the American educational system is to be truly democratic, some way must be found to enable those States in which the burden of child care is greatest and in which economic resources are most restricted to provide for their children a

fuller and richer educational experience. The only agency through which the necessary financial adjustments can be made for more nearly equalizing educational opportunity is the Federal Government. The conclusion appears inevitable that sound public policy requires increased Federal aid to education in the States.

7. Summary

During the past quarter of a century or more, basic changes in our economy and in the general pattern of our social arrangements have fundamentally altered the status of youth in American life. It is the force of social change playing directly on childhood and youth, and indirectly on the school, that has defined many of the major problems of American education. In one way or another, both school and college have felt an irresistible social pressure to modify their programs in order to meet new and enlarged responsibilities to the children and youth of the Nation.

The American educational system is undergoing a fundamental reorganization in response to new conditions. Experimentation with curriculum content and methods of instruction is being carried forward vigorously, and the structural organization of the system is being modified in an attempt to make it conform to the changing demands of a democratic society. In this country, educational opportunities at the secondary and college level are extended to young people far more liberally than in any of the other leading nations of the world. As yet, however, we have failed signally to provide equality of educational opportunity. In communities where the ratio of children to adults is low, the burden of child care and education light, economic resources most abundant, cultural resources rich, and the cultural-intellectual status of parents high, the financial support of education is liberal. In communities where the birth rate is high and the supporting adult population is carrying a disproportionately heavy child population, where income per child is much below the national norm, where the level of living is low, and where the home has least to contribute to cultural and intellectual growth, the financial support granted to education is niggardly. The consequences of this policy would not be of such vital concern were it not for the fact that a large percentage of the Nation's children are being reared in the less favored communities. Approximately a third of the Nation's children live on farms and nearly half of them attend rural schools. And, in general, it is the rural child whose formal education has been most neglected. Nor can the fact be overlooked that at present the advantages of education are extended most liberally in those areas where the birth rate is lowest. In more than half the States where the rate of natural increase is high enough to maintain the present

---

[25] On the basis of Chism's data, the Pearson coefficient of correlation between effort and adequacy is $r=0.11 \pm 0.10$; on the basis of Newcomer's data, it is $r=-0.23 \pm 0.09$. *Ibid.*, p. 43.

population permanently, the annual school expenditure per pupil is less than the national norm.

The inequalities of educational opportunity that exist between rural and urban communities constitute a challenge to our ideal of democracy. Education can be made a force to equalize the condition of men; it is no less true that it can be made a force to create class, race, and sectional distinctions. The evidence indicates clearly that continuance of present practices creates grave danger that our schools, which we have heretofore regarded as the bulwark of democracy, may in fact become an instrument for creating those very inequalities they were designed to prevent.

Differentials in reproduction and disparities in income contribute to inequality of educational opportunity. There is, however, another cause and perhaps a more fundamental one, namely, the local character of school support. In practical operation, the principle of local support results in inequalities of educational opportunity which at present cannot be avoided. In most States, failure to support an adequate program of education is due primarily to lack of taxable resources. The States ranking lowest in adequacy of financial support of education are in general the ones that put forth the greatest effort. There may be reasons why the Federal Government should not participate in the support of education in the States, but these reasons should be weighed against the certainty that if the States are left to their own resources the existing inequalities of educational opportunity will be perpetuated for a generation, if not indefinitely.

No one familiar with the facts can doubt that much has been accomplished in recent years toward making the American educational system more effective as an instrument of social adjustment. It is equally clear that much remains to be done. The truth is there was never a time when the problems of education were more baffling or the challenge to educational statesmanship greater than at present. How can education be made to contribute more effectively to the adjustment of the population to economic resources? How can an integrated curriculum, which enables the pupil to achieve a comprehensive view of the accomplishments of civilization, be substituted for the numerous and only partially related courses that now comprise the curriculums of school and college? By what means can we develop the social insight necessary for the passing of intelligent judgment on public issues? How can education be adjusted to the capacities and needs of the individual and by what processes can leaders be discovered and developed? What kind of occupational training is required to develop in the worker the degree of adaptability required by modern industry, and can this training be provided most economically and efficiently in the school or in the factory? What methods of teaching and what principles of curriculum organization can best be employed to overthrow the formalism of the traditional recitation, and how can we develop in pupils a genuine independence of intellect? Are the American people ready to "undertake that high adventure of mastering through trained intelligence the problems of human life?" And, if so, what policies should be adopted and what means employed to implement the ideal of "an all-inclusive cultural democracy"? These constitute the challenge of American education.

IX. CULTURAL DIVERSITY IN AMERICAN LIFE

1. Introduction

If people were all formed in one mold and were all motivated by the same interests and ideals, population study would be relieved of some of its most difficult and fascinating aspects. Obviously this is not the case. Everyone is aware of distinctions between the genius of various nationalities, races, communities, and classes. Moreover, any nation, studied over a long period, shows changes in its distinctive characteristics which result from changes in the composition of its population and in its social institutions.

In the course of its experience every continuing group—set off by geographical isolation, physical characteristics that serve as a "racial uniform," language, religion, or economic functions—develops and cherishes a set of social values particular to itself. The attitudes engendered by these values become the distinctive qualities in the personality structure of its members. This complex of values and attitudes may be called the cultural heritage of the group. The uniqueness of each heritage is a source of displeasure, prejudice, and moral disapproval when races and cultures come in contact. There is a common tendency for diverse groups to be accepted only to the degree that their cultures possess similar elements or that they have prestige from historical and artistic associations.[1] Among the more adventurous and sophisticated members of society there is a counter tendency to welcome such cultural diversity as a means of enlarging individual experience. A more conservative but no less sophisticated point of view directs attention to the social disorganization, conflicts, and confusion that result from the shock of contradictory cultures and rapid social changes. The great variety of cultural heritages among different groups in the United States, their interactions and transitions, defines the problems of this chapter.

Historically, the cultural diversity in American civilization has arisen as the byproduct of movements and policies that were largely controlled by quite different aims or by the blind force of geographic and historic circumstance. The meeting of English, Spanish, and Indian cultures in the Southwest may be spiritually stimulating, but it was not arranged on this account. The Negro may make an important cultural contribution to American life, but he was not brought here for this purpose. The positive encouragement of immigration to the United States, beginning in the sixties—which at first went to the length of legalizing the importation of contract laborers—was primarily motivated by expectation of profits to entrepreneurs and landowners from the influx of laborers. The early modifications of this immigration policy—the repeal of the legislation favoring contract labor and the exclusion of Chinese settlers—were dictated by organized labor groups to protect their own levels of living. It is true that opposition on cultural grounds to mass immigration had already been fostered by the "Know Nothing" faction, or American Party, a secret organization with ideas similar to those of the recent Ku Klux Klan; but the popular line of action found moral sanction in the more generous ideal of America, "Asylum for the Oppressed of Every Land."[2]

The same mixture of conflicting economic motives and conflicting cultural interests marked the discussions that preceded the passage of the legislation now in force for the restriction of overseas immigration. By this time a strong reaction had developed against the further introduction of groups with cultures very different from those of the dominant groups in this country. It is significant that the new legislation was based on the "quota principle," explicitly formulated to limit immigration in proportion to the elements of different national origins already established on this soil. In general, however, cultural considerations have as yet played a

[1] See Thomas, William I., and Znaniecki (Florian). *The Polish Peasant in Europe and America*, 5 vols. (1918–20), I; also Park, Robert, and Miller, Herbert A., *Old World Traits Transplanted* (1921).

[2] See Beard, Charles A. and Mary, *The Rise of American Civilization*.

very minor role in shaping the nation's destiny; and where they have been invoked it has usually been on a rather meager scientific or theoretical basis.

From the biological standpoint the continued preponderance of the national stocks chiefly represented in the early settlement of this country seems to be assued—for better or worse. It is true that in many localities, especially in some industrial centers, the new immigrant stocks are tending to replace the older groups; but for the Nation as a whole this is not the case. Those drawn from the nations of northern and western Europe, including persons entering the United States from Canada, in 1920 still made up about 75 percent of the total population of the United States.[3] Furthermore, due to the preponderance of colonial stocks in rural areas (reinforced by Germans and Scandinavians in the Northwest) and due to the decline in the birth rates of urban immigrant groups as they become adapted to their new habitat, the former are certainly increasing more rapidly than the rest of the Nation. Some of the minor racial groups have high rates of natural increase, but their numbers at present are very small.[4]

Culturally, the situation is much more complex. For a variety of reasons, traditional ways of living are rapidly being replaced by new modes. These new cultural influences tend to originate in and to emanate from the centers where goods are designed, fashions set, copy written, entertainers trained, news and periodicals edited, movies produced, and programs broadcast, though some of the most important movements in *belles lettres* and the fine arts have their locus in the provinces. In the style and information centers, where the tempo of social change is apt to be most rapid, there is the greatest diversity of cultural heritages. For this reason and others some of the newer groups in American life have a cultural importance quite out of proportion to their numerical strength. Organized minority groups also exercise a political influence that is frequently more powerful than the unorganized will of the majority. Meanwhile, the increasingly complex organization of industry fosters the growth of class consciousness in both managerial and laboring groups. This conflict of cultural forces opens to the individual a wide range of alternatives and possibilities. At the same time it may leave him without guiding principles or sense of social support. It is, therefore, not surprising that urban populations should not be self-replacing at present, nor that many individuals are afflicted with a sense of frustration and conflict which not infrequently leads to complete mental break-down. Neither is it surprising that great advances are being made in science, art, education, and perhaps also in political organization.

Is a more rational and finer civilization emerging through the interplay of diverse cultural influences in the melting-pot of American life? Or will their net effect be the debasing of culture, the dominance of elemental passions, and destructive social conflict? No one can answer such a question. Nevertheless it is possible to take account of some of the cultural resources of the Nation, to examine the social values of the various groups, and to inquire into the relation of cultural processes to the changing population of the United States.

No conclusive findings can be expected from this brief excursion into so vast a field. We may at best hope to define certain problems and possibilities. The excursion, however, may at least serve to make clear that, in dealing with population problems, objectives other than mere increase or decrease in numbers must be considered. The ultimate tests by which population trends may be judged to be good or bad must be related to conditions affecting capacities and opportunities for individual development.

2. Cultural Contrasts in the United States

Cultural Diversity in Rural America

The cultural heritage of most rural groups in the United States involves few sharp breaks with tradition. Most of our cultural institutions have their ultimate roots in rural communities. And in spite of important changes in agricultural methods and increasing contact with city ways, materials, and ideas, social change has been fairly gradual in rural America. This has been true of the main immigrant groups in American villages and on farms as well as of the older native stocks. On the other hand, there has been much regional differentiation of culture in various parts of the country; and contact with the cultural changes of industrial society has varied in different areas from complete identification in some places to the almost absolute isolation of the Kentucky highlander (outside of the mining villages). Cultural isolation almost as complete has also characterized communities in other areas where physical distance has been reinforced by other conditions—by poverty as among poor white and Negro families in the Cotton and Tobacco Belt, or by language barriers as among Swedish, German, and Czech communities in some parts of the Northwest, or by religion as among the Mormons, or by the conditions of migratory labor characteristic of Mexicans in the Southwest. Such isolated rural groups are usually characterized by traditional folk practices, strong family loyalties, and fixed beliefs. The extremely high birth rates of such communities are one expression of cultural persistence. The decline in birth

---

[3] Lorimer, Frank, and Osborn, Frederick, *Dynamics of Population* (1934), 40.
[4] See ch. IV above.

rates recently recorded in most of these same groups is an index of the breaking down of this isolation and the revision of the traditional cultures. According to this index, cultural change is now proceeding rapidly in the Gulf and South Atlantic States, Utah, and the Far West.

Immigrants and natives in the Northwest.— The adjustment of immigrant families to established American institutions has usually involved less strain in rural than in urban areas. The earlier immigrants from northwest Europe arrived in time to take part in the frontier process, the Irish being the only large group from northern and western Europe that did not share to any great extent in this movement. They pushed out on the fringe of settlement and took up new lands which they soon made productive. They shared with old American neighbors the all-absorbing tasks of pioneer life. The cultural transition of the newcomers, accordingly, was relatively easy, and their assimilation proceeded as a matter of course.

A comparison of farm operators of immigrant stocks in the Middle and Northwestern States with old Americans in the same region shows that the former own farms equally large and equally fertile, and adopt as good or better farm-management practices.[5] Their incomes from agriculture equal or exceed those of native farmers.

The situation is somewhat different with respect to cultural participation. Certain communities which achieved competence and the respect of their neighbors are still set off by a certain amount of enforced isolation. In all these communities the amount of intermarriage between the immigrant families and the old American families was slight at first, but there is a pronounced tendency toward increase of mixed marriages in the later generations. In social life the chief barriers are those of language, indifference, and prejudice. The amount of social participation, however, is higher than might have been expected. Studies of 70 communities of 21 nationalities showed that they participate quite generally in American institutions, having joined more native organizations than they formed themselves. They secure more recognition in political organizations, however, than in those purely social. In intellectual achievement the children of immigrant farmers stand well. Their children generally make as high scores and reach as high grades as the native children in rural schools.

The pioneer experience of "starting from scratch"—immigrants from Europe and newcomers from the east meeting in the western plains on equal terms, passing from a tense struggle for existence to the mastery of the means of production in a fertile land, from the era of the sod house to the era of the mechanical reaper—led to an emphasis on action, common sense, and constructive enthusiasm. This has found expression in a vigorous literature dealing with the clearing of the wilderness, the struggle of man against nature, the growth of communities, and the whole epic of frontier movements, exploration, and settlements. The treatment varies from the simple, powerful folk realism of O. E. Rölvaag's *Giants in the Earth* to the lyric mysticism of Elizabeth Madox Roberts' *The Great Meadow* and Willa Cather's *O Pioneers! My Ántonia*, and *Death Comes for the Archbishop*.

Spanish-Americans in the Southwest.—The experience of the older Spanish-American settlers who became landowners in the Southwest is in many respects similar to that of farmers from northwestern Europe who settled in the Northern and Western States. But that of the agricultural migratory workers from Mexico has been very different.

It is difficult to estimate accurately the number of persons of Spanish-speaking ancestry in the United States, but altogether there are probably about 3,000,000. A majority of them still retain the Spanish language and Spanish traditions. Immigrants from Mexico and their children are the largest group in this total. Before 1900 there was relatively little immigration from Mexico to the United States, but the coming of the railroad and the attendant increased activity in industry and agriculture started a mass movement across the northern border of Mexico. There was pressing need for manual labor on the new railroads, in the mines, and in the extensive cultivation of crops now made profitable by cheap and rapid transportation. The coincidence of civil strife in Mexico with the development of economic opportunity combined to attract large numbers of Mexicans, rich and poor, skilled and unskilled, into the United States. With them they brought the Spanish language and their own customs, manifestations of Indian and Spanish cultures which they had inherited from colonial days and which they had continued to develop in republican Mexico.

Most Mexican immigrants enter into unskilled labor jobs. They serve as day laborers and tenants in the cotton lands of Texas, Arizona, and New Mexico. They are found on the beet farms of Colorado and in the fruit groves and garden fields of California. While they form the section gangs of western railroads, the "muckers" in the mines of the West, and are to be found in large numbers as laborers in the industrial region of Chicago and the Calumet area, the typical Mexican laborer is the migratory worker who follows seasonal farm crops. Chopping and picking cotton, thinning and cutting lettuce, transplanting and pulling onions, cutting and tying spinach and carrots, thinning sugar beets, and picking melons, the Mexican laborer moves over the States of the

---

[5] Brunner, Edmund de S., *Immigrant Farmers and Their Children* (1929).

Southwest with the growing seasons. He stays in one place only as long as there is crop work to be done and a few dollars to be earned. Although many Mexicans have settled permanently in various parts of the country, tens of thousands—men, women, and children—lead nomadic lives. Their situation raises many problems. The task of housing large groups of people who, overnight, have invaded a farming district is in itself a serious matter. Large families are obliged to live in overcrowded quarters in the poorer parts of town. Converted box cars, dilapidated tenements, and makeshift shacks are utilized by this mobile labor supply which, because of its very mobility, cannot afford more suitable housing. The education of the laborers' children is made extremely difficult by the seasonal migrations, by economic and racial prejudice, by inadequate school facilities, and by the system of family contract labor which practically compels all members of a family to labor in the fields.

The Mormons.—One of the most interesting large cultural groups in this country is strictly indigenous, stemming in culture as in descent from New England puritanism. Its distinctive institution, the Church of Jesus Christ of Latter-Day Saints, is an expression and development of the millennial zeal of the 1840's. Other social institutions and values represent original adaptations of early American and Old Testament patterns to the conditions of life in the Great Basin, including, of course, the famous institution of plural marriage, formally abrogated as a condition of admission to the Union. One distinctive adaptation, the location of the agricultural population in villages rather than on isolated farms, simulates, though it is not derived from, a feature of farm life in many parts of Europe, as well as in New England. As a characteristic feature of Mormon settlements, it has been attributed to a combination of three influences—sectarian ideology, particularly the plan of the "City of Zion"; marked solidarity, and the advantages of such a plan in the geographic environment encountered in the Great Basin.[6] The great emphasis on religion, moral discipline, and education still gives life in Mormon communities a strong similarity to that in old New England. We have already commented on the recent decline in birth rates in Utah. There is little doubt that the similarity of Mormon to Protestant traits will lead to a fairly rapid cultural convergence between this and other American groups.

Old Americans in the Southeast.—Among old American stocks, the effects of isolation— geographic, economic, and social—are most striking and far reaching in the Southeast. The white population of this whole region is derived, with little later admixture, from the colonial stocks that formed the dominant tra-

ditions of this country. Its outstanding qualities are strictly in line with the colonial tradition. If the southern people are characterized as Protestant, Sabbath observing, family loving, patriarchal, of religious intensity, quarreling with government, individualistic, taking their politics, their honor, and their liquor "hard", was not the Nation so characterized a century ago?[7]

In the popular mind this has come to be overlaid with romantic traditions of "a humanism over and above the basic puritanism of the early fathers; a setting of classical architecture, classical libraries, elegant furnishings, in the midst of groves and gardens and feudal settlements; dignity, polish, respect for form and amenities, pride of family, hospitality with merriment and conviviality abounding."[8] But this tradition was confined to a few; it hardly touched the great masses in southern life; little of it survives today.

Two main types predominate among the native white groups of the Southeast—(1) the small farmer, tenant, or sharecropper in the Cotton Belt and (2) the southern highlander. Many elements of cultural diversity in southern agricultural life can be traced back to the pattern of life set by cotton cultivation. The grower's flow of income is subject to the cycle of the seasons and to the fluctuations of cotton prices. His standard of living is low, not only because his family living is furnished on an expensive credit basis during the long growing season, but because changing cotton prices hinder, if they do not prevent, habits of thrift or a budgeting of the family income. The type of land tenure in itself engenders a shiftless attitude of the renter toward the land and the dwelling in which he lives. The common complaints of landowners are of houses allowed to go to ruin, fences torn down, and lands lacerated by erosion. Law gives the tenant no interest in his tenure and no claim for improvements made. He hopes to skim the most from the land with the least possible effort and then to move on to a new farm. To fix fences, clear land, stop gullies from washing, repair a shed, or shingle a roof is for him a foolish waste of time and energy. Moreover, the tenant is prone to move every 2 or 3 years or oftener. He swings around in a comparatively narrow circle, usually within his own or neighboring counties, in search of a better farm, better house, better school, or a better landlord. In normal times about a third of the tenants move each year; it often takes less than 5 years to change the composition of a whole neighborhood. The effect on retardation in schools, membership in community organizations, neighborhood status, credit, and even personal character is well known.

The labor of women and children for long hours in the fields during planting, chopping,

[6] Nelson, Lowry, *The Mormon Village: A Study in Social Origins,* Brigham Young University Studies, No. 3 (1930).

[7] The description is from Odum, Howard W., *Southern Regions of the United States* (1936), 227.
[8] *Ibid.,* 23.

and harvest periods; frequent absence from school; the typical diet of salt pork, corn meal, and molasses; the lack of home hygiene and adequate educational facilities are also well known. These things affect the health, training, and personalities of children growing up in these communities, and handicap them when they go elsewhere to seek employment. Such conditions have, naturally enough, not led to any great spontaneous movements in art, except in aristocratic circles as among writers and artists in Charleston, Atlanta, and New Orleans. But they are becoming a theme of increasing interest to authors, to both those of aristocratic and those of proletarian viewpoint.

The culture of the southern highlands has with good reason caught the imagination of "furriners" in other parts of the United States. Here are to be found the survivals of a backwoods America, in the coon hunting, folk songs, fiddling tunes, play parties, handicrafts, and the leisurely ways of mountain life. More than one observer has seen in the life of the Ozarks and the Appalachians the emergence of a genuinely indigenous American culture.

The true values of mountain life should not blind us to the economic dangers facing highland areas, since intriguing cultural diversity is no substitute for an adequate level of living. Soil leaching and erosion are year-round processes here, because of the abundant rainfall, steep slopes, relatively mild climate, and the type of soil. Saw timber has decreased tremendously, the peak of lumber production having passed in 1909. Primarily an area of small holdings, land in farms in the Appalachians has decreased since 1900, while the number of farms has increased. The dominant type of farm is self-sufficing, while many farmers must supplement their incomes by part-time employment, chiefly in the local mines. The irregularity of employment in coal mining has left many families in a situation worse than they formerly encountered on their hillside farms. Taxes on land are heavy in relation to income from land; but they still yield insufficient revenue to meet local needs.[9]

It must be remembered that conditions are not uniform throughout the Southeast. The cities and the prosperous limestone valleys frequently enjoy levels of living as high as those found elsewhere.

We will return to the consideration of other cultural aspects of southern life in later sections, including the agrarian movement in literature and cultural developments among Negro groups.

Cultural Diversity in Urban America

As industry and commerce have expanded, an increasing proportion of the whole population has been drawn into cities; the cities meanwhile have spread out and become more "citified", changing from trading towns to manufacturing areas and metropolitan districts with elaborate functional differentiation, social stratifications, and cross currents of diverse cultures.

For many of those nurtured in provincial traditions, transition to modern city living comes as a distinct cultural shock. It has been well said that "the modern machine-developed city is the man-made habitation of a race educated and trained to the open road. The problem of urban organization today is so to condition a thronging population that it can live under the most complex social conditions in the face of centuries of experience which developed habits, customs, and institutions."[10]

Rural-urban aspects of immigrant adjustment.—In America the problems of urban civilization have been intensified by the fact that rapid city growth has taken place through the attraction of successive waves of immigrants from many different sources. For most of these immigrants, transition from European provinces to American cities has involved a double shock: Transition to a new national culture, and transition from rural to urban modes of behavior. This rural-urban adjustment is an essential feature of the problem of immigrant assimilation. The high birth rates characteristic of the first generation of the foreign born in this country represent simply the persistence of the same sort of family traditions that are manifest in the high birth rates of typical rural groups in the native population. Similarly, the rapid drop in the fertility of the foreign-born population of the United States during the past 15 years is evidence of the same sort of cultural change that is found among various native rural groups, except that among immigrant families in American cities the tempo of such changes is more rapid, and in the case of the second-generation Americans they frequently involve even greater personal strain and conflict.

From the early years of the nineteenth century, the continuous drift of rural people into urban industrial communities has reflected the transformation of farmers or their children into factory hands. Relying first on a nearby supply, industries have had to seek their workers further and further afield, both in America and overseas. When unsuccessful in attracting the type of labor desired, they have changed their location to tap new areas. The history of the cotton textile industry illustrates this process. The earliest mills relied on the poorer farmers from the hills and stony fields of southern New England. As the industry expanded, this source became insufficient, and mill owners looked for ways to attract work-

---

[9] See *Economic and Social Problems and Conditions of the Southern Appalachians*, United States Department of Agriculture, Miscellaneous Publication No. 205 (January 1935).

[10] Dykstra, C. A., The Challenge of Urbanism, *Public Management*, 16 : 333 (November 1934). For an extensive treatment of this whole problem, see the forthcoming report of the Committee on Urbanism of the National Resources Committee.

ers from more distant and more substantial farms. The famous "boarding-house system" of the New England mills in the 1820's and 1830's, designed to attract farm girls into the mills, drew each year from a wider radius in northern New England. When the westward movement in the 1840's checked the native labor supply at the same time that the mills were expanding, the Irish, first of the peasant immigrants, were brought into the mills to fill the demand. As the industry grew, successive groups of immigrants took their places tending spindles and looms—French Canadians after the Civil War, Italians, Portuguese, Greeks, and others in the early years of the twentieth century. In its latest stage, the textile industry has turned to yet another source of rural labor. The cycle is being repeated in the migration of the industry to the Southeast to tap the reservoir of impoverished tenant farmers and mountain people.

In some industrial areas there has been a succession of different immigrant groups, each starting at the bottom of the industrial scale and occupying residential quarters abandoned by other groups that by this time were enjoying more favorable situations. These successive groups have gone through similar processes of economic and cultural conflict and adjustment.[11]

The occupational distribution of the foreign-born.—The majority of our newcomers were at first absorbed into industry as unskilled workers. "America at first has nothing for us

[11] See Cressey, Paul F., The Succession of Cultural Groups in the City of Chicago, doctoral dissertation, University of Chicago (1930).

but the shovel", is a common saying among immigrant groups. No satisfactory classification of gainful workers by social-economic classes and nativity is available except for 1930, so that a statistical analysis of trends in the occupational distribution of the foreign-born is impossible. The percentage distribution in 1930, however, is shown regionally in table 1 for native white and foreign-born males in all occupations except farming.

While it is true that considerable concentration in the unskilled group is still shown for the foreign-born, it is by no means true that they are restricted to the lowest unskilled jobs. They have a considerable representation in each group, although they are not so evenly distributed among the various classes as are the native whites. In most regions the foreign-born have a larger proportion who are unskilled laborers, and a smaller proportion who are clerks, skilled and semiskilled workers than is true of the native whites. Some interesting deviations appear in the regional comparison. In the Southeast and the Southwest, the proportion of foreign-born in the "proprietor" class is almost twice as great as the corresponding proportion among the native whites, and is also very much larger than the percentage of unskilled workers among the foreign-born in these two regions. The number of foreign-born whites in the South is relatively small, but the ones who are living there are professional workers and tradesmen rather than unskilled workers.

A vast body of information about the condition of immigrant groups around 1907 is available in an extensive study carried out under

TABLE 1.—*Percentage distribution by social-economic classes of native and foreign-born white male nonfarm workers, by regions, 1930*

| Region and group | Total nonfarm workers | | Professional persons | Proprietors, managers, and officials | Clerks and kindred workers | Skilled workers and foremen | Semiskilled workers | Unskilled workers |
	Number	Percent						
			Percent of total	*Percent of total*	*Percent of total*	*Percent of total*	*Percent of total*	*Percent of total*
United States	26,030,055							
Native	20,416,547	100	6.09	12.64	20.88	22.65	19.04	18.70
Foreign-born	5,613,508	100	3.42	13.44	9.41	24.36	21.03	28.34
Northeast	10,513,850							
Native	7,283,792	100	6.18	11.20	21.72	22.38	20.68	17.84
Foreign-born	3,230,058	100	3.17	13.35	9.17	23.32	23.53	27.46
Middle States	7,932,251							
Native	6,311,403	100	5.75	12.09	20.34	23.62	19.56	18.64
Foreign-born	1,620,848	100	3.17	11.64	8.83	27.24	19.23	29.89
Northwest	1,233,225							
Native	1,074,564	100	6.78	15.59	20.05	20.62	14.29	22.67
Foreign-born	158,661	100	4.41	15.99	9.31	22.72	10.63	36.94
Southeast	2,870,243							
Native	2,779,513	100	5.56	14.55	19.46	22.20	18.96	19.27
Foreign-born	90,730	100	6.39	32.59	12.44	19.30	16.33	12.95
Southwest	1,294,206							
Native	1,243,673	100	6.41	16.05	20.75	21.73	14.34	20.72
Foreign-born	50,533	100	7.23	28.31	12.92	21.98	11.23	18.33
Far West	2,186,280							
Native	1,723,602	100	7.14	13.42	22.18	22.85	16.65	17.76
Foreign-born	462,678	100	4.66	14.13	12.25	23.36	15.36	30.25

the auspices of the United States Immigration Commission.[12] In general, the Commission reported that the immigrant's lack of skill had encouraged further use of machinery and had affected the form of industrial organization by introducing subforemen and the "routing" of processes. This latter shift had tended to concentrate the more skilled and dangerous tasks that had previously been distributed throughout the workshop. Another result, it was felt, had been the spread of unsatisfactory working conditions. When the native workman protested and the immigrant acquiesced, it often meant that the immigrant replaced the native, under less satisfactory conditions. Finally, existing labor organization had been weakened; both the immigrant's lack of English and the native's prejudices were bars to either organization or participation.[13]

The Commission distinguished between two types of immigrant communities, the established industrial center and the single-industry town. The tendency to an informal segregation of immigrant families was found in both types of communities, but tended to be more serious in its effects in the single-industry town. In large centers many ethnic groups met, and it was but natural that the common denominator of their associations should in time come to be the English language, the public schools, and American institutions.

The living standards, housing conditions, and home hygiene of early immigrant groups offer valuable indices of adjustment. Here was largely a migration of peasants, unfamiliar with urban modes of life even in their own countries. The Commission found clear evidence that conditions of housing congestion and low standards improved with length of residence in the United States. This was a function both of improved economic status and of changes in culture and matters of taste. Conditions were found to be worse in single-industry towns, but the indications were that in all places the most miserable tenements were occupied by the newest arrivals.

For purposes of comparison with this early finding, recent census material is significant for its general implications. In 1930 it was found that the median monthly rental of urban nonfarm homes was slightly higher for foreign-born white ($35.13) than for all native white ($34.11). When the native white classification is further subdivided according to parentage, an even greater difference is seen. The figure for those of native parentage is $23.26, and for those of foreign or mixed parentage $37.74. In most cities the native white families pay somewhat higher median rentals, but the low rents characteristic of many cities with few foreign elements reduce the national average for the native white population.[14]

Available economic indices seem to point to the fact that, judged by externals, the immigrant is becoming assimilated. This may be due primarily to the fact that enormous numbers of migrants from abroad are no longer being poured at random into the American urban melting-pot. But whatever the reason, the immigrant is no longer restricted to the lowest unskilled jobs, and the conditions under which he lives do not differ greatly from those of the native American.

A recent special study of crime rates among native and foreign-born whites in the United States showed no significant differences between these two groups, when the data were controlled by elimination of differences in age composition and size of community.[15]

Statistics for the United States and Canada on intermarriage among groups of different national origin indicate that in the first generation there is usually a tendency to marry within the group, although this tendency is more pronounced in some groups than in others. Among all the groups, higher rates of intermarriage were found in later generations than in the first, indicating a definite trend toward cultural assimilation and intermingling.[16]

The new immigration.—With the virtual ceasing of foreign immigration, our cities are dependent on rural migration for population expansion or even stability. The northward wave of Negro migration in the war and postwar period marked one important phase of this movement. The cultural divergence of the Negro peasant who has turned cityward is obvious; his background of southern rural ways is greatly accented by his physical diversity. Both have operated to accord him a lower economic position involving rougher work, lower wages, and a large measure of exclusion from union organization. Housing is a primary problem for the transplanted Negro worker, as for the newly arrived immigrant. Practically

---

[12] See report of Immigration Commission, etc., in 28 volumes, Government Printing Office.

[13] Report of Immigration Commission, summarized in Jenks, Jeremiah W., and Lauck, W. Jett, *The Immigration Problem*, revised edition (1926), 194–200.

[14] From a census table showing median monthly rental values for the 93 cities of more than 100,000 population, regional differences are apparent. In 22 of these cities the foreign-born paid a higher median rental than the native white; of this number, only five were outside the two southern regions. In all these five (Evansville and Indianapolis, Ind., Flint, Mich., Washington, D. C., and Wichita, Kans.) the figures for the two groups were quite close together. The difference in no case exceeded $3.62. Of the 71 cities in which the native-born paid a higher median rental, only El Paso and San Antonio, Tex., and Tampa, Fla., were in the South. Here again the differences were small. The largest difference in these three cities between the rent paid by native- and foreign-born was $1.81. The reason for this regional distinction, as appears from the discussion of table 1, is chiefly occupational. The 7 cities where the native white group pays a higher median rent, and in which the difference is more than $10, all have relatively large numbers of recently arrived immigrants. Chicago, Ill., Elizabeth, N. J., the Borough of Manhattan, Utica and Yonkers, N. Y., New Haven, Conn., and Cambridge, Mass., appear in this group.

[15] National Commission on Law Observance and Enforcement, Publication No. 10. *Report on Crime and the Foreign-Born* (1931), 195–196.

[16] See vital statistics for Canada, New York State exclusive of New York City, and Massachusetts; also Drachsler, Julius, *Intermarriage in New York City* (1931); and Wessel, Bessie B., *An Ethnic Survey of Woonsocket, Rhode Island* (1931), 108, 110.

every city has one central district where half or more of its Negro population lives. As the Negro population expands, the structural community meets the line of dwellings held by white laborers, and spatial expansion is blocked. New Negro communities are started but the resulting crowding leaves the Negro with the highest percentage of concentration of any group in our cities.[17] Nevertheless, for one Negro group, those from the Sea Islands off the coast of South Carolina, Kiser has been able to show that they have bettered their economic status, kept something of their group cohesion, lost or partly lost attachment to their families, and found less prejudice and better economic opportunity. Some are found to complain of the tempo of work and the "coldness" of employers and associates.[18]

No studies comparable to those of Negroes have been made of recent white migration, but it is known that there has been a large movement of native whites from the cotton areas and the southern highlands both northward and into the expanding textile towns of the southeast. The difficulties of cultural diversity and conflicting standards created by this situation are especially pertinent to this discussion. Here the problem is particularly clear-cut, in that it is not one of biological heritage, physical diversity, or even language differences. We have here a native colonial stock, whose cultural diversity is based on retarded economic status, health, and educational opportunity. The genuine folk adaptations, which seem so quaint to the casual visitor and appear so satisfactory to those who sing ballads and hunt foxes, cannot hide the fact that here is a new immigrant substratum in our industrial cities.

No serious study has yet been given to what the newspapers call the problem of "hill-billy and poor white labor", but stereotypes familiar to students of immigration are already emerging. The common attitudes formerly shown the immigrants from southeastern Europe are now turned against the white native-born stock newly arrived in industrial centers.[19]

In the Far West the same problem of native migrants is met in agricultural labor. During the 4 months ending October 15, 1935, more than 30,500 men, women, and children in parties "needing manual employment" entered California in automobiles bearing out-of-State licenses. These "pea pickers" and "fruit tramps" build and live in squalid shanty towns, lacking the elements of sanitation and decent living. In many instances, the immigrants from the southeast are now casual laborers and odd-job men, performing the tasks once done by Mexicans.[20]

The problem of cultural assimilation in urban life is not merely that of immigrant and native. In fact, the primary adjustment necessary is that between fundamental rural patterns of living and contemporary urban ways—except that, where physical racial differences are involved, this process may be complicated by other, more persistent problems of cultural adjustment.

Social stratification and cultural diversity.—The problems of cultural diversity in urban society have even deeper roots in the complex differentiation and stratification of urban groups in accordance with economic functions, social status, and cultural interests. These problems persist in the more slowly developing older cities of this country and Europe, even where their populations are racially quite homogeneous. According to McKenzie, "The widest cultural differences, as judged by the spread of any cultural trait or complex of traits, are not between the country and the city but rather between residential areas within the city itself."[21] When tested by demographic indices, this statement does not seem to be verified in the case of birth rates, but it is supported by data on infant mortality. Certainly, studies of census tract data for Cleveland, Chicago, New York, and other large cities do reveal very great cultural distances between economic and social groups in the same city. There are sometimes equally great cultural distances between cities in specialized industrial, trading, or recreational areas. Such distinctions spell wide differences in social values, attitudes, and opportunity of life.

3. Some Indices of Variations in Cultural Level

Several sets of data on regional, State, or county variations in plane of living, income, value-productivity per worker, and occupational distribution were presented in chapter II. Indices of school attendance and school efficiency were presented in chapter VIII; these were found to show a close relation to the economic indices previously introduced. It is not surprising, therefore, to find similar geographical variations in indices of cultural facilities, cultural habits, and levels of cultural-intellectual development. Of course, none of these indices can be accepted as an absolute measure of cultural traits; but taken together they carry a significant story, and show that the conditions they reflect are closely associated with economic opportunity. This is not at all surprising in the case of newspapers, magazines, radios, and library usage, due to the direct influence of economic factors on these variables. (See figs. 1–4.) Similar regional variations in intelligence-test ratings are perhaps more surprising and significant, especially in view of the limitation of the

[17] Woofter, T. J., Jr., *Negro Problems in Cities* (1928).
[18] Kiser, Clyde V., *Sea Island to City* (1932).
[19] Some of these attitudes are suggested in an article by Louis Adamic, "Hill-billies Come to Detroit", in the *Nation* (Feb. 1935).
[20] Taylor, Paul S., "Synopsis of Survey of Migratory Labor Problem in California", Resettlement Administration, Berkeley, Calif. (1936).

[21] The New Regionalism. Round Table on Regionalism, Institute of Public Affairs, University of Virginia, July 1931.

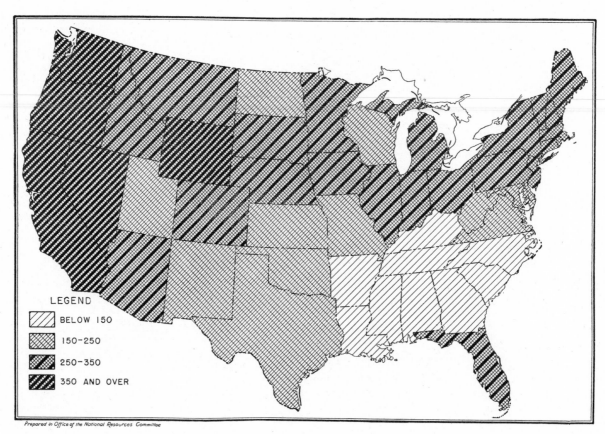

Prepared in Office of the National Resources Committee

FIGURE 1.—Net paid daily circulation of newspapers per 1,000 inhabitants, by States, 1930. Adapted from Odum, *Southern Regions*.

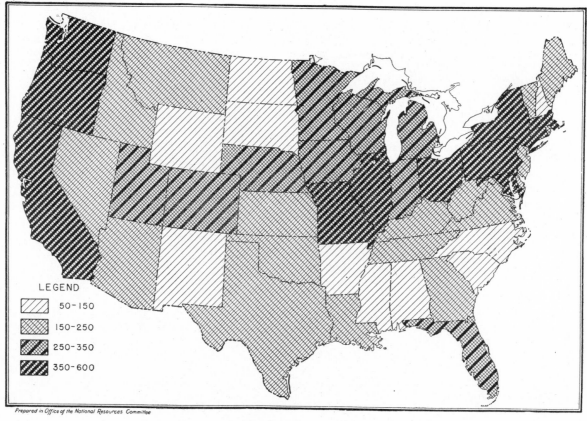

Prepared in Office of the National Resources Committee

FIGURE 2.—Circulation of 47 leading magazines per 1,000 inhabitants, by States, 1924. Adapted from Odum, *Southern Regions*.

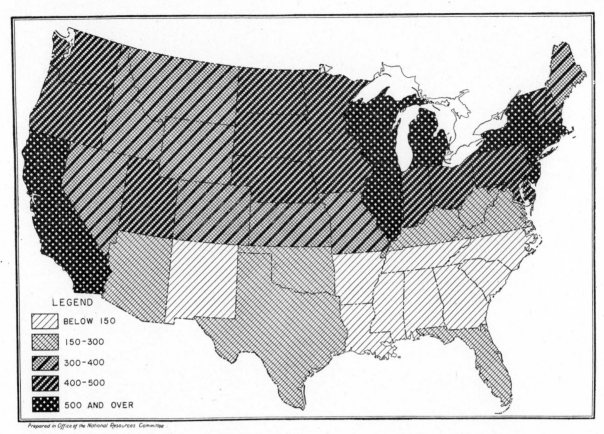

LEGEND
BELOW 150
150-300
300-400
400-500
500 AND OVER

Prepared in Office of the National Resources Committee

FIGURE 3.—Radios per 1,000 families, by States, 1930.

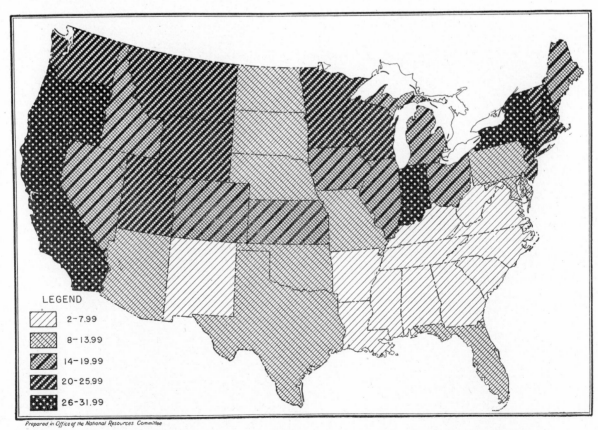

LEGEND
2-7.99
8-13.99
14-19.99
20-25.99
26-31.99

Prepared in Office of the National Resources Committee

FIGURE 4.—Percentage of population registered as library borrowers, by States, 1929. Adapted from Odum, *Southern Regions*.

sample in this case to white populations. (See figs. 5 and 6.)

Daily newspaper circulation is apparently strongly influenced by proximity to metropolitan centers, and interestingly enough the same seems to be true of radio distribution in 1930. Magazine circulation, according to the data for 47 leading periodicals in 1924, shows the highest frequencies in the Pacific States, Nevada, and Wyoming, with fairly high frequencies in most northern States, and in Arizona, Colorado, and Florida. The proportion of the population registered as library borrowers seems to be more directly related to the proportion of the population living in cities, with the maximum frequencies shown here for New York, New Hampshire, Indiana, California, and Oregon, and with high frequencies for Massachusetts, Rhode Island, Connecticut, New Jersey, Wisconsin, Minnesota, Utah, and Washington, as well as for several distinctly rural States, such as Vermont, Wyoming, and Montana.

Variations in intelligence-test ratings afford an even more penetrating index of cultural levels in different areas. Intelligence-test scores for individuals brought up in similar environments, as regards home, community, and school influences, are strongly influenced by hereditary factors. The same tests, however, when applied to groups matured in very different environmental conditions, exposed to diverse family traditions, and trained in different schools, may be used to measure differences in cultural opportunity. Intelligence tests vary in form and structure; they are chiefly tests of ability to manipulate words, numbers, and other symbols in solving simple problems, ability to remember and recall digits or nonsense syllables, and information about everyday affairs. The Army alpha examination was supposedly administered only to persons able to read and write English. State variations in median ratings and in percentages of persons with high scores (A and B ratings) for white drafted men are shown in figure 5. The Army tests were necessarily administered under conditions that were far from ideal for scientific purposes; the results have been subjected to much misinterpretation and consequent criticism. But used as an instrument for measuring variations in cultural level, as influenced by differences in opportunity, they indicate significant variations among large population groups.

Here, as is frequently the case, southern New England (and often, though not in this instance, New York) is matched with the Far West at one extreme. The cultural handicap of the South is again in evidence, quite as definitely as when data on school attendance or school efficiency are directly introduced. One of the most interesting features of this presentation is the high average intelligence ratings of the population in a block of sparsely set-tled rural States—Nebraska, Colorado, Wyoming, and Montana. It may also be significant that the lowest frequencies of mental deficiency, according to an entirely different set of Army data, are also found in the newer areas of the Northwest.[22]

Opportunity for cultural development is, of course, not merely a matter of regional situation but is affected by family background and social conditions making for participation in or exclusion from stimulating community activities. Such factors are undoubtedly responsible, at least in large measure, for the relatively unfavorable ratings made by Negroes in comparison with whites in the same localities. On the other hand, if the Army intelligence scores are used as an index of cultural level, the influences toward intellectual development affecting Negroes in some regions appear to be at least as effective as those reaching old native white stocks in other parts of the country. (See table 2.)

The Army intelligence ratings for various immigrant groups must, of course, be interpreted in accordance with the same canons applied in the analysis of regional variations. In their case, of course, the situation may be complicated by foreign-language handicaps in taking examinations, even nonverbal tests, administered in English. (See table 3.)

TABLE 2.—*Median alpha scores of white and Negro recruits, U. S. Army, 5 northern States, 8 south central States*[1]

	Median alpha score	
	White recruits	Negro recruits
5 northern States:		
New York	58.3	38.6
Pennsylvania	62.0	34.7
Ohio	62.2	45.5
Indiana	55.9	41.5
Illinois	61.6	42.2
8 south central States:		
Kentucky	41.5	23.9
Tennessee	44.0	29.7
Alabama	41.3	19.9
Mississippi	37.6	10.2
Arkansas	35.6	16.1
Louisiana	36.1	13.4
Oklahoma	42.9	31.4
Texas	43.4	12.1

[1] From data by Yerkes, Robert M., editor, Psychological Examining in the U. S. Army, *Memoirs of the National Academy of Sciences*, XV: 689, 730, tables 205, 266 (1921).

In the interpretation of intelligence-test results, it is possible to err either in accepting them at face value as measures of hereditary capacity or in dismissing them in flippant fashion as meaningless. Neither of these procedures does justice to the scientists in this field who have contributed to the development, standardization, and critical use of this important instrument of research. It should also be noted that major variations indicated here on the basis of the Army intelligence examinations have been confirmed, with important

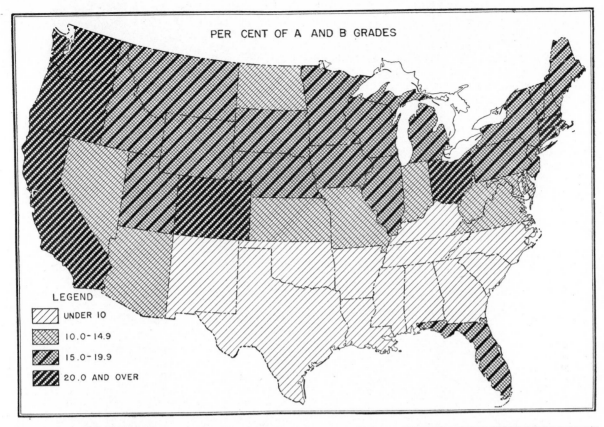

PER CENT OF A AND B GRADES

LEGEND
UNDER 10
10.0-14.9
15.0-19.9
20.0 AND OVER

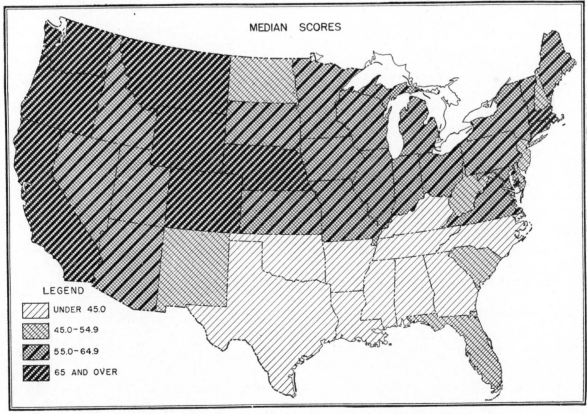

MEDIAN SCORES

LEGEND
UNDER 45.0
45.0-54.9
55.0-64.9
65 AND OVER

FIGURE 5.—Variations in army alpha examination ratings, white population only, by States.

TABLE 3.—*Percentage distribution by letter grades of foreign-born recruits, United States Army intelligence tests (alpha, beta, or individual examinations)*[1]

A. MEN FROM ENGLISH-SPEAKING COUNTRIES

Country by birth	Number of cases	A, B	C+, C, C−	D, D−, E
Canada	972	10.5	69.6	19.5
England	411	19.7	71.8	8.7
Ireland	658	4.1	56.0	39.4
Scotland	146	13.0	73.4	13.6

B. MEN FROM NON-ENGLISH-SPEAKING COUNTRIES

Austria	301	3.4	59.0	37.5
Belgium	129	.8	74.8	24.0
Denmark	325	5.4	81.6	13.4
Germany	299	8.3	77.2	15.0
Greece	572	2.1	54.5	43.6
Holland	140	10.7	80.1	9.2
Italy	4,007	.8	35.8	63.4
Norway	611	4.1	70.8	25.6
Poland	382	.5	29.9	69.9
Russia	2,340	2.7	37.4	60.4
Sweden	691	4.3	76.4	19.4
Turkey	423	3.4	54.8	42.0

[1] Adapted from Yerkes, *op. cit.*, 696, 698.

modifications and refinements, by later local experiments. Low scores on intelligence tests signify handicaps in managing machines, in the enjoyment of literature, in response to theatrical productions, in following the principal issues in political controversy, and in building a home background favorable to school progress and the later achievement of children. The usual positive relationship between indexes of cultural-intellectual development and of economic status, on the one hand, and the negative relationship between indexes of cultural-intellectual level and 'of fertility, on the other, raise questions regarding the trend of cultural forces in American life to which the answer is not clear, but which cannot be lightly dismissed.

Regional and other group variations in interests and behavior reflect, more than is sometimes realized, basic differences in opportunity for cultural-intellectual development. The levels of such development that are actually reached are not, for the most part, biologically determined but are subject to change through the improvement of institutional facilities for formal and informal education. It is possible that if environmental handicaps were removed, considerable group differences in mental capacity would remain; but it is impossible to know whether or not this is the case so long as the situation is obscured by the continuing force of such unequal opportunities for intellectual development as now exist in the United States.

4. The Role of Minority Groups in American Culture

Changing Attitudes Toward Cultural Diversity

The existence of diverse cultural heritages in American society has often been regarded as an evil, to be overcome as rapidly as possible. Movements initiated for the purpose of promoting harmony have sometimes tended, through excess of zeal, toward enforced assimilation or regimentation. They have tended toward the suppression of initiative, the destruction of traditional moral and artistic values, the fostering of feelings of inferiority and confusion, and toward personal and social conflict. "Assimilation if it takes place at all must be", as Fairchild has observed, "unenforced, primarily the product of natural spontaneous associations with those who embody the assimilating nationality. It was and is a great injustice to the immigrant to assume that he might assimilate himself by an act of the will. The first step in assimilation is the cultivation by native Americans of the greatest possible sympathy toward immigrant life and culture. The first step for the immigrant is that he must have an opportunity to 'live in America.'" [23] Blame of the immigrant for his lack of assimilation, probably the greatest hindrance to the old Americanization movement, completely prevents this sort of sympathy.

Amalgamation and adjustment are beyond the sphere of government; they are the function of society in its unofficial aspect. Cultural assimilation can be affected by education or thwarted by legislative interference; but above all it remains a matter of community process and of participation—economic, political and social. Accordingly, the waning enthusiasm for Americanization programs and the much-advertised failure of the melting-pot are to be accepted not as failure, but as a change in emphasis—a change away from attempts to enforce conformity and toward an understanding of the fundamental conditions and character of cultural processes.

This changing emphasis is in part a new appreciation of cultural diversity. Americans have come to realize that while we do not have a wealth of cathedrals, fine carvings, old family customs, or a national folk music and literature, we do possess an abundance of cultural resources in the heritage of many American groups. Such recognition is passing beyond the stage of antiquarian interest in curiosities and relics; it is becoming a spontaneous and wide-spread movement of great importance. It is significant that this has been announced as a major theme of the New York World Fair to be held in 1939.[24]

[23] Fairchild, Henry P., *Immigration*, rev, ed. (1930), pp. 422–424.
[24] To quote an informal statement by one of the Fair's executives, "The interest, in that respect, is to try to show at the Fair, particularly in Music, the Dance, the Theatre, and the graphic and applied arts—as well as in certain worthwhile characteristics of living—the richness of racial group source material, which should not be flattened out or commonplaced out of existence by a colorless uniformity. As one of my teachers put it many years ago, 'the simile of the Melting Pot is a detestable thing.' For that means a colorless mess. What we do want is a rich pattern full of variety, the variety which these various colonial sources can bring to it, not through imitation of the Old Country forms but through modification consistent with modern means and materials."

A change of attitude toward cultural diversity is also supported by the democratic and humanitarian impulse to make the ideal of equal opportunity for all a reality, even as affecting the lives of members of minority groups. It clearly follows, as a corollary to this ideal, that cultural diversity shall not prejudice personal or group development. In the well-established principle of religious tolerance, great diversity of belief and faith is cherished as a matter of public policy. It has been constitutionally established that race, color, or creed shall form no barrier to political participation. While not established by law, it is a quite definite popular conception that part of the promise of American life is participation in the community and the opportunity to earn and enjoy the "American standard of living." These criteria, if they are interpreted realistically, carry far-reaching implications.

The Cultural Experience of Immigrant Groups

The American community was not really visible to many of the immigrants coming to industrial towns and cities in this country.[25] By its separation of classes and ethnic groups, the American city showed the immigrant its worst aspect, the slums. His acquaintance with older Americans was often limited to the boss, the policeman, and the school teacher. He saw but little of the America described in his textbooks, and he saw only enough evidence of luxury to make him envious. The resulting sense of loneliness and frustration was frequently intense.

Even for the native-born, casual contacts are necessarily restricted in the crowded urban centers; the immigrant, of course, is even more intensely affected in this way.

Enforced isolation was not confined to unskilled laborers; it extended to middle-class intellectuals. Ludwig Lewisohn has vividly portrayed the effects of such isolation, as experienced by his parents. "They were", he says, "left in a state of solitariness which would have broken stronger and better-balanced natures. The strain of wild eccentricity in my father's character sharpened, my mother's brooding melancholy deepened from year to year. When after nearly 15 years in Queenshaven a breach was made in that inhuman wall, my father was hopelessly 'queer' as a social being; my mother—whose sweet and gracious presence atoned with people for his rasping ways—had become morbidly suspicious of this belated kindness."[26]

In many respects the experience of the second generation—the children of immigrants—has been even more difficult than that of their parents. Failure in their case cannot be accepted with resignation. They lack spiritual solidarity with old world culture; but in many cases they find little opportunity for participation in American culture. Part of the damage worked by the cruder sort of Americanization programs is that they destroy the loyalties and values that might have facilitated the cultural development of young people who otherwise find themselves between two worlds, without being quite a part of either. Many of the newcomers to the United States and many of their children have found opportunity for satisfying activity, and some have become leaders in all sorts of endeavor. But for millions of others, America has not been, in any significant sense, a "land of opportunity." Thus Louis Adamic writes: "The chief and most important fact * * * about the New Americans is that the majority of them are oppressed by feelings of inferiority in relation to their fellow citizens of older stock, to the main stream of American life, and to the problem of life as a whole; which, of course, is bad for them as individuals, but, since there are so many of them and their number is still rapidly increasing, even worse for the country."[27]

Appreciation of the nature of culture and the values of cultural diversity leads to a recognition of the important function of the spontaneous enterprises and institutions of minority groups, such as the foreign-language or race press, religious, artistic, and social organizations, cooperatives as among the Finnish, and other organizations that enlist the loyalty of individuals and minister to their needs. The monumental study of Polish culture in the United States by Thomas and Znaniecki gives a penetrating analysis of the role of such institutions as instruments of cultural adjustment.

The situation is really much more complicated than most of the popular American literature concerning immigration and Americanization sees it. It would seem *a priori* and it is generally assumed that the main problems concerning the immigrants can be stated in terms of individual assimilation or non-assimilation. * * * But, in fact, if we look at the Poles in America not from the standpoint of Polish or American national interests but from that of an objective sociological inquiry, we find that the problem of individual assimilation is at present an entirely secondary and unimportant issue. * * * The striking phenomenon * * * [is] the creation of a society which in structure and prevalent attitudes is neither Polish nor American but constitutes a specific, new product whose raw materials have been partly drawn from Polish traditions, partly from the new conditions in which the immigrants live and from American social values as the immigrant sees and interprets them. It is this Polish-American social milieu into which the immigrant who comes from Poland becomes incorporated and to whose standards and institutions he must adapt himself. * * * The imperfect development of this Polish-American social structure manifests itself most clearly in the fact that the combined influence of old and new institutions cannot prevent individual disorganization. * * * The only method which can check demoral-

---

[25] Commons, John R., *Races and Immigrants in America* (1907), p. 216.
[26] Lewisohn, Ludwig, *Up Stream* (1922), p. 59.
[27] Adamic, Louis, *Thirty Million New Americans, Harpers Magazine,* 169: 685 (November 1934).

ization, make of the immigrants—and particularly of their descendants—valuable and culturally productive members of the American society and imperceptibly, and without violence lead to their real Americanization, is to supplement the existing Polish-American institutions by others—many others—built on a similar foundation but in closer contact with American society. It must be always remembered that very little can be achieved by dealing with the immigrant sporadically and individually by the "case method." The Polish immigrant is an essentially social being * * * to be dealt with *in groups.*[28]

One school of thought among those who are conscious of a cultural heritage different from that of the dominant groups in American society tends to emphasize and develop the values of that heritage as a source of personal worth and as the means of distinctive contribution. This point of view, for example, is set forth by the editor of the *Menorah Journal*, in an article called "Chaos or Creation?" The writer points out that the Jews are modern minded; that economically, politically, and ethically they are a part of the modern world. But he insists that, however great their similarities, the division between Jew and Gentile remains. Accordingly, this spokesman feels that the Jew can achieve a fuller realization of his personal significance in terms of his distinctive heritage.

> The spiritual community of Jews lies not in creed: it lies, first of all, in Jewish history and culture * * *. In each one's identification of himself, to the limit of his knowledge and imagination, with the career of Israel in the world, one finds the means to intensify, enrich and transcend one's little self. One becomes a living part of a great tradition. The products of this tradition constitute our inherited Jewish culture. It is, of course, the inheritance of all mankind, to whatever extent mankind chooses to know it and live by it. It is the inheritance of the Jew in a personal and emotional way naturally different from the Gentile's.[29]

An entirely different type of response among those who have experienced limitation of opportunity, or felt themselves excluded from full participation in American enterprise and culture, ignores such distinctions in tradition, identifying their cause with that of the exploited everywhere. From this standpoint, Michael Gold's apostrophe of the workers' revolution stands in striking contrast to the religious consciousness of Lewisohn or Hurwitz: "O workers' Revolution, you brought hope to me, a lonely suicidal boy. You are the true Messiah. You will destroy the East Side when you come, and build there a garden for the human spirit."[30] The same contrast is found in current intellectual movements in many other fields, among artists and writers of the younger generation, among mountain whites in mill villages and mines, and among Negro leaders.

The importance of diverse cultural heritages as such is rapidly waning, except where these are tied up with racial distinctions or present

economic, religious, or other powerful and persistent interests. There is a natural tendency toward the assimilation of diverse cultures in the same communities. It is quite likely that this process has actually been forced too rapidly in the United States, with results that have often been personally and socially injurious.

But although it may be too late to save much of the vigor and richness of the new cultural resources brought to this country during the past half century by various immigrant groups, there still remains in the United States such a diversity of social values as to make renewed emphasis on tolerance and experimentation in the realm of social relations and ideas a matter of prime importance.

The Experience of Racial Minorities

Cultural adjustments are immensely complicated by the existence of racial differences, not merely because of possible biological differences in temperament and intellect (about which there is much controversy but little clear scientific evidence) but because physical differences serve as a persistent uniform of group identity and difference. We shall examine in some detail the situation of two distinct racial groups, Indians and Negroes. The Indians are selected for special treatment because of their peculiar position as wards of the Federal Government, and because recent governmental policy with respect to them represents an interesting and significant experiment in the recognition of cultural autonomy as a matter of public policy. Special attention is given to the Negroes because they are numerically the most important minority group in this country, and because their cultural status, not as yet finally determined, involves many complex and difficult problems.

The Chinese and Japanese and other minor racial groups in this country must be neglected, to avoid prolonging the treatment unduly. The number of Asiatics in this country is relatively small, the Japanese being the largest group. They have the advantage of entering American life from the background of another complex civilization. The evidence from a battery of widely different physical and mental tests shows the Japanese in America as very similar to the native whites in developed capacities.[31] The American-born Japanese have on the whole school records as good as or better than the children of Anglo-Saxon descent. They also show similar adaptability to a variety of occupations. In general, we may expect rapid approach to equality of status with other groups on the part of the Americans of Asiatic origin, although many cultural conflicts are likely to persist. Such conflicts may have international significance

[28] Thomas and Znaniecki, *op. cit.,* V: viii. x. xvi. 343, 344.
[29] Hurwitz, Henry, Chaos or Creation? *Menorah Journal,* XX: 11, spring, 1932.
[30] *Jews Without Money* (1930), 309.

[31] Strong, Edward K., *The Second-Generation Japanese Problem* (1934), 184.

beyond their immediate import in American communities. The development of an enlightened appreciation of cultural differences may therefore have special importance in this situation. Americans of Asiatic descent, if they can be encouraged to preserve their contact with the cultures of the East, may aid other Americans in understanding the complex civilization of the vast and increasing populations of Asia.

Cultural Aspects of Indian Administration

The aboriginies in America are the least "Americanized" of all groups, in the sense of assimilation to the dominant civilization in our society. Without daily contact with white culture, and effectively debarred from participation on equal footing in most enterprises, the Indian has remained a problem for political administration and evangelical enterprise. In many instances, tribal cultures have succumbed to the destruction of traditional economy and the impact of other influences. In other situations, indigenous institutions remain intact, or have been progressively developed.

Recent governmental policy in Indian affairs has made a radical departure from earlier practices. This represents the first conscious official attempt to preserve and creatively develop cultural traditions fundamentally divergent from those of the majority. The new respect for the integrity of Indian tribal life may be influenced by the possibility that anxiety concerning Indian raids on white settlements has been supplanted by anxiety concerning the economic costs of supporting a population that older methods have been forcing into chronic dependency. Such an interpretation of official policy would, however, be inadequate, if not wholly unjust. It is much more accurate to conceive of the policy as symbolizing the newer approach to the whole question of cultural diversity, mentioned in the opening paragraphs of this chapter. It seems worth-while, therefore, to give special attention to some of the issues raised and some of the problems encountered in this new procedure. It should be noted that a policy adapted to a group already largely isolated from other cultural groups is not directly applicable to groups in the main channels of national enterprise.

The present Indian population is composed of more than 330,000 individuals, living in scattered rural communities. In 1935 the full-blooded Indian population increased nearly twice as fast as the general population of the United States. No group in the country has a higher rate of natural increase.[32] The Indians in the United States are only one forty-fifth of all Indians. The fact that in some other countries, particularly Mexico, social experimentation by and through Indians is now

under way, gives an enhanced importance to present experiments in this country.

For this minority group, the Federal Government acts as guardian of tribal interests. Two radically different procedures are possible in this situation. One is to conceive as the desirable result the complete absorption of the Indian into the American scene; the other has as its purpose the separate economic and cultural continuance of the group, under conditions most favorable to Indian welfare. It is the latter point of view, generally speaking, that has come to prevail, as the Office of Indian Affairs has had to take the role of sociologist, anthropologist, land manager, educator, legal and business adviser. It has made positive attempts to meet the problems raised by the adjustments of a non-European culture within the American pattern.

The two major emphases in recent Indian policy are on the one hand a physical and on the other hand a spiritual reinforcement of Indian life and values. In contrast to the earlier policy of attempting to reconcile the Indian and white civilizations by the breakdown of geographic and cultural boundaries, the present aim is a consolidation of Indian resources and the maintenance of organic and traditional patterns. The Wheeler-Howard Indian Reorganization Act of 1934 and the Oklahoma Indian General Welfare Bill of 1936 are the legal implements of this policy. They assist tribes to organize for purposes of local self-government and economic cooperation, check the transfer of Indian acres to whites, provide credit to tribal corporations and to cooperative associations of Indians, and make mandatory the application of the principles of conservation to Indian timber and range areas. Thus far, 181 tribes have voted themselves under the Reorganization Act and 70 tribes have chosen to remain outside of its jurisdiction.

Economic aspects.—Since Indian income is derived largely from grazing, farming, and timber operations, land use is the essential problem of Indian economy. The object of the above legislation and the present land-use program is to make existing resources available so as to produce for the Indian, through the Indian's own work, the greatest permanent benefit.

Before this legislation was enacted, governmental policy had to meet the immediate rather than the eventual needs of the Indian. The following examples illustrate this earlier concept. Timber was sold outright to white companies at four reservations in Minnesota and on reservations generally. The Great Plains reservations leased their land to whites for grazing, with resulting depletion of the range. It is estimated that on the 37 million acres of Indian grazing land, more than 50 percent of the stock-bearing capacity has been lost through overgrazing and consequent

[32] See ch. IV.

115961°—38——16

erosion. The motive in all these instances was an immediate cash return, in preference to a smaller permanent income. The cash income itself was not invested for capital purposes, but was disbursed in per capita payments to Indians or used for administrative costs. Nor on millions of acres did Indians receive employment; instead, they subsisted as petty landlords. The end achieved was momentary gain, but ultimate destruction of natural resources. There were exceptions to this in many southwestern tribal areas, and to some extent in other parts of the country.

In the past few years measures have been taken to reverse this policy. Duck Valley, Nev., a small reservation of 800 people, has range land providing ample subsistence for summer months when pasture exists, but there is no feed for the long bitter winters. By the introduction of irrigation projects, hay is being grown to yield winter feed, and the resources of the reservation have been balanced. In general, the land-purchase program is directed toward a balanced economy in each tribe that secures land. Irrigation construction has been shifted from large, commercial farming projects to numerous smaller subsistence projects, and the Indians by their own labor will supply most of the maintenance.

Although accepted by the majority of tribes, the introduction of the present conservation methods has caused conflict. This has arisen from the clash of immediate economic interests with long-range planning. On the Navajo Reservation reduction in grazing, so vital to the preservation of the land, has not been accomplished without resistance by owners of large herds. The failure to accept the Reorganization Act by the Navajo Tribe may be attributed to this division of interests.

In addition to the encouragement of communal and individual responsibility for land use, the Indian Reorganization Act provides in other ways for group and individual self-help. It specifically gives preference to Indians as candidates for positions in the Indian Service. Through educational loans it assists Indians to receive professional and business training. The Office of Indian Affairs has increased its in-service employment of Indians from 30 percent of the total in 1933 to 59 percent in 1935. Other fields for Indian opportunity have been opened up. The extensive building operations of schools, hospitals, and community centers have been conducted with the express stipulation that Indians were to be employed wherever possible. Previous construction on the reservations had rarely been done by Indians, although they are good at such trades as masonry and carpentering. Conservation work (Indian emergency conservation work) has also been provided, and it has been found that the accomplishment of Indians compares favorably with that of whites.

Schools.—The goal of present Indian education is a rural and vocational schooling that will fit the pupil for a place within his own social environment, rather than to attempt to borrow from white education patterns. The Indian is helped to make adjustments through a knowledge of traditional organization, land use, health education, and traditional crafts. For instance, as a part of the curriculum in a Navajo day school, lessons are based on the problems of animal husbandry, erosion control, dry farming, and hygiene.

The earlier system was to send Indian children to boarding schools, often for from 4 to 8 years consecutively, including vacations. The enrollment in boarding schools (some of them supplanted by day schools) has dropped from 22,000 to 13,000 between 1933 and 1936, and the boarding schools are being converted into vocational schools. The unfortunate effects of the boarding school in alienating the child from his home is still felt in many communities today, for instance in the pueblos of the Southwest. The young men and women returning from the boarding schools have often looked upon their tribal life with scorn; the result has been in many cases a factional split between young and old.

Religion and ceremony.—The Office of Indian Affairs in current years has encouraged the practice of religious and traditional ceremonies. Indian superintendents are reminded of the right of all tribes to conduct their festivals and dances, a right previously denied. The official attitude is one of religious tolerance. This policy is summarized in the Bureau's bulletin of January 3, 1934: "The fullest constitutional liberty in all matters affecting religion, conscience, and culture is insisted on for all Indians." The Indian school child is not subjected to coercion; but the Bureau permits religious instruction, whether Christian or Indian, as desired by parental or personal choice.[33]

Apart from the ceremonial, viewed as the essential manifestation of the Indian's inner life, another expression more likely to be significant to white civilization is being given impetus by Government aid. The Indian shapes the clay of his earth, weaves the pattern of his experience in his baskets and his rugs, hammers silver into ornaments. These crafts are as old as Indian memory and are the concrete expression of Indian experience.

---

[33] The Bureau's religious policy has brought up an interesting question concerning the use of the drug, Peyote, a sacramental substance forming a part in the ceremony of the Native American Church cult. There are estimated to be 10,000 members of the church in this country, for the most part Indians. In one of the pueblo villages the presence of a fairly active Peyote group of Indians is the alleged cause of factional dispute. Certain Indians, it has appeared, may desire that the Government take sides in their religious differences. If this were to be done, it would be in conflict with the principles of the present Indian Bureau leadership, which maintains an attitude of noninterference as between competing religious groups. Peyote, a cactus product used immemorially for ceremonial purposes in Mexico, has been found by investigations not to be habit forming or injurious to health. Its physiological action is upon the centers of vision of the brain.

Arts and crafts.—The purpose of the Indian Bureau in fostering the development of arts and crafts is to tap possible sources of supplementary income for Indian communities. The Indian Arts and Crafts Act of 1935 is the Federal instrument designed, among other things, to assist in expansion of the Indian handicraft market. This bill encourages study of methods of production and merchandising and, what is more important, seeks to protect the Indian's creative integrity through the establishment of a governmental trade mark of genuineness and quality. What risks are involved to Indian art and ways of life by the encouragement of widening markets and the inevitable speeding up of increased production? The situation is confused, and a number of factors must be considered: craft economy, methods of production, existing and potential markets. In origin craft objects were utilitarian and functional. The traditional pueblo woman made "pots whose form, decoration, and function expressed her innate feeling as a primitive woman for her home, her connection with earth and its springs, her wonder before the earth mysteries and magical invocation of them."[34] Later, frontier commerce and barter led to the production of craft objects for trading purposes. Today the Indian receives, in exchange for his handiwork, either manufactured goods from the Indian trader or a cash income from trader and tourist. In most cases he produces solely for white markets, rarely for his own use.

Already the urgency of commercial economy has hastened the evolution of Indian craftsmanship, partly to its destruction. The Navajo silversmith still creates his silver and turquoise bracelet, the design conceived in his mind and carried out by his fingers. However, a similar but cheapened and standardized product is being stamped by machine in a factory in Albuquerque, N. Mex. Indian boys employed by a white proprietor make this less expensive jewelry. This threat to Indian creative art has raised a storm of protest, and has resulted in litigation. The labeling of such goods "Indian made" has caused much discussion about protection of fine products by trade mark.

The same sort of quantity manufacture is carried on in the Pueblo of San Ildefonso. Here the need for cash income has altered the pottery technique from an individual act of creation into a factory process. The ceramic type that pleases the white man is made in quantity and by a number of hands—one molding, another firing, another decorating and painting, and still another "slipping" and polishing. The design motifs are no longer traditional, nor is the pot water-tight. "The pot now symbolized not the connection of the potter with the deep spring of Indian life, but her connection with the white life."[35]

The impulses leading to cheap popularization in Indian artistic endeavors are forces difficult to combat. Perhaps the fact mainly responsible is that the existing craft market is a large tourist trade. Another market—minor and selective—is that of the Indian connoisseur. Products sold in that market have a small turnover; they reach the higher priced curio shop and the collector's home.

The dangers involved in the governmental attempt to guide the Indian arts and crafts movement are important. Insistence on the copying of traditional design stifles the imagination of the craftsman and takes vitality from his art. Similarly, a sentimental stressing of the use of obsolete techniques and primitive tools will handicap the Indian by laying him open to competition with craftsmen of other groups, such as the Mexicans, using more efficient methods. There may be a solution in the trade mark to protect standards of workmanship, as well as to prevent imitation by white manufacturers, which might take place if Indian products were popularized. The ultimate fate of the Indian handicraft is not known, nor can it be foretold.

Summary.—The present official policy toward the Indians is to accept permanence of divergent cultures, accompanied by the interaction of these cultures within the American system. This is expressed through a wide range of practical programs. Cooperative association for land management, based on tribal communal organization, and the fostering of self-reliance through improved opportunity and specialized training for individuals are among the goals desired. The organizations fostered may be ancient tribal systems, furnished now with such modern tools as credit and cooperative trade; or they may be wholly modern community organizations of "Americanized" Indians. The social anthropologist finds his place within the present Indian Service; so equally does the agricultural extension agent who transfers his experience from white rural life. But the stress is upon the small group, and where the group is culturally ancient this stress is in the direction of conservation, even revival of ancient values. For the Indian, this policy means the preservation of cherished traditions, and an increased sense of personal dignity; for the Nation as a whole it means an enlargement of interests and perspective.

Changing Aspects of Negro Culture

In contrast to the Indians, whose problems are those of an isolated people with unique institutions, Negroes even in the areas where they are culturally most isolated adhere to institutions that are Anglo-Saxon in origin. They

[34] *Tewa Basin Study, the Indian Pueblos,* by Indian Land Research Unit of the Office of Indian Affairs.

[35] *Ibid.*

live in more or less constant contact with, and dependence on, the organization of the dominant white society in their communities. Park thus pictures the lines of communication in one typical county of the deep South, Macon County, Ala.:

> Plantation, hamlet, and town, still rather widely displaced, are connected by a network of rural roads which, except for a few stretches of recently constructed thoroughfare, wind their way leisurely along rolling ridges in order to escape or as far as possible to escape the peril of the sometimes heavy spring rains. Closer observation of this same countryside discloses the existence of another narrower, and less obvious network of footpaths which—unplanned, unplotted and without official recognition—intersect, connect and supplement but never compete with the public highways.
>
> These two systems of transportation—the public highways connecting the towns and the plantations and the footpaths connecting the humbler habitations of the Negro tenant farmers—suggest and symbolize the complicated interrelations and divisions between the races in Macon County and in the South generally.[36]

For many Negroes, and their numbers may now be counted in millions, the whole basis of life has been suddenly altered by movement from areas where social relations are fixed, the tempo of living slow, and primitive culture traits persist, to areas of rapid social change in industrial and metropolitan districts. We have observed that in 1930 one out of every four American Negroes was living outside his native State and that the majority of these migrants were living in large cities.

It is also important to realize that the Negro population of the United States is by no means homogeneous biologically, economically, or culturally. The broad mass of the Negro population is still made up of persons of African descent, occupied as farm laborers or tenants in the South. But the Negro group, as socially defined, also includes persons who are predominantly Anglo-Saxon in race, some of whom pass into the white community permanently, others occasionally, others not at all. It also includes persons who occupy high administrative positions, some of whom have profited by the best educational opportunities in the United States. Some Negroes of superior social status are engaged in enterprises dissociated from Negro institutions, but most of them find their place through professional or commercial service to the Negro community.

One of the striking features about Negro culture in the United States is the complete absence of any carry-over of African language or institutions. This is to be explained as the result of the conditions under which the slaves worked. In some cases groups of Negroes coming from the same region in Africa were purposely separated in order to avoid opportunity for conspiracy. Their only medium of social exchange was the language and institutions of the dominant group that they served.

In its daily routine and character, life in the old slave areas has changed less than might have been expected. It is true that most Negroes have at least been taught to read and write and have acquired the rudiments of elementary education. But their economic and social outlook is still characterized by a dependence and fixity so profound that their life is "muffled with a vast apathy."

The weight of generations of habit holds the Negro tenant to his rut. Change is difficult, even in the face of the increasing struggle for survival under the old modes * * *. Year after year of this existence for many of them and the hopelessness crystallizes itself at times into despair. "Ain't make nothing, don't speck nothing no more till I die. Eleven bales of cotton and man take it all. We jest work for de other man. He git everything" * * *.

It is evident that all is not exploitation. The high level of illiteracy at times fuses its weight with a diffidence and an ignorance which not only invite exploitation but make misunderstandings inevitable. Some families did not know the acreage they were working; the work to be done; the terms under which they accepted the land; the weight of their cotton yield. They were just working; if they came out of debt they would spend the money from the very novelty of having it; if they stayed in the hole, it was only what they expected. "We always owe money and going to owe it too; jest one month after another always something. That's the way it goes."

The plantation in theory was a capital investment for large-scale production under a continuing routine. Its purpose was not the encouragement of peasant proprietorship. The social relations, labor, mentality, and discipline fostered by it are at the same time reflected in its surviving forms and traditions, and in the continuing selection and molding of its tenant types. It demands an unquestioning obedience to its managerial intelligence; it demands the right to dictate and control every stage of cultivation; it cannot and does not tolerate a suggestion of independent status. Those Negro tenants who have in spirit revolted against its implication, or who have with praiseworthy intent sought to detach themselves from its grip by attaining an independent status, have felt the full force of its remaining strength. Nothing remains but to succumb or to migrate * * *.

To the Negro tenant the white landlord is the system; to the white landlord the capital of the banks is the system. The landlord needs credit by which to advance credit to the tenants. The security of the landlord is the mortgages on his land; the security of the tenant is the mortgage on the crops which he will raise. Because cotton lends itself best to this arrangement, cotton is overproduced and debts descend to obscure still another year of labor, and the vicious cycle continues. In the desperate struggle both may lose, but the advantage is always with the white landlord. He dictates the terms and keeps the books. The demands of the system determine the social and economic relations, the weight of which falls heaviest upon those lowest down. There was a song which old women hummed as they hacked the earth with their hoes. The words were almost always indistinct but the mood of the same tune, dreary and listless, fitted as naturally to the movement of their bodies as it did to the slick and swish of the earth under the blows of their hoes. One verse was remembered by one of them, and it ran so:

> Trouble comes, trouble goes
> I done had my share of woes
> Times get better by'n'by
> But then my time will come to die.[37]

Neither the economic opportunities open to them nor the education made available to Ne-

---

[36] Robert E. Park's Introduction to Johnson, Charles S., *The Shadow of the Plantation* (1934), xviii.

[37] Johnson, *op. cit.*, 125–128.

groes in most rural areas has stimulated initiative or intellectual effort. In many of the schools the teachers themselves have had little education and must frequently get along without textbooks or other material aids, except perhaps a crude blackboard, benches, and primitive desks. Embree states that in the typical school from 60 to 90 percent of the students are in the first three grades.[38] Nevertheless, he points out that the teachers, ill equipped and ill trained as they are, often succeed, with their native wit and ingenuity, in carrying the children along. At bottom, the inadequacy of schools provided for Negroes is due to the small amount of funds allocated for this purpose. In some cases, counties even go so far as to appropriate a portion of supplementary State funds allocated on the basis of Negro pupil enrollment to aid in the support of the white schools.[39] The whole Negro educational system in most Southern States is marked by a degree of neglect and inefficiency that acts as a drag against cultural progress. Conditions making for retardation are also prevalent in many white communities, but to a less marked degree. The very low average intelligence scores made by Negroes from some Southern States and the low average scores made by white drafted men from those same States, noted above, register the effects of these backward school systems. There can be little doubt that the same retardation also affects the development of character and personality in its more subtle phases.

The movement from "the shadow of the plantation" to days and nights in city streets, employment in factories, restaurants, stores, and in the homes of prosperous white families must come as a distinct cultural shock to many Negroes nurtured in an isolated folk culture. Their situation is both mitigated and complicated by the presence, in most large cities, of a nucleus of Negro families long adapted to urban living. These older urban Negro families include a large proportion of mulattoes, and some of them have long enjoyed superior educational opportunities. It is important to understand the origin and status of this Negro upper class.[40]

Even in slave times, the Negro community did not long remain wholly undifferentiated. The position of the slave differed from locality to locality, and with the type of work performed. On the smaller plantations and in the towns conditions were milder and there was often much contact between slaves and the owners and their families. On the large plantations a slave might not see a white man any more frequently than he did in Africa, and thus had little opportunity to take over the culture of the white community.

The most important basis for the initial differentiation within the group was difference in color. There seems to be no historical exception to the rule that when peoples come into contact and occupy the same area, mixture of blood occurs, which results ultimately in the establishment of a new or modified ethnic type. Mixture between the Negroes, white indenture servants, and Indians took place from the time the first Africans landed in this country. As it was generally believed in the South during the slave period that the mulattoes were superior in intelligence to the blacks, they were most often chosen for the tasks which required skill and intelligence.

The favored classes among the slaves, as the numbers of the mulattoes increased, came more and more to be light-colored classes. The trained mechanics and the trusted servants were drawn from the most intelligent; these were always assumed to be mulattoes. Moreover, the mulattoes made a better appearance than the black Negro and were less offensive in close association, and so gravitated to those house and personal duties which brought them into personal association with the master class. The plantation slaves and the rough laborers in the cities and towns were the black men. The division was, of course, not everywhere equally marked and it was seldom a sharp and complete separation. There were many full-blooded blacks among the favored classes and there were mulattoes in considerable numbers among the lower classes of slaves, but the tendency was toward a more and more complete separation of the colors. Manumission further widened the breach that existed in bondage. The free Negro group at all times contained a preponderance of mulattoes; in some places it was, to all intent and purpose, a mulatto group. Such education of the Negro as existed before the war was almost entirely mulatto education; it was limited to the free Negroes and to certain favored individuals and groups among the slaves. All things tended to make the mulatto a superior man and to make the superior groups among the Negro race mulatto groups.[41]

With the emancipation it was inevitable that the Negro and mulatto individuals of education and refinement should desire association with persons of like culture. They had little in common with the illiterate laboring groups. Their whole cultural orientation was toward the white rather than the Negro group. In tastes and ideas, interests and ambitions, standards and education, they were drawn to the dominant cultural group, but they were largely excluded from such association by the caste line, which persisted culturally in spite of the destruction of slavery as a legal institution. The mulattoes developed a common body of sentiments and beliefs that fostered their closer association, and they held themselves more and

[38] Embree, Edwin R., *Brown America* (1931), 127.
[39] For example, in Limestone County, Ala., in 1930, $58,464 came to the county on account of a per capita appropriation from the State school fund. The 3,478 Negro children in the county were responsible for $15,442 of this total; an additional $2,717 was received, specifically for Negro education, from the Julius Rosenwald Fund; but the total payment for Negro schools was listed as $16,890. In this county, 50 percent of all the Negro children were enrolled in the first grade. In several of the communities there was no special school building but classes were held in churches or lodge buildings. (Based on unpublished survey of education in Limestone County, Ala., from Tennessee Valley studies, under the direction of Charles S. Johnson.)
[40] The treatment here is based on unpublished materials supplied by Horace R. Cayton of the University of Chicago.

[41] Reuter, E. B., *The Mulatto in the United States* (1918), p. 339.

more aloof from the backward Negroes. They became a "marginal" race group, occupying an extremely difficult social position.

During the reconstruction period the mulatto aristocrats were the leaders in politics, which at that time was the great profession for educated Negroes. Later on, as the Negroes were gradually shut out of the political life of the South, the educated mulattoes migrated in large numbers to the North, where they could enjoy a status in the community more in keeping with their conception of themselves. Those who remained in the South turned to business enterprises and the education of the masses. With the migration of large numbers of Negroes to cities, these "marginal" men between two ethnic groups— educated Negroes and city-bred mulattoes— became established as a distinct upper class within the Negro communities which they served and on which they were now dependent. By virtue of their position, these professional and business Negro leaders have an economic stake in the preservation of the biracial system. At the same time, they experience most acutely the stings associated with segregation, the frustration of cultural ambitions, and alternating favors and repulsions.

The existence of social stratification and cleavage within Negro society tends to destroy the cultural cohesion of the group. This lack of unity in Negro culture very greatly complicates the problem of Negro leadership. This is discussed by Guy B. Johnson of the University of North Carolina, who points out that Booker T. Washington is the only Negro who has ever had anything like a race-wide leadership and that, strange as it may seem, at first glance, "Washington was in some respects a greater leader of white opinion than he was of Negro opinion. * * * Washington was a peacemaker. He reassured the white people of the South and relieved the tension which they felt on three points in particular: political participation, education, and social relations." Speaking of the more militant movement against segregation led by W. E. B. Dubois and the National Association for the Advancement of Colored People, Johnson comments:

> Sociologically the weakness of the movement is inevitable and incurable: it attempts to undo the folkways and mores of the southern caste system by attacking the results and symptoms of the system. Paradoxically, if it leaves the attitudes and folkways of the white man out of its picture, it is doomed to fail; and if it takes those attitudes and folkways into account, it is either forced back to the gradualistic and conciliatory position of Booker Washington or forced forward into revolutionary tactics.[42]

Dubois himself has recently repudiated the ideals of the N. A. A. C. P., which developed under his leadership, and is now throwing his energies into the promotion of distinctive Negro institutions.[43] In this new turn, he has received little outspoken approval from other Negro intellectuals, although the immediate interests of the Negro upper class are for the most part tied up with separate social institutions and services. Ideally, most Negro leaders repudiate fixed social lines. Actually their own status is dependent on such distinctions; and in practice it often seems more important to effect the immediate mitigation of unhappy situations than to challenge the existing basic code.

The whole tone of Negro life in urban centers among professional workers, clerks, industrial workers, hotel and railway employees, and servants is very different from that of families living in plantation cabins or isolated farmhouses. The folk characteristics of the static rural culture no longer persist in the new situation; old loyalties are repudiated. The difference is perhaps in no way more vividly revealed than by the contrast between the "spirituals", the characteristic music of the primitive Negro communities, and the "blues" of the city Negroes:

> These blues, which, by the way, first gained recognition as a form of popular ballad in night clubs of Beale Street, Memphis, are the natural idiom of the Negro proletarian, just as the "spirituals" have been, and to a very considerable extent still are, the natural expression of the mind and mood of the plantation Negro. The distinction between the folk of the villages and the open country and the proletarians or populus of the city is expressed and symbolized in the difference between the folk song and the popular ballad, the spirituals and the blues.[44]

In the period immediately following the World War there came an extraordinary burst of Negro literature. This climaxed a long period of unconscious artistic creation, expressed in "spirituals", stories, exhortations, work songs, "blues", and in the literature of protest, plea, and controversy. There had all along been occasional formal contributions by individual Negroes, from Phyllis Wheatley (who composed poems on classical themes in the prerevolutionary period) to Braithwaite (a member of the editorial staff of *The Atlantic Monthly*), but their works did not for the most part have their roots in Negro culture. The post-war renaissance, on the other hand, may be interpreted as one phase of the influence of new environmental conditions on developing Negro life. It was led by poets—Claude McKay, Countée Cullen, Langston Hughes, Sterling Brown, and others—and by writers of short stories, sketches, and fiction, including Toomer, Walrond, Fisher, and Fausset, James Weldon Johnson, and Bontemps. The movement was undoubtedly spontaneous in its origin; but it was definitely stimulated and encouraged by the activity of the National Urban League, under the leadership of Charles S. Johnson, research director and editor of *Op-*

[42] Johnson, Guy B., "Negro Racial Movements and Leadership in the United States", to be published in the *American Journal of Sociology*, January 1937.

[43] Dubois is now a member of the faculty of Atlantic University. See "Does the Negro Need Separate Schools?" *The Journal of Negro Education*, 4 : 328–335 (July 1935).

[44] From Park's Introduction, *op. cit.*, p. xiv.

portunity. It brought forth considerable literature, some of it characterized by great beauty and brilliance. It covered a wide range of artistic experience; but much of the literature was burdened with race consciousness, pathos, and pride.[45] Johnson, in 1927, characterized the work of these writers as follows:

The Negro writers, removed by two generations from slavery, are now much less self-conscious, less interested in proving that they are just like white people, and in their excursions into the field of letters and art, seem to care less about what white people think, or are likely to think about the race. Relief from the stifling consciousness of being a problem has brought a certain superiority to it. . . . The taboos and racial ritual are less strict; there is more overt self-criticism, less of bitterness and appeals to sympathy . . . The return of the Negro writer to folk material has proved a new emancipation.[46]

The period represented by this movement may be characterized as the lyric period in American Negro literature. This movement is now definitely under eclipse through an increased sense of strain, economic and cultural conflict, and confusion. Even before the depression, a distinct shift of emphasis was drawing the attention of young Negro intellectuals from literary themes to economic and social issues. Most of the poets mentioned above have become writers of problem plays and novels. The experience of the depression has intensified the conflict that exists within the Negro cultural community.

The economic crisis of the present decade has shown the Negro more clearly than anything else has ever done that his economic position is marginal and insecure. In despair he has shown an increasing interest in the economic interpretation of his career in America and a disposition to believe that some mighty medicine like communism is the only alternative to a permanent status of insecurity.[47]

Of course the majority of the educated young Negroes today do not espouse the cause of communism, but it is very probably true that a majority of them do conceive the problems of race adjustment primarily in economic terms. They are frequently more concerned about the status of Negro workers in labor unions and their place in industry generally than about court decisions on questions affecting Negro institutions.

The effective cooperation of white and Negro workers in the same labor unions, as among miners in Birmingham and among share croppers in the South Central States, is hailed as marking a shift from a caste situation to a realignment in accordance with recognized economic interests.

The whole history of the development of Negro culture in America and the present conflict of issues experienced by Negro leaders reveals the way in which institutions, interests, and attitudes are shaped under the influence of particular economic and social conditions. Where race becomes associated with economic differentiation, the physical traits that make up the "racial uniform" of any group may serve to limit the opportunities open to its members for productive activity and intellectual advance. In different circumstances racial conflict may be translated into conflict between economic groups; but the persistence of racial distinctions may create further divisions and intensify the elements of conflict. The cultural adjustment of minority groups in such situations becomes extremely complicated, with traditional, economic, and psychological motives and ideals.

5. Cross Currents in American Culture

Metropolis and Provinces

There are two main currents in the interchange of cultural influences in our society: (1) The movement of people nurtured in rural backgrounds—peasants from Europe, Canadian French from Quebec, Mexicans, and whites and Negroes from farms and villages in this country—into industrial and commercial centers, bringing with them ideas, attitudes, abilities, personal resources shaped in relation to rural conditions and institutions; and (2) the diffusion of material design, styles, popular tastes, and ideas from metropolitan centers into all parts of the country. Across these currents run the forces of economic cooperation and conflict, the public school system, political organization and campaigns, religious activity, literary and artistic experiments. These movements are tending toward the gradual assimilation of variant traditional cultures into a complex, more or less homogeneous American civilization, with many diverse and conflicting motives. Some "cultural islands" persist, due to geographical or racial isolation, or both. But the forces of contemporary civilization are rapidly beating down the barriers that preserve such cultures intact.

There is some truth in the aphorism that manners originate in cities, character in the country. The influence of urban ways on standards of living, techniques of production, play habits, and morals is an obvious and cumulative force in American civilization. At the same time, inheritance and personality patterns formed in early childhood exert a profound influence on the character and qualities of a nation, and these forces are focused with special intensity in rural areas where reproduction rates are highest. Metropolis and provinces are complementary features of American society. The physical, economic, and cultural vitality of both are essential to its progress.

---

[45] See Anthologies: Locke, Alain: *The New Negro* (1925); Cullen, Countée, *Caroling Dusk* (1927); Johnson, Charles S., *Ebony and Topaz* (1927).
[46] Johnson, Charles S., *Ebony and Topaz*, p. 13.
[47] Johnson, Guy B., *op. cit.*

The Impact of Machine Technology

A new motif is now affecting all these cultural processes: the machine and its accompanying developments in science, art, and daily habits. It is the essence of a machine to do the same thing in the same way repeatedly, supplying mass production of identical products. The requirements of mechanical production necessitate the standardization of materials to be processed and parts to be fitted together or to be used interchangeably. Machines also make specifications, so to speak, about the character of the people who are to operate them: they must be quick, punctual, and subordinate to a complex industrial organization. The importance of quantity marketing reinforces the need for standard specifications in production, and leads to systematic campaigns to control consumer tastes. Thus mechanical mass production inevitably sets up forces that work against cultural diversity and in the direction of the regimentation of human affairs.

At the same time the new technology brings release from the limitations of the immediate physical environment. It provides new resources for the sustenance of life, a measure of control over pain, sickness, and death, regulation of reproduction, and the communication of ideas. Machinery makes possible new pragmatic tests of scientific theory, the collection, classification, and manipulation of mass data; the machine places a premium on accuracy and rationality. In some ways the machine also makes social organization more flexible, making possible direct communication between leaders and masses, and the quick registration of changes in situations and attitudes. It also brings new possibilities for the communication of aesthetic experience and new means of widening man's intellectual horizon.

The question of the significance of machinery for culture is a favorite topic of historians and social philosophers.[47] Here we can merely note this force as one that must constantly be reckoned with, bringing new problems and opening up new possibilities, establishing new class alinements, and introducing new cultural motifs.

Standardization Versus Diversity

We are led at once to a fundamental question of vital importance concerning contemporary American life: To what extent is American culture tending toward uniformity and standardization? And what forces are at work that make for spontaneity, initiative, and diversity among groups and individuals? We shall briefly examine tendencies in three fields of mass culture, not with any idea of obtaining a categorical answer to such questions, but in order to make the issue somewhat more explicit and concrete.

Industrial design.—At the beginning of the twentieth century the slowly evolving regional and local movements in arts and crafts met the full impact of machine methods, mass production, standardization, and quick turnover. The objects of interior decoration reveal the full force of these new tendencies; the materials which make up the furnishing of our homes are more intimately connected with our lives than most graphic forms; they most clearly reflect the taste of the household.

One result of the growth of mass production was a more definite and formal distinction between purchaser, distributor, and manufacturer than had existed before. At first the manufacturer governed the kind of product made available to the consumer. The merchandiser was merely the promoter, and accepted whatever products the makers provided. A change in this situation occurred with the development of the large department stores, 5- and 10-cent stores, and mail-order houses. These distributors, because of their enormous business resources, were able to dictate to the manufacturers. Their influence was as important in this respect as in its effect on the taste of the purchaser who was so dependent on their facilities.

Today there are unmistakable indications of an increased interest in improvement of design on the part of some of the large distributing concerns. This trend is said to be in direct response to new market demands. Manufacturers, partly in response to such pressure, are now putting greater emphasis than before on design. Possibly this reflects some improvement in public taste or the assertion of greater independence on the part of individual consumers.

Interior decoration began about 10 years ago to be influenced by a new interest in native design sources, perhaps in reaction against the first excesses of machine production and its shoddy results. At this time the American wing of the Metropolitan Museum in New York City was opened to the public. An American motif popularizing colonial forms developed, and is still in force. Such revivals as the rebuilding of the town of Williamsburg, Va., have brought about what may be considered a secondary style trend in contemporary house furnishing. But the tendency to turn to design sources is not confined to an exploitation of colonial motifs. Reference may appropriately be made again to the fact that the New York World Fair of 1939 will seek particularly to demonstrate the richness of the artistic contribution of racial and national groups that have given to the United States its colonial and old-country forms, as a major theme.[48]

---

[47] See, for example, Mumford, Lewis, *Technics and Civilization* (1934), and the treatment of this theme by Charles and Mary Beard, in *The Rise of American Civilization*.

[48] See footnote 24, p. 237.

There is also a growing appreciation of functionalism as a factor in design. An unconscious functionalism is characteristic of many primitive art forms; they show that design springs naturally from the orderly and efficient use of materials. Modern designers at first gave a false emphasis to this conception, mistaking the meaningless arrangement of geometric forms by zigzags and angular breaks for functionalism. This phase is happily on the wane; but the movement for more direct interpretation of material, structure, and use seems to be advancing.

In the field of applied design, the forces of standardization and mass production thus seem to be balanced by other forces which tend toward increased diversity and greater use of significant form in the decoration and furnishing of homes. The factors of machine production do not necessarily vitiate artistic perception, if restrained and directed by other cultural influences making for individual initiative and critical taste. Where they are not so directed, in place of the beauty and simplicity of traditional devices, our perceptions may be dulled by a succession of meaningless sensations and our houses cluttered up with tawdry and useless gadgets. Clearly there are strong tendencies in both directions at present.

The cinema.—At first, the motion picture was widely regarded as making for standardization at a vulgar level; now it is often hailed as a medium of cultural advance. Perhaps the truth lies between these extremes. In any case the trend toward standardization seems to be inherent in the processes involved and the organization required for this development, though the movies may contribute something to spontaneity by offering humor, relaxation, and new interests.

It is easy to see from even a cursory glance that the major thread in the history of the cinema is the development of technique. The most recent technical developments are the improvement of color photography and the revolution introduced by the talking picture; there were, of course, many others. It has always been true, however, that mere novelty of technical development was insufficient to hold public interest. Recourse to something more universal in appeal was necessary, and various expedients have been tried. One is the exploitation of personality, another is the development of the fiction film. Only spasmodically has recourse been had to what may be called the naturalistic technique. By that is meant dependence on subject and setting, rather than on plot or actor, to carry the burden of the production. There have been naturalistic films—successful, without exception—but they were for the most part not produced by American companies. Examples of this type of film are *Grass, Chang, The White Hell of Pitz Palu,* and *White Shadows in the South Seas.*

It is difficult to characterize trends in film content with any accuracy. The trend away from the merely vulgar is easy to see; the public agitation leading up to it is still fairly recent. Another obvious tendency is to film favorite novels of the past, and successful plays and novels of the moment. Such pictures as *Little Women, David Copperfield, and* The *Green Pastures* bring a high order of drama to neighborhoods in all parts of the country, of a quality quite different from that of the usual offerings. The best American movies are characterized by a high degree of technical excellence and an infinite amount of efficiently handled detail. More and more attention is being paid to excellence of acting and to economy and ingenuity of plot. The final product—the work of an enormous number of unseen persons, plus the visible and audible actors—at least provides its vast public with the "flight from reality." It provides also some imaginative stimulus of which we have heard so much. Some realization is also conveyed of the world's variety, in character and natural setting.

One thing that the commercial cinema has almost never done is to experiment in the realm of ideas. The path established as successful is the one the industry seeks to follow. It is perhaps better that the major emphasis in filmmaking should continue to be the purveying of entertainment, rather than that a conscious effort should be made to mold public opinion. Nevertheless, experiment with ideas and concepts is possible, and might be financially successful.

In the main, movies are designed to amuse everybody and offend nobody. At the same time, there are indications that the producers recognize the fact that their audience can be subdivided. The two major divisions are the small-town and the metropolitan movie-goers; they correspond roughly to the rural-urban distinctions indicated at many other points in this report. The distinction is recognized by the tendency to make more than one ending to a given film, as a convenient answer to the problem raised by the fact that small-town audiences do not like unhappy endings. This was done for the silent version of *Anna Karenina,* called *Love,* made in 1927. In one version, Anna fell under the railroad train, but in the other the lovers were reunited. *A Farewell to Arms* was treated in this way, and, more recently, *Hearts Divided.*

The significance of the cinema as a force tending to channelize existing manners, dress, ideas, and morals seems to be inherent in its essential character and organization. The capture of an enormous audience is required of every film in order to defray the mounting costs of production and bring the coveted reward for the risks involved. The primary emphasis is on immediate entertainment. It is, nevertheless, reasonable to expect of the cinema some real contribution to human spontaneity, relaxation, and imagination, and a measure of fidelity to the characters and events portrayed.

The radio.—The cultural significance of the other great instrument of mass art, the radio, is in many ways more complex. The presentation of single programs is far less expensive than the production of films, thus permitting greater experimentation. On the other hand, the commercial programs are dominated by the same drive to capture the maximum audience with every event. This major cultural force has been for the most part developed and directed in the United States as an instrument of sales promotion. Its cultural values, however, have not been wholly neglected; they have been accepted by the industry as an important, though necessarily secondary, consideration. The actual effects have, in many respects, been more salutary than might have been expected.

Even allowing a considerable margin of error in estimates of this sort, the tremendous cultural import of the radio for all classes in American society is revealed by figures on the average amount of daily listening by radio-owning families (see fig. 6).

If we confine our attention to the influence of the radio in the field of music, we find that broadcasting has contributed above all else to spreading the influence of music of all sorts to a large public. The primary objective of the companies that produce radio programs is, of course, to reach as large an audience and evoke as enthusiastic a response as possible. Determination of the magnitude of audience response is therefore of prime importance. An effort is made to discover the number and kind of listeners for a given program, station or hour; to find out what people do as a result of listening; to report the attitude on the part of the audience toward the program or advertiser, and to record a change of attitude; and finally to ascertain what people remember.[49]

The radio industry has no standard criteria for measuring audience response. When their views were solicited, officials of radio companies were unanimous in saying that fan mail is to be regarded with caution; its quality is more important than its quantity. They admitted that they are especially influenced by the criticisms of radio editors, radio periodicals and other journals. The reaction of individuals whose judgment is respected plays an important part in influencing the radio executive. There is, too, the response of the managers of local stations and their gauge of audience reaction in particular localities. Inquiry by telephone and personal interview, for sur-

veys on a large scale, are considered indicative but not sure tests.[50]

Most surveys show that good music, unfortunately, does not now evoke a large response. It is not surprising, therefore, that the radio networks do not succeed in selling much *commercial* time for serious music. One company has published figures that are indicative of the situation, showing that 4 percent of its total commercial programs are devoted to classical music, 11 percent to dance music, 16 percent to light music, 6 percent to comedy, 6 percent to news, 17 percent to variety, 30 percent to script and serial features.[51] On the other hand, a large portion of *sustaining* time is devoted to programs of high musical quality. There are a number of reasons for this. The prestige element is important, but there

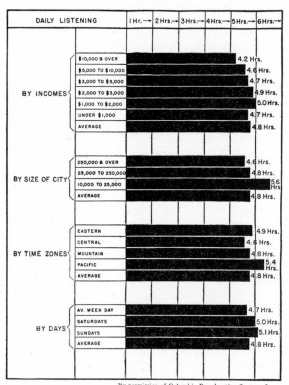

By permission of Columbia Broadcasting System, Inc.

FIGURE 6.—Estimated daily use of radio per radio-owning family, 1935, as estimated by Starch. From *Radio in 1936.*

[50] The Association of National Advertisers makes a confidential analysis of broadcasting by a telephone inquiry, issuing a biweekly report. The basis of a telephone survey is limited to those radio homes which are equipped with telephones. According to CBS, 43 percent of the radio homes in towns over 2,500 population have telephones. Other important data concerning radio ownership should be mentioned here. The 1930 Census listed the number of radio owners as 12,048,762, and since that time replacements and sales have been carefully noted. There are now approximately 22,869,000 radio homes, as determined by the Joint Committee on Radio Research. 93 percent of all families with incomes over $1,000, living in cities of over 10,000 population own radios. 96 percent of radio owners keep their sets in working order; 77 percent of the sets are in use some time daily, and 67 percent are in use after 6 p. m. The average daily amount of time devoted to listening is reported to be somewhat over 4 hours. These estimates are published by CBS in its book *Radio in 1936.* There is universal agreement among radio broadcast officials that the unreliable nature of tests is a serious handicap. A valuable contribution could be made to radio program improvement through a truer evaluation of listeners' reaction.

[51] *Variety,* Aug. 26, 1936.

[49] Lumley, F. H., Measuring Audience Reaction, *Yearbook of the Institute of Education by Radio* (1930 edition).

is also the fact that the radio is a medium which seeks to build public taste along the lines which it is naturally following. For this reason the radio presentations of more serious music express developments similar to those in music apart from radio.[52]

An investigation of educational and social music reveals a marked emphasis on programs of both types, in recognition of amateur interest, appreciative and participatory, in music. Best known of the programs in this category is NBC's "Music Appreciation Hour", directed by Walter Damrosch. This was started in 1928, as a commercial enterprise, and in later years has been carried as a sustaining program, with two half-hour periods weekly. It is estimated that 4 million school children are reached. Many other radio music appreciation lessons are offered. CBS provides instruction in its "American School of the Air" and an approach for the layman to a serious symphonic repertoire in the "Everybody's Music" program. In 1930, Joseph E. Maddy, in cooperation with the University of Michigan, taught the playing of band instruments to Michigan school children. Pupils responded so enthusiastically that the program has continued and expanded through successive years. Piano lessons directed by Sigmund Spaeth and Osbourne McConany were given some years ago under the sponsorship of NBC. A remarkable experiment among the teaching programs was attempted by NBC in the fall of 1936 by the introduction of the "Home Symphony." Arrangements were made for the audience of amateurs, either singly or in groups, to play with an orchestra broadcast from the studio. The officials of NBC say that this novel enterprise was undertaken as the culmination of many requests on the part of amateurs.

Amateur enjoyment and active response were encouraged in other broadcast programs. CBS maintained through the summer of 1936 a community sing. Its success has led to the taking over of the program by two commercial companies. Other instances of amateur radio programs are the broadcasts of the National Music Camp at Interlaken, Mich., and the "Music Is My Hobby" program. On the latter, persons from various walks of life have given performances on the air and recounted their music experiences. The responses by letter include requests for advice and other proofs that the program is of wide interest.

In the conflict between standardization and diversity, the new instruments of sight and sound reproduction exert direct influence far more on the side of standardization. The radio has, to be sure, recognized diversity and to some extent furthered it; but this development is somewhat impeded by the sheer magnitude of the audiences reached. The cinema is much more clearly a force tending toward cultural standardization. Both are instruments of mass communication, with primary emphasis on immediate entertainment. They may not crush individual initiative and spontaneous group enterprises, but they cannot be relied upon to bring new perspectives, or to provide for harmonious individual development.

The need for educational processes that deal intimately with individuals, induce critical thinking, and foster the orderly development of maturing personal interests is more than ever apparent. The instruments of sight and sound reproduction may prove a powerful supplement to such educational processes—providing emotional stimulus and release, and furthering the mutual appreciation and tolerance of diverse groups—but can never replace them. Apart from an adequate educational basis for individual development, the new means of mass production of goods and mass communication may tend to deaden rather than to quicken individual spontaneity and artistic experience.

Regionalism in Contemporary American Literature

It is possible to define four main types of literary regionalism—an inclusive term for a variety of movements to relate the artist to his region—in the United States, each associated with a particular area.[53]

The *Localist*, strongly represented in the Northwest—an empiric, matter-of-fact regionalist, interested in developing local or native materials in a specific soil;

The *Naturist*, typified by Mary Austin and her literary associates in the Southwest—the mystical, cosmic regionalist, with a philosophy of the land and the folk, of the good life and the indigenous, interested in developing native modes of expression mediating between man and the universe;

The *Traditionalist*, as represented by the agrarian movement in the Southeast—the humanist, interested in a usable past as the source of personal symbols and values, aesthetic and ethical; and

The *Culturist*, less conspicuously associated with any particular region in the United States, but well represented in the Southeast by Howard W. Odum and associates—a social, cosmopolitan regionalist, interested in shaping life as well as literature according to the needs and resources of interrelated regions.

The two movements last mentioned represent highly significant, contrasting types of

---

[52] A comparison of the summer of 1936 with preceding years will demonstrate an appreciable change in the field of broadcast concerts. A large number of summer symphony concerts were heard over the air in 1936 from Philadelphia, New York, Boston, Chicago, Cleveland, Portland, Seattle, San Diego, and San Francisco. Besides the broadcasting of symphonies, operas have been given time on the air. Concerts from numerous museums and libraries are broadcast, notably the excellent string ensembles from the Library of Congress in Washington. Festivals have provided occasions for radio presentation, such as the recent American Festival of the Westminster Choir School at Princeton, N. J. The radio industry has supported the tendency to encourage the playing of native compositions, in line with the efforts of the Federal Music Project.

[53] Botkin, B. A., We Talk About Regionalism—North, East, South, and West, *The Frontier*, May 1933.

imaginative response to the current problem of the relation of the traditional cultures of rural America, especially those of the rural South, to the industrial, commercial, and metropolitan forces now dominant in American life.

Agrarianism.—The agrarians are the most independent, consolidated, and articulate group produced by the regional movement. Theirs is both a secession from the "world-city" and a retreat into the memories of their forefathers. And, quoting Herbert Agar in *Land of the Free*, "it was natural the movement should start in the South, for southern culture has been deeper and more self-conscious than that of any other section."

The agrarian movement has passed through at least three stages. It began with a group of poets identified with *The Fugitive*, a magazine of verse published at Vanderbilt University from May 1922 to December 1925. One of their number saw the only hope for American poetry in the formation of groups, since "the American problem * * * is not national at all; it is sectional."

> The personal resources of the poet are capable of further intensification if they can be brought back to contact with the local cultures from which, in each instance, they originally sprang. Only a return to the provinces, to the small, self-contained centers of life, will put the all-destroying abstraction, America, safely to rest.[54]

In its first stage, then, agrarianism was a literary attempt to counteract and avoid the "aggressive Americanism" of the earlier middle western poets, Sandburg, Lindsay, and Masters. It was a direction, but "at least for the moment, quite negative."

But the movement was not long to remain negative and on the defensive. With the publication in 1930 of *I'll Take My Stand: The South and the Agrarian Tradition*, the attack on industrialism and metropolitan life was definitely launched. In an introductory "Statement of Principles", the "Twelve Southerners"[55] subscribed to their articles of faith, laid down the challenge, and defined the issues in no uncertain terms:

> * * * to support a Southern way of life against what may be called the American or prevailing way; * * * the best terms in which to represent the distinction are contained in the phrase, "Agrarian *versus* industrial". * * *
> But there are many other minority communities opposed to industrialism, and wanting a much simpler economy to live by. * * * Proper living is a matter of the intelligence and the will, does not depend on the local climate or geography, and is capable of a definition which is general and not Southern at all. * * * The members of the present group would be happy to be counted as members of a national agrarian movement.
> Opposed to the industrial society is the agrarian, which does not stand in particular need of definition.

> * * * The theory of agrarianism is that the culture of the soil is the best and most sensitive of vocations, and that therefore it should have the economic preference and enlist the maximum number of workers * * *.

The body of the book is devoted to the elaboration of the charges and the sharpening of the controversy.

In the third stage agrarianism set itself to the task of rebuttal, and, stating "what it stands for rather than what it is against", offered for national acceptance an economic program.

As agricultural economics, agrarianism does not concern us here. But in its insistence that literature is inseparable from a "way of life", including an economy and a defense of tradition, and that a writer must be a person and a citizen as well as an artist, it did much to bring regionalism to the "contemporary" stage of an "interest in the totality of a community's life and history" and to form "fresh objectives, political, economic, civic, cultural, on the basis, not of a servile restoration of the past, but of a growing integration of the new forces that have attached themselves to the main trunk of tradition."[56]

Constructive regionalism.—Odum takes decisive issue with the agrarians as perpetuating the undesirable features of the reactionary sectionalism of an earlier day. He says that "the substance of the nostalgic yearnings of this particular group of agrarians is little more than this: the culture of the Old South, if it had been what it was purported to be, which it was not, would have constituted a magnificent contribution to a richer civilization; therefore, go to let us turn back to that agrarian ideal as relief from the maladjusted industrialism of the new era. Manifestly, there is little realism here." Odum's desire is to substitute a new realistic regionalism, a view that permits of an interdependence of regions and of metropolitan as well as rural regions. It is a "geographic representation which recognizes the actualities of groups, occupations, aptitudes, cultures, and the special parts which they must play in the national drama." In reactionary regionalism, he points out, "only the local viewpoint, contacts, materials, and resources are utilized, while in the other [regionalism] local resources are utilized with reference to all other possible materials; and, if matters of social policy are involved, local resources are utilized and developed through skills made available through outside cooperation and cross fertilization of ideas. Sectionalism imbreeds to stagnation by ignoring time, technology, and collaboration; regionalism develops new strength from old power through progressive line breeding of new cultures, built upon the old."[57]

Regionalism marks a trend away from pure literature, abstract social and psychological

[54] Tate, Allen, American Poetry Since 1920, *The Bookman,* LXVIII: 508 (January 1929).
[55] John Crowe Ransom, Donald Davidson, Frank Lawrence Owsley, John Gould Fletcher, Lyle H. Lanier, Allen Tate, Herman Clarence Nixon, Andrew Nelson Lytle, Robert Penn Warren, John Donald Wade, Henry Blue Kline, and Stark Young.
[56] Mumford, *op. cit.*
[57] Odum, *op. cit.*, 55, 257.

studies, and decadent modernism toward a social and cultural art. In this development the regional movement has served to fix attention on the fact that, as individual character and action are inseparable from social structure, so geographical relationships tend to modify and diversify both. Regional variations and coherences exist, to be cultivated by the artist, not for a peculiar glamour of picturesqueness or quaintness, or for the false security of "limited solidarities", but as a means to social portraiture, the cultivation and expression of personality with its complex social, traditional, and geographic roots. In this literature, a natural division of labor exists between the provincial writer, on the side of the rural and agrarian, and the metropolitan writer, on the side of the urban and industrial. Both are essential to a complete picture of the diversified American scene and American folk and to the new ideology and mythology emerging alike from our buried cultures and our submerged minorities.

Industrialism undoubtedly brings grave cultural risks, and metropolitan life is characterized by much conflict and strain. The orderly development of individuals and the harmonious cooperation of social groups may be more difficult today than yesterday. But it is still possible that technical progress and social organization will supply the basis for finer personal living and peaceful relations among people—remote as this hope may appear at the moment.

In this situation there is naturally a good deal of nostalgia for the more "natural" life of earlier times; but little profit can be had from wishful agrarianism. Anaesthetics and automobiles and magazines and contraceptives and the radio are at our service, for better or worse. Even if it could be proved that the mechanic is a modern Pandora, it would still be impossible to put his tricks back into the box. Furthermore, the withholding of such goods from some rural groups through the maintenance of a class of "subsistence" farmers, for the good of their souls and the increase of the national population—while the rest of us endure these gadgets—might result in cultural patterns among those selected for rural poverty quite different from those characteristic of independent agrarian societies. The solution of the difficult social problems that the machine and the city have thrust upon us must be sought through more positive developments. The encouragement of creative regional movements in economic activity, politics, and art offers one constructive approach to this end.

Conclusion

To the first settlers and to the immigrants who followed later, America offered virgin mineral and forest resources, fertile valleys and wide plains, as the material support for a new life. On the spiritual side, there was the promise of freedom from rigid traditions and political tyranny. These hopes drew millions to the "land of opportunity." Those who came took pride in the thought that they and their sons and daughters were building a new nation. These hopes have not been without a measure of fulfillment. We have, however, reached a point in population growth and in economic and social development when the promise of American life must be restated if it is to have realistic meaning.

The natural resources of the United States still afford an ample basis for the development of a progressive economy; but direct exploitation of land, mines, forest, and game no longer suffices even to maintain all those now dependent on these industries at a satisfactory level of living. We have seen, for example, that the average annual value of products per male worker in agriculture is much lower in one of the principal farming regions of the United States than in England. At the same time, the depletion of natural resources through wasteful operations and soil erosion is assuming serious proportions. Future material progress must be founded less on wealth drawn from the earth than on goods and services that can be supplied through the efficient organization of human endeavor.

The new question of prime importance in population theory from the economic viewpoint is not the one that Malthus would have asked, "Has America land enough to support a further increase in population?" It is rather, "Can America develop an economy and culture that will promote the free development of individuals and the orderly progress of the Nation?"

It is apparent that cultural diversity among groups differentiated only by ancestral heritage or by spatial segregation, though still a vital factor in American life, is tending to disappear through processes of assimilation and the impact of mass production, distribution, and modern means of communication. On the other hand, divisions along functional lines, relative to economic status, occupation, education, and so forth, are perhaps becoming more pronounced; certainly there is no indication of a tendency for such distinctions to disappear—either as between agrarian, commercial, and industrial areas or as between economic groups within the same area. There is also a strong tendency for cultural distinctions associated with race to be reinterpreted along economic lines.

Meanwhile the impact of machine culture in production, consumption, and communication makes possible either cultural regimentation on a mass scale or the release of individual and group spontaneity and the accommodation of diverse interests on a new and higher level.

There are undoubtedly powerful influences working at present in these opposite directions. One set of forces tends toward "the totalitarian state", through the suppression of racial and cultural diversity and conflicting interests of all sorts. The other set of influences fosters cultural pluralism, the free adjustment of conflicting interests, local, group, and individual initiative, and thus makes for the preservation and furtherance of democracy.

The basis of democracy.—The previous course of population trends and institutional developments in the United States—the free opportunities afforded by a vast, undeveloped, and varied territory, the variety of cultural heritages, and the diversity of local interests—favored freedom and democracy. These conditions are no longer operative in the same way in our changing population. The future course of American culture cannot, therefore, be predicted on the basis of past experience. If democracy is to be preserved, it must be tempered by a high degree of tolerance and implemented by new cultural institutions designed to foster individual initiative, critical intelligence, and free cooperative adventure.

Democracy, where it is a vital force in modern life, is something more than a mechanism for registering votes on formulated issues at periodic polls. Accepting the existence of different economic and cultural interests, it is the essence of democracy to seek the furtherance of these interests and their mutual adjustment, through a wide variety of free associations and compacts. It is only through participation in democratic processes immediately affecting his own interests that the individual gains the experience of cooperative endeavor and acquires the democratic spirit.

Efficient economy and the adjustment of conflicting interests that are Nation-wide give peculiar importance to the task of the Federal Government, as economic processes increase in scope and complexity. But efficient government, responsive to public interests, is not a substitute, at least from the cultural angle, for local initiative and spontaneous cooperative activity in sports, art scholarship, production, marketing, politics, and all other fields in which individual initiative, loyalty, and enthusiasm are engendered.

Economic cooperation and competition.—Both cooperation and competition seem to be essential characteristics of any effective economy. Certainly both features are present in all national economic structures today—in fascist and socialist countries as well as in the economic regime of Scandinavian countries or of the United States—but in different proportions and in different relations. None of these structures, it may be assumed, has attained the ideal balance. There are few persons who do not recognize the need for further experimentation, though there are intense differences of opinion about the type and degree of changes to be sought. The definition of procedures in this field lies outside the scope of this report. It is appropriate at this point

only to call attention to the cultural as well as the material aspects of economic relations, and to insist that the former may be quite as important as the latter in evaluating alternative courses.

Producers' and consumers' cooperatives have been developed to a high degree in the Scandinavian countries. There they have fostered cultural trends that merit careful study. The same has been true in several other countries. Such cooperative groups are playing a very minor but an increasing role in the economy of the United States at the present time. It is impossible to say with certainty whether or not such movements are likely to have large significance in this country in the near future.

The labor movement may be expected to have increasing cultural significance in this country. The pioneer conditions of American life, the high degree of mobility among occupational classes, and the diverse backgrounds of industrial workers have led to an emphasis on immediate goals rather than on a broad labor program. "American labor still remains the most heterogeneous labor class in existence—ethnically, linguistically, religiously, and culturally—although the restriction of immigration will in time make it more homogeneous . . . Consequently the only acceptable 'consciousness' for American labor as a whole has been a 'job consciousness', with a 'limited' objective of wage and job control; which has not at all hindered American unionism from being the most hard hitting unionism in any country."[58] Individual unions, however, have entertained a wide variety of objectives and ideals. In the future the adjustment of conflicting philosophies within the labor movement and participation of union members in new forms of economic conflict and cooperation may be expected to afford a vital educational experience in the basic processes of democracy.

The issue with which we are here concerned takes many forms. For example, the National Industrial Recovery Act was essentially an attempt to meet the emergency of the depression by a reorganization of the spheres of cooperation and conflict in the traditional economy of the United States. It would, therefore, be quite as difficult to evaluate the cultural as the material effects of this experiment. The same considerations apply to proposals for meeting the problem of farm tenancy and many economic measures.

It is vital to the progressive development of the economy of the United States that we approach proposals for reconstruction in the spirit of critical inquiry regarding their remote and immediate effects, and with tolerance for divergent opinions, in order to bring about those changes that will release most fully the potentialities of the whole population for pro-

[58] Perlman, Selig, and Taft, Philip, *History of Labor in the United States, 1896–1932*, IV, Labor Movements, pp. 622–623 (1935).

ductive activity and free spiritual development.

The family.—The oldest, most universal, and most varied of all human institutions acquires a new importance in contemporary civilization. In a society characterized by kaleidoscopic events and the prevalence of conflicts, inferiority feelings, and anxiety neuroses, the family affords the primary foundation of emotional security and the orderly development of personality. In a civilization in which reproduction, among those enjoying sufficient resources to control family size, is insufficient for population replacement, there is need for establishing conditions more favorable to the voluntary formation and adequate support of moderately large families.

The primary need here is for a general recognition of the actual situation. Young people today are influenced by the modern reactions against involuntary reproduction. They are more impressed with the high fertility of their forebears and with the large families of the poor than with the trend toward infertility on the part of those with high school education and moderate incomes. As time goes on, an increasingly large proportion of children will come from parents who have emphasized the values associated with family life and borne a moderately large number of children voluntarily. It is by no means unlikely that there may be a spontaneous reaction toward family security and effective reproduction. It is also possible that public policy may lead to the establishment of economic and cultural conditions that will more effectively reinforce the spontaneous interest of human beings in reproduction and parenthood.

A shift of emphasis toward voluntary provision for somewhat larger families would have cultural values, apart from its significance for population trends. While there may be much excellence in the family that has its sole *raison d'etre* in the companionship of husband and wife and in the one-child or the two-child family, it may be doubted whether such families bring as great emotional satisfaction or afford such full development of personalities as the moderately large family, if the means of support are adequate to provide for such a family at an accepted standard of living.

Art.—There is increasing provision for the broadcasting of a wealth of stimulating, varied cultural material—along with a plethora of dull and vulgar exhibitions. The primary need in the field of art is the cultivation of individual taste through broad education and the encouragement of participatory arts that enrich individual experience and feed the springs of creative activity.

Scientific inquiry.—Democracy originated in face-to-face assemblies of citizens in tribal moots, town meetings, and state councils. In these meetings, "moot questions" were analyzed and relationships explored in leisurely fashion among neighbors. Truth was established through the logic of debate, which reached its highest theoretical expression in Greek dialectic. The institutions of representative republicanism widened the scope of political democracy, but trends in modern economic and social organization have put severe strain on these institutions. The controversial issues of modern civilization involve organized groups; their solution is effected through complex processes including specialized research, expensive publicity programs, and elaborate mechanisms of adjustment and administration. Defeat or the threat of defeat to the will of powerful groups, where vital issues are at stake, may bring resort to violence, or at least to abusive and deceptive propaganda, the forerunner of violence. Already these processes have superseded democracy in many parts of the world.

The old logic of debate is too cumbersome and inconclusive to meet effectively the impact of organized propaganda. There is need for a superior instrument of inquiry, namely, the logic of science, including the principles of physical experimentation, statistics, and objective historical research. It is less important that the people of the United States should believe the correct theory about any particular thing than that they should understand what constitutes evidence and be disciplined in the search for truth, so as to repudiate falsehood with ridicule even when it may seem to serve their own immediate ends. The ability or inability of American institutions to foster the spirit and methods of scientific inquiry may prove to be the decisive factor in the progress or decline of democracy.

Summary.—There is great diversity in the cultural influences at work in American civilization today. There is a definite tendency toward the assimilation of traditional, regional and ethnic cultures but toward the emergence of new lines of social conflict; toward standardization of culture but toward new motifs and experimentation with new ways of living; toward the disappearance of the patriarchal family and involuntary natural increase but, possibly, toward the emergence of a new recognition of the values of family life. These cultural influences reflect and in turn direct economic changes. These changing conditions will determine the future course of population and future opportunities for individual development. Recognition of these forces opens up a new field of social research, the study of culture and personality, which is both challenging and elusive. We cannot foretell or control the future; but we can, if we choose to do so, favor those conditions that appear to be most consistent with sound biological inheritance, economic progress, social harmony, and the orderly development and spontaneity of the individuals who together comprise our changing population.

APPENDIX A.
GOVERNMENTAL NEEDS AND
RESPONSIBILITIES FOR POPULATION
RESEARCH

Relation of Population Studies to Various Governmental Activities

Population research yields information that is, for the most part, of long-time rather than of short-time significance; its findings relate to the general welfare rather than to the profit of particular parties; its progress is dependent on the technical treatment of large masses of data. For these reasons, population research is primarily a field for organized effort by institutions with a public purpose, universities, foundations, State and local agencies, and the Federal Government. Some, though not all, aspects of this work can best be presented by governmental agencies. Moreover, the programs of some governmental agencies are vitally dependent on accurate population data and the systematic development of their implications.

Estimates of trends in crop production and food consumption by the United States Department of Agriculture must take account of changes in the farm and nonfarm population of different regions. In view of the shrinkage of exports in recent years, changes in the size of the nonfarm population largely determine the market for American agricultural products. Population studies also bear directly on land use and conservation programs, and accurate appreciation of the outlook for the farming population in different areas. Regional relations between population, land resources and markets, rates of natural increase, and the volume, direction, and character of migration movements are basic factors that influence levels of living for farm groups and types of land use. These factors need to be taken into account, and are being taken into account so far as the data that are available permit, in the agricultural program as it is actually taking shape.

Feeling the urgent need for more data concerning the large-scale population movements between farm and city, the Division of Farm Population and Rural Life, in the Department of Agriculture, has for some years been making annual estimates of farm-to-city and city-to-farm movements, on the basis of fig-

ures turned in by crop reporters. The Division is now sponsoring field studies in a number of States on rural population mobility, the field work being financed from Works Progress Administration funds. At the present time, however, students and administrators in the field of agriculture face a variety of questions which cannot be answered satisfactorily with the data at hand. What, for instance, have been the total changes in the farm population since 1930? County by county, how has migration since 1930 reinforced or counterbalanced the effects of natural increase on total farm population? How are changes in the farm population in recent years related to agricultural resources; have the better farming regions gained population and the poorer ones lost, or has the reverse been true? To what extent are selective factors operating in migration; are the families which are moving the ones which are most or least likely to make a success in their new locations? How are these movements affecting rural social life?

In the field of education the changing age distribution of the American population has already been reflected in a declining enrollment in the elementary schools (see ch. VIII), and this new situation will make itself felt, at varying rates in different regions, in the older school population. More thorough research on school needs in relation to population trends would prove helpful in shaping school curriculums, in planning teacher training, and in the development of school building programs. Much of this research must be intensive and local in character, and must be imaginatively related to educational objectives in different situations. There is need for extensive and realistic analysis of the costs of maintaining adequate school facilities in relation to the economic resources of different areas.

Complete data on school enrollments should, of course, be required from all private as well as from public schools. If such data covered the areas represented in census statistics, they would constitute very valuable material for postcensal population estimates. Greater coordination of school census and school enrollment data with other population statistics would increase their value and reliability, both for school administration and for general demographic use.

The increased emphasis in the past few years on social responsibility for the aged, the unemployed, the ill and handicapped, and the enactment of legislation, both State and Federal, embodying this philosophy, has created an additional need for population research. Estimates of the cost of insurance and pension systems must be based on forecasts of the future size and age distribution of the population. The framing of workable unemployment insurance systems calls for more accurate and detailed data on employment and occupational distribution than are now available. The whole philosophy of social security implies a measure of planning for the distribution of population in relation to economic opportunity which we have only very recently begun to undertake. The Social Security Board, in shaping its program, is taking cognizance of the relation of social security administration to migration. The effects of social security provisions on labor mobility and the influence of migration on occupational adjustments and employment have both been recognized. The Board is providing for studies of urban and rural migration in relation to social security problems.

The agencies formed to deal especially with problems relating to the economic emergency have felt acutely the need for various types of statistical data that were not at hand. Needing to make plans to meet rapidly changing situations, these agencies have organized special research divisions that may in some ways be compared with the "intelligence service" of the war emergency. In dealing with the economic emergency, however, the types of information needed relate more directly to ordinary demographic, economic, and social research. Special kinds of information have been needed, for example, about the movement of relief cases in different areas. But in order to measure the intensity of relief in different areas, it was necessary to estimate the base population. And in order to measure the relative incidence and effects of relief in different population groups it was necessary to compare the characteristics of those receiving relief with the general population, as regards age, sex, occupation, marital status, and so forth. In order to analyze rural relief trends efficiently it was found expedient to select a representative sample of rural counties, using a variety of statistical indices. In order to gain insight into the outlook for employment in different parts of the country, a special sectional economic analysis was instituted, using a variety of demographic and economic statistics. In dealing with special problems concerning transients seeking relief and the relation of relief to mobility, it was important to study these problems against the background

of previous trends in internal migration, on which very few data were available. Thus, although the emergency programs called in part for special data not needed at other times, these programs were quite as much dependent on regular sources of information for basic data for use in computing rates, making comparative studies, and analyzing trends—and the efficiency of these programs was in no small part limited by the adequacy, scope, and accuracy of these basic data.

In one line of emergency action relating most directly to population problems, that of directed migration or resettlement, there appeared to be serious danger at first that temporary disturbances and the lack of adequate information might lead to measures tending in some instances to intensify rather than to relieve maladjustment of population relative to economic resources. In this situation, the Social Science Research Council instituted the Study of Population Redistribution. The findings of this private body were welcomed and utilized by the administration, and led to a reconsideration of policies, associated with the establishment of the Resettlement Administration. Little more than a beginning, however, has yet been made in the analysis of the relation of distribution of population to economic opportunity. This is a field that cannot be ignored in governmental councils, although some lines of action initiated during the emergency period may need to be reformulated.

Many Government agencies in addition to the ones already mentioned are making increased use of population data: The Labor Department, especially the Bureau of Labor Statistics and the United States Employment Service; the Bureau of Foreign and Domestic Commerce; the Department of the Treasury, particularly the Public Health Service and the Bureau of Internal Revenue; the Department of Indian Affairs, and the Office of Education; and various other agencies concerned with housing, transportation, and communication, banking, administration of island possessions, and international relations.

The present report is in line with the surveys of potentialities and opportunities in the United States today, conducted by the National Resources Committee. It is also closely related to studies by the State planning boards, most of which have already given serious attention to population trends viewed in relation to changing needs and opportunities in different States. The work of these State boards may give a new impetus to population research through studying intensively the relation of demographic statistics to varying economic and social conditions in different situations.

Some Major Fields of Population Research

Caution in the use of estimates of future population has been emphasized throughout this report, while at the same time there has been an insistence on the importance of such estimates. Estimates of future population based on an extrapolation of previous population trends, without regard to changes in composition of population, age and sex structures, or economic conditions are particularly hazardous. The use of refined mathematical procedures sometimes tends to obscure the hypothetical character of such extrapolations. The most reliable estimates involve the detailed analysis of different demographic and economic factors in the past and present situation of a given area. This includes an analysis of age and sex distribution, age-specific birth and death rates, and trends in migration to and from the areas concerned.

All population estimates are dependent on arbitrary hypotheses, expressed or implied. The explicit statement of several hypotheses, with the presentation of alternative estimates, has the advantage of emphasizing the experimental character of all such estimates.

Estimates of the total population of the United States in the near future that have a fair degree of reliability can be made without taking hypothetical changes in economic conditions into account, because changes in birth and death rates follow long-time trends in social organization and personal habits. On the other hand, in preparing estimates of future population for regions and localities, demographic analysis should be supplemented by, and in part based on, economic analysis—in an effort to determine whether and how far the conditions controlling previous movements in these areas can be expected to continue into the future.

The almost total absence of data on internal mobility creates a problem transcending that of understanding the trends in mobility as such. It is no longer possible to make confident estimates of population between census dates for areas smaller than the Nation as a whole. Therefore, all per capita rates—such as rates of births, deaths, crimes, taxes, relief—become generally undependable except in a census year, or 1 or 2 years following the enumeration. The Bureau of the Census is cognizant of this problem and is attempting to secure adequate personnel and funds to enable it to arrive at a solution.

It is easy to understand why population estimates are unsatisfactory. The population of a city on July 1, 1936, consists of (1) all the residents as of the census of April 1, 1930, (2) plus births and people moving in, (3) less deaths and people moving out. If the mobility is great, as has been increasingly the case with the growth of easy transportation facilities, any effort to add (1) and (2) and subtract (3) is doomed to failure without a basis for estimating the mobility. In view of the slowing down of population growth, the filling up of

land in the West, and the restriction of immigration from abroad, population changes in different parts of the United States are increasingly affected by cross-currents of internal migration. This situation makes population estimates based on a projection of past trends less reliable than ever before. Reliable information regarding present numbers and useful forecasts of population change in different areas have therefore become increasingly dependent on frequent and accurate population data, and on systematic treatment of such data in relation to economic and social trends.

The growing public interest in the trend of the birth rate, the wide variations of reproductive tendencies now existing among population groups, and questions relating to their causes and significance, give rise to a need for refinement and extension of studies of differential fertility. In view of the apparent stabilization of the birth rate, prior to the influence of the depression, among native white stocks in New England and the Middle Atlantic States, data now available in the census schedules should be examined to determine whether or not this is true of the older native stocks (native white of native parentage) or whether the apparent stabilization merely represents the gradual infusion of immigrant stocks with initial tendency to higher fertility. It would also be interesting to know whether or not, within the same region, there is any tendency toward differential fertility among farm families comparable to that found among urban families, in relation to their economic status—a question on which we are almost completely ignorant. The two most extensive sources of basic data on differential fertility in the United States now available in published form are the studies of differential fertility in 1900 and in 1910 sponsored by the Milbank Memorial Fund and a census monograph, *Ratio of Children to Women, 1920.* The former of these is based on the question "Number of children ever born?" asked of each woman in the population schedules for 1900 and 1910, but omitted in the following censuses. The repetition of this question in 1940 would supply the basis for a very significant analysis of trends in differential fertility, by supplying data comparable with those for 1900 and 1910. Data throwing new light on certain aspects of the question of differential fertility are available from various inquiries primarily initiated for other purposes. An important study of fertility based on health survey data is now under way through the cooperation of the United States Public Health Service and the Milbank Fund.

We may expect continued research contributions by Federal and State agencies to studies of differential reproduction. Much of the responsibility for research in this field, however, must be carried by private agencies. This is particularly true with reference to the interpretative treatment of data on qualitative population trends, in which the demographic data must be related to the results of anthropological, psychological, and other social research. It is equally true with reference to the collection and analysis of data on causal factors in fertility, to medical findings and reports relating to sex practices, contraception, abortion, and to social conditions affecting family life.

The study of selective factors in migration, relative to age, sex, family, status, occupation, economic status, education, and personal characteristics offers a promising field for new research,[1] which may be largely developed by State, local, and private agencies but in which the Federal Government may also be expected to make important research contributions, especially in relation to problems of labor mobility, social security, and agriculture. The chief contributions made to this subject have come from the State agricultural experiment stations, in cooperation with the Division of Farm Population of the United States Department of Agriculture, and recently, with the Works Progress Administration; from other university departments; and from private sources.

Problems relating to international migrations still hold much interest, although emphasis has been shifted, in national outlook, to problems relating to internal migration and reproduction (reviewed in this report) and, in world outlook, to problems relating to variations among nations in net reproduction rates and in economic organization and resources.

In this section we have listed only a few of the major fields of population research, in its more limited demographic aspects. Beyond these lines of study, population research provides a foundation for, and leads into, a wide range of studies in biology, health, education, and the whole field of social science as it is concerned with conditions and opportunities for individual development.

Basic Data for Population Research

In all lines of population research, both those of immediate and those of more remote significance, the prime requisite is accurate and extensive basic data on numbers of persons, population changes, and composition and characteristics of population groups. Basic population data in this country are at present seriously defective and incomplete at many critical points. The data now available do not permit definite answers to certain important questions. For example, the answer to each of the following questions depends primarily on the research worker's guess as to correction factors for errors in the basic data used. Was there a net migration from farms to cities and

villages during the period 1930–35, or was there a net migration in the opposite direction? How many people in the United States are unemployed and seeking work at the present time? Is the frequency of mental disease in the United States increasing, decreasing, or remaining fairly constant?

In most cases the agencies concerned with collecting these data are fully cognizant of these difficulties; they have developed research programs to test the reliability of statistics of different types; and they are taking measures to enhance their value. They encounter two fundamental obstacles in this endeavor. In the first place, most of these agencies are handicapped by inadequate appropriations, especially for research related to administrative procedures. In the second place, social statistics are essentially dependent on public cooperation. They are subject to errors arising from indifference or ignorance. For example, inaccuracies in data on age distribution, which cause a good deal of difficulty and confusion, are primarily a matter of popular responsibility. Such errors can be overcome by continuous records and systems of cross checking and by educational campaigns that bring greater general understanding and appreciation of the value of such statistics. But both of these approaches are difficult, slow, and expensive. The educational approach is perhaps the most fundamental. As the American people become more keenly aware of the value of the scientific work of governmental agencies, and take increased pride in their development, such work will receive both more adequate financial support and more effective general cooperation.

The principal source of information on population is, as all are aware, the Federal census. Prior to 1900 a new staff was organized for each decennial census, and disbanded at the completion of its immediate task. The establishment of a permanent Bureau of the Census marks an important forward step in the systematic development of census procedures. During the last three decades there has been a specialization of functions within the Bureau of the Census, along with the establishment of a series of special periodic censuses for agriculture, business, manufactures, mining, institutional populations, financial statistics of cities, and religious bodies, in addition to the census of the population and the compilation and analysis of vital statistics.

The United States census of population, in the extent of detail in its tabulation and the method of organization of its vast materials, is, on the whole, an admirable product. That this should be true is all the more a tribute to the leaders in the Bureau of the Census since the conditions under which the census has been taken are far from ideal. An army of untrained enumerators and clerks, numbering, at the peak, more than 100,000, is recruited, trained, sent into the field, and quickly de-

---

[1] This field is now receiving the special attention of the Committee on Migration (Dorothy S. Thomas, chairman) of the Social Science Research Council.

mobilized. Political considerations rather than merit have too often determined the selection of field personnel. The district supervisors, generally, have been political appointees, and they in turn have selected the enumerators.

There are recognized inaccuracies in the census, arising in part from incomplete and inaccurate reporting by individuals regarding themselves and their relatives or neighbors. There is an apparent discrepancy of more than a million between the figure for the native population (native white and Negroes) in 1930, and that expected on the basis of the 1920 returns and death rates during the interval (see ch. I), apparently due to greater underenumeration in 1920 than in 1930. There is evidence that about 5 percent of all children under 5 years of age are usually not enumerated. The age data are sufficiently inaccurate to result in certain typical irregularities in the figures for single years of age and in the figures for aged persons. Many divorced people are reported as married, widowed, or single, instead of as divorced. Illiteracy figures are so undependable that they must be used with great caution. Occupational information as obtained by the enumerator is sometimes too incomplete for accurate classification.

The Bureau of the Census is to be congratulated for the readiness shown in recent years to admit the imperfections of the data presented, and for research on the extent of such errors and methods of obviating them, so far as is possible within the framework of the present type of decennial enumeration. For example, the Bureau is alert to the possibilities of using various sampling methods for checking up on some types of debatable figures, and progress is anticipated from such analyses.

The census has grown in usefulness along with the growing complexity of American life. This growth, as might be expected, has been irregular; but the general trend has clearly been in the direction of increased scientific service. The establishment of the Division of Statistical Research in the Bureau of the Census in 1933 and the plans, introduced in 1936, for basing postcensal estimates for States on available data from various sources rather than on results obtained through the application of a mechanical formula, denote the progress of the Bureau of the Census from an agency for the mere compilation of data to an agency for population research.

A few important innovations in the Fifteenth Census (1930) may be listed as follows:

The separate reporting of "rural-farm" and "rural-nonfarm" population.
Classification of owned homes by estimated value and of rented homes by monthly rental.
Separate tabulation of data by families.
The census of unemployment, supplemented by a special enumeration in 1931.

At the same time, the Bureau has taken active leadership in establishing census tracts in the cities of 250,000 or over, thus making possible detailed analysis of demographic and economic facts by so-called natural areas in a city, instead of by inconstant and artificial ward lines.

These advances are evidence of effort on the part of the Bureau of the Census to understand and even to anticipate the needs of other Government agencies and students of population problems.

Some of the important needs in the 1940 Census, in the opinion of population experts, are for data on mobility and on place of work (which often is not in the same community as place of residence), a repetition of the question regarding the number of children ever born to a mother (as in 1900 and 1910), and information on grade completed in school.

In addition to the collection of data on subjects such as these mentioned above, certain new and more detailed tabulations of regularly collected data have become essential. Particularly, occupational data need to be presented not only in the present industrial classification, but also in a "social-economic" classification, with distinction between employers, employed, and self-employed, in order to provide a population base for the comparison of important differentials with respect to health, fertility, mobility, and so forth. It has been urged that "employment" be coupled to "occupation", providing a basing point for current employment studies and a less ambiguous basis for estimating so-called "unemployment" than would direct questions on unemployment itself. Finally, there is need for detailed tabulation by metropolitan and other economic regions, since the political boundaries of States and cities are often unsatisfactory for statistical purposes.

While new problems in population come to the foreground, some older ones fade with changing conditions. Such items in the census as year of immigration of foreign born, mother tongue of foreign born, ability to speak English, and perhaps illiteracy are becoming less important and might well be dropped from the next census.

Provision of accurate estimates of the population in different localities at any time is a primary responsibility of the Federal Government. Any other course would involve great duplication of effort and lead to confusion in results. The development of reliable population estimates frequently requires the use of different types of data and coordination of materials collected in different localities and for different purposes.

The United States has lagged far behind most of the civilized world in meeting the need for frequent and reliable estimates of the population by geographic breakdowns. Until recently, the Bureau of the Census published annual population estimates based on the assumption that a community which had grown rapidly, in comparison with other communities in the State, in the 10 years prior to the last census, had continued to grow rapidly in comparison with others since the census. Unfortunately, this assumption in the years since 1930 was almost as likely to be false as to be true. Equally unfortunately, the census estimates, having the prestige of official Government figures, were too often accepted as if they were authentic. In 1936 the Bureau of the Census, keenly aware of this situation, made one of its most significant breaks with precedent. It gave up the mechanical method of estimates by mere arithmetic, and assembled instead a large amount of locally collected information, from school attendance records, city directories, and other sources. The new estimates are an improvement and deserve encouragement, but nobody appreciates better than the officials of the Bureau the fact that the new estimates are subject to understatements and overstatements. The census has been handicapped in this work by lack of sufficient funds to employ a permanent research staff and by the inadequacy of available data.

The political divisions of the United States (States, counties, municipalities, and townships) do not afford a satisfactory working basis for the analysis of population statistics. For many purposes the counties represent units too small for convenient manipulation of statistics. While for other purposes the use of statistics for counties and municipalities is expensive and frequently confusing, it is well recognized that metropolitan areas, which cross municipal lines and sometimes State lines as well, need separate study. The same statement applies to distinct agricultural and industrial regions. It is obvious that generalizations about New York State or Michigan or Colorado lack the refinement necessary in studying population trends or economic changes. Each of these States includes radically different economic regions, with different history and divergent present trends. Several standard types of statistical areas are needed for the efficient development of different kinds of social research. Economic and social conditions as well as political boundaries and conventional lines should be recognized in setting up such areas. Three main sets of such statistical areas, arranged according to size, are required.

The need for analysis by major regional divisions in the United States has been served in the past by the traditional nine census divisions. These divisions have been in use for many decades, but no longer afford the most significant differentiation of regional areas. The six regions of the Southern Regional Study have been used throughout this report, and are recommended as facilitating research

and presentation of data on population and related topics.[2]

There is need for the demarcation of useful statistical areas intermediate in size between regions and municipalities. There should be a standard series of some 250 to 350 sections, drawn within State boundaries. These State sections should be arranged so that they could be combined to cover regions stretching across State lines, such as the Great Lakes cut-over area, the New York metropolitan area, the Great Plains, or the southern Appalachians.[3] The principal metropolitan areas should be included as units in this third series. The question as to whether these metropolitan areas should be drawn in conformity to county lines or with greater refinement needs further investigation. No single series of sections could serve all the purposes of regional analysis. In particular, the areas needed for economic, social, and demographic study do not correspond to trade or administrative areas (the latter being regions which radiate from certain centers without regard to the characteristics of the subdivisions included). But except for trade or administrative purposes, many of the aims of health, industrial, occupational, demographic, and social studies could be served by such a standard series.

The geographer of the Bureau of the Census has now completed base maps for all States on the uniform scale of 1:500,000, showing the minor civil divisions as of 1930. Determination of the exact area of these divisions would make possible for the first time an accurate population density map of the United States. Studying the density of population in relation to the use of natural resources requires analysis of population dependent on major types of industry. This should be done with reference to base maps of land uses and mineral resources—at least with demarcation of deserts, swamps, and other areas unsuited to agriculture in any form. Population research would be furthered by more functional mapping of population in relation to physical and social data. Cartography is not merely a way of presenting facts already known in effective form; it is also a valuable instrument of research, revealing variations and relations that might otherwise remain undiscovered.

Statistics of births and deaths are collected by the States and forwarded to the Bureau of the Census. The history of vital statistics in the United States very well illustrates the difficulties involved in assembling from local sources data of Nation-wide concern. European nations generally have assumed central control over the collection of vital statistics, and consequently the European data in many

[2] On this problem see *Regional Factors in National Planning and Development*, National Resources Committee (1935).
[3] Much of the analytical work needed for the demarcation of such areas has already been carried out by various government agencies.

countries are far more complete and accurate than the American data. States and individual cities in which the omissions of births or deaths are estimated not to run above 10 percent are admitted to the "Birth" and "Death Registration Areas." Both areas became complete with the admission of Texas in 1933. Since that time every State in the Union has sent to Washington copies of its birth and death certificates.

Careful estimates suggest that even in 1930 about 8 percent of all births in reporting States were not registered, and that the percentage of infant deaths not registered was almost as large. Adult deaths have been much more completely reported. Beginning as of the year 1935, the Bureau of the Census is tabulating births both by place of residence of the mother and by place of occurrence, and deaths both by place of residence and by place of occurrence. This is a very important advance, because rates may be highly fictitious if deaths of rural people or births to rural women occurring in a city hospital are included with the deaths or births of those resident in that place. It is also planned to tabulate, beginning with the 1935 figures, death statistics to show, by State, county, and city of 10,000 population and over, deaths from tuberculosis, diseases of early infancy, maternal mortality, automobile accidents, and cancer, as well as total deaths. The most important present need in vital statistics is for the improvement of basic reporting in the States, under the leadership and stimulation of the Bureau of the Census and its field staff. Plans are already formulated for progress along these lines.

Collection of statistics of marriage and divorce was discontinued in 1932, and the United States is now the only advanced nation that does not supply current data on marriages. Since about 20 of the States collect no data from their county officials, the trends in marriage and divorce can only be estimated. Yet such data are vital to an interpretation of trends in reproduction, to estimates of housing needs, and to other social research. It is to be hoped that this obvious deficiency in basic data on population will soon be remedied.

The creation in 1919 of a Division of Farm Population and Rural Life in the Bureau of Agricultural Economics gave nominal recognition to the critical importance of population studies in agricultural economics and the vital relation of rural population trends to national welfare. "Nominal" is unfortunately a necessary qualification. This Division has never received sufficient appropriations to conduct field studies or to maintain proper statistical services. The allotted funds have been inadequate for the maintenance of a modern research unit. The Division, in attempting to estimate the annual movement of farm population to and from farms, has used data known to be biased, but available without cost from crop reporters' schedules, and has applied various correction factors in an attempt to secure the best results now possible. A more substantial basis is needed for these estimates and for related studies. An adequate research program in this field would include extensive studies of many problems that have been touched on in this report: relation of people to economic opportunity in different areas, economic balance of agricultural and industrial population, social conditions affecting child development in rural areas, selective migration, and other related topics.

Basic data for farm population and other agricultural studies would be greatly improved by an annual sample census of American agriculture. A bill along these lines—the Buchanan bill—was proposed in the last session of Congress. The idea received theoretical support in the report of a statistical conference held at Iowa State College, July 14–17, 1936, attended by 51 experts in this field:

Important needs for agricultural statistics, not now met, would be satisfied by an annual sample census of American agriculture yielding county data. Present county data, available at but 5-year intervals, and present annual data, available only by States, have proven inadequate for the requirements of the Government, of business, and of agriculture. To supplement and improve this information a sampling procedure, proven practical in other countries, would more effectively use available resources in satisfying these requirements than would a complete enumeration.

To be adequate, however, such a sample census must embody certain recent improvements in statistical technique. It is essential that the appropriate sampling design be found to insure such adequacy in the results.

It is equally vital to the success of a sample census that both administrative and field personnel be competently trained. The integrity derived from the understanding and appreciation of statistical procedures is required of enumerators. The facility in the solution of technical questions based on thorough knowledge of recent statistical developments is required of administrators. The development of such a corps of permanent statistical personnel would increase the accuracy and the economy of collection of all of the data now secured.

The preceding paragraphs provide a brief survey of the major sources of population data in the United States—with some appraisal of their usefulness, and some suggestions for their possible improvement. A guide to other governmental sources is presented in appendix B. Extensive data on other aspects of population research, e. g., sickness and death rates, fertility, and contraception, have been provided by some private agencies.

There are three possible approaches to the improvement of basic population data: (1) Improvement and extension of administrative procedures, including more rigid selection and training of census takers, improvement of local registration of births, deaths, and marriages, the establishment of a regular quinquennial census of population, an annual sample census of agriculture, and other systematic sampling procedures for postcensal estimates; (2) educational campaigns directed toward securing more general appreciation of the importance of accurate statistics on population, vital statistics and health, and more adequate public cooperation in such undertaking; and (3) the development of a continuous population accounting system, analogous to that developed in several European countries, notably in Holland, Belgium, and Sweden. Development of the last suggestion would obviously be expensive, but it may be the most adequate answer to the modern need for accurate and complete data on population. One of the essential features of the population accounting system, in contrast to separate registration and enumeration schemes, is that the former makes possible the checking of different items. A means would thereby be provided for increasing the accuracy of all statistics, or at least of measuring degrees of error with considerable exactness.[4] In countries in which the continuous accounting system is developed, there is a permanent registration of all inhabitants, somewhat similar to the registration of voters in some parts of the United States. If a person or family changes residence, that change is reported to the proper local officials. A record of the status of the population is then possible, at any time, by drawing a balance of the registers. Changes during any period of time can be measured.[5]

Some such procedure may eventually be adopted in the United States. The difficulties in the way are numerous, but such a procedure might be developed in relation to any one of several present institutions. Individual registration is already required of all operators of motor vehicles. The personnel of the Post Office Department covers practically every community in the country. At the present time one has to sign a form before the delivery of a registered letter or parcel. Rural mail carriers make annual reports on the numbers of families on their routes. There would be needed an additional postal regulation requiring each newcomer into a community to fill out a very brief form for himself and his family. Conceivably these records might be expanded into a continuous accounting system. Experiments along this line might be tried in some communities. Again, the registration needs of the social-security program, if extended to cover the entire population, would lead toward such a continuous population accounting system.

Population research is dependent on the support of the general public, and there is evidence of rising public interest. The United States Government shares responsibility for developing population research with State and local agencies, universities, and other private research agencies. The former has unique responsibility for supplying the reliable basic data in this field on which the work of all other agencies is dependent. The work of many Government bureaus is dependent on special lines of research on population problems. The Federal Government is most likely to meet effectively its primary responsibility for supplying accurate data on population if it also shares largely in the development, interpretation, and exposition of scientific findings in this field.

---

[4] See appendix C.

[5] Such an accounting system, with an accurate record of the age and changes of residence, serves to protect each citizen in his civic rights. These records could, of course, be maintained as confidential. It would be possible to allow change of name in certificates issued on the basis of these records, under conditions prescribed by legislation.

APPENDIX B.
GOVERNMENT SERIAL REPORTS AND
CURRENT POPULATION RESEARCH

I. REGULAR SERIES

Department of Agriculture
Bureau of Agricultural Economics
Division of Farm Population and Rural Life

FARM POPULATION
Annual, 1920–date
Special release; *Crops and Markets; The
Agricultural Situation*

Intercensal estimates of farm population by census
regions. Revised after each census.

MOVEMENTS TO AND FROM FARMS
Annual, 1920–date
Special release; *The Agricultural Situation*

Movements from farms to villages and cities, and
from villages and cities to farms, by census regions.
Estimated.

NATURAL INCREASE OF THE FARM POPULATION
Annual, 1920–date
Special release; *The Agricultural Situation*

Annual estimates by census regions.

Division of Crop and Livestock Estimates

FARM EMPLOYMENT
Monthly, October 1923–date
Mimeographed press release of the Bureau;
Crops and Markets

Questionnaire mailed to key list of crop reporters.
About 20,000 answers received. In the north, geographically in proportion to number of farms; not so
many in the south. Twenty-five percent turnover
monthly. Commercial-truck farms excluded; part-
time and subsistence practically excluded. Data includes operator, hired farm help, and paid and un-
paid family labor (excluding household workers).
Breakdown by geographic divisions of the Census.

Bureau of Home Economics

FARM-FAMILY LIVING DATA
Annual, 1933–date
Yearbook of Agriculture

Tabulated summaries of studies made in the field
of farm-family living in the United States. Tables
for 1936 printed in a separate from the Yearbook:
Agricultural Statistics, 1936.

FARM-FAMILY LIVING OUTLOOK
Annual, 1933–date

Agriculture Outlook (printed annually)
Farm Family Living Outlook chart book
and report (mimeographed).

Summaries of special studies of expense for farm-
family living and other available material in this
field, for use in the annual Outlook Conference of
the Department of Agriculture. Chart book and report published only since 1934; data have increased
greatly in scope since 1933.

FOOD COSTS OF DIETS AT FOUR NUTRITIVE
LEVELS
Quarterly, September 1935–date
Hectographed table available through the
Bureau of Home Economics.

Computation of cost of each of four diet plans (representing four levels of nutritive value and cost) set
up by the Bureau of Home Economics. Average retail food prices collected by the Bureau of Labor
Statistics are applied to the items of the diets and
total costs computed. Weekly costs of each diet for
individuals differing in age, sex, and activity, and
for families of three sizes are computed quarterly.
Same data, not strictly comparable, are available
for years earlier than 1935. An annual figure for
1934 and 1935 has been prepared.

FOOD COSTS OF DIETS AT TWO NUTRITIVE
LEVELS
Quarterly, September 1935–date
Table available through the Bureau of Home
Economics (typed)

Computation of costs in Washington, D. C., of the
two least expensive of the four diets set up by the
Bureau. Washington retail prices collected by the
Bureau of Labor Statistics are applied in computing
the costs, for use by local and nearby social service
agencies. Weekly costs are calculated for individuals
differing in sex, age, and activity. Some data, not
strictly comparable, are available for years earlier
than 1935.

Department of Commerce
Bureau of the Census
Division of Population

CHILDREN UNDER INSTITUTIONAL CARE AND IN
FOSTER HOMES
Decennial 1880, 1890, 1904, 1910, 1923, 1933
Press release, 9 months to 1 year after pe-
riod; final publication about 1½ years
after close of period

National survey; data collected by mail from 2,280 agencies. Coverage about 98 percent complete in 1933. Breakdown by States, color or race, sex, age, place of first residence, years under care, whereabouts of parents for children under care. Support by institutions.

Juvenile Delinquents in Public Institutions

Decennial 1880, 1890, 1904, 1910, 1923, 1933

Press release about 9 months after close of period; publication about 1½ years after close of period

National survey by mail questionnaire; coverage about 95 percent complete in 1935. Commitments by sex and type of institution for states; previous record, offense, length of term, education, type of family by age, color and sex.

Mental Defectives and Epileptics in Institutions

Annual, 1926–date; decennial, 1850–1890, 1904

Press release about 9 months after close of period; final publication about 1½ years after close of period

National survey by mail questionnaire; approximately complete coverage. By States; patients by sex, by mental status, for admission and discharge, mortality of patients, personnel and expenditures by institutions.

Patients in Hospitals for Mental Diseases

Annual, 1926–date; decennial 1880, 1890, 1904, 1914, 1923

Press release about 9 months after close of period; final publication about 1½ years after close of period

Mail questionnaire to Federal, State, county, city, private and veterans' hospitals; coverage approximately complete. By States; admissions and discharges by psychosis and sex, for State hospitals and private institutions. Mortality of patients. Personnel and expenditures by institutions.

Crime and Mental Disease or Deficiency

Annual, 1926–date; decennial, 1880, 1890, 1904, 1910, 1923

Press release of summary figures about 9 months after period; final publication about 1½ years after close of period

Mail questionnaire. Coverage: 8 Federal prisons, 44 State prisons, no city or county prisons or private institutions. By state: prisoners by institutions, age, sex, nativity or color, economic status, education, type of mental disease.

Prisoners in Jails and Other Penal Institutions under County or Municipal Jurisdiction

Decennial, 1850–1890; 1904, 1910, 1923, 1933

Press release about 1 year after close of period; final publication about 1½ years after close of period

National survey by mail questionnaire; about 90 percent of all sentenced prisoners covered 1933. Breakdown by States, giving the offense, sentence, fine, previous commitments by age, nativity or color, and sex by new and discharged cases.

Prisoners in State and Federal Prisons and Penitentiaries

Annual, 1926–date; decennial, 1850–1890, 1904, 1910, 1923

Press release of summary figures about 9 months after period; final publication about 1½ years after close of period

National survey by mail questionnaire. Coverage about 92 percent complete in all States except Delaware, Georgia, Alabama, Mississippi. By States: Prisoners received and discharged, by offense, nativity or color, age, sex, marital condition, length of sentence, previous record, parole and supervision.

Judicial Criminal Statistics

Annual 1932–date (1933)

Press release of summary figures 9 months to 1 year after close of period; final publication about 2 years after close of period

National survey by mail of State courts of general criminal procedure. Size of sample has increased each year (27 in 1934); probably 31 States in 1935. By States: Defendants by offense, procedural outcome, defendants found guilty by offense, sentence or treatment.

Division of Vital Statistics

Weekly Accident Bulletin (Fatalities from Automobile Accidents)

Weekly, September 5, 1936–date

Rotoprinted bulletin of the Division under this title

Mail and telegraph reports from 130 major cities over 50,000 (number of cities is increasing). Publication 6 days after week period, including cumulative totals for the year, weekly total (both compared with previous year); deaths in the city, deaths due to accidents in the city.

Summary of Mortality from Automobile Accidents

Four-week period, 1929–date

Rotoprinted bulletin of the Division under this title

Telegraphic reports from 86 cities (chiefly of 100,000 and over). The same as those covered in *Weekly Health Index*. Publication 2 weeks after close of period. Series being maintained temporarily until it can be coordinated with *Weekly Accident Bulletin* (above). Deaths in the city; deaths due to accidents in the city (both compared with previous period and year).

Summary of Mortality From Automobile Accidents

Annual, 1935–date

Vital Statistics, Special Reports (rotoprinted) by states

Transcripts of state records from the U. S. registration area. Data include calendar year plus trend over a period. Publication irregular, about 1 year after calendar year close. More detailed tables about 1 year later in published volumes.

Weekly Health Index

Weekly, 1918–date

Rotoprinted under this title. Also released to newspapers

Telegraphic reports from 86 cities, chiefly of 100,000 and over, the same as those covered in Summary of Mortality from Automobile Accidents. Publication 5 days after close of week, with subclassification of total infant mortality and breakdown by color.

Birth, Stillbirth, and Infant Mortality Statistics

Annual, 1915–date (1933)

Vital Statistics—Special Reports

Transcripts of state office records from U. S. registration area. Publication about 2 years after close of calendar year. Classification by States, cities, counties, sex, color or nativity, age of parents.

MORTALITY STATISTICS
Annual, 1900–date (1933)
Vital Statistics—Special Reports

Transcripts of State office records from U. S. death registration area. Publication about 2 years after close of calendar year. Causes of death by age, sex, nativity or color, States, cities, counties.

VITAL STATISTICS, SPECIAL REPORTS, VOL. 2 (VITAL STATISTICS SUMMARY FOR . . . . . [name of State])
Annual, 1935–date
Rotoprinted under title *Vital Statistics, Special Reports*

Transcripts of State records for U. S. registration area. Each report contains 22 tables on births, deaths by cause, age, sex, color or race, etc. Report for the calendar year, with trend over a period. More detailed tables appear about a year later in the published volumes *Mortality Statistics* and *Birth, Stillbirth, and Infant Mortality Statistics.*

Department of Interior

Office of Education

SCHOOL ENROLLMENTS
Biennial, 1918–date (annual, 1870–1916)
Biennial Survey of Education, 1918–present. (*Annual Report of the Commissioner of Education* to 1916)

Data collected from State and city school systems, public high schools, private high schools and academies, institutions for higher education, library schools, special schools for the handicapped, private commercial schools, and nurses' training schools. Enrollment by grade for elementary and secondary schools; total enrollment in institutions for higher education. Some of the current data are available for the years before 1916–18, but for the most part earlier tables are not comparable. The Office did attempt to get school census data, but found it impossible to secure comparable figures.

Department of Interior

Bureau of Mines

EMPLOYMENT, MAN-DAYS AND MAN-HOURS AT METAL AND NONMETAL MINES
Annual, 1911–34
Mimeographed release 12–18 months after close of year; *Minerals Year Book*

Coverage: all mining industries, including quarrying and production of lime and cement. Petroleum and natural gas covered for first time in 1935. Mail questionnaires, supplemented by personal interviews where necessary. Total number of men employed; average for the period during which the mine is in operation. Employment in copper, iron, lead and zinc, and gold, silver and miscellaneous metal mines.

Department of Labor

Bureau of Labor Statistics

ACCIDENTS IN 30 MANUFACTURING INDUSTRIES
Annual; iron and steel since 1910, manufacturing since 1926
Monthly Labor Review

State reports on accidents; firms report man-hours exposure by mail. Compensable accidents: death,

permanent total, permanent partial, and temporary total disability. Data not comparable for all States due to variations in State laws, e. g., the waiting period before the compensation begins. Breakdown by severity of injury, by frequency rate (number of accidents per 1,000,000 man-hours worked), by severity rate (number of days lost per 1,000 man-hours), by industry. Coverage to be expanded in collecting data for 1936, both in industries included and coverage within each industry.

INDEX OF EMPLOYMENT IN ANTHRACITE COAL INDUSTRY
Monthly 1929–date
Mimeographed release about 3 weeks after close of month. "Employment and Payrolls," about end of second month. *Monthly Labor Review* about opening of the third month. Also in *Survey of Current Business*

Base period 1929. Coverage about 95 percent complete.

INDEX OF EMPLOYMENT IN BITUMINOUS COAL INDUSTRY
Monthly, 1929–date
Mimeographed release about 3 weeks after close of month. "Employment and Payrolls," about end of second month. *Monthly Labor Review* about opening of third month. Also in *Survey of Current Business*

Base period 1929. Coverage about 50 percent complete.

INDEX NUMBERS OF FACTORY EMPLOYMENT
Monthly, 1919–date
Press release and newspapers about 3 weeks after close of month. "Employment and Payrolls," about end of second month. *Monthly Labor Review* about opening of third month. Also in *Federal Reserve Bulletin* and *Survey of Current Business*

Base period 1923–25. Coverage exceeds 50 percent of employment in the aggregate with larger coverage for certain industries. Adjustments to Census give accurate trend. Manufacturing group as defined by the Census. Current estimate also made of total number employed in each industry and in all manufactures. Index is a weighted aggregative, with weight given to component industries and industry groups as shown by the Census of Manufactures.

INDEX OF EMPLOYMENT IN METALLIFEROUS MINING INDUSTRIES
Monthly, 1929–date
Mimeographed release about 3 weeks after close of period; "Employment and Payrolls" about two months after close of period; *Monthly Labor Review* about beginning of third month. Also in *Survey of Current Business*

Base period 1929. Coverage about 60 percent. Not available separately for different kinds of metals.

INDEX OF EMPLOYMENT IN RETAIL TRADE
Monthly, 1929–date
Mimeographed release about 3 weeks after close of period; "Employment and Payrolls" about end of second month; *Monthly Labor Review* about beginning of third month. Also in *Survey of Current Business*

Base period 1929. Coverage about 27 percent of total employees. Two series: retail trade and general merchandising and retail trade other than general merchandising. Weighted by number of persons employed in these two groups, as shown by Census of Distribution. Index a weighted aggregative. Department stores and other large units heavily weighted in comparison with small stores and certain special types of trade.

INDEX OF EMPLOYMENT IN WHOLESALE TRADE
Monthly, 1929–date
Mimeographed release about 3 weeks after end of month. "Employment and Payrolls" about end of second month; *Monthly Labor Review* about beginning of third month. Also in *Survey of Current Business*

Base period 1929. Coverage about 22 percent. Unweighted aggregates.

Children's Bureau

EMPLOYMENT CERTIFICATE STATISTICS
Annual, 1920–date
Monthly Labor Review, and Children's Bureau press releases and annual reports

Work permits or employment certificates issued to children, 14–17 years of age, inclusive, in 18 States, the District of Columbia, and 78 cities in 17 other States.

SOCIAL AND HEALTH STATISTICS IN SELECTED URBAN AREAS
Quarterly, 1930–date
Supplement to *The Child*

Data from 18 types of health and welfare agencies in 43 cities.

RELIEF STATISTICS
Monthly, 1929–date
Social Statistics (quarterly bulletin)

Noninstitutional relief, public and private, for a registration area of 120 cities. Transferred to Social Security Board, July 1, 1936.

JUVENILE COURT STATISTICS
Annual, 1927–date
Juvenile Court Statistics

Reports from 326 courts, reports being secured from a number of States on a State-wide basis. About 30 percent of the total United States population is in the area included in these reports.

BIRTH RATES
Annual, 1915–date
Mimeographed releases

Trend of birth rates by States. Rates compiled on basis of data secured from Bureau of Census. Also trend of birth rates, in expanding birth registration area, in birth registration area of 1921, and in selected foreign countries. Based on official statistics.

INFANT MORTALITY RATES
Annual, 1915–date
Mimeographed releases

Trends in the birth registration area by States. Based on data from the Bureau of the Census. Trends by color in the birth registration area and in States having 1,500 or more Negro births in 1934. Trends in urban and rural districts of the birth registration area. Rates by specified causes in the birth registration area of 1921. Trends of rates in the expanding birth registration area, the area of 1921, and in selected foreign countries. Neonatal mortality in the United States birth registration area by States and in selected foreign countries.

MATERNAL MORTALITY
Annual, 1915–date
Mimeographed releases

Trends in the birth registration area by States, in urban and rural districts by States; by color in the birth registration area and in States having 1,500 or more Negro births in 1934; trends in the United States and certain foreign countries. Maternal mortality in the United States birth registration area of 1930, by specified causes.

United States Employment Service

APPLICATIONS TO SERVICE
Monthly, July 1, 1933–date
Preliminary mimeographed release; later in *Monthly Labor Review* and *Employment Service News*

Data by States. Industrial classification, with breakdowns by sex, up to July 1, 1934. Since then, industrial and occupational classification, age, length of unemployment, with breakdowns by sex, color, and veteran status. Since July 1, 1935, by relief status also.

PLACEMENTS
Monthly, July 1, 1933–date
Preliminary mimeographed release; later in *Monthly Labor Review* and *Employment Service News*

Data by States. Industrial classification, with breakdowns by sex and duration of employment, up to July 1, 1934. Since then, same breakdowns as in Applications to Service, with added breakdown of duration of employment.

REGISTRANTS ACTIVELY SEEKING WORK
Monthly, March 1934–date
Monthly Labor Review

Number of registrants with the Employment Service who are actually seeking employment.

RELIEF AND NONRELIEF REGISTRANTS
Intermittently, July 1, 1936–date
Monthly Labor Review and *Employment Service News*

Census of registrants, with breakdown by sex and by employed or unemployed status.

Immigration and Naturalization Service

IMMIGRATION STATISTICS
Annual by months, 1820–date
Mimeographed tables, annual report of the Secretary of Labor

Immigrant aliens admitted by countries (since 1820), races (since 1911), and occupations (since 1911). Data by sex, age, marital condition, literacy, state of intended residence, physical defects. Excess of immigrants over emigrants by countries, races, and States (since 1911). Immigration from northern and western Europe, southern and eastern Europe, with comparative percentage of total (since 1820). Nonimmigrant aliens admitted by principal countries of last permanent residence (since 1908).

EMIGRATION STATISTICS
Annual by months, 1908–date
Mimeographed tables, annual report of the Secretary of Labor

Emigrant aliens departed, by countries and races (since 1908), and by States and occupations (since 1911). Nonemigrant aliens departed by principal countries of future permanent residence (since 1908). United States citizens permanently departed by principal countries of future residence (since 1918).

Data on departures by sex, age, marital status, State of last permanent residence, length of last residence in United States, and literacy.

DEPORTATIONS
Annual by months, 1892–date
Mimeographed tables, annual report of Secretary of Labor

By race, sex, age, length of residence in the United States, cause for deportation, State from which deported, foreign country of destination, ports of arrival and departure.

NATURALIZATION STATISTICS
Annual, 1907–date
Mimeographed tables, annual report of Secretary of Labor

Number of declarations and petitions filed, and of certificates issued, by naturalization field districts, States, court, and sex. Also by nationality of aliens naturalized. Data on petitions denied show reasons for denial.

Department of the Treasury

Public Health Service

COMMUNICABLE DISEASES
Weekly, 1917–date
Health Officers Weekly Statement (mimeographed); *Public Health Reports*

Telegraphed reports on 8 specified diseases by State health officers. Subject to later revision; at 4-week intervals an analysis. Number of States has increased, now includes all except Nevada.

COMMUNICABLE DISEASES
Monthly, 1910–date
Public Health Reports

Summary of cases of 10 notifiable diseases reported by mail monthly by States. Published weekly for those States from which reports are received during the current week.

COMMUNICABLE DISEASES AND DEATHS BY CAUSE
Weekly, 1932–date
Public Health Reports

Reports from 140 selected cities showing cases of 7 specified diseases, deaths from 3 specified diseases, and deaths from all causes. Succeeds a table covering more cities and more diseases.

INCIDENCE OF ILLNESS AMONG WAGE EARNERS
Quarterly, 1918–date (at different times annual, semi-annual, and rates computed monthly)
Public Health Reports

Illness and nonindustrial accidents. Reports from sick benefit associations, industrial organizations, etc. Covers cases of 8 days' or more duration.

MORTALITY BY CAUSE
Quarterly, 1927–date (at different times annual and semi-annual)
Public Health Reports

Summary of mortality data reported monthly by States. Preliminary, for current information only. Reports from 25 States, 15–20 causes. Annual summary appears about 4 months after close of year.

Federal Emergency Relief Administration

VOLUME OF PUBLIC RELIEF AND NUMBER OF CASES
Monthly, 1933–1935
Monthly Report

Families and single individuals. Breakdown by type of relief abandoned after June 1935.

TRANSIENTS ON RELIEF
Monthly, 1933–1936
Monthly Report

Single persons and families. Census as of a given date in month. Breakdown by age and sex. Discontinued in 1936.

APPLICATIONS FOR RELIEF
Monthly, 1933–1936
Monthly Report

Number of applications received during month. Discontinued in 1936.

APPLICATIONS APPROVED
Monthly, 1933–1936
Monthly Report

Discontinued 1936.

CASES OPENED AND CLOSED
Monthly, 1933–1936
Monthly Report

Discontinued 1936.

EMPLOYMENT IN WORKS PROGRAM
Weekly, 1933–1935
Monthly Report

Number employed, earnings, man-hours. Discontinued after June, 1935.

AVERAGE RELIEF BENEFIT
Monthly, 1933–1936
Monthly Report

Monthly benefit per family and per case, by States.

Interstate Commerce Commission

INDEX OF RAILROAD EMPLOYMENT (CLASS I STEAM RAILWAYS, EXCLUDING SWITCHING AND TERMINAL)
Monthly, 1923–date
Mimeographed release about 10 days after close of month. Multilith release during third month after close of month

Base period 1923–25. Coverage complete. Aggregative index (unweighted), with seasonal adjustment on basis of seasonal factors relating to the years 1924–32 inclusive. Seven classifications of employees in original data (not in the form of an index) based on nature of the work.

Social Security Board

RELIEF IN URBAN AREAS
Monthly, January 1929–date
Special release of the Board

Series originally published by Russell Sage Foundation, transferred to the Children's Bureau in 1932 and to Social Security Board July 1, 1936. Includes data for 118 urban areas, shown separately for public and private agencies.

AID TO THE BLIND
Monthly, February 1, 1936–date
Public Assistance (issued monthly by Social Security Board)

Data by States for those States which have plans approved by the Social Security Board. Data for number of recipients and amount received.

AID TO DEPENDENT CHILDREN
Monthly, February 1, 1936–date
Public Assistance

Data by States for States which have plans approved by the Social Security Board. Data include number of families, number of children, amount received.

OLD-AGE ASSISTANCE
Monthly, February 1, 1936–date
Public Assistance

By States for States with plans approved by the Social Security Board. Data include number of recipients and amounts received.

TOTAL ANNUAL WAGES BY STATES FOR COVERED INDUSTRIES AND ESTABLISHMENTS
Annual, 1936 following (a year after close of period)
Not yet decided

Including estimates of cash value of certain payments in kind. Wages paid by employers of 8 or more individuals in industries covered by Title IX of the Act. Data can be tabulated in 9 broad industrial groups, following the present Treasury classification.

NUMBER ON THE PAYROLL WHO ARE SUBJECT TO THE ACT
Quarterly, 1936 following (a year after close of period)
Not yet decided

By States, for the pay period nearest March 15, June 15, September 15, and December 15. Data can be tabulated in 9 broad industrial groups, following the Treasury classification.

HOURS WORKED
Plans uncertain
Not yet decided

Data will be available for States having unemployment compensation laws for plants of employers subject to these laws. Definitions not yet uniform and methods of reporting not yet standardized.

TOTAL TAXABLE WAGES PAID BY EMPLOYERS SUBJECT TO TITLE VIII OF THE ACT
Monthly, 1936 following (a year after close of period)
Not yet decided

Wages up to $3,000 paid to each individual by each employer of 1 or more individuals in covered industries.

TAXABLE WAGES OF INDIVIDUALS UNDER TITLE VIII OF THE ACT
Quarterly, beginning 1937
Not yet decided

Areas and industries by which these data will be classified are as yet uncertain. These are strictly administrative statistics, of which annual or less frequent summaries may be published.

NUMBER OF INDIVIDUALS ON WHOSE ACCOUNT OLD-AGE BENEFIT TAXES ARE PAID
Quarterly, beginning 1937
Not yet decided

Areas and industries by which these data will be classified are as yet uncertain. These are strictly administrative statistics, of which annual or less frequent summaries may be published.

Works Progress Administration

WAGE RATES AND EARNINGS
Monthly, 1935–date

Average monthly wage rates and earnings.

EMPLOYMENT, HOURS AND EARNINGS ON W. P. A. PROJECTS
Semimonthly, 1935–date
Mimeographed release

By States. Breakdown by sex and type of project. Partly estimated. Subject to later revision.

EMPLOYMENT, HOURS AND EARNINGS ON STUDENT AID PROJECTS OF N. Y. A.
Semimonthly, 1935–date
Mimeographed release

By States. Breakdown by sex. Subject to later revision.

NUMBER EMPLOYED IN WORKS PROGRAM
Monthly, 1935–date
Report on the Works Program

By type of agency.

NUMBER EMPLOYED ON W. P. A. PROJECTS
Monthly, 1935–date
Report on the Works Program

By type of project, wage classes, sex, and previous relief status.

II. SPECIAL STUDIES

Department of Agriculture
Bureau of Agricultural Economics
Division of Farm Population and Rural Life

ANALYSIS OF POPULATION MOVEMENTS IN RESETTLEMENT ADMINISTRATION REGION 12 (DUST BOWL)
Begun: May 1, 1936. Completed: July 1, 1937
In charge: C. C. Taylor
Publication: Mimeographed bulletin by Resettlement Administration

To ascertain what movements have occurred, and whether Federal funds have retarded depopulation. Enumeration in sample areas in southwestern Kansas. In cooperation with Resettlement Administration. Field interviews with a mobility schedule.

SURVEY OF AMERICAN VILLAGES
Begun: 1936. Completed: Spring, 1937
In charge: E. de S. Brunner
Publication: Book

An analysis of changes in rural social life. 140 selected nationally distributed agricultural village communities, the same as those covered in C. Luther Fry's *Census Analysis of American Villages* (1924), and Brunner and DeKolb, *Rural Social Trends* (1933). The population of some of these villages was reenumerated; in other cases estimates of population were made. In cooperation with Carnegie Institution and Works Progress Administration. Field work and interviews in each village.

FAMILY LIVING AND MOBILITY IN THE APPALACHIAN REGION
Begun: April 1936. Completed: Spring, 1937

In charge: C. P. Loomis, Conrad Taeuber
Publication: Mimeographed or rotoprinted bulletin by Resettlement Administration

To secure a detailed picture of occupational changes, particularly among new farmers in the area. A total of 1,500 families interviewed in 2 counties in Kentucky and 2 in North Carolina, the mobility and family living schedules being used alternately. Study conducted in cooperation with Resettlement Administration. Field interviews with schedules of a sample population.

STUDY OF CONTEMPORARY COMMUNITIES
Begun: 1936. Completed: (field work) 1936
In charge: C. P. Loomis
Publication: Bulletin

To ascertain the level of living of families in the communities established by Federal agencies and of families living on the peripheries of these settlements; and to determine the factors involved in the formation of groups and the development of institutions. Field work completed in 4 communities, under way in 2 others, and is planned for other communities under the jurisdiction of the Resettlement Administration. In cooperation with the Resettlement Administration. Field interviews with selected families, using a standard of living and a community schedule.

LEVEL OF LIVING OF FARM FAMILIES
Begun: 1936. Completed: (field work) January 1, 1937
In charge: Charles P. Loomis
Publication: Bulletin

It is expected to secure schedules from 9,500 families, more than 7,000 from 4 States—Minnesota, South Dakota, Wisconsin, and Virginia. Schedules have also been taken in 4 Appalachian mountain counties. In cooperation with the Resettlement Administration; some of the field work being done by State agencies. Field interviews with a schedule.

RURAL POPULATION MOBILITY
Begun: 1936. Completed: Spring, 1937
In charge: C. E. Lively, Conrad Taeuber
Publication: Bulletins of the respective state colleges of agriculture or agricultural experimental stations; also a general summary

To determine: (1) The extent and nature of the mobility of the rural population; (2) the extent to which mobility is associated with relief problems in the rural districts; (3) the characteristics of mobility among rural relief families as compared with nonrelief families; and (4) the extent to which spatial and occupational mobility are associated in selected areas. A study of selected samples in Iowa, North Dakota, South Dakota, Kentucky, Maryland, North Carolina, Arizona, and Minnesota. Studies financed by Works Progress Administration; in cooperation with State agricultural colleges and Resettlement Administration. Field interview with mobility schedule.

Bureau of Home Economics

COMPILATION OF DATA ON FARM-FAMILY LIVING
Begun: 1935. Completed: Analysis in process (1936)
In charge: Day Monroe, Medora Ward, Hazel K. Stiebeling
Publication: Preliminary summaries of some items appeared in "Planning Farm Family Living" (mimeographed September 1935). Partial summaries (chiefly for

food and clothing) in "Farm-family living outlook charts and conference summaries for use with Agricultural Outlook for 1936" (November 1935). "Agricultural Outlook Charts for 1937; Farm Family Living" (November 1936), contains tabulated summaries of yearly per capita expense of 11 items of farm-family living; yearly per capita value of home-produced food also included

To bring together, classify, and summarize data from a number of separate studies of farm-family living. Data from 1920–35. Schedule estimates of approximately 19,700 families are included. Summaries have been or are being made of 11 items of family living, one of them being food, as a part of the Bureau's study of the economy and nutritive adequacy of American diets. In cooperation with State, Federal, and other agencies. Published studies, or data provided by cooperating agencies.

DISBURSEMENTS OF FAMILIES OF WAGE-EARNERS AND LOW-SALARIED WORKERS
Begun: 1934. Completed: Analysis in process (1936)
In charge: Hazel K. Stiebeling
Publication: Preliminary reports: (1) "Nutritive Value of Diets of Families of Wage-Earners and Clerical Workers in North Atlantic Cities", *Monthly Labor Review*, July 1936. (2) "Diets of Urban and Village Families in the United States, 1914–36" (multilithed). (3) "Food Consumption of Urban and Village Families at Different Levels of Expenditures for Food," *Journal of Home Economics*, January 1937

To evaluate nutritional adequacy and economy of diets of different population groups, as a basis for recommending diet plans at different economic levels. Records collected from approximately 3,000 families in conjunction with the 1934–35 study of the Bureau of Labor Statistics of disbursements of wage-earners and low-salaried workers. Weekly dietary records collected by field agents.

FARM-FAMILY LIVING IN APPALACHIAN HIGHLANDS
Begun: 1929. Completed: Preliminary 1935. Detailed analysis in process (1936)
In charge: Faith Williams, Day Monroe, Hazel K. Stiebeling
Publication: *Economic and Social Problems and Conditions of the Southern Appalachians*, Department of Agriculture, Miscellaneous Publication No. 205 (1935). Detailed analysis of Knott County data forthcoming

228 farm families in Knott County, Kentucky, and 331 farm families in Grayson County, Virginia, interviewed. The Knott County families furnished an estimate of their year's food supply (purchased and home-produced), 41 kept an accurate record of food consumption for one week in summer. Interviews by field agents with a schedule.

FARM HOUSING SURVEY
Begun: 1934. Completed: Analysis in process (1936)
In charge: Judith Clark, Louise Stanley, Mordecai Ezekiel

Publication: Mimeographed tables summarizing data for each of 43 States have been released to government agencies

To provide an estimate of rural housing needs for the use of economists, extension workers, business men, etc. 600,000 farm houses in 300 counties in 46 States were examined as to structure, condition, fixed equipment. House-to-house enumeration in selected areas by C. W. A. workers under supervision of state extension service.

STUDY OF CONSUMER PURCHASES (PRINCIPALLY IN RURAL AREAS)
Begun: October 1935. Completed: July 1937
In charge: Day Monroe
Publication: Preliminary publication, in bulletin or monograph, about January 1937; final publication in bulletin or monograph between July and December 1937

To secure information on expenditures and consumption habits of families of numerous types, defined according to income, occupation and composition. A random sample of families of selected major types canvassed for information on income, occupation, and composition. From the random sample, a controlled sample is selected and information on expenditures obtained. About 125,000 families in the random sample; 20,000 in the selected sample. About 18 small cities, 125 villages and 80 farm sections covered. Data on family composition include number, age, sex, and relationship of members of economic family; some data on education and rural-urban background. Data all related to family income and occupation. Study financed by Works Progress Administration; it is complementary to similar study by Bureau of Labor Statistics. Field interviews with schedule.

TIME STUDIES OF THE WORK OF HOMEMAKERS
Begun: 1924–1930. Complete: Analysis in process (1936)
In charge: Hildegarde Kneeland until March 1935; now under supervision of Day Monroe
Publication: Preliminary report: "Homemaking in this Modern Age," *Journal of the American Association of University Women*, January 1934

To show the distribution of time and energy of homemakers in different situations and under different conditions. Study made in 1,900 households (of which 900 were urban) of the work done, and its organization, in various types of homes. Housewives kept records on time study blanks, in cooperation with workers from State experiment stations and extension service.

STUDIES OF FAMILY LIVING IN THE UNITED STATES AND OTHER COUNTRIES: AN ANALYSIS OF MATERIAL AND METHOD
Begun: 1929. Completed: 1935
In charge: Faith Williams, Carle C. Zimmerman (the latter representing the Social Science Research Council)
Publication: Final report published as Miscellaneous Report No. 223 (December 1935) of the Department of Agriculture

To bring together references on family living studies, with an analysis of methods and findings. Annotated bibliography of nearly 1,500 studies of family living made in 52 counties. The references for the most part include studies made during a 100-year period, running through 1933. Analysis of published materials.

Department of Labor

Bureau of Labor Statistics

MONEY DISBURSEMENTS OF FAMILIES OF WAGE EARNERS AND LOWERED SALARIED CLERICAL WORKERS
Begun: October 1934. Completed: (Field work) November 1936
In charge: Faith Williams
Publication: Preliminary articles in *Monthly Labor Review* beginning March 1936. Regional bulletins and final summary bulletin planned

To secure data on incomes and expenditures for all items of family living and special data on food consumption. Nation-wide study including about 16,000 families in 55 industrial cities in all regions of the United States. Family interviews by trained agents using a detailed schedule.

STUDY OF CONSUMER PURCHASES (IN URBAN AREAS)
Begun: October 1935. Completed: July 1937
In charge: Faith Williams
Publication: Articles in *Monthly Labor Review;* possibly a bulletin of the Bureau. Final material will be available about July–December 1937

To secure information on expenditures and consumption habits of families of numerous types, defined according to income, occupation and composition. Will provide weights if the Bureau's cost of living indexes are extended. Will furnish data for Bureau of Home Economics work on nutrition. A random sample of families of selected major types is canvassed for information on income, occupation, and composition. From this random sample, a controlled sample is selected, from which information on expenditures is obtained. The random sample includes about 200,000 families; the controlled sample about 25,000, in 32 cities. Data on family composition include number, age, sex, and relationship of members of economic family (with some information on other members of household); some data on education and rural-urban background. All these data are related to family income and occupation. Study complementary to similar project being carried on by Bureau of Home Economics in small cities and rural areas. Financed by W. P. A. funds. Interviews with schedule.

Children's Bureau

STILLBIRTH STUDY
Begun: 1936. Completed: 1937
In charge: Elizabeth C. Tandy, Ethel C. Dunham
Publication: A special bulletin of the Bureau

The improvement of stillbirth statistics, including the furthering of a classification of causes of stillbirth and facilitating the introduction and use of a standard certificate for stillbirth. Plan is to secure complete individual records of 5,000 stillbirths from hospitals registering more than 500 live births annually and located in cities having hospitals registering 1,000 or more births annually. The base is about 275,000 live births annually, about 270 hospitals in 24 States cooperating in furnishing the data. A schedule is to be filled out for each stillborn fetus of 20 weeks or more gestation occurring in the cooperating hospitals over a period of several months.

United States Employment Service

OCCUPATIONAL INVENTORY OF REGISTERED JOB-SEEKERS

Begun: First inventory begun 1935. Completed: July 1936. Second inventory begun 1936. Completed: (Tabulation) November 1936.

In charge: William H. Stead

Publication: Results of the two inventories will be published together, as a special bulletin of Employment Service, late 1936 or early 1937

Inventory of occupational training and experience of all jobseekers registered with the Employment Service as of the close of 1935. District and State basis. Breakdowns by sex, color, veteran status, relief status, and age, industrial, and occupational classification. A similar inventory is under way as of July 1, 1936, on a county and State basis. It is hoped to make a similar inventory annually. Active files of district and branch employment offices.

JOB-ANALYSIS STUDY

Begun: 1935. Completed: 5 industries completed and descriptions are in process of publication; 28 industries will be studied during fiscal year 1936–37

In charge: William H. Stead

Publication: As job descriptions are completed for a given industry, they are published as monographs by the Employment Service

Studies conducted in each of 13 cities of 33 selected industries, certain establishments in each city being selected for study, and all jobs in these establishments analyzed and descriptions written. Schedules are filled out by field workers who observe job performance in the establishments selected.

Women's Bureau

THE AGE FACTOR AS IT RELATES TO WOMEN IN BUSINESS AND THE PROFESSIONS

Begun: May 1931. Completed: January 1934

In charge: Harriet A. Byrne

Publication: Women's Bureau Bulletin No. 117, published October 1934

Effects of age and other factors on the employment of women, the extent of unemployment among them, and other data useful in giving vocational advice. Questionnaires to 58,720 women, members of National Federation of Business and Professional Women's Clubs. Usable replies received from 20,168. Study made in cooperation with this Federation. Mailed questionnaires.

EFFECTS OF THE DEPRESSION ON WAGE EARNERS' FAMILIES

Begun: Fall, 1932. Completed: December 1935

In charge: Caroline Manning

Publication: Women's Bureau Bulletin No. 108, February 1936

To show the changes which the later phases of the depression brought about in employment, earnings, and the social and economic status of the families. 1,120 households visited; work histories of 1,468 women secured in South Bend, Mishawaka, Indiana. These

women were among 3,245 women interviewed in 1930, as a basis for Women's Bureau Bulletin No. 92. Home interviews and visits to plants.

THE EMPLOYED WOMAN HOMEMAKER, HER RESPONSIBILITY FOR FAMILY SUPPORT

Begun: July 1935. Completed: October 1936

In charge: Mary E. Pidgeon

Publication: Women's Bureau Bulletin No. 148

Unpublished data made available by the Census Bureau on 3,882,143 gainfully employed homemakers in 1930. Other surveys of the same problem in Women's Bureau Bulletins Nos. 30, 41, 75. Data from Bureau of the Census.

EMPLOYMENT OF WOMEN IN OFFICES

Begun: September 1931. Completed: July 1934

In charge: Ethel Erickson

Publication: Women's Bureau Bulletin No. 120

To secure data useful in vocational guidance. 314 offices visited in New York, Hartford, Philadelphia, Atlanta, Chicago, Des Moines, St. Louis. Records of 42,897 women secured. Data on type of office, occupation, salary, hours of work, mechanization, personnel policies. Other data in the same field in Women's Bureau Bulletins Nos. 96, 132. Visits to places of employment, personnel records.

GAINFUL EMPLOYMENT OF MARRIED WOMEN

Begun: August 1934. Completed: October 1934 (revised 1936)

In charge: Rachel Myswander

Publication: Mimeographed report October 1934; revised 1936

To indicate the extent and nature of such employment, the economic needs of such workers, and the problems resulting from discrimination against married women workers. Analysis of data from Census, 1890–1930; reports by various agencies and individuals, including the survey by the Office of Education of the legal status of married women teachers, and the survey made by the Women's Bureau of the effects on women in the federal service of Section 213 of the Economy Act of 1932. Various types of official data.

THE OCCUPATIONAL PROGRESS OF WOMEN, 1910–30

Begun: February 1932. Completed: January 1933

In charge: Mary V. Dempsey

Publication: Women's Bureau Bulletin No. 104, April 1933

Analysis of data from Bureau of the Census. A previous bulletin, covering the period 1910–20, published in 1922. Data from Bureau of the Census.

OCCUPATIONAL DISEASES, WITH A SURVEY OF PREVENTIVE LEGISLATION, 1932–34

Begun: February 1935. Completed: August 1936

In charge: Margaret T. Mettert

Publication: Women's Bureau Bulletin No. 147

Analysis of State reports and of special studies by government or other agencies; analysis of State legislation and International Labour Office reports. 9 States reporting data, 5 by sex. An earlier report on this subject is contained in Women's Bureau Bulletin No. 114. Data from various types of official reports.

TECHNOLOGICAL CHANGES IN RELATION TO WOMEN'S EMPLOYMENT
Begun: January 1930. Completed: July 1935
In charge: Ethel L. Best
Publication: Women's Bureau Bulletin No. 107, November 1935

115 plants visited in 32 cities in 9 states. 1,035 women interviewed to secure data on nativity, age, and marital status as well as jobs and earnings. Other studies dealing with the problems of hours and methods of production in Women's Bureau Bulletins Nos. 100, 105, 110, 116, 141. Data from interviews with employers and workers.

Department of the Treasury

Public Health Service

Office of Statistical Investigations

NATIONAL HEALTH INVENTORY
a. Begun: August 1, 1935. Completed: Field work May 1, 1936; coding and tabulation April 1, 1937
In charge: G. St. J. Perrott, Clark Tibbitts, Selwyn D. Collins, Rollo H. Britten
Publication: Preliminary reports in mimeographed form late in 1936; final reports in *Public Health Reports* beginning about July 1937

Chronic disease survey: The incidence of chronic diseases and physical handicaps in the general population, the duration of disability, medical services received, and the relation of these to occupation, employment status, income, housing, and other environmental factors. House to house canvass of 750,000 families in 91 cities in 19 states, selected to be representative of the population of the country in cities of 25,000 and over. Smaller cities and rural areas included, but not in proportion to their representation in the population. Data for the year 1935. Breakdown by age, sex, color, nativity, marital status, school attendance, family relationship, occupation and industry, chronic diseases and physical handicaps, medical care, health services, family income, rental 1929 and 1936, housing and sanitary facilities. Cities under 100,000 enumerated completely; cities over 100,000 sampled by a random selection of enumeration districts.

b. Begun: August 1, 1935. Completed: Field work May 1, 1936; coding and tabulation April 1, 1937
In charge: G. St. J. Perrott, Clark Tibbitts, D. K. Brundage
Publication: Preliminary reports in mimeographed form late in 1936; final reports in *Public Health Reports* beginning about July 1937

Occupational morbidity and mortality study: Amount of time lost due to illness among industrial workers and the relation of illness to occupation and the hazards of the occupational environment. Transcription of the records of industrial sick benefit associations including 700,000 individuals in 105 cities in 17 states, including 64 industries and 421 plants. Breakdown by age, sex, occupation, industry, nature of illness, days disabled, occupational hazards. Data apply to period January 1930–January 1935. Records of industrial sick benefit associations.

c. Begun: August 1, 1935. Completed: Field work May 1, 1936; coding and tabulation April 1, 1937
In charge: G. St. J. Perrott, Clark Tibbitts, J. M. Mountin, Elliot H. Pennell, Wilhelm Reitz
Publication: Preliminary reports in mimeographed form late in 1936; final reports in *Public Health Reports* beginning about July 1937

Health facilities study: Census of public health facilities in terms of expenditures, personnel and services rendered. Census of all hospitals in cooperation with the Census of Business; survey of hospital out-patient departments. Survey of all health agencies in 100 counties. Survey to be extended to the 48 States. Schedule covers type of agency, population served, income, expense, personnel, services rendered, payrolls, plant assets, endowment funds, indebtedness. Data for year 1935. Study financed by W. P. A. (Federal Project). Field survey with schedule.

d. Begun: March 1, 1936. Completed: Field work June 15, 1936; coding and tabulation August 1, 1937
In charge: G. St. J. Perrott, Clark Tibbitts, Selwyn D. Collins, Helen C. Griffin
Publication: Late in 1937

Communicable disease: To determine the incidence of 13 common and rare communicable diseases among all children, with no prior attacks, among children with no prior immunization as compared to those with an immunization, among children exposed to a case in the household—all of the above items to be related to family income, crowding, type and rental of house, etc. To determine the completeness of reporting to the health departments of various kinds of cases. House-to-house canvass in 200,000 families in 38 cities of 100,000 or more population. No cities enumerated completely—cities sampled by random sample of enumeration districts.

HEALTH AND THE ECONOMIC DEPRESSION
a. Begun: March 1, 1933. Completed: Field work June 1, 1933; coding and tabulation about April 1, 1934
In charge: Selwyn D. Collins, G. St. J. Perrott
Publication: Numerous preliminary papers have been published in the *Milbank Memorial Fund Quarterly* and elsewhere and 3 papers in a final series have appeared in the *Public Health Reports*. At least 3 others are (1936) in preparation.

Incidence of illness during 3 months early in 1933 among persons classified according to their income history during the 4 years 1929–32. (1) House-to-house canvass of 1,000 families in each of 10 localities. The areas were not selected to be representative of the cities but to include districts that were hard hit by the depression. Eight of the areas were large cities and 2 were small towns. Breakdown by age and sex (all white), employment status and income history during 1929–32. (2) Special study of diets of about one-tenth of the total families canvassed in each locality. (3) Height and weight records of school children from the canvassed families were copied from school records and analyzed in relation to the family's income history. (4) Facts about housing were gathered along with the diet information. House-to-house canvass as described above.

b. Begun: September 1, 1934. Completed: Field work February 1, 1935; coding and tabulation August 1, 1935
In charge: Selwyn D. Collins, G. St. J. Perrott, Arthur St. Clair, Bess A. Cheney
Publication: April 1, 1937

Mortality in relation to income history among 30,000 families in the poorer districts of San Francisco. House-to-house canvass of 30,000 families in the poorer districts in San Francisco to obtain an income record for the years 1929–34 and a record of all deaths that occurred in the canvassed families and in all families in which any member of the present household had lived since 1929. This method was intended to pick up deaths of parents of orphaned children, deaths of the spouses of widows, widowers, etc. House-to-house canvass and a check of the health department records.

NEGRO MORTALITY
Begun: March 1, 1935. Completed: December 1, 1936
In charge: Mary Gover
Publication: Early in 1937

Systematic study of mortality among Negroes as compared with whites in the same States—supplement to Public Health Bulletin No. 174, which was published in 1928. This study considers death rates from specific causes at specific ages among Negroes and whites in 14 southern States, with some supplementary data for northern states. It also considers trends of death rates among white and colored in a group of 10 southern States that have been in the registration area since 1920. Trends are considered by age and sex for all causes and by cause for all ages. Mortality statistics from the Bureau of the Census and population statistics.

SICKNESS IN URBAN AND RURAL AREAS
Begun: Field work relate to years from 1928 to 1933. Completed: January 1, 1937
In charge: Selwyn D. Collins
Publication: Late in 1937

To determine sickness rates in rural as compared with urban areas, including case incidence, time lost, mentary data for northern States. It also considers office and to be used in this study include (a) records for 1 year on 9,000 families living in 130 communities of 18 States, including both urban and rural areas, (b) records for 3 years on 1,500 families living in 5 towns in Cattaraugus County, mostly rural but including 1 village of 900 population, (c) records for 18 months on 1,500 families living in Syracuse, New York (population 200,000). Breakdown by age, sex, occupation, nature of illness, days disabled, etc. House-to-house canvasses as outlined above.

SICKNESS AND MEDICAL CARE AND PREVENTIVE SERVICES IN THE GENERAL POPULATION
Begun: Canvassing applies to the period 1928–32. Completed: Field work about 1932; data now (1936) all on punch cards
In charge: Selwyn D. Collins
Publication: 9 papers have been published in the *Public Health Reports* as a series which will include a total of at least 15

To determine (a) the amount and kind of sickness in the general population, (b) the duration in terms of days lost, days in bed and the total duration of symptoms, (c) the extent of medical care in terms of hospital days and physicians' calls per case of a specific diagnosis, (d) the extent of the use of preventive and related services, such as vaccinations and immunizations against various diseases, physical examinations,

eye refractions and specific dental services. Sickness records for 1 year on 9,000 families living in 130 localities in 18 States. Breakdown by age, sex, cause of illness, etc. House-to-house canvasses covering a 12-month period.

Department of Commerce

Bureau of the Census

Division of Population

INDEX OF UNPUBLISHED POPULATION MATERIAL
Begun: 1933. Completed: Before 1938
In charge: Olive M. Riddleberger
Publication: 1930 index will be released first

To acquaint those interested in population problems with the amount of data tabulated but not published. Data available for the 1910, 1920, and 1930 censuses will be presented in tabular form. Bureau of Census.

EXPERIMENTS IN ESTIMATING STATE POPULATIONS FOR INTERCENSAL PERIODS
Begun: October 1935. Completed: 1937
In charge: Henry Shryock
Publication: Preliminary press releases of estimates February and May 1936; final evaluation of methods in a Ph. D. thesis by Shryock at University of Wisconsin

To test various methods of estimating and determine the best method or methods to be used. Use of birth and death rates, school attendance and enrollment data, and State school censuses. Estimates made by States. State school data, birth, and death rates.

GAINFULLY EMPLOYED HOMEMAKERS
Begun: 1932. Completed: Tabulation complete (1936)
In charge: Leon E. Truesdell
Publication: Uncertain

To make an analysis of the characteristics of employed women who are also homemakers. All gainfully employed homemakers except those in the minor races—Japanese, Chinese, etc. Tabulation by size of community, color or nativity, occupation and age of homemaker by (1) number of gainful workers by size of family, (2) size of family, (3) number of children by size of family, (4) marital condition of head, (5) number of lodgers. Family cards of 1930 Census (4th count).

RELATION OF OCCUPATION OF HEAD OF FAMILY TO RENTAL OR VALUE OF HOME
Begun: 1932. Completed: Tabulation complete (1936)
In charge: Leon E. Truesdell
Publication: Uncertain

Sample of about 715,000 native white male heads of families in Missouri. Occupation by value or rental of home for male heads by (1) age of male head, (2) number of children under 10, (3) gainful workers in family. Family cards of 1930 Census (6th count).

TYPES OF FAMILY COMPOSITION
Begun: 1932. Completed: Tabulation complete (1936)
In charge: Leon E. Truesdell
Publication: Preliminary press release of summary for United States August 1935. Final publication uncertain

A social-economic analysis of families. Family heads in the United States (except minor races), by color or nativity, size of community, and 37 "types" based on sex and marital condition of head of family and number of children under 21, classified by (1) value or rental of home, (2) size of family, (3) age of head, (4) gainful workers, (5) lodgers, (6) children under 10. Family cards of 1930 Census (5th count).

RELATION BETWEEN FERTILITY AND CERTAIN POPULATION CHARACTERISTICS
Begun: 1932. Completed: Tabulation complete (1936)
In charge: Leon E. Truesdell
Publication: Uncertain

The most extensive study of differential fertility ever made in United States. First, marriage families (except minor races). Color or nativity, size of community and value or rental of home by (1) number of children by age of wife and of husband and duration of marriage; (2) age at marriage, and (3) employment status of homemakers. East North Central Census division. Family cards of 1930 Census (6th count).

Division of Vital Statistics

EFFECT OF RESIDENT ALLOCATION OF BIRTHS AND DEATHS
Begun: October, 1935. Completed: Uncertain
In charge: H. L. Dunn
Publication: Preliminary, beginning 1937 in *Vital Statistics, Special Reports*, vol 3, (1937)

To compare tabulation of nonresident with resident births and deaths. Tabulation of 1935 data by states, counties, and cities. Mechanical tabulation and analysis following a special coding of transcripts. Birth and death statistics of the Division.

METHODS AND TECHNIQUES OF STATE COLLECTION OF VITAL STATISTICS
Begun: July 1936. Completed: January 1937
In charge: H. L. Dunn
Publication: Preliminary in *Vital Statistics, Special Reports*, vol. 3 (1937)

Comparison of state procedures used in handling birth and death certificates. Mail questionnaire to state registrars of all states, 1936. Results to be presented in tabular form. State registrars.

MORTALITY AMONG AMERICAN INDIANS, 1934
Begun: April 1936. Completed: July 1937
In charge: H. L. Dunn
Publication: Preliminary, in *Vital Statistics, Special Reports*, vol. 3 (1937)

Analysis of causes of death. Causes of death by age, sex, tribe, reservation. Machine tabulation of data in Division, with field checking to secure transcripts.

MULTIPLE CAUSES OF DEATH
Begun: October, 1935. Completed: Uncertain
In charge: Dr. H. L. Dunn
Publication: Preliminary, beginning Spring 1937, in *Vital Statistics, Special Reports*, vol. 3 (1937)

To clarify the effect of joint causes of death, and to discover what "complicated causes" are most frequent. Tabulation of 1935 data for Maryland for all causes of death; all states for material causes. Recoding and retabulation of death transcripts.

SUICIDAL AND ACCIDENTAL POISONINGS
Begun: August 1936. Completed: July 1937
In charge: H. L. Dunn

Publication: Preliminary in *Vital Statistics, Special Reports*, vol. 3 (1937)

To provide a basis for more logical classification in International List. Tabulation of 1925-35 data for the United States, with detailed breakdown by type of drug used. Recoding and retabulation of data in the Division.

SPECIAL REPORTS, VOL. 1
In charge: H. L. Dunn
Publication: At irregular intervals by the Division of Vital Statistics

Publication of special studies of interest to persons in the field. Special analyses of data on births, deaths, infant mortality and stillbirths. Reports published at frequent intervals, 1–6 per month. Data in the Division.

Division of Statistical Research

UNITED STATES LIFE TABLES
Begun: 1934. Completed: June 1936
In charge: Elbertie Foudray
Publication: Preliminary press release July 27, 1936. Final publication in a bulletin of the Census Bureau, November, 1936

To present the "life expectancy at birth and each year of life." Total United States, 1929–31; 1920 registration states 1919–21, 1920–29, 1929–31; original registration states 1900–09; 1910–19, 1920–29, 1929–31. Each period has 4 tables (color by sex) showing expectancy of life at each year of life. 1920–1930 census data, and births and deaths 1919–31 inclusive.

Federal Emergency Relief Administration and Works Progress Administration*

Division of Research, Statistics, and Finance

SIX RURAL PROBLEM AREAS—RELIEF—RESOURCES—REHABILITATION
Begun: 1934. Completed: 1935
In charge: Dwight Sanderson, E. D. Tetreau, J. O. Babcock, P. G. Beck
Publication: Published as Research Monograph I under title: *Six Rural Problem Areas—Relief—Resources — Rehabilitation*

An analysis of the human and material resources in six rural areas with high relief rates. 65 counties were surveyed in 6 areas which included approximately one-half the rural families receiving relief. The counties were selected to represent the range of social and economic conditions in each area. In each county all, or a random sample, of the population on relief in June 1934 was studied. Data secured from case records and through interviews with local relief workers and families concerned. Household schedule was used.

Division of Social Research

MIGRANT FAMILY STUDY
Begun: 1935. Completed: 1936
In charge: John N. Webb
Publication: Research bulletins TR–10, TR–11. Final report in preparation.

To determine the personal, economic, and social characteristics of migrant families; reasons for migration; origins and destinations; and residence history prior to migration. Country-wide sample study covering about 5,500 cases from 85 cities. Attempt made to secure a representative sample by taking cases from cities of different sizes; number of cases selected from each city was roughly proportional to the number of transient cases. Survey made in 1935; residence his-

---

*See also Rural Population Mobilization, p. 269.

tory secured either since 1929 or since formation of the family. Sample selected from the monthly census made by the Transient Division. Data secured on a 4-page questionnaire.

Labor Inventory March 1935
Begun: 1935. Completed: 1936
In charge: P. M. Hauser
Publication: Rotoprinted tables. Final report in preparation

A census of usual occupations of persons on relief. Census taken as of March 1935 of 6,100,000 workers on relief rolls. Data tabulated for: the United States, each state, cities of over 100,000 population, counties with a relief case load of over 5,000, and in condensed form for counties with a relief case load of less than 5,000. Workers classified by usual occupation, by color, sex, age groups, rural-urban residence, and priority ranking for work on the Works Program. Occupational classification can be converted in broad terms to the Census classification. From files of local relief offices transcription sheets were sent to 6 district coding and editing offices; from them to 2 tabulating offices.

Labor Inventory January 15, 1936
Begun: January 1936. Completed: March 1936
In charge: P. M. Hauser
Publication: Rotoprinted tables. Final report in preparation

Census of usual occupations of persons certified as eligible for the Works Program. Another census taken as of January 15, 1936, using the same occupational classification, with breakdowns by sex and priority ranking for work on the Works Program for each county, district and state. Since a uniform filing system was used in Works Progress Administration district offices, county tables were sent to 11 area statistical offices for tabulation.

Study of Public Assistance Extended to Families in Drought Area
Monthly, July to December 1936. May be continued thereafter in limited number of counties
In charge: F. D. Cronin and T. J. Woofter, Jr.
Publication: To be decided

A reporting system to give a complete, unduplicated count of families receiving public assistance in 65 sample counties in Colorado, Iowa, Kansas, Montana, Nebraska, New Mexico, North Dakota, Oklahoma, South Dakota, and Texas. Data include types and amounts of assistance to families aided; incidence of relief by occupation of household head; duplication of assistance; and relief turn-over. Separate files set up for all agencies in each county surveyed. Summary sheets transmitted to Washington office.

Survey of Opened and Closed Rural Relief Cases
Begun: 1934. Completed: 1935
In charge: C. E. Lively and Conrad Taeuber
Publication: Research bulletins, Series II, Nos. 2, 3, 4, 5

To ascertain the extent to which the relief population was affected by the various opportunities for employment, especially C. W. A.; changes in the characteristics of the population coming on and going off rural relief rolls; the reasons families came on relief; the methods by which they were transferred from relief to self-maintenance; and the representation of the different rural occupational groups in the relief

population. Household schedules taken of all cases that came on and went off relief rolls in 49 counties from November 1, 1933, through April 30, 1934. Supplemented the information obtained in the Unemployment Relief Census of October 1933. Case records.

Survey of the Plantation-Tenant Situation in the South
Begun: 1935. Completed: 1936
In charge: T. J. Woofter, Jr.
Publication: Published as Research Monograph V under title: *Landlord and Tenant on the Cotton Plantation*

An analysis of the cotton plantation, emphasizing the plantation rather than the individual tenant as the unit. Report contains sections on plantation areas and tenant classes; ownership; plantation organization and management; the one-crop system; credit; income; tenant's standard of living; mobility; education; and relief and rehabilitation. The survey included 40 counties in which large plantations dominate in Alabama, Arkansas, Georgia, Louisiana, Mississippi, and North Carolina. 646 plantations were studied; 5,171 tenants and laborers were interviewed. Data taken on separate schedules for landlords and for tenants and laborers were for the year 1934.

Survey of Rural Households on Relief in June and Closed Prior to December 1, 1935
Begun: 1936. Completed: 1937
In charge: A. R. Mangus, T. J. Woofter, Jr.
Publication: Report now (1937) in preparation

To show the extent to which rural relief families have been affected by the various government emergency work programs, by the Resettlement Administration, by private employment, and by State and local relief agencies. 72 sample counties in Georgia, Iowa, Montana, North Carolina, South Dakota, West Virginia, and Wisconsin. Designed to supplement information obtained by Survey of Current Changes in the Rural Relief Population. Case records and interviews. Household schedule used.

Youth and Employment
Begun: 1934. Completed: Late in 1937
In charge: Bruce L. Melvin
Publication: Monograph in preparation

A study of the extent to which the United States Employment Service reaches rural and urban youth. For comparative purposes 96 industrial and 134 rural counties have been selected. Data include age, sex, and employment characteristics of youth and types of industries and occupations in which they find employment. Information available on punch cards of U. S. Employment Service.

Survey of Village Youth
Begun: 1936. Completed: November 1, 1936
In charge: Bruce L. Melvin
Publication: A monograph

To ascertain social and economic characteristics of the youth in some of the villages included in the resurvey of American villages. Detailed study of all youth 15–29 years of age in 45 of the 140 villages in the large survey, distributed among the following states: New York, Pennsylvania, Virginia, North and South Carolina, Mississippi, Arkansas, Texas, Indiana, Illinois, Wisconsin, Minnesota, Iowa, Missouri, Nebraska, Kansas, Colorado, Washington, Oregon, and California. 16,000–18,000 households will be included in the study. Field interview with schedule containing sections on education, residential mobility, employment history, economic situation, participation in social organizations, and use of leisure time.

Farm Rehabilitation Prospects in the Drought Area

Begun: 1935. Completed: 1936
In charge: R. S. Kifer, T. J. Woofter, Jr.
Publication: 9 bulletins have been published: Research Bulletins K–1 to K–9, inclusive. Others are (1936) in preparation

To determine the basic causes of the rural distress in the drought areas, in order to assist in the development of rehabilitation programs adapted to the different areas. A study of the natural factors which affect productivity; of the organization of the factors of production and farm practices followed; of the present financial condition of farmers; and the problem of rehabilitation "in place" or reestablishment. Detailed information secured, in 13 representative counties in Colorado, Nebraska, New Mexico, North and South Dakota, Texas, and Wyoming, on farm organization, crops, livestock and crop production, and financial conditions of farmers. In cooperation with the Bureau of Agricultural Economics. Field work in the areas studied, and data from the Department of Agriculture, state statisticians, and records of production control contracts.

Survey of Combined Farming and Industrial Employment

Begun: 1935. Completed: 1936
In charge: W. W. Troxell, L. S. Cottrell, Jr., A. D. Edwards, R. H. Allen
Publication: Research Bulletins J–1—J–6

To describe existing types of combined farming-industrial employment, appraise their benefits and disadvantages, and determine the possibilities for further development of desirable types. Also to estimate the possibilities for rehabilitation of rural relief families. 7 counties in the eastern cotton area of Alabama, Georgia, and South Carolina in which the cotton industry is important were studied intensively. Special tabulations of Census data were supplemented by an extensive field survey. A sample of 1,400 part-time farm families and of 1,500 non-farming industrial employees were interviewed with a schedule including items on family composition, employment, income, agricultural production, housing, and level of living. In cooperation with Resettlement Administration. Bureau of the Census, studies by agricultural experiment stations, industrial surveys, field survey with a schedule, interviews with employers, public officials, etc.

Urban Relief Survey, May 1934

Begun: Survey taken as of May 1934. Completed: 1936
In charge: Clark Tibbitts, George Lundberg, Henry B. Arthur, Gladys L. Palmer, Kathryn D. Wood
Publication: Research Monograph IV, *Urban Workers on Relief*, May 1934

To determine the occupational characteristics of workers on relief, to provide basic social and economic information concerning the urban relief load. Approximately 165,000 households selected at random from the relief cases in 79 cities which varied in size, geographic location, and economic background. Size of sample in each city determined by size of city and of case load; sampling ratio varied from one in 30 cases in New York City to 100 percent in cities under 50,000 population. Household schedule used included items concerning race, sex, age, schooling for all persons, questions applicable only to employable persons (defined as persons 16–64 working or seeking work), and for unemployed workers, usual occupation and industry, length of experience, length of unemployment, longest job with one employer, and alternate occupation. For workers on nonrelief jobs, present occupation and industry, hours worked and weekly earnings. Household schedule. Occupation and industry codes of the Bureau of the Census were used.

Survey of Current Changes in the Urban Relief Population, 13 Cities

Begun: November 1934. Completed: December, 1935
In charge: F. L. Carmichael
Publication: "Changing Aspects of Urban Relief" now (1936) in preparation. Monthly bulletins, Research Bulletins, Series I, Nos. 4, 5, 7, 8, 10, 12, 14, 17

Planned to answer the following questions: (1) what proportion of the families coming on relief have never before received relief; (2) the major causes bringing them to relief; (3) the relationship between the varying number of families coming on and going off relief and seasonal and industrial activities; (4) the occupational level of families coming on relief, as it affects the program designed to care for them. Study conducted in 13 cities, selected with reference to size, geographic location, economic characteristics, relief problems: Atlanta, Baltimore, Bridgeport, Butte, Chicago, Houston, Manchester, Omaha, Paterson, St. Louis, San Francisco, Wilkes-Barre. Attempt was made to secure schedules for approximately 1,000 cases of each type (opened, closed, reopened) in each city for each month. Information secured included: reasons for granting relief, reasons for discontinuing relief, duration of unemployment of workers, occupation of last usual employment, weekly earnings and hours worked in the case of employed members, cases having no employable members, prior relief status. Schedules filled out from records in relief agencies.

Study of Transient, Homeless, and Nonresident and Nonfamily Persons and Study of Transient Bureau Cases

Begun: October 1934. Complete: April 1935
In charge: John N. Webb
Publication: Monthly bulletins, Research Bulletins Nos. TR–1 through TR–8. Final report, Research Monograph III, *The Transient Unemployed*

An analysis of the characteristics of the transient relief population, their movements, reasons for migration, and problems involved in their reabsorption into private industrial employment. Cases registered in Transient Service Bureaus of 13 cities, selected because of importance as transient centers and because they represented the areas in which they were located: Boston, Chicago, Dallas, Denver, Jacksonville (Fla.), Kansas City (Mo.), Los Angeles, Minneapolis, New Orleans, Phoenix, Pittsburgh, Seattle. Data received each month. Data transferred to schedules from record cards kept for each applicant for relief in the Transient Service Bureaus.

Comparative Study of Rural Relief and Nonrelief Households

Begun: Winter 1933–34. Completed: 1935
In charge: E. D. Tetreau, T. C. McCormick
Publication: Preliminary in Research Bulletins Nos. G–1 through G–7. Final report: *Rural Households, Relief and Nonrelief*, Research Monograph II

To show in what ways and to what extent the rural households receiving public emergency relief in October 1933 differed from their nearest neighbors who had not received relief. 47 sample counties selected in 19 States falling within 13 types of farming areas. Household schedules called for data on household composition, occupational history, farm tenure, mobility of head of household, employment status of other members of household, economic status of household, types and sources of public and private relief. Design to supplement information from Unemployment Relief Census, October 1933. Case records and interviews. Household schedule used.

Survey of Current Changes in the Rural Relief Population

Begun: February 1935. Completed: 1936

In charge: A. R. Mangus, T. J. Woofter, Jr.

Publication: Preliminary in Research Bulletins H–1 through H–7. Final report: "Changing Aspects of Rural Relief", now (1936) in preparation, as well as "The Farmer on Relief and Rehabilitation", and "The Rural Family in the Depression"

Analysis of rural relief cases in terms of mobility, family composition, occupational shifts, changes in relief loads, reasons for opening and closing cases. Selected sample of 331 counties in 33 States, and 138 counties in 9 agricultural areas. Cross-section surveys made in February, June, and October 1935, analysis of cases coming on and going off relief rolls made for the intervening months. Relief records of cases in the open country and in villages of from 50 to 2,500 inhabitants.

Needed Standards of Living for Rural Resettlement

Begun: 1935. Completed: Published 1936

In charge: E. L. Kirkpatrick

Publication: Mimeographed report, "Needed Standards of Living for Rural Resettlement, released by Wisconsin Rural Rehabilitation Division of the Resettlement Administration, Madison, Wisconsin

To throw light on the best policies to be following in developing rehabilitation programs. The first special family living study made in an area which is to be evacuated for reforestation. An analysis of 290 families living in the Crandon, Wisconsin, Federal Land Purchase Area, divided among the following groups: (1) Those whose land had been appraised or optioned for purchase by the Land Policy Section of A. A. A.; (2) those who had applied to the Wisconsin Rehabilitation Corporation; (3) those dwelling in three typically stranded villages in "cut-over" area. Field interview with a schedule covering items of family expenditure (including items furnished from the farm) and indexes of participation in home and community activities.

Rural Population Mobility and Standard of Living in Southern Appalachians

Begun: April 1, 1936. Complete: Tabulation in progress (1936)

In charge: C. P. Loomis, Conrad Taeuber

Publication: Will be published as a bulletin of the United States Department of Agriculture

Sample area of 4 counties: Avery and Haywood, North Carolina; Magoffin and Morgan, Kentucky. Every family (1,500) in sample area was interviewed, using 2 schedules (rural population mobility and standard of living) alternately. In cooperation with the Department of Agriculture. Field interviews with schedules.

Sectional Economic Research

National Research Project

Involves the Evaluation and Selection of Statistical and Technological Informa-

tion on Industries and Agriculture, Their Analysis and Representation as Indicators of Employment and Income Stability, Especially From a Sectional Viewpoint

Begun: 1934. Completed: In process (1936)

In charge: Col. J. M. S. Waring

Publication: Preliminary releases have been made of several special studies: *The Bituminous Coal Industry with a Survey of Competing Fuels* (December 1935); *The Employment Situation in the Pennsylvania Anthracite Region* (October 1935)

(1) To develop uniform and simplified methods of procedure by which a general picture of the changing economy of industries or homogeneous sections of the country might be continuously measured and evaluated; and (2) to correlate with the general picture all other pertinent information which might affect the ultimate aim of correct forecasting. The formulation of homogeneous economic sections; the determination of the vital productive industries in these sections; the classification of services into responsive and extra-service groups; the determination and calculation of inherent stability indexes for the sections—urban and rural; differentiation between secular and transitory reactions; determination of vital and focal products of the vital industries; determination of the vital factors responsible for major changes in the vital industries; determination of the effects of corporate and governmental policies on the stability of sections and industries; development of methods for ascertaining the spending characteristics of sections and political units. Statistical data from Bureau of the Census, Bureau of Labor, and other official sources. Also industry consultants and private research groups.

Resettlement Administration

Migratory Farm Labor in California

Begun: June 1, 1935. Completed: April 1937

In charge: Paul S. Taylor

Publication: Preliminary articles in *Monthly Labor Review*, February (1936) and *Rural Sociology* (September 1936)

To secure data on the origins and history of migratory laborers. 407 schedules were secured from labor camps in 20 counties of the State. Personal interviews with men in labor camps.

Land Use Planning Section

Development and Characteristics of Farm Tenancy

Begun: January 1, 1936. Completed: July 1, 1936

In charge: James G. Maddox

Publication: Bulletin

An historical analysis of tenancy in different regions in relation to size and value of farm, type of land use, cropping practices, and other factors. 4 cropping areas were selected (cotton, corn, wheat, and tobacco areas) and special tabulations made of 1,500–2,000 farm schedules from each of about 20 local sub-regions in these areas. The sample chosen constituted a homogeneous group of farms for each sub-region. Conducted in cooperation with the Department of Agriculture. Special tabulations of census material.

Reconnaissance Survey of Recent and Current Land Occupancy, With Special Reference to Land Use

Begun: February 1, 1936. Completed: 1937
In charge: E. H. Wiecking, Davis McEntire
Publication: Bulletin

To obtain a general picture of the volume and distribution of land settlement activities, origins of the people; types of land occupied; types of farming done and the manner by which settlement has taken place; the effects on the economic situation of the families affected, and to make an analysis of the social and economic factors operating. Nation-wide study, with emphasis on areas where settlement is now taking place in considerable volume. Field work by the State Land Planning Specialists.

Social Research Section

SOCIAL CORRELATIVES OF FARM TENURE

Begun: December 1, 1936. Completed: Uncertain. Field work March 1, 1937
In charge: Edgar A. Schuler
Publication: Bulletin

To determine the relationship between the forms of farm land tenure and family composition and characteristics; family living and social participation; attitudes toward farm land tenure and mode of living; tenure and migration history of heads of farm households; relationships between tenants and landlords, and between farm laborers and their employers; social status in the community. Representative local areas in the cotton belt, the corn belt, and the southeastern tobacco area will be studied. A schedule will be taken from each farm family in the selected local area for the crop year 1936. Supplementary schedules may be developed for such families or individuals as county agents, bankers, lawyers, merchants, ministers, teachers. Field interviews with schedule.

CAPACITY OF CERTAIN AREAS (IN OHIO) TO SUPPORT A DENSER POPULATION

Begun: April 1936. Completed: July 1937
In charge: C. E. Lively
Publication: Bulletin

Analysis of available material, the findings to be tested by field work. Printed sources and material at Ohio State College.

CAPACITY OF A CERTAIN AREA (IN MISSOURI) TO SUPPORT A DENSER POPULATION

Begun: April 1936. Completed: July 1937
In charge: E. L. Morgan
Publication: Bulletin

A schedule will be used to determine residential, occupational, and income history of the group, and community organization, with a view to prophesying what will occur if the resettlement now planned in this community is carried out. Field work in a selected area, with a schedule.

Social Security Board [1]

SOCIAL DATA ABOUT RECIPIENTS OF AID TO THE BLIND

---

[1] The Social Security Board will conduct a number of special studies, plans for which are not yet completed, which will involve population analysis. Large bodies of statistical data will be collected as a part of the administration of the Act, and to further the work of the Board, which will make possible analyses of the age, sex, and color composition of the workers in covered industries, data on the mobility of these workers, and similar data of social significance.

Begun: November 1, 1936. Completed: June 30, 1937
In charge: Helen R. Jeter
Publication: Annual report of the Board for fiscal year 1936–37

Analysis of sources and characteristics of the case load for aid to the blind. Detailed information outlined by Social Security Board to be reported by investigators in local departments of public welfare, filed and tabulated in office of State departments of public welfare. Report on each case accepted and each case closed on or after November 1, 1936.

SOCIAL DATA ABOUT RECIPIENTS OF AID TO DEPENDENT CHILDREN

Begun: November 1, 1936. Completed: June 30, 1937
In charge: Helen R. Jeter
Publication: Annual report of the Board for fiscal year 1936–37

Analysis of sources and characteristics of the case load for aid to dependent children. Detailed information outlined by Social Security Board to be reported by investigators in local departments of public welfare, filed and tabulated in office of State departments of public welfare. Report on each case accepted and each case closed on or after November 1, 1936.

SOCIAL DATA ABOUT RECIPIENTS OF OLD-AGE ASSISTANCE

Begun: November 1, 1936. Completed June 30, 1937
In charge: Helen R. Jeter
Publication: Annual report of the Board for fiscal year 1936–37

Analysis of sources and characteristics of the case load for old-age assistance. Detailed information outlined by Social Security Board to be reported by investigators in local departments of public welfare, filed and tabulated in office of State departments of public welfare. Report on each case accepted and each case closed on or after November 1, 1936.

Tennessee Valley Authority

Research Section, Social and Economic Division

POPULATION CHARACTERISTICS OF THE TENNESSEE VALLEY AREA

Begun: November 1936. Completed: 1937
In charge: Hershal L. Macon
Publication: After June 1937

To present a picture of population characteristics, migrations, etc., in the Tennessee Valley. 121 counties in the Tennessee River drainage basin. Census and other secondary sources.

Works Progress Administration

(See Federal Emergency Relief Administration)

APPENDIX C.
THE CONTINUOUS REGISTER SYSTEM
OF POPULATION ACCOUNTING[1]

Introduction

Accurate population accounting is the basis on which the science of social demography has been built. Effective legislation and planning and efficient administration are to a great extent dependent on the knowledge of the composition, status, and movement of the population. This is equally true whether compulsion is involved, as in the administration of a compulsory education law, or privilege extended, as in the determination of the classes of people (of certain age, citizenship, and residence qualifications) who are entitled to governmental protection and benefits of various sorts. Emergency action in regard to particular population groups and measures for immediate relief as well as long-range planning for the rational control of unemployment and for the adjustment of the interrelationships between agriculture and industry—in so far as such action and planning proceed on a sounder basis than trial and error—are intimately dependent on a record of the changes in population distribution and composition. Not only the government but the governed are directly benefited by systems of accounting which establish the various rights, claims, and exemptions of individuals under the laws of the government and the rules of the courts—particularly in regard to matters of social insurance, of relief, and of inheritance.

The situation in the United States at present—a highly mobile population and a highly dynamic economic situation—has led to a rather general appreciation of the fact that a decennial census alone cannot give an adequate accounting of the population. The census is continually being supplemented as a matter of necessity by surveys of special groups (e. g., an unemployment relief census), and various efforts have been made to record the rapidly changing distribution and composition of the population, but there is considerable dissatisfaction as to the adequacy of the results. (See chapter X.)

This appendix will present a detailed description of the systems of population accounting developed in certain European countries (Holland, Belgium, and Sweden) and in the city of Stockholm, where population accounting has been grounded on so-called community registers. These systems have been of relatively long duration, the technical procedures have been formulated in specific rules and definitions, and the results obtained can now be evaluated. These systems have in common that every person is registered at birth in his community of residence, a record is made at the time of occurrence of all changes in his civil status and family composition during his period of residence in this community, and, when he leaves the community, an official transcript of his birth (place and date), his civil status and family status at this time, accompanies him or is sent to the community where he is establishing a new residence. Thus, for the individual, birth or in-migration, marriage, dissolution of marriage, death, or out-migration becomes a matter of authentic record when and where it occurs. For the family, a record of changes in its composition during the residence of any of its members in a given community is obtained. With these systems of accounting, a balance sheet can be drawn at any point of time indicating the status and characteristics of the residents of any area, a periodic summary of changes in status can be prepared (persons reaching school age, voting age, pension age, etc.), the rate and direction of migration readily determined, and the factors producing movement in the population evaluated.

Historically, these systems were, in the main, founded on the old parish registers, which were kept by the pastors. The first traces of

[1] Prepared by Dorothy Swaine Thomas of the Institute of Human Relations, Yale University. She acknowledges her indebtedness to J. L. Lentz of The Hague and J. Gustav Kollberg of Stockholm for information, criticism, and advice; also to H. W. Methorst of The Hague, E. Höijer of Stockholm, and M. Steyaert, E. Lesoir, and R. Warans of Brussels.

276

the systems described here are found at the end of the seventeenth century in Sweden and the Netherlands and about 100 years later in Belgium.[2] The secular importance of population accounting brought registration under the control of the State during the nineteenth century.

In the Netherlands, civil registration of the population has been universal since 1850, and a consistent policy in regard to the determination of residence has been followed since 1861.[3] Population registers are required, by law, in every community. They are kept by special functionaries connected with the local government, and are under the general control and inspection of the Department of Interior. The registers are continuous, i. e., a record is made of each demographic change (birth or migration into the community, marriage or dissolution of marriage, death or migration from the community) at the time it occurs. The data relating to birth, death, and marriage are transferred to the registers from compulsory reports sent in by the registrar of births, deaths, and marriages; the data relating to migration are obtained through a similar requirement on the population to notify the authorities regarding a contemplated change of residence and to present a certificate from the community of last residence when taking up residence in a new community. The community registers are arranged in terms of family or coresident groups and make possible a summing up of the present and past "human resources" of any community in terms of the characteristics and status of the population. The developmental history of the population, in terms of its progress during the lifespan, is represented very inadequately in the community registers, except for those classes of the population whose whole development, from birth to death, has taken place within a single community. The most that is known about a migrant into a community is where and when he was born, where he resided before migrating, what his civil status, family connections, and occupation are upon entrance to the community. It is impossible to determine the intermediate stages between birth and present inmigration, or the subsequent changes between out-migration and death. In other words, population accounting based on community registers is bound to be cross-sectional, and de-

velopment can be studied only in terms of abstract statistical averages, and not in terms of the actual units contributing to this change.

As early as 1890, the desirability of modifying the system of population accounting to allow for the developmental aspects was recognized and the chief of the population bureau in Rotterdam (de Voogt) proposed to substitute for the community registers a system of individual cards, which would follow the individual from birth to death or emigration from the country, and would include notations of changes at the time and place they occurred. This proposal was not carried through, largely because it was recognized that the substitution of an individual card for the family register would lose sight of one of the most important sociodemographic factors; i. e., the individual's place as a member of a family group. In other words, individual development could be traced by this method only at the expense of losing track of the family groupings, which might also be expected to show important changes over time, and to react strongly upon the social and demographic development of the country.

In 1909, a commission met to consider the matter, and recommended the use of the individual card, but only if the conventional population register, with family groupings, was maintained at the same time. The administrative burden of carrying two systems of registration alongside each other probably explains the fact that this recommendation was not acted upon.

In 1928, a new commission was appointed and a plan was developed by H. W. Methorst and J. L. Lentz for a card which would follow the individual through life or residence in the country, but which would contain, in the case of every family head, all relevant data about the members of the family. Every person was to have an individual card, and the card of every family head was to contain additional data about the members of his or her family. Upon emigration or death, the cards were to be deposited in the central archives. In addition, the community entity was to be preserved through the development of a series of archives containing the history of all persons who had left the community or died in the community up to the time of migration or death. This proposal of this commission was accepted, and the new system was introduced in a few communities in 1930. At the present time, it has been extended to include about 14 percent of all the communities (having, together, a population of over 1,000,000—Utrecht being the only large city in the list). It is planned to extend the system in easy stages, accompanied by the necessary education of the authorities in accepting and carrying out the details.

[2] Amnéus, G., Folkeregistrering, *Nordisk Statistik Tidskrift*, Band 8: 370–386 (1929).
[3] Methorst, H. W., and Lentz, J. L., Die Volksregistrierung und das neue in den Niederlanden eingeführte einheitliche System, *Allgemeines Statistisches Archiv*, Band 26: 59–84 (1936).
Besluit Bevolkings-Boekhouding 1936, Staatsblad No. 342. *Handleidnig Bevolkings-Boekhouding.* Departement van Binnenlandsche Zaken, No. 16300 (1936).
These last two references are the handbooks of the law and the instructions regarding the keeping of population registers. After this appendix went to press, an excellent comprehensive account of population registration in The Netherlands appears: Lentz, J. L., *De Bevolkings-boekhouding*, Zwolle: De Erven J. T. Tijl N. V. (1936).

In Belgium [4] civil registration of the population has been compulsory since 1856. As in Holland, the community is the administrative unit, and the registers are kept by local civil authorities and are subject to control and inspection by the Department of the Interior. The registers include all persons, natives and foreigners, adults and minors, who, at the time of the decennial census, have their habitual residence in the community. The household is the unit in the main register. The registers are kept continuously between censuses; all births, deaths, changes in civil status and migrations to and from the community are noted upon occurrence.

Demographers can thank the Swedish State Church for providing the basis on which the excellent Swedish system of population accounting is founded.[5] The church law of 1686 made general for all parishes a system of population accounting which had been developed in some parishes by the beginning of the century. According to this law, every pastor was required to keep continuously lists of persons belonging in the parish (residents), of married couples, of children born (legitimate and illegitimate) of persons dying (or rather, at that time, of persons buried in the churchyard) and of migrants to and from the parish. As Arosenius has expressed it, "Quite unconsciously, these church laws provided the basis for some of the most important elements in population statistics, but it took considerable time for the State to realize their utility for administrative purposes." In 1748, these lists were made the basis of the Swedish official statistics, but not until 1856 was a complete and thoroughly organized set of administrative rules determined.

The pastors of the church have to this date continued to function as registrars of population and of vital statistics. They now exercise these functions partly in the capacity of church officials, partly in the capacity of civil officials.

The unit for population registration is the parish, which corresponds generally to the civil administrative unit, the community. Many large towns comprise several parishes; in such cases the unit is the parish. In Stockholm, as will be described, there has been developed a

highly organized civil system of population registration, although the pastors still function as registrars of vital statistics.

Population accounting in Sweden at present represents a combination of two systems: Continuous registration in the communities of actual residence (Kyrkobokföring), and an annual registration in the community of residence at the end of the year for purposes of tax assessment (Mantalsskrivning). The purpose of the latter is to determine where the individual may exercise his civil rights (voting, etc.), where he may obtain social benefits (relief, etc.), and where he is subject to taxation for the ensuing year. The details of the several systems are described below.

Population Accounting in the Netherlands

The general situation with regard to registration in the Netherlands is at present rather complicated by the fact that the older system of registration exists in most communities, the new system in a few. The same data are, of course, collected by means of the two systems, but the bookkeeping technique is quite different. All registrars must be acquainted with both systems, for people are continually migrating from an old-register community to a new-register community, and vice versa.

A. The Responsibility for Registration

Registration is compulsory. The head of every family or coresident group and all non-family persons, who give up residence in one community and take up residence in another, are required by law to present themselves to the civil registration authorities within 5 days of arrival for registration. Immigrants from other countries must have with them their passports; in-migrants from other places in Holland must show identification papers (moving certificate) from the community of previous residence. Everyone born outside the Netherlands is required to produce, within 3 months after the demand is made, a birth certificate, baptism certificate, or some equivalent attested document.

To become a bona fide resident of a Dutch community depends initially on the *intention* of the migrant, as evidenced by the giving up of residence in the community of previous residence and the presenting of the moving certificate in the new community, but also upon *fact*. A person who, though registered in one community, habitually lodges in another community, must give up his official residence in the first and become registered as a resident of the second. In case of a choice between two communities, habitual residence is determined on the basis of the community in which the

[4] Lesoir, Edm., Les registres de population, *Révue de l'Institut International de Statistique*, 3 année livraison 1: 14–39 (1935).
Piron, Th., *Des registres de population en Belgique*. Gand, Vanderpoorten (1922).
Jacquart, Camille, *Statistiques démographiques et sanitaires de la Belgique* (Extrait du tome XXII du Bulletin de la Commission centrale de statistique) Gand, Société Coopérative "Volksdrukkerij" (1925).
Piron contains the law and an interpretation of the rules for keeping population registers.
[5] Arosenius, E., *Bidrag till det Svenska Tabellverkets Historia*. Stockholm, P. A. Norstedt och Söner (1928).
Lysander, A. och Forkman, G., *Kyrkobokföringen*. Stockholm, Svenska Kyrkans Diakonistyrelses Bokförlag (1929).
Norrman, Sune, *Mantalsskrivning*. Stockholm, P. A. Norstedt och Söner, 1933.
The last two references give the law and rules for the keeping of the community books (parish registers) and for the preparation of the annual assessment declarations, respectively.

FAMILY REGISTER (OLD SYSTEM)- THE NETHERLANDS

| No. | Family Name | Given Names | Sex | Rel. to Head of Family | Born | | Civil Status | |
					Date	Place	at inscription	changes and date of same
1	2	3	4	5	6	7	8	9

PLATE I

1. Consecutive number of entries on this page.
2. Family name; family name of spouse may in each case be indicated in parentheses.
3. Given names (same rule as above about spouses).
4. Sex.
5. Relationship to family head.
6. Date of birth.
7. Place of birth.
8. Civil status. In case of doubt, indication in column 20.

9. Date of marriage, divorce, separation, annulment, and name of community where such certificates are recorded. If unknown, indication in column 20.
10. Religious affiliation.
11. Nationality.
12. Occupation, and standing in occupation. Indication if employer or employee.
13. Changes in occupation and date of changes.
14. Consecutive addresses within the community and dates of moves. If a card system is used, and a child moves to another address than that of parent, the child is placed on a special card and a note of change is made in column 17 of the family card.

person has spent the greater number of the previous 360 nights.

Other factors are, however, taken into consideration in doubtful cases, and include the following: Community in which the other members of the family are registered, the place where the person is registered for personal taxes, where he is required to live in order to carry on his main occupation, where he has to perform his regular duties, etc. In all other cases of doubt, the question is referred to the Ministry of the Interior.

All persons must be registered in one (and only one) community, except those in the country "temporarily", and persons who have no fixed residence. The former will be entered in a transients' register, the latter in the central register of the Ministry of the Interior. Temporary residents are defined, in the case of natives, as those who within 90 days of registered arrival have spent not more than 30 days in the country, in the case of foreigners 180 out of 360 days.

B. The Old System of Community Registers

Communities having the old system of registration are required to have—

1. A family register.
2. An identification register.
3. A dwelling register.

The *family register*, arranged in terms of family or coresident groups[6] is the basis of population accounting. It shows the status of the population at any point of time, is reorganized and checked after each decennial census, and entries are made continuously of all demographic changes between censuses. After 1940 this register must be kept on cards; at present, ledgers are extensively used and are renewed after each census. Plate I indicates the arrangement of the currently used registers.

The *identification register* must be either loose-leaf or a card system, and indicates in alphabetical order the names of all family heads and other persons in the community, provided the family register is not kept in

[6] The definitions of various terms used in applying the registration rules are as follows:
A *family* is either a married couple living together, or a married couple living together with their common unmarried children or step-children, or a father or a mother living with his or her unmarried children ("broken family" type).
Coresidents are all groups of persons forming a household together not included under the definition of family.
The *family head* is the husband in the first type of family mentioned above; the father or the mother in the broken-family type; in coresident groups, the man, if such a group consists of one man and one woman; if a coresident group consists of one or more men and of one or more women, the man or the woman who acts in the capacity of head and is treated as such by the other members. In coresident groups where there is difficulty in assigning headship according to the previous definition, the oldest person is considered the head.
Children are the own and stepchildren of the head.
A *nonfamily person* is a person who cannot, in accordance with the above definitions, be considered as part of either a family or a coresident group.

Religious affiliation	Nation-ality	Occupation		Address	Inscription in this Register		Removal from this Register		Death	Remarks
					Date	Place of previous registration	Date	Place of subsequent residence	Date	
		at Inscription	changes and date of same							
10	11	12	13	14	15	16	17	18	19	20

15. Date of inscription in the population register.
16. Community of last previous residence and address in that community.
17. Date of removal from population register. Date of removal is the same as that of inscription in the new community, and is determined upon receipt of notification from that community.
18. Community of destination and address.
19. Community in which death occurred, and number of death certificate.
20. Other data required from time to time by the Minister of the Interior, and including:

For every man 20 years of age and older, his status in regard to compulsory military service.
For every person receiving a decoration or order of the Netherlands, an indication of this.
For every person receiving state insurance or benefit, indication of nature and reference to file number (invalidity, accident, old age, etc.).
For every person holding a Dutch passport, number and date of issue.
Indication of permit to possess firearms.
Indication of guardianship, both for guardians and wards.

alphabetical order, in which case family heads may be omitted from this register. This identification register must include at least the family name, given name, birth year, and under what name the person is inscribed in the family register. Widows and separated women who are registered under their maiden names in the population register are here placed under their husbands' names; wives who are registered under their husbands' names in the population register are here placed under their maiden names. The previous names of persons who have legally changed their names are entered here.

The *dwelling register* (see plate II) lists all buildings capable of being used, or actually being used, for dwelling purposes arranged in order according to house number (the communal authorities are required to assign house numbers). This file can be either loose-leaf or card system. Every card includes for the building in question the name of the head of every family, of every person in a coresident group, and of every nonfamily person resident in the building. Buildings which have many families moving in and out can have a separate register. The importance of having the dwelling register arranged for maximum accessibility and usefulness is emphasized.

In addition to these registers, a *transient register* must be kept in every community. Persons in this register are not to be counted as belonging to the population of the community. When a person is removed from this register, a record is made as to the cause of removal (death, migration, or inscription in the population register of the community).

C. The New System of Individual-Family Cards

Communities having the new system of registration are required to have—

1. An individual-family card register.
2. An archive register.
3. A dwelling register.

The *individual-family card register* consists of a collection of cards, one for every person in the community. These cards are furnished by the Ministry of the Interior (yellow cards for males, gray for females). They include essentially the same data as the family register. As indicated above, a card is filled in for each person at birth or migration into a community using this system. The family groupings are recorded on the card of each person who is, at the time of record, a family head. The collection of such cards in any community at any given time represents the resident, living population. When a person migrates to another Dutch community, his card is sent to that community. Upon death, emigration, or "disappearance", the card is deposited in the central files in The Hague. Plate III (face) shows the arrangement of the card for every person in the

DWELLING REGISTER   THE NETHERLANDS

(Face of Card)

Street_____   No._____

Name of Family Head Date of birth (in parentheses)	Previous address and date of inscription at this address	Succeeding address and date of removal from this address	Remarks (No. of family members)	Special Annotations regarding billeting of soldiers, care of state wards, etc.			
1							
2							
18							

(Back of Card)

Names of							
No. on face of card	Persons living with head of family (not servants)	Previous address and date of inscription at this address	Succeeding address and date of removal from this address	No. on face of card	Servants living in household	Previous address and date of inscription at this address	Succeeding address and date of removal from this address

PLATE II.—Dwelling register, The Netherlands.

community and plate III (back) shows the additional data entered on the card of each family head.

On the individual card of a family member who is not the head of the family, a notation is made as to relationship to the head on whose card this person is also recorded (father, mother, husband), and, in case of a different name, the name of the head (entry 2). When, and if, this person no longer belongs to the family, or becomes a member of another family, or himself becomes a family head, the previous notation is stricken and the appropriate new notation entered. These cards must be filled in on a typewriter or with blocked letters in ink, except that entries 17, 24, 33, and 34, which are considered to be temporary factors, are to be filled in with pencil, and erased when they no longer apply.

The *archive register* is obligatory for communities having this individual-family register, and includes a record of all persons who have migrated to another community within the country, emigrated or migrated to an unknown destination or died while registered in the community. No card may be sent out either to another community or to the central files until an abstract is made for the archive register. The form for the archive register is exactly the same as that for the individual-family card, and all data are copied, except that, in the case of migrants, the address in the new community is entered in the dwelling register. Spaces are left in the archive register to be filled in when the same person reenters and departs again from the community. An alphabetical index is provided.

The *identification register* is of the same type as for communities using the old system, unless the individual-family cards are arranged in

PLATE III (RIGHT)

3 (a). Family name.
3 (b). Given names.
4. Date of birth. Place of birth.
5. Nationality.
6. Religious affiliation.
7. Occupation and status in occupation.
8. Name, date of birth, and place of birth of the father and the mother (maiden name).
9-12. Names of all spouses, in order, with place and date of birth.
13. Date and place of all marriages, in order.
14-16. Date of dissolution of marriages, indication of whether dissolution was caused by death, by divorce, by 5-year separation from bed and board, by nullification. Place where certificate of dissolution is recorded.
17. If spouse left the family (not by divorce or death) date of such temporary desertion is entered.
21. Date of taking out moving certificate to another community or of moving within community.
22. Name of community to which migration is made and addresses, in order, in this community.
23. When beginning an individual card at any point other than birth, notation is made of community from which person last came, name of community in which card is begun and address at that time; also notations required from time to time by Minister of the Interior. (Same as in column 20 of Family Register.)
24. Communal authorities may note special features of interest to themselves but not obligatory.
27. If child leaves family, notation as to whether by move within community, migration from community, marriage, or death. Notation of date of such move or migration, also date of marriage or of death, if relevant. If by marriage, name of spouse.
28-29. Family name and given names of each child.
30-31. Date of birth and place of birth of each child.
32. Sex of child, and whether own or stepchild.
33-34. Any specific requirements of Minister of Interior.
35. Details of the legitimization of an illegitimate child; changes of name. Death, in what community and when, the number of the death certificate, name of physician, cause of death.

INDIVIDUAL-FAMILY CARD (NEW SYSTEM) THE NETHERLANDS
(Face of Card)

3) Fam. Name a _____ Given Name b _____	1) Birth Certif. Attested No. of certif. 4) on comm. div. or country 5) nat.	2) Family Head _____ 6) Rel. / 7) Occ. (Employ-er-ee)

| 8) Son of _____ and of _____ | Born on _____ at _____
Born on _____ at _____ |

9) Fam. name and 10) Given name	11-12) Born	13) Marr. performed	14-15-16) Marr. dissolved	17) Separation comm. and date
Married to I _____	on / at	on / at	on / at by	
II _____	on / at	on / at	on / at by	

21) Date inscribed	22) Community and address	21)	22)	21)	22)

23) Required annotations	24) Voluntary annotations

(Back of Card)

26) own and step-children (on card of fam. head only)				
27 (moved, marr., died)	28) Fam. name and 29) Given name	30-31) Born	32) Rel. to Head	33-34) Remarks
I		on / at		
II		on / at		
III		on / at		
IV		on / at		
V		on / at		
VI		on / at		
VII		on / at		
VIII		on / at		
IX		on / at		
X		on / at		
XI		on / at		
XII		on / at		
35)				

PLATE III.—Individual-family card (new system), The Netherlands.

alphabetical order, in which case the identification register may be greatly simplified.

The *dwelling register* is the same as for communities using the old system, except that it is required that the name of the community of previous residence and of subsequent residence be entered here in every case, as well as the previous and subsequent addresses within the community.

The *transient register* is precisely the same for the two types of registration.

D. Registers Kept at the Minstry of the Interior

The *central register*, containing a card for each person who is a resident of the Netherlands but who has no fixed residence in any particular community (nomads, vagabonds, etc.).

The *central archives*, containing cards for all residents who have died, emigrated, or are untraceable.

The *link register*, containing reference cards, arranged in alphabetical order, of all persons who have emigrated, immigrated, or whose residence is unknown (the untraceables). This register is so called because it serves as a link in the chain of registration: persons who turn up for registration in a community (with or without identifying papers) coming from a foreign country, or from some other community, can be traced through this file. No new card is issued for such a person until a thorough search of this register has been made. If he has been registered previously and emigrated or become "untraceable", there must be a card concerning him in this file, which supplies the missing link as to his identity and whereabouts.

A notation is then made on the reference card, and when the individual-family card is found it is sent to the community of residence. If there is no link card, there are two possibilities: (1) the person has never lived in Holland before or (2) he is still registered in some community. If the first alternative can be shown to be probable, the community is given permission to issue an individual-family card; if there is a suspicion that the second alternative is true, an investigation is made before a card may be issued. If a new card has been issued, and, after some time, the old card is sent in by another community, the link register once more serves the purpose of "closing the chain."

This register is intended to safeguard the system from the possibility of double registration, and to insure the tracing of each resident from one community to another from birth or immigration to death or emigration.

E. The Keeping of the Population Registers

The local community government is responsible for the keeping of the population registers and every community must keep such registers. The registrar of births, deaths, and marriages is required to notify the population registrar within 24 hours of all changes which occur. He must also give, free of charge, all information requested by the population registrar within 3 days of such request. Similar regulations apply to other departments (the law courts, etc.) where data necessary for the completion of population registration are recorded. The same rule applies to all institutions where sentences are served, where communal guardianship is assumed, etc. These latter data are entered in (20) of the family register, or (35) of the individual-family card.

Every birth, except a stillbirth, is recorded immediately after the report is received. A legitimate child is entered on the father's card, and an illegitimate child on the mother's card at the same time that an individual card is made out for the child. After the birth is recorded on the individual-family card, the card is sent to the registrar of births, deaths, and marriages for verification and the date of verification and the number of the birth certificate are entered in (1). These rules, of course, apply only to the new system. Under the old system, the birth is entered in the appropriate place in the family register. Births to persons temporarily in the community are noted, and the card or a notification is sent to the community of residence.

Every death is noted, not only on the card of the deceased but also on the card of the spouse, and in the case of a family member, on the card of the head of the family. The cause of death, the number of the death certificate, and the name of the physician are entered on the card of the deceased. If death occurred in a community other than that in which the person was registered, notification is sent to the community of residence, or, if this is unknown, to the Department of the Interior. Under the new system, cards of persons who have died are sent every month to the central bureau of statistics, where they are kept for 2 years and then deposited in the archives of the Department of the Interior. Under the old system, the same data noted above are entered in the family register.

A moving certificate is to be issued upon demand to every person leaving the community. A duplicate of this certificate is sent to the community mentioned as destination. Under the new system, the card itself is sent to this community, or, in the case of an emigrant, to the central register. If a person is leaving a community where the old system has been in force for a community where the new system exists, an individual-family card must be filled in for such a person, and in the case of persons born in the community from which they are migrating, the date of birth must be attested by the registrar of births, deaths and marriages. Upon the registration of a migrant (which, as mentioned before, must occur within 5 days of arrival), the authorities in this community must send back the moving certificate, stamped by the registrar, to the community from which the migrant has come. The cards of persons leaving a community for an unknown destination are sent to the Department of the Interior, as are those of persons who do not turn up in the community for which they have taken out moving certificate. Persons turning up in a community without a certificate must give the name of the last community of residence, an investigation must be made, and the Department of the Interior notified.

Details about marriage, divorce, and annulment are entered from reports sent in by the registrar of births, deaths, and marriages.

Changes of residence within a community must be noted. The communal authorities must decide under which residence to list a person who has several addresses in a single community.

Persons are entered in the population registers upon birth or upon taking up residence in the community. Persons are taken out of the registers upon death, or upon giving up (intentionally or factually) residence in a community or the country, with the exception that persons temporarily out of the community, or temporarily out of the country are not removed from the registers. "Temporary" is here defined as not usually out of the country more than 270 of 360 consecutive days, or not out of the country at any one time more than 360 days (for seamen, 720 days). Cases difficult to classify are decided by the Ministry of the Interior.

The following are listed specifically for removal from the registers: Those who die or whose death may be assumed on reasonable grounds; all persons leaving the community or the Netherlands with the intent to remain away permanently or in accordance with the time rules discussed above; all persons who have left a community after taking out a moving certificate but who have not turned up in the community of declared destination (these persons are entered in the central register as "unknowns"); all persons who have left a community without taking out a moving certificate and have not been traced for 360 days.

Under special circumstances, migrants are entered in the registers by official action, either when their factual residence does not correspond to their registration or when the community of last residence cannot be determined and identification papers cannot be secured. Similarly and more frequently, they are removed by official action when they have left their community of residence without taking out a certificate and their destination is unknown, or when the registration does not correspond to the factual residence.

The communal authorities are required to check the population registers once a year, either by a direct approach to the population or by mail.

The Inspector of Population Registers has access to the registers of a community at any time and interprets the specific rules.

An advisory committee with the function of interpreting and recommending is appointed by the Minister of the Interior.

Population Accounting in Sweden (Excluding Stockholm)

In Sweden as in Holland the registered population is defined as those persons habitually residing in a community. Habitual residence is determined on the basis of where a person is assessable for taxes (see sec. D, below).

All persons, whether members of the State Church or not, foreigners or citizens, minors or adults, are registered in the community books. Persons out of their community of residence temporarily (such as children or adults attending educational institutions, persons away on recognized professional pursuits, members of parliament, persons in institutions, hospitals, sanitoria, etc.), are not removed from the registers in the community of habitual residence unless, in the case of minors or legally irresponsible persons, persons in institutions, etc., their families or guardians migrate from this community.

Registration is in terms of family or household groups arranged according to the address in the community. But certain persons may be registered as belonging to the community even though they have no address or residence there, e. g., persons in prisons or institutions, seamen, etc.

A person becomes statistically "nonexistent" (obefintlig) if he is known to have emigrated without taking out papers, or if his whereabouts are unknown for 2 consecutive years at the time the assessment lists are drawn up. Such persons are not reckoned as either registered in the community or as migrating from the community but are recorded in a special "book of the nonexistent", from which they are removed when and if they go through the formalities necessary to register in some other community, or when they return to the community of habitual residence.

A. The Responsibility for Registration

The pastors are responsible for keeping registers of all residents, of all movements in the population (births, deaths, migrations) and of all changes in civil and legal status. All heads of families and all persons 15 years of age or over except wives migrating with their husbands, must, before migrating from one Swedish community to another, declare their intention and take out a moving certificate. Upon presentation of this certificate in the commu-

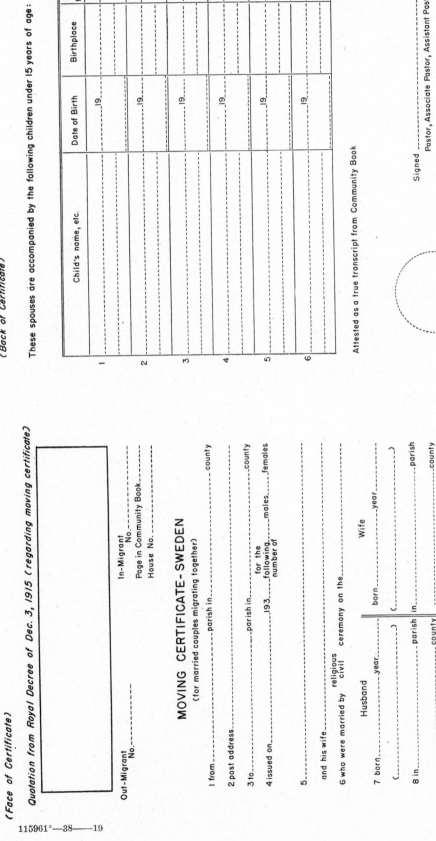

PLATE IV.—Moving certificate, Sweden.

nity of new residence, registration is accomplished and a notification is sent to the community of previous residence. Until this notification is received, no migration is considered to have taken place, and the person concerned is not removed from the register. The certificate must be presented within a month of migration (in the autumn, within a week; in Stockholm within 2 weeks at all times). The employer is responsible for the registration of servants. The migrant must personally present his moving certificate to the pastor to accomplish registration. See plate IV.

B. The Population Registers (The Church Books)

The pastor in every community or parish is required to keep the following set of books, which serve as a basis of population accounting.

1. The community book.
2. The book of the non-existent.
3. The book of in-migrants.
4. The book of out-migrants.
5. The book of births.
6. The book of marriages.
7. The book of deaths.

These books fulfill all the technical secular requirements. In addition, matters of interest to the church are cared for by the inclusion of a record of baptisms in the birth book, of burials in the death book, of banns in the marriage book, and so forth.

The community book.—The community or parish book is arranged according to dwellings in the community (except in larger communities where this would be inconvenient) in a bound volume. The entries are made either in chronological order (according to time of migration) or in alphabetical order. If the arrangement is other than in order of dwellings, a separate dwelling register must be kept indicating under each address for the family or household head (and for nonfamily persons) the name and occupation of the head, and the names of servants and other members of the household, if these are not registered with the family head in the community book.

If the arrangement in the community book is by dwellings (which is usual) the families or households occupying each dwelling are listed in order, the head of each family first, then his wife, his children in order of age, other family members and servants. If a family member marries, the new family is recorded separately, even if the spouses continue to live with the other family members. The form is indicated in plate V.

The book of the non-existent.—This book is arranged exactly the same as the community book, and all data referring to persons transferred to this book are transcribed exactly from the community book.

The book of in-migrants (and immigrants).—This book contains, in chronological order, a record of all persons entering the com-

munity. Each person who has a moving certificate is entered separately, but wives and children under 15 migrating with the husband and father, or children under 15 migrating with either parent, are simply indicated by sex as accompanying the head of a family. The record includes date of in-migration, occupation and sex of head of family or of person holding moving certificate, and his date of birth, the number of male and female persons included on the certificate of the head of a family, the community of origin, the address in the present community, and a reference to the page in the community book where the complete record will be found.

The book of out-migrants (and emigrants) is organized on a similar basis, but two dates are given: the date of taking out the certificate and the date of notification of registration from the community of destination. This latter is considered the date of migration.

The other books kept by the pastor are concerned with the details of vital statistics, civil status, and matters pertaining to the church. The community book contains a summary of all such data, which are entered immediately both in the special book and in the community book.

C. The Keeping of the Population Registers

As indicated, the registers are kept by the pastors of the State Church, subject to control and regular inspection of the central statistical bureau. The parish registers are renewed every 10 years, after the decennial census, and are checked every year against assessment lists.

The various departments and individuals concerned with collecting data essential to the keeping of the registers are required to send reports to the pastors (e. g., midwives, doctors, hospitals, institutions, the courts, child-care committees, etc.). Since births and deaths are allocated to the community of registration, reports of all such events occurring in other communities must be sent to the pastor in the community of registration.

D. The Assessment Lists (Mantalsskrivning)

Once a year, registration of all the residents of Sweden is carried through for tax assessment purposes and for the determination of the residence of communal rights and duties for the ensuing year. This registration is under the control of the Finance Department. Its essential features are:

1. An obligatory declaration by every householder.
2. The checking of the householder's declarations against the community book, involving cooperation between the church and civil officials.
3. The completing of the declarations from the data in the community books (regarding in-migrants during the year) and from other sources.
4. The determination of the actual residence of each person as of the time of assessment, this resi-

COMMUNITY BOOK (PARISH REGISTER)- SWEDEN

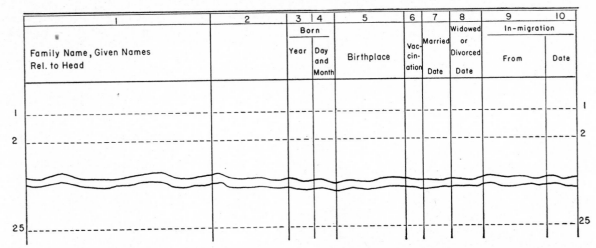

1	2	3 Born Year	4 Born Day and Month	5 Birthplace	6 Vaccination	7 Married Date	8 Widowed or Divorced Date	9 In-migration From	10 In-migration Date
Family Name, Given Names Rel. to Head									

PLATE V

1. Family name and given name; for married women, divorced and separated and widows, the maiden name also. In cases of legally changed names, the former name is indicated in parentheses. Family status, i. e., relationship to head, or in the case of a wife's children by another marriage, or before marriage by another man than the husband, an indication of this situation. For persons whose whereabouts are unknown at the time the assessment lists are made out, an indication is made here. (If such an indication is made in 2 consecutive years, the person is removed to the book of the nonexistent.)

2. Occupation: Chief occupation in all cases; indication of position and function.

> Occupation is to be recorded for all heads of families and all other family members usually employed; widows having no occupation are described in terms of their deceased husband's occupation, e. g. "widow of a carpenter"; for persons having no occupation, an attempt is made to indicate their status in terms of a previous occupation, e. g. former soldier, in the case of persons on relief, this is noted here.
> Race, noted in cases of Finns, Lapps, Gypsies, etc.

Defects; indication if insane, feebleminded, blind, deaf, dumb, and epileptic.

3-4. Date of birth (year, month, day).

5. Place of birth; actual birthplace, not place to which birth is assigned for statistical purposes (births are assigned to the community where the mother was registered at the time of delivery, not necessarily the community where the delivery took place. But the latter is recorded as place of birth).

6. Indication of vaccination, or recovery from smallpox.

7. Date of marriage; indication of whether religious or civil ceremony.

8. Indication if widowed or divorced, and date of same.

9. For in-migrants since the renewal of book, community of origin. For residents at time of renewal of book, reference to page in preceding book.

10. Date of in-migration.

11-12-13. Special data regarding church status and participation.

14. Special annotations:

> In the case of foreign-born to a mother who was registered in a Swedish community at the time of delivery, name of Swedish community.
> In the case of minors not registered with parents or registered with only one parent, the name, occupation, and place of residence of

dence to serve as his locus for the performance of duties and the receipt of social benefits during the ensuing year, irrespective of migrations during the year.

5. The completion of the community book in terms of the residence as determined by the assessment lists, and a final comparison of the community books and the assessment lists.

The responsibility for self-declaration is placed upon every Swedish citizen and every foreigner resident in Sweden, provided such persons are not included in the declaration of a householder. This declaration includes name, occupation, birthdate, birthplace, civil status and address, and details of property ownership. Employers are required to send in similar reports of all employees as are military authorities, etc. In Stockholm and Gothenburg, every house owner or agent must send in lists of tenants. Pastors are required to make the community books accessible, to be present at the time the declarations are checked and to give information about persons who, in their knowledge, are resident in the community without registration (i. e., who have not handed in moving certificates).

The determination of residence for the ensuing year is made on the basis of where a person is actually living, where he carries on his occupation and where he has his family. In the case of multiple residences, some degree

of choice is left to the person concerned, but under no circumstances can anyone be inscribed on the lists of two communities at the same time. A married woman has the same right as a man to determine her residence in these doubtful cases, and is not listed with her husband unless she shares a household with him (or is absent only temporarily). In cases of multiple residence, where the man works and lives certain days during a part of the year in one place and his family in another, his residence is usually determined as that of his family.

Particularly important is the role played by these lists in bringing the community registers up to date. As mentioned above, they are the basis on which the book of the nonexistent is built.

Population Accounting in Stockholm

With the development of the metropolis, the parish registers proved inadequate as a complete check on the population. In both Stockholm and Gothenburg, registration of migrants has been taken over by the office concerned with the annual compulsory registration for tax assessment purposes. But whereas in Gothenburg this system is limited entirely to records of in- and out-migrants and the com-

11	12	13	14	15	16	17	18
					Out- Migration		
	Religious participation		Special Annotations	Military Service	To	Date	Death Date
1							1
2							2
25							25

parents or parent with whom child is not registered; in the case of adopted children, this rule applies to adoptives. In the case of illegitimate children, name of father if father has recognized child, or if father was engaged to mother at time of conception (such a child, a "trolovnings-barn", has special rights of inheritance).

In the case of a man who has legally recognized an illegitimate child, or of a man who was engaged to the mother of the child at the time of conception, the name, birthplace, and birthdate of such a child is indicated here.

In the case of persons declared legally irresponsible or of legally irresponsible persons later declared responsible, annotation of situation is made.

In the case of persons taking out marriage certificates, this fact is noted; also the date and place or publication of banns. In the case of children brought up in other religion than that of the Swedish church, the sect is indicated.

In the case only one of two spouses is registered in the community, the name and address of the other spouse.

For the widowed, the deceased spouse's name and occupation; if a spouse has been legally declared dead, reference to the court's decision.

In the case of persons temporarily absent for long periods, their temporary residence, and reason for considering it temporary (attending school, at sea, in jail, etc.).

In the case of persons of other sects who have announced their intention of joining the state church, an annotation of this intention and date of acceptance in the church, if this occurs. In the case of citizens of any other country, name of such country. In the case of Swedish naturalization, indication of this.

In case of moving certificate is applied for, date of such application and any other features required from time to time.

15. Status in regard to compulsory military service.

16. For out-migrants; community of destination.

For persons removed to the book of the nonexistent date and reference.

For residents at time of renewal of book, reference to page in new book.

17. Date of out-migration: for internal migrants, date on receipt of notice of in-migration in community of destination; for emigrants, date of taking out moving certificate.

18 Date of death.

munity books are still kept by the pastors, in Stockholm a civil population register has supplanted the community register and the function of the pastors is now limited to the recording of vital statistics. The Registration Bureau in Stockholm was reorganized by Gustav Kollberg in 1926–27 and, under his direction, has attained a high degree of efficiency.

The essential features of the Civil Registration Bureau in Stockholm are as follows:

1. Compulsory and continuous reports of all changes of residence by persons moving into, out of, or within the city;

2. Compulsory annual declarations by all householders; and

3. The continual clearing of information from the parish records and other sources.

Everyone who moves into Stockholm, moves from one residence to another within the city, or moves out of the city is required by law to apply to the registration bureau for a moving certificate or to present the certificate from the place of last residence. The data thus obtained are supplemented by records of births, deaths, and marriages which the pastors from each of the city's parishes send in currently. Reports of changes of residence are obtained not only from the persons concerned but also from the income-tax authorities, the poor law institutions, the maternity hospitals, the elec-

tric works (which report all changes of meters), and other sources. Reports are sent out from the registration bureau to the communities of destination of all persons leaving Stockholm, and to the pastors of the various parishes for all persons moving within the city.

The plan of organization is indicated by the following lists of records kept by the registration bureau, institutions from which information is regularly and currently received and cleared, and institutions to which information is regularly and currently sent.

A. Records Kept by the Registration Bureau

The population register.—This is an active card file of everyone living in Stockholm. The cards are arranged according to address (parish, block, and dwelling), and, under each address, all inhabitants are arranged alphabetically. A separate card is issued for every person over 15 years of age, except wives living together with their husbands. Children under 15 (own or foster) are entered on the card of the parents or parent with whom they live. The card includes information as to family name, given names, occupation, foreign nationality, birth date and birthplace, civil status, vaccination, dates of registration for assessment, in-migration, out-migration, or death, and changes of address within Stockholm.

POPULATION REGISTER - STOCKHOLM

(Face of Card)

Family Name		Military Service	Extraterritorial Parish	Foreign Nationality

Given Name,	Title or Occupation	Birth Year	Date Month	Day	Birthplace	Civil Status	Vaccin- ation
1 Registered for assessment							
2							
3							
4							
5							
6							
7							
8							

In-migration to Stockholm	Other Family Data

(Back of Card)

Inscribed in Parish Register		Address	Pop. Register's real estate annotation	Remarks
Date	Parish			

PLATE VI.—Population register, Stockholm.

The card is shifted with each change of address within the city. See plate VI.

The alphabetical register.—This is also an active card file, arranged according to names, and including the birth date and occupation, the consecutive addresses in Stockholm, and a reference to the population register. Women married within 2 years of migrating to Stockholm have cards under their maiden names, as do widows and women separated from their husbands. See plate VII.

Current in-migration lists of all persons moving into Stockholm, with dates and community of origin (chronological order), and of immigrants.

Current out-migration lists of all persons moving out of Stockholm, with date of migration and name of community of destination (chronological order), and of emigrants.

Birth book.—A record of all births in Stockholm, and births to women inscribed in Stockholm.

Death book.—A record of all deaths in Stockholm, and deaths of persons inscribed in Stockholm.

Migration book.—The complete record of all in- and out-migrants. The current lists are merely abstracts from this book.

Search register.—Names and identifying data regarding all persons who have moved without notification from the address indicated in the register, and who are being sought by some public authority.

Register of the nonexistent.—Persons who have not been traced at two consecutive assessment registrations.

The archives.—The cards of persons who have migrated from Stockholm and of Stockholm residents who have died are placed in the archive files. Before 1927 (back to 1878) these archives are in ledgers.

General register.—An alphabetical list, made annually, of all persons and families in Stockholm at the end of the year.

B. Sources of Information

The population register is made up on the basis of information received from—

1. Parishes within or outside of Stockholm. The pastors send a complete record regarding migrants whose destination is Stockholm and Stockholm residents regarding:
   a. Marriages.
   b. Separations from marriage.
   c. Changes of name.
   d. Baptisms (for obtaining names).
   e. Births.
   f. Adoptions.
   g. Mentally diseased persons.
   h. Declarations regarding minors.
   i. Criminal judgments.
   j. Established fatherhood in the case of illegitimate children.

2. Government reports on all persons admitted to Swedish citizenship.
3. Lists from military authorities of persons in military service.
4. Reports from various institutions, including all insane asylums, homes for vagabonds, poor-law houses, unemployment-dole committees, maternity hospitals, etc.
5. Pension bureau reports on all receiving old age or disability pension.
6. State physicians' reports of all vaccinations.
7. Prison reports on all persons incarcerated or freed.
8. Naval reports on all seamen entering or leaving service, etc.
9. Reports from the electric works regarding residence meter changes.

C. Reports Sent Out by Registration Bureau

1. To the parishes outside of Stockholm, continuous reports of migrants.
2. To the parishes within Stockholm, reports of changes of residence, continuously; once a year, a list of all persons transferred to the book of the nonexistent.
3. To the military authorities, once a year, names of all persons eligible for military service, and current lists of in-migrants, out-migrants, and emigrants who are eligible but have not fulfilled the requirements for military service.
4. To the tax authorities, at the time when the assessment declarations are due, a list of births, deaths, marriages, adoptions, divorces, and other demographic changes, which may be used as a basis for preparing the new assessment lists through additions or subtractions from the previous lists.
5. To the Stockholm school board, once a year, a list of all resident children of school age, and of all who, during the year, have moved into or out of Stockholm or who have died.
6. To the internal revenue department, once a year, a list of all deaths.
7. To the old-age pension bureau, persons eligible for the pension.
8. To the central statistical bureau, lists of immigrants, emigrants, etc.
9. To the Stockholm city statistical bureau, monthly reports of in- and out-migrants, and, once a year, a report of persons transferred to or from the book of the nonexistent.
10. To the Government offices, once a year, lists of Swedish citizens who have attained the age of 23 years during the year (the age of eligibility for voting).

The functioning of the registration bureau as a demographic clearing house is facilitated by a triple-plate addressograph system, which will soon be in full swing. Each resident will then have an addressograph card with three plates: on the main plate are included unchanging factors (birth date, birth place, etc.) and infrequently changing factors (name, civil status, etc.); on the other two smaller plates more frequently changing factors, address on the one, and place of employment on the other. Any one of the three plates may be readily removed and a new one substituted when a change occurs. These plates are tabbed for identification of various classes of persons (children of school age, persons eligible for old-age pension, persons subject to military service, etc.) and the required lists can be prepared quickly and efficiently by this system.

ALPHABETICAL REGISTER - STOCKHOLM
(Face of Card)

Name ....

Birth Date ....

Title or
Occupation ....

Address	Date of notification of moving	Reference to Population Register

(Back of Card)

Address	Date of notification of moving	Reference to Population Register

PLATE VII.—Alphabetical register, Stockholm.

Population Accounting in Belgium

The Belgian system of population accounting is similar to the "old system" in the Netherlands in respect to civil registration, continuous reports from the registrar of births, deaths and marriages, and the general form of the population register. It is similar to the Swedish system in that a series of special books relating to migrants are kept alongside the main register. As in both Holland and Sweden, the community is the unit of registration, the responsibility for registration is placed upon the population, moving certificates are sent from the community of last residence to the community of intended residence, and all demographic events are recorded as they occur.

Features peculiar to the Belgian system are: (1) The requirement, in the case of multiple residence, of registration in every community where residence is maintained. For statistical purposes, a principal residence must, however, be determined. Hence an elaborate series of definitions have been derived to differentiate between "principal residence", "secondary residence", and "legal domicile." (2) The requirement that every person aged 15 years or over carry in his possession a sort of internal passport (the so-called identification card).

These two features make the Belgian system somewhat more complicated administratively than either the Dutch or the Swedish. For this reason, as well as the fact that this system has been described in great detail by both Piron and Lesoir, no description of the details of registration will be given here. To indicate the features of similarity of the principal population register with those of the other systems, plate VIII is presented, with explanatory notes. This shows the form of the population register currently used. This register is arranged in terms of households by address in the community. One page is used for every household, except that several may be entered on the same page in the case of a house containing many small households. This register is kept in bound volumes. For every household, the following order of inscription is preserved: first the head of the family, then his wife, then the children in order of age, then the parents or other related or unrelated persons who are habitually a part of the household. If a member of the household marries, but does not leave the household, the spouses are entered after the other family members, after the former member has been stricken from the line where his name was previously written. If the married couple forms a new household, the spouses are inscribed on a new page. At the top of each page is a reference to the preceding and following register where each family is recorded.

At the bottom of the page are two sections. In the first are indicated all movements of the household or any of its members within the community, including the new address and the date of the move.

The second section indicates, in order, all the heads of families or nonfamily persons who have successively inhabited the dwelling on this page, with the name, first address in community, date of entering this address, date of leaving it, number of persons concerned in the move.

In addition to this principal register each community keeps a register of in-migrants and immigrants, a register of out-migrants and emigrants and an alphabetical index.

Summary

Essentially similar systems of population accounting are at present in operation in Belgium, Sweden, and the greater part of the Netherlands. These systems have the following common features:

1. Each country utilizes the smallest local governmental unit (the parish or community) as the basis of population registration.

2. The following data affecting the residents of each unit are recorded *continuously* (at the time of occurrence or shortly thereafter):

> Birth (in the community or to a woman registered in the community).
> Out-migration (to another community in the same country).
> Immigration (from a foreign country).
> Marriage.
> Dissolution of marriage.
> Out-migration (to another community in the same country).
> Emigration (to a foreign country).
> Death (in the community or of a person registered in the community).

3. Although registration is in terms of individuals, the data are entered in terms of family or household groupings by address in the community, and the relationship of the individual to a family head is indicated.

4. Upon out-migration a transcript of the individual's demographic history and status is sent to the community of destination.

5. In the case of a birth or a death occurring in a community to a resident of another community, a record of this occurrence is sent to the community of residence.

6. So far as internal migrants are concerned, these are "closed" systems: An out-migration is not considered to have occurred until the fact of in-migration into another community has been attested. For each country as a whole the sum of in-migrants during any period should equal the sum of out-migrants.

7. These registers represent the actual resident population of each community at any point of time. Residence is determined in accordance with specific rules.

Persons having no fixed residence (vagabonds, gypsies, etc.) are usually registered cen-

POPULATION REGISTER (EXPANDED FORM) BELGIUM

Inscription in preceding register Volume_____ Page_____

Quarter _____   Street _____

Number	PERSONS COMPOSING HOUSEHOLD						A. Principal Residence B. Secondary Residence C. Legal Domicile	Identity Card	Foreign Register	A. Military Service B. Court Record C. Old Age Pension D. War Pension
	1 Family Name 2 Given Names 3 Place and Date of Birth 2	Rela-tion to Head of House 3	Civil Status Parentage 4	Nationality 5	Occupation 6		7	8	9	10
1	1_____ 2_____ 3_____									A____ B____ C____ D____
2	1_____ 2_____ 3_____									A____ B____ C____ D____

etc. to 10

Changes of Residence within Community

No.	Persons involved in change 2	Street and No. of new residence 3	Vol. 4	Page 5	Date of change 6		1	2	3	4	5	6
1						13						
2						14						
3						15						
4						16						
5						17						
6						18						
7						19						
8						20						
9						21						
10						22						
11						23						
12						24						

PLATE VIII

1. Consecutive numbers.
2. Family name and given names; for wives and widows also the maiden name; if sex is not obvious from name, annotation of sex.
   Place and date of birth.
3. Relationship to head of family or position in household; not the legal status but the commonly used terms, son, daughter, uncle, etc. If a man is cohabiting with a widow or with an unmarried woman, there is assumed to be no relationship, and this column is left blank; if such a woman has children by a previous marriage, the relation of children to her is indicated, and she is placed as head of family, as is the case of an unmarried woman with unrecognized illegitimate children. The position in the household of persons not related by blood or marriage to the head is noted, e. g., secretary, governess.

4. Civil status: Left blank for the unmarried. All changes noted which affect civil status, i. e., marriage, divorce, death of spouse, remarriage, legitimization, recognition (of illegitimates) or adoption. In case of married, divorced, and widowed, name of spouse.
   Parentage: Not obligatory, but considered desirable to note.
5. Nationality: Also changes noted which affect nationality, as marriage, naturalization, etc.
6. Occupation and status in occupation; noted for all heads of household and all persons having a personal income. Note changes. Persons dependent on the head are considered without occupation (column is left blank). Persons on relief are noted as "indigents."
7. Legal domicile; name of guardian.
   Secondary residence.
   Principal residence.

trally. The unregistered population is considered to have no statistical existence.

8. The responsibility for registration is placed, in the case of migration, upon the population itself. On the basis of such registration social benefits and duties are determined. The responsibility for keeping the population registers is placed upon local government functionaries (in Sweden, however, upon the pastors of the State Church).

The responsibility for completing the registers is placed upon various authorities (registrars of vital statistics, institutions, doctors, midwives, etc.). The final control of the registers and the final interpretation of the rules of registration is placed upon some central government department. Inspection is carried out by the representatives of this department at regular intervals.

This might be described as the standard system of population registration. The new system in the Netherlands, while built upon and following most of the traditions of the standard system, makes a radical and important innovation: the continuity of demographic experience is preserved for every individual by the simple device of starting a registration card at birth or immigration and letting this card follow him through all his migrations within the country until he dies or emigrates. At the same time, a record of shifting family groupings is obtained by recording relevant data about other family members on the card of each person who is at any time a family head. The community entity is preserved by a series of archives in which the history of all persons at any time resident in a given community is recorded up to the time of migration from the community or death. The regional

No. of House _____   ---------

Inscription in succeeding register
Volume _____ page _____

Inscriptions						Removals							Changes	Remarks	
Preceding Residences	Street	No.	Date of Declaration of Departure from Preced. Residence	Date of Inscription	Inscription by Official Action	Subsequent Residence / Place of Death / Removal by Official Action	Street	No.	Date of Declaration of Moving	Date of Death	Date of Removal from Register	A. Preceding Vol. & Page / B. Succeeding Vol. & Page	Remarks	
11	12	13	14	15	16	17	18	19	20	21	22	23	24	25
1												A		
2														
3														1
4														
5												B		
1												A		
2														
3														2
4														
5												B		

etc. to 10

Successive Inhabitants of this Dwelling

No. 1	Name of Family Head or persons changing residence 2	1st inscription in community — Street & No. 3	Vol 4	Page 5	No. of Persons 6	Date of inscription 7	Date of removal 8		1	2	3	4	5	6	7	8
1									13							
2									14							
3									15							
4									16							
5									17							
6									18							
7									19							
8									20							
9									21							
10									22							
11									23							
12									24							

8. Identification card: Number of card, date of issue; annotations regarding renewal.

9. Reference to register of foreigners.

10. Status regarding compulsory military service. Reference to criminal sentences (page in register where details are recorded). Old-age pension, war pension.

11–13. Preceding residence: Name of community where person was registered as having habitual residence before migration.

14–16. Date of declaration of departure from previous community; for persons born in community, word "born" is written here (i. e. for persons who have not migrated). Date of inscription; i. e., date moving certificate was delivered upon declaration of arrival.

17–19. Subsequent residence; name of community to which habitual residence is transferred upon out-migration. For persons removed from register upon death, word "deceased" is written here.

20. Date of declaration of out-migration.

21. Date of death or Date of removal from register, i. e., date on receipt of inscription in new community.

22. Date of removal by official action, with annotation of decision thereto.

23. Reference to preceding and following page in same register where person has been or is later inscribed.

24. Remarks. Following facts must be noted: Return of a family previously migrating from community; change of name; conferring title of nobility; suspension of electoral rights; name of institution in cases of persons confined for various reasons; etc. Following facts may be noted: Education, defects, details regarding State pensioners, etc.

demography within a community is enlightened by a record of the persons and families living successively in the same dwelling. This system represents the most important demographic invention of our times by making possible an authenticated life history of every individual, by capturing the elements of that shifting and unstable unit, the family, and by throwing the demographic factor into constant relationship with community and regional structure.

The Utility of the Continuous Register System of Population Accounting

The practical utility of population registers has been implied in the preceding section; the individual establishes his rights and claims on the basis of an authenticated record; planning by the government and by private enterprises is made possible with heightened efficiency when an accurate record of the status and changes in the population is at hand; administration (of school regulations, social insurance, etc.) is facilitated by current reports of relevant changes in the composition and characteristics of the population.

The research needs that might be met by the development of such a system in the United States may be summarized briefly as follows:

1. The determination of mere numbers of people, regionally, at shorter intervals than a decennium. This is a necessary basis for computing all the crude rates (birth rates, death rates, unemployment rates, relief rates, etc.) which are needed to throw light on population trends.

2. The determination of the varying composition and characteristics of the population, likewise regionally, and likewise at shorter intervals than a decennium. This is particularly important if interrelationships in the factors producing population change

are to be evaluated with a view to prediction of future trends.

3. A more precise determination of the role of internal migrations in producing population change and an evaluation of their social effects. At present, in America, this problem can be approached only inferentially in terms of the end result of such migrations (e. g., by a comparative analysis of state of birth and state of residence, or by an analysis of the regional migration balance between two censuses), or by a few isolated primary investigations (e. g., those of the Department of Agriculture, the Works Progress Administration, the Agricultural Experiment Stations, etc.). It is recognized that we have no adequate information as to the extent and direction of the streams of migration, the demographic, social and economic differentials of the migrants, or the degree of success or failure in their assimilation to a new environment.

4. A more adequate approach to the analysis of differential fertility and mortality, depending partly on the development of the three preceding points, partly on the allocation of these factors to the actual region of residence, and partly on the preservation of the continuity of individual experience.

5. A better basis for estimating the reliability of our main sources of population data, particularly the census, for it is admitted that, at present, the use of many of these data for scientific studies is vitiated by the necessity of making guesses and crude estimates of the degree of error involved in the primary data.

6. A better basis for sampling procedures, which are recognized as the most efficient and satisfactory means of throwing light on problems of immediate importance, and of estimating complicated interrelationships.

The direction of the application of the continuous register system of population accounting may be indicated for each of these six points:

1. Since the registers are continuous, the determination of numbers by regions at short intervals can be readily made. Given a population base as of any point of time, either by complete enumeration or by drawing a balance from preexisting registers, the population at any desired point can be derived by the simple addition of births, in-migrants and immigrants to this base and the subtraction of deaths, out-migrants, and emigrants for the appropriate time period.

2. A similar tabulation of the characteristics of persons born, dying, and migrating (e. g., their age, sex, civil status) can be applied by addition and subtraction to the basic composition data to derive any required trends in these factors.

3. Since all changes of residence are recorded at the time they occur, the trends of migration can be easily studied by a very simple tabulation of the number of such changes. The registration data lend themselves to an analysis of the direction and distance of migration, the economic type of migrations (farm to city, farm to farm, city to farm) and to the characteristics of the migrants (age, sex, family status, etc.), without the collection of any additional data. Since the same data are collected both for the stable and the mobile population, migration differentials can be readily determined. Since the data on births, deaths, and migrants are recorded in the same registers by family groupings, a more adequate analysis of the interrelationship of these factors in producing total population change is possible.

4. The allocation of all births and deaths to community of residence under both the standard system and the new Dutch system is an invaluable aid in all studies of vital processes, as is the unquestioned reliability of the data on age and civil status. The standard population registers, however, do not lend themselves to a direct approach to the problems of differential fertility, for there is no continuous record, except in the case of the stable part of the population, of the number of children ever born, but the new Dutch system will make possible accurate studies of the fertility of marriages through the records of all the children ever born to persons who are heads of families.

5. It is impossible to exaggerate the importance of population registers in producing accurate demographic data. The ordinary census, based on a schedule or questionnaire, has all the uncertainties and defects of testimony and varies in reliability with the honesty, intelligence, and knowledge of the informant. To the extent that population registers are built upon the basis of attested demographic facts at the time of their occurrence, they minimize, and, in some respects, avoid entirely the chance of errors. Population registers are not, however, a panacea for all statistical ills, nor can they, at their best, entirely replace a census. A census is obviously needed at the point at which population registers are set up as a basis from which to proceed. In Belgium, Holland, and Sweden, regular decennial censuses are taken both as a safeguard against a possible cumulative "loss" of population and to obtain data not readily available in the registers. In Belgium and Holland, these censuses are by direct enumeration; in Sweden (with the exception of the special census of 1935–36) these have been by an indirect method, i. e., a combination of abstracts from the registers, checked against tax assessment records, with additional information filled in by the informants without direct questioning. The general procedure in all these countries involves a cross-checking of the census by the registers, and the completion and revision of the registers on the basis of the census returns. The technique varies somewhat in each country but is, in general terms, as follows: A canvass is made, in terms of addresses, to determine the factual population. The schedules of the factual population are compared with the registers which comprise the legal ("habitual" or "resident" population) and necessary revisions are made, i. e., excluding from the resident population persons whose residential status has actually changed or whose whereabouts are definitely unknown, and adding those who are actually residents but who have, for various reasons, not previously been entered in the registers. In checking errors, the registers are taken as the standard in cases of disagreements on demographic facts, but on points where the registers are known to be of questionable accuracy (e. g., in regard to occupation, which is usually entered in the registers only at the time of in-migration and which may have changed) the informant or some other source (e. g., the employer) is taken as the standard. Data relating to the continuity of individual experience (e. g., the number of children ever born) must usually be accepted from the informant, for the standard registers are not complete in this respect except for persons who have never migrated.

On the basis of the officially published statistics, the registers in Holland and Sweden seem to have attained a remarkable degree of accounting efficiency. One criterion of this efficiency can be taken as the proportions of persons lost to the registers, i. e., those removed by official action (in Sweden, those transferred to the book of the nonexistent) compared with the proportion reentered in the registers after being lost. The migration data for Holland and Sweden for recent years are shown in the following table on page 299.

If the inscriptions and removals by official action are expressed as a percent of the total inscriptions of migrants and removals of migrants respectively, the proportions for Holland for inscriptions vary from about 0.5 to 1 percent, for Sweden slightly higher than 1 percent. Removals vary, for Holland, from 0.5 to 2.5 percent (the latter for the census year 1930); for Sweden, from 1 to 1.5 percent (the latter again for the census year).[7]

---

[7] The situation is apparently not so favorable in Belgium, the removal by official action amounting in 1934 (a non-census year) to 3.5 percent of all removals. See *Relevé officiel du chiffre de la population du Royaume á la date du 31 décembre 1934,* Bruxelles (1935), 2–3.

	In-mi-grants	Out-mi-grants	Immi-grants [1]	Emi-grants [1]	In-scribed by official action	Re-moved by official action
Holland: [2]						
1929	488,781	489,421	57,772	45,831	5,830	9,525
1930	509,175	509,380	66,725	48,055	6,251	14,885
1931	439,843	442,167	62,650	37,364	5,319	2,614
1932	423,130	424,084	55,621	38,423	4,560	4,449
1933	414,877	415,196	49,629	38,780	2,668	5,394
1934	431,187	430,822	43,700	41,878	1,830	4,430
					From book of nonex-istent	To book of nonex-istent
Sweden: [3]						
1929	482,705	480,206	6,336	11,019	6,729	7,247
1930	526,166	523,674	7,515	5,682	7,773	8,081
1931	477,388	475,470	8,390	2,971	6,140	5,865
1932	481,479	478,938	8,990	2,117	6,504	5,349
1933	463,270	460,927	7,256	2,417	6,154	4,892

[1] Including, for Holland, colonial migrants.
[2] *Statistiek van den Loop der Bevolking van Nederland over het jaar 1934,* Central Bureau voor de Statistiek, 's Gravenhage (1935), 54–55.
[3] *Befolkningsrörelsen år 1933 av Statistiska Centralbyrån,* Stockholm (1936), 41.

If this is a valid index of reliability, the registers seem to function remarkably well in keeping track of population movements.

It will be noted also that although the in-migrants and out-migrants should be exactly the same, there are discrepancies, but that these, again, are negligible.

In Stockholm, where the mobility is exceptionally high, the registration system has reached such a high degree of efficiency, due to the constant checking of the registers from other sources, that for every year since 1928 (including the census year) there have been more people "found" (from the cumulative losses of past years) than "lost." The data are as follows: [8]

	Entered in book of non-exist-ent "lost"	Removed from book of non-existent "found"
1928	2,478	2,654
1929	2,632	2,639
1930	1,972	2,824
1931	1,877	2,250
1932	1,549	2,142
1933	1,478	1,776
1934	1,182	1,478
1935	1,034	1,284

This is impressive evidence of the workability of registration in a relatively large and complicated city.

6. Population registers afford an excellent basis for sampling, for, if they are kept properly, they represent the statistical universe and a sample can be drawn quickly and efficiently. Thus, analyses of particular problems which can be solved only by the collection of new data are possible, and questioning on points included in the registers is avoided. The recent Swedish census of 1935–36 is a case in point. A population commission appointed by the Riksdag needed information as the basis of developing a rational population policy. Their general problem was to combine demographic with social and economic factors to indicate the environmental situations which might be operating on the people's will and capacity to marry and bear children. The data that could be derived from the population registers alone were not relevant to the solution of this problem, and a rather complicated schedule was necessary. By an ingenious combination of an indirect census, based on the registers and covering the statis-

tical universe, and a sample drawn from the schedules of this indirect census, data bearing directly on the problem were obtained. The technique used in this census illustrates very well the possibilities of sampling on the basis of population registers and should be capable of application to many other problems. It is, therefore, of some interest to quote the following description of its method of operation.

"The indirect census of 1935–36 represented a complete enumeration of the population, and was directed toward two ends, (1) the determination of the age distribution by sex and civil status for each community and (2) through the identification of all the population in terms of name and residence to serve as a basis from which samples could be drawn for the direct census. The chief reasons for sampling rather than complete enumeration in the direct census were practical considerations, the necessity of getting the data as quickly and cheaply as possible, and the necessity of using only qualified enumerators because of the complexity of the questions.

"The indirect census was merely a simplified form of the usual decennial census and the procedure was the same as that used since 1860. This census is a balance sheet drawn from the population registers by the pastors of the Swedish State Church, who are charged with the keeping of the registers. [9] It indicates the legal population of each community as of December 31, 1935. A schedule was filled in for every household and included the following data for each member of the household: Name, family status (relationship to head of household), sex, occupation, physical defects (blind, deaf and dumb, imbecile, insane, epileptic), date of birth, place of birth, civil status, date of marriage, date of dissolution of marriage, whether the person was temporarily absent from the community of residence, and the address of the spouse in case of marriage separation.

"After these schedules were assembled, samples were drawn from them for the direct enumeration. For the larger cities (population 20,000 or more) every fifth household was selected from the indirect schedules which were arranged in the order in which they had been filled in from the population registers, i. e., according to addresses. Lots were drawn separately for each city to indicate which household among the first five should be taken as the first household in the sample, and thereafter each fifth household was selected. Of the smaller towns and rural communities (which numbered about 2,500), one in every five communities was selected and every household investigated. The sampling of rural communities was made after the communities had first been stratified into three classes according to the occupational distribution of the population at the time of the 1930 census: Agricultural communities in which at least 75 percent of the population was occupied in or dependent upon farming, rural mixed communities in which the proportions engaged in farming were from 50 to 75 percent, and rural industrial communities in which the proportion engaged in farming represented less than 50 percent. Within each stratum of each county (Sweden is divided into 24 counties or *län*) the communities were arranged in order according to their geographical position in the county, and every fifth community in each stratum selected for the sample, lots being drawn for each group to determine which community should be the first to be drawn within the group. It was recognized that it might have been theoretically more desirable to sample one in every five households for all rural communities, but practical considerations of time and money dictated this other plan. One of the interesting by-products will be an empirical test of the validity of this sampling procedure by comparing the sample with the known universe.

"After the sample for the direct enumeration had been drawn, the details obtained through the indirect census were entered on the new schedules. Thus the

[8] Communication from Gustav Kollberg.

[9] Civil registration exists only in Stockholm.

accuracy of the purely demographic data was insured and direct questioning on this point, except for purposes of identification, was avoided. The only exception to this rule was in regard to occupation, on which point the population registers are known to be incomplete and unreliable.

"The questions on the direct schedule were organized around three main points: economic status and occupational history, children born to spouses living together at the time of the census, and housing conditions.

"The questions on economic status included: chief occupation, status in occupation, industry (and, in the case of employers, the number of persons employed), whether the occupation was carried on in or away from home, subsidiary occupations (in the case of married women, whether they acted as assistants to their husbands), occupation and occupational status in 1930. In addition, there were extra questions for special classes of persons: for spouses living together at the time of the census, occupation and status in occupation at the time of or shortly before marriage; for all persons over 15 years of age, education and vocational training; for all persons aged 16–66 years, occupational disability (whole or partial), whether unemployed on March 2, 1936, and total number of weeks unemployed during 1935; for all women whose present marriages were contracted after 1900 and who were living with their husbands at the time of the census, whether they gave up their jobs upon marrying, whether they migrated in connection with marriage, and the details of their occupational history since marriage.

"The questions relating to the number of children ever born were limited to married spouses living together at the time of the census. Demographic details were entered for children who had died or left home. Children of the husband and wife (in common) born before marriage were entered on the schedule as well as those born during marriage.

"The questions relating to housing conditions included: the number of "real" living rooms (defined as of a minimum size, with windows or ventilation, a door that can be closed, and some sort of heating); the number of "other" living rooms; the nature of the kitchen; the existence of bath room, shower room, hall, vestibule; the number of lodgers and the quarters occupied by them; the existence of a kitchen garden.

"The direct census was taken in the cities from March 16 to March 31; in rural communities from March 6 to March 13, 1936. Before the enumeration began, duplicate schedules were sent out to every household included in the sample. At the same time, nation-wide propaganda was carried on, and two radio talks were held, one indicating the purpose of the census, the other explaining in detail what the separate questions meant. Thus, by the time the enumerators arrived, many of the duplicate schedules had already been completely filled in, and the enumerator's function was in these cases limited to checking up on the more difficult points.

"Data on income and property for the year 1935 were entered directly on the schedules by the county tax authorities.

"Taken as a whole, this census is one of the most interesting experiments in the collection of mass statistics that has ever been carried out. It was motivated by the need for information bearing on an important social problem, the questions were organized around this problem, and all available resources were used to get the desired information quickly, efficiently, and reliably. The usually troublesome data on age, civil status, etc., were taken from the parish registers, the accuracy of which is unquestioned on purely demographic lines; the developmental data, relating to occupational history and the number of children ever born were obtained from the only possible source, the people themselves, and they were prepared in advance for the questions that would be asked; the housing data were checked by the observing enumerators, and the income tax data were entered from the official tax records. The combination of the direct and indirect methods of enumeration should, to some extent, act as a check on both. The combination of a sampling procedure with a complete enumeration will make possible a test of the representative nature of the sample and has a theoretical interest as well as a practical utility as a guide to the type of inference that can be drawn from the sample."[10]

It is clear that the continuous register system of population accounting would go far toward solving the many difficulties in the way of obtaining reliable population data in the United States and would give an impetus to a more scientific approach in this field. It can be justified both from the administrative and the research point of view. With the application of the American talent for organization and of the currently used mechanical techniques of tabulation to the long and successful experience of these European countries, neither the practical difficulties nor the cost should be great, and the initiation of such a system at the present time would represent an investment, dividends on which would quickly repay the cost of installation and upkeep.

[10] Thomas, Dorothy Swaine, The Swedish Census of 1935–36, *Journal of the American Statistical Association*, 31: 542–544 (September 1936). By permission.

INDEX

302